Exploring the Collective Unconscious in the Age of Digital Media

Stephen Brock Schafer
Digipen Institute of Technology, USA

A volume in the Advances in Psychology, Mental Health, and Behavioral Studies (APMHBS) Book Series

Information Science REFERENCE
An Imprint of IGI Global

Published in the United States of America by
Information Science Reference (an imprint of IGI Global)
701 E. Chocolate Avenue
Hershey PA, USA 17033
Tel: 717-533-8845
Fax: 717-533-8661
E-mail: cust@igi-global.com
Web site: http://www.igi-global.com

Library of Congress Cataloging-in-Publication Data

Names: Schafer, Stephen Brock, 1942- editor.
Title: Exploring the collective unconscious in the age of digital media / Stephen Brock Schafer, editor.
Description: Hershey : Information Science Reference, 2016. | Includes bibliographical references and index.
Identifiers: LCCN 2015046872| ISBN 9781466698918 (hardcover) | ISBN 9781466698925 (ebook)
Subjects: LCSH: Subconsciousness. | Archetype (Psychology) | Digital media. | Cognitive psychology.
Classification: LCC BF1001 .E97 2016 | DDC 154.2--dc23 LC record available at http://lccn.loc.gov/2015046872

This book is published in the IGI Global book series Advances in Psychology, Mental Health, and Behavioral Studies (APMHBS) (ISSN: pending; eISSN: pending)

British Cataloguing in Publication Data
A Cataloguing in Publication record for this book is available from the British Library.

For electronic access to this publication, please contact: eresources@igi-global.com.

Advances in Psychology, Mental Health, and Behavioral Studies (APMHBS) Book Series

Bryan Christiansen
PryMarke, LLC, USA

ISSN: pending
EISSN: pending

Mission

The complexity of the human mind has puzzled researchers and physicians for centuries. While widely studied, the brain still remains largely misunderstood.

The **Advances in Psychology, Mental Health, and Behavioral Studies (APMHBS)** book series presents comprehensive research publications focusing on topics relating to the human psyche, cognition, psychiatric care, mental and developmental disorders, as well as human behavior and interaction. Featuring diverse and innovative research, publications within APMHBS are ideally designed for use by mental health professionals, academicians, researchers, and upper-level students.

Coverage

- Eating Disorders
- Developmental Disorders
- Mental Health & Disorders
- Substance Abuse
- Neurological Disorders
- Personality Disorders
- Psychiatry
- Socialization
- Emotional Health
- Addiction

IGI Global is currently accepting manuscripts for publication within this series. To submit a proposal for a volume in this series, please contact our Acquisition Editors at Acquisitions@igi-global.com or visit: http://www.igi-global.com/publish/.

The Advances in Psychology, Mental Health, and Behavioral Studies (APMHBS) Book Series (ISSN pending) is published by IGI Global, 701 E. Chocolate Avenue, Hershey, PA 17033-1240, USA, www.igi-global.com. This series is composed of titles available for purchase individually; each title is edited to be contextually exclusive from any other title within the series. For pricing and ordering information please visit http://www.igi-global.com/book-series/advances-psychology-mental-health-behavioral/110200. Postmaster: Send all address changes to above address.

Titles in this Series

For a list of additional titles in this series, please visit: www.igi-global.com

Psychosocial Studies of the Individual's Changing Perspectives in Alzheimer's Disease
Cordula Dick-Muehlke (University of California, Irvine, USA) Ruobing Li (University of California, Irvine, USA) and Myron Orleans (California State University, Fullerton, USA)
Medical Information Science Reference • copyright 2015 • 434pp • H/C (ISBN: 9781466684782) • US $225.00 (our price)

Psychological and Social Implications Surrounding Internet and Gaming Addiction
Jonathan Bishop (Centre for Research into Online Communities and E-Learning Systems, Swansea, UK)
Information Science Reference • copyright 2015 • 335pp • H/C (ISBN: 9781466685956) • US $195.00 (our price)

Handbook of Research on Innovations in the Diagnosis and Treatment of Dementia
Panagiotis D. Bamidis (Aristotle University of Thessaloniki, Greece) Ioannis Tarnanas (Aristotle University of Thessaloniki, Greece) Leontios Hadjileontiadis (Aristotle University of Thessaloniki, Greece) and Magda Tsolaki (Aristotle University of Thessaloniki, Greece)
Medical Information Science Reference • copyright 2015 • 511pp • H/C (ISBN: 9781466682344) • US $245.00 (our price)

Exploring Implicit Cognition Learning, Memory, and Social Cognitive Processes
Zheng Jin (Zhengzhou Normal University, China & University of California, Davis, USA)
Information Science Reference • copyright 2015 • 371pp • H/C (ISBN: 9781466665996) • US $195.00 (our price)

IGI GLOBAL
DISSEMINATOR OF KNOWLEDGE
www.igi-global.com

701 E. Chocolate Ave., Hershey, PA 17033
Order online at www.igi-global.com or call 717-533-8845 x100
To place a standing order for titles released in this series, contact: cust@igi-global.com
Mon-Fri 8:00 am - 5:00 pm (est) or fax 24 hours a day 717-533-8661

Editorial Advisory Board

Table of Contents

Detailed Table of Contents

are real. This suggests that virtual realities may be analyzed according to Carl Jung's compensational dynamics of dream analysis. The objective of such analysis would be discovery of contextual (target group) meaning in unconscious dimensions. Such discovery could lead to the use of mediated biofeedback to engineer Earth-sustainable media content in order to promote coherent frequencies on correlated electromagnetic scales. This chapter will emphasize the authenticity of research on the collective unconscious as projected into the metaverse. Based on fundamental correlations in structure, function, and purpose of dreams as defined by Carl Jung, drama-based video games can be understood as a genre that may serve as an unprecedented, interactive dream analog for purposes of cognitive research.

Just as our dreaming reality is constructed, our waking reality may also be constructed. While our waking reality influences our lives the most, other constructed realities also have impact. Yet, never before has such a large part of the population been so widely affected by another constructed reality beyond dreaming; specifically, our technologically constructed digital reality through video game play. One potential consequence of video game play is breaking the illusion or 'frame' of our dreams as reality through various dream experiences. Many of the world's wisdom traditions believe that waking reality is an illusion, and now this idea is supported by modern digital physics. While being aware of the illusory nature of waking reality is difficult, it may be easier to break the framework of perception or 'wake up' to the true nature of reality in alternative realities, such as digital and dreaming. This chapter will review the evidence collected in the video game and dream laboratory to explore how video game play is breaking the frame within dreaming realities.

Humans utilize sensory and motor systems developed genetically, physically and socially for interfacing with our external environment. We use these same systems to interface in our interactions with artificial intelligence. There are other functioning central nervous system (CNS) systems, however, involved in cognitive processing for which the function and environmental interface is less clear. The synchronous physiologic electrical field system utilizes broadcast extracellular electrical fields for a wide variety of CNS functions. The operations of this system are usually non-conscious and most apparent during sleep (especially the conscious states of sleep that include dreaming), and un-focused waking. The electrical fields of this system are altered and affected by both internal and external stimuli. These fields can be monitored and analyzed by artificial intelligence (AI) systems, and independently of human input, AI systems can utilize similar frequency based electrical potentials to convey data, communicate, supply power, and to store memory. From both human and AI perspectives, these systems have the potential to function more fully in human/machine interaction. This chapter reviews our current knowledge as to function, current interactive approaches, and interface potential for these physiological electrical fields.

Section 2
Exponentials for Exploring the Psychological Metaverse

Section 2 represents directions for continued research upon the concept that the Metaverse is energetically correlated with the Psychecology (unified field) and dream structure according to Carl Jung. Chapter five explores film and video games relative to Jungian principles of dream structure. Chapter six amplifies the concept of archetypal projection of the cognitive unconscious as understood by exponents of Jungian dream principles. Chapter seven focuses on coherence or "Flow" as cognitive relationships that exist between dreams and the serious sport of mountaineering. Chapter eight emphasizes principles of Jungian archetypal projection as it relates to healing potentials in South African film. Chapter nine speculates on the archetypal hero's journey from the standpoint of an emergent understanding of psychological group contexts in the media-sphere. Chapter ten discusses the synchronous (entangled) relationship that exists between two contextual groups: Terrorists and media professionals. Finally, Chapter 11 provides an extensive discussion of the neurobiological Psychecology as it impacts the global ionosphere.

This chapter shows the attempt to use narrative projections of the unconscious in video games (and film) for transgressing into a virtual world. It demonstrates the conceptual development from C.G. Jung's theories via Joseph Campbell and Hollywood's screenwriters to Video Game mythologies. It shows that a visual approach by game artists often leads to stereotypical implementation of archetypes and archeplot in video games that illustrates a lack of reflection and flexibility of mind and creativity. It further shows that a conscious implementation of individual patterns and archetypes as seen in Adventure Games and recent Indie Games may obtain narrative depth for a game and contribute to exploring the collective unconscious in new media. Gaming is rapidly changing and aims towards the ideal of a Holodeck. New Virtual Reality experiments and gadgets prepare the ground for new ways to engage in imagined (conscious and unconscious) realities. The chapter concludes with an example of an attempt to build a virtual dream world with the project Birdly (2014) and Oculus Rift.

Knowingly or unknowingly, games manifest archetypal forces from the unconscious. Through play and fantasy, unconscious content of the psyche is able to express its deep longings. Hypnogogic landscapes of videogames provide immersive realms in which players enact psychological dramas. Game designers reside on a unique axis from which their work with the imaginary realm can create profound psychic containers. At this pivotal point in our culture, digital games hold tremendous influence over the creation of new myths, lore, and possibilities. This chapter investigates archetypal psychology concepts of Carl

Foreword

ASCENT OF THE COLLECTIVE MIND

When Worlds Collide

Starting in 1998, I was in charge of a two-year research program at Interval Research Corporation, a private Silicon Valley think-tank funded by Microsoft co-founder, Paul Allen. At the time, my project was one of a handful in the world engaged in the scientific investigation of psi (psychic) phenomena, with a healthy budget and a research team. We were mainly interested in the phenomenon of precognition, which we were studying in a variety of ways (Radin D.I., 2004; Radin D., 2006).

My budget was sufficient to include computer scientists, psychologists, a mathematician, a statistician, a psychophysiologist, and a journalist. Three members of the project were especially notable: computer scientist Richard Shoup, creator of Interval's psi program and winner of both an Emmy and an Academy Award for developing methods leading to the ubiquitous use of CGI (computer graphics effects) in television and movies; physicist Russell Targ, co-founder of the US government's classified "StarGate" research program on psychic espionage; and physicist Edwin May, director of the StarGate program from 1985 to 1995 (May E.C., Marwaha S.B., 2014). Given Interval's insistence on secrecy, few people outside of the company had any idea what we were up to.

In early 2000, when my contract with Interval was ending, Richard Shoup and I decided to create a nonprofit lab to continue our work. At the time, rents for office space in Silicon Valley were more stratospheric than usual because Y2K had come and gone without incident, and technology investors were still living in a state of irrational exuberance. Also, the impending implosion of the dot-com boom wasn't yet on the radar (Radin, 2004). So we spent several weeks scouting for an affordable space.

We finally settled on a suitable place in Los Altos, on the outskirts of Silicon Valley. It was an end-unit in a simple office complex housing accountants, psychotherapists, dentists, real estate agents, and a few small companies. We moved a few personal items into our new office, and I went about ordering furniture and planning our research program for the coming year. One of my first tasks was to design the laboratory that I wanted to build. I envisioned that it would consist of a large electromagnetically shielded chamber plus a variety of devices used to test for mind-matter interactions, some psychophysiological monitoring gear, a comfortable reclining chair, and so on. As my plan grew I started to worry about the price tag, but I was caught up in the post-Y2K enthusiasm and decided to dream big.

A month later our offices had taken shape, but I was still fussing over the details of the laboratory. I had drawn a sketch of the lab on a white board, which I had hung on a wall that separated our space from our neighboring office, next door.

I had walked past that office a few times and peeked in the window. It was smartly furnished, reminiscent of a therapist's waiting room, but no one was in sight. I decided that the next time I saw someone there I would introduce myself.

A few weeks later I noticed to my surprise a small sign next to our neighbor's door. It read, "PSI Quest Labs." I thought this was a delightful coincidence given that our new organization was one of only a handful of labs in the world devoted to the scientific exploration of psi phenomena, and given the exclusivity of our club we were all well aware of each other. So I naturally assumed that the "PSI" in our neighbor's name was an acronym for something like Personnel Services Incorporated. But then I wondered what a personnel office would be doing with a laboratory. I imaged that they must be running focus groups to discuss topics in human resources or some other workplace issue.

The next week I decided to walk through the office complex by a route I hadn't taken before. To my surprise I noticed an office with a sign near the door which read, "PSI Quest Inc." Now my curiosity was doubly piqued, because the "I" in PSI Quest Labs must have meant something other than "incorporated." With renewed interest I peeked into both of those offices every day.

A week went by. Finally one day I noticed movement in the PSI Quest Labs office. I knocked on the door and a man opened it. He was neatly dressed and my first impression was that he might be an accountant. I held out my hand and said, "Hi, I'm your neighbor in the office next door. My name is Dean …."

The man suddenly turned ashen gray and croaked, "Dean Radin?" Given his sudden pallor, I thought he might be having a stroke, but I was also puzzled how he knew my name. The only sign outside our office read, "Boundary Institute." Our names were not listed anywhere.

Perplexed, I replied, "Yes, but …." Again he interrupted me, looking even more dazed. "Dean Radin?" he said with a strange mixture of terror and hope.

I didn't know whether to call 911 or to offer my hand again. Fortunately, he gestured for me to enter the office. I saw an attractive coffee table, fashionable chrome lamps, and a plush leather couch. No one else appeared to be around.

To avoid further agitating the man, I adopted a soothing tone and quietly said, "Yes, I'm Dean Radin. I'm glad to meet you, but how do you know who I am?"

He replied, "Because you wrote *The Conscious Universe*."

"Well, yes," I said, "but …."

He interrupted, "And I was looking for you, to ask you to be on my Board."

"Your Board?"

"I was using a Tibetan Dream Yoga technique to manifest you."

"Manifest me?" I said sluggishly, my head starting to spin.

He continued, "I'm doing psi research and I want to build up my Board of Directors to help raise funds for my lab, PSI Quest."

My sense of stability began to dissolve. The walls melted and the ground turned into quicksand. I had to sit down.

Then Jon's eyes narrowed and he said, "Did you just say you're my neighbor?"

With my head still spinning, I explained that I was starting a new research institute with a couple of colleagues, and our offices were right next door to his. We shared a common wall, and we were engaged in exactly the same type of work.

Neither of us could speak for a few minutes. The coincidence of two psi labs ending up in exactly the same location, with neither aware of the other, was just too extreme.

It turned out that our neighbor, Jon, was a prominent Apple employee, one of the designers of the Apple Powerbook laptop. He decided to cash out and do what he always wanted to do – psi research. About 9 months before Richard Shoup and I were thinking about forming the Boundary Institute, Jon started PSI Quest to follow his dream.

About a month before I showed up at his door, Jon decided that he wanted to expand his efforts. To do so he felt that I would be an ideal candidate for his company's Board of Directors, but he had no idea how to contact me. In my book *The Conscious Universe* I mentioned my lab at the University of Nevada, but that was before I moved to Silicon Valley, and since then I had essentially disappeared from public view due to Interval's secrecy policy.

But Jon was determined to find me, so each day for a month he was using a lucid dreaming technique whereby intense mental imagery is used to "dream" a desired outcome into physical being. At the same time, I was intently focusing on the laboratory that I wanted to build, but I hadn't purchased anything yet because of the projected costs. When I mentioned this to Jon, he calmly said, "Follow me." We left the reception area and went around the corner. We stood at the entrance to a large electromagnetically shielded chamber, *exactly* the type of lab I had been envisioning about over the past month. The same size, the same shielding, the same reclining chair, the physiological equipment. All of it.

In short, Jon manifested me through his dream, and I manifested the lab through my dream. We were literally next door to each other, dreaming each other's wishes into existence.

This synchronicity was so outrageous that to confirm if it really happened I rechecked the details with Jon several times over the next few years. I also asked Jon to tell his side of the story to other members of the Boundary Institute. We verified that this wasn't a hallucination or a confabulation. It was real.

Coincidence?

But *how* could it be real? Maybe it was just a fluke; coincidences do happen. But in this case the odds against chance were ridiculously unlikely. With a mere handful of laboratories in the entire world engaged in the scientific study of psi phenomena, the chances that two of them would accidentally show up next to each other, when neither had any idea of the other's existence, and where in each case a highly motivated need was solved by the appearance of the other, was just preposterous. This was not a case where billions of people were dreaming similar dreams, and where a rich set of random overlaps in those dreams could have accidentally caused what an amazing coincidence. Instead, this involved two one-in-a-billion events colliding in spacetime.

So if it wasn't chance, perhaps it signaled what synchronicities, psychic and mystical experiences are trying to reveal to us, namely that mind and matter – Rene Descartes' dualistic conception of reality – are actually reflections of a deeper reality. That reality has three underlying principles: First, mind and matter are two sides of the same coin; second, this particular coin is a monistic reality that transcends common sense boundaries of space and time; and third, that separation is fundamentally an illusion.

That is, experiences of mind-to-mind communication (telepathy) tell us that your sense of self, your *mind*, is not strictly separated from another person's sense of self, regardless of where you are both located. Verifiably correct impressions of distant events (clairvoyance) indicate that our minds are not separate from the material world, even if those events are in the future or the past (precognition and retrocognition). And further, mind can influence matter (psychokinesis) as in the synchronicity Jon and I experienced, because they intimately linked through the same underlying source.

These three aspects of mind-matter interaction are wound into the core message of the perennial philosophy of Western and Eastern esoteric lore, the teachings of the Gnostics, the Rosicrucians, the Theosophists, and so on (Huxley A., 2004; Horowitz M., 2009; Fish S., 1996; Brenner E.M., 1990). This is the domain of *mundus imaginalis*, the Imaginal World so-named by French scholar Henry Corbin based on his analysis of Islamic thought, and then advanced into the notion of archetypes by Swiss psychiatrist Carl Jung (Jung C. G., 1959; Rowan J., 2005).

How is the imaginal world related to two psi labs colliding in Los Altos in the year 2000? As a quasi-scientific metaphor, we may think of it in this way: Einstein's Theory of General Relativity says that gravity may be considered a warping of spacetime due to the presence of mass, which in turn may be thought of as a highly dense form of energy (Stachel J.J., 2005). These spacetime warps will attract objects moving through otherwise "flat" space, causing them to orbit each other, like a whirlpool. If the warping is sufficiently strong, the objects will eventually be forced together, and in extreme circumstances they can be completely swallowed up by a black hole at the center of the whirlpool.

With that imagery in mind, what if strong mental intention, imbued with exceptional "gravity" of purpose and importance, influences a primordial universal substance from which mind and matter emerge? Let's call that hypothetical substance, the fabric from which the tapestry of the imaginal realm is woven, *mindmatter*. This strange substance is exquisitely sensitive to, shapes, and is shaped by, both material and mental efforts. This allows minds to precipitate unexpected events in the material world. Jon and I both exercised free will to dream our dreams, but in so doing we were apparently caught up in a collective imaginal whirlpool larger than either of us, which literally bent spatial and temporal realities and caused our worlds to collide.

While a *mundus imaginalis* explanation may seem a bit too marvelous, on the micro scale something like this is already known to occur. That is, it is well known that when quanta (elementary particles, like photons or electrons) are observed that their behavior changes from a distribution of wavelike, potential outcomes to a single, particle-like, actual event. (Herbert N., 1995; Radin 2006; Green B., 2004) When Jon and I tightly focused on a strongly desired, mutually compatible outcome, those acts of observation may have constrained the potential directions that each of us could have independently taken in our lives, and in so doing our orbits were affected to such an extent that we had no choice but to end up in the same location.

Scientific Evidence

Such speculations are all well and good, but besides stories of odd synchronicities, of which there are many, is there any objective, scientific evidence validating the idea that mind and matter are intimately related? The answer is yes: Systematic laboratory studies investigating mind-matter interactions have been conducted since the 1930s, and experiments studying collective mind-matter interactions have been conducted since the 1990s (Radin 1997; Radon D., 2013). In both cases there is empirical evidence for mind-matter ("psychokinetic" or PK) effects, collected under rigorously controlled conditions by numerous, independent researchers. We will review some of that evidence shortly.

When we add to the empirical PK database a century of additional laboratory evidence for other psi phenomena, including telepathy, clairvoyance, and precognition, and then consider the preponderance of that evidence against legitimate concerns over biased reviews both pro and con, claims of fraud, and distortions in how these topics are presented in college textbooks, a strong case can be made that while mind-matter interactions are chronically controversial, from a fact-like, empirical perspective, we are justified in maintaining strong confidence that they do indeed exist, and that fraud can be traced almost exclusively to con artists masquerading as psychics or mediums. It is extremely rare among scientists, with just one known case of experimenter fraud and a handful of suspected cases, over a period of 150 years.

A thorough review of this extensive literature is beyond the scope of this chapter, but two topics are worth mentioning briefly. Both involve use of random physical systems as targets of PK influences. The basic tool used in these studies is called the random number generator (RNG), an electronic "coin flipper" circuit designed to quickly generate sequences of truly random bits (0's and 1's), and where the source of randomness is considered fundamentally unpredictable, like electronic noise based on quantum processes.

The RNG has proven to be a useful PK target because by design it is impervious to mundane environmental influences like fluctuations in electromagnetic fields, and it is assumed that to influence a random bit to become a 0 or a 1 would require an exceedingly small amount of energy or force. Metaphorically speaking, influencing an RNG output would only require a "feather touch." Randomness is also a convenient target of influence because the statistical behavior of random variables is well understood and is easily evaluated.

Over the past 50 years, hundreds of PK tests using RNGs have been reported, and the combined results have been published in several meta-analyses. Princeton University psychologist Roger Nelson and I published the first meta-analysis in the journal *Foundations of Physics,* in 1989. After reviewing some 800 relevant experiments, we concluded that,

The overall effect size obtained in experimental conditions cannot be adequately explained by methodological flaws or selective reporting practices. Therefore, after considering all of the retrievable evidence, published and unpublished, tempered by all legitimate criticisms raised to date, it is difficult to avoid the conclusion that under certain circumstances, consciousness interacts with random physical systems. (Radin D, Nelson R., 1989 p. 1512)

A more recent meta-analysis was published in 2006 in the journal *Psychological Bulletin* by Holger Bösch from the University Hospital in Freiburg, Germany, and his colleagues (Bosch H., Steinkamp F., Boller E., 2006). Unlike the earlier analysis that Nelson and I published, which considered all known RNG experiments, Bösch et al. excluded over 200 studies that involved animals, plants, or babies as participants, indirect forms of intention, the use of hidden targets, and experimental designs studying possible future influences. But even after excluding hundreds of those studies, Bösch et al. confirmed our conclusion that there was a significant overall effect, that the studies were generally judged to be of high quality, and that the database was heterogeneous, meaning that there was a wide range of effects reported. The only thing we disagreed upon was the *source* of that heterogeneity. Bösch et al. proposed that the heterogeneity reflected a selective reporting problem, which can inflate the results of a meta-analysis. My colleagues and I investigated why Bösch et al. had reached that conclusion, and we soon discovered why: They assumed that the effect size in RNG experiments was independent of the sample size.

This may sound like an exotic technical argument, but it's really quite simple. Here's how my colleagues and I explained it in *Psychological Bulletin*:

[Imagine] that we conduct a study involving 1,000 experienced meditators, each of whom is selected on the basis of his or her performance on a previous, similar [PK] task. Each participant is asked by a cordial, enthusiastic investigator to engage in a daily intention-focusing practice for 4 weeks in prepa-

ration for the experiment, in which he or she will be asked to intentionally influence the generation of a single random bit. Participants are told that the outcome of that random decision will determine the outcome of a meaningful bonus, such as winning a scholarship. Now consider a second study in which a bored student investigator indifferently recruits an arbitrarily selected college sophomore, who is asked to mentally influence 1,000 random bits generated in a millisecond, with no feedback of the results and no consequences regardless of the outcome.

The physical context of these two studies may be identical, using the same [RNG] and statistics to evaluate the resulting data sets, each of which consists of a total of 1,000 randomly generated bits. But it is clear that the psychological contexts differ radically. If we presume that the only important factor in this type of experiment is the number of bits generated, then the two studies should provide about the same results. But if a significant variable is the amount of time or effort one can apply in focusing mental intention toward each random event, then the former study might result in an effect size orders of magnitude larger than the latter. (Radin D., Nelson R., Dobyns Y., Houtkooper J., 2006 p. 529)

Besides the problem with Bösch et al.'s assumption about heterogeneity, we also found that they excluded three large-scale experiments as "outliers" (meaning they were much larger in size than the other studies), even though those experiments had *extremely* significant outcomes. In fact, those three studies alone contained over 210 times as much data as all of the remaining studies combined. Failing to include those successful experiments in an assessment of PK was puzzling.

Without belaboring this discussion and devolving into technical minutia, my assessment is that the evidence for PK effects on RNGs is quite clear. I have conducted many such studies and have seen positive results first-hand. The hypothesized effects don't always occur on demand because the mind side of mind-matter interactions is very difficult to control. This should not be surprising, because what form of human performance is *not* variable? Indeed, we would not pay much attention to games of sport, even if the players were the best in the world, if there wasn't some uncertainty in how they would perform. Those very same uncertainties reduce the size and reliability of effects observed in PK studies, but fortunately by collecting enough data we can gain confidence that the effects are quite real.

Implications for the Digital Age

If mind-matter interactions do exist at the individual level, then what happens when many minds focus their attention *en masse*? This brings us to the topic of the present volume.

The world in the digital age is rapidly approaching Teilhard de Chardin's concept of the noosphere: a world-wide mind, supported by the Internet and interconnected by billions of minds and their smartphones (Teilhard de Chardin P., 1959). News events which once took weeks to travel to a few people by pony express, and then days by telegraph to small groups, then hours by newspapers to thousands, and then minutes by television to millions, are now available in seconds to billions, simultaneously. This massive form of instant connection is a new phenomenon in human history.

Are these massive mental interconnections affecting the world? In a trivial way, of course they are. On the negative side, it makes the masses more easily manipulated by the media and by advertising. On the positive side, tragedies like racially motivated shootings and terrorist attacks can now spark dramatic political reactions in hours. Once rigidly held social norms, like rejection of same-sex marriage, public display of the Confederate flag, and prohibition of marijuana, are all being swept away at an unprecedented rate.

But what about nontrivial effects? Is the noosphere actually awakening, as Teilhard de Chardin predicted? One way to find out is to conduct RNG experiments on a mass scale to see if there are global-level mind-matter interactions. Such studies, dubbed "field consciousness" experiments, were started by Roger Nelson in the early 1990s.

These experiments were inspired by the observation of groups experiencing moments of being "in the zone," or "in the flow," or "on the same wavelength." During numinous religious rituals, meditating at sacred sites, resonating with emotionally stirring speeches, engaging in team sports and singing in choruses, we find that the normally scattered attentions of individuals seem to gel into a single mind. People who have experienced being in "the zone" instantly recognize the feeling. Experiments in field consciousness explore whether such mentally felt shifts are associated with measurable *physical* changes in the environment. That is, these studies ask: If mind and matter are really relational rather than absolutely separate, then when many minds become unusually coherent, does matter also become more coherent?

To find out, RNGs are used for the same reason they have been used in testing the effects of individuals' intention -- because they are physical systems that designed to produce maximum entropy (randomness), and as such if unexpected moments of mental order appear, that order can be easily detected.

Over a hundred field consciousness experiments have been reported in contexts ranging from mediation groups to theatrical presentations, sports games to religious festivals; all of which are events where moments of mass attention can be inferred (Nelson R.D., Radin D.I., Shoup R., Bancel P., 2002; Radin D.I., 2002; Nelson R.D., Jahn R.G., Dunne B.J., Dobyns Y.H., Bradish G.J., 1998). The cumulative evidence strongly supports the existence of a genuine mass-mind-matter interaction. All of those studies were conducted by simply placing one or more RNGs in the vicinity of a group, and then analyzing the resulting data afterwards. In most of those studies the individuals in the groups had no idea that RNGs were present.

Global Consciousness Project

In 1998, Roger Nelson proposed to take the next step in these studies and create what he called the Global Consciousness Project (Nelson, R., Bancel, P., 2011) which, since 2015, has been known as the Global-Mind Project (Nelson R., Bancel P., 2011). This effort was designed to expand the field consciousness experiment from the study of small groups engaged in one-off events, to large-scale occurrences that attracted global attention, including events that were not publicly known or planned in advance. This was made possible by the Internet, which allowed us to create a network of dozens of continuously running time-synchronized RNGs located in major cities around the world.

The testable hypothesis of the GCP was that during a major event, a sizable fraction of the world's attention – millions to billions of people – could be inferred to focus their attention on that event. As a result of that sudden rise in mental coherence, which might last from a few minutes to hours, we could predict that RNGs located around the world would begin to exhibit coherent behavior as well, reflected by a change in the outputs of the RNGs, from random to orderly.

As a metaphor, the GCP may be thought of as a "mental tsunami" detector. To detect tsunamis in the ocean, scores of buoys are scattered around to dance upon the waves. Each buoy has the equivalent of a bell attached to it. The sounds made by each buoy's bell are transmitted to a land-based central receiving station, which receives all of the radio transmissions and consolidates them to form a single collective tone reflecting the ocean's grand dance. Most of the time that sound is unpatterned, similar to the random tinkling one might hear from a set of wind chimes swinging in the breeze. But every so often the buoys unexpectedly synchronize and their tones swell into a great harmonic chord. When that happens, we know that something big has affected the entire ocean.

Buoys record movements on the ocean's surface, but the ocean is deep. So the "something big" might be due to an earthquake, or to a meteorite landing in the ocean, or even to something quite subtle stirring in the depths. Likewise, occasionally the world-wide network of RNGs will spontaneously shift into a coherent state. As a result – and this is a very important point – it would not be a legitimate experiment to attempt to match unexpected deviations in randomness to world events. That would be much too open to potential bias of the part of the analysts. So instead, in a rigorously predefined way *before* any of the GCP data are examined, a period of time is established that clearly defines the world-wide event of interest (typically a few hours before to a few hours after the event), and only then are the data examined using a standardized method to see if it deviates from chance expectation.

Between August 1998 and August 2015, a total of 493 events of global interest had been defined by the GCP (May & Marwaha, 2014). The data during these events were analyzed and then double-checked by independent analysts. The events included New Year celebrations, natural disasters, terrorist activity, mass meditations, sports events, outbreaks of war, outbreaks of peace, deaths of celebrities, and so on. The overall results show an unambiguous deviation from chance, with odds against chance of nearly 3 trillion to 1. This means that when a sizable proportion of the planet's population focuses their attention toward the same event, a measure of physical coherence in the world definitely changes.

The Quickening Noosphere

Given the accelerating spread of instant connectivity around the world, mass-mind moments are becoming increasingly common. How will this affect the physical world? We don't know, yet. But, if the GCP results are correct, and so far multiple analyses suggest that they are, then the global mind is indeed reshaping the world around us in extraordinary ways.

Just as most climate scientists now agree that the global climate is being influenced by human activities, and just as a host of cultural beliefs and habits are being influenced by mass social attention, more subtle aspects of the environment are also being influenced. At this point it is not entirely clear what effect these physical changes may have on humanity as a whole, or on the planet. But that *something* is stirring is becoming more apparent, day by day.

Looking toward the future, in 1959 Teilhard de Chardin wrote,

Under the increasing tension of the mind on the surface of the globe, we may begin by asking seriously whether life will not perhaps one day succeed in ingeniously forcing the bars of its earthly prison, either by finding the means to invade other inhabited planets or (a still more giddy perspective) by getting into psychical touch with other focal points of consciousness across the abysses of space. The meeting and mutual fecundation of two noospheres is a supposition which may seem at first crazy, but which after all is merely extending to psychical phenomena a scope no-one would think of denying to material phenomena. Consciousness would thus finally construct itself by a synthesis of planetary units. (1959 p. 286)

To which we might add, thereby leading ultimately to a conscious universe, whose imaginal capabilities might, if it wished, create whole new universes. Perhaps the clearest depiction of this idea is in Isaac Asimov's short story, "The Last Question." Given the results of a century of research on psychic phenomena, and the accumulating results of the GCP experiment, Teilhard de Chardin's giddy vision no longer seems so crazy.

Dean Radin
Institute of Noetic Sciences (IONS), USA & Sonoma State University, USA
August 27, 2015

Dean Radin, *PhD, is Chief Scientist at the Institute of Noetic Sciences (IONS) and Volunteer Faculty in the Department of Psychology at Sonoma State University. His original career track as a concert violinist shifted into science after earning a BSEE degree in electrical engineering, magna cum laude with honors in physics, from the University of Massachusetts, Amherst, and then an MS in electrical engineering and a PhD in psychology from the University of Illinois, Urbana-Champaign. For a decade he worked on advanced telecommunications R&D at AT&T Bell Laboratories and GTE Laboratories. For over two decades he has been engaged in frontiers research on the nature of consciousness. Before joining the research staff at IONS in 2001, he held appointments at Princeton University, University of Edinburgh, University of Nevada, Interval Research Corporation, and SRI International. He is author or coauthor of over 200 technical and popular articles, a dozen book chapters, and several books including the award-winning and bestselling The Conscious Universe (HarperOne, 1997), Entangled Minds (Simon & Schuster, 2006), and a 2014 Silver Nautilus Book Award, Supernormal (Random House, 2013). These books have been translated into a dozen foreign languages. His technical articles have appeared in journals ranging from Foundations of Physics and Physics Essays to Psychological Bulletin and Journal of Consciousness Studies; he was featured in a New York Times Magazine article; and he has appeared on dozens of television shows ranging from the BBC's Horizon and PBS's Closer to Truth to Oprah and Larry King Live. He has given over 350 interviews and talks, including invited presentations at Harvard, Stanford, Cambridge, Princeton, and the Sorbonne, for industries including Google and Johnson & Johnson, and for US government organizations including the US Navy and DARPA. In 2010, he spent a month lecturing in India as the National Visiting Professor of the Indian Council of Philosophical Research, a program within the Indian government's Ministry of Human Resource Development. In 2013 and 2014, he gave invited lectures in Kuala Lumpur at the International Center for Leadership and Governance, an organization supported by the Central Bank of Malaysia. In 2015 he spoke at the Australian Leadership Retreat, a program "designed to present participants, drawn from the highest levels of business and other sectors, with broader insights to inform their strategies, through a series of exclusive and confidential briefings and discussions led by a distinguished group of Australian and international speakers."*

REFERENCES

Asimov, I. (2015). *The Last Question*. Retrieved from http://www.physics.princeton.edu/ph115/LQ.pdf

Bosch, H., Steinkamp, F., & Boller, E. (2006). Examining psychokinesis: The interaction of human intention with random number generators—a meta-analysis. *Psychological Bulletin, 132*(4), 497–523. doi:10.1037/0033-2909.132.4.497 PMID:16822162

Brenner, E. M. (1990). Gnosticism and psychology. Jung's Septem sermones ad mortuos. *The Journal of Analytical Psychology*, *35*(4), 397–419. doi:10.1111/j.1465-5922.1990.00397.x PMID:2283345

Colman, W. (2011). Synchronicity and the meaning-making psyche. *The Journal of Analytical Psychology*, *56*(4), 471–491. doi:10.1111/j.1468-5922.2011.01924.x PMID:21884094

Feather, S. R., & Schmicker, M. (2005). *The gift: ESP, the extraordinary experiences of ordinary people* (1st ed.). New York: St. Martin's Press.

Fish, S. (1996). A brief history of theosophy. *Journal of Christian Nursing, 13*(3), 12–13. PMID:9362808

Graff, D. E. (2003). *Tracks in the psychic wilderness: an exploration of ESP, remote viewing, precognitive dreaming and synchronicity*. London: Vega.

Greene, B. (2004). *The fabric of the cosmos: space, time, and the texture of reality* (1st ed.). New York: A.A. Knopf.

Herbert, N. (1985). *Quantum reality: beyond the new physics*. Garden City, N.Y.: Anchor Press/Doubleday.

Horowitz, M. (2009). *Occult America: the secret history of how mysticism shaped our nation* (1st ed.). New York: Bantam Books.

Huxley, A. (2004). The perennial philosophy (1st Perennial Classics ed.). New York: Perennial Classics.

Jung, C. G. (1959). *The archetypes and the collective unconscious*. New York: Pantheon Books.

May, E. C., & Marwaha, S. B. (2014). *Anomalous cognition: remote viewing research and theory*. Jefferson, North Carolina: McFarland & Company, Inc.

Nelson, R., & Bancel, P. (2004). Effects of Mass Consciousness: Changes in Random Data during Global Events. *Explore (New York, N.Y.), 7*(6), 373–383. PMID:22051562

Nelson, R. D., Jahn, R. G., Dunne, B. J., Dobyns, Y. H., & Bradish, G. J. (1998). FieldREG II: Consciousness Field Effects: Replications and Explorations. *Journal of Scientific Exploration, 12*(3), 425–454.

Nelson, R. D., Radin, D. I., Shoup, R., & Bancel, P. (2002). Correlation of continuous random data with major world events. *Foundations of Physics Letters, 15*(6), 537–550. doi:10.1023/A:1023981519179

Radin, D. (2006). *Entangled Minds*. New York: Simon & Schuster.

Radin, D. (2006). Experiments Testing Models of Mind-Matter Interaction. *Journal of Scientific Exploration, 20*(3), 375–401.

Radin, D. (2013). *Supernormal*. New York: Random House.

Radin, D., & Nelson, R. (1989). Evidence for consciousness-related anomalies in random physical systems. *Foundations of Physics, 19*(12), 1499–1514. doi:10.1007/BF00732509

Radin, D., Nelson, R., Dobyns, Y., & Houtkooper, J. (2006). Reexamining psychokinesis: Commentary on the Bösch, Steinkamp and Boller meta-analysis. *Psychological Bulletin, 2006*, 529–532. doi:10.1037/0033-2909.132.4.529 PMID:16822164

Radin, D. I. (1997). *The conscious universe*. San Francisco, CA: HarperOne.

Radin, D. I. (2002). Exploring relationships between random physical events and mass human attention: Asking for whom the bell tolls. *Journal of Scientific Exploration, 16*(4), 533–548.

Radin, D. I. (2004). Electrodermal presentiments of future emotions. *Journal of Scientific Exploration, 18*, 253–274.

Rowan, J. (2005). *The transpersonal: spirituality in psychotherapy and counselling* (2nd ed.). New York: Routledge.

Stachel, J. J. (2005). Einstein's miraculous year: five papers that changed the face of physics (Centenary ed.). Princeton, NJ: Princeton University Press.

Teilhard de Chardin, P. (1959). *The phenomenon of man*. New York: Harper.

Wallace, B. A., & Hodel, B. (2012). *Dreaming yourself awake: lucid dreaming and Tibetan dream yoga for insight and transformation* (1st ed.). Boston: Shambhala.

Zabriskie, B. (2005). Synchronicity and the I Ching: Jung, Pauli, and the Chinese woman. *The Journal of Analytical Psychology*, *50*(2), 223–235. doi:10.1111/j.0021-8774.2005.00525.x PMID:15817044

Preface

PREPARING FOR THE AGE OF VIRTUAL ILLUSION

In 1962, Thomas Kuhn defined a paradigm shift as a change of basic assumptions within the ruling theory of science. According to Kuhn, an epistemological *paradigm shift* or a "scientific revolution" occurs when scientists encounter anomalies that cannot be explained by the universally accepted paradigm within which scientific progress has thereto been made. In Kuhn's view, the paradigm constitutes a worldview and all of the implications that come with it—all features in the landscape of knowledge that scientists can identify. The so-called atomic age presaged such a shift, but that was only the beginning. For decades we have witnessed the emergence of a media age of illusion—a virtual reality as unified field of energy and information—that is based on correlations between principles of physics— multi-dimensionality, immateriality, and non-locality—and the principles of myth—psychology, symbolic meaning, and linguistic structure. The incipient stage of the paradigm shift has already reframed the cognitive unconscious of individuals and collectives and generated a worldview in which mediated illusion prevails in nearly every field of human endeavor. Though professional opinion and—increasingly—research in computer science, cognition, artificial intelligence, and psycho-energetics is contributing to the understanding of reality as illusion, the significance of this demonstrable fact is still unappreciated, and it is not factored into personal and collective behavior nor policy decisions in such critical areas as government, environment, education, and commerce.

The literature—both academic and popular—addressing this virtual reality is longstanding and literally vast. The purpose of this book is not to document all these arguments, but to provide a timely and manageable focus for research on the strange and paradoxical nature of virtual reality—reality as illusion. The book includes an array of informed opinion and research from diverse fields relative to this paradigm shift in perceived reality. Chapters focus on the neuro-electrical dynamics at work in dreams and Psychecology Games (PEG). Video games are a good place to start when addressing cognitive-perceptual reality because they are prime exemplars of the nature of the paradigm shift. The Target audience includes anyone who may inhabit the impending virtual reality, but the critical audience includes policy makers and creative workers in the fields of government, education, media, video games, film, the arts, and commerce.

Exploring the Collective Unconscious in a Digital Age investigates the cognitive significance of an altered mediated reality that appears to have all the dimensions of a dreamscape. The hypothesis is that the psychological nature of the global electronic media environment is dreamlike and can be analyzed like dreams using the dream analog of *Psych*ecology video games (PEG). In other words, if the digital media-sphere proves to be structurally and functionally analogous to a Jungian dreamscape, the Collective Unconscious researched by Carl Jung and the Cognitive Unconscious researched by George Lakoff are susceptible to research according to parameters of hard science. Neuro-electrical cognitive patterns simulated by sophisticated algorithms in the digital unconscious—virtual realities—are not only based on what is known about the structure of the brain and nervous system but what is known about molecular levels of Psyche. In other words, the connections between computational reality and perceptual-cognitive reality have already been established, but a great deal of ongoing research will be necessary in order to begin addressing the scope of the paradigm shift.

The thesis of the book is essentially holistic, and this is daunting because the term holistic is unacceptable to many even though the physical principles of holography are experiencing an explosion within the realm of the mediated holographic reality—the virtual reality. Wholeness is very difficult to contemplate because the term is redolent of mysticism, magic, and incense. Even though modern hard science is indisputably holistic, the ramifications of such a fact go well beyond the comfort zone of many. One objective of this book is to provide diverse and convincing expert perspectives on the suggestion that there exists a practical and manageable process for researching the illusion and for fostering benign wholeness or healing throughout the planet. In order to make such a suggestion viable, an effort is made to outline the general parameters of the challenge without losing the audience.

In a nutshell, the argument is that *Psych*ecology games have all of the structural and functional aspects of Jungian dreams, and that Jungian dreams as archetypal projections of unconscious psyche are directly analogous to media dreams as archetypal projections of the collective unconscious. Because they are dream analogs, PEG can provide access to meaningful "archetypal" patterns existing in unconscious molecular dimensions of psyche that are projected as "archetypal representations" or virtual illusions in the mediated reality. Such study of the unconscious psychological dynamics of the media-sphere could provide benign insight in order to discover its neurobiological dynamics and to promote *meaningful insight and coherent states* within contextual collectives using mediated biofeedback.

Arguments in the various chapters are addressed to a focus on what has been called the *Psychecology, Metaverse,* or *Media Sphere* that has been defined as an ecology of the world's media including newspapers, journals, television, radio, books, novels, advertising, press releases, publicity and the blogosphere—any and all media both broadcast and published. Observation clearly suggests the veracity of the shift. However, there is a paucity of recommendations as to practical accommodations for the paradox of the absolute—of wholeness. Carl Jung was one of the first and the few philosopher-scientists to grapple with the cognitive dimensions of illusion and its source in unconscious dimensions, and though Jung has been recognized as one of the world's greatest psychiatrists, it is only in the light of modern physics that the scope of his genius and prescience can be assessed.

What are these cognitive dimensions of the unconscious and how can PEG access meaning in benign ways without violating human autonomy? The first of Jung's keys to cognitive dimension is "interactivity". Jung's entire theory and practice depends upon interactivity—the fact that the symbolic dream language changes as the cognitive state of the "patient" changes. In the game industry, interactivity is generally understood as choice-making by the player in order to alter the progression of the game—as represented by symbolic images on the computer monitor. Video games constitute an interactive breakthrough that enables dream research. Apparently, these contextual archetypal images on the game monitor comport with the archetypal images in dreams, and—as in dreams—the images change according to interactive choices. This constitutes the dynamic essence of both healing and learning, cause and effect, trial and error, meaningful insight based on "stored" collateral patterns of metaphorical frequency, and the achievement of coherent states such as Flow or transcendence. In the case of dreams, Jung researched the interactivity in terms of multi-functionality (sensing, feeling, thinking, intuiting). Today, this multi-functionality can be tracked technologically (EEG, ECG, fMRI, MEG) as neuro-energetic signatures. Interactive choices made during gameplay reflect unconscious cognitive patterns that ultimately lead to learning or healing. The dramatic structure of dream-games (explained in various chapters) provides an unprecedented scope and authenticity for the study of dramatic interactivity. Due to the dynamic scope of game-choices, as experience they could prove to be equally as authentic as autonomous choices in so-called "real life" experience.

We now know that advertisements are real-life experiences. It may be stipulated that advertising and now "neuro-marketing" is based on the principle of psychological association. Representative (contextual) focus groups are researched in order to discover their inclinations, and the discovery is applied to the creation of symbolic advertisements targeted to and associated with inclinations of well-defined contextual collectives. Since Edward Bernase fostered Freudian dynamics in advertising (Curtis, 2002), it has been so effective that the advertising industry has changed cultural reality from a needs-based to a wants-based cultural dynamic that is known as consumerism. It may be argued that this consumerism is both highly manipulative and naturally unsustainable. Psychological association as employed in traditional advertising has always been essentially manipulative and limited to one objective—financial profit. The Jungian-Lakoffian dynamics recommended in the book are not manipulative because they are multi-functional and their systematized motives are self-realization and healing as opposed to simplistic financial profit. Jungian-Lakoffian objectives prove to foster multi-functional coherence or harmony that has healing-teaching potential, is natural, and is highly sustainable. Moreover, the dramatic context is much more comprehensive and authentic than simple association. These dynamics are addressed in the book.

The virtual worldview has many names including metaverse, media-sphere, and *Psych*ecology which are attempts to nominalize the emergent reality of illusion. Materialistic science has long associated the phenomena of the illusory-energetic worldview with primitivism, or "fringe science". However, as hard science, physics has prevailed and the reality of virtual illusions that physics has bequeathed humanity in the form of media, artificial intelligence, and virtual realities has become accepted fact. Ancient mythic and scientific knowledge are merging. Many scientists—especially physicists—have correlated the nature of physics with the nature of myth, and this has created a stage upon which the paradigm shift is being played. The language of myth and science has been merging. A case in point is the Doctrine of Avatars that—from an informed understanding—is a psycho-energetic phenomenon (Paladin, 2015). The great avatar teachers (Christ, Buddha, Gandhi, et al.) are central to mythology, and Avatars may be understood as personifications of energy patterns understood as principles such as "Compassion" and "love". Avatars are exemplars of evolutionary principles or frequency shifts (spirit) which initiate comprehensive reality shifts that lead to greater coherence and sustainability. In the game industry, the term is applied to the protagonist through which a player makes choices and wins or loses the game. Perhaps unknowingly, the term avatar is correctly used: a higher being (player) employs a virtual image (avatar/game protagonist) as a simulation in the virtual reality of the game which—like dreams—has an evolutionary purpose.

The informed understanding that the symbolic languages of myth and modern science are closely related has not yet been fully appreciated. Such applications as Jungian dream analysis—with its comprehensive theory and clinical data—has not yet been employed by scientific researchers though it has been cited by a plethora of top scientists—mostly physicists –Chopra, Radin, Capra, Eddington, Jeans, Oppenheimer, Russel, Whitehead, Schrödinger, et al. (Foster, David, 1985).

The meaningful relationship between myth and science arises from the resurgent understanding that both may be understood as representations of psycho-energetic phenomena. Chi, mana, Ginungegap, and alchemy may be understood in terms of psycho-energetics, and the structure of the Tao, Tetractys, dreams, Pleroma, and Ain Soph, may be understood as archetypal energy patterns within the framework of a unified field. Due to the diversity and scope of this statement, documentation is impossible; however, it may be stipulated that the materialist worldview is now archaic and the study of psycho-energetics is becoming the focus of hard scientific attention—especially robotics, artificial intelligence, and cognition-based algorithms.

According to ancient precedents and medieval science, classical *aether*--also called the *quintessence* or *spirit*—may be understood in terms of sub-atomic dimensions—"the non-material that fills the region of the universe above the terrestrial or material sphere." It may be deduced that the concept of aether was used by philosophers and metaphysicians as a default to explain several natural phenomena, such as gravity. In the late 19th century, physicists postulated that aether permeated space and provided a medium through which light could travel in a vacuum. This sounds similar to spin 1 particles. The concept of non-material aether can now be revisited in terms of energy and information, archetypes of the unconscious, a vital unified field, or the collective unconscious from which the human perceptual reality is generated.

Today, other terms such as energetics and virtual realities have replaced aether and spirit, but in the process, subjective psyche has been demoted and a phantom objectivity has become paramount in the hard-scientific understanding of "reality". What humans have learned over a period spanning millennia is still largely unacknowledged by modern science. Not fully aware of this neglect, modern science has been engaged in the process of validating ancient principles of multidimensional, multifunctional unified cosmic psyche in terms of algorithms, artificial intelligence and virtual reality—but without the overview. Nevertheless, from a growing array of perspectives—neuro-marketing to robotics—tens of thousands of books and academic papers already deal with this unified field of sentience, and researchers are making incredible progress as they discover the "scientific" basis for the ancient mysteries and begin to contemplate the nature and dynamics of what this book calls the "*Psych*ecology."

Due to the quantum leap in digital media technology, a paradigm shift in human reality concepts is well underway, and it is not uncommon to hear that the emergent technologically mediated reality is dreamlike. It may be that the key to welcoming this avatar—this transcendent guest—is to appreciate its gifts. It may be that the emergent gifts of the paradigm shift have to do with actualizing the human perception of "reality" as a self-engendered living dream. The idea that human reality is an illusion has been pervasive for millennia—"What we think is real is not real, and what we think is not real is real." (Lao Tzu) So too, the transcendent value of dreams has been a staple throughout the history of diverse cultures; however, the more advanced our physics and cognitive research become, the more the ghostly unreality of dreams becomes a viable worldview. The opportunity—the gifts—being proffered by our digital media may be related to the dramatic structure of dreams as understood by Carl Jung and of the cognitive unconscious as understood by George Lakoff. Moreover, because it may be argued that *Psych*ecology video games (PEG) are structurally analogous to Jungian dreams, PEG may be used as a cognitive research instrument for investigating and mapping the psychological "territory" and dynamics of this long-awaited guest—this Messiah, this Imam Mahdi, this Maitreya, this returning Christ.

Beyond investigation, research will lead to insight as to meaning, and this insight may lead to coherent choices and then to resolution of what seem to be intractable global problems. For nearly a century, the human worldview has been shaped by media advertising and propaganda that changes our values, alters our choices, and tends to emphasize human separateness. Increasingly, the media model for cognitive framing has been co-opted for primarily commercial purposes. *Exploring the Collective Unconscious in a Digital Age* is intended to generate a coherent discussion of a much more comprehensively understood and sustainable future based on human integrity and the connectedness of all life.

It may be argued that the holographic *psych*ecology is patterned according to four human functions that have both mythic precedence and current scientific adherence. These functions represent the four human "bodies" with which humans function: physical, mental, emotional, and spiritual. Jung called these functions: Sensing, Thinking, Feeling, and Intuiting. They are integrated, inseparable, but definable as discreet. Within a unified field of energy and information Jung's Psyche seems essentially the same as the unified field of physics. For this reason alone, Jungian theory was far ahead of most scientific thinkers of his era.

However, the significance of his research efforts is far more specific, and more scientifically relevant today than ever. Jung is known primarily for his *Analytical Psychology* that is based on analysis of dreams. Jung's basis for analysis was his empirical observation that dreams have the same structure as "good drama" as defined by Aristotle, and this dramatic framework provided a context for interpreting a series of dreams according to the symbols imbedded in them. In this clinical context, the psychiatrist serves as a highly empathetic "mentor" who provided feedback to patients in a process that can be understood as metaphorical extension. Listening with empathy to a patient's dreams over a period of time, Jung was able to discover symbolic dream motifs within the unique psychological context of a patient and to make suggestions to the patient as to the meaning of these symbols. When a patient developed insight as to the meaning of the symbols and, therefore, the meaning of his/her dreams, the patient could experience a degree of healing—release from psychological/physical disharmony. Jung developed his principles of Analytical Psychology—in great scope and detail—based on thousands of empirical observations, and explains dream dynamics in terms of coherent energy. (Jacoby) From both mythic and scientific perspectives, no one is better qualified to contemplate relevance than Dr. Dean Radin.

Dean Radin, PhD provides the Introduction to *Exploring the Collective Unconscious in a Digital Age* and—as a generative thinker of the age—supports the authenticity of its content and underlying hypothesis. Chief Scientist at the Institute of Noetic Sciences (IONS) and Volunteer Faculty in the Department of Psychology at Sonoma, Dr. Radin is author or coauthor of over 200 technical and popular articles, a dozen book chapters, and several books including the award-winning and bestselling *The Conscious Universe* (HarperOne, 1997), *Entangled Minds* (Simon & Schuster, 2006), and a 2014 Silver Nautilus Book Award, *Supernormal* (Random House, 2013). These books have been translated into a dozen foreign languages. His technical articles have appeared in journals ranging from *Foundations of Physics* and *Physics Essays* to *Psychological Bulletin* and *Journal of Consciousness Studies*; he was featured in a *New York Times Magazine* article; and he has appeared on dozens of television shows ranging from the BBC's *Horizon* and PBS's *Closer to Truth* to *Oprah* and *Larry King Live*. He has given over 350 interviews and talks, including invited presentations at Harvard, Stanford, Cambridge, Princeton, and the Sorbonne, for industries including Google and Johnson & Johnson, and for US government organizations including the US Navy and DARPA.

In his introduction, Dr. Radin describes his personal experiences with the conscious universe and the collective mind. A salient experience details a complex case of Jungian synchronicity that goes far beyond coincidence and verifies the power of mental "manifestation"—specifically with the use of "a dream yoga technique whereby intense imagery is used to 'dream' a desired outcome into being." The story Radin tells convincingly demonstrates the complexity of such manifestation and shows how it relates to the theme of the book. Implicitly, his story illustrates the dynamic discussed throughout *Exploring the Collective Unconscious in a Digital Age*—the mediated Metaverse is manifesting like a dream from the collective unconscious.

He goes on to review the scientific evidence validating the idea that mind and matter are intimately related. "This is the domain of *mundus imaginalis*, the Imaginal World so-named by French scholar Henry Corbin based on his analysis of Islamic thought, and then advanced into the notion of archetypes by Swiss psychiatrist Carl Jung." He goes on to ask he fundamental question addressed in the book, "If mind-matter interactions do exist at the individual level, then what happens when minds are focused *en masse*? This brings us to the topic of the present volume."

The world in the digital age is rapidly approaching Teilhard de Chardin's concept of the noosphere: a world-wide mind, supported by the Internet and connected by billions of smartphones. News events which once took weeks to travel to a few people by pony express, and then days by telegraph to small groups, then hours by newspapers to thousands, and then minutes by television to millions, are now available in seconds to billions, simultaneously. This massive form of instant connection is a new phenomenon in human history.

Sections

The book is divided into two sections: Section 1, *Fundamentals for Exploring the Psychological Metaverse,* establishes parameters for study of the *Psych*ecology and the correlated Metaverse, media-sphere, or collective mediated dreamscape. Section 2, *Exponentials for Exploring the Psychological Metaverse*, represents directions for continued research upon the concept that the Metaverse is energetically correlated with the *Psych*ecology (unified field) and dream structure according to Carl Jung.

Chapters

In section 1, *Chapter One* explores the dimensions of the media dream relative to synchronous dynamics in cognitive psychology and the digital Metaverse. *Chapter Two* establishes the basis for *Psych*ecology games as analog for dreams. *Chapter Three* discusses the cognitive framing of the collective unconscious and its projections in the waking dream. *Chapter Four* established the electrophyiological basis for contemplating the Metaverse as dream analog.

In section 2, *Chapter Five* explores film and video games relative to Jungian principles of dream structure. *Chapter Six* amplifies the concept of archetypal projection of the cognitive unconscious as understood by exponents of Jungian dream principles. *Chapter Seven* focuses on coherence or "Flow" as cognitive relationships that exist between dreams and the serious sport of mountaineering. *Chapter Eight* emphasizes principles of Jungian archetypal projection as it relates to healing potentials in South African film. *Chapter Nine* speculates on the archetypal hero's journey from the standpoint of an emergent understanding of psychological group contexts in the media-sphere. *Chapter Ten* provides an extensive discussion of the neurobiological *Psych*ecology as it impacts the global ionosphere.

Objectives of the Book

The objective of this book is to tap expert insight from diverse fields of research in order to establish parameters for discussion and extended research based on the assumption that cognitive correlations exist among the emergent mediated reality, dreams as defined by Carl G. Jung, the cognitive unconscious, the non-material reality of quantum physics (holography), and drama-based video games. If "dreams have a purpose" (Jung), and the above correlations truly exist, the purpose of the mediated "dreamscape" can be understood as the establishment of harmony or coherence in the human psyche (both individual and collective). Research based on these assumptions would have enormous impact on education, global media policy, and planetary coherence.

Target Audience

The target audience of this book includes anyone who hopes for the creation of sustainable social patterns in the emergent reality of energy and information. It includes professionals and researchers working in the fields of cognitive psychology, psychiatry, video game design, and various disciples of information and knowledge management, e.g. library, information and communication sciences, administrative sciences and management, education, adult education, environmental sciences, sociology, computer science, and information technology/management. Moreover, the book will provide insights that support innovators in such diverse fields as the environment, commerce, education, law, and entertainment.

REFERENCES

Bateson, G. (1972). *Steps to an ecology of mind: Collected essays in anthropology, psychiatry, evolution, and epistemology*. University Of Chicago Press.

Curtis, A. (2009). *Century of the self: Happiness machines for free. British Broadcasting Corporation, Freedocumentaries.com*. Retrieved from http://freedocumentaries.org/film.php?id=140

Foster, D. (1985). *The philosophical scientists*. USA: Dorset Press.

Jacobi, J. (1973). *The psychology of C. G. Jung*. USA: Yale University Press.

Jung, C. G. (1933). *Modern man in search of a soul*. San Diego: Harcourt Brace & Company.

Paladin. (2015). *The doctrine of avatars*. Retrieved from http://www.scam.com/showthread.php?31078-The-Doctrine-of-Avatars

Section 1

Fundamentals for Exploring the Psychological Metaverse

Section 1 establishes parameters for study of the Psychecology and the correlated Metaverse, media-sphere, or collective mediated dreamscape. Chapter one explores the dimensions of the media dream relative to synchronous dynamics in cognitive psychology and the digital Metaverse. Chapter two establishes the basis for Psychecology games as analog for dreams. Chapter three discusses the cognitive framing of the collective unconscious and its projections in the waking dream. Chapter four established the electrophyiological basis for contemplating the Metaverse as dream analog.

Chapter 1
Exploring Dimensions of the Media Dream:
Functional Context in Collective Personae

Rollin McCraty
Institute of HeartMath, USA

Stephen Brock Schafer
Pacific Rim Enterprises, USA

ABSTRACT

The earth's magnetic fields are carriers of biologically relevant information that connects all living systems. The electromagnetic coupling of the human brain, cardiovascular and nervous systems, and geomagnetic frequencies supports the hypothesis that the mediated reality of electromagnetic bandwidths can be correlated with bio-energetic and geomagnetic frequencies. Understood as bio-energetic functions (Thinking, Feeling, Sensing, & Intuiting), the media-sphere becomes measurable according to principles of coherency (measured as heart-rate variability, HRV) and principles of Jungian dream analysis (compensation and dramatic structure). It has been demonstrated that the rhythmic patterns in beat-to-beat heart rate variability reflect emotional functions, permeate every bodily cell, and play a central role in the generation and transmission of system-wide information via the electromagnetic field. So, the "media dream" becomes susceptible to psychological analysis leading to a better understanding of unconscious cognitive archetypal patterns of contextual collectives.

INTRODUCTION

If the degree of harmony and coherence between conscious and unconscious dimensions of human cognition can be increased and attuned to biochemical, digital, and geomagnetic frequencies in the Earth- ionosphere, it is probable that such harmonious energetic fields would improve the quality of life on earth. Happily, the principles and tools for researching the dreamscape are available. (Schafer, Stephen, and Yu, Gino (2011; Schafer, Stephen, 2007; Schafer, Stephen, 2011; Schafer, Stephen, 2012) *Fourier transforms* are the mathematical key to correlating these diverse dimensions. This type of cal-

DOI: 10.4018/978-1-4666-9891-8.ch001

culus, invented by an eighteenth century Frenchman named Jean B. J. Fourier, is a mathematical way of "converting any pattern, no matter how complex, into a language of simple waves. He also showed how these wave forms could be converted back into the original pattern." (Talbot, 1991, p.27)

Fourier transforms enabled the theoretical formulation of holograms in 1947 by Dennis Gabor (who later won a Nobel Prize for his work). Holograms are illusions that seem to have extension in space. This is accomplished by converting a picture of an object into a blur of interference patterns on a piece of holographic film and back into an image of the original objects. The hologram is a virtual image that possesses no more extension in space than does the three dimensional image you see of yourself in a mirror. (Talbot, p 24) In other words, holograms are illusions that employ the same mathematical principles that generate the digital media-sphere. Increasingly, scientific evidence confirms the relationships among different scales in the unified field of energy and information. Researching the media-sphere according to principles of cognitive processes could lead to a better understanding of ethical, coherent behavior in collective dimensions. (Schafer, Stephen and Palamides, Thomas (2011)

One of the byproducts of holographic research has been the realization that—when an image or pattern is translated into the Fourier language of wave forms—the whole exists within every part. This realization has set the stage for using holography to model the transition—the paradigm shift—into a mediated reality. Ironically, the existence of the whole within the part has ancient precedent. It was a fundamental principle of Alchemy as represented metaphorically as *the seed*. (Hall, 2003, pp. 494-524) Interestingly, the alchemical metaphor of translating base metal into gold can also be understood in terms of experimentation with energetic frequencies. Based on the discovery of the DNA molecule, the principle of wholeness within the part has become fundamental to the science of genetic manipulation.

Since frequency is a measure of the number of oscillations a wave undergoes per second, mathematical conversion of the holographic principle into the domain of neurobiology became feasible. Advances in magnetic resonance imaging have become increasingly non-intrusive. Recent studies have reported successful classification of patients with multiple sclerosis, Alzheimer's disease, schizophrenia, Sjögren's syndrome, chronic alcoholism, and facial pain with the use of a promising new technology known as magnetoencephalography (MEG). Using a very sensitive magnetometer, MEG is a functional neuroimaging technique for neurofeedback and for mapping brain activity by recording magnetic fields produced by electrical currents occurring naturally in the brain and. Arrays of SQUIDs (superconducting quantum interference devices) are currently the most common magnetometer, while the SERF (spin exchange relaxation-free) magnetometer is being investigated for future machines.

MEG can be used to distinguish these patients from healthy control subjects, suggesting a future role of MEG in diagnostics. (Georgopoulos, et al, 2007; Montez, et al, 2009) Synchronized neuronal currents induce weak magnetic fields, and synchronicity is an important aspect of coherence relative to heart-rate variability (HRV) as well as Jungian Compensation. Such measurements during real-time game-play are feasible in order to provide information relative to frequency patterns that can then be applied to the media-sphere.

MEG determines the location of electric activity within the brain from the induced magnetic fields outside the head. MEG can resolve events with a precision of 10 milliseconds or faster, while functional magnetic resonance imaging (fMRI), which depends on changes in blood flow, can at best resolve events with a precision of several hundred milliseconds. MEG also accurately pinpoints sources in primary auditory, somatosensory, and motor areas. For creating functional maps of human cortex during more complex cognitive tasks, MEG is most often combined with fMRI, as the methods complement each other. (Ibid) Psychologists are also taking advantage of MEG neuroimaging to better understand relationships between brain function and behavior. For example, a number of studies have been done comparing the MEG responses of patients with psychological troubles to control patients. There has been great success isolating unique responses in patients with schizophrenia, such as auditory gating deficits to human voices (Hirano, et al, 2010). MEG is also being used to correlate standard psychological responses, such as the emotional dependence of language comprehension (Ihara, et al, 2012).

So, cognitive research is based on mathematics of Fourier transforms (FT) and holography in order to correlate neurobiological functions with imaging technology, and it is well-understood that FT articulate dimensions (bandwidths) of the media-sphere. Recent discovery of orchestrated vibrations in synaptic microtubules (Hameroff & Penrose) strengthens the potential for discovery relative to quantum-molecular relationships. If geomagnetic frequencies are also based on FT, the mathematics may be used to establish multi-dimensional coherence and to research the *Psych*ecology with drama-based video games. (Schafer, 2008)

With the advance of the technological media age, a Khunian paradigm shift in ontology and epistemology is altering the human worldview. The human reality is becoming more dreamlike. According to common sense, observation, and scientific research, the extraordinary degree to which modern technological development has changed human reality seems obvious. Stephen Kosslyn's Image and Brain (Kosslyn, 1994) focuses on "seeing with the mind's eye"—the internal representation that is used in information processing.

Theories about the role of imagery in information processing took a leap forward when researchers began to think about how one could program a computer to produce specific behavior. To program a computer to mimic imagery, one must specify an image representation with particular properties; a representation is a type of code, a way of specifying information. (Kosslyn, 1994 pp. 3-4)

But in spite of the other-worldly miracles of the digital reality and its offspring, the Metaverse or media-sphere, the vast potential of this altered reality of illusion has barely begun to be addressed. Relevant research discussing the impacts of sex and violence in the media—especially video games—is longstanding, and a recent extensively documented publication titled, "Video Games Do Affect Social Outcomes" is available. (Greitemeyer & Mügge, 2015)

However, though fundamental principles and tools for researching the media-sphere as dreamscape are available, the cognitive significance of this illusory reality is not being researched or realized in a timely way. A cursory survey of the media (Internet, television, film, and video games), confirms that they are saturated with sensationalism, trivia, sex, violence, disinformation, commercialism, wars and rumors of wars. Though all knowledge seems available only a finger's touch away, the cognitive faculties that allow for integration of this massive data into meaningful insight are yet to be effectively addressed. Even worse, beyond the skin of sensationalist trivia exist real threats of catastrophic misuse of the powers of illusion—universal surveillance, militarism, lies and propaganda, and the fostering of a global fear, terror, delusion, and psychological defensiveness. Such misuse of media has been extensively documented by Adam Curtis in such works as the BBC's Happiness Machines, The Power of Nightmares, and The Trap (Curtis, Adam, 2002).

BACKGROUND

According to Carl Jung, the unconscious aspect of *psyche* is much like a *unified field*:

Sooner or later nuclear physics and the psychology of the unconscious will draw closer together as both of them, independently of one another and from opposite directions, push forward into transcendental territory, the one with the concept of the atom, the other with that of the archetype. (Aion, p. 69, from Jacoby, 1973)

Video games generated from the unified field of the media-sphere appear to provide an appropriate connection between physics and psychology. A video game is an electronic game that involves human interaction with a user interface to generate visual feedback on a video device. Video games typically use additional sensory means such as speakers and headphones for audio and haptic peripherals that employ vibration to simulate force feedback. The word *video* in *video game* traditionally referred to a raster display device, but display devices have evolved and now produce two- or three-dimensional images. The electronic systems used to play video games are known as platforms; examples of these are personal computers and video game consoles. Today, platforms range from large mainframe computers to smart phones. Since the early days of arcade games, video games have evolved to become a global industry. In order to "play" video games, input devices for manipulating screen content have become diverse and ubiquitous. A few of the most common game controllers are game pads, mouses, keyboards, and joysticks. In recent years, additional methods of input have emerged such as camera-based player observation for video game consoles and touch screens on mobile devices.

Interactive influence on game images comports with the fundamental Jungian principles based on the "interactivity" of dreams; i.e. symbolic patterns in a patient's dreams change as the patient gains insight as to their meaning. (Jacoby, 1973, p. 10) Dreams employ a symbolic language that communicates messages between that part of the dreamer's brain that is conscious and that part that is unconscious. Because the interactive button-pushing in games translates a complex cognitive process into a monitor image, the interactive process articulates the psychological process. This interactivity represents an important breakthrough that incorporates total functionality in the mediating process. In the sense that players make psychological choices and take action based on the images (and other sensory data) in their perceived reality, psychecology games can be understood as simulations of "real" experience in which causal behavior is generated and consequences of the behavior materializes as images. So doing, psychecology games are simulating a psychological "multi-functional" reality based on a repository if unconscious memories and interpretations of their experience that Jung calls the personal and collective unconscious. (Schafer, 2012) Unconscious cognitive dimensions may be correlated with technological software that is measurably generative and unconscious relative to the user.

Using interactive feedback—primarily images—Psychecology games are employing cognitive alchemy, mathematics, and symbolic language to translate the unknown into the known. This can lead to meaningful insight into dimensions of the unknown, and this dynamic is the basis for learning and healing. Increasing use of interactivity in the paraphernalia of mediation has added new urgency to the need for addressing the psychological dimensions of the media-sphere. It should not be long before a large percentage of the population makes the connection between interactivity, the unconscious dynamics (such as non-locality) of psyche-physics, and the fact of influence at a distance. It is probable that unless coherence is fostered in the initial stages of realization, the magic of human functionality in the media-sphere (action, thought, intuition, and feeling at a distance) will be characterized by large scale misuse and negativity.

This chapter will provide evidence that because multi-functionality is standard in personality profiling such as Myers-Briggs and Big 5, functions may be correlated with frequencies of energy in a unified field of psyche-physics. Also, employing linguistic principles such as dramatic unities and the archetypal model of the hero's journey to analyze the media-sphere and to provide mediated biofeedback could enhance potentials for achieving coherent states in collective personae. (Schafer, 2012)

The chapter, *The Dream Analog*, argues the efficacy of researching the cognitive unconscious with psychecology games. In this chapter, we expand on data supporting the hypothesis that the earth's magnetic fields are carriers of biologically relevant information that connects all living systems. Such interconnectedness implies that our attitudes, emotions and intentions are highly significant and that coherent, cooperative intent can impact global events and the quality of life on Earth.

The proposed research instrument for addressing the cognitive dynamics of Psyche is psychecology video games. In order to integrate human potential with the new ontological and epistemological order introduced by an impending age of illusion, the multi-functional cognitive unconscious must be addressed. Viewing the media-sphere as a dreamscape according to parameters of Jungian dream analysis is by far the most comprehensive—and practical—strategy available. Though it remains to be proven, dream analysis incorporates the dynamics necessary to address the practical issues of global social pathology and to foster multi-dimensional coherence.

EXPLORING DIMENSIONS OF THE MEDIA DREAM

The Global Information Field

For millennia, human activities have been associated with astrological observations that are based in the mathematics and empirical observations of the great cultures of all ages. Currently data from solar and geomagnetic field detectors and human nervous system activity as reflected in heart rate variability (HRV) show that human physiological rhythms and collective behaviors are not only synchronized with solar and geomagnetic activity, but disruptions in these fields can create adverse multi-functional mental, emotional and physiological effects, while other solar and magnetic indices are correlated with improved HRV and mental and emotional states.

The convergence of several independent lines of evidence provides strong support for the existence of a global information field that connects all living systems and contributes to a type of global consciousness. Every cell in our body is bathed in an external and internal environment of fluctuating invisible magnetic forces that can affect virtually every cell and circuit in biological systems. Therefore, it should not be surprising that numerous physiological rhythms in humans and global collective behaviors are not only synchronized with solar and geomagnetic activity, but disruptions in these fields can create adverse effects on human health and behavior.

The most likely mechanism for explaining how solar and geomagnetic influences affect human health and behavior are a coupling between the human nervous system and resonating geomagnetic frequencies called Schumann resonances, Alven Waves and other very low frequency resonances which occur in the earth-ionosphere resonant cavity. It is well established that these resonant frequencies directly overlap with those of the human brain, cardiovascular and autonomic nervous systems. Overwhelming scientific-environmental evidence supports the hypothesis that all living systems are interconnected via the earth's magnetic field, which can act as a carrier wave of biologically relevant and pattered information. In order to advance this research, a global network of 12 to 14 ultrasensitive magnetic field detectors, specifically designed to measure the earth's magnetic resonances, are being installed strategically around the planet. An important goal of the project is to motivate as many people as possible to work together in a more coherent and collaborative manor to lift the collective human consciousness.

If we are persuaded by both ancient precedent and current science that not only external fields of solar and cosmic origins, but also human consciousness and emotion projected into the media-sphere can affect the mental and emotional states of others, it broadens our view of what interconnectedness means and how it can be intentionally utilized to shape the future of the world we live in. Observing the Media-sphere as a dreamscape and correlating psychological data with bio-energetic data may provide additional proof of the quality and meaning of human/cultural attitudes, emotions, and intentions—especially as it is projected into the media dream. As to these projections, they are available to conscious/unconscious perception by way of images on an array of media devices. Research by Reeves and Nass in The Media Equation, proved the hypothesis that—at unconscious levels—people experience such images in the same way they experience "reality." (Reeves & Nass, 1996) This is not surprising in the emergent mediated reality where, clearly, the interactive media become a significant aspect of reality that influences functional behavior. Based on accordance with an array of such research, it becomes possible to research the holographic nature of the *Psych*ecology. With a better understanding of the dynamics of image perception, the correlations among perceptual, holographic, cognitive, neurobiological, and geomantic energies may lead to a global, mediated effort to evoke coherent collective behaviors. Providing media bio-feedback to foster coherent cognitive patterns might result in collective insight, peak experience, or even experience of transcendent states.

An excellent example of existing research is The Global Coherence Initiative (GCI) which was launched by the Institute of HeartMath, a non-profit research and education organization, in 2008. It is a science-based, co-creative initiative that has the goal to unite millions of people globally in heart-focused care and intention. Many people perceive that humanity has reached a critical juncture in the 21st century (McCraty R, Deyhle, A., Childre, D., 2012). Worldwide, people are experiencing mounting concerns about climate change, natural disasters, extreme weather, terrorism, energy and water shortages, food and product safety and economic instability. Also, there has been an increase in social unrest, revolutions, insurrections and uprisings. The most prominent example of current times is the Arab Spring that started in December 2010. By December 2013, rulers have been forced from power in Tunisia, Egypt, Libya and Yemen. Civil uprisings have erupted in Bahrain and Syria. Also Algeria, Iraq, Jordan, Kuwait, Morocco and Sudan have experienced major protests (Wikipedia. Arab Spring 2013). The path to transition to more stability globally is not certain, and yet, there is an urgent need to replace archaic structures that do not serve humanity, all living beings, and the environment. Hence, we are on the threshold of a new stage of social, spiritual, and cultural evolution (McCraty R, Childre, D., 2010) that could be interpreted to reflect the final tests of the collective persona in the archetypal Hero's Journey. We have the chance to evolve into a more interconnected, information-based social, economic, and cultural system that spans the entire planet (Deyhle A., 2010)—a system that could be equated to a manifestation of the human Soul.

GCI employs several strategies to help increase personal, social and global coherence. An internet-based network connects people globally, who want to participate in creating a shift in global consciousness. Currently, participants of 154 countries and over 150,000 people are involved in the GCI initiative.

Members of GCI receive regular updates that inform the participants where to direct their energetic contributions of heart-focused care and intention. GCI also helps to educate the global community by providing tools and technologies for increasing individual, social and global coherence. Furthermore, scientific data is gathered that allows monitoring of earth's electromagnetic fields with state-of-the-art magnetometers that are placed globally in suitable locations. (GCI) Additionally, to further investigate the interactions between solar activity and the earth's geomagnetic field environment and human health and behaviors, scientific studies such as the Interconnectedness Study (Deyhle A., 2010) and studies on heart rate variability (HRV) are being conducted. (Deyhle A., 2013)

Mechanisms for measuring geo-magnetic fluctuations and correlating them with psychological markers in cultural media content already exist. Also, research on correlating qualitatively coherent collective energy, has been studied for decades and has generated global data relative to the "Maharishi Effect." (Orme-Johnson, 2002)

A dynamic influence on integrated fields that has not yet been researched is the impact of *psyche*cology games. In order to illustrate the potential of *psych*ecology games for electro-magnetic impact, recent data includes this bit of information about player numbers of the most popular video game in the world—the multiplayer online battle arena video game, *League of Legends,* developed and published by Riot Games for Microsoft Windows.

League of Legends was generally well received at release, and it has grown in popularity in the years since. By July 2012, League of Legends was the most played PC game in North America and Europe in terms of the number of hours played. As of January 2014, over 67 million people play League of Legends per month, 27 million per day, and over 7.5 million concurrently during peak hours. (Sheer, 2014)

The dramatic structure of *LoL* is relatively sophisticated, such that the story exposition could lend itself to contextualization according to Jungian parameters. In *League of Legends*, players assume the role of a character, called a "champion", who has unique abilities (contextualization), and, in cooperation with a team, battles against other player or computer-controlled champions. Psychologically, the battles can be understood as symbolic challenges emerging (as in dreams) from player contexts of the personal and collective unconscious. In the most popular game modes, each team's goal is to destroy the opposing team's nexus, a building which lies at the heart of a base protected by defensive structures. Psychologically, the nexus could be understood as a symbolic focus, the destruction of which gradually leads to the at-one-ment at the end of the Hero's Journey. (Campbell, 1973) Each *League of Legends* (LoL) game is discrete, with all champions starting off each game fairly weak and progressing by accumulating gold and experience over the course of the game. (New player guide, 2014) Understood symbolically, such acquisitions could represent evolution toward self-realization. In terms of the media dreamscape, LoL constitutes a contextual dream. Whatever the profiles of constituent players may be, they can be analyzed according to symbolic patterns projected by the game in order to disclose unconscious patterns of their collective persona.

Such games could be designed to promote coherent states. Using sophisticated psychological character profiling such as Myers-Briggs Profiling and correlating the personality profile with coherence fostering choice patterns that lead to a game-win could lead to the discovery of rubrics that could be applied to media-sphere dynamics. Winning a video game requires repetitive problem solving. It is well known that repetition alters frames of the cognitive unconscious (Lakoff, 2008), and repetition is not only fundamental to rote learning but to success in advertising. Recent research in neuro-marketing reaffirms the fact in a post titled, Repeat, Repeat, Repeat…and Sell. (Dooley, Roger, 2015) Like any experience, repetition alters frames of the cognitive unconscious, has the potential to provide meaningful insight, and the potential to foster coherent states. With estimates that three billion hours per week are spent playing digital games, repeating coherence fostering rubrics in contextual game design could have awe inspiring impact on the Earth's ionosphere.

How can coherence be designed into drama-based video games and why? We have established that human functionality provides a metaphorical template for understanding everything human. The multi-functional *psych*ecology game dream analogue has the potential for researching multi-dimensional human functionality using algorithms for increasing functional coherence in the process of achieving a game-win (see Schafer, *The Dream Analog*). In bio-energetic notation, the dream analog could track patterns of the cognitive unconscious in order to correlate archetypal patterns with digital patterns, and to translate the patterns into media-sphere images.

At archetypal levels, information is communicated non-locally between people at the subconscious level—the collective unconscious—which links all living systems and is projected into collective consciousness as sensory "images." Thus, a feedback loop exists between all human beings and the earth's energetic systems. It is further proposed that when coherently aligned individuals intentionally create physiologically coherent waves, they more effectively resonate with and encode information in the planetary magnetic fields. These magnetic fields act as a carrier wave, thereby positively impacting all living systems contained within the field environment and the collective consciousness (McCraty R, Deyhle, A., Childre, D., 2012).

Ultimately, such research will open a window into specific human impacts on the geomagnetic dimension and help us understand how human emotions and consciousness interact with and encode information in the geomagnetic field. Most importantly, the research may provide authentic parameters of human morality, ethics, and responsibilities within global-planetary function understood as a *Psych*ecology. This discovery is essential as we progress further on the path into an altered reality of mediated illusion.

Coherence is a term that can be used in many different contexts but we will focus on the definitions relevant for this chapter. The HeartMath Institute (HMI) has identified a psychophysiological state that is the underpinning of optimal function, termed *heart coherence* (McCraty & Childre, 2010, pp. 10-24). Practical techniques, tools, and technologies were developed by HMI that help the practitioner learn to get into and maintain a state of heart coherence. These tools and technologies help empower people to better manage stress, increase performance and connect with a deeper self-awareness and intuitive intelligence (McCraty, Atkinson, Tomasino, & Bradley, 2009, pp. 10-115; Bradley, McCraty, Atkinson, & Gillin, editor, 2008; Bradley, Murray, McCraty, & Atkinson, 2011). Also, improvements in cognitive performance, focus and effectiveness, self-responsibility and social cohesion were demonstrated (McCraty & Childre, 2010; McCraty, et al., 2009). At the individual level, a person's level of heart coherence can be assessed by monitoring the rhythmic patterns that are reflected in their heart rate variability (HRV), the beat-to-beat change in heart rate. Positive emotions such as love, appreciation, and compassion generate a heart rhythm pattern that is more ordered and coherent, whereas negative emotions such as anxiety, anger and fear generate a disordered, incoherent heart-rhythm pattern (McCraty, et al., 2009). Ongoing feelings of impatience, frustration, irritation, worry or blame throw our inner rhythms out of sync and have a negative carryover effect on our hormonal and nervous systems.

It is likely that based on this research on coherent biofeedback, *psych*ecology games could be designed to foster multi-functional coherent states. In order to do so, less coherent choice options would also need to be incorporated into the dramatic process. Another way to look at the same "healing" dynamic is that coherent feedback is analogous to Jungian Compensation, and the process (response to images) is analogous to the Jungian Amplification process of dream analysis. As emWave research has already demonstrated, the emotions experienced by a winning game player can be expanded to other functions in order to enhance understanding of deeper, more specific neurobiological function and to foster response patterns of a more coherent "healing" nature. Studies have found that the combination of emotional self-regulation techniques with heart rhythm coherence monitoring technology (emWave or Inner Balance) has proven to be highly successful for reducing stress, anxiety, anger, chronic pain, fatigue and burnout, as well as many other stress-related conditions (McCraty & Childre, 2010; McCraty, et al., 2009, pp. 11-14).

Global Coherence Monitoring System

GCI uses the Global Coherence Monitoring System to measure and explore fluctuations and resonances in the earth's magnetic field and in the earth-ionosphere resonant cavity in order to conduct research on the mechanisms of how the earth's fields affect human mental and emotional processes, health, and collective behavior. In addition, the hope is to investigate if changes in the earth's magnetic fields occur prior to natural catastrophes such as earthquakes, volcanic eruptions and human events such as social unrest and terrorist attacks.

This system is the first global network of GPS time stamped detectors designed to continuously measure magnetic signals that occur in the same range as human physiological frequencies such as the brain and cardiovascular systems. Each site, shown in Figure 1, includes ultrasensitive magnetic field detectors specifically designed to measure the magnetic resonances in the earth/ionosphere cavity, resonances that are generated by the vibrations of the earth's geomagnetic field lines, and ultra-low frequencies that occur in the earth's magnetic field. All of these have been shown to impact human functions: health, mental and emotional processes and behaviors. Each monitoring site detects the local alternating magnetic field

Figure 1.

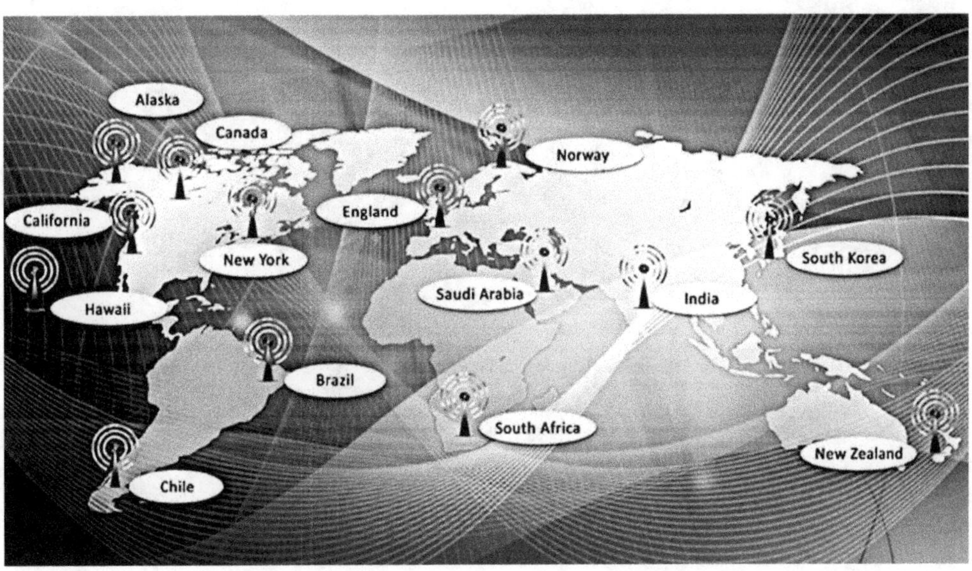

strengths in 3 dimensions over a relatively wide frequency range (0.01-300 Hz) while maintaining a flat frequency response. In addition to several space weather satellites, there are several networks of ground-based fluxgate magnetometers around the world, which measure the strength of the earth magnetic field and geomagnetic disturbances (Kp). The GCI monitoring system adds a missing component required to better understand how people and animals are affected by the rhythms and resonant frequencies in earth's magnetic fields and to enable further research on the interconnections between solar and other external forces on the planetary magnetic field environment. They make their data freely available to other research groups who may wish to explore how it may be utilized to predict earthquakes and other events. Thus, the network will provide a significant research tool to further understand how solar and geomagnetic disturbances and rhythms affect human health, emotions, behaviors and consciousness and vice versa.

Figure 2 show a photo of the monitoring site located in Boulder Creek, California. At of the beginning of 2014, 5 sites—one at the HeartMath Research Center in northern California, one in the eastern province of Saudi Arabia, one in Lithuania, one in Canada, and one in New Zealand and South Africa—are operational.

The data acquisition infrastructure captures, stamps with time and global positioning data, and transmits the data to a common server. In addition, each site has a random number generator (RNG) that is part of the Global Consciousness Project (GCP) network (described below). The monitoring system tracks changes in geomagnetic activity due to solar storms, changes in solar wind speed, disruption of Schumann resonances (SR) and, potentially, the signatures of major global events that have a strong emotional component. A growing body of data also suggests that changes occur in ionospheric activity prior to earthquake activity (Gousheva MN, Georgieva KY, Kirov BB, Antanasov D, editors, 2003; Odintsov S, Boyarchuk K, Georgieva K, Kirov B, Atanasov D., 2006, pp 88-93).

Figure 2.

Earth's Energetic Systems and Human Health and Behavior

Every cell in our bodies is bathed in an external and internal environment of fluctuating invisible magnetic forces (Halberg F, Cornelissen G, Otsuka K, Watanabe Y, Katinas GS, Burioka N, et al., 2000, pp.233-58). Because fluctuations in magnetic fields can affect virtually every circuit in biological systems (McCraty, R. et al. 2009, pp. 10-115; Halberg F., et al. (2000); Cornelissen G, Halberg F, Schwartkopff O, Delmore P, Katinas G, Hunter D, et al., 1999, pp. 152-87) human physiological rhythms and global behaviors are not only synchronized with solar and geomagnetic activity, but disruptions in these fields can create adverse effects on human health and behavior (Doronin VN, Parfentev, V.A., Tleulin, S.Zh, .Namvar, R.A., Somsikov, V.M., Drobzhev, V.I. & Chemeris, A.V., 1998, pp. 647-53; Mikulecký M, 2007, pp. 749-56).

Research confirms that whole body changes occur in conjunction with geomagnetic activity by changing heart and brain patterns. EEG patterns, heart rate, blood pressure and reaction times were measured in a group of people by Doronin et al. (1998) The authors noted that the oscillations in the Kp index had identical periods in the monitored EEG Alpha-Rhythm.

The human body is designed to adapt to daily and seasonal climatic and geomagnetic variations. Environmental factors alter the hormone balance of the body, specifically the melatonin/ serotonin balance, which affect many physiological functions, e.g. blood pressure, breathing, immune system, reproductive, cardiac and neurological processes (Bartsch H, Bartsch, C., Mecke, D. & Lippert, T.H., 1994, pp. 21-6; Bergiannaki J-D, Paparrigopoulos, T.J., Stefanis, C.N., 1996, pp. 253-8; Burch JB, Reif, J.S., Yost, M.G., 1999, pp. 209-12; Cernouss S, Vinogradov, A., Vlassova, E., 2001, pp. 121–35; Cherry N., 2002, pp 279-331; Ghione S, Mazzasalma, L., Del Seppia, C., Papi, F., 1998, pp. 749-54; Hamer JR., 1965, pp. 65-199.

Research by Burch et al. (Burch, et al.) and Rapoport et al. (Rapoport SI, Blodypakova, T.D., Malinovskaia, N.K., Oraevskii, V.N., Meshcheriakova, S.A., Breus, T.K. and Sosnovskii, A.M., 1998, pp. 632-9) provides evidence that the melatonin levels are reduced during increased solar and geomagnetic activity. Diseases like cancer, neurological disease, acute heart disease and heart attacks are all related to melatonin levels that are too low, as is accelerated aging. In the daily cycle, the blood pressure, heart rate, neurological, cardiopulmonary and reproductive functions are affected (Doronin, et al. 1998, pp. 647-53; Bartsch, et al.; Bergiannaki, et al.; Cernouss, et al.; Ghione, et al.; Belov DR, Kanunikov, I. E., and Kiselev, B. V.; Ross Fiziol Zh Im I M Sechenova, 1998, pp. 761–74; Berk M, Dodd, S., Henry, M., 2006, pp. 151-5; Dolgato K, M., and Kholodov, Y., A. M., 1987, pp. 133; Knox EG, Armstrong, E., Lancashire, R., Wall, M. and Hayes R., 1979, pp. 281:564-5; Malin SRCaS, B.J., 1979, pp. 277:646-8.; Oraevskii VN, Breus, T.K., Baevskii, R.M., Rapoport, S.I., Petrov, V.M., Barsukova, Zh.V., Gurfinkel' IuI, and Rogoza, A.T., 1998, pp. 43(5):819-26). In addition, clinical measurements have identified significant changes in blood pressure, blood flow, aggregation and coagulation, cardiac arrhythmia and heart rate variability during increased geomagnetic activity events, all of which are influenced by melatonin levels (Doronin, et al.; Halberg F, Cornelissen G, McCraty R, A.Al-Abdulgader A.; 2011, pp.3(1):1-40).

Another study by Pobachenko et al.(2006) monitored the Schumann resonances (SR) of the environment and the EEG in a frequency range between 6-16 Hz simultaneously. During a daily cycle, individuals studied showed variations in the EEG similar to changes in the SR. Hence, the biological EEG rhythm is characteristic of the daily rhythm of the SR (Pobachenko, et al.) The lowest frequency SR is approximately 7.83 hertz (Hz), with a daily variation of about ± 0.5 Hz. The other frequencies are ~ 14, 20, 26, 33, 39 and 45 Hz. Figure 3 shows the frequencies of the SR, which are closely overlapping with alpha

Figure 3.

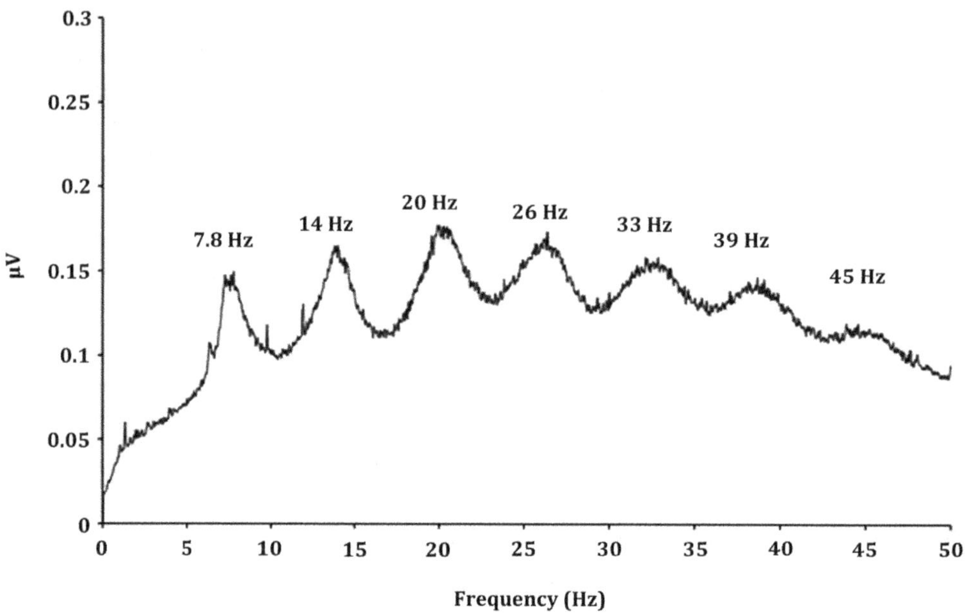

(8-12 Hz), beta (12-30 Hz) and gamma (30-100Hz) brain waves. Because the brain is a very sensitive electromagnetic organ, changes in geomagnetic activity and SR intensities appear to alter brain wave and neuro-hormone responses. Geomagnetic storms are also related to human health effects and death. Altered EEG rhythms have been observed by Belov et al. (Belov, et al.), while low frequency magnetic oscillations (around 3 Hz) had a sedative effect, stronger oscillations, around 10 Hz signal, stresses and stimulates people (Belov, et al.).

Using such sophisticated detail to monitor massive use of specific DBG and to explore fluctuations in the earth's magnetic field may prove susceptible to greater experimental control and neurobiological neurlinguistic specificity. Eventually, such control and specificity may allow researchers to address collective motives and functionality of contextual collectives in order to foster coherence in their affect on designated geomagnetic frequencies.

Benefits of Coherence

Coherence confers a number of benefits to the system in terms of both physiological and psychological functioning. Practicing certain techniques that increase physiological coherence is associated with both short-term and long-term improvement in several objective health-related measures, including enhanced humoral immunity (Tiller, W.A., J. W E Dibble, and M.J. Kohane, 2001, pp. 201-202; Bradley, R.T., 2007, pp. 61-97) and an increased DHEA/cortisol ratio. Increased physiological coherence is similarly associated with psychological benefits, including improvements in cognitive performance and mental clarity as well as increased emotional stability and well-being (Laszlo, E., 1995; Marcer, P. and W. Schempp, 1998, pp. 231-248).

Studies conducted in diverse populations have documented significant reductions in stress and negative affect and increases in positive mood and attitudes in individuals using coherence-building techniques (McCraty, R., R.T. Bradley, and D. Tomasino, 2004, pp. 15-19; McCraty, R. and D. Childre, 2004, pp. 230-255; Bradley, R.T, 2007, pp. 61-97; Marcer & Schempp, 1998, pp. 231-248; Pribram, K.H. and R.T. Bradley, 1998, pp. 273-307) improvements in clinical status, emotional well-being and quality of life have also been demonstrated in various medical patient populations in intervention programs using coherence-building approaches. For example, significant blood pressure reductions have been demonstrated in individuals with hypertension (Schempp, W., 1992 pp. 109-164; Umetani, K., et al., 1998d, pp. 593-601) improved functional capacity and reduced depression in congestive heart failure patients (Levy, B.R., et al., 2002 pp. 261-270) improved psychological health and quality of life in patients with diabetes (Arrone, L.J., et al., 1997, pp. 354-9) and improvements in asthma (Lindmark, S., J. Buren, and J.W. Eriksson, 2006. pp. 301-9) Another study reported reductions in pathological symptoms and anxiety and significant improvements in positive affect, physical vitality, and general well-being in individuals with HIV infection and AIDS (Luthar, et al., 2000, pp. 543-62; Umetani, et al., 1998, pp. 593-601; Lindmark, et al., 2005, pp. 717-28; Lindmark, S., et al., 2003, pp. 399-405).

Increasing Coherence

Although physiological coherence is a natural state that can occur spontaneously during sleep and deep relaxation, sustained episodes during normal daily activities are generally rare. While specific rhythmic breathing methods can induce coherence for brief periods, paced breathing is difficult for many people to maintain. On the other hand, HeartMath's findings indicate that individuals can produce extended periods of physiological coherence by actively generating and sustaining a feeling of appreciation or other positive emotions. Sincere positive feelings appear to excite the system at its resonant frequency, allowing the coherent mode to emerge naturally. This typically makes it easier for people to sustain a positive emotion for much longer periods, thus facilitating the process of establishing and reinforcing coherent patterns in the neural architecture as the familiar reference. Once a new pattern is established, the brain strives to maintain a match with the new program, thus increasing the probability of maintaining coherence and reducing stress, even during challenging situations. (McCraty, R., et al., 2009, pp. 10-115)

Doc Childre, founder of HMI, has developed a number of practical positive emotion refocusing and emotional restructuring techniques that allow people to quickly self-generate coherence at will (Saul, J.P., 1988, pp. 1292-1299; Beauchaine, T., 2001. pp. 183-214). Known as the HeartMath system, these techniques utilize the heart as a point of entry into the psychophysiological networks that connect the physiological, mental, and emotional systems. In essence, because the heart is a primary generator of rhythmic neural and energetic patterns in the body, it influences brain processes that control the ANS, cognitive function, and emotion. It also provides an access point from which system-wide dynamics can be quickly and profoundly affected. Research studies and the experience of numerous health care professionals indicate that HeartMath coherence-building techniques are easily learned, have a high rate of compliance, and are highly adaptable to a wide range of demographic [contextual] groups (Thayer, J.F., et al., 2009, pp. 141-53.; Lehrer, P., et al., 2006, pp. 278-84). Incorporated into *psych*ecology game research, the HeartMath system could provide important information relative to promoting functional coherence in game players.

Heart Rhythm Coherence Feedback

Used in conjunction with positive emotion-based coherence-building techniques, heart rhythm feedback training can be a powerful tool to assist people in learning how to self-generate increased physiological coherence (Foreman, R., 1997, pp. 663-683). HMI has developed a portable heart rhythm monitoring and feedback system that enables physiological coherence to be objectively monitored and quantified. Known as the emWave Pro, emWave2, and Inner Balance Trainer (HeartMath LLC, Boulder Creek, CA), these interactive systems monitor and display individuals' heart rate variability patterns in real time as they practice the self-regulation techniques. Using an ear or fingertip sensor to record the pulse wave, the emWave plots changes in heart rate on a beat-to-beat basis. HeartMath feedback procedures could be easily applied to DBG.

As people practice the coherence-building techniques, they can readily see and experience the changes in their heart rhythm patterns, which generally become more ordered, smoother, and more sine wave-like as they experience positive emotions. This process reinforces the natural association between the physiological coherence mode and positive feelings. The real-time physiological feedback essentially takes the guesswork and randomness out of the process of self-inducing a coherent state, resulting in greater consistency, focus, and effectiveness in shifting to a beneficial psychophysiological mode. Heart rhythm coherence feedback training has been successfully used in clinical settings by physicians, mental health professionals to facilitate health improvements in patients with numerous physical and psychological disorders (Siegel, G., et al., 1984, pp. 319-38; Langhorst, P., G. Schulz, and M. Lambertz, 1984, pp. 257-275). It is also increasingly being utilized in corporate, military, law enforcement, and educational settings to enhance physical and emotional health and improve performance (Luthar, S.S., D. Cicchetti, and B. Becker, 2000, pp. 543-62; Lehrer, P.M., et al., 2003. p. 796-805; Baselli, G., et al., 1994, pp. 143-152).

Biomagnetic Information Patterns

The first biomagnetic signal was demonstrated in 1963 by Gerhard Baule and Richard McFee in a magnetocardiogram (MCG) that used magnetic induction coils to detect fields generated by the human heart. (deBoer, R.W., J.M. Karemaker, and J. Strackee, 1987, pp. H680-H689). A remarkable increase in the sensitivity of biomagnetic measurements was achieved with the introduction of the Superconducting Quantum Interference Device (SQUID) in the early 1970s, and the ECG and MCG have since been shown to closely parallel one another (Cameron, O.G., 2002).

The heart generates a series of electromagnetic pulses in which the time interval between each beat varies in a complex manner. These pulsing waves of electromagnetic energy give rise to interference patterns when they interact with magnetically polarizable tissues and substances. Figure 4 shows two different power spectra derived from an average of 12 individual 10-second epochs of ECG data recorded during differing psychophysiological modes. The plot on the left was produced while the subject was in a state of deep appreciation, whereas the plot on the right was generated while the subject experienced recalled feelings of anger. The difference in the patterns, and thus the information they contain, can be clearly seen. There is a direct correlation between the patterns in the heart rate variability rhythm and the frequency patterns in the spectrum of the ECG or MCG. Experiments such as these indicate that psychophysiological information can be encoded into the electromagnetic fields produced by the heart (McCraty, R., 2004, pp. 541-562; Frysinger, R.C. and R.M. Harper, 1990. pp. 162-171).

Figure 4.

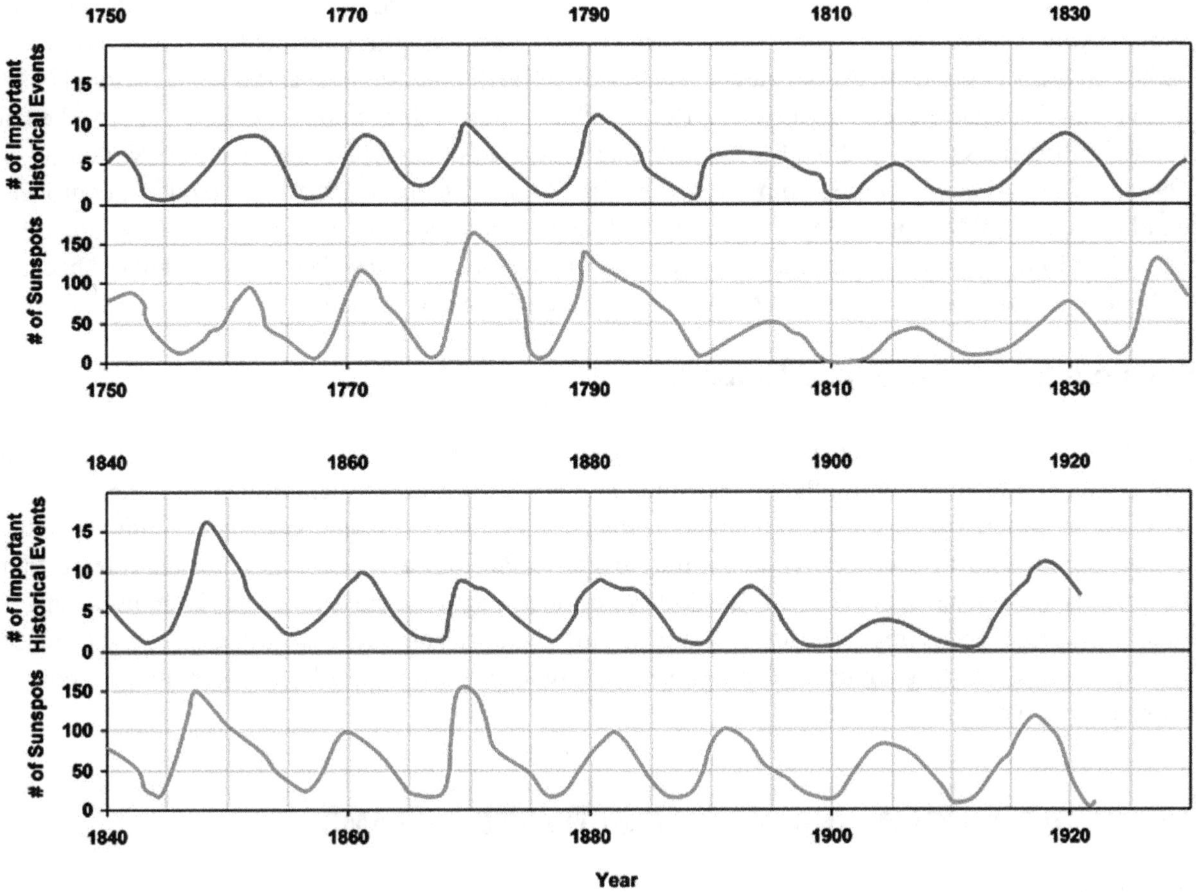

Biomagnetic Communication between People

The human body is replete with mechanisms for detecting its external environment. Sense organs, the most obvious example, are specifically geared to react to touch, temperature, select ranges of light and sound waves, etc. These organs are acutely sensitive to external stimuli. The nose, for example, can detect one molecule of gas, while a cell in the retina of the eye can detect a single photon of light. If the ear were any more sensitive, it would pick up the sound of the random vibrations of its own molecules (Oppenheimer, S. and D. Hopkins, 1994, pp. 309-341). The interaction between two human beings, for example, the consultation between a patient and her clinician, is a very sophisticated dance that involves many subtle factors. Most people tend to think of communication solely in terms of overt signals expressed through facial movements, voice qualities, gestures and body movements. However, evidence now supports the perspective that a subtle yet influential electromagnetic or "energetic" communication system operates just below our conscious level of awareness. The following section will discuss data suggesting that this energetic system contributes to the "magnetic" attractions or repulsions that occur between individuals. It is also quite plausible that these energetic interactions can affect the therapeutic process.

The concept of energy or information exchange between individuals is central to many of the Eastern healing arts, but its acceptance in Western medicine has been hampered by the lack of a plausible mechanism to explain the nature of this "energy information" or how it is communicated. However, numerous studies investigating the effects of healers, Therapeutic Touch practitioners, and other individuals have demonstrated a wide range of significant effects including the influence of "energetic" approaches on wound healing rates (Zhang, J.X., R.M. Harper, and R.C. Frysinger, 1986, pp. 193-207; Armour, J.A., 1994, pp. 219-244), pain hemoglobin levels (Cantin, M. and J. Genest, 1985, pp. 107-127., conformational changes of DNA and water structure as well as psychological states (Huang, M.H., et al., 1996, pp. 1298-1303). Although these reports show beneficial results, they have been largely ignored because of the lack of any scientific rationale to explain how the effects are achieved.

Physiological Linkage and Empathy

The ability to sense what other people are feeling is an important factor in allowing us to connect or communicate effectively with others. The smoothness or flow in any social interaction depends to a great extent on the establishment of a spontaneous entrainment or linkage between individuals. When people are engaged in deep conversation, they begin to fall into a subtle dance, synchronizing their movements and postures, vocal pitch, speaking rates, and length of pauses between responses, and, as we are now discovering, important aspects of their physiology can also become linked and synchronized. Such linkage is probably significant in terms of the importance Jung attributes to creating a sense of empathy with a patient.

BIOMETRIC JUNGIAN ANALYSIS OF MEDIATED DREAMS

Collective Personae

We citizens of the modern world have become accustomed to think of ourselves in collective terms. In addition to our citizenship in a national collective—due to advertising, the media, and common experience—we think of ourselves as parts of many demographics: target groups (those who would buy a Land Rover or quiche), political parties, religions, genders, races, and nationalities. As George Lakoff says, "We live our narratives," and could not understand ourselves or others without them. (Lakoff, 2008) Collectivity has been imbedded in our psyche from our first experiences with family, clan, tribe, or community on any scale including nation states and the fundamental assumptions of the social contract.

Without the sense of the collective as a point of reference, the individual does not exist. However, collective humanity has yet to understand that "collectivity" must be understood in terms of other life forms and alternate realities—a more inclusive framework than human-centered ontology that extends from cosmos to sub-atomic dimensions. This view was common to the wisdom of antiquity, but it has been dismissed as primitive by many orthodox scientists during the age of materialism. Ironically, the paradigm shift has reintroduced humanity to this ancient wisdom, but it s ramifications have yet to be fully realized by modern science. One researcher who has recognized the unconscious influence of the media is George Lakoff who has denominated the unconscious political metaphors that define fundamental collective personae in terms of conservative or progressive tendencies. (Lakoff, 2008) Like Jung, Lakoff emphasizes narrative structure and functions of the cognitive unconscious.

In "Toward a Computational Model of Narrative" (Lakoff & Narayanan, 2010), the authors expand on Lakoff's research on unconscious cognitive frameworks and the idea that the structure of narrative shapes our understanding of the world and ourselves. As he says, narratives (drama), "Exploit the shared cognitive structures of human motivations, goals, actions, events, and outcomes. We report on a computational model that is motivated by results in neural computation and capture fine-grained, context sensitive information about human goals, processes, actions, policies and outcomes. (Lakoff & Narayanan, 2010, p. 1) The term "fine-grained" applies to the qualitative nature of language. Furthermore, "Language routinely involves imagining alternative goals, resources, outcomes, and actions (or inactions)." All of these components are directly relevant to our recommended *psych*ecology model for researching the contextual, collective unconscious.

The Myers-Briggs attributes for personality profiling define functional personality according to a synthesis of Jungian dynamics including contextuality. (Myers-Briggs, 2015) When we watch a sports event, we watch it as a fan, a statistical entity that is defined computationally and, for awhile, becomes more fan than person. The individual may wear many masks and play many roles among which being a sports fan is only one. Latent aspects of the individual personality only emerge in certain contexts, but when they do they dominate the persona and other aspects become submerged. In religious rituals or outpourings of generosity and heroism such as those we witnessed in selfless humanitarian acts of New Yorkers after the September 11 attack, we can see collective personae at work. Even in the depths of scientific materialism, Carl Jung fully recognized this fact.

Now the doctor in me refuses point blank to consider the life of a people as something that does not conform to psychological law. A people, in the doctor's eyes, presents only a somewhat more complex picture of psychic life than the individual...has not a poet spoken of the 'nations' of his soul? And quite correctly, as it seems to me, for in one of its aspects the psyche is not individual, but is derived from the nation, from collectivity, or from humanity even. In some way or other we are part of an all-embracing psychic life, of a single 'greatest' man, to quote Swedenborg. And so we can draw a parallel: just as in me, a single human being, the darkness calls forth the helpful light, so does it also in the psychic life of a people." (Jung 1933, p 209-210)

FUNCTIONAL DIMENSIONS OF THE MEDIA DREAM

It may be stipulated that, according to both conscious and unconscious parameters, illusory multi-functional cultural personae exist. This assumption has ancient precedent and modern application. There is no need to detail the significance of the universally understood four classical human functions that included the physical, emotional, mental, and spiritual. The primary metaphorical expressions of these functions are earth, water, air, and fire which Jung correlated with Sensing, Feeling, Thinking, and Intuiting.

The idea of this selfsame functionality pervades modern research, and examples of the existence of collective personas are implicit in: Marketing to target groups; assessing opinions with statistical opinion polls; narrow-casting to target groups; political advertising; propaganda; the scapegoat syndrome; principles underlying demographic research; civil rights laws; tax laws; foreign policy; poverty programs; social services; social security; and law itself assume the existence of definable collectives. But does a collective constitute a collective persona? At least in the virtual reality, the answer is yes. The classical pattern for the human persona is that it exists on three, four, or five levels that, today, may be understood as bandwidths, and these frequencies could be designed to correspond with levels of nested masks (Glassner, 2004, pp. 43-45) in a cultural entity. Glassner's Nested Masks are summarized as follows:

- **True Self:** Correlated to intuitive function and the concept of Soul.
- **Conscience:** Correlated to mental function and value formation.
- **Self Image:** Correlated to feeling function and conversion of values into desire.
- **World Mask:** Correlated to sensing function, physical action and metaphorical action as reflected in the consequences of behavior It.

Of the many new scientific perspectives that emerged from the twentieth century, one of the most profound is that the universe is wholly and enduringly interconnected and *coherent*. Complex living systems, including human beings, are composed of numerous dynamic, interconnected networks of biological structures and processes. Coherence implies order, structure, harmony and alignment within and amongst systems - whether in atoms, organisms, social groups, planets or galaxies. Thus every whole has a relationship with and is a part of a greater whole, which is again part of something greater. In this context, nothing can be considered as separate, alone or lacking relationships. One of the more surprising findings that has emerged from physics is quantum coherence, which has given rise to the prediction of non-locality and instantaneous communication between subatomic particles separated by vast distances. (McCraty R, Deyhle, A., Childre, D., 2012).

Most people know what it feels like to be in harmonious state, the place where our hearts, minds and bodies are united in a feeling of wholeness. This state is often referred to as "the zone," "flow," "oneness," etc. When we are in such states we typically feel connected not only to our deepest selves but to others, even to the earth itself. We call this state of internal and external connectedness "coherence." The following overview discusses how increased personal coherence can be achieved as people learn to more consistently self-regulate their emotions from a more intuitive, intelligent and balanced inner reference and how this state is directly associated with increased intuition, improved health and cognitive functioning. The overview also describes how coherence is reflected in physiology and objectively measured. The discussion then expands to coherence in the context of families, workplaces, and communities. The discussion concludes with the perspective that being responsible for and increasing our personal coherence is not only reflected in improved personal health and happiness, but is also feeds into and is reflected in a global field environment. It is postulated that as increasing numbers of people add coherent energy to the global field, it helps strengthen and stabilize mutually beneficial feedback loops between human beings and the earth itself.

Concept of Coherence

The various concepts and measurements embraced under the term coherence have become central to fields as diverse as quantum physics, cosmology, physiology, and brain and consciousness research. Coherence has several related definitions, all of which are applicable to the study of human physiology, social interactions and global affairs. The most common dictionary definition is "the quality of being logically integrated, consistent and intelligible," as in a coherent statement. (Deyhle A., 2010) A related meaning is the logical, orderly and aesthetically consistent relationship among parts. (Deyhle A., 2010) Coherence always implies correlations, connectedness, consistency and efficient energy utilization. We refer to people's speech or thoughts as coherent if the words fit together well, and incoherent if they are uttering meaningless nonsense or presenting ideas that make no sense as a whole. Thus, coherence refers to wholeness and global order, where the whole is greater than the sum of its individual parts. In the example of organizing words into a coherent sentence, the meaning and purpose conveyed by the arrangement of the words is greater than the individual meaning of each word. For any system to produce a function, it must have the property of global coherence, and this is also true for our physical, mental, emotional and social systems. However, the energy efficiency and degree of coordinated action of any given system can vary widely and does not necessarily result in a coherent output or flow of behavior.

Coherence is also used to describe the coupling and degree of synchronization between different oscillating systems. In some cases, where two or more oscillatory systems operate at the same basic frequency, they can become either phase or frequency-locked as occurs between the photons in a laser. (Deyhle A., 2013) This type of coherence is called cross-coherence and this is the type of coherence that most scientists think of when they use the term. In physiology, cross-coherence occurs when two or more of the body's oscillatory systems, such as respiration and heart rhythms, become entrained and operate at the same frequency. However, global coherence does not mean that everyone or all the parts are doing the same thing simultaneously. In complex globally coherent systems, such as human beings, there is an incredible amount of activity at every level of magnification or scale that spans more than two thirds of the 73 known octaves of the electromagnetic spectrum. (McCraty R, Atkinson, M., Tomasino, D., & Bradley, R. T., 2009) It can appear at one level of scale that a given system is operating autonomously, yet it is perfectly coordinated within the whole. In living systems, there are micro-level systems, molecular machines, protons and electrons, organs and glands each functioning autonomously, doing very different things at different rates, yet all working together in a complex harmoniously coordinated and synchronized manner. If this were not the case, it would be a free-for-all among the body's independent systems, rather than a coordinated federation of interdependent systems and functions. Biologist Mae-Won Ho, has suggested that coherence is the defining quality of living systems and accounts for their most characteristic properties, such as long range order and coordination, rapid and efficient energy transfer, and extreme sensitivity to specific signals. (McCraty R, Atkinson, M., Tomasino, D., & Bradley, R. T., 2009)

Many contemporary scientists believe that it is the underlying state of our physiological processes that determines the quality and stability of the feelings and emotion we experience. The feelings we label as "positive" actually reflect body states in which "the regulation of life processes become efficient, or even optimal, free-flowing and easy." (McCraty R, Childre D., 2004) Indeed, it appears that synchronized activity underlies conscious experience itself. For the brain and nervous system to function, the neural activity, which encodes information, must be stable and coordinated and the various centers within the brain must be able to dynamically synchronize their activity in order for information to be smoothly processed and perceived.

Our "coherent" perception of an object in the external world actually comes from millions of neurons involved in processing sensory information that are made globally coherent by being brought together and organized into a global conscious experience. (Tiller WA, McCraty R, Atkinson M., 1996) We are not only conscious of external inputs, but of ourselves as a coherent whole. In fact, it is estimated that 40 to 65% of all activities in the brain are phase synchronized at any given time. (Bradley RT, R. McCraty, M. Atkinson, & M. Gillin, editor, 2008) Coherence in this context is a measure of the correlated activity between brain regions which is orchestrated (Hameroff, Stuart & Penrose, Sir Roger., 2014) from direct neural connections between the regions, common input from the thalamus or other neocortical regions. (Bradley RT, Murray G, McCraty R, Atkinson M., 2011) Cross-coherence, however, also occurs between distant cortical structures that are not interconnected anatomically. (Bradley RT, McCraty, R., Atkinson, M., Tomasino., D., 2010) The degree of coupling, which regulates synchronized activity in the networks, varies depending on the needs of the moment. It is this flexibility that allows us to quickly adapt to changing demands, such as focusing on external sensory input or an internal process. However, if the networks become either excessively coupled or are too loosely coupled, the system is less able to dynamically marshal the appropriate neural support systems it needs to respond to a particular demand. (Tiller WA, McCraty R, Atkinson M., 1996) This is reflected in the alpha rhythm, which increases in amplitude and distribution when the neural populations are more tightly coupled and are not involved in processing information. Under these circumstances cognitive performance is reduced, especially tasks involving the processing of external sensory information. In terms of optimizing performance, this usually means that one should not be too relaxed (increased coupling) or overly stimulated (decreased coupling) when performing important cognitive tasks.

There are also many examples in physiology where synchronized activity occurs across different time scales, which is characteristic of a globally coherent system. The brain rhythms operate over a wide range of frequencies, yet most of these frequencies exhibit various degrees of synchronized activity with the heart, which has much slower rhythms than the brain. For example, when heart rate increases, the activity and amplitude of the brain waves also tends to increase. When the heart rhythm is coherent, as described below, there also tends to be an increase in heart-brain synchronization. (Ginsberg JP, Berry, M.E., Powell, D.A., 2010) These are examples of a phase-amplitude relationship between macroscopic physiological rhythms, which reflect the constant intercommunication between different biological rhythms that take place in healthy organisms. (McCraty et al, 2009)

Another aspect of coherence relates to the dynamic rhythms produced by a single oscillatory system. The term *auto-coherence* describes coherent activity within a single system. An ideal example is a system that exhibits sine wave like oscillations; the more stable the frequency, amplitude and shape, the higher the degree of coherence. When coherence is increased in a system that is coupled to other systems, it can pull the other systems into increased synchronization and more efficient function. For example, frequency pulling and entrainment can easily be seen between the heart, respiratory and blood-pressure rhythms as well as between very low frequency brain rhythms, craniosacral rhythms, and electrical potentials measured across the skin. (Lloyd A, Brett, D., Wesnes, K., 2010; McCraty R, Atkinson M, Lipsenthal L, Arguelles aL., 2009)

The Coherent Heart Rhythm of Positive Emotions

We introduced the term physiological coherence to describe the degree of order, harmony and stability in the various rhythmic activities within living systems over any given time period. (Lloyd & Wesnes, 2010) This harmonious order signifies a coherent system, whose efficient or optimal function is directly related to the ease and flow in life processes. By contrast, an erratic, discordant pattern of activity denotes an incoherent system whose function reflects stress and inefficient utilization of energy in life processes. Interestingly, we have found that positive emotions such as appreciation and compassion, as opposed to negative emotions such as anxiety, anger, and fear, are reflected in a heart rhythm pattern that is more coherent (see Figure 1). (Gousheva MN, Georgieva KY, Kirov BB, Antanasov D, editors, 2003; Odintsov S, Boyarchuk K, Georgieva K, Kirov B, Atanasov D., 2006; Halberg F, Cornelissen G, Otsuka K, Watanabe Y, Katinas GS, Burioka N, et al, 2000; Cornelissen G, Halberg F, Schwartkopff O, Delmore P, Katinas G, Hunter D, et al, 1999; Doronin VN, Parfentev, V.A., Tleulin, S.Zh, Namvar,

Figure 5.

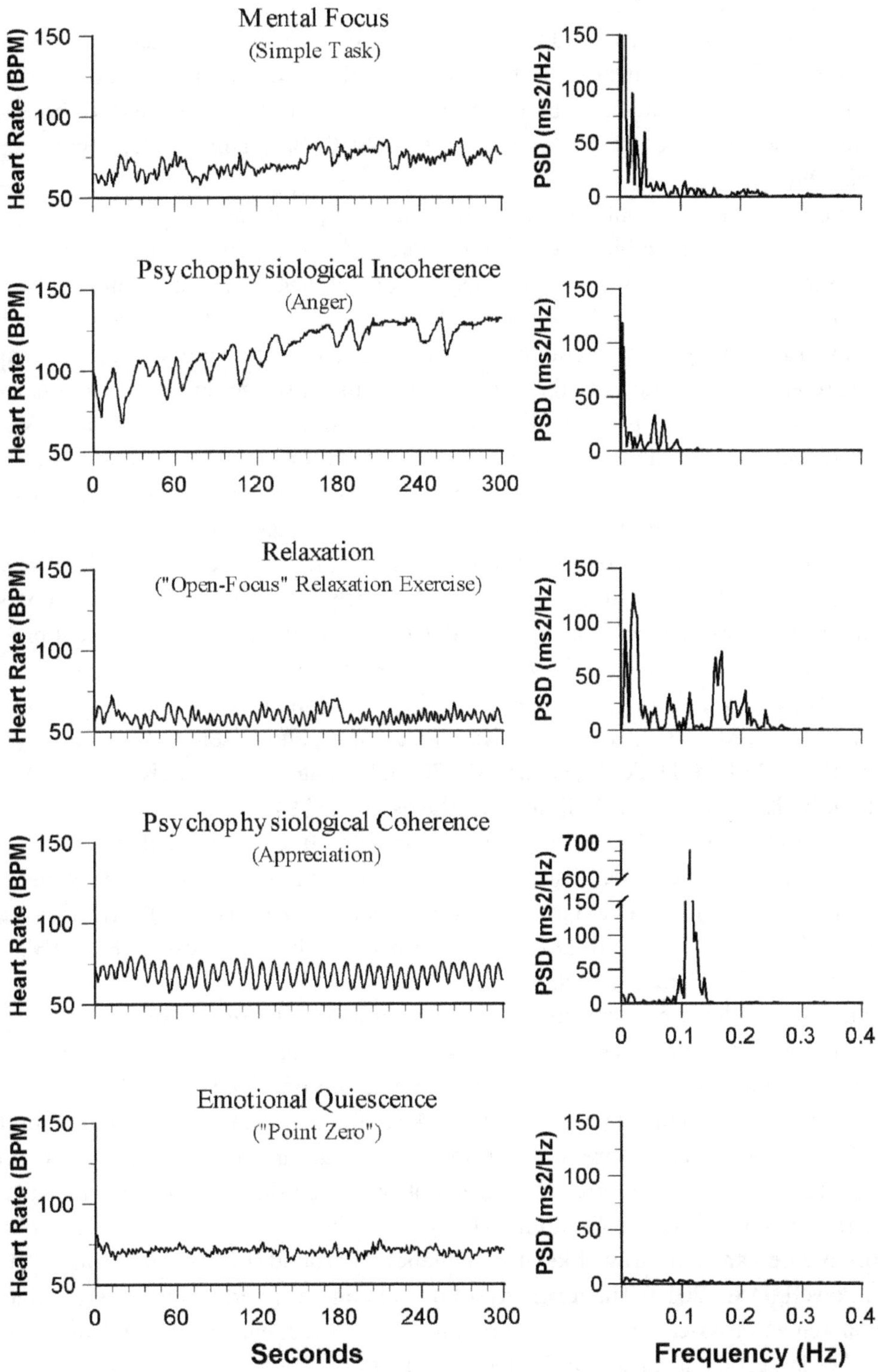
Mental Focus
(Simple Task)
Psychophysiological Incoherence
(Anger)
Relaxation
("Open-Focus" Relaxation Exercise)
Psychophysiological Coherence
(Appreciation)
Emotional Quiescence
("Point Zero")
Heart Rate (BPM)
PSD (ms2/Hz)
Seconds
Frequency (Hz)

R.A., Somsikov, V.M., Drobzhev, V.I. and Chemeris, A.V., 1998; Kay RW., 1994; Mikulecký M., 2007; Bartsch H, Bartsch, C., Mecke, D. and Lippert, T.H., 1994)

The coherent state has been correlated with a general sense of well-being, and improvements in cognitive, social and physical performance. We have observed this association between emotions and heart rhythm patterns in studies conducted in both laboratory and natural settings, and for both spontaneous and intentionally generated emotions. (Lloyd & Wesnes, 2010; Bergiannaki J-D, Paparrigopoulos, T.J., Stefanis, C.N., 1996)

There is abundant evidence that emotions alter the activity of the body's physiological systems, and that beyond their pleasant subjective feeling, heart-felt positive emotions and attitudes provide a number of benefits that enhance physiological, psychological, and social functioning. (Burch JB, Reif, J.S., Yost, M.G., 1999; Cernouss S, Vinogradov, A., Vlassova, E., 2001; Cherry N., 2002) As coherence tends to naturally emerge with the activation of heart-felt positive emotions such as appreciation, compassion, care and love, it suggests that such feelings increase the coherence and harmony in our energetic systems which are the primary drivers of our physiological systems. (Kay, RW, 1994) This increased coherence and alignment in turn facilitate the body's natural regenerative processes. In this context the term energetic systems refers to the functions we cannot directly measure, touch or see, such as our emotions, thoughts and intuitions. Although these functions have loose correlations with biological activity patterns, they nevertheless remain covert and hidden from direct observation. Several notable scientists have proposed that such functions operate primarily in the frequency domain outside of time and space and have suggested mechanisms as to how they can interact with biological processes. (McCraty R, Childre, D., 2010; Ghione S, Mazzasalma, L., Del Seppia, C., Papi, F., 1998; Hamer JR, 1965; Rapoport SI, Blodypakova, T.D., Malinovskaia, N.K., Oraevskii, V.N., Meshcheriakova, S.A., Breus, T.K. and Sosnovskii, A.M., 1998; Belov DR, Kanunikov, I. E., and Kiselev, B. V., Ross Fiziol Zh Im I M Sechenova. 1998; Berk M, Dodd, S., Henry, M., 2006; Dolgato K, M., and Kholodov, Y., `187; Knox EG, Armstrong, E., Lancashire, R., Wall, M. and Hayes, R., 1979)

It is important to note that although changes in heart rate often covary with emotions, our research has found that it is the pattern of the heart's rhythm that is primarily reflective of the emotional state, especially emotions that do not lead to large autonomic nervous system (ANS) activations or withdrawals. (Ginsberg JP, Berry, M.E., Powell, D.A., 2010; Lloyd A, Brett, D., Wesnes, K., 2010; Bergiannaki J-D, Paparrigopoulos, T.J., Stefanis, C.N., 1996)

These changes in rhythmic patterns are independent of heart rate; that is, one can have a coherent or incoherent pattern at higher or lower heart rates. Thus, it is the pattern of the rhythm (the ordering of changes in rate overtime), rather than the rate (at any point in time) that is most directly related to emotional dynamics and physiological synchronization. Also, the coherent state is fundamentally different from a state of relaxation which requires only a lowered heart rate and not necessarily a coherent rhythm.

Physiological coherence, also referred to as heart coherence, cardiac coherence or resonance is a functional mode, measured by heart rate variability (HRV) analysis wherein a person's heart rhythm pattern becomes more ordered and sine-wave like at a frequency of around 0.1 Hz (10 seconds). (Ginsberg JP, Berry, M.E., Powell, D.A., 2010) The term physiological coherence embraces several related phenomena—auto-coherence, cross-coherence, synchronization, and resonance—all of which are associated with increased order, efficiency, and harmony in the functioning of the body's systems. When one is in a coherent state, it reflects increased synchronization and resonance in higher-level brain systems and in the activity occurring in the two branches of the autonomic nervous system (ANS), as well as a shift in autonomic balance toward increased parasympathetic activity.

In terms of psychological functionality, coherence reflects increased emotional and perceptual stability and alignment among the physical, cognitive, and emotional systems (Figure 2). Coherence and resilience are closely related as each has the quality of being both a process and an outcome as they rely on physiological and psychological processes that create resilient outcomes. In addition, both are states rather then traits that vary over time as demands, circumstances and level of maturity change (Malin SRCaS, B.J., 1979).

Because multi-functional Resilience is related to self-management and efficient utilization of energy resources across four domains; physical, emotional, mental and spiritual (Figure 3) it can be correlated with Jungian Individuation or Maslow's stage of self-actualization. Physical resilience is basically reflected in physical flexibility, endurance and strength, while emotional resilience is reflected in one's ability to self-regulate the degree of emotional flexibility, positive emotions and relationships. Mental resilience is reflected in our attention span, mental flexibility, an optimistic world view and ability to integrate multiple points of view. Spiritual resilience is typically associated with our commitment to core values, intuition, and tolerance of others' values and beliefs. These dimensions of resilience can be programmed for increasingly coherent states relative to the exposition of a story in a *psych*ecology game and the premise of protagonists in the drama. According to Aristotle, Exposition in good drama is the statement of the story problem, while *lysis* is the resolution of the problem. Character premise is defined as "what a character learns." (Glassner, 2004; Schafer, 2007) If a game-win depends on resolution of the story problem and is associated with exposition and character premise, the game-win would also be associated with increased coherence in the in the framing of the player's cognitive unconscious.

When a coherent state is maintained, the increased physiological efficiency and alignment of the mental and emotional systems accumulates resilience (energy) across all four energetic domains. Having a high level of resilience is important for not only recouping from challenging situations, but for preventing unnecessary stress reactions (frustration, impatience, anxiety) that deplete our physical and psychological resources. As explained above, winning a coherently structured *psych*ecology game would result in energy efficiencies that have an impact on the global field.

Figure 6.

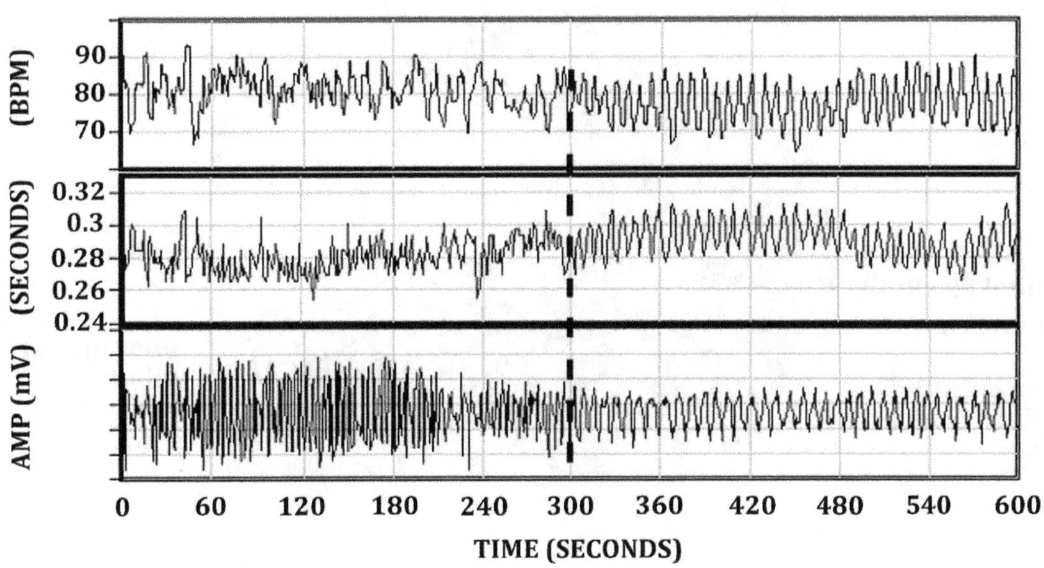

Figure 7.

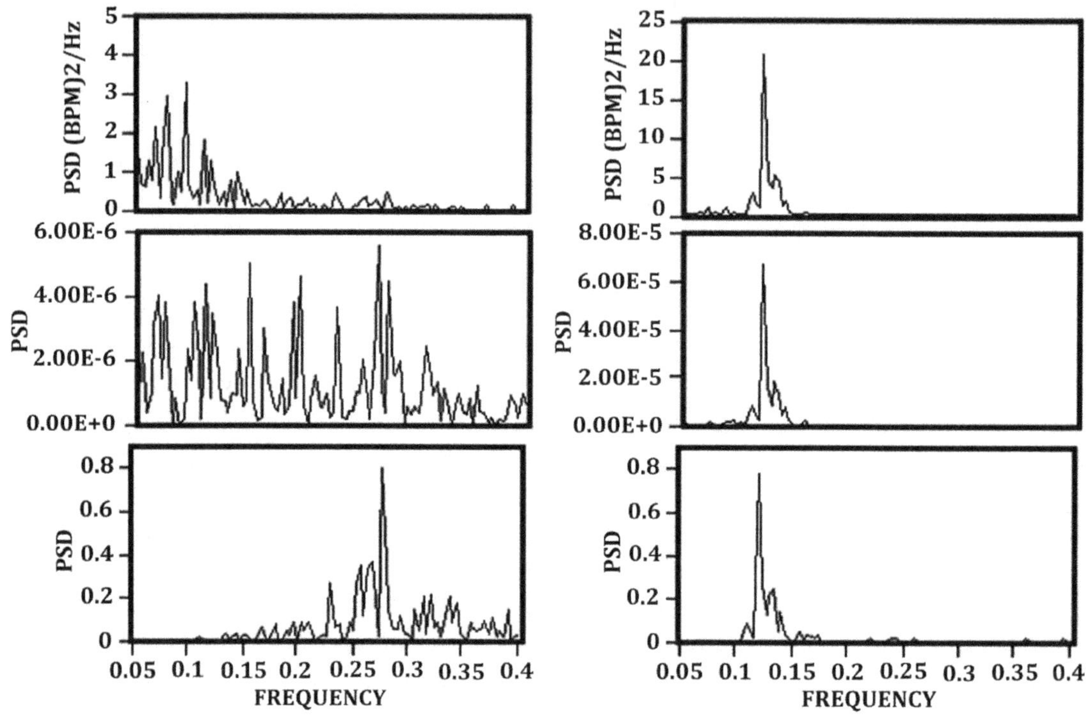

Figure 8.

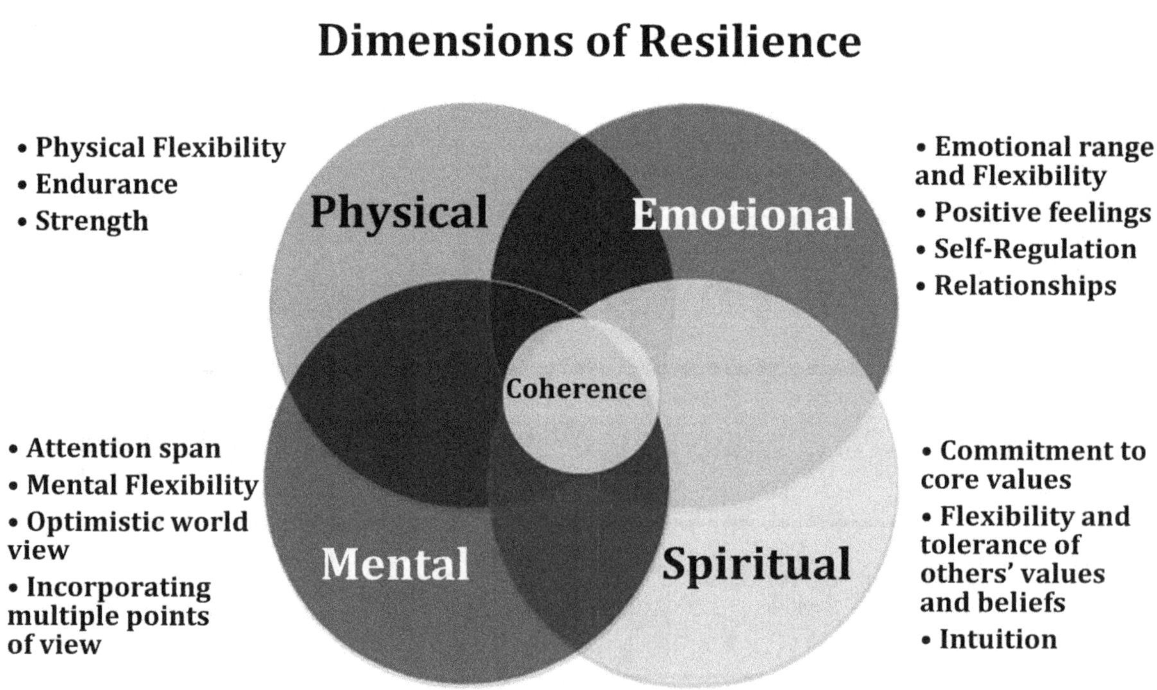

Heart Rate Variability Coherence

HRV is widely considered a measure of neurocardiac function that reflects heart–brain interactions and ANS dynamics. All HRV measures are derived from the assessment of the naturally occurring changes in beat-to-beat heart rate. HRV is much more than an assessment of heart rate since it reflects the complex interactions of the heart with multiple body systems. (Ginsberg JP, Berry, M.E., Powell, D.A., 2010) An optimal level of variability within an organism's key regulatory systems is critical to the inherent flexibility and adaptability or resilience that epitomizes healthy coherent function and well-being. While too much instability is detrimental to efficient physiological functioning and energy utilization, too little variation indicates depletion or pathology. (Oraevskii VN, Breus, T.K., Baevskii, R.M., Rapoport, S.I., Petrov, V.M., Barsukova, Zh.V., Gurfinkel' IuI, and Rogoza, A.T., 1998) The amount or range of overall HRV is related to our age, with younger people having higher levels than older ones. (Oraevskii VN, Breus, T.K., Baevskii, R.M., Rapoport, S.I., Petrov, V.M., Barsukova, Zh.V., Gurfinkel' IuI, and Rogoza, A.T., 1998) Low HRV is a strong and independent predictor of future health problems, including all causes of mortality, (Halberg F, Cornelissen G, McCraty R, A.Al-Abdulgader A., 2011) and it is associated with numerous medical conditions. (Pobachenko SV, Kolesnik, A. G., Borodin, A. S., Kalyuzhin, V. V., 2006; Persinger MA., 1995; Stoupel E., 1993; Villoresi G, Ptitsyna, N.G., Tiasto, M.I. and Iucci, N., 1998; Gordon C, Berk, M., 2003) HRV is also an important indicator of psychological resiliency and behavioral flexibility as well as the ability to effectively adapt to changing social or environmental demands. (Kay RW, 2004) In addition, resting levels of HRV are associated with individual differences in cognitive performance on tasks requiring utilization of executive functions. (Nikolaev YS, Rudakov, Y.Y., Mansurov, S.M. and Mansurova, L.G, 1976) Heart rhythm coherence is reflected in the HRV power spectrum as a large increase in power in the low frequency (LF) band (typically around 0.1 Hz) and a decrease in power in the very low frequency (VLF) and high frequency (HF) bands. (Ginsberg JP, Berry, M.E., Powell, D.A., 2010; Lloyd A, Brett, D., Wesnes, K., 2010)

A coherent heart rhythm can therefore be defined as a relatively harmonic (sine-wave-like) signal with a very narrow, high-amplitude peak in the LF region of the HRV power spectrum with no major peaks in the VLF or HF regions. Coherence thus approximates the LF/(VLF + HF) ratio (see Figure 1). (Lloyd A, Brett, D., Wesnes, K., 2010) More specifically, coherence is assessed by identifying the maximum peak in the 0.04–0.26 Hz range of the HRV power spectrum, calculating the integral in a window 0.030 Hz wide centered on the highest peak in that region, then calculating the total power of the entire spectrum. The Coherence ratio is formulated as: (Peak Power / (Total Power – Peak Power).

Heart coherence is a highly efficient functional mode that is associated with efficient utilization of energy resources and numerous health related benefits. These include: (1) resetting of baroreceptor sensitivity, which is related to short-term blood pressure control and increased respiratory efficiency; (Zaitseva SAaP, M. I., 1995) (2) increased vagal afferent traffic, which is involved in the inhibition of pain signals and sympathetic outflow; (Persinger MA., 1999) (3) increased cardiac output in conjunction with increased efficiency in fluid exchange, filtration, and absorption between the capillaries and tissues; (Kleimenova N, Kozyreva O., 2007) (4) increased ability of the cardiovascular system to adapt to circulatory requirements; (5) increased temporal synchronization of cells throughout the body; (Subrahmanyam S, Narayan P, Srinivasan T., 1985) and (6) increased synchronization in the reciprocal activity of the branches of the ANS. (Ginsberg JP, Berry, M.E., Powell, D.A.d, 2010) Thus, coherence results in increased system-wide energy efficiency and metabolic energy savings. (Kleimenova N, Kozyreva

O., 2007; Subrahmanyam S, Narayan P, Srinivasan T., 1985; Halberg F, Cornelissen G, Sothern RB, Katinas GS, Schwartkopff O, Otsuka K., 2008).

Another aspect of the coherence mode is the phenomenon of resonance. Resonance occurs in an oscillatory system when there is a large sudden increase in amplitude at a specific frequency. The frequency at which this large increase in amplitude occurs is defined as the resonance frequency of the system. Most mathematical models show that the resonance frequency of the human cardiovascular system is determined by the feedback loops between the heart and brain. (Otsuka K, Cornelissen G, Norboo T, Takasugi E, Halberg F., 2008; Persinger MA., 1987) In humans and in many animals, the resonance frequency of the system is approximately 0.1 Hz. It is reasonable to conclude that coherence and resonance are characteristic of the natural physiological state associated with heart-felt positive emotions.

The Central Role of the Heart

There is substantial evidence that the heart plays a unique role in synchronizing the activity across multiple [functional] systems and levels of organization. (Ginsberg JP, Berry, M.E., Powell, D.A., 2010; Kleimenova N, Kozyreva O., 2007; Subrahmanyam S, Narayan P, Srinivasan T., 1985) As the most powerful and consistent generator of rhythmic information patterns in the body, the heart is in continuous communication with the brain and body through multiple pathways: *neurologically*, (through the ANS) *biochemically* (through hormones), *biophysically* (through pressure and sound waves), and *energetically* (through electromagnetic field interactions). The heart is uniquely well positioned to act as the "global coordinator" in the body's symphony of functions to bind and synchronize the system as a whole. Because of the extensiveness of the heart's influence on functional physiological, cognitive, and emotional systems, the heart provides a central point of reference from which the dynamics of such processes can be regulated.

Although most discussions of the ANS focus on the efferent (descending) pathways, the afferent (ascending) nerves play a critical role in creating the heart rhythm and thus the coherent state. Although not well known, 85% to 90% of the nerves in the vagus nerve are afferents and the cardiovascular afferents send signals to the brain to a much greater extent than other major organs. (Dimitrova S, Stoilova, I. and Cholakov, I., 2004) While it is generally known that these afferent signals have a regulatory influence on many aspects of the efferent signals that flow to the heart, blood vessels, and other glands and organs, it is less commonly appreciated that they also have profound affects on the higher brain centers. Cardiovascular afferents have numerous connections to such brain centers as the thalamus, hypothalamus, and amygdala, and they play an important role in determining emotional experience (Figure 4). (Odintsov S, Boyarchuk K, Georgieva K, Kirov B, Atanasov D., 2006; Dimitrova S, Stoilova, I. and Cholakov, I., 2004; Rapoport SI, Malinovskaia, N.K., Oraevskii, V.N., Komarov, F.I., Nosovskii, A.M. and Vetterberg, L., 1997; Ertel S. 1996; Grigoryev P, Rozanov, V., Vaiserman, A., Vladimirskiy, B., 2009)

SURVEY OF DYNAMICS FOR CREATING COHERENCE WITH DBG PLAY

By all indications, Jungian Compensation is synonymous with coherence. As detailed above, researchers have studied systemic-biological coherence intensively. The resulting understanding of global coherence comports with the Jungian process of *compensation* in psyche made possible by analyzing metaphors projected in dream symbolism. So, compensation and coherence can be understood as fundamental

Figure 9. Diagram of the currently known afferent pathways by which information from the heart and cardiovascular system modulates brain activity. Note the direct connections from the NTS to the amygdala, hypothalamus, and thalamus. Although not shown, there is also evidence emerging of a pathway from the dorsal vagal complex that travels directly to the frontal cortex.

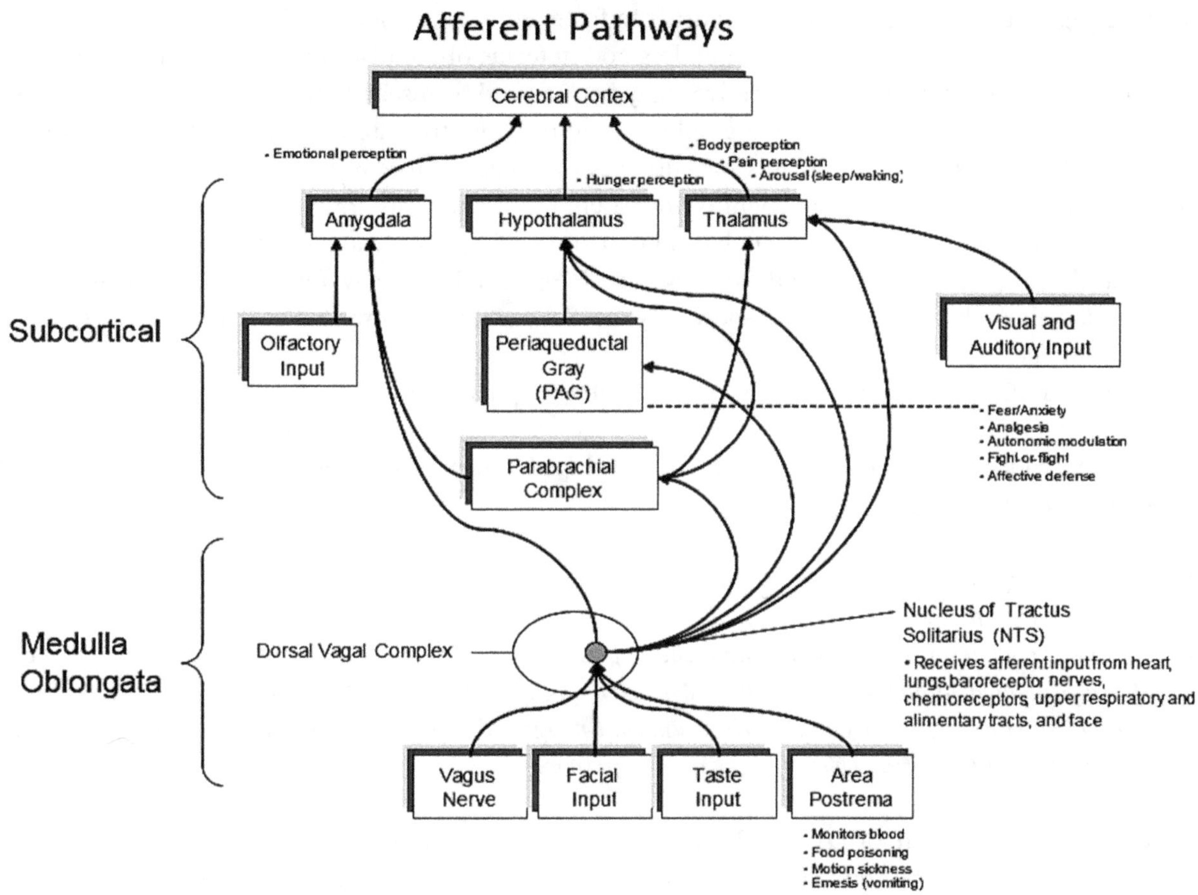

objectives in Jung's *Amplification Method* of clinical treatment. For additional verification, the harmonious states of coherence and compensation have the same characteristics as those experiencing the multi-functional "Flow" phenomena: feelings of involvement, serenity, oneness, ecstasy, timelessness, intrinsic worth, and control. (Csíkszentmihályi, 1990) Jung explains the dynamic as follows:

For every piece of conscious life that loses its importance and value—so runs the law—there arises a compensation in the unconscious. We may see in this an analogy to the conservation of energy in the physical world, for our psychic processes have a quantitative aspect also. No psychic value can disappear without being replaced by another of equivalent intensity. (Jung, 1933 p. 209-210)

It is our contention that with the application of Jungian principles to *psych*ecology game (PG) research, findings relative to cognitive dynamics could be applied to the Media Dream. Therefore, based on PG research, coherent psychological states could be induced in collective personae by researching how target groups can be predisposed to coherent states in both collectives and distributive individuals. The above discussion of research relevant to the nature of coherence, how it can be measured and reinforced with biofeedback, and how it can be applied to harmonization of psyche in all its functions—physical, emotional, rational, and spiritual—demonstrates that the functions cited above correspond to the Jungian functions of psyche—sensing, feeling, thinking, and intuiting. These principles and functions can be integrated into experimental design in order to foster coherence (Schafer, 2015, p. 9).

Compensation and coherence can be understood in terms of the discovery of meaning. Potentially, cognitive meaning for contextual collectives may be accessed by researching the media-sphere with the PG model in terms of its dramatic-holographic structure. This structure is directly correlated with Carl Jung's context and analysis of dreams for purposes of healing. Moreover, Jung's theories are entirely consistent and predictive of recent cognitive research. Employing this array of theoretical and practical frameworks in game design and research design, it should be possible to analyze the collective unconscious as the incipient digital age of illusion evolves. PG research model would provide robust and timely information about this altered reality, and verify the electromagnetic impact of the human collective on the dreamscape.

In order to illustrate the potential of PG for electro-magnetic impact, recent data includes this bit of information about player numbers of the most popular video game in the world—the multiplayer online battle arena video game, *League of Legends,* developed and published by Riot Games for Microsoft Windows (Sheer, 2014).

In League of Legends, players assume the role of a character, called a "champion", with unique abilities, battling with a team against other player or computer-controlled champions. In the most popular game modes, each team's goal is to destroy the opposing team's nexus, a building which lies at the heart of a base protected by defensive structures. Each League of Legends (LOL) game is discrete, with all champions starting off each game fairly weak and progressing by accumulating gold and experience over the course of the game. (New player guide, 2014)

The dramatic structure of *LoL* is relatively sophisticated, such that the story exposition would lend itself to contextualization (unique abilities) according to Jungian parameters (dramatic unities of the Hero's Journey). In terms of the media dreamscape, LoL constitutes a contextual dream. Whatever the profiles of constituent players may be, they can be analyzed according to symbolic patterns projected by the game in order to disclose unconscious patterns of their collective persona.

The fact that each game is discrete suggests that LoL has a wide target group appeal. Its basic structure is evolutionary and acquisitive—players learn from experience and are motivated by accumulating gold. If focus groups of players were profiled with existing Myers-Briggs algorithms, more refined psychological motives symbolized by the basic context of the game (growth and acquisition) might be discovered and addressed within the choice patterns proffered to the contextual group by the game. Each distributive refinement would result in collective refinement. When game-wins are associated with increased functional group coherency in various contexts, insights become possible relative to patterns that could lead to increased coherence in collective personae.

Our hypothesis is that Jungian principles of dream analysis may be extended to the dreamlike images in the digital media-sphere in order to discover meaningful patterns of unconscious motivation in contextual individuals and collectives. In other words, due to dynamic correspondences between the collective unconscious and the digital unconscious, analysis of symbolic patterns in contextual media images can provide meaningful information relative to unconscious contextual patterns of collective personae. If this information can be measured in terms of coherent psychological states, the affordances reflected by the contextual media would provide a degree of predictability for fostering coherence (healing and learning) in cognitive states of collective personae. A fundamental aspect of Jungian principle is that dreams have dramatic structure—Aristotle's dramatic unity, characters, plot, exposition (statement of the dramatic problem), and *lysis* (resolution of the dramatic problem)—that serves as a reference point for the analytical process.

Aristotle's dramatic unities can be understood in terms of holography. The dramatic unities of time, place, and action are called unities because—like time, space, and what happens there—they cannot be separated. In his analytical system of dream analysis, Carl Jung applies Aristotle's definition to the dramatic structure of dreams in order to probe the personal unconscious of patients. However, the dynamics of his analysis may also be applied to collectives. (Jung 1933, p 209-210) Extrapolating, it becomes possible to apply the same dynamics to the media dreamscape in order to probe the collective unconscious of contextual groups.

For purposes of cognitive research, drama-based video games have all of the Aristotelian dramatic dimensions as well as the Jungian dynamics of Psyche. Therefore, according to their unique character profile (context), player choices may be designed to access unconscious contextual problems and to resolve them by associating *lysis* (solution of the contextual premise) with a game win. Essentially, this interactive process in game play constitutes the well-known learning dynamic of repetition whereby choice patterns strengthen neural synapses. Such patterns could reinforce meaningful insight and learning on the part of the player in the direction of Jungian individuation and coherence. In the field of neuro-marketing, similar assumptions underlie research. However, most of this research tends to employ Freudian principles that are unlike Jungian principles.

In drama, character is multidimensional as measured in terms of four Jungian functions (sensing, feeling, thinking, and intuiting) These are the classical four functions symbolized by the four elements (earth, water, air, and fire) pervasive in myth and philosophy. The functions and other dynamics of Jungian analysis such as introversion and extroversion have been incorporated into Myers-Briggs personality profiling algorithms that have proven to be quite accurate and relatively easy to administer with short tests. Such profiling applied to target group demographics could prove to be much more effective at accessing unconscious dimensions of personality than existing focus group profiling as applied in advertising. Psychological profiling could also establish the character *premise* (what the character needs to learn). Premise could be integrated into the exposition (statement of the story problem) and lysis (resolution of the problem) of the drama.

Plot is determined by interactive contextual character/player choices. As in Jungian dreams, a patient/player's agency and interaction with the dream images/monitor images reflects psychological changes and progress toward individuation. Dramatic choices occur within the fundamental archetypal pattern known as the hero's journey. Based on these archetypal-dramatic parameters, the potential for contextual choices become infinite, and such potentials are within reach because of advances in artificial intelligence (AI) algorithms. In short, PG constitute a dream analogue as well as a metaphorical model of so-called "reality".

Dramatic action resides within narrative-metaphorical parameters and can be designed in accordance with sophisticated personality profiling and cognitive research. Profiling can pinpoint the character premise (what needs to be learned) in order to incorporate authentic, predictive target group (player) opportunities for authentic choice-making. Authentic choice patterns can be associated with a game-win in order to alter unconscious neural synapses according to contextually defined psychologically coherent states.

Like dreams, myths are replete with symbolic messages from the realms of what Carl Jung called the personal and collective unconscious. Dreams are the quintessential medium for accessing the contents of the unconscious and giving that content conscious form. Given this parallel between dream and myth, the great scholar of myth, Joseph Campbell, espoused the revolutionary idea that myth should be understood as psychology: "The patterns and logic of fairy tale and myth correspond to those of dream" and "symbolic expression is given to the unconscious desires, fears, and tension that underlie the conscious patterns of human behavior. Mythology, in other words, is psychology misread as biography; history, and cosmology." Campbell goes on to say that, "Dream is the personalized myth, myth the depersonalized dream; both myth and dream are symbolic in the same general way of the dynamics of the psyche. But in the dream the forms are quirked by the peculiar troubles of the dreamer, whereas in myth the problems and solutions shown are directly valid for all mankind." So, "The modern psychologist can translate it back to its proper denotations and thus rescue for the contemporary world a rich and eloquent document of the profoundest depths of human character." (Campbell, 1968, pp. 19)

Campbell was referring specifically to the psychology of Carl G. Jung, and by making the connection between psychology and myth he provided a clue to the healing potential in video games. A basic structural reference for analyzing dreams is the archetypal Journey of the Hero which Campbell named and defined as a fundamental parallel among the world's myths. (Jung understood the journey as a process he called Individuation or self-realization.) Campbell meant that myths should be interpreted according to the principles of Jungian dream analysis: functions of psyche, attitude types, complexes, archetypes, projection, compensation, libido, amplification, symbol, pictorial expressions, the shadow, and individuation. According to Jung:

The dream has a certain purpose, namely to disclose a fact of which the dreamer was not or did not want to be aware....Such a warning is the expression of a dynamic tendency in the unconscious. This dynamic tendency, the force behind the dream and its utterances, sends new contents into consciousness which in turn—if they have been assimilated by the personality—react upon and modify the unconscious field of forces....Once understood and elaborated, they can exert an extraordinary and even liberating effect on the dreamer whose problem they express and illuminate.'" (Jacoby, pp. 88-89)

This narrative-metaphorical dynamic is the common denominator between dream analysis and design of Drama-based Games—a popular genre that was originally known as *Role-playing games*. Narrative structure is an important aspect of the *amplification method* of dream analysis that Jung employed to cure his patients.

The subjective, individual meaning of the dream is supplied by subjective amplification; i.e., the analyst asks the dreamer what each dream element means to him personally. Then the collective meaning is obtained by objective amplification; i.e., the dream elements are enriched with the universal, symbolic material of fairy tales, myths, etc., which illuminate the universal aspect of the problem that concerns every human being (Jacobi, p. 89).

So, psychological parallels exist in the psychological patterns of the mythic Journey and the patterns of dream analysis. "This amplification, in contrast to the Freudian method of [reduction]...is not an unbroken chain of causally connected associations leading backward, but a process by which the dream content is broadened and enriched with the help of analogous images." (Jacobi, p. 84) In Jungian analysis, the psychiatrist employs *the dynamics of metaphor* to gain insight and plays the role of guide and mentor, assisting the patient with metaphorical amplifications as to the subliminal content of the dreamer's psyche. Dreams are stories in which the patient is the protagonist. If a series of dreams is analyzed like a story, insight about the premise of the story (what the character learns) is generated from the unconscious psyche of the patient. Dreams constitute a symbolic narrative in which the images are the medium with which the unconscious aspects of a patient's psyche can be accessed. Though it is only a paraphrase of Jung's methodology, it is accurate to say that he employed the skills of literary exegesis to analyze a patient's story. Invariably, the subject's story has the elements of the Hero Journey, and its symbols and archetypes were mythical.

An important correspondence between narrative role-playing games or DBG and the Jungian psychiatrist is that both healer and game software adopt the role of archetypal Mentor. Assume that game software is programmed to remember Jungian principles and practices; given the sophistication of today's big-data algorithms, machine intelligence might actually perform in a manner superior to the trained Jungian analyst. In no way do I intend to diminish the value of an authentic intuitive healer, but such healers can be influenced by their own cognitive frameworks, and that may skew the mentoring process. Verifying this assumption will require research, but considered as analytical process it seems feasible that a game could be programmed with a degree of psychological integrity. Just as dreams adjust to the process of analysis, or atoms (wave vs. particle) adjust to the structure of an experiment the game could adjust to player inputs within a well defined personality profile such as Myers-Briggs personality types. Player responses would be remembered by the software in order to invoke a steady stream of dream scenarios embedded with symbolism attuned to foster psychological coherence in the contextual player.

CONCLUSION AND RECOMMENDATIONS

Just as dreams and game-wins divulge meaning, research on the content of the media dream could lead to biologically relevant information about the nature and significance of illusion in preparation for an age of illusion. Methods for fostering coherent states within the *Psych*ecology could be developed by providing meaningful choice patterns during *psych*ecology game play that lead to increased coherence in collective cognitive states. Employing this methodology, a coupling among functions of the human brain, cardiovascular and nervous systems, and resonating geomagnetic frequencies would provide experimental support for the hypothesis that the emergent mediated reality of electromagnetic bandwidths can be correlated with bio-energetic and geomagnetic frequencies.

Conscious-unconscious, interactive player choice patterns could divulge robust data relative to bio-energetic impacts of collective "personae" on the media-sphere and, ultimately, their impact on the biosphere. A salient factor in the unified field of Psyche is the impact of electromagnetic fields generated by the heart. This field is essential to the body's function as a coherent whole, and it permeates every cell and plays a central role in the generation and transmission of system-wide information. Abundant research has demonstrated that the rhythmic patterns in beat-to-beat heart rate variability reflect emotional functions and encode and transmit biologically relevant information via the electromagnetic field radiated into the environment.

Because coherent functional states and Jungian compensational states are correlated, the "media dream" becomes susceptible to psychological analysis leading to a better understanding of unconscious cognitive patterns in order to address "healing" of contextual collectives. Amplification of this hypothesis suggests that research on the patterns of energetic impacts of contextual collectives will divulge authentic ways—using mediated biofeedback—to foster coherent cognitive states in collective personae. Such research using the PG model can provide robust data relative to the functional impact that human energies have on the ionosphere of the planet.

REFERENCES

Aronne, L. J., Mackintosh, R., Rosenbaum, M., Leibel, R. L., & Hirsch, J. (1997). Cardiac autonomic nervous system activity in obese and never-obese young men. *Obesity Research*, *5*(4), 354–359. doi:10.1002/j.1550-8528.1997.tb00564.x PMID:9285844

Bartsch, H., Bartsch, C., Mecke, D., & Lippert, T. H. (1994). Seasonality of pineal melatonin production in the rat: Possible synchronization by the geomagnetic field. *Chronobiology International*, *11*(1), 21–26. doi:10.3109/07420529409057227 PMID:8013047

Baselli, G. et al.. (1994). Model for the assessment of heart period variability interactions of respiration influences. *Medical and Biological Engineering and Computing*, 32(2), 143-152.

Belov, D. R., Kanunikov, I. E., & Kiselev, B. V. (1998). Dependence of human EEGsynchronization on the geomagnetic activity on the day of experiment. *Rossiiskii Fiziologicheskii Zhurnal Imeni I. M. Sechenova*, *84*(8), 761–774.

Bergiannaki, J.-D., Paparrigopoulos, T. J., & Stefanis, C. N. (1996). Seasonal pattern of melatonin excretion in humans: Relationship to day length variation rate and geomagnetic field fluctuations. *Experientia*, *52*(3), 253–258. doi:10.1007/BF01920718 PMID:8631397

Berk, M., Dodd, S., & Henry, M. (2006). Do ambient electromagnetic fields affect behaviour? A demonstration of the relationship between geomagnetic storm activity and suicide. *Bioelectromagnetics*, *27*(2), 151–155. doi:10.1002/bem.20190 PMID:16304696

Bohm, D., & Hiley, B. J. (1993). *The Undivided Universe*. London: Routledge.

Bradley, R. T., Gillin, M., McCraty, R., & Atkinson, M. (2011). Nonlocal Intuition in Entrepreneurs and Non-entrepreneurs: Results of Two Experiments Using Electrophysiological Measures. *International Journal of Entrepreneurship and Small Business*, *12*(3), 343–372. doi:10.1504/IJESB.2011.039012

Bradley, R. T., McCraty, R., Atkinson, M., & Gillin, M. (2007). Reducing Test Anxiety and Improving Test Performance in America's Schools: Results from the TestEdge National Demonstration StudyBoulder Creek, CA: HeartMath Research Center, Institute of HeartMath, Publication No. 07-09-01.

Bradley, R. T., McCraty, R., Atkinson, M., & Gillin, M. (Eds.). (2008). Nonlocal Intuition in Entrepreneurs and Nonentrepreneurs: An Experimental Comparison Using Electrophysiological Measures. Regional Frontiers of Entrepreneurship Research, Hawthorne, Australia.

Bradley, R. T., McCraty, R., Atkinson, M., Tomasino, D., Daugherty, A., & Arguelles, L. (2010). Emotion Self-Regulation, Psychophysiological Coherence, and Test Anxiety: Results from an Experiment Using Electrophysiological Measures. *Applied Psychophysiology and Biofeedback*, *35*(4), 261–283. doi:10.1007/s10484-010-9134-x PMID:20559707

Burch, J. B., Reif, J. S., & Yost, M. G. (1999). Geomagnetic disturbances are associated with reduced nocturnal excretion of a melatonin metabolite in humans. *Neuroscience Letters*, *266*(3), 209–212. doi:10.1016/S0304-3940(99)00308-0 PMID:10465710

Campbell, J. (1973). *The hero with a thousand faces*. Princeton, NJ: First Princeton/Bolingen.

Cernouss, S., Vinogradov, A., & Vlassova, E. (2001). Geophysical Hazard for Human Health in the Circumpolar Auroral Belt: Evidence of a Relationship between Heart Rate Variation and Electromagnetic Disturbances. *Natural Hazards*, *23*(2/3), 121–135. doi:10.1023/A:1011108723374

Cherry, N. (2002). Schumann Resonances, a plausible biophysical mechanism for the human health effects of Solar/Geomagnetic Activity. *Natural Hazards*, *26*(3), 279–331. doi:10.1023/A:1015637127504

Cornelissen, G., Halberg, F., Schwartkopff, O., Delmore, P., Katinas, G., & Hunter, D. et al.. (1993). Chronomes, Time Structures, for Chronobioengineering for "A Full Life". *Biomedical Instrumentation & Technology*, *1999*(33), 152–187. PMID:10194568

Csíkszentmihályi, M. (1990). *Flow: The Psychology of Optimal Experience*. Harper & Row.

Curtis, A. (2002). The century of self. *BBC*. Retrieved from http://topdocumentaryfilms.com/the-century-of-the-self/

deBoer, R. W., Karemaker, J. M., & Strackee, J. (1987). Hemodynamic fluctuations and baroreflex sensitivity in humans: A beat-to-beat model. *The American Journal of Physiology*, *253*(3 Pt 2), H680–H689. PMID:3631301

Deyhle, A. (2010) Interconnectedness. *Global Coherence Initiative Commentary*. Retrieved from http://www.glcoherence.org/monitoring-system/commentaries.html

Deyhle, A. (2013). Solar Activity, Global Coherence Monitoring System and Saudi Arabia HRVStudy. *Global Coherence Initiative Commentary*. Retrieved from http://www.glcoherence.org/monitoring-system/commentaries.html

Dimitrova, S., Stoilova, I., & Cholakov, I. (2004). Influence of Local Geomagnetic Storms on Arterial Blood Pressure. *Bioelectromagnetics*, *25*(6), 408–414. doi:10.1002/bem.20009 PMID:15300726

Dolgato, K. M., & Kholodov, Y. A. (1987). Magnetic fields and brain. *Future Science*, *20*, 133.

Dooley, R. (2015). Repeat, repeat, repeat…and sell. *Neuromarketing*. Retrieved from http://www.neurosciencemarketing.com/blog/articles/repetition.htm

Doronin, V. N., Parfentev, V. A., & Tleulin, S. Zh., Namvar, R.A., Somsikov, V.M., Drobzhev, V.I. & Chemeris (1998). A.V. Effect of variations of the geomagnetic field and solar activity on human physiological indicators. *Biofizika*, *43*(4), 647–653. PMID:9783072

Ertel, S. (1996). Space weather and revolutions: Chizhevsky's heliobiological claim scrutinized. *Studia Psychologica*, *39*, 3–22.

Frysinger, R. C., & Harper, R. M. (1990). Cardiac and respiratory correlations with unit discharge in epileptic human temporal lobe. *Epilepsia*, *31*(2), 162–171. doi:10.1111/j.1528-1167.1990.tb06301.x PMID:2318169

Georgopoulos, A. P., Karageorgiou, E., Leuthold, A. C., Lewis, S. M., Lynch, J. K., Alonso, A. A., & Westermeyer, J. J. et al. (2007, December). Synchronous neural interactions assessed by magnetoencephalography: A functional biomarker for brain disorders. *Journal of Neural Engineering*, *4*(4), 349–355. doi:10.1088/1741-2560/4/4/001 PMID:18057502

Ghione, S., Mazzasalma, L., Del Seppia, C., & Papi, F. (1998). Do geomagnetic disturbances of solar origin affect arterial blood pressure? *Journal of Human Hypertension*, *12*(11), 749–754. doi:10.1038/sj.jhh.1000708 PMID:9844945

Ginsberg,, J.P., Berry, M.E., & Powell, D.A. (2010). Cardiac Coherence and PTSD in Combat Veterans. *Alternative Therapies in Health and Medicine*, *16*(4), 52–60. PMID:20653296

Glassner, A. (2004). *Interactive storytelling*. Natick, Massachusetts: A.K. Peters.

Gordon, C., & Berk, M. (2003). The effect of geomagnetic storms on suicide. *South African Psychiatry Review*, *6*, 24–27.

Gousheva, M. N., Georgieva, K. Y., Kirov, B. B., & Antanasov, D. (Eds.), (2003, November 20-22). On the relation between solar activity and seismicity. *Proceedings of International Conference on Recent Advances in Space Technologies RAST '03*. doi:10.1109/RAST.2003.1303913

Grigoryev, P., Rozanov, V., Vaiserman, A., & Vladimirskiy, B. (2009). Heliogeophysical factors as possible triggers of suicide terroristic acts. *Health*, *1*(4), 294–297. doi:10.4236/health.2009.14048

Halberg, F., Cornelissen, G., McCraty, R. A., & Al-Abdulgader, A. (2011). Time Structures (Chronomes) of the Blood Circulation, Populations' Health, Human Affairs and Space Weather. *World Heart Journal*, *3*(1), 1–40. PMID:24511305

Halberg, F., Cornelissen, G., Otsuka, K., Watanabe, Y., Katinas, G. S., & Burioka, N. et al.. (2000). Cross-spectrally coherent ~10.5- and 21-year biological and physical cycles, magnetic storms and myocardial infarctions. *Neuroendocrinology*, *21*, 233–258. PMID:11455355

Halberg, F., Cornélissen, G., Sothern, R. B., Katinas, G. S., Schwartzkopff, O., & Otsuka, K. (2008). Cycles Tipping the Scale between Death and Survival (="Life"). *Progress ofTheoretical Physics Supplement*, *173*, 153–181. doi:10.1143/PTPS.173.153

Hamer, J. R. (1965). Biological entrainment of the human brain by low frequency radiation. *Northrop Space Labs.*, *1965*, 65–199.

Hameroff, S., & Penrose, S. R. (2014). Discovery of quantum vibrations in 'mocrotubules' corroborates theory of consciousness. Retrieved from http://phys.org/news/2014-01-discovery-quantum-vibrations-microtubules-corroborates.html)

Jacobi, J. (1973). *The Psychology of CG Jung*. London, USA: Yale University Press.

Jung, C. G. (1933). *Modern man in search of a soul*. USA: Harcourt Brace & Company.

Kay, R. W. (1994). Geomagnetic Storms: Association with Incidence of Depression as Measured by Hospital Admission. *The British Journal of Psychiatry*, *164*(3), 403–409. doi:10.1192/bjp.164.3.403 PMID:8199794

Kay, R. W. (2004). Schizophrenia and season of birth: Relationship to geomagnetic storms. *Schizophrenia Research*, *66*(1), 7–20. doi:10.1016/S0920-9964(02)00495-4 PMID:14693348

Kleimenova N, Kozyreva O. (2005). Daytime quasiperiodic geomagnetic pulsations during the recovery phase of the strong magnetic storm of May 15, 2005. *Geomagnetism and Aeronomy,* 47(5), 580-7.

Knox, E. G., Armstrong, E., Lancashire, R., Wall, M., & Haynes, R. (1979). Heart attacks and geomagnetic activity. *Nature*, *281*(5732), 564–565. doi:10.1038/281564a0 PMID:492317

Kosslyn, S. (1994). *Image and brain*. PA: Massachusetts Institute of Technology.

Lakoff, G. (2008). *The Political Mind*. New York, NY: Viking Penguin.

Lakoff, G., & Narayanan, S. (2010). *Toward a Computational Model of Narrative*. Association for the Advancement of Artificial Intelligence. Retrieved from http://www1.icsi.berkeley.edu/~snarayan/narrative-aaai-fs2010.pdf

Lakoff, G. (2002). *Moral Politics*. University of Chicago Press: Chicago

Laszlo, E. (1995). *The Interconnected Universe: Conceptual Foundations of Transdiciplinary Unified Theroy*. Singapore: World Scientific.

Laszlo, E. (2008). *Quantum Shift in the Global Brain: how the new scientific reality can change us and our world*. Rochester, VT: Inner Traditions.

Lehrer, P. M., Vaschillo, E., Vaschillo, B., Lu, S.-E., Eckberg, D. L., Edelberg, R., & Hamer, R. M. et al. (2003). Heart rate variability biofeedback increases baroreflex gain and peak expiratory flow. *Psychosomatic Medicine*, *65*(5), 796–805. doi:10.1097/01.PSY.0000089200.81962.19 PMID:14508023

Levy, B. R., Slade, M. D., Kunkel, S. R., & Kasl, S. V. (2002). Longevity increased by positive self-perceptions of aging. *Journal of Personality and Social Psychology*, *83*(2), 261–270. doi:10.1037/0022-3514.83.2.261 PMID:12150226

Levy, B. R., Slade, M. D., Kunkel, S. R., & Kasl, S. V. (2002). Longevity increased by positive self-perceptions of aging. *Journal of Personality and Social Psychology*, *83*(2), 261–270. doi:10.1037/0022-3514.83.2.261 PMID:12150226

Lindmark, S., Buren, J., & Eriksson, J. W. (2006). Insulin resistance, endocrine function and adipokines in type 2 diabetes patients at different glycaemic levels: Potential impact for glucotoxicity in vivo. *Horumon To Rinsho*, *65*(3), 301–309. doi:10.1111/j.1365-2265.2006.02593.x PMID:16918948

Lindmark, S., Lönn, L., Wiklund, U., Tufvesson, M., Olsson, T., & Eriksson, J. W. (2005). Dysregulation of the autonomic nervous system can be a link between visceral adiposity and insulin resistance. *Obesity Research*, *13*(4), 717–728. doi:10.1038/oby.2005.81 PMID:15897481

Lindmark, S., Wiklund, U., Bjerle, P., & Eriksson, J. W. (2003). Does the autonomic nervous system play a role in the development of insulin resistance? A study on heart rate variability in first-degree relatives of Type 2 diabetes patients and control subjects. *Diabetic Medicine*, *20*(5), 399–405. doi:10.1046/j.1464-5491.2003.00920.x PMID:12752490

Lloyd, A., Brett, D., & Wesnes, K. (2010). Coherence Training Improves Cognitive Functions and Behavior In Children with ADHD. *Alternative Therapies in Health and Medicine*, *16*(4), 34–42. PMID:20653294

Luthar, S. S., Cicchetti, D., & Becker, B. (2000). The construct of resilience: A critical evaluation and guidelines for future work. *Child Development*, *71*(3), 543–562. doi:10.1111/1467-8624.00164 PMID:10953923

Luthar, S. S., Cicchetti, D., & Becker, B. (2000). The construct of resilience: A critical evaluation and guidelines for future work. *Child Development*, *71*(3), 543–562. doi:10.1111/1467-8624.00164 PMID:10953923

Malin, S. R. C., & Srivastava, B. J.Malin SRCaS. (1979). B.J. (1979). Correlation between heart attacks and magnetic activity. *Nature*, *277*(5698), 646–648. doi:10.1038/277646a0 PMID:423962

Marcer, P., & Schempp, W. (1998). The brain as a conscious system. *International Journal of General Systems*, *27*(1-3), 231–248. doi:10.1080/03081079808962066

McCraty, R., Atkinson, M., Lipsenthal, L., & Arguelles, L. (2009). Arguelles aL. (2009). New Hope for Correctional Officers: An Innovative Program for Reducing Stress and Health Risks. *Appl Psych and Biofeedback*, *34*(4), 251–272. doi:10.1007/s10484-009-9087-0

McCraty, R., Atkinson, M., Tomasino, D., & Bradley, R. T. (2009). The coherent heart: Heart-brain interactions, psychophysiological coherence, and the emergence of system-wide order. *Integral Review.*, *5*(2), 10–115.

McCraty, R., & Childre, D. (2004). The grateful heart: The psychophysiology of appreciation. In R. A. Emmons & M. E. McCullough (Eds.), *The Psychology of Gratitude* (pp. 230–255). New York: Oxford University Press.

McCraty, R., & Childre, D. (2010). Coherence: Bridging Personal, Social and Global Health. *Alternative Therapies in Health and Medicine*, *16*(4), 10–24. PMID:20653292

McCraty, R., Deyhle, A., & Childre, D. (2012). The Global Coherence Initiative: Creating a Coherent Planetary Standing Wave. *Global Advances in Health and Medicine*, *1*(1), 64–77. doi:10.7453/gahmj.2012.1.1.013 PMID:24278803

Mikulecký, M. (2007). Solar activity, revolutions and cultural prime in the history of mankind. *Neuroendocrinology Letters*, *28*(6), 749–756. PMID:18063926

Montez, T., Poil, S.-S., Jones, B. F., Manshanden, I., Verbunt, J. P. A., van Dijk, B. W., & Linkenkaer-Hansen, K. et al. (2009). Altered temporal correlations in parietal alpha and prefrontal theta oscillations in early-stage Alzheimer disease. *Proceedings of the National Academy of Sciences of the United States of America*, *106*(5), 1614–1619. doi:10.1073/pnas.0811699106

New Player Guide. (2014). League of Legends. *Riot Games*. Retrieved from http://en.wikipedia.org/wiki/League_of_Legends

Nikolaev, Y. S., Rudakov, Y. Y., Mansurov, S. M., & Mansurova, L. G. (1976). Interplanetary magnetic field sector structure and disturbances of the central nervous system activity. Reprint N 17a, Acad Sci USSR. *IZMIRAN, Moscow*, *1976*, 29.

Odintsov, S., Boyarchuk, K., Georgieva, K., Kirov, B., & Atanasov, D. (2006). Long-period trends in global seismic and geomagnetic activity and their relation to solar activity. *Physics and Chemistry of the Earth Parts A/B/C*, *31*(1–3), 88–93. doi:10.1016/j.pce.2005.03.004

Odintsov, S., Boyarchuk, K., Georgieva, K., Kirov, B., & Atanasov, D. (2006). Long-period trends in global seismic and geomagnetic activity and their relation to solar activity. *Physics and Chemistry of the Earth Parts A/B/C*, *31*(1–3), 88–93. doi:10.1016/j.pce.2005.03.004

Oppenheimer, S., & Hopkins, D. (1994). Suprabulbar neuronal regulation of the heart. In J. A. Armour & J. L. Ardell (Eds.), *Neurocardiology* (pp. 309–341). New York: Oxford University Press.

Oraevskii VN, Breus, T.K., Baevskii, R.M., Rapoport, S.I., Petrov, V.M., Barsukova, Zh.V., Gurfinkel' IuI, & Rogoza, A.T. (1998). Effect of geomagnetic activity on the functional status of the body. *Biofizika*, 43(5), 819-826.

Orme-Johnson, D. W. (2002). Quantifying the field effects of consciousness: From increased EEG coherence to reduced international terrorism. *Proceedings: Bridging.*

Otsuka, K., Cornelissen, G., Norboo, T., Takasugi, E., & Halberg, F. (2008). Chronomics and "Glocal" (Combined Global and Local) Assessment of Human Life. *Progress of Theoretical Physics Supplement.*, *173*, 134–152. doi:10.1143/PTPS.173.134

Persinger, M. A. (1987). Geopsychology and geopsychopathology: Mental processes and disorders associated with geochemical and geophysical factors. *Experientia*, *43*(1), 92–104. doi:10.1007/BF01940360 PMID:3792507

Persinger MA. (1998). Sudden unexpected death in epileptics following sudden, intense, increases in geomagnetic activity: prevalence of effect and potential mechanisms. *Int J Biometeorol.* 43(5), 819-826.

Persinger, M. A. (1999). Wars and increased solar-geomagnetic activity: Aggression or change in intraspecies dominance? *Perceptual and Motor Skills*, *88*(3 Pt. 2), 1351–1355. doi:10.2466/pms.1999.88.3c.1351 PMID:10485122

Pobachenko, S. V., Kolesnik, A. G., Borodin, A. S., & Kalyuzhin, V. V. (2006). The Contigency of Parameters of Human Encephalograms and Schumann Resonance Electromagnetic Fields Revealed in Monitoring Studies. *Complex Systems Biophysics.*, *51*(3), 480–483.

Pribram, K. H., & Bradley, R. T. (1998). The brain, the me and the I. In M. Ferrari & R. Sternberg (Eds.), *Self-Awareness: Its Nature and Development* (pp. 273–307). New York: The Guilford Press.

Rapoport, S. I., & Blodypakova, T. (1998). D., Malinovskaia, N.K., Oraevskii, V.N., Meshcheriakova, S.A., Breus, T.K. and Sosnovskii, A.M. (1998). Magnetic storms as a stress factor. *Biofizika*, *43*(4), 632–639. PMID:9783070

Rapoport, S. I., Malinovskaia, N. K., Oraevskii, V. N., Komarov, F. I., Nosovskii, A. M., & Vetterberg, L. (1997). Effects of disturbances of natural magnetic field of the Earth on melatonin production in patients with coronary heart disease. *Klinicheskaia Meditsina*, *75*(6), 24–26. PMID:9273394

Reeves, B., & Nass, C. (1996). The media equation. Stanford: Center For the study of Language and Information & Cambridge University Press.

Schafer, S. (2006). Curriculum and The dream Paradigm. Retrieved from http://www.gmecareerguide.com/features/288/curriculum_and_the_dream_paradigm.php

Schafer, S. (2007). Premise: The Key to Interactive Storytelling. *Game Career Guide*. Retrieved from http://www.gamecareerguide.com/features/357/premise_the_key_to_interactive_.php?page=1

Schafer, S. (2008). The *Psych*ecology Game I-V; Using Story-based Video Games to Capture Veridical Data on Subliminal States of Being. (The computational Resonance of Jungian Synchronicity) *Toward a Science of Consciousness 2008*, sponsored by the Consciousness Center & the University of Arizona. Retrieved from https://bandura.sbs.arizona.edu/login/consciousness/pubreport.aspx?aid=2761

Schafer, S. (2011). *Book Chapter: Articulating the paradigm shift: Serious games for psychological healing of the collective persona.* Business Social Networking: Organizational, Managerial, and Technological Dimensions. IGI Global. Retrieved from http://www.igi-global.com/book/handbook-research-serious-games-educational/5

Schafer, S. (2012). Optimizing Cognitive Coherence, Learning, and Psychological Healing with Drama-based Games. In J. Gackenbach (Ed.), *Video Game Play and Consciousness*. Nova Science Publishers. http://www.facebook.com/insights/?sk=po_261980910540561#!/pages/Video-Game-Play-and-Consciousness/261980910540561?sk=wall

Schafer, S., & Palamides, T. (2011) Designing an Ethical structure for Social Influence Marketing. In M.M. Cruz-Cunha, P. Gonçalves, N. Lopes, & G.D. Putnik (Eds.), *School Handbook of Research on Business Social Networking: Organizational, Managerial, and Technological Dimensions*. Hershey, PA, USA: IGI Global. Retrieved from www.igi-global.com

Schafer, S., & Yu, G. (2011) Meaningful Video Games: Drama-Based video Games as transformational experience. In M.M. Cruz-Cunha, & V.H. Varvalho, & P. Tavares (Eds.), *Business, Technological, and Social Dimensions to Video Games: Multidisciplinary Approach*. Hershey, PA, USA: IGI Global. Retrieved from http://resources.igi-global.com/Marketing/discountforms/FillableGenericBookDiscountForm.pdf

Schempp, W. (1992). Quantum holography and neurocomputer architectures. *Journal of Mathematical Imaging and Vision*, *2*(4), 279–326. doi:10.1007/BF00121876

Sheer, I. (2014). Player Tally for 'League of Legends' Surges. *Wsj.com*. Retrieved from http://en.wikipedia.org/wiki/League_of_Legends

Stoupel, E. (1993). Sudden cardiac deaths and ventricular extrasystoles on days of four levels of geomagnetic activity. *J Basic Physiol Pharmacol.*, *4*(4), 357–366. PMID:8664252

Subrahmanyam, S., Narayan, P., & Srinivasan, T. (1985). Effect of magnetic micropulsations on the biological systems — A bioenvironmental study. *International Journal of Biometeorology*, *29*(3), 293–305. doi:10.1007/BF02189660 PMID:3902670

Talbot, M. (1991). *The Holographic Universe*. New York, NY: Harper Collins Publishers.

Tiller, W. A., Dibble, J. W. E., & Kohane, M. J. (2001). *Conscious Acts of Creation: The Emergence of a New Physics. 2001* (pp. 201–202). Walnut Creek, CA: Pavior Publishing.

Tiller, W. A., McCraty, R., & Atkinson, M. (1996). Cardiac coherence: A new, noninvasive measure of autonomic nervous system order. *Alternative Therapies in Health and Medicine*, *2*(1), 52–65. PMID:8795873

Umetani, K., Singer, D. H., McCraty, R., & Atkinson, M. (1998). Twenty-four hour time domain heart rate variability and heart rate: Relations to age and gender over nine decades. *Journal of the American College of Cardiology*, *31*(3), 593–601. doi:10.1016/S0735-1097(97)00554-8 PMID:9502641

Villoresi, G., Ptitsyna, N. G., Tiasto, M. I., & Iucci, N. (1998). Myocardial infarct and geomagnetic disturbances: Analysis of data on morbidity and mortality [In Russian]. *Biofizika*, *43*(4), 623–631. PMID:9783069

Zaitseva SAaP. (1995). M. I. (1995). Effect of solar and geomagnetic activity on population dynamics among residents of Russia [In Russian]. *Biofizika*, *40*(4), 861–864. PMID:7495913

Chapter 2
The Dream Analog: *Psych*ecology Video Games

Stephen Brock Schafer
Pacific Rim Enterprises, USA

ABSTRACT

Increasingly, human perceptions of reality are based on virtual illusions. This altered reality called the metaverse is dreamlike. If reality, the metaverse, and dreams are virtual illusions, the metaverse and dreams are real. This suggests that virtual realities may be analyzed according to Carl Jung's compensational dynamics of dream analysis. The objective of such analysis would be discovery of contextual (target group) meaning in unconscious dimensions. Such discovery could lead to the use of mediated biofeedback to engineer Earth-sustainable media content in order to promote coherent frequencies on correlated electro-magnetic scales. This chapter will emphasize the authenticity of research on the collective unconscious as projected into the metaverse. Based on fundamental correlations in structure, function, and purpose of dreams as defined by Carl Jung, drama-based video games can be understood as a genre that may serve as an unprecedented, interactive dream analog for purposes of cognitive research.

INTRODUCTION

Since Edward Bernays created "Public Relations", the advertising industry has been employing techniques that stimulate unconscious association with products in order to promote sales and political agendas (Curtis, Adam, 2009). Focus groups have been a mainstay in the discovery process. With similar limited motives, the modern neuromarketing industry is probing the virtual unconscious of target groups based largely on Freudian principles that are "reductive" and view the unconscious in negative terms. (Curtis). Moreover, there has been an explosion of interest in exploiting video games and "gamefication" in research and engagement for tapping "buy buttons" in selected target groups. (Claes, 2014) This trend has been associated with ever more sophisticated use of "pseudo-spiritual" messages that promote their own worldviews and cult-like adherence to brands. (Goodman, Barak & Rushkoff, Douglas, 2004) Ultimately, the drama-based game research model based on Jungian/Lakoffian principles would provide more authentic research that would go far beyond marketing motivations in order to foster individual

DOI: 10.4018/978-1-4666-9891-8.ch002

and collective self-realization and healing. Such an expansion of consciousness would have profound positive impact on all aspects of human "reality"—education, commerce, healthcare, and law.

Unlike "reductive" Freudian principles, amplification principles and dynamics underlying Jungian therapy are "not an unbroken chain of causally connected associations leading backward, but a process by which the dream content is broadened and enriched with the help of analogous images." (Jacobi, 1973, pp. 84-87, 103) The Jungian Amplification Process emphasizes contextuality, empowerment, and empathy with the patient on multifunctional psychic levels. Therefore, adhering to authentic Jungian principles should dictate against misuse or manipulation of powerful subconscious forces. The same is true of George Lakoff's (2008) work. Lakoff says: "American values are progressive values," (2008, pp. 77-82), and it is critically important to verbalize this truth relative to the collective persona of the USA. Lakoff emphasizes that saying it matters. It matters because language works by mental simulation. Here, Lakoff cites Feldman: "'Words evoke whole frames—whole mental structures. Those mental structures activate an embodied mental simulation, giving the words meaning.'" (Feldman, 2006; Lakoff, 2008, p. 240) Metaphorically amplified Jungian symbols can also be understood as "whole frames".

In other words, according to Lakoff's reasoning, progressive thinking (according to the Nurturant Parent model) is in harmony with the greater symphony of American cultural ideologies. The term "progressive" denotes values based on the "common good", egalitarianism, and mutual respect that pervade theories of the Social Contract including John Locke (Locke, 1991, p. 5) and Jean-Jaques Rousseau (1754) who have argued that obtaining civil rights is dependent on accepting the obligation to respect and defend the rights of others, giving up some freedoms to do so. John Stuart Mill's Principle of Utility (Mill, John Stuart 1909, p. 258) and Harold Lasswell's Functional Analysis. (1948 pp. 203-243; Wright, W. R., 1960, pp. 610-613) Among his many contributions, Lasswell studied social structure as patterned social arrangements in society and the media that are both emergent from and determinant of the actions of individuals. His prescient work set the stage for modern discussions of the interactive metaverse.

Both Jung and Lakoff understand the collective unconscious with reference to dramatic structure as fundamentally defined by Aristotle. (Aristotle, 350 B.C.E.; O'Donnell, 2010) This subject will be expanded in the section on dramatic structure. In the dramatic context, "dramatis personae" may be defined in terms of human "function" (thinking, sensing, feeling, and intuiting) and purpose (learning and healing). A character's purpose may be understood as what s/he learns from experience in the drama, and this learning process may be understood in terms of character "premise" (Schafer, Stephen, 2007; Glassner, Andrew, 2004, p. 69) and psychological plot-exposition-and-resolution of the dramatic "problem"—exposition leading to *lysis*. Using modern technologies such as EEG, ECG, fMRI, and MEG to track neural electro-magnetic activity during game-play could provide real-time tracking of neuro-functional dynamics in order to disclose contextual meaning at levels of the cognitive unconscious. Relative to unconscious cognitive frames, Lakoff cites Feldman who points out that:

Combinations of simple "triangle nodes" are sufficient to characterize the neural computational properties of frames. Each "node" is a relatively small connection of neurons forming a circuit, and the firing of any two activates the third. In addition there is a control node, a simple circuit that accomplishes this. (Lakoff, 2008, p.275)

Whether the supposition is based on neuro-chemical imaging research or on "spooky action at a distance", it may be stipulated that significant correlations exist between the unified energy fields of cognition and physics. As the concept of reality as a unified field of energy and information espoused by such seers as Deepak Chopra (1995), Dean Radin (2006; 2009), and Michael Talbot (1991) is verified, the impacts of the metavese on human perceptions of reality must be explored more fully.

Though the universe of modern technological media has many names, the term metaverse is well-suited to discussion of virtual realities. The metaverse has been defined as a virtual shared space—a collective—created by the convergence of virtually enhanced physical reality and "physically persistent virtual space, including the sum of all virtual worlds, augmented reality, and the internet. The word *metaverse* is used to describe the concept of a future iteration of the internet, made up of persistent, shared, 3D virtual spaces linked into a perceived virtual universe. The term was coined in Neal Stephenson's 1992 science fiction novel *Snow Crash*, in which humans, as avatars, interact with each other and software agents, in a three-dimensional space that employs the real world as metaphor. Stephenson used the term to describe a virtual reality-based successor to the Internet (Smart, J.M., Cascio, J. and Paffendorf, J., 2007).

The metaverse can be understood as an integral part of the human psychological reality. The implicit concept underlying the metaverse is that real life is a metaphor and that virtual life is reality. This sounds typically nerdish except that Stanford researchers Byron Reeves and Clifford Nass laid a foundation for the concept in their book, The Media Equation (1996). The content of The Media Equation describes research methodology in thirty-five experiments that come to a unanimous conclusion: at unconscious levels, media is perceived by all demographics as "real." Their research has had a significant impact on the subsequent development of user-friendly computers. As Bill Gates said, "Nass and Reeves have spent the last decade working in the area of social responses to technology. We brought them into our team, and they have shown us some amazing things" (ibid.).

The unconscious perception that illusion is real has, therefore, been verified in fields of sociology and psychology as well as physics. Yet—though common sense dictates that being an aspect of everyday experience—human experience with the media is psychologically "real", the significance of this fact has been generally overlooked by researchers still unconsciously invested in the context of scientific materialism. Though many philosophers and academics would deny this accusation, in the frames of their cognitive unconscious, distrust of anything non-material persists and prevents efficient study of a non-material reality that has already been proven beyond doubt.

Though it is beyond the scope of this chapter, the argument relative to the dream analog is based on research in quantum physics, so a cursory background is provided in the background section. The reason that drama-based video games can be considered a dream analog is due to apparent correlations between principles of physics and psychiatry or energy and information components of communication and information technologies (ICTs). A case in point is the correlation between quantum entanglement and Jungian synchronicity. Another is the seeming correlation between coherence and Jungian compensation. Another is the direct correlation between Jungian "contextuality" and the profiling of target groups.

The hypothesis of this chapter is unprecedented; According to correlations between Jungian dynamics of dream analysis and video game dynamics, drama-based video games may serve as a dream analog. This is important because it suggests that—like dreams—drama-based video games have powerful potentials for discovery of unconscious meaning (learning) and multi-functional healing. Jung's work—usually unattributed—accords with current cognitive research, and though research on consciousness and quantum communication is vast, we refer to the work of George Lakoff because of its obvious similarities to Jungian research. However, as Lakoff's references indicate, primary assumptions have been developed in research fields for decades (2008).

Discussion of the hypothesis depends on allusions to diverse and complex fields of research including physics, holography, psychiatry, psychology, quantum communication, consciousness, and video games that cannot possibly be fully developed and referenced in a single chapter. Other chapters in the book expand on key concepts, but the emphasis here is on the dream analog with specific reference to structural continuities between video games and dreams as understood by Carl Jung. Of course, all dream research is not based on Jung's work, and researchers have a wide range of perspectives on the nature of dreams, but it cannot be doubted that Carl Jung has had a profound effect on dream research. A standout study is Robert Van de Castle's Our Dreaming Mind (1994). Related research has been accruing on the subject of lucid dreaming. Perhaps the best known researcher in this field is Stephen LaBerg (1980), but many others have contemplated the subject dating back to Aristotle. (Mavrematis, Andreas, 1987, p. 96). No matter what perspective researchers and theorists may have regarding the illusions of reality, much post-Jungian research is not inconsistent with Jungian insights; so, for the purposes of this chapter, Jungian principles are emphasized.

Beyond research on dreams, perspectives on ***why*** narrative-dramatic dynamics are practical and useful in various fields such as narrative therapy, witness reliability, interrogation, game theory, etc. is not always known. Though Freud is more often cited than Jung, the reasons why drama constitutes a framework for cognitive reference can best be explained in Jungian terms. Just as perspectives on dream analysis and the psychology of drama vary, so do definitions of coherence vary among scientific fields. The discussion of how coherence relates to Jungian compensation is based on its measurability as heart rate variability—explained more fully later. In this chapter, the significant correlations between video games and Jungian dreams are discussed in terms of: 1) agency, 2) dramatic structure, 3) coherence, 4) context & personality functions, and 5) individuation.

BACKGROUND

For the purposes of this chapter, it is not necessary to cite copious sources in physics, mathematics, and computer science, but only to summarize known principles. Within our intended context, excessive citations in these fields could be counter-productive., so moving forward: In the area of quantum communication, *quantum information science* is based on the idea that information science depends on quantum effects in physics. It includes theoretical issues in computational models as well as more experimental topics in quantum physics. There are numerous subsidiary fields among which the most relevant to this chapter are quantum computing and quantum entanglement.

In the field of *quantum computing* theoretical computation systems (quantum computers which are different from digital computers) are studied that make direct use of quantum-mechanical phenomena to perform operations on data. Such quantum-mechanical phenomena are *superposition* and *entanglement*. Whereas digital computers require data to be encoded into binary digits (bits), each of which is always in one of two definite states (0 or 1), quantum computation uses qubits (quantum bits), which can be in *superpositions* of states. While opinions vary as to the efficacy of quantum computing (Rincon, Paul, 2014), one form of quantum computing, "spintronics" or spin-based electronics (Kirk, Paul, 2014) promises the potential to create a new generation of super-fast computers, capable of processing vast amounts of data in an energy-efficient way. However opinions may differ, Microsoft has taken enough interest in quantum computing to bet on it as the next breakthrough in computation. (Simonite, Tom, 2014b; Markoff, John, 2014)

The concept of quantum entanglement is important to research on quantum computing. In physics, *quantum entanglement* is a physical phenomenon that occurs when pairs or groups of particles are generated or interact in such ways that the quantum state of each particle cannot be described independently—instead, a quantum state may be given for the system as a whole. Without going into the details of quantum measurement, entangled particles are *correlated*, and in this usage, correlation refers to any of a broad class of statistical relationships involving dependence. Such phenomena were the subject of a paper by Albert Einstein, Boris Podolsky, and Nathan Rosen (1935). Subsequently, Erwin Schrödinger (1935, pp. 555-563) dealt with what came to be known as the EPR paradox. Because it violated the local realist view of causality, Einstein and others considered such behavior to be impossible. Einstein referred to it as "spooky action at a distance". *Local realism* combines the principle of locality with the assumption that something must have a pre-existing value in order to measure it. According to the formalism of quantum theory, the effect of measurement happens instantly. Since 1935, the counterintuitive predictions of quantum mechanics have been verified experimentally. Experiments have been performed involving measuring the polarization or spin of entangled particles in different directions, which—by producing violations of Bell's inequality—demonstrate statistically that the local realist view cannot be correct. From 1996 to the present, Quantum entanglement has been an area of extremely active research by the physics community; to name a few: Roger Penrose (2004), Olaf Nair, Markus Arndt, and Anton Zeilinger (2003), and Markus Arndt, Olaf Nairz, Julian Vos-Andreae, Claudia Keller, Gerbrand van der Zouw & Anton Zeilinger (1999).

Though additional research is necessary to verify many assumptions, this chapter advocates researching the use of Jungian principles applied to design of dramatic video games in order to verify correlations in the fields of Quantum Information Science and cognitive science. Given the above context, and in view of the virtual dreamlike nature of our emergent mediated reality—the metaverse—it may be possible to apply Jungian psychological healing methods to contextual collective (target groups). Already, AI neural network algorithms can understand videos (Simonite, Tom, 2015), and Haier, a global brand for major appliances, has broadcast a call for proposals to use image recognition to distinguish foods Inside refrigerators. Haier's vision is to become the customer's first choice for household appliances. (Geril, Philippe (2014c) Also, neuromorphic chips have been tested in drone aircraft:

Academic and corporate labs have been experimenting with "neuromorphic" chips modeled on features seen in brains. These chips have networks of "neurons" that communicate in spikes of electricity. They can be significantly more energy-efficient than conventional chips, and some can even automatically reprogram themselves to learn new skills. (Simonite, Tom 2014)

The following research is so relevant to dream simulation in games that mentioning it is irresistible.

A team of researchers in Japan lead by Akira Asano of Burton Inc. have developed a 3D aerial display capable of projecting text and imagery in mid-air. The Aerial Burton works by firing a 1kHz infrared pulse directly into a 3D scanner which in turn focuses and reflects the laser to a specific point in the air. Molecules at the end of the laser then ionize, releasing energy in the form of photons. While the full potential for such a display has yet to be seen, Asano suggests it could be used as a communication aid in the event of a disaster by communicating evacuation routes or broadcasting the location of emergency supplies. (Jobson, Christopher 2014)

Once the dream simulation programming is established, advanced algorithms for image recognition software could be applied to video games. Such image recognition algorithms are presently being intensively researched Simonite, Tom (2014c), and—in the same way pixel imagery is devised to be meaningful--symbolically contextual images can be designed according to cognitive frameworks that are meaningful to game-playing demographics. If propaganda, advertising, sex, violence, and the media-in-general can be studied within the context of dream analysis, perhaps insight as to their meaning could have powerfully benign influences. The reader need not be reminded that the evolution of human civilization can be directly attributed to the evolution of its media from the spoken word to the Internet. Like our ancestors, we are again questing beyond the known into that unknown land where illusion reigns and reality is understood to be virtual.

Future researchers will be probing virtual reality empirically using the proven patterns of the known reality. Like Jung, their "psychology… [will] not investigate for investigation's sake, but for the immediate purpose of giving help (Jacobi, p. 2 quoted from Jung, *Education*, pp 86, 90, 93) ... [Jung's] edifice is no abstract theory born of the speculative intellect, but a structure resting entirely upon the solid foundation of experience. Its two main pillars are: 1. The principle of psychic totality; 2. the principle of psychic *energism* (Jacobi, 1973, p. 2).

If a culture can be psychologically sick, psychosis/neurosis may be more than "just" metaphorical. If human reality is entirely based on metaphor, the psychotic metaphor becomes reality. Therefore, it becomes a research mandate to address virtual psychosis. Ontological issues are discussed elsewhere. (Schafer & Yu, 2011; Schafer, Stephen, 2012; Schafer, Stephen, 2015) However, in this age of communication, many aspects of the media are perceived as negative and debated ad-infinitum in diverse fields of inquiry. If—as in dream analysis—the negative characteristics are understood to be messages from the unconscious, negatives suddenly become positive. So called "negative" characteristics could be considered interpreted as elements of the archetypal shadow—the evolutionary mentor.

The dream speaks in images, and gives expression to instincts, that are derived from the most primitive levels of nature. Consciousness all too easily departs from the law of nature; but it can be brought again into harmony [coherence] with the latter by the assimilation of unconscious contents. By fostering this process we lead the patient to the rediscovery of the law of his own being. ...The way of successive assimilations reaches far beyond the curative results that specifically concern the doctor. It leads in the end to that distant goal (which may perhaps have been the first urge to life), the bringing into reality of the whole human being—that is, individuation. (Jung 1933, p. 26)

It may be stipulated that for many decades, research on the cognitive unconscious has been for purposes of marketing or politics where the overwhelming motive is profit or power. These limited motives for employing psychic potentials has permeated politics, law, morality, and has even become the raison detré of the incipient metaverse in which the sale of virtual goods for real money provided initial interest and impetus. Industrial monetization and manipulation from unconscious levels of target group collectives have provided the primary motivations for much current research. (Curtis, Adam, 2009)

Collective susceptibility to use of Freudian defense mechanisms is rampant in the metaverse and the *Psych*ecology. (See below for definitions) The *Spirit of the Age* has been traumatized first by a radical shift from a basically mystical worldview to the worldview of scientific materialism (Jung, 1933, pp. 173-185), and now by a second shift into the virtual illusory worldview of modern technology. It is understandable why—with the hope of returning to the "solid" world of the past—repression of the fact that scientific reality appears to have become a godless illusion is a primary source of collective pathology. A cursory suggestion of the existence of collective psychosis/neurosis may be seen in the following illustrations:

- **Denial:** There is no poverty in the United States, and if the poor exist, their condition is their own fault.
- **Rationalization:** Torture is good because it protects us from the terrorists.
- **Reaction Formation:** Buccaneering sub-optimizing capitalism is an exercise of the free market.
- **Displacement:** Contributing money to environmental causes dispels guilt for living environmentally destructive lifestyles.
- **Projection:** Decades of covert U.S. terrorist activities are projected onto a vague conspiracy of international terrorism.
- **Sublimation:** Transmuting a tendency to dominate with an overwhelming taste for mediated dramas about the military, police, lawyers, violence, and sexuality.

If such messages were understood as dreams with compensational potential, insights provided by these mediated patterns could lead to compensation or harmonization-through-insight. The psychological healing model suggested in this study is intended to address problems deriving from the alternate reality of dreamlike illusion—a fact as yet unrecognized by the cultural persona. Because the problem has not been defined, it has not been recognized, and it cannot be addressed realistically if it is not recognized for what it is. The fact is that human culture (specifically the culture of the United States) is facing a psychological catastrophe that is directly related to its unwillingness to understand the Psychecology as reality. Because we are at war with ourselves (won't admit dangerous realizations into consciousness) the problem complex seems intractable. Salient indicators of the pervasive psychotic syndrome include the following:

- **Privacy:** Problems of domestic spying and unauthorized information sharing, and the inability to deal with them according to principles of law.
- **Misuse of Information:** Problems of propaganda, mind control, patents, and copyrights.
- **Politics Based on Principles of Advertisement and Lies:** Problems of loss of freedom, democracy (the oft repeated complaint, "We no longer consider the issues."), and misinformation.
- **Negative Cognitive Effects of Mediated Sex and Violence:** The problem is that most citizens are ignorant of the psychological issues underlying the problem, and tend to address them reactively with "holier than though" attitudes.
- **Defensive Military Action throughout the World:** The problem is usually one of psychological defensiveness that cannot be effectively addressed on the basis of physical reaction. Citizens don't realize that physical political boundaries, national self-righteousness, and isolationism are delusions when it comes to dealing with problems in a virtual reality. In a unified field of psyche, ideas are more real than borders or armaments.
- **Propaganda and the War on Terrorism:** The problem is that the collective persona doesn't realize that terrorism is a deeply psychological condition that cannot be addressed on physical levels.

- **Genetic Research:** With little ethical consideration, research is being conducted entirely on the rudimentary so-called physical level and with absolutely no consideration of psychological or multi-functional (earth, water, air, and vitality) ramifications.
- **Geocide:** The problem is that the cultural persona believes its purpose is to dominate earth instead of providing stewardship. This may apply not only to issues of animal and human cloning, euthanasia, animal rights, and species endangerment, but to pollution and decimation of the plant kingdom in such forms as deforestation, loss of wetlands, "Fracking," and the unconscionable plethora of careless killing by illegal pollution.

The delusion that humans are somehow safe from the consequences of their poisoning is no less than psychotic. Humans carelessly kill not only with pesticides, herbicides, chemical warfare, contamination from bombing and industrial, petrochemical use, but from dysfunctional thought-forms and associated emotional forms of murder, hatred, genocide, torture, sadism, sexual and gender domination, profiteering, and the plethora of related bandwidths.

- **Life in the Universe and Space Travel:** Reminiscent of the geocentric, flat earth delusion, the main problem is that the cultural persona believes it is isolated and alone in a material universe that is antagonistic. This perception alone is reason enough for severe psychosis.
- **Abortion Rights:** Among related problems is the lack of definitions of terms. How is the human defined, where does the human begin, and what rights does it have in a psychologically entangled virtual reality?

Presently, instead of looking for real solutions, the most advanced psychological-media science is being used to understand and manipulate the cognitive unconscious of consumers and voters, thereby altering cultural values, personal choices, collective perspectives and policies in limited and unrealistic ways. In an emergent media age, it is time to begin applying the same science to education, media policy, and cultural healing. Our premise is that due to structural synchronicities among cognitive models and Psychecology games, drama-based video games can be used as research instruments in the development of software and technology that can probe the cognitive unconscious proactively for veridical data relative to the structure of the individual and cultural psyche. Ensuing knowledge will contribute to analysis of a culture's media dream, define any neurotic or psychotic symptoms, and enable a therapeutic re-design of media content. He who controls the content of the airways controls the future.

THE DREAM ANALOG

Since its inception when Edward Bernays created "Public Relations", the advertising industry has been employing techniques intended to limit personal and collective agency with the use of psychological dynamics. Generally speaking, advertising for purposes of selling products or candidates is based on the psychological dynamic of association. If frameworks of unconscious target group predispositions can be associated with products (Curtis, Adam, 2009), sales and political agendas will be promoted and agency will be diminished.

Focus groups have been a mainstay in the discovery process. Increasingly, but with the same motives the modern neuromarketing industry is probing the virtual unconscious of target groups based largely on Freudian principles that are "reductive" and view the unconscious in negative terms. (Curtis, Adam, 2009). Moreover, video games and "gamefication" (Claes, 2014) are being recognized as research instruments for tapping "buy buttons" in selected target groups. (Barr, Alistaire and Winkler, Rolfe, 2015; Lindsay, Rowen, 2015) This trend has been associated with ever more sophisticated use of "pseudo-spiritual" messages that promote their own worldviews and cult-like adherence to brands. (Goodman, Barak & Rushkoff, Douglas, 2004) Ultimately, the drama-based game research model based on Jungian/Lakoffian principles would provide more authentic research that would go far beyond marketing motivations in order to foster individual and collective self-realization and healing. Such an expansion of consciousness would have profound impact on all aspects of human "reality"—education, commerce, healthcare, and law.

Unlike "reductive" Freudian principles, amplification principles and dynamics underlying Jungian therapy are "not an unbroken chain of causally connected associations leading backward, but a process by which the dream content is broadened and enriched with the help of analogous images." (Jacobi, 1973, pp. 84-87, 103) The Jungian Amplification Process emphasizes empathy, contextuality, and empowerment. Therefore, adhering to authentic Jungian principles should dictate against misuse or manipulation of powerful subconscious forces. The same is true of George Lakoff's work which is motivated by "progressive" values. Lakoff says: "American values are progressive values," (2008, pp. 77-82), and it is critically important to verbalize this truth relative to the collective persona of the USA. Lakoff emphasizes that saying it matters. It matters because language works by mental simulation. Here, Lakoff cites Feldman: "'Words evoke whole frames—whole mental structures. Those mental structures activate an embodied mental simulation, giving the words meaning.'" (Feldman, 2006; Lakoff, 2008, p. 240) In other words, according to Lakoff's reasoning, progressive thinking (according to the Nurturant Parent model) is in harmony with the greater symphony of American cultural ideologies. The term "progressive" denotes values based on the "common good", egalitarianism, and mutual respect that pervade theories of the Social Contract including John Stuart Mill's Principle of Utility and Harold Lasswell's Functional Analysis. Metaphorically amplified Jungian symbols can also be understood as "whole frames".

Both Jung and Lakoff understand the collective unconscious with reference to dramatic structure as fundamentally defined by Aristotle. (Aristotle, 350 B.C.E.; O'Donnell, 2010) This subject will be expanded in the section on dramatic structure. In the dramatic context, "dramatis personae" may be defined in terms of human "function" (thinking, sensing, feeling, and intuiting) and purpose (learning and healing). A character's purpose may be understood as what s/he learns from experience in the drama, and this learning process may be understood in terms of character "premise" (Schafer, Stephen, 2007) and psychological plot-statement-and-resolution of the dramatic "problem" (exposition/*lysis*). Using modern technologies such as EEG, ECG, fMRI, and MEG to track neural electromagnetic activity during game-play could provide real-time tracking of neuro-functional dynamics in order to disclose contextual meaning at levels of the cognitive unconscious

As energetic activity in the cognitive unconscious is correlated with dramatic dynamics of its "contextual" projections into the emergent media environment; like dreams, the metaverse will disclose the potentials for learning and healing with symbolic patterns projected from the collective unconscious. As the dream dynamics of the holographic metaverse are recognized, they can be incorporated into simulations of Jungian/Lakoffian Psyche. Ultimately, such simulations could provide significant insight not only as to cognitive dynamics of learning, healing, and self realization, but to the fostering of coherent states for improvement of global harmony.

Scientific modeling and the use of simulations is a longstanding practice in scientific research. This chapter recommends a new model--Psychecology video games as dream analog—for simulating unconscious cognitive functions. The recommended model is based on a combination of the functional model of Psyche employed by Carl Jung, who anticipated current research, and the Family Metaphor model defined by George Lakoff. Relative to the dramatic structure and function of unconscious dimensions, primary correlations exist between the two models. It is also important to understand that—unlike some research models—both Jung and Lakoff foster empathy, cognitive harmony, and self-empowerment. *Coherence* is a measure of harmony, and Jungian *Compensation* appears to be synonymous with coherence. Given these correlations and the nearly incredible advances in simulation technology, the cognitive-dramatic model should prove to be practical for accessing robust data relative to unconscious neuro-biological function.

Simulations made possible by advances in algorithms for artificial intelligence are being used increasingly to imitate or model key characteristics or behavioral functions of selected physical or abstract systems or processes. (Barker, Longman, 1992) Often, computer experiments are used to study simulation models. Simulation is also used with scientific modeling (Cartwright, 1983) of natural systems or human systems to gain insight into their functioning. (Hacking, 1983) Simulations such as conceptual, operational, mathematical or graphical models can be used to show the eventual real effects of alternative conditions and courses of action, or when the real system cannot be engaged because it may not be accessible. "Philosophers are acknowledging the importance of models with increasing attention and are probing the assorted roles that models play in scientific practice" (Frigg & Hartman, 2009).

Essentially, like dreams, simulations are virtual illusions, but they have proven to be very practical in such contexts as safety engineering, testing, training, and education. A well-known context relative to the use of simulation is in video games and computer experiments. For the purposes of this chapter, a video game is an electronic game that involves human interaction with a user interface to generate visual feedback on a video device. The word *video* in *video game* traditionally referred to a raster (Leblanc, 1880) display device, but it now implies any type of display device that can produce two- or three-dimensional images. The electronic systems used to play video games are known as platforms; examples of these are personal computers and video game consoles. These platforms range from large mainframe computers to small handheld devices. As technology has evolved during the last twenty years, video games have become increasingly sophisticated, have surpassed film in global profit, and now engage millions of people in simultaneous game-play. Technologically, video games have become an art form and industry.

At great cost throughout the world, the virtual reality of the metaverse is already being intensively explored with sophisticated algorithms based on cognitive structure. Suddenly, there is an unprecedented interest on the part of government and industry to "map" the brain. Their motives are open to speculation. As opposed to tapping unconscious dimensions of target populations for marketing and industrial management purposes (Geril, Philippe; 2014a; Geril, Philippe, 2014b; Claes, Zane, 2014), the motivation for the DBG model is to empower people and harmonize planetary energy.

As humanity leaps into the abyss of virtual illusion, it may be wise to contemplate the metaverse as a dreamscape. This chapter recommends the DBG dream simulation model as a tool for neurobiological research in the emergent age of illusion where the dreamscape of the metaverse is directly correlated to the Jungian dreamscape of Psyche and to Lakoff's cognitive unconscious. For purposes of definition, the following terms are similar but not synonymous:

- **Psychecology:** The term Psychecology alludes to the existence of an ecology of psyche that exists both macrocosmically and microcosmically. The implication is that—based on research in diverse scientific fields—the universe can be understood in terms of bio-energetic life-forms and extrapolated to dimensions not usually considered biological. This ontology that has its roots in the mythologies of most cultures, is re-emergent—a sort of scientific pantheism. New media technologies have begun generating a paradigm shift in human understanding of reality—and life—through advances in Artificial Intelligence (AI), robotics, and a whole array of super intelligences within the "singularity". The term suggests a vital reality in which mathematics, the media, the unified field of physics, and the unified field of Jungian Psyche can be researched using the most advanced cognitive parameters and technology.
- **Metaverse:** The Metaverse is a virtual shared space—a collective—created by the convergence of virtually enhanced physical reality and "physically persistent virtual space, including the sum of all virtual worlds, augmented reality, and the internet. The word *metaverse* is a portmanteau of the prefix "meta" (meaning "beyond") and "universe" and is typically used to describe the concept of a future iteration of the internet, made up of persistent, shared, 3D virtual spaces linked into a perceived virtual universe. The term was coined in Neal Stephenson's 1992 science fiction novel *Snow Crash*, in which humans, as avatars, interact with each other and software agents, in a three-dimensional space that employs the real world as metaphor. Stephenson used the term to describe a virtual reality-based successor to the Internet. Concepts similar to the Metaverse have appeared under a variety of names in the cyberpunk genre of fiction as far back as 1981 in the novella *True Names*, Stephenson stated in the afterword to *Snow Crash* that after finishing the novel he learned about *Habitat*, an early MMORPG which resembled the Metaverse." (Smart, J.M., Cascio, J. and Paffendorf, J., 2007)
- **Media Dream:** The media dream, a term coined by the author, goes beyond the technologically generated virtual realities called the metaverse and provides a comprehensive framework for correlating fundamental dimensions of reality by including multi-functional dynamics of Jungian dreams.
- **Psychecology (Drama-Based) Video Games:** These games should not be unduly associated with video games in their present state of development. Rather, they constitute an emergent game genre that is characterized by advanced principles of cognitive dynamics and story-telling art. These games have all the components of dreams, physics, the media, and interactivity with which to research the fourth dimension.

Hypothetically, Jungian principles of dream analysis may be extended to the dreamlike images in the virtual metaverse in order to discover meaningful patterns of unconscious motivation in contextual individuals and collectives. In other words, due to dynamic correspondences between the collective unconscious and the virtual unconscious, analysis of symbolic patterns in contextual media images can provide meaningful information relative to unconscious contextual patterns of collective personae. If this information can be measured in terms of coherent psychological states, the affordances reflected by the contextual media would provide a degree of predictability for fostering coherence (healing and learning) in the age of virtual illusion.

This chapter will argue the functional correlations that exist on multiple scales. Psychecology games can employ Jungian principles to research individual and collective dynamics of insight as to the meaning of media dreams in order to heal individual and collective psychosis. Then, this insight can be applied to the metaverse. This might lead to a spontaneous psychic harmonization or healing of human collectives: ethnic, racial, and national.

Agency

Webster's New World Dictionary defines *agency* as 1. action; power. 2. means; instrumentality. In this chapter, agency is the characteristic of video games that is known as interactivity. Agency or interactivity is the fundamental dynamic for learning that involves the capacity to make choices, observe consequences, and adjust subsequent choices.

In the early days of video gaming, the term interactivity was applied to simple manipulations—button pushing--that was so engaging to players in rudimentary arcade games. Even then, interactivity was wireless. A game player would aim his rifle at the button on the moving bear, and—if the aim was somewhat accurate—the button would light up, the bear would roar, and change direction. Today, interactivity must be understood as a multi-functional psychological process that—applied to human choice-making—includes both conscious and unconscious dynamics. Shooting the bear in the arcade game was a primarily unconscious action. Current cognitive research indicates that our choices, actions and behaviors are generated primarily—an estimated 98 percent—from unconscious dimensions. (Lakoff, 2008, p. 11) Much of our mediated reality has become interactive as indicated by Wi-Fi and remote control. Wi-Fi is the name of a popular wireless networking technology that uses radio waves to provide wireless high-speed Internet and network connections. That this amazing fact of wireless interactivity is rarely interrogated by users is ample indication of its unconscious sources. Whether the concept of agency is applied within contexts of neuro-biological wetware or technological software, it constitutes a fundamental learning dynamic that can be logically correlated with evolutionary dynamics.

In his book, Psychological Agency, Roger Frie (2008) summarizes the concept. Frie says, agency does not adhere to traditional definitions of free will. Rather, it conforms to affective, embodied, and relational processing of human experience.

Agency is dependent on the biological, social, and cultural contexts that inform and shape who we are. Yet agency also involves the creation of meaning and the capacity for imagining new and different ways of being and acting and cannot be entirely reduced to biology or culture. This generative potential of agency is central to the process of psychotherapy and to psychological change and development. (Frie, Roger, 2008)

In the social sciences there is a standing debate over the primacy of structure or agency in shaping human behavior. Structure is the recurrent patterned arrangements which influence or limit the choices and opportunities available. Agency is the capacity of individuals to act independently and to make their own free choices. The structure versus agency debate may be understood as an issue of socialization vs. autonomy in determining whether an individual acts as a free agent or in a manner dictated by social structure. (Barker, Chris, 2005 p. 448)

For the purposes of this chapter, structure and agency are inseparable, and they must be considered from both conscious and unconscious cognitive contexts. For example, both Jungian archetypes of the unconscious and Lakoffian frames of the cognitive unconscious can be understood as structural patterns that are projected into contexts in which perceptions form the basis for consciousness choice-making or agency. All these projections—what Jung would call archetypal representations—function as illusions that are susceptible to contextual perception. So agency becomes infinitely contextual but is also fundamentally dependent on structure. Correlated—fractal—patterns or structures extend into diverse illusory dimensions including but not limited to the biosphere, the neuro-chemical sphere, the geo-sphere, the genomic–sphere, and the media-sphere. Clearly, the ontological and epistemological arguments related to this statement cannot be addressed in a chapter, but a degree of familiarity with the logic of such contexts may be assumed in the reader. If the complexities of the hypothesis are contemplated, a good way to research them is with the patterns of Jungian functionality.

Research with Psychecology video games could contribute significant data relative to psychological dynamics at work in the "reality" of the metaverse. The trajectory of argument in this chapter focuses on energetic activity (Jungian archetypes) in two correlated contexts. The first context is dream images that have an interactive life of their own, and the second context is interactive computer monitor images that have a life of their own. Though correlations between images are emphasized, all the classic human functions (thinking, sensing, feeling, and intuiting), because they are integrated or "entangled", appear to be projected in the same way. Therefore, the term "image" can be understood as multi-functional, and both of the "illusions"—dream images and monitor images—can be understood as archetypal representations (projections). Consequently, just as unconscious cognitive frames can be changed with the biofeedback of experience, patterns in algorithms can be adjusted according to the experience of mediated biofeedback. In other words, images in dreams can be correlated with images in the metaverse.

A primary virtue of Psychecology games as dream analogs is their dramatic multi-functionality. The four "cognitive" functions are universal. They have classical—mythic— precedents as well as modern usages. In personality profiling such as Myers-Briggs, Big 5, and other contexts such as Timothy Leary's circumplex the four functions are represented as polarities on a virtual matrix or grid. Within the contexts of dreams and computer monitors, these four functions can be integrated due to "interactivity". Jungian principles of dream analysis are based on the factor of interactivity; i.e. dream images change as a patient gains insight as to the meaning of symbols in dreams. This correlates exactly with interactivity in video games where changing image-symbols on the computer monitor provide insight to the player as to how to win a game. Associating a game-win with meaning culminates the learning process. In each case conscious-unconscious dynamics are at work, and these dynamics can be tracked with neuro-imaging techniques in order to discover multi-functional dynamics. The objective of game-play is the same as the objective of experience—to xpand consciousness—to bring what is unknown into the realm of the known. The interactive process—though it is multi-dimensional—can be understood in terms of agency.

Hypothetically, software based on multi-functionality has the same scope of potential to teach and to heal as proffered by dreams. Scope of agency potential may be expanded with the same advertising dynamic that associates unconscious psychological characteristics of target groups with some product. A game-win can be associated with almost anything (empathy, algebra, self-empowerment) in order to increase psychological coherence. In this case the end product of the game drama is learning and healing.

Jung understood that psychological dynamics of dreams—both personal and collective—are the same. "Now the doctor in me refuses point blank to consider the life of a people as something that does not conform to psychological law. "A people, in the doctor's eyes, presents only a somewhat more complex picture of psychic life than the individual. (Jung, Carl, 1933, p 209-210). For present purposes, this may be the most important pronouncement made by Jung because it provides a uniquely comprehensive framework for study of the paradigm shift represented by the metaverse. The psychological dynamics of a people—contextual collectives (race, gender, nationality, politics, etc.)—can be analyzed according to Jungian principles, and addressed with his Amplification principles.

As the dream dynamics of the holographic metaverse are better appreciated, game simulation algorithms can be designed in accord with principles of Jungian/Lakoffian Psyche. Ultimately, such simulations could provide significant insight not only as to cognitive dynamics of learning, healing, and self-realization, but to the fostering of coherent psychological states leading to improvement of global harmony.

Holographic-Dramatic Structure

Due to the relative complexity of the argument, every idea mentioned cannot be cited. Therefore, concepts that are generally accepted in certain fields are not cited. The reason that quotes are sometimes long is to convey subtleties of concept to readers who may not be familiar with them. The objective is to activate intuitive insight as well as so-called reason. Without this insight, the logical correlations relative to holography, dreams, the metaverse, and virtual realities that are fundamental to the argument will seem strange.

Dreams form a self-contained whole, a dramatic action which can meaningfully be broken down into the elements of a Greek play. (1) Place, time, dramatis personae: this is the beginning of the dream, which often indicates the scene of action and the cast of characters; (2) Exposition or statement of the problem. Here is presented the central content: the unconscious frames the question to which it will reply in the course of the dream; (3) Peripety: this is the 'backbone' of the dream; the plot is woven, the action moves toward a climax, transformation, or catastrophe; (4) Lysis, the solution, the outcome of the dream, its meaningful conclusion and the disclosure of its compensatory message. This rough pattern, on which most dreams are constructed, forms a suitable basis for interpretation. *(Jacobi, 1973, p. 83)*

A fundamental aspect of Jungian principle is that dramatic structure provides a basis for dream interpretation. One of the most important aspects of the Aristotelian definition is dramatic unity. Historically, there have been many attempts to interpret his meaning. One of these attempts was the idea that a play must take place in real time and place, but this was not right; for example, Aristotle often refers to Greek epic poetry to exemplify what is "good", and epics don't take place in real time and space. It is much more likely that Aristotle used the term dramatic unity in the same sense that physicists use the term unified field. This subject cannot be fully addressed in this chapter, but it must be mentioned because it is a significant factor for understanding how drama may be used as a basis for dream interpretation.

A fundamental correlation between the work of Jung and Lakoff is this idea that unconscious cognitive dimensions have dramatic structure. Though the idea of "non-existent" unconscious states with "structure" seems paradoxical, modern science has verified the paradox. Moreover, modern physics-based science is full of paradoxes. This is the character of the paradigm shift. Applied to psychology, Jung says, "Nothing influences our conduct ***less*** than do intellectual ideas…for such ideas represent forces that are beyond logical justification and moral sanction." (Jung, 1933, p. 174-175) George Lakoff would agree with Jung. For example, contrary to what Lakoff calls the "rational enlightenment metaphor" which is based on an assumption of human rationality, he cites statistical estimates that 98% of human mental function resides in the "cognitive unconscious"—that our embodied (neurobiological) minds reside below the level of consciousness and our moral and political thought is patterned as narrative-metaphorical frames that determine how we function in both the physical and social worlds. (Lakoff, 2008, p. 11)

Aristotle's dramatic unities can be understood in terms of holography. The dramatic unities of time, place, and action are called unities because—like holographic time, space, and what happens there—they cannot be separated. Also—a characteristic of holography—due to metaphorical resonance, the whole drama exists in every part. In conjunction with principles of the unified field of physics, the existence of dramatic structural unities suggest an underlying unity or integrity among dimensions of physics, cognition, media-sphere, and Psychecology games. The probability is that these different states can be thought of in terms of bandwidth and measured according to the mathematics of Fourier Transforms; so, the dramatic unities constitute a metaphor relative to mathematically defined patterns of the unified field of energy and information. The dramatic metaphor can also be understood to correspond with principles of holography.

- Cast of characters = space
- Plot = time
- Action or *peripety* = infinite potential of player choices and interaction

As documented by Michael Talbot (1991), the concept of a holographic universe has been explored by many, but correlations between the cosmos and the Holonomic brain was developed primarily through the collaboration between David Bohm and Karl Pribram. Bohm and Pribram developed the theory that in accordance with quantum mathematical principles and the characteristics of wave patterns, the brain is structured like a hologram. From *Brain and Perception,* this functional model is explained:

In addition to the circuitry accomplished by the large fiber tracts in the brain, processing also occurs in webs of fine fiber branches (for instance, dendrites) that form webs, as well as in the dynamic electrical fields that surround these denritic "trees". In addition, the processing occurring around these dendritic trees can influence that occurring in those trees of nearby neurons … whose dendrites are entangled but not in direct contact. In this way, processing in the brain can occur in a non-localized manner. This type of processing is properly described by Dennis Gabor, the inventor of the hologram, as quanta of information he called a "holon", an energy based concept of information. These wavelets are used in quantum holography, the basis of MRI, Pet scans and other image processing procedures. (Pribram, 1991)

Substantial research has been addressed to these holographic concepts, but research on correspondences to the media-sphere has been primarily focused on sub categories of quantum holography such as artificial intelligence, mathematical algorithms, processing big data, and neuromarketing. Recent research on social networks has been kept secret (The Hidden World of Facebook "Like Farms"), and it is primarily motivated by marketing concerns. Nevertheless, a trend is evident. Research in diverse fields is producing abundant scientific evidence relative to the holographic-cognitive nature of the media dream illusion of reality.

The research is still compartmentalized and largely limited by sophisticated but anachronistic expectations inherited from "materialistic" science. However, key research is salient and appears to be consistent with Jungian views. For example, on October 31, 2014, "A review and update of a controversial 20-year-old theory of consciousness published in *Physics of Life Reviews* claims that consciousness derives from deeper level, finer scale activities inside brain neurons." The recent discovery of quantum vibrations in 'microtubules' inside brain neurons corroborates the theory called 'orchestrated objective reduction' (Orch or Or) that was put forward in the mid-1990s and suggested that quantum vibrational computations in microtubules were 'orchestrated' (Orch) by synaptic inputs and memory stored in microtubules. According to *MIT Review* authors, Stuart Hameroff and Sir Roger Penrose (2014), "EEG rhythms (brain waves) also derive from deeper level microtubule vibrations, and that from a practical standpoint, treating brain microtubule vibrations could benefit a host of mental, neurobiological, and cognitive conditions." (Schafer, 2015, p. 12)

The existence of such vibrations in synaptic microtubules expands recent neurobiological research into quantum dimensions and tends to verify earlier research on Carl Jung's collective unconscious, David Boehm's holographic universe, and Carl Pribram's holonomic mind, the "Maharishi Effect, the perennial philosophy, Fechner's measurement of sensory thresholds, and Durkheim's concept of the collective consciousness." (Orme-Johnson, D. W. 2002) All of these approaches establish and support the ontological assumption of the paradigm shift in which the phenomenal world is a dreamlike illusion—the manifestation of an unmanifest transcendental ground.

Cast of characters: For purposes of cognitive research, Psychecology video games have all of the Aristotelian dramatic dimensions as well as the (unified-energetic) Jungian dynamics of Psyche and the unified-energetic field of physics. Therefore, according to their unique character profile (context), player choices may be designed to access unconscious cognitive problems associated with dramatic problems in the game story and to resolve them. The dramatic problem or "exposition" is resolved according to dramatic *lysis*—the dynamic that represents resolution of a story problem—that is associated with a game win. Essentially, this interactive process in game play constitutes the well-known learning dynamic of repetition whereby choice patterns strengthen neural synapses. Such patterns could reinforce meaningful insight and learning on the part of the player in the direction of Jungian individuation and individuation can be correlated with coherence (see below).

In drama, character is multidimensional as measured in terms of four Jungian functions, (see section on functions) and these are the classical four functions symbolized by the four elements (earth, water, air, and fire) symbolically pervasive in myth and philosophy. The functions and other dynamics of Jungian analysis such as introversion and extroversion have been incorporated into Myers-Briggs personality profiling algorithms that have proven to be quite accurate and relatively easy to administer with short tests. (Myers-Briggs, 2015) The application of fully functional profiling of target group demographics could prove to be much more effective for accessing unconscious dimensions of personality than existing focus group profiling as applied in advertising. Psychological profiling could also establish the character *premise* (what the character needs to learn). Therefore, premise could be integrated into the exposition (statement of the story problem) and *lysis* (resolution of the problem) of the drama in order to foster individuation of the game player or collective.

Plot: is determined by interactive contextual character/player choices. As with Jungian dreams, a patient/player's agency and interaction with the dream images/monitor images reflects psychological changes and progress toward individuation. Dramatic choices occur within the fundamental archetypal process known as the hero's journey. Based on these archetypal-dramatic parameters, the potential for contextual choices becomes infinite, but such potentials are within reach due to advances in artificial intelligence (AI) algorithms. In short, Psychecology games constitute dream analogs as well as metaphorical models of so-called "reality".

Action: Dramatic action resides within narrative-metaphorical parameters and can be designed in accordance with sophisticated personality profiling and cognitive research. Profiling can pinpoint the character premise (what needs to be learned) in order to incorporate authentic, predictive target group (player) opportunities for authentic choice-making. Authentic choice patterns can be associated with a game-win in order to alter unconscious neural synapses according to contextually pre-defined psychologically coherent states. Such research would lead to better understanding of unconscious collective meaning as it is symbolically projected into the metaverse.

Basics of neurolinguistic framing. The research of neurolinguistic expert, George Lakoff, is especially relevant to Jung's research in that it emphasizes both the narrative structure and multi-functionality of the cognitive unconscious. Lakoff observes that, "The neural circuitry needed to create frame structures [in the cognitive unconscious] is relatively simple [neural binding circuitry, neural signatures, event structures] and so frames tend to structure a huge amount of our thought…Each frame has roles (like a cast of characters), relations between the roles, and scenarios carried out by those playing the roles." (Lakoff, 2008, p. 22; Goffman, 1974) "There is a protagonist, the person whose point of view is being taken. The events are good and bad things that happen. And there are appropriate emotions that fit certain kinds of events in the scenarios." (Lakoff, 2008, p. 23; Schafer, 2015, p. 5) Such observations relative to the dramatic, neurobiological basis for the structure of the cognitive unconscious are thoroughly developed in Lakoff's *The Political Mind,* and they comport precisely with Carl Jung's Aristotelian-based explanation of the dramatic structure of dreams. Taken together, their research and that of McCraty & Childre (p. 5) on functionally coherent states strongly suggests the efficacy of Psychecology research on contextual collectives.

Psychecology games may provide a key for navigating the challenges posed by the paradigm shift into an age of illusions. Jung called dream images *archetypal representations* (AR). ARs have the same form as archetypes of the unconscious, but they are relatively conscious—as in dreams. Therefore, we can probe for unconscious meaning due to the recursive congruities between generative archetypes and projected archetypal representations. Analyzing digital images of the metaverse as AR, game research may provide answers to some of the many unconsciously generated problems presently facing humanity and the planet—especially in areas of education reform and healing of what Jung called the *Spirit of the Age*. (1933, p. 175)

State-of-the-art cognitive research models employ a narrative-metaphorical common denominator to provide structure to their research. Because of their narrative-metaphorical structure and interactive-immersive dramatic potential, the medium of Psychecology games can simulate the fundamental dynamics of psyche according to the psychic functions and the amplification method of dream analysis defined by Carl Jung. Formerly known as Role Playing Games (RPGs), drama-based games can be used to simulate the dramatic dimensions of the *Theatre Model* of *Global Workspace*, and the narrative-metaphorical structural context of Jungian amplification, contrastive analysis (Baars, 1997), and cognitive framing (Lakoff, 2008). Programmed as an analog to simulate cognitive structure according to these existing research parameters, drama-based games could be employed as a research instrument for exploration of embodied (neurobiological) criteria related to normative-conceptual (value formation) levels of cognition at both personal and cultural levels.

Narrative structures of the cognitive unconscious, says Lakoff, "Exist outside the body—in our culture—and inside the body—in the very building blocks of our brains." In the following quote, Lakoff implies the functionality of these dramatic structures:

Simple narratives have the form of frame-based scenarios, but with extra structure. There is a protagonist, the person whose point of view is being taken. The events are good and bad things that happen. And there are appropriate emotions that fit certain kinds of events in the scenarios. In a simple Rags-to-Riches scenario, for example, the initial state of the Protagonist is poverty, where the appropriate emotion is sadness; then there are intermediate states of hard work with varying emotions of frustration and satisfaction; and finally a state of wealth, with the emotions of joy and pride. (Lakoff, 2008, p. 21-23)

Designing narrative software to fit the personality of defined target groups in drama-based games has been discussed in detail (Schafer, 2012). Relative to semantic "scripts," the writing of Lakoff is again highly relevant. Lakoff cites Roger Shank and Robert Abelson (Ibid. p. 249) in his paraphrase, "Complex narratives—the kinds we find in everyone's life story, as well as in fairy tales, novels, and dramas—are made up of smaller narratives with very simple structures." Chapter 18 of Political Mind goes into detail regarding cognitive framing of the nervous system. Lakoff says, "The neural circuitry needed to create frame structures is relatively simple [neural binding circuitry, neural signatures, event structures] and so frames tend to structure a huge amount of our thought." Lakoff explains that each frame has roles (like a cast of characters), relations between the roles (plot as both plot and view sequence), and scenarios carried out by those playing the roles." (Lakoff, 2008, p. 22; Goffman) Within the cognitive frames, "There is a protagonist, the person whose point of view is being taken. The events are good and bad things that happen. And there are appropriate emotions that fit certain kinds of events in the scenarios." (Lakoff, 2008, p. 23) Citing Goffman, Dr. Lakoff also observes that words are all defined relative to conceptual frames: "Groups of related words, called 'semantic fields,' are defined with respect to the same frame. Thus words like 'cost,' sell,' 'goods,' price,' buy,' and so on are defined with respect to a single frame," (Lakoff, 2008, p 22; Goffman, 1974) and the roles of Buyer, Seller, Goods, and Money, form a narrative field context for the unconscious frame.

Much current neurobiological research—being yet limited by materialistic frames of the unconscious—only tentatively addresses issues of spirit. Jung addresses the intuitive or "spiritual" function (that he calls intuition) in the following way:

There is nothing to prevent the speculative intellect from treating the psyche, on the one hand, as a complicated biochemical phenomenon, and [essentially] a mere play of electrons, or, on the other, from regarding the unpredictable behavior of electrons as the sign of mental life even in them. The fact that a metaphysics of the mind was supplanted in the nineteenth century by a metaphysics of matter, is a mere trick if we consider it as a question for the intellect; yet regarded from the standpoint of psychology, it is an unexampled revolution in man's outlook upon the world. Other-worldliness is converted into matter-of-factness; empirical boundaries are set to man's discussion of every problem, to his choice of purposes, and even to what he calls "meaning." Intangible inner happenings seem to have to yield place to things in the external, tangible world, and no value exists if it is not founded on a so-called fact....Just as formerly the assumption was unquestionable that everything that exists takes its rise from the creative will of a God who is spirit, so the nineteenth century discovered the equally unquestionable truth that everything arises from material causes. Today the psyche does not build itself a body, but on the contrary, matter, by chemical action, produces the psyche. (Jung 1933, p. 174-175)

Jung discusses how "deep narratives" are related to sleeping dreams and waking dreams. Projected images are susceptible to interrogation in order to discover unconscious meaning. "The dream speaks in images," that give expression to contents of unconscious dimensions. "Consciousness all too easily departs from the law of nature; but it can be brought again into harmony with the latter by the assimilation of unconscious contents. By fostering this process we lead the patient to the rediscovery of the law of his own being. …The way of successive assimilations reaches far beyond the curative results that specifically concern the doctor. It leads in the end to that distant goal … the bringing into reality of the whole human being—that is, individuation." (Jung 1933, p 26)

In Moral Politics (2008, p.63), Lakoff defines the functional connection between symbolic-metaphorical framing and value formation. He explains in detail how "much of moral reasoning is metaphorical reasoning." An example of how narrative-metaphorical resonance can influence morality is discussed by Lakoff in terms of the core metaphor of moral accounting. According to this fundamental metaphor, a syllogism is established: well-being is good; well-being is moral; wealth contributes to well-being; to be wealthy is moral. According to this *Moral Accounting metaphor*, economic words like *owe, debt,* and *pay* are used in a moral context. The result is a logical framework in which the metaphorical resonance suggests that wealth is better than poverty (good), so being wealthy is moral (good). Lakoff explains further:

A conceptual metaphor is a correspondence between concepts across conceptual domains, allowing forms of reasoning and words from one domain (in this case, the economic domain) to be used in the other (in this case, the moral domain)…Thousands of such metaphors contribute to our everyday modes of thought, [and] play an enormous role in characterizing our worldviews. (2002, p. 63)

Reminiscent of the Jungian Amplification Method, Lakoff describes *radial conceptual categories* as the most common form of metaphorical structure. "The radial categories show how the coherent ideologies in each category fit together and what the relationships among them are." (Lakoff, 2002, p. 14) Radial categories are structured according to variations on a central model. As an example, he uses the category *mother* and explains that the term is characterized by four metaphorical sub-models: The birth model, the genetic model, the nurturance model, and the marriage model. (p. 8) All of the frames in the radial categories are couched in little metaphorical stories within stories. Presumably, if "mother" is the prototype and sub-model variants of the "mother metaphor" constitute radial categories or variations on the central model, discovering how the categories fit together and how they are related in a contextual field would result in discovery of meaning.

Carl Jung's Model for analysis (Jacobi, 1973, p. 85) of metaphorical dream motifs is essentially a diagram of metaphorical extension—similar to a choice tree in computation—which may be correlated with radial categories. In Jung's model of dream motifs, recurring symbols form the basis for multifunctional extension of the metaphors. This may be understood in terms of Lakoff's research. Corresponding points in the models can be employed to determine, "how the coherent ideologies in each [functional] category fit together." Stories within stories that are related holographically to Jungian metaphorical extension with the objective of achieving coherent functionality may be translated into digital-algorithmic form. Research informs us that functional modalities are based on Fourier Transforms.

In view of Jungian and more recent neurobiological intelligence, defining target groups and designing game stories that encompass their unconscious requirements for evolution toward individuation becomes feasible. Moreover, instead of being motivated only by profit, such game design would be motivated by empathy, and a desire to teach, heal, and empower the target group. "Dramatic event structures are carried out by brain circuitry. The same event structure circuitry can be used to live out an action or a narrative, or to understand the actions of others or the structure of a story" (Lakoff, 2008, p. 27).

Lakoff, who has the research advantage of modern technology, discusses neuro-chemical detail in order to explain dramatic-cognitive structure. Jung employs more general terms such as "value intensity and constellation" (Jacobi, p. 58), but recent theories and findings tend to agree with Jung. For example, Jung defines the term *libido* as psychic energy that, "pulses through all the forms and activities of the psychic system and establishes a communication between them." (p. 52) Jungian libido is not limited to sexuality, "It is nothing other than the intensity of the psychic process, its psychological value, which can be determined only by psychic manifestations and effects." (p. 52) Among these psychic manifestations are dreams that can be analyzed and "measured" according to their symbolic motifs. Relative to how Jung uses the term energy, Jacobi explains that energy is "a concept similar to that employed in physics." Jungian *energy*, "is fundamentally different from the Aristotelian concept of energy as a 'formative principle.' (p. 522)

Neither is Jung's concept of energy metaphysical. "When he speaks of an 'undifferentiated libido', he is stating not a premise from which something is supposed to follow but an empirical finding." (p. 52) "When an empirical scientist says 'energy', he is postulating nothing, but merely drawing an inference from the facts at hand." (p. 52) Jacobi goes on to clarify the term energy saying, "There are two kinds of 'concept': first, the concept postulated as an idea (or model), such as the Aristotelian or scholastic concept of 'energy'; and second the empirical concept as an a posteriori principle of order, an example of which is the Jungian concept of 'libido'." (p. 52)

Returning to Lakoff's discussion of neurochemical dramatic form:

What in the brain allows a general narrative form, say a Rags-to-Riches narrative to be applied in a special case? ...The answer is 'neural binding.' Neural signals go from downstream to upstream and back. Neural pathways from downstream regions 'converge' on their way upstream at what are called 'convergence zones.' Information from downstream and upstream is 'integrated' at the convergence zones via neural binding. There are theories of how binding works, but we do not know for sure. The most prominent theory is that binding is "time locking"–neurons firing simultaneously in different parts of the brain along connecting pathways....Another current theory is based on the coordination of so-called neural signatures—small collections of individual neurons together forming distinct firing patterns. (Lakoff, 2008, p. 25)

Lakoff goes on to explain that, "Binding circuitry consists just of neurons and connections, but has a special effect: it creates new experiences." (p. 26) James Gee has reiterated the same thing relative to the learning potential inherent to video games. (Shapiro, 2014)

Neural binding can create emotional experiences. In the area of the limbic system, the oldest part of the brain in terms of evolution, there are two emotional pathways with different neurotransmitters: one for positive emotions (happiness, satisfaction)—the dopamine circuit—and one for negative emotions (fear, anxiety, and anger)—the norepinephrine circuit. There are pathways in the brain linking these emotional pathways to the forebrain, where dramatic structure circuitry seems most likely to be located. (p. 28)

Neurochemistry seems to mirror dramatic unities that Lakoff denominates "somatic markers" and "event structures."

Activations of such convergent pathways are called "somatic markers." It is they that neutrally bind the emotions (downstream, near the brainstem) to event sequences [plot] in a narrative (upstream, apparently in the prefrontal cortex, at the front and top of the brain). The somatic markers allow the right emotions to go where they should [plot] in a story. They are the binding circuits responsible for the emotional content of everyday experiences. ...emotional content can be bound to a narrative, yielding a melodrama—a narrative with heightened emotional content. (p. 28)

Lakoff adds, "We understand events in the world in terms of what our bodies can do. As a result, every simple narrative has such an 'event structure.' In the field of computational neural modeling, the technical term is an 'executing schema,' or 'X-schema' for short." (p. 27) Neural binding is also crucial to the plot structure of a narrative. (p. 26 & p. 29) The narrative stages of the frame, *Pull-Yourself-up-by-Your Bootstraps,* are as follows:

- **Preconditions:** Hero/heroine starts out poor and unknown.
- **Buildup:** Undergo a series of hardships; odds against.
- **Main Event:** Through exercise of will and discipline, he/she does something extraordinary.
- **Purpose:** Achieves success.
- **Result:** Achieves recognition.
- **Consequences:** Gains respect, fame, and/or wealth (p. 26 & p. 29).

The details relative to the neurobiology of drama are directly related to Jungian theory and practice. However, the correlations are not always explicit. They are implied. According to Lakoff:

We live our narratives. The lived story is at the center of modern personality theory. The theory of neural computation...shows how our brains not only permit this, but favor it. The typical roles played in narratives include Hero, Victim, and Helper...The roles in narratives that you understand yourself as fitting give meaning to your life, including the emotional color that is inherent in narrative structures. (p. 33)

It should also be understood that when we use the term media dream, it is in the Jungian sense—both a dramatic sequence and a spontaneous emergence from a unified field. Viewed as a whole—unlike the pony express and more like a dream—the modern technological media is not imprisoned by time; instead, it is emergent, nonlocal, and insubstantial. The media-sphere exists in a non-local present moment, but—depending on a particular earth-surface perspective—that moment can be simultaneously interpreted as night or day, here or there, yesterday or tomorrow. Jung did not presume to understand the meaning of a patient's every fleeting dream. That would have been impossible. Relative to the existence of dramatic structure, it should also be noted that:

An obscure dream, taken by itself, can rarely be interpreted with any certainty, so that I attach little importance to the interpretation of single dreams. With a series of dreams we can have more confidence in our interpretations, for the latter dreams correct the mistakes [interactivity] we have made in handling those that went before. (Jung, 1933, p. 14)

Plot sequence (unconscious Territory) & View sequence (conscious map). Instead Jung read a patient's dreams like a holographic story that has both a *view sequence* and a *plot sequence*. In drama, view sequence can be understood in symbolic-metaphorical terms to represent narrative patterns as they are consciously experienced. View sequence is nonlinear and may include flashback (memory) and flash-forward (what Jung would call a *prospective* view of the future). On the other hand, plot sequence is linear, causal, and unconscious until meaningful insight evolves in the patient/dreamer in much the same way as it evolves in a viewer while experiencing a mystery film. (Schafer, 2007)

I use the term plot sequence to refer to the chain of events that make up the plot of a story. As we've seen, stories always have a beginning, where the hero is confronted with a problem, a middle where he tries to address it, and an end, where he makes a final attempt and then deals with the consequences. In contrast to this plot sequence, I use the term view sequence to refer to the order in which those events are presented to the audience. (Glassner, 2004, p. 117)

Like dreams, the media can be understood in terms of compensation; i.e. like all experience, mediated experience mirrors meaning for the purposes of psychological growth through experience. This ancient axiom has far too much precedent to detail in this chapter, but it is well documented by Ray Grasse (1996, pp. 127-146). Jungian Compensation may be understood as "learning" through experience—again, a subject that is vast, but one that should be self-evident. Compensation is largely dependent on discovery or insight as to meaning—through psychological experience and the significance of symbols—and is consummated with the realization of personal and collective individuation (Jung 1933, p 26). In view of the dreamlike nature of our emergent mediated reality, it may be possible to apply Jungian psychological healing methods to cultures. Once the simulation programming is understood, algorithms for software can be devised to predict image recognition in the same way that pixel imagery is devised to be meaningful to a contextual game-playing demographic. If propaganda, advertising, and the media-in- general can have powerfully negative influence on civilization, perhaps they can also have powerfully benign influence. I need not remind the reader that the evolution of human civilization may be directly attributed to the evolution of its media from the spoken word to the Internet. Like our ancestors, we are again going beyond the known into that unknown land where illusion reigns and reality is understood to be virtual.

Like Jung, researching the unknown reality of the metavers is based on empirically proven patterns of the known reality. Jacoby quotes Jung, "Our psychology…does not investigate for investigation's sake, but for the immediate purpose of giving help." (Jung, *Education*, pp 86, 90, 93) "[Jung's] edifice is no abstract theory born of the speculative intellect, but a structure resting entirely upon the solid foundation of experience. Its two main pillars are: 1. The principle of psychic totality; 2. the principle of psychic energism." (Jacoby 1973, p.2).

Seen as messages with compensational potential, insights provided by mediated patterns in the metaverse could lead to compensation. The psychological healing model suggested in this study is intended to address a problem that is a logical development of the realization that human reality on every scale is virtual—a fact as yet unrecognized by the cultural persona. Because the problem has not been defined, it has not been recognized, and it cannot be addressed realistically if it is not recognized for what it is. The fact is that human culture (specifically the culture of the United States) is facing a psychological catastrophe that is directly related to our unwillingness to understand the Psychecology as our reality. Because we are at war with ourselves (won't admit dangerous realizations into consciousness) the problem complex seems intractable. Salient indicators of the pervasive psychotic syndrome were introduced in the BACKGROUND section.

Context and Personality Functions

Contextual collective personae. Citizens of the modern world have become accustomed to think of themselves in terms of "contextual" collectives. In addition to our membership in a national collective, they think of themselves as parts of many demographics: target groups (those who would buy a Land Rover or 4 by 4), political parties, religions, genders, races, and nationalities. When they watch a sports event, they watch it as fans, statistical entities that, for awhile, become dominant in their expression of persona. The individual may wear many masks and play many roles among which being a sports fan is only one. Latent aspects of the individual personality only emerge at certain times, but when they do they dominate the persona and other cognitive aspects become submerged. Mob mentality and the true believer syndrome are pejorative illustrations of the same principle. Individuals in the mob are diverse, but when their latent mob persona emerges, it dominates other aspects of their natures.

The existence of the collective psyche may clearly be revealed in riots, political conventions, religious extravaganzas, and concerts as well as outpourings of generosity and heroism such as those we saw in New Yorkers after the September 11 attack. The collective psyche can manifest in positive and negative ways. Understanding the unconscious patterns and motivations for such phenomena could contribute to fostering psychologically coherent states. Thus considered, the assumption that there are psychic parameters for contextual collectives and that they are projected as such in the media becomes a truism. As quoted above, according to Jung, a collective persona has a psychic life.

A salient feature of the Jungian reality is the existence of contextual collective personae. In *Modern Man in Search of a Soul*, Jung develops the idea of the existence of cultural personae that is paraphrased in the following quote:

Now the doctor in me refuses point blank to consider the life of a people as something that does not conform to psychological law. A people, in the doctor's eyes, presents only a somewhat more complex picture of psychic life than the individual. Moreover, taking it the other way round, has not a poet spoken of the 'nations' of his soul? And quite correctly, as it seems to me, for in one of its aspects the psyche is not individual, but is derived from the nation, from collectivity, or from humanity even. In some way or other we are part of an all-embracing psychic life, of a single 'greatest' man, to quote Swedenborg. And so we can draw a parallel: just as in me, a single human being, the darkness calls forth the helpful light, so does it also in the psychic life of a people. (Jung 1933, p. 209-210)

Relative to the existence of collective personae, Lakoff's family metaphors—Strict Father (SFM) and Nurturant Parent (NPM) (Lakoff, 2008)—are explicit references to the existence of these patterns in the nervous system and their projections into the media-sphere.

In the language of the brain—its very building blocks—words and thoughts are defined relative to narrative frames and conceptual metaphors. The very fact that we recognize these cultural narratives and frames means that they are instantiated physically in our brains. We are not born with them, but we start growing them soon, and as we acquire the deep narratives, our synapses change and become fixed. A large number of deep narratives can be activated together. We cannot understand other people without such cultural narratives. But more important, we cannot understand ourselves—who we are, who we have been, and where we want to go—without recognizing and seeing how we fit into cultural narratives. (Lakoff, 2008, p. 33-34)

In Jungian terminology, "context" includes as much of a patient's psychological condition as possible. Not only culture, religion, politics, gender, age, education, profession, nationality, but unique experiences, attitudes, personality types, etc. In Jungian principle, the purpose for understanding all these things is to develop empathy and harmony with the psychological context of a patient. The first accomplishment of a Jungian counselor is to be empathetic; next is to contemplate the symbols and patterns in a series of dreams from the patient's unique perspective. In this way, the psychiatrist can have insight about contextual symbolic meaning and—by metaphorical extension—can provide valuable feedback to the patient. Jung did not presume to heal a patient. Rather, he devised a method with which a patient could heal self. Jung called it the Amplification Method with which the psychiatrist provides feedback as to possible meanings of dream symbolism. Only with empathy can a healer provide the feedback and reinforcement necessary for the patient to achieve insight. DBG could be designed to follow the same method, and though the help of an intuitive counselor is critically important, it may be that sophisticated algorithms could accomplish even more.

The Amplification Method incorporates both learning and healing dynamics, so using the term "patient" is not necessarily accurate. In the sense that everyone has something unique to learn, we are all patients. The precipitous alteration in personal and cultural perspectives relative to what is real constitutes a scientific revolution, but research on education and healing—even research on the media—has not progressed apace with the psychological, normative, and substantive implications of an incipient media age that is more like a dream than an objective thing.

An American cultural persona exists. Examples of the existence of collective personae are implicit not only in generalized identification with the cultural state, but in: Marketing to target groups; assessing opinions with statistical opinion polls; narrow-casting to target groups; political advertising; propaganda; the scapegoat syndrome; principles of demographics; civil rights laws; tax laws; foreign policy; poverty programs; social services; and social security to name a few. In its various interpretations, the social contract, itself, assumes the existence of definable (contextual) collectives.

But does a collective constitute a collective persona? The answer is yes. The classical pattern for the human persona is that it exists on four definable functional levels or frequencies, and these levels correspond to levels of nested masks in a cultural entity (see below).

That the US persona exhibits symptoms of social pathology is self-evident. Such pathologies are only part of the story, but they tend to be over-emphasized in the media, so they become more prominent. Superficial symptoms include rampant graft, violence, immorality, injustice, inconsistency, crudity—even treason in high places. Collectives that reflect these symptoms express predictably hysterical responses relative to nearly any critical issue of planetary survival. On deeper levels, symptoms of fear and self-loathing are evident in the defense mechanisms that rule our collective choices, empower unqualified leadership, and perpetrate worldwide injustice in the name of human freedom and civility. (Curtis; Lakoff) The reasons for societal trauma are many, but perhaps like the individual persona, the collective persona employs defense mechanisms to protect its self-image from psychological-emotional wounds, fears, guilt, and lack of integrity or coherence. Usually, such reliance on defense mechanisms is counterproductive because it diverts attention and hides symptoms of dis-ease. Rather than dealing with problems realistically, the persona avoids them and refuses to learn from experience. On a collective level, several examples of collective repression are, US guilt for the Viet Nam war, German guilt for WWII, and American guilt for genocide in dealing with Native Americans and slaves.

Such guilt influences the entire culture in ways that range from foreign policy to domestic law. Until the source of the guilt is faced, rationalization ensues and misdirection snowballs. Examples of collective projection (sacrificing a scapegoat) are legion. Of course, the most recent case is Sadam Hussain and Al Queda in general. Political manipulation of the media fostered this projection, but images of death and destruction during the Iraq War constitute affordances that, if recognized as such, proffer the possibility of collective healing. All of a nation's covert operations and secret aggression constitute an aspect of the collective unconscious that wreaks havoc in the cultural psyche. Until the culture owns its responsibility, its psyche becomes increasingly unbalanced. In order to heal the collective persona, its distributive citizenry (individuals as integrated parts of the whole) must experience insight as to the problem, make amends, and take responsibility for both personal and collective transgressions in thought, word, and deed. Of course, these are just the obvious symptoms of social pathology. On the other hand, the great American persona must be viewed as the mythic Hero suffering the road of trials. Perhaps s/he is the hope of the world, but the American persona has many masks and many tests to pass before it achieves atonement (at-one-ment). S/he has greatness of soul, but that soul needs professional help in order to manifest complete coherence.

Whether in dreams or the metaverse, the importance of monstrous imagery is that it alerts a patient to psychological problems. Our objective should not be—as in the past—either to ban them from the airways or to repress them. Rather, our objective must be to strive for insight as to their meaning and source. Jungian methodology for achieving such meaningful insight would tend to dispel problems through compensation. It is important to remember that:

The unconscious is not a demonic monster, but a thing of nature that is perfectly neutral as far as moral sense, aesthetic taste and intellectual judgments go...the overwhelming of consciousness by the unconscious—is most likely to occur when the unconscious is excluded from life by repressions, or is misunderstood and depreciated...It is always helpful, when we set out to interpret a dream, to ask: What conscious attitude does it compensate? (Jung, 1933, p 17)

Having started down this road of dreams, this unified field of psyche, we must adapt to the environment or perish. Because dreams are a powerful component of psychic life, it is not so difficult to extrapolate that collectives, like individuals, have dreams, and that these dreams may be projected as media dreams. The American dream is palpable. It has been very real to generations of immigrants from the Pilgrims to refugees from all parts of the modern world. The hope of winning Olympic prizes is real. National fantasies of superiority are real and have consequences in the real world (Curtis, 2009). The wars humans have fought for king and country, tribe and clan, home and family are numberless. We will not belabor the point. However, it may be possible to analyze the media dreams of collective personae just as psychiatrists analyze the dreams of individual patients. When we refer to the *media dream*, we mean the spontaneous holographic articulations of the kaleidoscopic regime of information and energy exchange which, in this paper, is called the ***Psychecology***. We are referring to the media as a non-local *stream of consciousness*—a series of seemingly unrelated emergent images that constitute memories, perceptions, and fantasies of collective personae.

Humans have been perceiving their reality psychologically and in terms of contextual collectives since time immemorial—them vs. us—and in modern mediated terms, statistics, advertising, and the structures of symbolic language establish a fundamental correspondence between individual and collective personae. Using media biofeedback methods, these correspondences can be applied to the design of a genre of video games that has the potential both to teach and to cure collective personae of neurotic/psychotic symptoms.

Human Function

Psychological correspondences between collective and individual personae. A valuable perspective on human functionality is defined according to Andrew Glassner's discussion of "nested masks" in his *Interactive Storytelling*. (Glassner, p. 43; Schafer, 2007) This definition provides practical parameters for designing complex characters for interactive games:

- True self = a character's soul
- Conscience = mind and value structures
- Self-image = emotion/desires
- World mask = physical experience within an interactive-reflective environment

A well-established approach to defining contextual personalities is provided by Myers-Briggs profiling (MBTI). The MBTI Functions: Sensing (S) / iNtuition (N) and Thinking (T) / Feeling (F) are based on a synthesis of Jungian principles of function but include such additional parameters as Jung's dichotomous pairs of cognitive functions:

- The "rational" (judging) functions: *thinking* and *feeling*
- The "irrational" (perceiving) functions: *sensing* and *intuition*

Jung went on to suggest that these functional components are expressed in either an introverted or extraverted form. As defined in the MBTI context, extroverts prefer outward-directed action while introverts prefer inward-directed reflection. From Jung's original concepts, Briggs and Myers developed an effective model for profiling personality according to a classification of psychological differences into four opposite pairs, called types or "dichotomies".

- *E*xtraversion → *I*ntroversion
- *S*ensing → i*N*tuition
- *T*hinking → *F*eeling
- *J*udging → Perceiving

The four dichotomies and their 16 factors (generally known by an abbreviation of four letters) are not to be understood as "better" or "worse". They are simply contextual preferences similar to left/right hand contextual preference. In the same way that writing with the left hand is hard work for a right-hander, so people tend to find using their opposite psychological preferences more difficult.

According to the Myers-Briggs typology model, though all four functions are available for use, each person uses one of these four functions more dominantly and proficiently than the other three. According to Wikipedia:

- *Jung's sensing* and *intuition* are the information-gathering (perceiving) functions that describe how new information is understood and interpreted—sensing may be correlated with earth or the world mask, and intuition may be correlated with fire or the Soul. For example, individuals who prefer *sensing* are more likely to trust information that is in the present, tangible and concrete—understandable with the five senses. They tend to distrust hunches and prefer to look for details and facts. On the other hand, those who prefer *intuition* tend to trust information that is more abstract or theoretical, that can be associated with other information (either remembered or discovered by seeking a wider context or pattern). They may be more interested in future possibilities. They tend to trust those flashes of insight that seem to bubble up from the unconscious mind. The meaning is in how the data relates to the pattern or theory.

- *Jung's thinking* and *feeling* are the decision-making (judging) functions. The thinking and feeling functions are both used to make rational decisions, based on the data received from their information-gathering functions (sensing or intuition). Those who prefer *thinking* tend to decide things from a more detached standpoint, measuring the decision by what seems reasonable, logical, causal, consistent and matching a given set of rules. Those who prefer *feeling* tend to come to decisions by associating or empathizing with the situation, looking at it 'from the inside' and weighing the situation to achieve, on balance, the greatest harmony, consensus and fit, considering the needs of the people involved. MBTI assessment is a measure of preference, not ability.
- **Dominant Function:** Although people use all four cognitive functions, one function is generally used in a more conscious and confident way. This dominant function is supported by the secondary (auxiliary) function, and to a lesser degree the tertiary function. The fourth and least conscious function is always the opposite of the dominant function. Myers called this inferior function the *shadow*. (Myers-Briggs, 1995)
- **Attitudes:** The four functions operate in conjunction with the attitudes (extraversion and introversion). Each function is used in either an extraverted or introverted way. A person whose dominant function is extraverted intuition, for example, uses intuition very differently from someone whose dominant function is introverted intuition. (Wikipedia, Myers-Briggs, 2015)

Compensation and Coherence

The coherent state has been correlated with a general sense of well-being, and improvements in cognitive, social and physical performance." (McCraty & Childre, 2010, p. 5) The various concepts and measurements embraced under the term coherence have become central to fields as diverse as quantum physics, cosmology, physiology, and brain and consciousness research. Coherence has several related definitions, all of which are applicable to the study of human physiology, social interactions and global affairs. The most common dictionary definition is "the quality of being logically integrated, consistent and intelligible. (McCraty & Childre, 2010, p. 2)

By all indications, Jungian Compensation is synonymous with coherence. Researchers at the Institute of HeartMath have studied systemic-biological coherence intensively:

Of the many new scientific perspectives that emerged from the twentieth century, one of the most profound is that the universe is wholly and enduringly interconnected and coherent. (Boehm, Laszlo) Complex living systems, including human beings, are composed of numerous dynamic, interconnected networks of biological structures and processes. Coherence implies order, structure, harmony and alignment within and amongst systems - whether in atoms, organisms, social groups, planets or galaxies. Thus every whole has a relationship with and is a part of a greater whole, which is again part of something greater. In this context, nothing can be considered as separate, alone or lacking relationships. One of the more surprising findings that has emerged from physics is quantum coherence, which has given rise to the prediction of non-locality and instantaneous communication between subatomic particles separated by vast distances. (Ibid, p. 1)

This understanding of global coherence comports with the Jungian concept of compensation—a state of which is the objective of his Amplification Method of clinical treatment.

For every piece of conscious life that loses its importance and value—so runs the law—there arises a compensation in the unconscious. We may see in this an analogy to the conservation of energy in the physical world, for our psychic processes have a quantitative aspect also. No psychic value can disappear without being replaced by another of equivalent intensity. (Jung, 1933 p. 209-210)

The harmonious states of coherence and compensation have the same characteristics as one who experiences multi-functional "Flow" phenomena: feelings of involvement, serenity, oneness, ecstasy, timelessness, intrinsic worth, and control (Csíkszentmihályi, 1990).

With the application of Jungian principles to the Metaverse, coherent psychological states can be induced in collective personae by researching how target groups can be predisposed to coherent states in both collectives and distributive individuals. McCraty and Childre discuss the nature of coherence, how it can be measured and reinforced with biofeedback, and how it can be applied to harmonization of psyche in all its functions—physical, emotional, rational, and spiritual. "In globally coherent systems such as human beings, there is an incredible amount of activity at every level of magnification or scale that spans more than two-thirds of the 73 known octaves of the electromagnetic spectrum" (2010). The functions cited by McCraty and Childre correspond to the Jungian functions of psyche—sensing, feeling, thinking, and intuiting. These principles and functions can be integrated into experimental design in order to foster coherence (Schafer, 2015, p. 9).

Cognitive meaning may be accessed by understanding both drama-based video games and the media-sphere in terms of their dramatic-holographic structure. That structure is directly correlated with Carl Jung's context and analysis of dreams for purposes of healing. Moreover, Jung's theories are entirely consistent and predictive of recent cognitive research. Employing this array of theoretical and practical frameworks in game design and research design, it should be possible to analyze the collective unconscious in an incipient digital age of illusion. The drama-based game research model would provide robust and timely information about this altered reality, as well as the electromagnetic impact of humans on the dreamscape.

In order to illustrate the potential of video games for electro-magnetic impact, recent data includes this bit of information about player numbers of the most popular video game in the world—the multi-player online battle arena video game, *League of Legends,* developed and published by Riot Games for Microsoft Windows.

League of Legends was generally well received at release, and it has grown in popularity in the years since. By July 2012, League of Legends was the most played PC game in North America and Europe in terms of the number of hours played. As of January 2014, over 67 million people play League of Legends per month, 27 million per day, and over 7.5 million concurrently during peak hours. (Sheer, 2014)

The game exhibits the orthodox dramatic-archetypal elements such as the hero, the shadow, the journey, purpose, and individuation. If these dramatic elements are understood as metaphors, they acquire a psychological-functional depth that would be useful in cognitive research.

In League of Legends, players assume the role of a character, called a "champion", with unique abilities, battling with a team against other player or computer-controlled champions. In the most popular game modes, each team's goal is to destroy the opposing team's nexus, a building which lies at the heart of a base protected by defensive structures. Each League of Legends (LOL) game is discrete, with all champions starting off each game fairly weak and progressing by accumulating gold and experience over the course of the game. (New player guide, 2014)

The dramatic structure of *LoL* is relatively sophisticated, such that the story exposition would lend itself to contextualization (unique abilities) according to Jungian parameters. In terms of the media dreamscape, LoL constitutes a contextual dream. Whatever the profiles of constituent players may be, they can be analyzed according to symbolic patterns projected by the game in order to disclose unconscious patterns of their collective persona. The following quote from Jung might as well be applied to LOL as to dreams:

We must see to it that the conscious personality [champion] remains intact, for we can only turn the unconscious compensations [discreet/contextual] to good account when the conscious personality cooperates in the venture. When it comes to the assimilation of content it is never a question of 'this or that,' but of 'this and that.' Just as the interpretation of dreams requires exact knowledge of the conscious status quo, so the treatment of dream symbolism demands that we take into account the dreamer's philosophical, religious and moral convictions. It is far wiser in practice not to regard the dream symbols as signs or symptoms of a fixed character. We should rather take them as true symbols—that is to say, as expressions of something not yet consciously recognized or conceptually formulated [nexus]. In addition to this, they must be considered in relation to the dreamer's immediate [real time] state of consciousness. I emphasize that this way of treating the dream-symbols is advisable in practice because theoretically there do exist relatively fixed symbols whose meaning must on no account be referred to anything whose content is known, or to anything that can be formulated in concepts. If there were no relatively fixed symbols, it would be impossible to determine the structure of the unconscious. (Jung 1933, p. 21)

The fact that each game is discrete suggests that LoL has a wide target group appeal. Its basic structure is evolutionary and acquisitive—players learn from experience and are motivated by accumulating gold. If focus groups of players were profiled with existing Myers-Briggs algorithms, more refined psychological motives symbolized by the basic context of the game (growth and acquisition) might be discovered and addressed within the choice patterns proffered by the game. Each distributive refinement would result in collective refinement. When game-wins are associated with increased functional group coherency in various contexts, insights become possible relative to patterns that could lead to increased coherence in collective personae.

Just as dreams and game-wins divulge meaning, the content of the media dream could point to meaningful choice patterns leading to increased coherence in collective cognitive states. The conscious-unconscious, interactive player choice patterns could divulge robust data relative to bio-energetic impacts of collective "personae" on the media-sphere. Amplification of this hypothesis suggests that research on the patterns of energetic impacts of contextual collectives will divulge authentic ways—using mediated biofeedback—to foster coherent cognitive states in collective personae. Such research using the psychecology game model can provide robust data relative to the functional impact that human energies have on the ionosphere of the planet.

Individuation

In Jungian terminology, individuation is synonymous with contextual harmony that leads to transcendence that can be achieved through completion of the learning experiences offered by the archetypal hero's journey. "The archetypal image which leads from...polarity to a union of the two psychic systems—consciousness and the unconscious—through a midpoint common to both is the SELF. It is the last station on the path of individuation, which Jung also calls *self-realization*." (Jacobi, 1973, p. 127) Also, "The way of individuation, as postulated by Jung, may be regarded as a serious endeavor to counter the disorientation of modern man by activating the creative forces of his unconscious and by consciously integrating them into the whole of the psyche. It means a 'liberation' from the snares of instinctual nature, an *opus contra naturum*." (Jacobi, 1973, p. 133) Therefore, individuation accords with the transcendence of the personality to become the true self or Soul (see nested masks above). In more orthodox terms, this transcendental experience can be understood in terms of coherence leading to learning and healing.

Humans occupy a dual reality that consists of the known and the unknown, the conscious and the unconscious, the self and the not self, the persona and the shadow. Some say this is a punishment (the fall of man). Others say it is an opportunity for humans to learn about themselves. Psychology teaches us that human rationality is only one aspect of their cognitive capacity; and, at subliminal or supraliminal levels, humans are in touch with other dimensions of awareness—other functional/fractal dimensions. However, some form of the media is necessary for any translation of information from one dimension to another—to transform the unknown into the known. On its simplest levels this process is understood as the acquisition of knowledge. Through experience—the making of choices and the contemplation of consequences—knowledge eventually becomes wisdom that may be understood in terms of more cocmplex neural connectivity. Ultimately, according to the archetypal pattern known as the Hero's Journey, wisdom leads to transcendence of the human condition.

If the ultimate human *premise* is to overcome the illusion of separation, individuation can be translated to "transcending" the illusion, and transcendence can be understood in terms of a personal and collective "integrity" that is synonymous with coherence, harmony, self-actualization, individuation, and at-one-ment at the culmination of the journey. Winning the game of life requires the player to learn and apply the rules of dual reality, to explore the unknown, and to understand that s/he is both a particle and a wave function. At this particular juncture in human development, the rules of the game seem directly related to the dynamics of dreams. The dreamscape exists within a unified field of psyche, and the human mandate to actualize the "self" is the premise (what the character needs to learn) of the interactive, experiential story. Each individual and every human collective shares the evolutionary learning objective that is related to the metaphor "achievement of more light," more coherent consciousness, or at-one-ment. Atonement is the objective of the psychological hero's journey. In less exalted contexts, this is the same process that a game player undergoes in order to win a game. To the degree a player projects his/her self-image on a hero and immerses self in the game, s/he has the potential to learn something about self and to move closer to atonement or self-actualization. S/he has the potential to become more whole—hale and sound.

Learning to become whole is the same as learning to heal oneself, so learning and healing may be understood as the same dynamic. Due to the structure of dreams—defined as the dramatic dynamic of the archetypal Hero's Journey—this essentially linguistic-metaphorical archetype constitutes a common denominator between the energy patterns of physics and information patterns of psyche. These patterns of physics are translated into neurobiological patterns, and then into the mediated "sensory" patterns of the media-sphere—all of which can be interrogated as correspondences using principles of Fourier transforms. During the "dramatically structured" journey, the mythic hero accrues conscious meaningful insights that integrate archetypal energy patterns and experiential information patterns in a process of expanding consciousness. This process of meaningful insights eventually leads to a state of knowing that transcends the human state—what Joseph Campbell calls atonement (at-one-ment). The Journey of the Hero is employed as a universal storytelling structure in literature, film, games, and the general media. The Journey is a template for human evolution and development from the condition of the divisive dissonant *personality* to the more coherent state of the integrated *Soul*. The symbolic nature of the Journey is not lost on writers, but often the psychological ramifications of the mythic mentor are ignored.

During drama-based game-play—understood as a dream analog—the evolutionary-transcendental patterns can be technologically traced relative to their impacts on the nervous system, correlated with percepts and affordances of player choice patterns, and reinforced in order to associate psychologically coherent choices (on whatever subject) with a game-win. Associating a game–win with functional, multi-dimensional insights constitutes the universal dynamic understood as "learning." Following are some of the correlates that should be researched in order to qualify drama-based games as dream analogs:

- Dreamer = Game player
- Cognitive/dramatic dream structure = Cognitive/dramatic DBG structure
- Journey of the hero = DBG game play
- Images = Symbolic language for compensation between conscious and unconscious states
- Archetypal representations (conscious patterns of energy/information as image) = Game monitor images (Consciously perceived patterns of energy and information as pixel patterns)
- Dream images = Game monitor images
- Coherent states = Compensational states & Flow
- Associative-cognitive-discovery leading to dreamer insight as to the symbolic meaning of dreams (images) = associative-cognitive-discovery leading player to insight as to game win--symbolic language of DBG (images/pixels)
- Interactivity/choices resulting in changes in dream images due to insights on the part of the dreamer = Interactivity/choices resulting in changes in computer monitor images due to conscious/unconscious insight on the part of the player
- Jungian amplification method (compensational biofeedback) = Dramatic choices (digital biofeedback)
- Archetypal psychic frames of the Collective Unconscious = cognitive frames of the cognitive unconscious
- Patient insight leading to learning/healing due to Psychiatric feedback relative to meaning = Player insight leading to learning/healing due to digital feedback.

- Dreamer has meaningful insight/problem solving/healing due to interactive biofeedback process = Game player has meaningful insight/problem solving/healing due to interactive association of a pattern of choices resulting in a game win.
- Complex contextual Jungian persona = Complex multi-functional DBG characters (Myers-Briggs personality profiles)
- Jungian Functions = Myers-Briggs attributes
- Fourier Transforms = Calibration of functions
- Family metaphors of cognitive framing (Lakoff, 2008) = mythic Jungian archetypes
- Cognitive dynamics of individual persona = cognitive dynamics of collective persona

Based upon the above analogies, physiological data gleaned from DBG research may point the direction for understanding the distributive (individual) dynamics of collective personae. Such understanding may be applied to methods for reframing the cognitive unconscious with feedback from the Media Dream. Research with DBG would address the following points:

1. Correlations among personal and distributive (individual) physiological dynamics in order to address cognitive dynamics of collective personae.
2. Protocol development in order to analyze the holographic media dream for evidence of cognitive correlations between individual & collective personae.
3. Examination of the mediated dreamscape as a psychological projection from the distributive unconscious of collective personae in order to apply Jungian Amplification to coherent feedback modalities in the media.
4. Exploration of the *Psych*ecology in order to research cognitive dimensions of distributive personae.

It is well known that the use of media in the form of advertising and propaganda alters collective values, choices, and behaviors (Curtis, 2009). If protocols for coherent feedback can be researched with DBG, perhaps the Media Dream—understood as a holographic version of the Hero's Journey—can be employed to reframe the distributive cognitive patterns of collective personae into the more coherent cognitive patterns of the collective *Soul*. Perhaps the media dream could be employed as feedback to provoke human transcendence.

CONCLUSION AND RECOMMENDATIONS

For the first time, due to advances in technology and neurological research, the mediated dreamscape can be studied scientifically. Advances in both spheres have been rapid. In 2004, the latest news was that soon we would be using brain waves to control video games. At the MIT Media Lab Europe, "Mind Balance" was demonstrated for the first time using a new wireless headset. That the "Mind Balance" demonstration followed so soon after the release of Nintendo's Wii clearly suggested that *video games are becoming a medium for direct contact* between the human nervous system and the electro-magnetic fields of the *virtual reality*. During the last few years our understanding of virtual illusion has been enhanced to the point that the dreamlike metaverse is becoming reality.

Right now, touted as "the future of entertainment," the youtube advertisement for the newest Star Trek-based video game reads, "The Void, where dreams become reality":

At THE VOID you will walk into new dimensions and experience worlds without limits. From fighting intergalactic wars on alien planets, to casting spells in the darkest of dungeons, THE VOID presents the future of entertainment. Only limited by imagination,, our advanced Virtual-Reality technologies allow you to see, move, and feel our digital worlds in a completely immersive and realistic way. (youtube, 2015)

As usual, state-of-the-art technology leaps beyond research. Today, almost all media is interactive. Influence at a distance is taken for granted, and the idea that thought, emotion, and bio-electro-magnetism have impact at a distant—an aspect of non-locality in physics—has already re-directed research and become a fundamental aspect of our scientific worldview. Suddenly everyone from the European Union to Google has been investing heavily in brain-mapping. However, as yet, the implications of this worldview are unrealized except for misguided efforts to understand the mechanisms of psychological control and the invasion of privacy. The real scope and potential of this paradigm shift will alter the known reality. Issues related to implied sentience (both conscious and unconscious) in the virtual metaverse constitutes a priority concern of scientific research. This chapter introduces a framework for research, summarizes existing research in related fields, and argues for the potential of drama-based video games as a research instrument.

It is only a matter of time before research provides a better understanding of the power of the media—especially the interactivity of games—as a palpable neuro-psychological phenomenon; however, the span of time is critical. Such power as represented by the metaverse should be based on a degree of wisdom. Though research on artificial intelligence based on some understanding of cognitive patterns of the brain has proliferated for decades and "consciousness research" has generated thousands of papers from diverse academic fields and ontological perspectives, the research has rarely—if ever—been addressed to what Carl Jung called *Psyche*. Moreover, the structural-functional correlations that exist among different scales of Psyche, the metaverse, dreams, and video games, has never been addressed. If human beings are made in the image of deity, their creative potentials go beyond creating with thought, feeling, and symbols. If we know anything about divinity, it is that creativity requires comprehensive responsibility.

Due to the many correspondences between video games and dreams as researched by Carl Jung, video games qualify as the medium of dreams. First among these correlations is the idea of context. In a superficial way, context is synonymous with the idea of target groups. With increasing success, advertisers have been defining context with focus groups and applying the context to target groups. High concept ads are becoming more multi-functional without actually knowing it. Meanwhile, psychological advertising has extended to every aspect of the holographic global media.

However, Jung employed this term in reference to a patient's entire psyche as far as the psychiatrist could know it. Jung was explicit in his advocacy of knowing the patient thoroughly in order to increase empathy and to guide a patient to heal him/her self. Family, age, gender, religion, nationality, profession, etc. were, to Jung, all aspects of a patient's psychological context. Using similar but more sophisticated dynamics as advertising, Jungian context can be applied not only to individual patients but to contextual collectives.

As we have seen, Jungian functional contextuality in conjunction with dramatic structure—especially exposition and *lysis*—in dreams and video games constitute a fundamental learning/healing CREATIVE dynamic that can be applied to both individuals and collectives. Dramatic context is becoming a functional matrix for exploration of multiple psychic dimensions.

REFERENCES

Arbib, M. A. (1985). In Search of the Person: Philosophical Explorations in Cognitive Science (November 1, 1985)

Arbib, M. A., & Hesse, M. B. (1986). *The Construction of Reality*. Cambridge Studies in Philosophy. doi:10.1017/CBO9780511527234

Aristotle (350 B.C.E.). *Poetics*. Translated by S. H. Butcher. Retrieved April 22, 2015 from http://classics.mit.edu/Aristotle/poetics.1.1.html

Arndt, M., Nairz, O., Vos-Andreae, J., Keller, C., Van der Zouw, G., & Zeilinger, A. (1999, October 14). Nature: Wave–particle duality of C_{60} molecules.

Baars, B.J. (1997). In the theatre of consciousness: global workspace theory, a rigorous scientific theory of consciousness. *Journal of Consciousness Studies*, 4(4), 292.

Barker, C. (2005). *Cultural Studies: Theory and Practice* (p. 448). London: Sage.

Barker, R., & Longman, C. (1992). *Case Method: Function and Process Modeling*. Addison-Wesley Professional.

Barr, A., & Winkler, R. (2015). Can Google Outsell Amazon and eBay? Company will launch buy buttons on its search-results pages in coming weeks. *Wall Street Journal*. Retrieved from http://www.wsj.com/articles/can-google-outsell-amazon-and-ebay-1431730741

Bell, J. S. (1987). *Speakable and Unspeakable in Quantum Mechanics*. CERN.

Bohm, D., & Hiley, B. J. (1993). *The Undivided Universe*. London: Routledge.

Cartwright, N. (1983). *How the Laws of Physics Lie*. Oxford University Press. doi:10.1093/0198247044.001.0001

Chopra, D. (1995). Body, mind, and soul: The mystery and the magic. Atlanta, GA: Turner Home Entertainment; Public Broadcasting Service.

Claes, Z. (2014). Three neuromarketing lessons derived from video games. *Neuromarketing*. Retrieved from http://www.neurosciencemarketing.com/blog/articles/neuromarketing-video-games.html

Curtis, A. (2009). Century of the self: Happiness machines for free. *Freedocumentaries.com*. Retrieved from http://freedocumentaries.org/film.php?id=140

Einstein, A., Podolsky, B., & Rosen, N. (1935). Can Quantum-Mechanical Description of Physical Reality Be Considered Complete? *Physical Review*, *47*(10), 777–780. doi:10.1103/PhysRev.47.777

Fable 2. (n. d.). *Microsoft Corporation*. Retrieved from http://www.lionhead.com/Fable2/About.aspx

Feldman, J. (2006). From molecule to metaphor. Cambridge, MA: MIT ress.

Frie, R. (2008). Psychological agency: Theory, practice, and culture. Cambridge, MA: The MIT Press; Retrieved from http://mitpress.mit.edu/books/psychological-agency

Frigg & Hartman. (2009). Models in Science. In E.N. Zalta (Ed.), The Stanford Encyclopedia of Philosophy (Summer 2009 ed.).

Geril, P. (2014a). Startup Europe- Capacity building for Business Angels (BAs) in ICT/ A digital Agenda for Europe. Retrieved from https://ec.europa.eu/digital-agenda/en/news/startup-europe-capacity-building-business-angels-bas-ict

Geril, P. (2014b). Crowdfunding innovative ventures in Europe - The financial ecosystem and regulatory landscape (SMART 2013/0074) Digital Agenda for Europe. Retrieved from https://ec.europa.eu/digital-agenda/en/news/crowdfunding-innovative-ventures-europe-financial-ecosystem-and-regulatory-landscape-smart

Geril, P. (2014c). Project proposal: Image Recognition to Distinguish Foods inside Refrigerator. *EUROSIS - The European Multidisciplinary Society for Modelling and Simulation Technology* Retrieved from https://www.linkedin.com/grp/post/1039687-5902320911746375684

Glassner, A. (2004). *Interactive storytelling*. Natick, Massachusetts: A.K. Peters.

Goffman, E. (1974). *Frame analysis: An essay on the organization of experience*. New York: Harper and Row.

Goodman, B., & Rushkoff, D. (2004). *The Persuaders*. Arlington, VA: WGBH Educational Foundation & PBS Home Video.

Grasse, R. (1996). *The waking dream*. Wheaton, IL: The Theosophical Publishihng House.

New Player Guide. (2014). *League of Legends*. Riot Games.

Hacking, I. (1983). *Representing and Intervening. Introductory Topics in the Philosophy of Natural Science*. Cambridge University Press. doi:10.1017/CBO9780511814563

Hameroff, S., & Penrose, S. R. (2014). Discovery of quantum vibrations in 'mocrotubules' corroborates theory of consciousness. Retrieved from http://phys.org/news/2014-01-discovery-quantum-vibrations-microtubules-corroborates.html)

Myers-Briggs Type Indicator. (2015, February 21). Wikipedia. Retrieved from http://en.wikipedia.org/wiki/Myers%E2%80%93Briggs_Type_Indicator

Jacobi, J. (1973). *The psychology of CG Jung*. London, USA: Yale University Press.

Jobson, C. (2014). An Aerial Laser Display Capable of Projecting 3D Objects in Mid-Air. *EUROSIS - The European Multidisciplinary Society for Modelling and Simulation Technology.* Retrieved from http://www.thisiscolossal.com/2014/11/an-aerial-laser-display-capable-of-projecting-3d-objects-in-mid-air/

Jung, C. G. (1933). *Modern man in search of a soul*. USA: Harcourt Brace & Company.

Kelly, M. (2015). The social contract. Retrieved from http://americanhistory.about.com/od/usconstitution/g/social_contract.htm

Kirk, T. (2014). Superconducting spintronics pave way for next-generation computing. *Nature Communications.* Retrieved from http://phys.org/news/2014-01-superconducting-spintronics-pave-next-generation.html

Laberge, S. (1980). Lucid dreaming: An exploratory study of consciousness during sleep [PhD thesis]. Stanford University.

Laberge, S. (1980). *Lucid dreaming: An exploratory study of consciousness during sleep* [PhD thesis]. Stanford University.

Lakoff, G. (2008). *The political mind. Viking Penguin, USA.*

Lakoff, G., & Narayanan, S. (2010). *Toward a computational model of narrative. Association for the Advancement of Artificial Intelligence.* Berkeley, CA: International Computer Science Institute and University of California at Berkeley.

Laswell, H. (1948). *The structure and function of communication and society: The communication of ideas* (pp. 203–243). Institute for Religious and Social Studies.

Laszlo, E. (1995). *The Interconnected Universe: Conceptual Foundations of Transdiciplinary Unified Theory.* Singapore: World Scientific.

Leblanc, M. (1880, December 1). Etude sur la transmission électrique des impressions lumineuses (Study on electrical transmission of luminous impressions). *La Lumière électrique* (Electric light).

Lindsay, R. (2015). Google to add "buy" buttons to some research. *Christian Science Monitor* Retrieved from http://www.csmonitor.com/Technology/2015/0517/Google-to-add-buy-buttons-to-some-search-results-video

Locke, J. (1991). A Letter Concerning Toleration (p. 5) [Introduction]. New York: Routledge.

Markoff, J. (2014). Microsoft Makes Bet Quantum Computing Is Next Breakthrough. *The New York Times* retrieved from http://www.nytimes.com/2014/06/24/technology/microsoft-makes-a-bet-on-quantum-computing-research.html

Mavrematis, A. (1987). *Hypnogogia: The Unique State of Consciousness Between Wakefullness and Sleep.* Routledge, Chapman & Hall, Incorporated.

McCraty, R., & Childre, D. (2010). Coherence: bridging personal, social, and global health. *Alternative Therapies, 16*(4).

Metaverse. (2011, May 1). *Wikipedia.* Retrieved from http://en.wikipedia.org/wiki/Metaverse

Mill, J. S. (1909). *On Liberty, Harvard Classics* (Vol. 25, p. 258). New York: PF Collier & Sons Company.

Minsky, M. (1961). Steps toward Artificial Intelligence. *Proceedings of the IRE, 49*(1), 8–1. doi:10.1109/JRPROC.1961.287775

Nairz, O., Arndt, M., & Zeilinger, A. (2003, April). Quantum interference experiments with large molecules. *American Journal of Physics, 71*(4), 319–325.

Nairz, O., Arndt, M., & Zeilinger, A. (2003, April). Quantum interference experiments with large molecules. *American Journal of Physics*, *71*(4), 319–325. doi:10.1119/1.1531580

Nielsen, M., & Chuang, I. (2000). *Quantum Computation and Quantum Information*. Cambridge University Press.

O'Donnell, M. (2010). *The dramatic structure of dreams*.

Orme-Johnson, D. W. (2002). Quantifying the field effects of consciousness: From increased EEG coherence to reduced international terrorism. In R.A. Chez (Ed.), Proceedings of Bridging Worlds and Filling Gaps in the Science of Healing. Corona del Mar, CA: Samueli Institute for Informational Biology (pp. 326-346).

Penrose, R. (2004). *The Road to Reality: A Complete Guide to the Laws of the Universe* (p. 603). London.

Pribram, K. (1991). *Brain and perception: holonomy and structure in figural processing*. Hillsdale, N.J.: Lawrence Erlbaum Associates.

Radin, D. (2006). *Entangled minds: Extrasensory experiences in a quantum reality*. New York: Paraview Pocket Books.

Radin, D. (2009). The conscious universe: The scientific truth of psychic phenomena. New York: Harper One.

Reeves, B., & Nass, C. (1996). The media equation. Stanford: Center For the study of Language and Information & Cambridge University Press.

Rincon, P. (2014). Study doubts quantum computer speed. *BBC News website*. Retrieved from http://www.bbc.com/news/science-environment-25787226

Rousseau, J.-J. (1754). *Discourse on the Origin of Inequality, Part Two. The Basic Political Writings*. Hackett Publishing Company.

Schafer, S. (2012). *Optimizing cognitive coherence, learning, and psychological healing with drama-based video games. Video game play and consciousness*. New York: Nova Science Publishers, Inc.

Schafer, S. (2015). *The Mediasphere as Dream: Exploring the media dream*. Hershy, PA: IGIGlobal.

Schafer, S. (2007, April). Premise: The key to interactive storytelling. *Gamasutra*. Retrieved from http://www.gamecareerguide.com/features/357/premise_the_key_to_interactive_.php?page=1

Schafer, S. (2006, October). Curriculum and the dream paradigm. *Gamasutra*. Retrieved from http://www.gmecareerguide.com/features/288/curriculum_and_the_dream_paradigm.php

Schafer, S., & Yu, G. (2011). Meaningful video games: drama-based video games as transformational experience. In M. M. Cruz-Cunha, V. H. Valvalho, & P. Tavares (Eds.), *Business, Technological, and Social Dimensions of Computer Games: Multidisciplinary Developments* (pp. 312–329). Hershey, PA, USA: IGI Global.

Schrödinger, E., & Born, M. (1935). Discussion of probability relations between separated systems. *Mathematical Proceedings of the Cambridge Philosophical Society*, *31*(4), 555–563. doi:10.1017/S0305004100013554

Shapiro, J. (2014). Games Can Advance Education: A Conversation With James Paul Gee. *MindShift*. Retrieved from http://ww2.kqed.org/mindshift/2014/07/03/games-can-advance-education-a-conversation-with-james-paul-gee/

Sheer, I. (2014, January 27). Player Tally for 'League of Legends' Surges. *Wsj.com.*

Simonite, T. (2014a). An experiment involving a chip on a small drone shows how hardware modeled on the brain could provide useful intelligence. *MIT Technology Review*. Retrieved from http://www.technologyreview.com/news/532176/a-brain-inspired-chip-takes-to-the-sky/?utm_campaign=newsletters&utm_source=newsletter-daily-all&utm_medium=email&utm_content=20141111

Simonite, T. (2014b). Digital Summit: Microsoft's Quantum Search for the "Next Transistor". *MIT Technology Review*. Retrieved from http://www.technologyreview.com/news/528256/digital-summit-microsofts-quantum-search-for-the-next-transistor/

Simonite, T. (2014c). Google's Brain-Inspired Software Describes What It Sees in Complex Images. *MIT Technology Review*. Retrieved from http://www.technologyreview.com/news/532666/googles-brain-inspired-software-describes-what-it-sees-in-complex images/?utm_campaign=newsletters&utm_source=newsletter-daily-all&utm_medium=email&utm_content=20141119

Simonite, T. (2015). A startup's neural network can understand video. *MIT Technology Review.* Retrieved from http://www.technologyreview.com/news/534631/a-startups-neural-network-can-understand-video/

Sloman, A. (2008). Why scientists and philosophers of science should teach intelligent design alongside the theory of evolution.

Smart, J. M., Cascio, J., & Paffendorf, J. (2007). Metaverse Roadmap Overview. *Accelerated Studies Foundation*. Retrieved from http://en.wikipedia.org/wiki/Metaverse

StarCraft 2: Legacy of the Void [YouTube video]. (2014). YouTube.com. Retrieved from https://www.youtube.com/watch?v=cML814JD09g&feature=share

Strickland, J. (2014). What is predictive modeling? *LindedIn Pulse.* Retrieved from https://www.linkedin.com/pulse/what-predictive-modeling-jeffrey-strickland-ph-d-cmsp-asep

Sun, R., & Bookman, L. (1994). Computational Architectures Integrating Neural and Symbolic Processes. Needham, MA: Kluwer Academic Publishers. Retrieved from http://www.cogsci.rpi.edu/~rsun/book2-ann.html doi:10.1007/b102608

Talbot, M. (1991). *The holographic universe*. New York: Harper.

The Hidden World of Facebook "Like Farms". (n. d.). *MIT Technology Review*. Retrieved from http://www.technologyreview.com/view/530961/the-hidden-world-of-facebook-like-farms/

Van de Castle, R. L. (1994). *Our dreaming mind*. New York: Random House.

Wright, W. R. (1960). Functional analysis and mass communication. *Public Opinion Quarterly*, (24): 610–613.

Zyga, L. (2013). Maxwell's demon can use quantum information to generate work. *Phys.org*. Retrieved from http://phys.org/news/2013-12-maxwell-demon-quantum.html

Chapter 3
Breaking the Frame of Digital, Dream, and Waking Realities

Jayne I. Gackenbach
MacEwan University, Canada

Sarkis Hakopdjanian
MacEwan University, Canada

ABSTRACT

Just as our dreaming reality is constructed, our waking reality may also be constructed. While our waking reality influences our lives the most, other constructed realities also have impact. Yet, never before has such a large part of the population been so widely affected by another constructed reality beyond dreaming; specifically, our technologically constructed digital reality through video game play. One potential consequence of video game play is breaking the illusion or 'frame' of our dreams as reality through various dream experiences. Many of the world's wisdom traditions believe that waking reality is an illusion, and now this idea is supported by modern digital physics. While being aware of the illusory nature of waking reality is difficult, it may be easier to break the framework of perception or 'wake up' to the true nature of reality in alternative realities, such as digital and dreaming. This chapter will review the evidence collected in the video game and dream laboratory to explore how video game play is breaking the frame within dreaming realities.

INTRODUCTION

Once upon a time, Zhuang Zhou dreamed he was a butterfly, a butterfly flitting about happily enjoying himself. He did not know that he was Zhou. Suddenly he awoke, and was palpably Zhou. He did not know whether he was Zhou, who had dreamed of being a butterfly, or a butterfly dreaming that he was Zhou. (Zhuangzi, as cited in Mair, 1998)

Our experience of life is subjective and may be a constructed reality (Blackmore, 2012). Within this experience, there exist various other constructed realities or states of consciousness. One such state is experienced by everyone while we sleep: our constructed dreaming reality. Dreams may have been

DOI: 10.4018/978-1-4666-9891-8.ch003

one of the first realizations of an alternative reality by our early ancestors. Zhuang Zhou's parable is over 2,000 years old, and it is one of the earliest instances in recorded history where we question the boundaries of reality through dreams. These boundaries can be broken or transcended through various techniques, which can result in altered, and perhaps even higher states of consciousness. In traditional, indigenous societies, psychoactive plants and fungi, as well as drumming, vision quests, and sweat lodges were used by our early ancestors to alter their consciousness and access states of non-physical reality (Schultes, Hofmann, & Rätsch, 2001). In modern, industrialized societies, digital technology is used to access various constructions of reality. These digital technologies are not only interacting with people and societies but are also influencing ideas and philosophies. As a result, our theories of mind and reality are being informed by these technologies and evolving into various theories on mind/machine relationships, digital philosophy, digital physics, and simulated reality.

Our intention in this chapter is to explore the relationship between various constructions of reality, focusing on our biologically constructed dreaming reality and our technologically constructed digital reality. These realities exist within a framework of perception and this frame can be broken in various ways, which may result in a phenomenon often called "waking up" in the transpersonal literature. For instance, in a lucid dream the dreamer is aware that they are in a dream. This awareness breaks the frame of the dreaming reality by allowing the dreamer to become simultaneously aware of the true nature of their dreamt reality as well as their waking reality. Thus, the dreamer is "waking up" in their dream while still remaining asleep. In this chapter, we investigate ways in which the frame can be broken in dreaming realities, but also in digital realities, and perhaps even in waking reality. Some of the newest theories in physics, while long espoused in the wisdom traditions, have philosophical implications on the nature of our waking reality as perhaps a simulated construction within a framework of perception. Ultimately, we are exploring how breaking the frame, within these constructions of reality, affects the nature of consciousness itself.

MEDIATED COMMUNICATION AND COGNITION

We have been creating, interacting with, and influencing technology since the beginning of our existence. In turn, these technologies have been influencing us biologically, psychologically, culturally, socially, and even philosophically, by informing our ontological theories of mind and reality. Theories of mind that consider the relationship between the human mind and machines have a long history. Sternberg and Preiss (2005) argue that mediated communication, whether it is through modern electronic technologies or through simple lines on a cave wall, has long affected how we think. They broadly conceptualize the development of technology as "the building of artifacts or procedures—tools—to help people accomplish their goals" (p. xvii) and thus note technology's longstanding influence on human development.

Sternberg and Preiss (2005) present two dimensions of technological influence: frequency of use and degree of dissemination. High and low classification along each of these two dimensions yields a four–part taxonomy. The degree of influence on the human mind by mediated communication ranges from the rarely used, but nonetheless widely influential (e.g. aptitude tests), to the widely used and widely influential (e.g. alphabets). In this taxonomy, digital worlds in computers, the Internet, and video gaming are moving from the very rare, if influential (e.g. early computer use by mainframe computers), to the widely used and widely disseminated (e.g. today's use of the Internet as a mass medium or the wide use of video games). The growth curve of technologies and their subsequent absorption into society is nicely articulated by Preiss and Sternberg (2005):

Cultural tools are invented historically and transmitted from one generation to the next and acquired ontogenetically. Some tools that are commonplace to one generation were created only through a great intellectual struggle by the previous generation. As these tools become commonplace and shared by a larger group of people, cognition becomes increasingly technological. (p. 203)

Similarly, Cole and Derry (2005) view "tool use as both amplifier of human action and transformative of human mind" (p. 221). Specifically, they note that:

Writing relates progressively less to the cultivation of expression on paper and more to effective computer use . . . this change restructures the writing process as planning and reviewing with word processors involves more cognitive effort than does working in longhand. (p. xiii)

Likewise, in mathematics, the use of calculators and computers allows more time for complex problem–solving, since computation is performed by the machine. A related development has been observed in people who play video games as they demonstrate higher levels of nonverbal problem–solving in the specialized cognitive ability of visuo–spatial information processing because of their game–playing experience (Greenfield, 1996). An important issue in evaluating the effects of such experiences is the increasing ability to couple our internal representational systems with technological systems that augment input data. There are many examples of such couplings, such as absorption in a movie, chatting on a cell phone, or playing a video game. It is becoming increasingly likely that we are not only immersing ourselves in and enjoying these augmented realities but also that our mental functions are being altered as we experience them (Sternberg & Preiss, 2005).

Certain types of media exposure provide a largely passive observer experience. Television, videos, and radio, for example, are organized for one–way communication. Although users can change channels, the content of each experience is fixed. This is not the case with video game play, where the player is an active participant, and sometimes creator, of the emerging experience. Video game play is arguably the most absorbing, and thus, immersive experience of technological mediation. It appears that mental functions are affected, and perhaps even consciousness may also be affected. As noted by Greenfield (1996), "video games make it possible for the first time to actively navigate through representational space" (p. 91).

NATURE OF REALITY

We are suggesting that perhaps reality itself is representational, literally; in other words, a simulation. Many philosophies on the nature of reality have posited the existence of a fundamental substance or essence that pervades the universe, such as monads, matter, mind, or God. Pre-Socratic philosophers postulated that elemental forces, such as water or air, compose the essence of the universe (Abernethy & Langford, 1970). Post-Socratic philosophers, such as the Pythagoreans, believed the first thing to come into existence was the monad, the Divine totality of all beings (Fairbanks, 1898). Various beliefs of the pervasiveness of mind or soul were prevalent throughout the ancient world, from indigenous religions such as paganism and shamanism to Eastern religions of Taoism, Shintoism, Buddhism and Hinduism (Clarke, 2004). In Western philosophy, Leibniz borrowed the term "monad" to describe the substance that builds the universe, or perhaps more specifically, the "perpetual living mirror of the universe" (Rescher, 1991).

In our recent history, we believe that the fundamental substance of reality is matter, composed of atoms, but we later discovered sub-atomic particles in the form of protons, neutrons, and electrons. As atomic theory continued to evolve, Schrödinger (1926) published a paper that described the electron as a wave-function, instead of a point particle, returning to deterministic classical physics. Born (1926), however, disagreed and published an interpretation of Schrödinger's wave-function by proposing that it does not to describe the electron itself but rather all of its possible states. This suggests that Schrödinger's wave-function can be used to calculate the probability of finding an electron around its nucleus. Born's interpretation reconciled the duality of the electron refracting like a wave but having the mass of a particle and thus, introduced the theory of wave-particle duality. This modern model of the atom and Heisenberg's uncertainty principle (Heisenberg, 1927) describes the position of electrons in terms of probabilities because it is mathematically impossible to derive the position and momentum of an electron. In the decades that followed, additional particles were proposed and subsequently detected inside of sub-atomic particles, such as matter and anti-matter particles, called fermions, as well as force particles, called bosons. Collectively, these were called elementary particles; "The atoms or the elementary particles themselves are not as real; they form a world of potentialities or possibilities rather than one of things or facts" (Heisenberg, 1958).

These new theories of physics, collectively called quantum physics, have significant philosophical implications with regards to the nature of reality. The universe no longer seems deterministic, as described by Newton's classical physics, but instead appears to be probabilistic, composed of elementary particles that exist in a wave of potentialities. This new physics provides a probability distribution for the outcome, calculated as a wave function, and the ultimate form of this distribution is determined by the quantum state and a measurable operator or observable describing the system. When one of these elementary particles switches from one quantum state to another, it is comparable to a binary digit changing from one value (e.g. 0) to another (e.g. 1). Since the universe is composed of elementary particles, it follows that the universe can be described as binary digits, changing from one quantum state to another, and existing in a field or wave of quantum probabilities. These changes in quantum states are changes in information, such as binary changes from one to zero. Consequently, the fundamental substance of the universe is ultimately information. This idea is further supported by loop quantum gravity (Rovelli, 1997), which proposes that space-time itself is quantized. If space-time is quantized, it may be computable. Furthermore, since information can be computable, perhaps the universe itself is being computed as a simulation. This hypothesis is at the core of various theories on digital physics and digital philosophy. Specifically,

Every it — every particle, every field of force, even the space-time continuum itself — derives its function, its meaning, its very existence entirely... from... binary choices, bits... What we call reality arises in the last analysis from the posing of yes-no questions. (Wheeler, 1989)

VIRTUAL REALITY

If the essence of our physical, material reality is information, this is analogous to our constructions of digital reality, which is also composed of binary digits of information. As we continue to develop interesting and exotic technologies, we are not only developing and influencing society and ourselves but also glimpsing into the very nature of reality. Our interaction with technology is also evolving. We are no longer content to simply observe and participate with technology on a screen in front of us. As a result, we are inventing ways to *enter* technology by creating a virtually simulated environment or a virtual reality. One of the most recent manifestations of our desire to *enter* technology is the highly anticipated Oculus Rift virtual reality head-mounted display.

Virtual reality (VR) is a digitally simulated environment that replicates the experience of being present in another location, a phenomenon known as presence. The developers of VR claim that users will perceive objects found in the virtual world as being equally present to those found in the "real" world. The extent to which one feels present in another location depends on how well the perceptual systems of the user are submerged in the computer-generated stimuli. The more the system captivates the senses and blocks out stimuli from the "real" world, the more the system is considered immersive, which in turn allows the user to experience presence. The easiest way to capture these experiences is by wearing a high quality VR head-mounted display. Until recently, high quality VR head-mounted displays have been too expensive for the average user. This changed, however, with the introduction of the Oculus Rift. Industry experts have been claiming for over a decade that in the near future, VR will reach a greater number of consumers and subsequently revolutionize the online world as we know it (Biocca, Kim, & Levy, 1995).

One of the key elements for presence in VR is engagement of the vestibular system. More specifically, the vestibular system contributes to our sense of spatial orientation by relying on visual and auditory feedback. Various systems have been and are currently being developed, which include haptic vests, VR gloves, and body placement recognition through feedback loops, such as Microsoft's Kinect for Xbox One. Following Facebook's acquisition of Oculus Rift in March of 2014, various other large corporations have announced that they are also entering the consumer retail market for VR interface. Some of the most anticipated new entrants into this market are creating holographic technology to augment our physical, material reality, such as Microsoft's HoloLens and Google's investment in the start-up Magic Leap. Other companies are competing directly with Oculus, such as Sony's Project Morpheus, which is a VR head-mounted display that is also geared for gaming and argued to be equally sophisticated. Other competing systems include Samsung's Gear VR, which is a head-mounted display made by Oculus, but powered by their phone-tablet, the Galaxy Note. The most recent addition to this market is a partnership between HTC, the smartphone manufacturer, and Valve, who run the social gaming platform Steam. The two have partnered to create the HTC Vivé VR, which is another competitor in this emerging new market. Mark Zuckerberg, the founder and CEO of Facebook, anticipates a huge shift occurring in society with the emergence of these new VR technologies. He believes that "one day… this kind of immersive, augmented reality will become a part of daily life for billions of people" (Zuckerberg, 2014).

Although VR has successfully captured the public's imagination, to truly capture the user's sense of presence, additional improvements still need to be made. For instance, Wlassoff (2015) argues that the brain is not actually fully convinced of the visual/auditory VR stimulus. He has pointed out that some of the newest research on place cells, neurons that create and control cognitive maps by taking input from the environment, claims that the brain can tell the difference between virtual reality and waking reality. Wlassoff explains that the relatively minor senses actually play a role in presence. While the soon to be released gamer-focused VR technologies do not include these minor senses, recent research has finally found a way to digitally reproduce them (Strickland, 2015). Thus, we believe that as VR becomes more widely dispersed, and the technology improves, the user will become completely immersed and perhaps the brain will be fully convinced.

Although, the capabilities and limitations of VR are a constant point of contention, immersion into virtual worlds is already happening without head-mounted displays as a result of the explosion of the Internet. The objective of VR is to create a mediated experience that appears to be non-mediated or "real", in order to create a sense of presence. However, a recent and reverse phenomenon, known as inverse presence, has emerged in which a real experience appears to be mediated:

Drawing on news reports and an online survey, we identify 3 categories of this "illusion of mediation": positive (when people perceive natural beauty as mediated), negative (when people perceive a disaster, crime, or other tragedy such as the events of September 11, 2001, as mediated), and unusual (when close connections between people's "real life" activities and mediated experiences lead them to confuse the former with the latter). (Timmins & Lombard, 2005, p. 492)

The exchange of real and virtual realities, consequently, seems to have come full cycle. Some industry experts have suggested that this VR transformation is comparable to the way that the Internet revolutionized the distribution of information in the 1990s (Zuckerberg, 2014). In fact, beyond the obvious application of VR to entertainment, Kaplan (2015) suggests that "as virtual reality headsets and the necessary enabling technologies improve and catch on, huge opportunities in journalism, business, education, medicine, mental health, and more, will start to appear." We are suggesting that it is not only the entertainment industry that are about to change but also education, healthcare, and even society-at-large. Furthermore, we posit that these industries are about to be radically transformed by emerging VR technologies, which will fundamentally shift human consciousness.

DREAMS AND TECHNOLOGY

In our research, we investigate the relationship between our technologically constructed digital realities and our biologically constructed dreaming realities, which exist within our consciousness. Dreams have been studied and interpreted since before our recorded history. Perhaps dreams are simply our mental experiences of the brain's activity while we are sleeping. Yet while asleep, the cognitive experience of dreaming is separated from most external stimuli and the dreamer experiences a biologically constructed virtual reality. The dreaming reality is composed of imagined perceptions that often feel very real, thus, it is a true virtual reality:

The dream world is thus 'virtual' for precisely the same reason as a computer-generated synthetic environment is: in both cases I feel physically present (i.e., I am phenomenologically present!) in an unreal place where my physical body is not really present at all. (Revonsuo, 2006, p. 114)

In our research laboratory, we have been investigating the relationship between digitally constructed online reality, such as social media or video game play, and another construction of reality, dreams. Dream research has progressed over the last century following Freud's (1900) classic opus publication, *The Interpretation of Dreams*. This research has clearly demonstrated that we regularly function in this biologically constructed realm, which is seemingly not as "real" as our waking reality appears to be. Our dreaming reality exists in a realm between our conscious awareness and our unconscious mind. For as long as we have dreamt, we have been postulating the purpose of those dreams, a realm rich in mythologies, archetypes, and narratives, which, according to Jung (1933), exist in our collective unconscious. This realm has been a source of inspiration for our visions of insight, elaborate storytelling, and expressions of art for thousands of years. Our forms of storytelling and artistic expression have evolved as well, based on the mediums available for expression. One such medium used today is digital media, such as television, cinema, video games, and the Internet. Thus, it follows that our dreams are a source of inspiration for this digital media as a result of the high levels of interactivity in today's media environment. This digital media, in turn, is also influencing our dreams, almost as a positive feedback loop. We propose that we have a push/pull relationship between digital media and night-time dreams.

Our early ancestors lived in tribal societies and experienced archetypes through shared rituals, dreams, and altered states of consciousness. These shared experiences are what held these societies together in terms of their collectivity of consciousness (Durkheim, 1961). Our modern Western society values autonomy and extreme individualism. We lack the collective societal nature traditionally seen in societies that value higher states of consciousness and absorptive states. Interestingly, we have unwittingly re-created this shared or collective social reality through our digital media, particularly interactive media, such as the Internet and video games. Interacting with others online and in video games serves some of the same societal functions as explicit mythological systems have served in indigenous cultures. Both offer fully available and explicit mythological imagery and narrative as part of a daily engaged virtual life. The sense of being part of the VR world and influencing it, such as in video games, achieves a level of immersion that cannot be attained with traditional storytelling. Furthermore, this experience ultimately evokes an emotional response, which may be unobtainable by any other means.

This immersion in a constructed reality, be it digitally or biologically created, occurs because the boundaries of these realities are permeable. In other words, it is difficult, arguably impossible, to know where one reality ends and another reality begins. Perhaps there are no boundaries at all; no lines of demarcation that clearly separate one construction of reality as being wholly distinct from another. Various physiological parallels of digital and dreaming reality have been observed along with their associated psychological importance. Practice in one alternative reality, VR, informs another alternative reality, dreams. But such practice can also change the very structure and function of these biologically constructed dreams (Gackenbach, 2012). Might this phenomenon also occur in waking reality, especially if waking reality is also constructed? That is, if our waking reality is constructed, might our digitally constructed reality (i.e. life online) also change the structure and function of our waking reality, as it seems to do so for our dreaming reality?

The boundaries of reality are often blurred because our constructions of them are fragile. Our susceptibility to illusion is well documented in the perception literature and makes for fun activities online. Beyond this susceptibility, however, is the phenomena of change blindness or inattentional blindness. That is, we may miss information in our visual field that is not necessarily subtle. One famous example of this is the gorilla in our midst experiment. In this experiment, a few people dressed in white or black are shown passing a basketball back and forth. The viewer is instructed to focus on the players dressed in white and count the number of passes. In the midst of passing the ball, a person dressed in a black gorilla costume walks directly through the visual field of the observer. Many people miss seeing the gorilla completely. Change blindness is a version of inattentional blindness where something in a picture changes and is not subsequently noticed by observers (Mack & Rock, 2000). These changes can be large or obvious, such as a person in a gorilla costume. The easily distracted nature of our attention is the stock and trade of the magician. Mack and Rock claim that these phenomena are a function of attention. Various techniques have been argued to focus attention, including meditation (Weinstein & Smith, 1992; Holzel & Ott, 2006). We have found that gamers are less susceptible to change blindness effects than either a control group or a group that claims high levels of prayer or meditation (Gackenbach, Swanston, & Stark, 2015). In either VR or prayer/meditation, one can argue that breaking the fragile frame of reality, in this case, not seeing all that is there, is a rather common occurrence that can be improved with various practices.

This fragility of reality is also spoken of by Jung (1933). He speaks extensively of the archaic man relative to the modern man and points out that each has a set of assumptions upon which his reality is based. The former intones sorcery while the latter relies on natural consequences to explain the world around him. Jung stresses that both have an explanatory system, which satisfies their need to understand and be in the world safely. The absolute truth of the matter either does not exist or does not matter, suggesting there is no objective reality. He goes on to argue that the supernatural explanatory system of the archaic man helps him embrace the clustering of apparently coincidental events as omens rather than events which occur together by chance. Thus, the archaic man's explanatory system allows for a wider range of "natural" events than the modern man's. Jung (1933) explains:

It is a rational presupposition of ours that everything has a natural and perceptible cause. We are convinced of this right from the start. Causality is one of our most sacred dogmas. There is no legitimate place in our world for invisible, arbitrary, and so-called supernatural powers – unless, indeed, we descend with the modern physicist into the obscure, microcosmic world inside the atom, where it appears, some very curious things happen. But that lies far from the beaten track. We distinctly resent the idea of invisible and arbitrary forces, for it is not so long ago that we made our escape from that frightening world of dreams and superstitions, and constructed for ourselves a picture of the cosmos worthy of our rational consciousness – that latest and greatest achievement of man. (p. 113)

Empirical evidence supporting these distinct ways of viewing the world comes from Drinkwater (1976). Specifically, Drinkwater reported a superiority for natural object placement among moderately integrated Australian aboriginal children relative to their European ancestry peers. The children of European ancestry, conversely, were superior in the placement of household objects found in traditional Western society. Staying within this tone of relative reality, Jung argued that the aboriginal framing of reality, which included causal attributions of witchcraft when anomalous but "natural" events occurred, gave way to modern views of the range of "normal".

Similarly, our mass immersion in technologically created realms is again changing our views of causal mechanisms for reality. Is the digital physics theory of reality as a simulation mentioned earlier, simply speculative new science or is it an idea whose time has come? At the 2011 New York Science Festival, various physicists discussed whether the universe is the ultimate computer simulation. One digital physics philosopher, Nick Bostrom (2011), pointed out that the time is right as simulations are now sophisticated enough that the scientist can imagine an alternative reality hypothesis. Bostrom went on to suggest that in 30 years technology will be sophisticated enough that we will not be able to tell the difference between our virtual and "real" world realms. Certainly, we have seen enough progress in the last two decades, with the advent and mass dissemination of the Internet, that this implication is plausible.

MERGING WAKING REALITIES

Computer-based systems for entertainment, communication, and productivity are so deeply enmeshed in human lives that it is difficult to imagine modern society without them. However, with the incorporation of these technologically constructed alternative realities into daily routines, our perceptions of our waking reality are also changing. Sometimes these changes are quite distinct, as immersing oneself in a video game, but sometimes they merge seamlessly with our behavior, like texting as one walks. These technological integrations also overlap in a more perceptually profound way, as in the work on the Game Transfer Phenomenon (GTP). GTP examines how video game play experiences are transferred to the real world, resulting in automatic mental processes, altered perceptions, and changes in behaviours influenced by video games (Ortiz de Gortari & Griffiths, 2012). Some of the experiences may blur the boundaries of reality to such an extent that they may be misinterpreted as hallucinations. The incidence of these experiences are self-reported by 92% of the participants observed, with 20% of those reporting distress and the remainder feeling the urge to do something (Ortiz de Gortari & Griffiths, 2014). Although the concept of playing video games may seem trivial to some to others they:

become a matter of emotional touch, evoking not just sensations, but lasting emotive imprints, which hold for the gamer many of the same characteristics as memorable real life experiences. (Ortiz de Gortari, 2007)

In a parallel and confirming series of studies, Poels and colleagues (Poels, Ijsselsteijn, & de Kort, 2010; 2014) explain that the:

phenomenon of game-biased perceptions and associations, or how, through intensive game play, elements from the game world can trigger thoughts and imagery outside the game world, influencing the perception and interpretation of stimuli in everyday life. (p. 1)

They further posit that these game transfer experiences increase with more play time and narrative involvement. It is reasonable to assume, accordingly, that with the imminent release of a variety of affordable VR head-mounted displays, that presence, and thus game transfer to reality, may increase. Supporting this assumption is early data collection where we found that presence, but not enjoyment, was higher after playing a video game with the Oculus Rift VR head-mounted display than after playing the same game on a computer screen (Gackenbach, Sinyard, Hakopdjanian, in press).

Just as it has often been pointed out that dreams are a constructed reality, it can also be argued that waking reality is constructed. While our waking reality influences our lives the most, other constructed realities, whether they occur during drug use, illness, hypnosis or meditation (Blackmore, 2012), also impact our lives. Yet, never before has such a large part of the population been so widely affected by another constructed reality beyond dreaming, specifically, our technologically constructed digital reality. We are able to break the frame of our dreaming reality through various dream experiences and these dreams affect our overall consciousness development. Relative to nighttime dreams, however, it is rather easy to break the frame of VR as we remain continuously awake upon entering and leaving it. Although as shown with game transfer effects, VR also seems to be affecting our consciousness. Thus, is it possible that we may also be able to break the frame of our physical, material reality, especially if this is a simulation as well? If this is the case, what will we find outside of the frame?

Alexander, Boyer, and Alexander (1987) have argued that the first signs of enlightenment (i.e. the growth or evolution of consciousness) first appear in sleep, and especially in dreams. Their argument is based upon the teachings of Maharishi Mahesh Yogi and their formidable research program (Alexander et al., 1990; Chalmers, 2015), which examines physiological, sociological and psychological parallels to the transcendent experience. Alexander et al. (1987) suggest that these signs of enlightenment take the form of lucid dreams initially while the ego is still "caught" by the excitement and fun of the experience. Eventually, as one's consciousness continues to develop, one can experience a state of transcendental consciousness or "witnessing", a silent state of pure awareness devoid of mental content (Mason, Alexander, Travis, Gackenbach & Orm-Johnson, 1995). "Witnessing" first appears and spreads throughout the dream, then progresses into 'dreamless' sleep and, finally, into waking as a state of restful alertness. As this state becomes more prevalent and stable it becomes a silent witness or observer, which is considered the first classical state of enlightenment in many Eastern ideologies. The practice of transcendence is the mechanism that this meditation research group has empirically shown is needed in order to attain this awakening in dreams, as lucidity, then eventually to the illusion of our waking reality.

Breaking the frame, or waking up to the true nature of "reality", initially happens in dreams because dreams are less driven, if at all, by external stimuli. Yet dreams are a regular experience of an altered reality that occurs for about two hours out of every 24 nearly universally, with the exception of brain damage (Solms, 2011). Our physical, material reality or "real" world has quite a stranglehold on our senses because we use our senses to process input data (sights, sounds, tastes, etc.). Thus, noticing the illusory nature of waking reality becomes quite difficult. When one moves to alternative realities, in this case digital and dream, or even drug-, hypnotic-, or fever-based, then it is much easier to break the frame or "wake up" to the reality of the frame whether induced by a video game, dream, or so forth.

While transcendence of dreams, then sleep, then waking is arguably the best way to "break the frame", it is not the only way. Although there is a long list of practices that may or may not create transcendence, many do seem to push consciousness to a more awake and present state. These are, increasingly, mindfulness practices. Gackenbach (2008; & Bown, 2011) has been arguing for years that exposure to digital realms of an alternative reality in general, especially in video game play, parallels a meditative state. Gackenbach suggests that the deep absorption of meditation is comparable to the same deep absorption in virtual realms that gamers experience. This absorption is associated with improvements in attention that also parallel meditative states. In some instances, they are better. Gackenbach, Swanston, and Stark (in press) found gamers outperformed those who pray/meditate on change blindness tasks. Following this logic, then gaming, and especially VR gaming with a head-mounted display, can be considered practice or training for waking up to the true nature of reality, or breaking the frame.

DREAMS AND VIDEO GAME PLAY

Our prior research efforts have focused primarily on the merging of digital and dreaming realities. More specifically, the relationship between video game play and dreams (reviewed in Gackenbach, 2012) and more recently non-gaming digital life, especially social media use, and its relationship to night time dreams (Gackenbach & Boyes, 2014a). We have examined the dreams of 'expert' video game players who have played approximately 10,000 hours since childhood to determine if there is an overlap of realities, convergence of realities, or a change in realities. Our research has shown that at the very least we dream about gaming, but that the more important impact is potentially on the structure and function of dreaming affected by gaming. Several lines of inquiry will be reviewed to make this case. Namely, higher lucidity/control in dreams, more nightmare protection, and more bizarreness/creativity in gamers. Each of these advantages in gamers' dreams extends the reach of dreaming in terms of negative emotional regulation and potentially into expanded states of consciousness.

Video gamers' dreams show incorporation of game content, which is consistent with the continuity hypothesis and suggests that there is a continuum between waking activities and dreamt activities (Shredl, 2003). Here is an example of simple incorporation of gaming into a dream consistent with the continuity hypothesis:

I had played a game called Bomber Man where you just run around and put bombs down and explode areas so that you can leap past.... There's, like, monsters running around that can kill you or you have to blow them up, and I remember in the dream I was down like in 3D, I was the bomber man type guy, and there were these monsters on these blocks, and I was running around, and my whole family was there actually, and we were running away from them as fast as we could. (Gackenbach et al., 2009)

While the game is not in the dream most of the time, when the game is the dream the content is not only a game being represented but rather the entire dreamt sequence is thought to be a game (Gackenbach, Sample, & Mandel, 2011). Thus, the dreamer's choices are affected by the attribution of "this is a game". In one gamer's dream, for instance, he wondered what it would be like to burn to death and, subsequently, chose to stay in a burning car to find out (Gackenbach & Hunt, 2014). Dying as a personal choice is a common occurrence in video games but in dreaming it is quite rare. In addition to incorporating game content in a dream or misattributing the state of the dream, such as believing the dream is a game, there are certain dream types that suggest breaking the frame of the dreaming reality.

LUCID/CONTROL DREAMING

Our dreaming reality is composed of imagined perceptions that often feel very real. Accordingly, it can be argued that our dreaming reality represents a true virtual reality (Revonsuo, 2006). Even if the dreamer realizes that they are within a dream, the felt experience remains, and this is called a lucid dream. While virtual gaming dreams are sometimes lucid, in that the gamer knows they are in a dream, what is more consistent in our research is the felt sense by the gamer that they can control the events and outcomes of the dreamt scenario (Gackenbach, 2012). This is often referred to as a "control dream". Unlike a lucid dream, in a control dream, the metacognitive component of awareness is somewhat missing but the dreamer can still exert some control over the dream. Deliberate decision making is present and is even allowed to violate the physics of waking reality. The degree of control a dreamer has can be measured on a continuum and varies between aspects of the dream.

In several studies, we discovered that high frequency gamers have more lucid dreams than those who rarely game (Gackenbach 2006; 2009; Gackenbach & Kuruvilla, 2008). This association between video game play and lucid dreaming is not unexpected. Video games are a technologically constructed alternative reality, while dreams are a biologically constructed alternative reality and thus, there may be a carryover learning effect. If you are in an artificial reality for hours a day, it follows that you might recognize something similar when you are in another one at night. As Revonsuo (2006) pointed out, in both the dream world and the virtual world, there is a sense of presence. In order to examine this perceived presence, Gackenbach and Rosie (2011) compared ratings of presence after playing a video game to presence after having a dream about that video game. Their results indicated that there were few differences between dreaming and gaming with regards to participants' felt sense of "being there". This supports the idea that there are similarities between virtual and dream states and thus the potential for a learning transfer.

Additionally, lucid dreaming has been characterized as presenting with a heightened meta-cognitive capacity (Kahan & LaBerge 1994). Koriat (2007) defines meta-cognition as the

process by which people self-reflect on their own cognitive and memory processes (monitoring) and how they put their meta-knowledge to use in regulating their information processing and behaviour (control). (p.289)

This meta-cognitive capacity can also be viewed as a type of self-reflective awareness (Kahan, 1994). LaBerge and DeGracia (2000) point out that while non-lucid dreams can have a meta-cognitive element,

meta-cognition during lucid dreams is not confined to events occurring in the dream, but references, either explicitly or implicitly, waking experience as well . . . hence, lucidity in the context of dreaming, implies meta-cognition framed by consciously accessible memories of waking experience. (p.275)

Another reason we might expect to find an association between lucidity and gaming is that both video game play and lucid dreaming have been associated with improved spatial skills (Gackenbach, Heilman, Boyt, & LaBerge, 1985; Sims & Mayer 2002; Subrahmanyam & Greenfield 1994). Furthermore, some resistance to motion sickness is needed to play video games for extensive periods of time (Preston, 1998) and, correspondingly, lucid dreamers have better vestibular systems (Gackenbach et al., 1986), which render them insusceptible to motion sickness. Additionally, the high attention and absorption reported by gamers (Glicksohn & Avnon 1997-98) and research on gaming (Gackenbach 2007) is reminiscent of the same qualities associated with meditation (Holzel & Ott, 2006; Weinstein & Smith, 1992). To this end, meditators have been found to have very high levels of lucidity in sleep (Gackenbach & Bosveld 1989; Hunt 1989; Mason et al., 1995).

A natural question that follows from this comparison is: are there self-selection factors in gaming that account for lucidity? The answer is yes and no. Yes, because to be a serious player you need to not suffer motion sickness. For serious game play, spatial skills are an advantage. The games most serious gamers play cater to boys and those who are able to get absorbed should do better. No, because today almost all children through to young adults play some form of video game. In the last decade, developers have been creating video games to capture a wider market, which has increased the number of girls playing as well as adults of all ages. The average gamer is now 35 years old and people of all ages and cultural backgrounds are playing games on various platforms, from computers and consoles, to phones and tablets.

Gackenbach (2008) has also argued that video game play specifically, and perhaps all electronically mediated interactions, can become a sort of meditative experience. Her argument is based on the similarities she has identified between video game play and meditation. These similarities include improved attentional skills, deep absorption, flow experiences, improved spatial skills, and increased lucid dreaming all of which are characteristic of both meditation and video game play (for a review of each of these areas see Gackenbach, 2012). Gackenbach posits that gaming allows an entry into states of consciousness typically accessed by meditators while not claiming that the effects of gaming are as profound or far reaching as meditation.

In addition to its heightened meta-cognitive self-monitoring, lucid dreaming bears a direct phenomenological and cognitive resemblance to the states sought in traditional meditation, and has been further developed within both Transcendental Meditation and Tibetan Buddhist practices. In both dream lucidity and meditation, participants experience an enhanced self-awareness. The full emergence of this awareness is marked by feelings of a vivid kinesthetically enhanced presence and feelings of awe, fascination, and at times, bliss. These feelings are similar to that in Maslow's peak experience and Otto's descriptive phenomenology of a numinous feeling of the felt sense of the sacred (Gackenbach & Bosveld, 1989; Hunt, 1989).

Hunt (1989) points out that when combined with enhanced mythic-archetypal content, lucid dreams have similarities to accounts of shamanistic vision-trance or sacred dreams of tribal societies. These sacred dreams were also of interest to Jung and were themselves crucial in confirming a directly felt sense of a shared or collective social reality. This sense of collective social reality explains the clans and other groups that emerge in long-term, committed gaming experiences, specifically in online role-playing games.

Gackenbach et al. (in press) examined lucidity and control dreams in two groups, a gaming group versus meditation/prayer group. Their research also considered a high activity versus low activity manipulation. That is, participants were asked to report a dream after a day of high activity (i.e. gaming or meditation/prayer) and after a day of low activity (i.e. little/no gaming or meditation/prayer). While the meditating/prayer group self-reported more lucid dreams overall, the gaming group reported the most control dreams across conditions. Internal commentary item on the metacognition scale was highest in the gamer group after a high activity day and lowest in the meditation/prayer group after high meditation/prayer activity. The opposite was the case after a low activity day. In terms of thwarted intention, the gamer group reported less thwarted intention in their dreams after a high activity day, while the meditation/prayer group reported more thwarted intention after a day of high activity and less thwarted intention in their dreams after a day of low activity.

Gackenbach et al.'s (in press) study also compared attention performance in the laboratory. Performance on the waking attention task was superior for gamers, while self-reports of positive effects of their chosen activity were highest for the meditation/prayer group. These findings imply that while gaming and meditation/prayer have unique differences, the absorbing qualities of both may share a similar role in their effects on consciousness. This combination of practicing control in the altered reality of gaming explains the transfer of skills of dream control for gamers into dreams. The lower lucidity, relative to meditation/prayer among gamers (although higher than the control group), however, points to an orthogonal relationship between lucidity and control, as has been noted in previous research (Levitan & LaBerge, 1993). Furthermore, it seems to be consistent with the nightmare protection hypothesis of gaming effects on dreams (Gackenbach, Ellerman, & Hall, 2011).

We make the argument that lucidity, and to some extent dream control, break the frame of the dreaming mind. Breaking the frame occurs when one is aware that they are no longer contained by the dream but are able to move within and between dreams at will. It is these moments that can also result in attributions of the dream as an out-of-body experience. Other states of consciousness confusion attributions include false awakenings, the belief that the dreamer has woken up while still asleep, and various pre-lucid experiences.

NIGHTMARE PROTECTION HYPOTHESIS

We have found that one result of personal dream control is nightmare protection. Our early ancestors evolved from primitive times where daily threats to survival were abundant. Those that were able to rehearse the perception and avoidance of threatening elements safely in the virtual reality of dreams had an evolutionary advantage for survival (Revonsuo & Valli, 2000). Thus, from an evolutionary perspective, one function of nighttime dreams may be threat simulation (Revonsuo & Valli, 2000). It therefore follows that playing combat-centric video games might serve that same function in an altered reality. Less threat should appear in dreams because that function has been served in combat-centric game play while awake. This effect is what we have found in several studies with male gamers. This adaptive response to threats in dreams is developed when a gamer fights threats for many hours over many years in a video game. Early in our work, we found some indications of how nightmares were differentially responded to by high end gamers, with comments like 'they were fun' or they reported fewer of them (reviewed in Gackenbach, et al, 2009). In our first content analysis of high versus low end gamers[1], we found a smaller number of dreams with aggression, yet more intense aggression (namely physical aggression), in those dreams that did contain violence (Gackenbach, et al, 2009) for the high end gamers relative to the lows. Here is an example of the intensity of violence:

so I went outside with my cat and shot these criminals that were trying to eat my dad and they were on top of my dad trying to eat his arms and he was fighting them off, and they were trying to hold him down and bite his shoulders and there was blood and stuff. (Gackenbach et al., 2009)

The respondent commented about this dream, "and it was a very graphic shootout for a dream; it was very blood and guts ya know?" Thus, it's important to keep in mind that while this can happen in gamers' dreams it is uncommon, not only statistically but also in the eyes of the dreamer. Further, it has been replicated in other such content analyses of gamers' dreams (Gackenbach & Boyes, 2014b; Boyes & Gackenbach, 2015; Gahr, 2015).

Our first focused look at the threat simulation hypothesis was in a 2008 study by Gackenbach and Kurvilla. In that study, we examined Revonsuo and Valli's (2000) threat simulation evolutionary theory of dream function, and hypothesized that high end gamers would report less threat in their nighttime dreams. While support of the hypothesis was correlational, the strength of this study was the selection of dreams as "all occurring last night", "after a full night's sleep", "feeling rested", and "having had played a video game the day before." Our inquiries continued with two subsequent studies (Gackenbach, Ellerman, & Hall, 2011; Gackenbach, & Flockhart, 2013) that examined populations more likely to experience threat in waking life compared to student samples, namely military and first responders.

In the first study, Gackenbach, Ellerman, and Hall (2011) solicited responses from soldiers who played at least some video games. They also prescreened out soldiers reporting symptoms of current post traumatic stress. Thus, their results apply to relatively healthy military personnel. In addition to collecting dreams that were from the soldier's military experience, Gackenbach et al. (2011) collected a recent dream. In a review of the nightmare literature, Levin and Nielsen (2009) reported that two predictors of susceptibly to nightmares are emotional reactivity and previous history of trauma. Thus, in the military study we inquired about these predictors, and held them constant in our threat simulation content analysis of the soldiers' dreams. We then examined two groups of almost entirely male soldiers who differed in video game play frequency. Soldiers reporting more play, as hypothesized, were found to have less threat in their dreams and more personal control. The following dreams illustrate the difference. The first is the military themed dream of a low frequency player:

I couldn't find my rifle and something was chasing me. I searched the entire forest until I did find my weapon. As I turned around to shoot what was hunting me - the trigger felt like it was a 1,000 lbs trigger pull. The rounds I was shooting were delayed and where not hitting where I was aiming (Subject #21). (Gackenbach et al., 2011)

This dream was coded as high in threat. In contrast, from a high frequency player, here is the second military themed dream:

I was told by my old Sargent to load up on the humvv in my gunners spot. he said we were going to roll out to fight some were in Baghdad. we drove down to the combat area where there was a brutal fight me and quite a few men against the insergants. i remember shooting and seeing men fall on both sides. i saw the faces of the dead eyes wide and staring at the sky soulless faces of friends. i walked dazed back to the humvv and woke up (Subject #115).

While both dreams contained high threat levels, the second dreamer is clearly able to fight back and thus is less victimized by his dreamt circumstances. Relatedly, in coding for war motifs in these dreams, the lower frequency gamers were found to report significantly more such content than the high gamers. This is noteworthy because there were no differences in such motifs in their recent dreams and there were no gamer group differences in deployment history.

In a subsequent study on first responders with the same design, we found that males who play video games frequently had fewer objective threats in their dreams (Gackenbach & Flockhart, 2013). In this study, we had enough women to identify a sex difference among high end gamers and nightmare protection. Specifically, high end female gamers did not appear to get the same advantage as their male counterparts in being protected from their nightmares by frequent game play. We went on to replicate these findings using the same study design on a student sample (Gackenbach, Darlington, Ferguson, & Boyes, 2013). We concluded that male high end gamers seem to be less troubled by nightmares than female high end gamers. We suggested three reasons for this: game genre, game sociability, and sex-role conflict. This is illustrated in another follow-up study from our laboratory examining nightmare protection. We found that chases and attacks in male gamers' dreams are more likely to result in a fight rather than a flight response (Boyes & Gackenbach, 2014). In addition, although the dreamt chases and attacks may remain frightening and threatening, male gamers also report that they are fun and empowering.

In two subsequent studies (Boyes & Gackenbach, 2014; Ditner, 2015), we examined these differences in responses to nightmares among high end male and female gamers. Our results, which are consistent with previous research (Gackenbach, Darlington, Ferguson, & Boyes, 2013), indicate that male and female gamers are playing different types of video games. Males played more combat centric games, which may be nightmare inoculating. Females, conversely, play primarily casual games, which may not be providing the nightmare protection found in males. No support was found for the stereotype threat hypothesis, which is that gaming women may not be fighting back in their dreams because it contradicted traditional sex roles. Early support was found for differences in coping styles in both waking and in dreaming. In our most recent inquiry into this gender disparity (Ditner, 2015), we examined high frequency and low frequency female gamers who favored either the combat centric or noncombat centric genres. Ditner (2015) reported that female high end gamers who favored combat centric games reported less fear in terms of fear experienced in the nightmare and immediately thereafter. In addition, she found that the sex role identity of masculinity was more associated with women who prefer combat centric games. Thus, we are beginning to better understand the apparent reversal of the nightmare protection hypothesis in women and see that it is a function of genre history and preference as well as gender role identity.

Under the right circumstances, both genders can break the frame of nightmares with video game play. From a clinical perspective, this may or may not be healthy as Jung has indicated that the nightmare is the psyche's invitation. From the perspective of the potential evolution of consciousness, however, such effects of gaming may be functional.

BIZARRENESS AND CREATIVITY

One of the most often assumed characteristics of dreams is that they can be so bizarre. Even when to an outside judge a dream may not appear bizarre (Domhoff, 2007), the dreamer may perceive it as bizarre. For instance, if a car is colored yellow in a dream, the dreamer may consider that very element to be bizarre. They may hate the color yellow, which is why they thought it was so bizarre to see the yellow car in their dream. Early in our work, we found bizarre elements in gamers' dreams (Gackenbachet al., 2009). In this study, the male norms for content analysis of low end gamers' dreams reported no inclusion of dead and imaginary characters, while among these high end gamers' dreams, in this sample, 22% had such characters. Here is an example of an imaginary dream character from that study:

I dreamt I was a character in Underworld 2; it was a werewolf character, and then I became a third person. It was the two main characters; it was the vampire girl and a hybrid werewolf character.

This was taken up as the focus of a study examining video game play history and dream bizarreness by Gackenbach, Kuruvilla, and Dopko in 2009. Consistent with Domhoff's (2007) findings, they found that gamers, both high and low end, had more non-bizarre elements than bizarre ones. However, of the bizarre elements, high frequency gamers' dreams were coded as containing more incongruent and vague elements than low end gamers. High end gamers report a greater amount of some types of dream bizarreness. Why does this occur? The first and most likely reason is because gamers are immersed in digitally constructed unusual worlds, often filled with fantasy and mythology, during their game play. Thus, what we may be observing is the direct incorporation of daytime activities into dreams. However, the participants in the Gackenbach, Kuruvilla and Dopko study, rated themselves as to whether there was any reference to digital media in their dreams. There were no gamer group differences. This finding is especially interesting in the context of the significantly higher digital media exposure that the high end gamers reported from the day prior to the dream. One might conclude that despite high end gamers being exposed to more bizarre media elements while awake, there were no group differences in morning after reports of media content in their dreams. This weakens the argument that bizarre dream content is purely a function of waking exposure to bizarre media (Gackenbach, Kuruvilla, & Dopko, 2009).

An alternative explanation for the higher bizarreness in gamers' dreams may be due to the nature of their semantic networks. Specifically, Revonsuo and Salmivalli (1995) state that:

One possible way to understand the underlying mechanisms of dream incongruity is to think of them in terms of connectionist networks . . . During dreaming there is no sensory input to constrain the possible combinations of activation patterns, which may result in an atypical configuration of activation in the network. Such activation could be reflected in subjective experience as incongruous dream imagery. (p. 183-184)

They argue that more diverse networks allow for more incongruous dream bizarreness. This interpretation is consistent with other research on high end video game players who have demonstrated a variety of cognitive and attentional type skills, which in turn may implicate more diverse neural networks (Green & Bavelier, 2003).

Diverse neural networks may be due to differences in creativity, which is "the ability to produce work that is both novel (i.e., original, unexpected) and appropriate (i.e., useful, adaptive concerning task constraints)" (Sternberg & Lubart, 1999, p. 3). Several studies link the degree of bizarreness in dreams to creativity. Specifically, Adelson (1974) found that college girls who had more creative dreams were also advanced students in creative writing classes. Schecter, Schmeidler, and Staal (1965) found that university students in an arts program recalled more imaginative dreams compared to students enrolled in science or engineering.

In a further study on dream bizarreness and creativity, Gackenbach and Dopko (2012) investigated this finding and also observed that the bizarreness occurrence associated with gaming was somewhat replicated by their study. This time, the number of hours playing a video game the day before was controlled. They also found that video game play history was related to figural creativity. The positive bizarreness, gaming, and creativity association was partially confirmed for males, while video game play was associated negatively with bizarreness for females, with no creativity link. In separate and joint factor analyses of the major variable clusters (i.e., media use, including gaming, bizarreness, and creativity), it was clear that any associations were to gaming and not to other media use the day before the dream.

Revonsuo and Salmivalli (1995) studied the frequency of three types of dream bizarreness. They found that incongruity is a more common form of bizarreness than vagueness or discontinuity. More specifically, they found that language and cognition were the most incongruent content and that the self was the least incongruent content. This indicates that the self is well preserved in dreams and rarely affected by features incongruous with waking reality. Early in our work, we found changes to the self, already noted, as related to gaming characters (Gackenbach et al., 2009), or to activities the self is not normally engaged in, such as choosing to burn to death (Gackenbach & Hunt, 2014). These deeper transformations in gamers' dream selves that occur due to the transfer of self into the avatar in gaming, can be interpreted as a form of breaking the frame in dreams. In other words, since the gamer is entering an avatar in the game, there is a separation between their actual self and their perceived self through the eyes of their avatar. This separation makes it more likely to undergo a metamorphosis of self, which has been observed in gamers' dreams.

We have explored three types of dreams that are affected by video game play and result in the frame of the dreamt reality being broken. Next, we explore two situational constraints and how they may also break the frame of the dream reality, due to exposure to digital reality.

SOCIAL MEDIA, CULTURE, AND DREAMS

Being present in digitally constructed realities is not limited to video game play and includes life online. The number of people using the Internet has grown exponentially, with over three billion users, transferring up to eight zettabytes of information in the digital universe in 2015. A zettabyte is one trillion gigabytes! The majority of Internet users reside in China, which has become the dominant population online. While North America has deep penetration of the Internet into its population (78 percent) and China has only 42 percent penetration, because of China's huge population, it has 15 times more users. Comparatively, India has five times the number of users in North America but its penetration is significantly lower than China's at only 11 percent of its population. Thus, it seems that the future direction of Internet growth will occur in the East (ITU, 2011; World Bank, 2012).

The move to mobile devices to reach the Internet is especially prevalent in developing countries. It is cheaper to buy or use a cell phone online at villages along a coastline than to buy a computer when trying to get the best market price for fish. While the trend internationally is towards more mobile Internet access, this trend is strongest in North America. North Americans, however, are using their mobile phones to get online information and the most common use internationally is to text others, followed by taking pictures and video.

Another new component of life online is the prevalence of social media networks. Although Facebook remains the undisputed market leader, in terms of total number of users with over 1.39 billion monthly users as of December 2014 (Facebook, 2014), other social media websites are also growing quickly. In 2013, 71 percent of adults in the United States used Facebook, while only 22 percent used LinkedIn, 21 percent used Pinterest, 18 percent used Twitter, and 17 percent used Instagram. Among the Chinese, there are also a high number of users of social media but not of the same websites. They have their own versions of each of these types of social media networks. Demographics of Facebook users in 2013 were largely even across gender, income, and education, but age evidenced a big drop in usage among those 65 and over (Duggan & Smith, 2014).

Given the prevalence of social media and our increasing time spent online it is prudent to ask whether these non-gaming digital reality experiences can also lead to breaking the frame? In our laboratory, we have begun an exploration of social media and culture effects on dreams. We propose that both of these have a potential effect of also breaking the frame, if not as strong as video game play.

In a preliminary study on the association between non-gaming digital life and dreams, Gackenbach and Boyes (2014a) asked students to indicate if they had played computer games or used their computer for non-gaming purposes during the day prior to a recent dream they reported. They then answered questions regarding their confidence about the type of dream they reported and their emotions during said dream. There was some indication that the high end non-gaming computer-use group had more lucid dreams (females only) and control dreams, but less bizarre dreams. All three of these dream types had previously been found to occur in gamers and can be seen as examples of breaking the frame (Gackenbach, 2012). However, in that data collection effort, the varieties of non-gaming computer-use were not inquired about.

In a second study (Gackenbach & Boyes, 2014b), this group compared the self-perceptions of typical dreams and reports of a recent dream from non-gaming and gaming electronic media users. They focused particularly on social media use, both on computers and on computer-like devices, such as smart phones. Gackenbach and Boyes found many similarities between high end gamers and high end social media users[2] in their nighttime dreams. Furthermore, the high end gamers and high end social media users had the thinnest psychological boundaries. That is, they were more susceptible to fantasy, hallucinations, were more creative (Hartmann & Kunzendorf, 2006-2007) and thus, were perhaps most susceptible to media effects. Will these be the first candidates to break the frame of dreaming into higher consciousness, due to their thin psychological boundaries?

In their 2015 study, Gackenbach and Gahr, had Canadian students of varying cultural backgrounds take an online survey to examine their dream experiences (Dream Intensity Scale, DIS; Yu, 2010) and history of media use, i.e., social media and video game play. Regression analyses found that the role of gender and culture, relative to history of media use, was the strongest in predicting total DIS scores as well as dream recall and nightmare information, which is often reported in the literature for females. Media use was also a component of these two dimensions, but its role in predicting self-reported dream experiences was stronger for the other types of DIS information. In general, the findings with media use predicting dream types seem to fall around the age the subject began using social media or gaming as well as their use of MySpace, one of the first social media sites and thus, presumably the longest one used.

Gahr (2015) has gone on to further explore ethnic differences within a Canadian sample and its relationship to video game play both in terms of a recent dream and scores on the DIS. She found that ethnic self-identification, collectivist versus individualistic, was associated with bad dreams sub-scale on the DIS as a function of gaming history. Specifically, bad dream history and fear associated with a recent dream report were higher for female individualistic high end gamers than their male contemporaries. The low end gamers of individualistic ethnic identity had little differences in these dream concepts. This largely replicates the findings from our laboratory on the same participant pool. The effect of culture was demonstrated among those who self-identified as from a collectivist culture. In a three way interaction between gender, self-identification of ethnic identity, and gaming history, culture seemed to not make any difference for the high end gamers. Conversely, for those participants who rarely gamed, culture was a major factor. Specifically, there was no gender difference in self-reported fear in a dream among the individualistic low end gamers but there was a large difference in fear, with women reporting more than men, among the collectivists low end gamers. Thus, gaming seems to have had a differential association to gender and ethnic identity.

Likewise, when Ditner, Hakopdjanian and Gackenbach (2015) administered many of the same scales as were administered in Canada in collectivist China, they found that the effects of the two media types we investigated were considered separately as there are differences among the high end video game players and social media users from different cultures. In short, the surrounding culture's embrace of collectivism, China, or individualism, Canada, informs the self-perceived constraints of the individual along traditional gender roles. In China, for instance, we observed that males did not report any differences in the bad dream intensity sub-scale, regardless of the frequency of video game play. This may be attributed to males not wanting to report any threats or nightmares, which may be perceived signs of weakness and vulnerability. For females, we observed a decrease in dream threats as video game play increased, adding support to our nightmare protection hypothesis. However, females with a low frequency of video game play did report more bad dreams as there were no effects from nightmare protection or from the male self-identity bias. Since Chinese females in this sample were found to be more collectivist than Chinese males, in an already collectivist culture, it may be that this further increased their vulnerability to threats in dreams. Carrying the burden of connecting with others may result in a lot of pressure for them, which in turn, is expressed in their dreams.

In Canada, we observed that males did report a decrease in dream threats as video game play increased, again, adding support to our nightmare protection hypothesis. However, females showed an increase in dream threats associated with video game play increases, inconsistent with our findings from several previous studies. For females, this may be from increased anxiety of an internal conflict of their self-identity as nurturers in an individualist culture, playing video games with violence.

A similar analysis can be applied to the social media use of respondents as was to the video game play history. This Chinese study from our laboratory was conducted to investigate the relationship between cultures, media use, and dreams, specifically, nightmares. We subsequently observed that males appear to be protected from our nightmare protection hypothesis in Canada, an individualist culture. Chinese females, however, seem to be more vulnerable to social pressures to conform to their expected gender role and show increased anxiety, and therefore nightmares and threats in dreams, when they do not conform. These findings allow us to better understand the effects that our technologically constructed digital world is having on our biologically constructed dream world.

We have made an argument that two immersive media experiences, video game play and social media use, have an effect on dreams such that they seem to break the frame of dreams in various ways. This is somewhat moderated by culture and gender, but at least for gender, when conditions like genre are taken into account the same frame breaking nightmare protection is possible. Culture seems to have a more nuanced effect depending in part on the degree of individualism versus collectivism.

CONCLUSION

Our research efforts have focused on the impact of our technologically constructed digital reality on our biologically constructed dreaming reality as an example of one form of naturally occurring consciousness. Specifically, we have investigated video game play and social media use and are beginning to investigate virtual reality technology as tools to break the frame of the digital reality these technologies partially construct. We have observed that these technologies are changing the structure and function of our consciousness, which we have measured by analyzing dreams, such as by affecting lucidity/dream control, nightmare protection, and bizarreness/creativity. For instance, playing video games seems to shift the gamer's consciousness into a digitally constructed virtual reality that is a more contracted state of consciousness. When the gamer emerges back to our physical, material reality, they experience a shift up into a more broad state of consciousness (Highland, 2012). This repeated shifting down into a more contracted state and then shifting up into a more broad state seems to train the gamer to break the frames of reality, thus, resulting in increased lucidity, control, nightmare protection, and bizarreness.

Never before in our human history have such a large part of the population been so widely affected by another constructed reality as the one we are currently digitally experiencing, with the exception of our dreaming reality. If we are able to break the frame of this digital reality, which seems to also have an effect in breaking the frame of our dreaming reality, does it also affect our waking reality? Our waking reality is certainly affected in a minor way with the game transfer phenomena, but we are suggesting a more profound change. Specifically, exposure to these digital realms parallels a meditative state, which has often been revered by Eastern ideologies as one of the most effective practices to transcend into a higher, transcendental consciousness. Transcending during these meditative states of consciousness facilitates an awakening in dreams, initially seen as lucidity, which will eventually lead to an awakening to the illusion of our waking reality.

Ancient Hindu and Buddhist texts describe the concept of *Maya* where the universe and our perception of reality is an illusion (Hiriyanna, 2000; Lochtefeld, 2002). The Upanishads describe the universe and the nature of reality as an interaction between the eternal consciousness, Atman, and the material world, Maya (Hiriyanna, 2000). Thus, Maya is our perception of reality and "it is not what it seems to be, that it is something constantly being made" (O'Flaherty, 1986). In Mayahana Buddhism, Maya is a magical illusion that is experienced differently depending on the state of consciousness of the individual (Rinpoche, 2002).

Today, there are a growing number of scientific researchers and scholars that are coming to a similar conclusion about the nature of reality. Evidence from parapsychology (i.e., the presentiment work of Radin (2009)), engineering (i.e., quantum voltage fluctuations associated with large human events of Nelson (2004)), sociology (i.e., Maharishi Effect of group meditations on peace by Orhm-Johnson, Alexander, Davis, Chandler & Larimore (1988)), and psychology (i.e., near-death experience research of Van Lommel (2011)) is pointing to consciousness as not local to the brain. That is, not resulting as epiphenomena of brain processes although it is likely affected by the same processes. This sets a fertile ground for the relatively new hypothesis from digital physics that reality is simulated.

The Church-Turing Thesis proposed that every function that would be regarded as computable is computable, if it is computable by a Turing machine (Davis, 1965). A Turing machine is a device that manipulates symbols according to a rule set, an early pre-cursor to the logic of a computer algorithm (Hodges, 2012). Since space, time, and energy is quantized, it is made up of individual binary units of information, which means it is computable. So it follows that reality itself is also computable. Perhaps the universe is a digital computer that computes its own evolution and uses a universal cellular automaton (Zuse, 1967), which replicates the emergence and self-organization of life based on a predetermined rule set, or by a universal Turing machine (Schmidhuber, 1997). Wolfram (2002) believes that the universe is digital and operates on fundamental laws that can be described as programs or algorithms. The Holographic Principle postulates that the three-dimensional universe emerges from information processing on a two-dimensional surface (Susskind, 1995). The information from the three-dimensional objects is carried on a distant two-dimensional cosmological horizon that surrounds us and we are a holographic projection of that distant data. Bostrom (2003) later extrapolated these ideas to suggest the probability that reality is a simulacrum, a representation of something else, in this case, inside a computer simulation.

Many physicists propose that the existence of matter is dependent on observation, which means that this simulation is rendered by an observer. In other words, consciousness creates reality (Campbell, 2007; Radin et al, 2012; Groeblacher et al., 2007). These physicists rely on the famous double-slit experiment to provide an interpretation that consciousness is required to collapse the wave function, which means changing the nature of an elementary particle from a wave of probabilities to a deterministic particle in existence. Although this is still a controversial debate, one of the founders of early quantum physics proposed that an observer is necessary to the observation:

The interaction between observer and object causes uncontrollable and large changes in the [atomic] system being observed... (Heisenberg, 1930).

Since our brains cannot distinguish between our waking reality and our dreaming reality, if our waking reality were simulated, it would seem just as real as it does to the dreamer in a dream, except it would be to the waking person while awake. Furthermore, our perception of reality is subjective, therefore, objective reality may not exist (Campbell, 2007). We may be constructing our physical, material reality based on a pre-determined rule set or perhaps our consciousness is rendering our reality. Just as we have a set of rules for virtual reality, we also have a set of rules for our dreaming reality and another set for our waking reality. But if the totality of the cosmos, our physical material reality, is being simulated, then who is the simulator?

Reality is merely an illusion, albeit a very persistent one. Albert Einstein (Einstein, as cited in Calaprice, 2005)

REFERENCES

Abernethy, G. L., & Langford, T. A. (1970). *Introduction to Western philosophy: Pre-Socratics to Mill.* Belmont, CA: Dickenson.

Adelson, J. (1974). The dreams of creative college girls. In R. Woods & H. Greenhouse (Eds.), *The new world of dreams.* New York: Macmillan.

Alexander, C., Boyer, R., & Alexander, V. (1987). Higher states of consciousness in the Vedic psychology of Maharishi Mahesh yogi: A theoretical introduction and research review. *Modern Science and Vedic Science, 1*(1), 89–126.

Alexander, C. N., Davies, J. L., Dixon, C. A., Dillbeck, M. C., Ortzel, R. M., Muehlman, J. M., & Orme-Johnson, D. W. (1990). Higher stages of consciousness beyond formal operations: The Vedic psychology of human development. In C. N. Alexander & E. J. Langer (Eds.), *Higher stages of human development: Adult growth beyond formal operations.* New York, NY: Oxford University Press.

Biocca, F., Kim, T., & Levy, M. R. (1995). The vision of virtual reality. In F. Biocca (Ed.), *Communication in the age of virtual reality* (pp. 3–14). Hillsdale, NJ: Erlbaum.

Blackmore, S. (2012). *Consciousness: An introduction* (2nd ed.). Oxford, UK: Oxford University Press.

Born, M. (1926). Zur quantenmechanik der stoßvorgänge. *Zeitschrift fur Physik, 37*(12), 863–867. doi:10.1007/BF01397477

Bostrom, N. (2003). Are you living in a computer simulation? *The Philosophical Quarterly, 53*(211), 243–255. doi:10.1111/1467-9213.00309

Bostrom, N. (2011). *World Science Festival Video Are We Living in a Simulation?* Retrieved from https://www.youtube.com/watch?v=iq1vly0HHo

Boyes, A., & Gackenbach, J. I. (2014, June). Nightmare protection hypothesis and female gamers. *Paper presented at the annual meeting of the International Association for the Study of Dreams*, Berkley, CA.

Campbell, T. (2007). *My big TOE: The complete trilogy.* Huntsville, AL: Lighting Strike Books.

Chalmers, R. (2015). *Summary of scientific research on Maharishi's Transcendental Meditation and Transcendental Meditation-Sidhi program.* Retrieved from http://www.truthabouttm.org/truth/TMResearch/TMResearchSummary/index.cfm

Clarke, D. S. (2004). *Panpsychism: Past and recent selected readings.* New York, NY: State University of New York Press.

Cole, M., & Derry, J. (2005). We have met technology and it is us. In R. J. Sternberg & D. D. Preiss (Eds.), *Intelligence and technology: The impact of tools on the nature and development of human abilities* (pp. 209–228). Mahwah, NJ: Erlbaum.

Davis, M. (1965). *The undecidable, basic papers on undecidable propositions, unsolvable problems and computable functions.* New York, NY: Raven Press.

Ditner, A. (2015, January). Female gamers and the nightmare protection thesis: A further exploration. *Paper presented at the MacEwan Student Research Showcase*, Edmonton, Alberta.

Ditner, A., Hakopdjanian, S., & Gackenbach, J. (2015, June). Video game play and nightmare protection hypothesis: A cross cultural analysis. *Poster presented at the International Association for the Study of Dreams conference*, Virginia Beach, VA.

Domhoff, G. W. (2007). Realistic simulation and bizarreness in dream content: Past findings and suggestions for future research. In D. Barrett & P. McNamara (Eds.), The new science of dreaming: Vol. 2. *Content recall, and personality characteristics* (pp. 1–27). Westport, CT: Praeger Press.

Drinkwater, B. A. (1976). Visual memory skills of medium contact aboriginal children. *Australian Journal of Psychology*, *28*(1), 37–43. doi:10.1080/00049537608255261

Duggan, M., & Smith, A. (2014, December 30). Social media update 2013. Retrieved from http://pewinternet.org/Reports/2013/Social-Media-Update.aspx

Durkheim, E. (1961). *The elementary forms of the religious life*. New York, NY: Collier Books.

Facebook, Inc. (2014). Stats. Retrieved from http://newsroom.fb.com/company-info/

Fairbanks, A. (1898). *The first philosophers of Greece*. London, UK: Kegan Paul, Trench, Trübner & Co. Ltd.

Freud, S. (1899). *The interpretation of dreams*. Bellingham, WA: Barnes & Noble.

Gackenbach, J. I. (2006). Video game play and lucid dreams: Implications for the development of consciousness. *Dreaming*, *16*(2), 96–110. doi:10.1037/1053-0797.16.2.96

Gackenbach, J. I. (2008). Video game play and consciousness development: A transpersonal perspective. *Journal of Transpersonal Psychology*, *40*(1), 60–87.

Gackenbach, J. I. (2009). Electronic media and lucid-control dreams: Morning after reports. *Dreaming*, *19*(1), 1–6. doi:10.1037/a0013781

Gackenbach, J. I. (2012). Video game play and dreams. In D. Barrett & P. McNamara (Eds.), *Encyclopedia of sleep and dreams* (pp. 795–800). Santa Barbara, CA: ABC-CLIO.

Gackenbach, J. I., & Bosveld, J. (1989). *Control your dreams*. New York, NY: Harper and Row.

Gackenbach, J. I., & Bown, J. (2011). Mindfulness and video game play: A preliminary inquiry. *Mindfulness*, *2*(2), 114–122. http://www.springerlink.com/content/p26n3h1uq1w00771/ doi:10.1007/s12671-011-0049-2

Gackenbach, J. I., & Boyes, A. (2014a). Non-gaming computer use relationship to type of dream. *International Journal of Dream Research*, *7*(2), 95–104.

Gackenbach, J. I., & Boyes, A. (2014b). Social media versus gaming associations with typical and recent dreams. *Dreaming*, *24*(3), 182–202. doi:10.1037/a0037616

Gackenbach, J. I., Darlington, M., Ferguson, M. L., & Boyes, A. (2013). Video game play as nightmare protection: A replication and extension. *Dreaming*, *23*(2), 97–111. doi:10.1037/a0032455

Gackenbach, J. I., & Dopko, R. (2012). The relationship between video game play, dream bizarreness, and creativity. *International Journal of Dream Research, 5*(1), 23–36.

Gackenbach, J. I., Ellerman, E., & Hall, C. (2011). Video game play as nightmare protection: A preliminary inquiry in military gamers. *Dreaming, 21*(4), 221–245. doi:10.1037/a0024972

Gackenbach, J. I., & Flockhart, C. (2013). Nightmare protection thesis of video game play in first responders. *International Journal of Dream Research: Supplement* (pdf). doi: 10.11588/ijodr.2013.0.10874

Gackenbach, J. I., & Gahr, S. (2015). Media use and dreams associations between Canadians of differing cultural backgrounds. *International Journal of Dream Research, 8*(1).

Gackenbach, J. I., Heilman, N., Boyt, S., & LaBerge, S. (1985). The relationship between field independence and lucid dreaming ability. *Journal of Mental Imagery, 9*, 9–20.

Gackenbach, J. I., & Hunt, H. (2014). A deeper inquiry into the association between lucid dreams and video game play. In R. Hurd & K. Buckeley (Eds.), *Lucid dreaming cross cultural understandings of consciousness in the dream state*. Santa Barbara, CA: ABC-CLIO.

Gackenbach, J. I., & Kuruvilla, B. (2008). The relationship between video game play and threat simulation dreams. *Dreaming, 18*(4), 236–256. doi:10.1037/a0013782

Gackenbach, J. I., Kuruvilla, B., & Dopko, R. (2009). Video game play and dream bizarreness. *Dreaming, 19*(4), 218–231. doi:10.1037/a0018145

Gackenbach, J. I., Matty, I., Kuruvilla, B., Samaha, A. N., Zederayko, A., Olischefski, J., & Von Stackelberg, H. (2009). Video game play: Waking and dreaming consciousness. In S. Krippner & D. Ellis (Eds.), *Perchance to dream* (pp. 239–253). Hauppauge, NY: Nova Science Publishers.

Gackenbach, J. I., & Rosie, M. (2011). Presence in video game play and nighttime dreams: An empirical inquiry. *International Journal of Dream Research, 4*(2), 98–109.

Gackenbach, J. I., Sample, T., & Mandel, G. (2011). The continuity versus discontinuity hypotheses: A consideration of issues for coding video game incorporation. *International Journal of Dream Research, 4*(2), 63–76.

Gackenbach, J. I., Swanston, D., & Stark, H. (in press). Effects of video game play versus meditation/prayer in waking and dreaming experiences. Paper under editorial consideration. *Journal of Transpersonal Psychology.*

Gahr, S. (2015, June). The relationship between dreaming and self-construals, sex role orientation and media use in Canadians of differing ethnic backgrounds. Paper to be presented at the International Association for the Study of Dreams, Virginia Beach, VA.

Green, C. S., & Bavelier, D. (2003). Action video games modifies visual selective attention. *Nature, 423*(6939), 534–537. doi:10.1038/nature01647 PMID:12774121

Greenfield, P. M. (1996). Video games as cultural artifacts. In P. M. Greenfield & R. R. Cocking (Eds.), *Interacting with video: Advances in applied developmental psychology* (Vol. 11, pp. 85–94). Norwood, NJ: Ablex.

Gröblacher, S., Paterek, T., Kaltenbaek, R., Brukner, C., Zukowski, M., Aspelmeyer, M., & Zeilinger, A. (2007). An experimental test of non-local realism. *Nature*, *446*(7138), 871–875. doi:10.1038/nature05677 PMID:17443179

Hand, M. M., Thomas, D., Buboltz, W. C., Deemer, E. D., & Buyanjargal, M. (2013). Facebook and romantic relationships: Intimacy and couple satisfaction associated with online social network use. *Cyberpsychology, Behavior, and Social Networking*, *16*(1), 8–13. doi:10.1089/cyber.2012.0038 PMID:23101932

Hartmann, E., & Kunzendorf, R. G. (2006-2007). Boundaries and dreams. *Imagination, Cognition and Personality*, *26*(1-2), 101–115. doi:10.2190/HK76-038K-407M-8670

Heisenberg, W. (1927). Über den anschaulichen inhalt der quantentheoretischen kinematik und mechanik. *Zeitschrift fur Physik*, *43*(3–4), 172–198. doi:10.1007/BF01397280

Heisenberg, W. (1958). *Physics and philosophy: The revolution in modern science*. New York, NY: Harper & Row Publishers, Inc.

Hiriyanna, M. (2000). *The essentials of Indian philosophy*. Delhi, India: Motilal Banarsidass.

Hodges, A. (2012). *Alan Turing: The enigma*. Princeton, NJ: Princeton University Press. doi:10.1515/9781400844975

Holzel, B., & Ott, U. (2006). Relationships between meditation depth, absorption, meditation practice, and mindfulness: A latent variable approach. *Journal of Transpersonal Psychology*, *38*(2), 179–199.

Hunt, H. (1989). *Multiplicity of dreams: Memory, imagination, and consciousness*. Westford, MA: Yale University Press.

ITU (International Telecommunication Union). (2011). *World Telecommunication/ICT Indicators Database*. Retrieved from http://www.itu.int/ITU-D/ict/statistics/

Jung, C. G. (1933). *Modern Man in Search of a Soul*. Oxon: Routledge.

Kahan, T., & LaBerge, S. (1994). Lucid dreaming as metacognition: Implications for cognitive science. *Consciousness and Cognition*, *3*(2), 246–264. doi:10.1006/ccog.1994.1014

Kahan, T. L., & LaBerge, S. (1996). Cognition and metacognition in dreaming and waking: Comparisons of first and third-person ratings. *Dreaming*, *6*(4), 235–249. doi:10.1037/h0094459

Kaplan, D. (2015). Facebook, Oculus, and the future of virtual reality. *TechCrunch*. Retrieved from http://techcrunch.com/2015/03/15/facebook-oculus-and-the-future-of-virtual-reality/

Koriat, A. (2007). Metacognition and consciousness. In P. D. Zelazo, M. Moscovitch, & E. Thompson (Eds.), *The Cambridge handbook of consciousness* (pp. 289–325). Cambridge, NY: Cambridge University Press. doi:10.1017/CBO9780511816789.012

LaBerge, S. & DeGracia, D.J. (2000). Varieties of lucid dreaming experience. *Individual Differences in Conscious Experience*, 269-307.

Levin, R., & Nielsen, T. A. (2009). Nightmares, bad dreams, and emotional dysregulation: A review and new neurocognitive model of dreaming. *Current Directions in Psychological Science, 18*(2), 84–88. doi:10.1111/j.1467-8721.2009.01614.x

Levitan, L. & LaBerge, S. (1993). Testing the limits of dream control: The light and mirror experiment. *Nightlight, 5*(2).

Lochtefeld, J. (2002). Maya. In *The illustrated encyclopedia of Hinduism* (Vol. 1, p. 433). New York, NY: Rosen Publishing.

Mack, A., & Rock, I. (2000). *Inattentional Blindness.* Cambridge, MA: MIT Press.

Mair, V. H. (1998). Chuang-tzu. In W. Nienhauser (Ed.), *The Indiana companion to traditional Chinese literature* (Vol. 2, pp. 20–26). Bloomington: Indiana University Press.

Mason, L., Alexander, C. N., Travis, F., Gackenbach, J. I., & Orme-Johnson, D. (1995). EEG correlates of "higher states of consciousness" during sleep. *Sleep, 24*, 152.

Nelson, R. (2004). Questions and explorations probing the GCP database: What matters, what doesn't, what questions we can ask. *Paper presented at the annual meeting of the Society for Scientific Exploration*, Las Vegas, NV.

O'Flaherty, W. D. (1986). *Dreams, Illusion, and Other Realities.* Chigaco, IL: University of Chicago Press.

Orhm-Johnson, D., Alexander, C., Davis, J., Chandler, H., & Larimore, W. (1988). The international peace project in the Middle East: The effects of the Maharishi technology of the unified field. *The Journal of Conflict Resolution, 32*(4), 776–812. doi:10.1177/0022002788032004009

Ortiz de Gortari, A. B. (2007). Psychosocial implications of online video gaming. *Paper presented at Game in Action*, Gothenburg, Sweden.

Ortiz de Gortari, A. B., & Griffiths, M. D. (2012). An introduction to game transfer phenomena in video game playing. In J. I. Gackenbach (Ed.), *Video game play and consciousness* (pp. 217–244). NY: Nova Science Publishers.

Ortiz de Gortari, A. B., & Griffiths, M. D. (2014). Auditory experiences in Game Transfer Phenomena: An empirical self-report study. *International Journal of Cyber Behavior, Psychology and Learning, 4*(1), 59–68. doi:10.4018/ijcbpl.2014010105

Poels, K., IJsselsteijn, W. A., & de Kort, Y. A. W. (2010). Digital games, the aftermath: Qualitative insights into post game experiences. In R. Bernhaupt (Ed.), *Evaluating user experience in games* (pp. 149–164). Berlin, Germany: Springer. doi:10.1007/978-1-84882-963-3_9

Poels, K., IJsselsteijn, W. A., & de Kort, Y. A. W. (2014). World of Warcraft, the aftermath: How game elements transfer into perceptions, associations and (day) dreams in the everyday life of massively multiplayer online role-playing game players. *New Media & Society.* doi:10.1177/1461444814521596

Preiss, D. D., & Sternberg, R. J. (2005). Technologies for working intelligence. In R. J. Sternberg & D. D. Preiss (Eds.), *Intelligence and technology: The impact of tools on the nature and development of human abilities* (pp. 183–208). Mahwah, NJ: Erlbaum.

Radin, D., Michel, L., Galdamez, K., Wendland, P., Rickenbach, R., & Delorme, A. (2012). Consciousness and the double-slit interference pattern: Six experiments. *Physics Essays Publication*, *25*(2), 157–171. doi:10.4006/0836-1398-25.2.157

Radin, D. I. (2009). *The conscious universe: The scientific truth of psychic phenomena* (1st ed.). New York, NY: HarperOne.

Rescher, N. (1991). *G. W. Leibniz's Monadology*. Pittsburgh, PA: University of Pittsburgh Press.

Revonsuo, A. (2006). *Inner presence: Consciousness as a biological phenomenon*. Cambridge, MA: MIT Press.

Revonsuo, A., & Salmivalli, C. (1995). A content analysis of bizarre elements in dreams. *Dreaming*, *5*(3), 160–187. doi:10.1037/h0094433

Revonsuo, A., & Valli, K. (2000). Dreaming and consciousness: Testing the threat stimulation theory of the function of dreaming. *Psyche*, *6*, 1–25.

Schecter, N., Schmeidler, G. R., & Staal, M. (1965). Dream reports and creative tendencies in students of the arts, sciences, engineering. *Journal of Consulting Psychology*, *29*(5), 415–421. doi:10.1037/h0022463 PMID:5827514

Schmidhuber, J. (2002). Algorithmic theories of everything. *International Journal of Foundations of Computer Science*, *13*(4).

Schmidt, M. B. (2002). *Thinley Norbe Rinpoche in the Dzogchen Primer*. Boston, MA: Shambala.

Schredl, M. (2003). Continuity between waking and dreaming: A proposal for a mathematical model. *Sleep and Hypnosis*, *5*(1), 26–39.

Schrödinger, E. (1926). Quantisation as an eigenvalue problem. *Annalen der Physik*, *81*(18), 109–139. doi:10.1002/andp.19263861802

Schultes, R. E., Hofmann, A., & Rätsch, C. (2001). *Plants of the Gods: Their sacred, healing and hallucinogenic powers*. Rochester, VT: Inner Traditions/Bear & Company.

Sims, V., & Mayer, R. (2002). Domain specificity of spatial expertise: The case of video game players. *Applied Cognitive Psychology*, *16*(1), 97–115. doi:10.1002/acp.759

Sinyard, A. (2015, June). Emerging implications of virtual reality game play on dreams. *Paper to be presented at Towards a Science of Consciousness*, Helsinki, Finland.

Solms, M. (2011). Neurobiology and the neurological basis of dreaming. In P. Montagna & S. Chokroverty (Eds.), *Handbook of clinical neurology* (3rd ed., pp. 519–544). New York, NY: Elsevier. doi:10.1016/B978-0-444-52006-7.00034-4

Sternberg, R. J., & Lubart, T. I. (1999). The concept of creativity: prospects and paradigms. In R. J. Sternberg (Ed.), *Handbook of creativity* (pp. 3–15). Cambridge, UK: Cambridge University Press.

Sternberg, R. J., & Preiss, D. D. (2005). *Intelligence and technology: The impact of tools on the nature and development of human abilities*. Mahwah, NJ: Erlbaum.

Strickland, D. (2015). FeelReal brings sense of smell to virtual reality. *VR World*. Retrieved from http://www.vrworld.com/2015/03/11/feelreal-brings-sense-of-smell-to-virtual-reality/

Subrahmanyam, K., & Greenfield, P. M. (1994). Effect of video game practice on spatial skills in girls and boys. *Journal of Applied Developmental Psychology*, *15*(1), 13–32. doi:10.1016/0193-3973(94)90004-3

Susskind, L. (1995). The world as a hologram. *Journal of Mathematical Physics*, *36*(11), 6377–6396. doi:10.1063/1.531249

Timmins, L. R., & Lombard, M. (2005). When 'real' seems mediated: Inverse presence. *Presence (Cambridge, Mass.)*, *14*(4), 492–500. doi:10.1162/105474605774785307

van Lommel, P. (2011). Near-death experiences: The experience of the self as real and not as an illusion. *Annals of the New York Academy of Sciences*, *1234*(1), 19–28. doi:10.1111/j.1749-6632.2011.06080.x PMID:21988246

Weinstein, M., & Smith, J. (1992). Isometric squeeze relaxation (progressive relaxation) vs. meditation: Absorption and focusing as predictors of state effects. *Perceptual and Motor Skills*, *75*(12), 63–71. PMID:1484796

Wheeler, J. A. (1990). Information, physics, quantum: The search for links. In W. H. Zurek (Ed.), *Complexity, Entropy, and the physics of information*. Redwood City, CA: Addison-Wesley.

Wlassoff, V. (2015). Brains aren't fooled by virtual reality. *ISPR Presence News*. Retrieved from http://ispr.info/2015/03/

Wolfram, S. (2002). *A New Kind of Science*. Champaign, IL: Wolfram Media, Inc.

World Bank. (2012). *International Internet bandwidth (bits per person)*. Retrieved from http://www.tradingeconomics.com/country-list/international-internet-bandwidth-bits-per-person-wb-data.html

Zuckerberg, M. (2014). Blog message. Retrieved from https://www.facebook.com/zuck

Zuse, K. (1967). Rechnender Raum. *Elektronische Datenverarbeitung*, *8*, 336–344.

ENDNOTES

1 The idea of gamers as low versus high end means that they fall along a continuation of either frequency of play alone or more often along a variety of game play queries. These have included number of games played, age begun gaming, with younger ages being rated higher, number of hours gaming, reading about gaming, talking with others about gaming, engaging in gaming social media to name a few.

2 As with gaming, social media use identified as high or low end includes most often a summary frequency of use of about a half dozen social media website of the most popular. These include Facebook, Pinterest, Tumblr, Instagram, Myspace, to name a few. In some studies estimates of cell phone texting were also included and in the Chinese studies Chinese social media sites were asked about.

Chapter 4
Synchronous Physiological Electrical Fields:
Function and Interface Potential

J.F. Pagel
University Of Colorado, USA

ABSTRACT

Humans utilize sensory and motor systems developed genetically, physically and socially for interfacing with our external environment. We use these same systems to interface in our interactions with artificial intelligence. There are other functioning central nervous system (CNS) systems, however, involved in cognitive processing for which the function and environmental interface is less clear. The synchronous physiologic electrical field system utilizes broadcast extracellular electrical fields for a wide variety of CNS functions. The operations of this system are usually non-conscious and most apparent during sleep (especially the conscious states of sleep that include dreaming), and un-focused waking. The electrical fields of this system are altered and affected by both internal and external stimuli. These fields can be monitored and analyzed by artificial intelligence (AI) systems, and independently of human input, AI systems can utilize similar frequency based electrical potentials to convey data, communicate, supply power, and to store memory. From both human and AI perspectives, these systems have the potential to function more fully in human/machine interaction. This chapter reviews our current knowledge as to function, current interactive approaches, and interface potential for these physiological electrical fields.

INTRODUCTION

In the first decade after Freud's publication of the "Interpretation of Dreams," the alpha rhythm was discovered, the first CNS electrical signal apparent on turn of the century monitoring systems (Berger H, 1931; Freud, 1903). Later and more sensitive equipment detected other physiologic frequencies (sigma, theta, delta, and gamma/beta) using scalp electrodes in humans and implanted electrodes in animal models (Elul, 1971). These specific frequencies were then utilized to define and characterize the various stages of sleep (Rechtschaffen & Kales, 1968). These frequencies, also present during wake, are a background

DOI: 10.4018/978-1-4666-9891-8.ch004

component of any electric or magnetic approach used for CNS monitoring. Recently, other rhythms at frequencies less than 1 Hertz (delta) have been described, occurring in both sleep and wake (Domhoff, 2003). These frequency modulated electrical fields are propagated extracellularly, in most cases apparent on monitoring systems attached outside the actual CNS such as scalp and facial electrodes.

In all species studied, occillatory (synchronous) brain activity has been shown to be a characteristic CNS property (Cantero & Atienza, 2005). While postulated to reflect CNS the spike potentials of neurons firing, it has been difficult to demonstrate how individual spike potentials might summate to create propagated frequency-based global rhythms (Christakos, 1986; Buzsaki, 2006). It is likely that the specific physiologic frequencies are linked to metabolic oscillators at the neural membrane, occurring secondary to oscillatory opening and closing of ionic gateways and channels (potassium for alpha, calcium for sigma) (Buzsaki, 2005, Pagel, 2005, Steriade, 2001). Such EEG rythmicity requires many neurons to fire in sequence, most likely secondary to repetitive changes in ion concentrations at the synaptic junction. Oscillation frequency is also modulated by inhibitory neurotransmitter (GABA) activity affecting the chloride channels essential for the synchronization of individual neurons in the CNS (Liu & Reppert, 2000, Buzsaki, 2006).

There was considerable debate as to whether the synchronous electrical fields of the CNS had actual function. It was postulated that these electric fields might rather be a non-functional externally observable side-effect of neural activity (Hobson, Pace-Schott & Stickgold, 2000). Even early after the discovery of this system, however, it was noted that could alter the tendency of individual neurons to form spike potentials (John, 1968). From the electo-neurochemical perspective these fields had the capacity to alter ionic concentrations at the neural membrane affecting any individual cell's tendency to form a spike potential (Formula 1). Any frequency based change in electrical potential would also affect cellular kinetics though ATP production (Formula 2). There is considerable recent data, indicating functional capacities of this electrophysiologic system in affecting the tendency of neurons to fire, cellular equilibrium, signal-to-noise ratio, neural communication, and cellular messaging systems (Pagel, 2005; Axmaker, Mormann, Fernandez, Eger & Fell, 2006; Anastassiou, Perin, Markam & Koch 2011, Cash, Halgren, Dehghani, Rosetti, Thesen & Wang 2009). EEG synchronization is now viewed by many neuroscientists as an important mechanism utilized by the CNS to attain functional cerebral integration between widely spaced neuronal populations (Singer, 1999; Salinas & Sejnowski, 2001; Cantero & Atienza, 2005). This system affects electrically sensitive neuromessaging systems at the neural cell membrane, potentially affecting expression and access to memory systems stored in electricochemically biological systems including cellular DNA (Pagel, 2005).

Formula 1: The classic Hodgkin, Katz, Goldman equation for the interaction of potassium, sodium, and chloride ions involved in inducing a neural spike potential (Hodgkin & Horowicz 1959). $\Delta\Theta$ the change in electrical membrane potential alters in a frequency based system inducing a resultant frequency based change at the neural membrane.

$$\Delta\Theta = \frac{2.3RT\log}{\mathrm{f}} \frac{\mathrm{Pk}\left[\mathrm{k}^{+}\right]\mathrm{o} + \mathrm{Pna}\left[\mathrm{na}^{+}\right]\mathrm{o} + \mathrm{Pcl}\left[\mathrm{cl}^{-}\right]\mathrm{o}}{\mathrm{Pk}\left[\mathrm{k}^{+}\right]\mathrm{i} + \mathrm{Pna}\left[\mathrm{na}^{+}\right]\mathrm{o} + \mathrm{Pcl}\left[\mathrm{cl}^{-}\right]\mathrm{I}}$$

F= Faraday's constant
P=ion permeability constraints

k+=potassium
T= degrees Kelvin
ΔΘ=change in membrane potential
na+=sodium
o=outside membrane
i=inside membrane
cl-=chloride

Formula 2: Describes the effects of membrane potential changes on cellular kinetics. Physiologic electrical fields changing with frequency based changing potential (ΔΘ) can supply energy through cyclic-AMP and ATP production at the cellular membrane (Harold 1986):

$$\Delta Gp = n\left(-\Delta^2 H^+\right) = F\left(\Delta\Theta\right) - 2.3RT \ \ Ph$$

ΔGp = Kilocalorie/mole (free energy available for ATP synthesis)
ΔβH+ = difference in electrochemical potential of protons inside/outside cell membrane
n = number of protons transiting the membrane per cycle

Quantitative EEG (QEEG) analysis has been utilized to characterize EEG frequency characteristics, location, and power. QEEG analysis has proven useful in mapping synchronous EEG activity, however this technique also has significant technical limitations. Artifact based on other electophysiological events such as eye blinks, motor activity, arousals, or the change to another EEG stage, can lead to interference, requiring the EEG data to be retrieved in discrete limited time samples – generally < 5 second recordings. The various analytic algorithms in current use are not standardized so that spectra based on different modeling criteria can differ markedly (Coburn, Lauterbach, Boutros, Black, Arciniegas & Coffey, 2006). Current real-time techniques of EEG topography and electromagnetic monitoring (MEG) mapping currently denote the limits of electrophysiological research. Despite their limitations, these techniques demonstrate that the electrical potentials of the CNS are highly multivariate, constantly fluxing and changing millisecond to millisecond across the CNS (Besserve, Jerbi, Laurent, Baillet, Martinerie & Garnero, 2007; Kiebel, Garrido, Moran, Chen & Friston, 2009). fMRI data suggests that blood oxygen levels in the CNS fluctuate at set frequencies in association with these physiologic EEG rhythms (Fox & Raichle, 2007; Leopold, Murayama & Logothetis, 2003).

The EEG of Consciousness

Recent studies of CNS activity recorded with fMRI, MEG, and EEG topographic mapping suggest that the synchronous EEG frequencies are correlated with specific states of waking and sleep consciousness (Cantero & Atienza, 05; Steriade, 06). Cognitive states with consistent patterns of associated electrophysiology share psycho-physiological attributes (Ioannides, Kostopoulos, Liu & Fenwick, 08). The presence and type of this synchronous EEG activity denotes a baseline electrophysiological "form" for each state. Several authors have proposed that consciousness itself has an electophysiologic signature in the beta/gamma frequency (30-80 Hz) that can be associated with cognitive states of attention (Hobson, 1999). The proposed electrophysiological correlates of attention, coupled with the experimental defini-

Table 1. Comparative behavioral and synchronous EEG characteristics for waking and associated states

	Perceptual Isolation	Thought -Attention	Associated EEG Frequencies
Focused wake	Lowest	Focused	Beta/gamma
Self-referential (default) wake	Low	Self-focused	Beta/gamma, delta, 0.5 HZ activity
Drowsy wake	Low	Un-focused	Alpha
Imagery	Low - moderate	Focused	NS
Hypnosis	Moderate	Var.	NS
Focused meditation	Moderate	Focused	Gamma, alpha
Unfocused Meditation	Moderate	Focused/un-focused	Alpha, theta

Note: Quantitative changes in EEG frequencies are correlated with changes in phenomenological aspects in perceptual isolation and attention normally used to compare conscious behavioral states.

tion of consciousness as attention, has led some authors to propose that electrophysiological correlates of attention can be utilized to define consciousness and model consciousness states (Crick, 1994; Bhala, 2000). Quantitative electrophysiology correlates with phenomenological aspects of thought and attention can be utilized in behaviorally comparing conscious states.

BACKGROUND

This chapter presents an overview of the proven and prospective functions of the frequency modulated electrophysiologic fields in the CNS, as well as the factors that can alter and affect the functional expressions of this system. Primary findings can be summarized as follows:

1. There is strong and convincing evidence for physiological frequency based electrical fields being an important and active functioning component of CNS processing during wake and sleep. These fields clearly affect the potentials of neurons to fire, affect ion-equilibrium at the cell membranes and intra-cellular kinetics. Extracellularly, these fields define the activity of widely separated neural networks such as the default systems.
2. This electrophysiological system is affected and altered by externally applied chemicals and electrical fields. Psychoactive medications and disease processes produce consistent alterations in these fields. The induced changes in these physiologic fields are associated with changes in wake and sleep functioning.
3. These electrophysiological systems can be affected and altered by biofeedback and training in different approaches of meditative practice. These alterations can be frequency specific, based on the technique utilized in training. Such induced alterations in this system can be used to affect waking cognitive function and performance. These induced alterations may affect some disease processes.
4. When applied in the supra-physiologic range electrically as ECT or magnetically as TMS, alterations in memory and sensory systems can be induced. The application of electrical fields in this manner is known to alter cognitive processing and the course of a variety of psychiatric illnesses.

5. Externally applied electrical fields in the physiological range can be demonstrated to induce alterations in this system as determined by electrophysiological monitoring. These fields are likely to affect neural electrolyte equilibrium and cellular kinetics.
6. Externally applied cognitive interventions (hypnotherapy and hypnopedia) have been shown to induce alterations in sleep electrophysiology. During the lighter stages of sleep, some cognitive stimuli (name-calling and sounds) as well as aversive physical stimuli, can incorporated into dream content.

THE SYNCHRONOUS PHYSIOLOGICAL ELECTRICAL FIELDS

Electrophysiologic States of Waking Consciousness

Waking can be viewed as the best described yet most poorly classified state of consciousness. Waking is behaviorally characterized by the integration and utilization of perceptual input. The EEG of wake, much like a storm wracked ocean, is characterized by asynchronous activity. In the background, however, the waking EEG includes synchronous waveforms – most often short duration high frequency gamma/beta activity during periods of "attention" and long runs of alpha activity during eyes-closed drowsiness. Short lived but highly coherent oscillations in the gamma/beta frequency has been reported to occur as a correlate to attentional input in the human CNS (Buzsaki, 2005; Schack, Klimesch & Syuseng, 2005). Gamma is postulated as a "binding" frequency resulting in a temporal synchronicity of neurons involved in a specific cognitive process (Buzsaki, 2005). Such gamma oscillations may be involved in the process of "working memory" that enables us to keep non-current memories available for cognitive processing (Axmaker, Mormann, Fernandez, Eger & Fell, 2006; Corsi-Cabrerra, Guerva & Rio-Portella, 2008; Lisman & Idiart,1995). Studies suggest that the slower neuronal oscillation frequencies, as well as the gamma frequency, are associated with increased response gain for task relevant events and increased response times, particularly when those tasks are rhythmatic in nature (Buzsaki, 2005; Lakatos, Karmos, Mehta, Ulbert & Schroeder, 2008; Plava & Karla, 2005). Waking varies throughout the day with different processes of thought, levels of focus and alertness, memory access and time sense associated with different types of waking (Hartmann, 1998). Waking includes a variety of "non-attentive" conscious states in which available perceptual input is de-emphasized.

The Default Network

Only a portion of our waking is spent in focused awareness of our environment. When individuals are left undisturbed, their waking thought process is often internally oriented to what has generally described as mind wandering, tasks such as autobiographical memory retrieval, envisioning possible futures and conceiving the perspectives of others (Buckner, Andrews-Hausa & Schacter, 08; Raichle, MacLeod, Snyder, Powers & Gusnard, 2001). This system is active during large portions of waking. In studies that include a prescribed and focused task, individuals report mind wandering and being off task more than 40% of the time (Christoff, Gordon, Smallwood, Smith & Schooler, 2009). Recent PET and fMRI data indicates that specific brain regions primarily in the medial prefrontal regions, which some authors refer to as the "default network," are consistently activated during such self-referential cognitive processing (Buckner & Carrol, 07; Gusner & Raiche, 01). In addition to this default network area, mind-wandering is also associated with executive network recruitment, particularly during periods of decreasing external task demands (Christoff, Gordon, Smallwood, Smith & Schooler, 2009). The default network anatomic area has been shown to have EEG based functional coherence based on EEG topography mapping of the alpha frequency (Fingelhurts A & Fingelhurts A, 2011). Low frequency fluctuations in the sub-delta range (0.5-1.5 Hz) are also associated with default network activity (De Luca, Beckmann, De Stafino, Matthews & Smith, 2006; Fox & Raichle 2007). During default network modes of cognition these synchronous frequency systems integrate and coalesce into an active system (Andrews-Hanna, 2011; Fox & Raichle 2007; Finglehurts A & Finglehurts A, 2011). Synchronous EEG rhythms often reflect activity within the default network – the introspective and adaptive mental activities in which humans spontaneously and deliberately engage in every day (Andrews-Hanna 2011). Diagnoses leading to a decrease in synchronous EEG activity as well as alterations in default network activity include schizophrenia, autism, and Alzheimer's disease (Andrews-Hanna, 2011, Buckner & Carroll, 2008, Daoust, Lusignan, Braun, Mottron & Godbout, 2008).

The Electrophysiologic States of Sleep

In the sleep laboratory, polysomnography is used to define the presence or absence of sleep, utilizing EEG in concert with EMG, EOG and other telemetry. Polysomnography is used to classify sleep into four stages – Rapid eye movement sleep (REMS), sleep onset (Stage 1), Stage 2, and deep sleep (Stage 3) (Iber, Ancoli-Israel, Chesson & Quan, 2007). These sleep stages are considered to be states of consciousness due to the presence of dreaming. Post-Freud multiple versions of activation-synthesis theory have postulated that the electrophysiological activity recorded in the brain as rapid-eye movement (REM) sleep was dreaming. (McCarley and Hobson, 1972; Hobson, Pace-Schott & Stickgold 2000; 2003). According to these theories, what we recall on waking integration as dreaming is a modulation of a primitive brain stem of activation that occurs during episodes of REM sleep (Hobson, 1999). However, REM sleep can occur without dreaming and dreaming clearly occurs without REM sleep (Solms, 2003). Dreaming is reported from approximately 80% REMS and sleep onset, and from approximately 40% of Stage 2 and deep sleep (Stage 3) awakenings (Foulks, 1985). While rare, non-dreamers who report never having experienced dreaming do exist, despite having electrophysiologically normal sleep, including REMS (Pagel, 2003). The REMS = dreaming correlate proved to be inordinately simplistic and restrictive, as well as inconsistent with the empiric findings that REMS and dream sleep were doubly dissociable (Solms, 2003; Pagel 2008). Dreaming - the basic criteria for the presence or absence of consciousness in sleep - occurs in association with all sleep and sleep-associated states (Domhoff, 2003). Today there is little evidence supporting the perspective that any special relationship exists between REM sleep and dreaming (Pagel 2011). It is clear however, that phenomnenologically characteristic dreaming occurs in association with the different electrophysiologiclly frequency defined states of sleep (Pagel 2014). One way of viewing dreams is as cognitive feedback on the process and functioning of this system (Pagel 2005). Independently of the REM sleep equals dreaming supposition, it is clear that dream-associated neuroconsciousness is tied to expressions and changes in brain electrophysiology.

The sleep EEG is dominated by the presence synchronous physiologic EEG potentials -- the primary difference between the sleep and waking EEG (Rechtschaffen & Kales, 1968). Drowsy awake with eyes closed, and Stage 1 (Sleep onset) are defined by the presence of alpha (9-11 Hz.) – the frequency with the most power on spectral analysis. The development of Stage 2 of sleep is denoted by bursts of sleep spindles at sigma frequency (11-16 Hz.) and K-complex events – electrophysiological down states known to negatively affect the general tendency of neurons to develop spike potential activity (Cash, Halgren, Dehghani, Rossetti, Thesen & Wang; 2009). Deep sleep (stage 3) occurs in association with delta frequency oscillations (0.5-1.5 Hz). REM sleep has been described by some authors as "desynchronized" (Walker, 2005). This perspective is artifactual, affected by the need in humans to record from the surface of the skin using high impedance skin electrodes on face and scalp to record the low voltage physiologic EEG potentials (< 50 mv.). When intracerebral electrodes are utilized in humans like those used in animal studies, REM sleep can be considered the most synchronous of the sleep stages, dominated by runs of hippocampal theta, gamma and slow wave activity (Cantero, Atienza, Stickgold, Kahana, Madsen & Kocsis, 2003; Cantero & Atienza, 05; Hangya, Tihanyi, Entz, Fabo, Eross & Wittner, 2011). During both REM sleep and non-REM sleep stages, increased theta, alpha and gamma activity is associated with an increased frequency of dream recall (Marzano, Ferrara, Mauro, Moroni, Gorgoni, Tempesta, Cipolli & DeGennaro, 2011). The occurrence of specific EEG frequencies throughout the night may be better correlated with specific states of brain activity than classic polysomnographic sleep staging (Cantero & Atienza, 05; Ioannides, Kostopoulos, Liu & Fenwick, 08; Steriade, 06). EEG frequency and distribution characteristics can be utilized to provide an alternative and neurophysiologically—potentially more informative—characterization of sleep staging. (Shultz, 2008)

Electrophysiology Correlates for Conscious States

All of the wake- and sleep-associated conscious states that have been studied demonstrate state-consistent patterns of synchronous EEG activity. The presence and type of synchronous EEG activity denotes a baseline "form" for each state (Table 2 & 3). The particular frequency effect may be less important than the fact that a change in synchronous activity is associated with the state, particularly if as previously suggested, synchronous EEG activity has active effects on CNS functioning (Axmaker, Mormann, Fernandez, Eger & Fell, 2006; Anastassiou, Perin, Markam & Koch 2011; Fingelhurts A & Fingelhurts A, 2011; Pagel 1990; 2005; 2008). The primary specific EEG frequency correlate for conscious states is alpha - the dominate EEG frequency in the human CNS and was the characteristic findings even of the first EEG's ever recorded (Berger H, 1931). Since alpha is the EEG frequency with by far the highest power in the human CNS, it is perhaps not surprising that a majority of synchronous EEG correlates for conscious states have an associated increased occurrence of this rhythm. Dreaming defined as sleep associated mentation reported on awaking from sleep, shows clear correlation with this alpha rhythm associated with daydreaming, REMS dreaming, lucid dreaming and sleep onset dreaming (Table 3). The gamma EEG frequency is associated with focused and default wake, focused meditation, REM sleep dreaming, and lucid dreaming. The EEG correlates between the wake-based states and lucid dreaming are particularly interesting since all are teachable states of focused consciousness under conscious control, with similarities in reported effects on cognitive processing, attention, and recall (Table 2) (Chiesa, 2009; Hunt, 1989; Lehman, Faber, Achermann, Jeanmonod D, Gianotti L & Pizzagalli, 2001). Lucid dreaming from an electrophysiological standpoint may be better viewed as a border-line wake state in which the perceptual and motor isolation typical of other sleep states is not present (LaBerge, Nagel, Dement & Zarcone, 1981; Voss, Holzmann, Tuin & Hobson, 2009).

Table 2. Comparative behavioral and EEG characteristics for sleeping associated states

	Perceptual Isolation	Thought -Attention	Memory Access	Mentation (Dream) Recall	Control	Teach-ability	Associated EEG Frequencies
Hypnogognic states	Moderate	Un-focused	High/ Disass-ciated	High	Low	No	Alpha
Sleep onset dreaming	High	Associative	High/ Disass-ciated	80%	Low	Low	Alpha
Rems dreaming	High	Associative	High	80%	Low	Low	Alpha, beta
Deep sleep dreaming	Very high	Un-focused	Low	40%	Low	No	Delta, sigma
Lucid dreaming	High	Focused Associative	High	High	High-var.	Mod.	Alpha, beta/ gamma
Sleep meditation	High	Focused/ Un-focused	High	High	High-var.	Mod. High	NS

Note: Changes in quantitative electrophysiology are correlated with changes in phenomenological aspects of perceptual isolation, thought-attention, memory access, dream recall frequency, volitional control, and teachability – behavioral aspects characterizing each sleep associated conscious states.

Key: NS = not studied

Table 3. Consistent quantitative alteration in physiologic EEG frequencies induced by major classes of psychoactive medications with treatment indications (Pagel 1993, 1996; Blume 2006)

	Delta –0.5-1.5 Hz.	Theta – 5.5-8.5 Hz.	Alpha - 8.5-11 Hz.	Sigma - 12-16 Hz.	Beta/Gamma - 21-32 Hz.	Treatment Indications
Benzodiazepines			Decrease	Increase	Increase	Anxiety Sedation
Barbiturates				Increase	Increase	Anxiety Sedation Epilepsy
Tricyclic Antidepressants	decrease	Decrease			Increase	Depression
SSRI Antidepressants	decrease		Increase			Depression Anxiety OCD
Amphetamines	decrease	Decrease			increase	Somnolence Narcolepsy AD/HD
Opiates	increase		decrease			Pain
Anticonvulsants Phenytoin, valpoate, carbamazapine		increase				Epilepsy
Gamma hydroxy butyrate	increase					Cataplexy Narcolepsy
Classic Neuroleptics		increase	decrease	decrease		Schizophrenia Psychosis

Interfacing with CNS Electrophysiologic Systems

Psychoactive Drugs

Neurochemically active drugs affect background EEG frequencies (Mandema & Danhof, 1992). In most cases, drug induced modulation in EEG frequency produces a consistent pattern of behavioral change (Herrmann & Schaerer 1986; Pagel 1993). CNS-active pharmacological agents alter CNS electrophysiology and produce typical alterations of the physiologic EEG across the therapeutic classification. (Pagel, 1993; 1996; Blume, 2006) (Table 4). Such neurochemical effects on synchronous electrophysiological systems can be used to describe the mode of activity for these agents in treating a variety of psychiatric and neurological illness.

Meditation and Lucid Dreaming

Lucid dreaming is most often defined as the experience of achieving conscious awareness of dreaming while asleep (Voss, Holzmann, Tuin & Hobson, 2009). During episodes of lucid dreaming, some individuals can consciously move or fix their gaze, using this change in gaze to signal an external observer (Holzinger, LaRerge &Levitan, 2006; La Berge, Nagel, Dement & Zarcone,1981; Tholey,1983; Voss; Holzmann, Tuin & Hobson, 2009). Experimentally, such signaling is often associated with an episode of electrophysiologic arousal. (Tholey, 1983; Voss, Holzmann, Tuin & Hobson, 2009). QEEG analysis indicates a high level of alpha and/or beta/gamma frequency activity during lucid dreaming episodes, suggestive of an "in-between" state between resting wake with eyes closed and REM sleep (Holzinger, LaRerge, Levitan 2006, Voss, Holzmann, Tuin & Hobson, 2009).

Table 4. Described conscious states and medications associated with quantitative alterations in physiologic EEG frequencies

	Decreased Delta – 0.5-1.5 Hz.	**Decreased Theta – 5.5-8.5 Hz.**	**Decreased Alpha - 8.5-11 Hz.**	**Decreased Sigma - 12-16 Hz.**	**Decreased Beta/Gamma - 21-32 Hz.**
Medications	Tricyclic & SSRI -Antidepressant Amphetamines	Tricyclic - Antidepressant Amphetamines	Benzodiazepines Opiates	Neuroleptics	
	Increased Delta – 0.5-1.5 Hz.	**Increased Theta – 5.5-8.5 Hz.**	**Increased Alpha - 8.5-11 Hz.**	**Increased Sigma - 12-16 Hz.**	**Increased Beta/Gamma - 21-32 Hz.**
Conscious States	Default Wake Arousal-disorders	REMS- Dreaming Sleep Paralysis	Drowsy Wake - daydreaming Hypnogognic-phenomena Sleep onset Dreaming REMS Dreaming Lucid Dreaming Unfocused-meditation		Focused Wake Default Wake Lucid Dreaming Focused- Meditation
Medications	GABA-Hydroxy-Butyrate Opiates	Anticonvulsant Neuroleptics	SSRI-Antidepressants	Barbiturates Benzodiaze-pines	Amphetamines Benzodiazepines Barbiturates Tricyclic- Antidepressants

Long term meditative practice induces changes in synchronous EEG activity, however, there is little consistent characterization of these changes across techniques (Fell, Axmacher & HH Haupt, 2010). Long-term Buddhist practitioners have a higher ratio of beta/gamma (25-42 Hz) band activity to theta/alpha activity (4-13 Hz.) (Lutz, Greischar, Rawlings, Richard & Davidson, 2004; Huang & Lo, 2009; Cahn, Delorme & Polich, 2010). Some types of yoga have been shown to induce high-frequency bi-phasic ripples of gamma waves during meditation (Vialatte, Bakardjian, Prasad & Cichochi, 2009). Increases in frontal alpha/theta activity are demonstrated by experienced Zen meditators (Huang & Lo, 2009; Chiesa, 2009). Studies of meditation-induced relaxation have demonstrated an increase in frontal midline theta (4-8 Hz.) activity when compared to subjects relaxing while listening to music (Chan, Han, & Chueng, 2008). The pattern of beta/gamma (33-44 Hz) band activity differs in focused meditators from what is found in individuals practicing unfocused meditation styles (Lehman, Faber, Achermann, Jeanmonod D, Gianotti L & Pizzagalli, 2001). Increased frontal theta and posterior alpha are apparently characteristic of unfocused meditative techniques (Lagopoulos, Xu, Rasmussen, Vik, Malhi, Eliassen, Arntsen, Saether, Hollup, Holen, Davanger & Ellingsen, 2009; Cahn, Delorme & Polich 2010). This confusion of data clearly suggests that meditation techniques can be used to alter CNS electrophysiology, with that change is in a variety of different frequency patterns depending on the technique utilized. Meditation initiated at sleep onset and continuing into behavioral sleep is utilized in some Tibetan Buddhist meditative traditions (Rinpoche, 1998). Some authors have proposed that sleep associated meditation is a form of lucid dreaming (Olgivie, Hunt, Tyson, Lucescu, Jeankin, 1978; Wallace, 2007). This formulation fits with modern concepts of lucid dreaming as a state of assuming conscious volitional control during sleep (Hunt, 1989). Based on associated electrophysiology, lucid dreaming may be best conceptualized as a meditation like state occurring during sleep rather than wake (Pagel, 2013)

Biofeedback

Since the early 1970's electrophysiological biofeedback systems have been successfully used to train individuals to develop different frequency patterns of the physiologic brain rhythms. Theta and alpha frequency systems have been utilized to induce relaxation, and drowsiness (Jacobs & Friedman, 2004). EEG biofeedback training has proven beneficial for some patients in the treatment of epileptic seizures, learning disability, PTSD, chronic fatigue, tobacco dependence and AD/HD (Linden, Habib & Radojevich, 1996) Frequency based biofeedback systems are used in sports, performance, military and artistic training in the attempt to assist individuals to develop task focus (Table 5). While many studies have shown individually positive results using this approach, a lack of technique consistency, patent controls of result outcome, and underdeveloped methodology has made it difficult to determine the efficacy of

Table 5. Attention process components

Components	Description
Focused attention	The ability to respond to specific stimuli
Sustained attention	The ability to maintain consistent concentration on performing a task
Selective attention	The ability not to be distracted by interfering or competing stimuli
Alternating attention	The ability to alternate the focus of attention
Divided attention	The ability to respond to two or more kinds of stimuli simultaneously

this approach (Vernon, 2005). EEG feedback has been incorporated with apparent benefit into in to virtual reality systems (Cho, Lee, Ku, & Jang, 2002;).

Hypnosis

The EEG changes that can be induced with hypnosis resemble those seen at sleep onset and with meditation states (Katayama et al 2007). Despite a plethora of attempts using a multiplicity of sampling, measuring and instrumental methodologies, no consistent pattern of electrophysiological changes has been identified for either the hypnotic state or for hypnotic tendency (Pascalis, 1999). Current approaches addressing the possibility of hypnosis-associated microstates (75-120 ms) have proved disappointing as well (Katayama, Gianotti, Isotani, Faber, Sasada, Kinoshita & Lehmann, 2007). Currently, based on limited study, it is unclear whether hypnosis induces state specific alterations in CNS electrophysiology.

Hypnopedia

Sleep associated learning/teaching or hypnopedia has been attempted for many years with minimal success (Hoskovek, 1966). There is good evidence, however, that some stimuli externally applied during sleep can affect both sleep-associated electrophysiology and dreaming. During lighter sleep (Stage 1, 2 and REM sleep) the externally vocalized expression of the individual's name can induce either a micro-arousal or a K-complex in monitored sleep (Berger R, 1963). Aversive stimuli (the tightening of a blood pressure cuff, sounds, flashing lights) are sometimes incorporated into reported dream content (Dement & Wolport, 1958). It has been difficult to demonstrate the capacity for hypnopedia to induce more complex alterations of cognitive processing. Despite the limited evidence for interface capacity, hypnopedia remains a plot mainstay in science fiction novels.

EXTERNALLY APPLIED ELECTRICAL FIELDS

Alternating Currents

Over the last century, without preparation and with little if any testing as to the potential physiologic and psychological effects, the human species has subjected itself to strong externally applied frequency modulated electrical fields in the physiologic range. We have become a 'plugged-in' species, and today it is the rare human who does not interface with 60 hz. alternating electric current on a full-time basis. Sixty-hertz current, like all frequency based electrical fields, is broadcast into the surrounding space, extending well beyond the various components, wires, and systems that use it as a power source. In the hospital setting, EEG monitoring is sometimes utilized in the attempt to assess whether brain death has occurred as determined by a lack of brain electrical activity. In many cases, this differential has become difficult to accomplish. In our modern hospitals, background electrical activity (60 Hz.) is invariably present as an 'artifact' on EEG and polysomnography recordings. It can only be eliminated by the use of wedge blocking filters that also technically eliminate some of the EEG frequencies in the physiologic range (beta and gamma), the same frequencies that have been proposed as markers for consciousness.

Despite some concern expressed by individuals living in close contact with high-voltage power lines, there has been little evidence for physiologic harm based on our ubiquitous exposure to the 60 HZ, frequency. Epidemiologically, there remain questions as to whether common diagnoses in our modern world such as cancer, Alzheimer's disease, and psychiatric diagnoses such as anxiety and mood disorders might be in some way tied to back ground electrical field exposure. There is minimal evidence, however, supporting this possibility (Oak Ridge Associated Universities Panel, 1992).

Other Externally Applied Frequencies in the Physiologic Range

We are subjected somewhat less to other externally propogated frequencies in the physiologic range. Frequencies ranging from 1-30 HZ. can be 'heard' by our auditory sensorium. Discrete beat patterns in lower frequency ranges can be achieved on percussion instruments. The normal frequency that can be accomplished with rapid finger tapping is 10 beats per minute (alpha) (Konvalinka, Bauer, Stahlhut, Roepstorff & Frith, 2005). Beats and frequencies in the physiologic range comprise much of what we refer to as 'music,' sounds that electronically modulated fill the soundscape of our modern world.

The physiological importance and potential interface potential of these frequency based CNS electrical fields also suggested the possibility for aversive weapon systems of potential use to warring governments and armies. During the 'Cold War' massive broadcast systems were built within the soviet block nations designed to broadcast alpha and other physiologic frequencies towards North America and Western Europe in the attempts to develop an "over-the-horizon" radar system with both offensive and defensive capacities. The largest of these systems, called 'Duga' was constructed in the Chernobyl Complex in what is now the Ukraine. This immensely powerful broadcast system was constantly active during the ten years leading up to the Chernobyl nuclear disaster. Described effects included European shortwave and emergency SOS call interference in the 10 Hz. range. In response, short wave sets were designed with blocking filters to eliminate this strong and irritating interference, referred to in the popular press as the "Russian Wood-Pecker" (Headrick, 1990). There is little evidence for any adverse health or other physiologic effects induced by exposure of millions of people to the continuous external application of external alpha frequency - the most dominate of our physiologic rhythms.

Externally Applied Supra-Physiological Fields

Electroconvulsive therapy (ECT) has been used for many years as a treatment modality for depression and psychosis. The applied electrical fields are in excess of the physiologic range, usually 800 milli-amps, up to several hundred watts, with current flows for between one and 6 seconds. ECT is usually applied as a pulsed direct current since frequency modulated currents are apparently more likely to result in memory disturbance (Lock, 1995). Transcranial magnetic stimulation (TMS) is a more recently developed approach for the treatment of psychiatric disorders. The magnetic field is applied externally, passing unimpeded through the skin and skull, inducing an oppositely directed current in the brain that activates nearby nerve cells in much the same way as currents applied directly to the cortical surface (Cacioppo, Tassinary & Berntson, 2007). Single or paired pulse TMS causes neurons under the site of stimulation to depolarize and discharge an action potential. If used in the primary motor cortex, it can produces a motor evoked potential which can be recorded. If used on the occipital cortex, 'phosphenes' (flashes of light) might be perceived by the subject. In most other areas of the cortex, the participant does not consciously experience any effect, but his or her behavior may be slightly altered (e.g., slower reaction time on a cognitive task), or changes in brain activity may be detected (Pascual-Leone, Davey, Rothwell, Wassermann & Puri, 2002). Both ECT and TMS have a treatment efficacy for selected psychiatric disorders that rivals the effects that can be achieved with medication. Both approaches can produce confusion and disturbances in memory.

SUMMARY AND RECOMMENDATIONS

While the CNS electrophysiological systems generally operate in a non-conscious manner, they are active during the conscious states of sleep (dreaming) and during non-focused waking. These systems have important functions including involvement in associative memory processing, creativity, and the integration of emotional experience (Pagel, 2014). These systems can be altered and affected by external factors, with the internal modulation of this system amenable to training such as meditation and lucidity.

Each of us commonly experience environmental electrical and magnetic fields in the physiological ranges. Yet even after almost constant exposure, the functional effects induced by external and internal alterations of these fields are limited, especially when compared to the effects that can be induced by cognitive interface interactions during waking. Human perspectives and attitudes are far more amenable to alterations induced by the interaction with visual and auditory sensory interface systems such as television, video gaming and film (Gackenback, 2013). To this point, there are no significant proven and consistent physiological or psychological consequences demonstrated that occur secondary to intense environmental exposure to these fields. It is unclear as to how the CNS electrophysiological system is able to protect itself from or ignore the environmental fields affecting these systems. To this point, there is little evidence demonstrating the capacity for external cognitive interventions to affect CNS electrophysiological systems by inducing complex or pervasive alterations of cognitive processing such as learning and/or memory alteration during sleep.

DISCUSSION: THE POTENTIAL FOR A HUMAN/MACHINE INTERFACE BASED ON FREQUENCY MODULATED ELECTRICAL FIELDS IN THE PHYSIOLOGIC RANGE

Both AI and biological systems utilize these physiological range electrical fields in their functioning. A human/machine interface utilizing this system is likely to differ from currently utilized approaches in at least the following ways:

1. The development of such an interface would require the development in both biologic and AI systems of a non-sensory based interaction. This interaction would occur in an electrophysiolgical system that is currently poorly understood, described, and defined.
2. This system operates primarily in a non-conscious manner. Any interface-induced alteration in this system is likely to also have a primarily non-conscious expression.
3. Such a system would be most likely to be useful in interfacing between the biologic and AI systems that utilize these electrical fields in their function. Such systems include those involved in supplying energy, establishing ionic equilibrium, storing information, and communicating between widely separated or otherwise unconnected networks.
4. This system is minimally or alternatively utilized in focused thought based cognitive functioning. A majority of our cognitive tests address parameters of waking attention and thought. Based on such

cognitive testing, it will be difficult to demonstrate waking cognitive effects induced by interactive alterations in this system.

5. Any cognitive changes induced by such an interface interaction are likely to be in those cognitive systems that utilize elecrophysiological systems in their functioning: waking mind-wandering, emotional and creative processing, and sleep associated conscious processing (dreaming).

While this chapter presents the scientific logic for such an interface, this interface may be better viewed metaphorically using archetypes and models. Independently of the REM sleep equals dreaming supposition, dream-associated neuroconsciousness is tied to expressions and changes in brain electrophysiology. Phenomenologically, dream content as well as brain electrophysiology can be altered in the user by machine interface interactions (Cho, Lee, Ku, & Jang, 2002; Gackenback, 2014). Conceptually and empirically, the potential exists for further developing external interfaces with CNS electrophysiologic systems. But that potential is likely not to be primarily expressed as alterations or effects on conscious waking thought. The electrophysiologically described CNS systems and the frequency-based electrical systems utilized by AI function are part of different cognitive processes from those that utilize typical neural and AI "transmission-line" interconnections. Any interface based on changes in electrophysiological systems is most likely to affect non-conscious or alternatively-conscious systems, inducing changes in energy, ionic equilibrium, and information storage. Cognitively, the processes that utilize the electrophysiological system in their functioning are primarily those involved in dreaming and dream-like states in both sleep and wake. Almost all dreams utilize the CNS processes of associative memory, intrinsic imagery, and emotions, in order to function in the processing if emotions and creative problem solving (Pagel, 2014). These CNS systems should be amenable to interaction based on an electrophysiology-based interface. The prospects for such an alternatively-conscious interface system are potentially profound.

REFERENCES

Anastassiou, C., Perin, R., Markam, H., & Koch, C. (2011). Emphatic coupling of cortical neurons. *Nature Neuroscience*, *14*(2), 217–223. doi:10.1038/nn.2727 PMID:21240273

Andrews-Hanna, J. (2011). The brain's default network and its adaptive role in internal mentation. *The Neuroscientist*, *XX*, 1–20. PMID:21677128

Axmacher, N., Mormann, F., Fernandez, G., Elger, C., & Fell, J. (2006). Memory formation by neuronal synchronization. *Brain Research. Brain Research Reviews*, *52*(1), 170–182. doi:10.1016/j.brainresrev.2006.01.007 PMID:16545463

Berger, H. (1931/1969). On the electroencephalogram of man: Third report. *Electroencephalography and Clinical Neurophysiology. Supplement*, *28*, 95–132. PMID:4188920

Berger, R. (1963). Experimental modification of dream content by meaningful verbal stimuli. *The British Journal of Psychiatry*, *109*(463), 722–740. doi:10.1192/bjp.109.463.722 PMID:14080566

Besserve, M., Jerbi, K., Laurent, F., Baillet, S., Martinerie, J., & Garnero, L. (2007). Classification methods for ongoing EEG and MEG signals. *Biological Research*, *20*, 415–437. PMID:18575676

Blaha, S. (2000). *Cosmos and Consciousness*. New Hampshire: Price Hill Publishing.

Blume, W. (2006). Drug effects on EEG. *Journal of Clinical Neurophysiology*, *23*(4), 306–311. doi:10.1097/01.wnp.0000229137.94384.fa PMID:16885705

Buckner, R., Andrews-Hanna, J., & Schacter, D. (2008). The brain's default network – Anatomy, function and relevance to disease. *Annals of the New York Academy of Sciences*, *1124*(1), 1–38. doi:10.1196/annals.1440.011 PMID:18400922

Buckner, R., & Carroll, D. (2007). Self projection and the brain. *Trends in Cognitive Sciences*, *11*(2), 49–57. doi:10.1016/j.tics.2006.11.004 PMID:17188554

Buzsaki, G. (2005). Theta rhythm of navigation: Link between path integration and landmark navigation, episodic and semantic memory. *Hippocampus*, *15*(7), 827–840. doi:10.1002/hipo.20113 PMID:16149082

Buzsaki, G. (2006). *Rhythms of the Brain*. Oxford: Oxford University Press. doi:10.1093/acprof:oso/9780195301069.001.0001

Cacioppo, J. T., Tassinary, L. G., & Berntson, G. G. (Eds.). (2007). *Handbook of psychophysiology* (3rd ed., p. 121). New York: Cambridge Univ. Press. doi:10.1017/CBO9780511546396

Cahn, B., Delorme, A., & Polich, J. (2010). Occipital gamma activation during Vipassana meditation. *Cognitive Processing*, *11*(1), 39–56. doi:10.1007/s10339-009-0352-1 PMID:20013298

Cantero, J., & Atienza, M. (2005). The role of neural synchronization n the emergence of cognition across the wake-sleep cycle. *Reviews in the Neurosciences*, *16*(1), 69–83. doi:10.1515/REVNEURO.2005.16.1.69 PMID:15810655

Cantero, J., Atienza, M., Stickgold, R., Kahana, M., Madsen, J., & Kocsis, B. (2003). Sleep dependent theta occilations in the human hippocampus and neocortex. *The Journal of Neuroscience*, *23*, 10897–10903. PMID:14645485

Cash, S., Halgren, E., Dehghani, N., Rossetti, A., Thesen, T., Wang, C., & Ulbert, I. et al. (2009). The human K-complex represents an isolated cortical down state. *Science*, *324*(5930), 1084–1087. doi:10.1126/science.1169626 PMID:19461004

Chan, A., Han, Y., & Chueng, M. (2008). Electroencephalographic (EEG) measurements of mindfulness-based Trirchic body-pathway relaxation technique: A pilot study. *Applied Psychophysiology and Biofeedback*, *33*(1), 39–47. doi:10.1007/s10484-008-9050-5 PMID:18214668

Cheek, T. R. (1989). Spatial aspects of calcium signaling. *Journal of Cell Science*, *93*, 211–216. PMID:2613762

Chiesa, A. (2009). Zen meditation: An integration of current evidence. *Journal of Alternative and Complementary Medicine (New York, N.Y.)*, *15*(5), 585–592. doi:10.1089/acm.2008.0416 PMID:19422285

Cho, B., & Lee, J. K. U. J Jang D, et al. (2002), Attention Enhancement System using Virtual Reality and EEG Biofeedback. *Proceedings of the IEEE Virtual Reality*.

Christakos, C. N. (1986). The mathematical basis of population rhythms in nervous and neuromuscular systems. *The International Journal of Neuroscience*, *29*(1-2), 103–107. doi:10.3109/00207458608985640 PMID:3699995

Christoff, K., Gordon, A., Smallwood, J., Smith, R., & Schooler, W. (2009). Experience sampling during fMRI reveals default network and executive system contributions to mind wandering. *Proceedings of the National Academy of Sciences of the United States of America*, 106(21), 8719-8724. PMID:19433790

Coburn, K., Lauterbach, E., Boutros, N., Black, K., Arciniegas, D., & Coffey, C. (2006). The value of quantitative electroencephalography in clinical psychiatry: A report by the committee on research of the American Neuropsychiatic Association. *The Journal of Neuropsychiatry and Clinical Neurosciences*, *18*(4), 460–500. doi:10.1176/jnp.2006.18.4.460 PMID:17135374

Corsi-Cabrerra, M., Guevara, M., & Rio-Portilla, Y. (2008). Brain activity and temporal coupling related to eye movements during REM sleep: EEG and MEG results. *Brain Research*, *1235*, 82–91. doi:10.1016/j.brainres.2008.06.052 PMID:18625213

Crick, F. (1994). *The Astonishing Hypothesis: The Scientific Search for the Soul*. New York: Charles Scribner's Sons.

Daoust, A., Lusignan, F., Braun, C., Mottron, L., & Godbout, R. (2008). EEG correlates of emotions in dream narratives from typical young adults and individuals with autistic spectrum disorders. *Psychophysiology*, *45*(2), 299–308. doi:10.1111/j.1469-8986.2007.00626.x PMID:18047484

DeLuca, M., Beckmann, C., DeStafano, N., Matthews, P., & Smith, S. (2006). fMRI resting state networks define distinct modes of long-distant interactions in the human brain. *NeuroImage*, *29*(4), 1359–1367. doi:10.1016/j.neuroimage.2005.08.035 PMID:16260155

Dement, W., & Wolpert, E. (1958). The relation of eye movements, body motility, and external stimuli to dream content. *Journal of Experimental Psychology*, *55*(6), 543–553. doi:10.1037/h0040031 PMID:13563767

Domhoff, W. (2003). *The Scientific Study of Dreams*. Washington, DC: American Psychological Association.

Elul, R. (1971). The genesis of the EEG. *International Review of Neurobiology*, *15*, 227–272. doi:10.1016/S0074-7742(08)60333-5 PMID:4949975

Fell, J., Axmacher, N., & Haupt, S. (2010). From alpha to gamma: Electrophysiological correlates of meditation-related states of consciousness. *Medical Hypotheses*, *75*(2), 218–224. doi:10.1016/j.mehy.2010.02.025 PMID:20227193

Finglehurts, A., & Finglehurts, A. (2011). Persistent operational synchrony within brain default-mode network and self processing operations in healthy subjects. *Brain and Cognition*, *75*(2), 79–90. doi:10.1016/j.bandc.2010.11.015 PMID:21172727

Foulkes, D. (1985). *Dreaming: A Cognitive-Psychological Analysis*. Hillsdale, NJ: Lawrence Erlbaum Associates.

Fox, M., & Raichle, M. (2007). Spontaneous fluctuations in brain activity observed with functional magnetic resonance imaging. *Nature Reviews. Neuroscience*, *8*(9), 700–711. doi:10.1038/nrn2201 PMID:17704812

Freud, S. (1903). The Interpretation of Dreams. In J. Strachey (Ed.), The Standard Editions of the Complete Psychological Works of Sigmund Freud (Vol. IV and V). London, England: Hogarth Press (1953).

Gackenback, J., & Kurville, B. (2013). Cognitive structure associated with the lucid features of gamer's dreams. *Dreaming*, *23*(4), 256–267. doi:10.1037/a0034817

Gusner, D., & Raichle, M. (2001). Searching for a baseline: Functional imaging and the resting human brain. *Nature Reviews. Neuroscience*, *2*(10), 685–694. doi:10.1038/35094500 PMID:11584306

Hangya, B., Tihanyi, B., Entz, L., Fabo, D., ErFss, L., Wittner, L., & Ulbert, I. et al. (2011). Complex propagation patterns characterize human cortical activity during slow-wave sleep. *The Journal of Neuroscience*, *31*(24), 8770–8779. doi:10.1523/JNEUROSCI.1498-11.2011 PMID:21677161

Harold, F. M. (1986). *The vital force: A study of Bioenergetics*. New York: WH Freeman & Co.

Hartmann, E. (1998). *Dreams and Nightmares – the New Theory on the Origin and Meaning of Dreams*. New York: Plenum Trade.

Headrick. (1990). Looking over the horizon (HF radar). *IEEE Spectrum*, 27, 36-39.

Herrmann, W. M., & Schaerer, E. (1986). Pharmaco-EEG: Computer EEG analysis to describe the projection of drug effects on a functional cerebral level in humans. In Lopes et al. (Eds.), Clinical application of computer analysis of EEG and other neurophysiological signals, EEG Handbook (Vol. 2, Rev. ed., pp. 385-445). Amsterdam: Elsevier.

Hobson, J., Pace-Schott, E., & Stickgold, R. (2003). Dreaming and the brain: Toward a cognitive neuroscience of conscious states. In E. Pace-Schott, M. Solms, M. Blagrove, & S. Harnad (Eds.), *Sleep and Dreaming: Scientific Advances and Reconsiderations* (pp. 1–50). Cambridge, UK: Cambridge University Press.

Hobson, J. A. (1999). *Consciousness*. New York: Scientific American Press.

Hobson, J. A., Pace-Schott, E. F., & Stickgold, R. (2000). Dreaming and the brain: Toward a cognitive neuroscience of conscious states. *BBS*, *23*(6), 793–842. doi:10.1017/S0140525X00003976 PMID:11515143

Hodgkin, A., & Horowicz, P. (1959). The influence of potassium and chloride ions on the membrane potential of single muscle fibers. *The Journal of Physiology*, *148*(1), 127–160. doi:10.1113/jphysiol.1959.sp006278 PMID:14402240

Holzinger, B., LaBerge, S., & Levitan, L. (2006). Psychophysiological correlates of lucid dreaming. *Dreaming*, *16*(2), 88–95. doi:10.1037/1053-0797.16.2.88

Hoskovek, J. (1966). Hypnopedia in the Soviet Union: A critical review of recent major experiments. *The International Journal of Clinical and Experimental Hypnosis*, *14*, 305–315. PMID:5977010

Huang, H., & Lo, P. (2009). EEG dynamics of experienced Zen meditation practitioners probed by complexity index and spectral measure. *Journal of Medical Engineering & Technology*, *33*(4), 314–321. doi:10.1080/03091900802602677 PMID:19384707

Hunt, H. (1989). *The Multiplicity of Dreams: Memory, Imagination, and Consciousness*. New Haven: Yale University Press.

Iber, C., Ancoli-Israel, S., Chesson, A., & Quan, S. (2007). *The AASM Manuel for the Scoring of Sleep and Associated Events. Westchester, Il.* American Academy of Sleep Medicine.

Ioannides, A., Kostopoulos, G., Liu, L., & Fenwick, P. (2008). MEG identifies dorsal medial brain activations during sleep. *NeuroImage*, *44*(2), 455–468. doi:10.1016/j.neuroimage.2008.09.030 PMID:18950718

Itil, T. M. (1981). The discovery of psychotrophic drugs by computer analyzed cerebral bioelectrical potentials (CEEG). *Drug Development Research*, *1*(4), 373–407. doi:10.1002/ddr.430010407

Jacobs G.D., Friedman R. (2004). EEG spectral analysis of relaxation techniques. Appl Psyclophysiol biofeedback 29,245-54

John, E. (1968). Mechanisms of Memory (Vol. 1 & 2). New York: Academic Press.

Jung, C. (1965). *Memories, Dreams, Reflections*. New York: Vintage.

Katayama, H., Gianotti, L., Isotani, T., Faber, P., Sasada, K., Kinoshita, T., & Lehmann, D. (2007). Classes of multichannel EEG microstates in light and deep hypnotic conditions. *Brain Topography*, *20*(1), 7–14. doi:10.1007/s10548-007-0024-3 PMID:17587166

Kiebel, S., Garrido, M., Moran, R., Chen, C., & Friston, K. (2009). Dynamic causal modeling for EEG and EMG. *Human Brain Mapping*, *30*(6), 1866–1876. doi:10.1002/hbm.20775 PMID:19360734

Konvalinka, I., Bauer, M., Stahlhut, C., Hansen, C. K., Roepstorff, A., & Frith, C. D. (2005). Frontal alpha oscillations distinguish leaders from followers: Multivariate decoding of mutually interactive brains. *NeuroImage*, *94*, 79–88. doi:10.1016/j.neuroimage.2014.03.003 PMID:24631790

Koulack, D. (1969). Effects of somatosensory stimulation on dream content. *Archives of General Psychiatry*, *120*, 71–80. PMID:4306322

LaBerge, S. (1985). *Lucid Dreaming*. Los Angeles, CA: JP Tarcher.

LaBerge, S., Nagel, L., Dement, W., & Zarcone, V. Jr. (1981). Lucid dreaming verified by volitional communication during REM sleep. *Perceptual and Motor Skills*, *52*(3), 727–732. doi:10.2466/pms.1981.52.3.727 PMID:24171230

Lagopoulos, J., Xu, J., Rasmussen, I., Vik, A., Malhi, G., Eliassen, C., & Ellingsen, O. et al. (2009). Increased theta and alpha activity during nondirective meditation. *Journal of Alternative and Complementary Medicine (New York, N.Y.)*, *15*(11), 1187–1192. doi:10.1089/acm.2009.0113 PMID:19922249

Lakatos, P., Karmos, G., Mehta, A., Ulbert, I., & Schroeder, C. (2008). Entrainment of neuronal occilations as a mechanism of attentional selection. *Science*, *320*(5872), 110–113. doi:10.1126/science.1154735 PMID:18388295

Lehmann, D., Faber, P., Achermann, P., Jeanmonod, D., Gianotti, L., & Pizzagalli, D. (2001). Brain sources of EEG gamma frequency during volitionally meditation-induced, altered states of consciousness, and experience of the self. *Psychiatry Research*, *108*(2), 111–121. doi:10.1016/S0925-4927(01)00116-0 PMID:11738545

Leopold, D., Murayama, Y., & Logothetis, N. (2003). Very slow activity fluctuations in monkey visual cortex: Implications for functional brain imaging. *Cereb Cortex*, *13*(4), 423–433. doi:10.1093/cercor/13.4.422 PMID:12631571

Linden, M., Habib, T., & Radojevich, V. (1996). A controlled study of the effects of EEG biofeedback on cognition and behavior of children with attention deficit disorder and learning disabilities. *Biofeedback and Self-Regulation*, *21*(1), 35–49. doi:10.1007/BF02214148 PMID:8833315

Lisman, J. E., & Idiart, M. A. (1995). Storage of 7 + 2 short term memories in oscillatory subcycles. *Science*, *267*(5203), 1512–1515. doi:10.1126/science.7878473 PMID:7878473

Liu, C., & Reppert, S. M. (2000). GABA synchronizes clock cells within the suprachiasmatic circadian clock. *Neuron*, *25*(1), 123–128. doi:10.1016/S0896-6273(00)80876-4 PMID:10707977

Lock, T. (1995). Stimulus dosing. In C. Freeman (Ed.), *The ECT Handbook* (pp. 72–87). London: Royal College of Psychiatrists.

Lutz, A., Greischar, L., Rawlings, N., Richard, M., & Davidson, R. (2004). Long-term meditators self-induce high-amplitude gamma synchrony during mental practice. *Proceedings of the National Academy of Sciences of the United States of America*, *101*(46), 16369–16373. doi:10.1073/pnas.0407401101 PMID:15534199

Mandema, J. W., & Danhof, M. (1992). Electroencephalogram effect measures and relationships between pharmackinetics and pharmacodynamics of centrally acting drugs. *Clinical Pharmacokinetics*, *23*(3), 191–215. doi:10.2165/00003088-199223030-00003 PMID:1511536

Marzano, C., Ferrara, M., Mauro, F., Moroni, F., Gorgoni, M., Tempesta, D., & DeGennaro, L. et al. (2011). Recalling and forgetting dreams: Theta and alpha oscillations during sleep predict subsequent dream recall. *The Journal of Neuroscience*, *31*(18), 6674–6683. doi:10.1523/JNEUROSCI.0412-11.2011 PMID:21543596

McCarley, R., & Hobson, J. (1975). Neuronal excitability modulation over the sleep cycle: A structural and mathematical model. *Science*, *189*(4196), 58–60. doi:10.1126/science.1135627 PMID:1135627

Oak Ridge Associated Universities Panel for the Committee on Interagency Radiation Research and Policy Commission. (1992). Health Effects of Low-Frequency Electric and Magnetic Fiels. Washington, D.C., Oak Ridge Associated Universities (US Government).

Olgivie, R., Hunt, H., Tyson, P., Lucescu, M., & Jeankin, D. (1978). Searching for lucid dreams. *Sleep Research*, *7*, 165.

Pagel J. (2013). Lucid Dreaming as Sleep Offset Waking – Sleep 34- Abstract supplement.

Pagel, J. F. (1990). *Proposing an Electrophysiology for State Dependent Sleep and Dream Mentation*. APSS Abstracts.

Pagel, J. F. (1993). Modeling drug actions on electrophysiologic effects produced by EEG modulated potentials. *Human Psychopharmacology*, *8*(3), 211–216. doi:10.1002/hup.470080307

Pagel, J. F. (1996). Pharmacologic alteration of sleep and dreams - a clinical framework medications. *Human Psychopharmacology, 11*, 217–224. doi:10.1002/(SICI)1099-1077(199605)11:3<217::AID-HUP790>3.0.CO;2-0

Pagel, J. F. (2003). Non-dreamers. *Sleep Medicine, 4*(3), 235–241. doi:10.1016/S1389-9457(02)00255-1 PMID:14592328

Pagel, J. F. (2005). Neurosignals – Incorporating CNS electrophysiology into cognitive process. *Behavioral and Brain Sciences, 28*(01), 75–76. doi:10.1017/S0140525X05330020

Pagel, J. F. (2008). *The Limits of Dream: A Scientific Exploration of the Mind/brain Interface*. Oxford, UK: Academic Press. doi:10.1016/B978-012374215-5.50033-7

Pagel, J. F. (2011). REMS and Dreaming – Historical Perspectives. In B.N. Mallick, S.R. Pandi Perumal, R.W. McCarley, A.R. Morrison (Eds.), Rapid Eye Movement Sleep – Regulation and Function (pp. 1-14). Cambridge University Press.

Pagel, J. F. (2014). Dream Science: Exploring the Forms of Consciousness. Oxford UK: Academic Press (Elsiever).

Palva, J., Palva, S., & Kaila, K. (2005). Phase synchrony among neuronal oscillations in the human cortex. *The Journal of Neuroscience, 24*(15), 3962–3972. doi:10.1523/JNEUROSCI.4250-04.2005 PMID:15829648

Pascalis, V. (1999). Psychophysiological correlates of hypnosis and hypnotic susceptibility. *The International Journal of Clinical and Experimental Hypnosis, 47*(2), 117–143. doi:10.1080/00207149908410026 PMID:10208074

Pascual-Leone, A., Davey, N., Rothwell, J., Wassermann, E. M., & Puri, B. K. (2002). *Handbook of Transcranial Magnetic Stimulation*. London: Edward Arnold.

Raichle, M., MacLeod, A., Snyder, A., Powers, W., Gusnard, D., & Shulman, G. L. (2001). A default mode of brain function. *Proceedings of the National Academy of Sciences of the United States of America, 98*(2), 676–682. doi:10.1073/pnas.98.2.676 PMID:11209064

Rechtschaffen Kales. (1968). *AASM Manual for Sleep and Associated Events*. Rochester, Minnesota: American Academy of Sleep Medicine.

Rinpoche, T. W. (1998). *The Tibetian Yogas of Dream and Sleep*. Ithaca, NY: Snow Lion Publications.

Salinas, E., & Sejnowski, T. (2001). Correlated neuronal activity and the flow of neural information. *Nat Rev Neurosicence, 2*(8), 539–550. doi:10.1038/35086012 PMID:11483997

Schack, B., Klimesch, W., & Sauseng, P. (2005). Phase synchronization between theta snd upper alpha occilations in a working memory task. *International Journal of Psychophysiology, 57*(2), 105–114. doi:10.1016/j.ijpsycho.2005.03.016 PMID:15949859

Searle, J. R. (1998). *The Rediscovery of the Mind*. Cambridge, Massachusetts: The MIT Press.

Shultz, H. (2008). Rethinking sleep analysis: Comment on the AASM manual for the scoring of sleep and associated events. *Journal of Clinical Sleep Medicine, 15*, 99–103.

Siegel, J. M. (2000). Brainstem Mechanisms generating REM sleep. In M.H. Kryger, T. Roth, W.C. Dement (Eds.), Principles and Practice of Sleep Medicine (3rd ed., pp.112-114). Philadelphia: WB Saunders.

Singer, W. (1999). Neuronal synchrony: A versatile code for the definition of relations? *Neuron, 24*(1), 49–65. doi:10.1016/S0896-6273(00)80821-1 PMID:10677026

Solms, M. (2003). Dreaming and REM sleep are controlled by different brain mechanisms. In E. Pace-Schott, M. Solms, M. Blagrove, & S. Harnad (Eds.), *Sleep and Dreaming: Scientific Advances and Reconsiderations* (pp. 51–58). Cambridge, UK: Cambridge University Press.

Steriade, M. (2001). *The Intact and Sliced Brain*. Massachusetts: MIT Press.

Steriade, M. (2006). Grouping of brain rhythms in corticothalamic systems. *Neuroscience, 137*(4), 1086–1106. doi:10.1016/j.neuroscience.2005.10.029 PMID:16343791

Tholey, P. (1983). Relation between dream content and eye movements tested by lucid dreams. *Perceptual and Motor Skills, 56*(3), 875–878. doi:10.2466/pms.1983.56.3.875 PMID:6877973

Vernon, D. (2005). Can Neurofeedback Training Enhance Performance? *An Evaluation of the Evidence with Implications for Future Research Applied Psychophysiology and Biofeedback, 30*, 165–205. PMID:16385423

Vialatte, F., Bakardjian, H., Prasad, R., & Cichocki, A. (2009). EEG paroxysmal gamma waves during Bhramari Pranayama: A yoga breathing technique. *Consciousness and Cognition, 18*(4), 977–988. doi:10.1016/j.concog.2008.01.004 PMID:18299208

Voss, U., Holzmann, R., Tuin, I., & Hobson, J. A. (2009). Lucid dreaming: A state of consciousness with features of both waking and non-lucid dreaming. *Sleep, 32*, 1191–1200. PMID:19750924

Walker, M. P. (2005). A refined model of sleep and the time course of memory consolidation. *Behavioral and Brain Sciences, 28*(01), 51–104. doi:10.1017/S0140525X05000026 PMID:16047457

Wallace, B. A. (2006). *The Attention Revolution: Unlocking the power of the Focused Mind*. Boston: Wisdom Publications.

Section 2

Exponentials for Exploring the Psychological Metaverse

Section 2 represents directions for continued research upon the concept that the Metaverse is energetically correlated with the Psychecology (unified field) and dream structure according to Carl Jung. Chapter five explores film and video games relative to Jungian principles of dream structure. Chapter six amplifies the concept of archetypal projection of the cognitive unconscious as understood by exponents of Jungian dream principles. Chapter seven focuses on coherence or "Flow" as cognitive relationships that exist between dreams and the serious sport of mountaineering. Chapter eight emphasizes principles of Jungian archetypal projection as it relates to healing potentials in South African film. Chapter nine speculates on the archetypal hero's journey from the standpoint of an emergent understanding of psychological group contexts in the media-sphere. Chapter ten discusses the synchronous (entangled) relationship that exists between two contextual groups: Terrorists and media professionals. Finally, Chapter 11 provides an extensive discussion of the neurobiological Psychecology as it impacts the global ionosphere.

Chapter 5
The Collective Unconscious as Culprit:
Archetypal Projections from the Unconscious in Video Games (and Film)

Beat Suter
University of the Arts Zurich, Switzerland

ABSTRACT

This chapter shows the attempt to use narrative projections of the unconscious in video games (and film) for transgressing into a virtual world. It demonstrates the conceptual development from C.G. Jung's theories via Joseph Campbell and Hollywood's screenwriters to Video Game mythologies. It shows that a visual approach by game artists often leads to stereotypical implementation of archetypes and archeplot in video games that illustrates a lack of reflection and flexibility of mind and creativity. It further shows that a conscious implementation of individual patterns and archetypes as seen in Adventure Games and recent Indie Games may obtain narrative depth for a game and contribute to exploring the collective unconscious in new media. Gaming is rapidly changing and aims towards the ideal of a Holodeck. New Virtual Reality experiments and gadgets prepare the ground for new ways to engage in imagined (conscious and unconscious) realities. The chapter concludes with an example of an attempt to build a virtual dream world with the project Birdly (2014) and Oculus Rift.

INTRODUCTION

Carl Jung reminds us that, "Consciousness is a very recent acquisition of nature, and it is still in an "experimental" state." (Jung, 1964, p.6) More recently in the film, Matrix, Neo raises the question of consciousness as dream. "Have you ever had that feeling, where you're not sure if you're awake or still dreaming?" The concept of reality-as-dream is longstanding—reaching back to mythic origins and beyond. Today, in the orthodox understanding, the metaphor of the monomyth is a common idea, but its significance is largely unknown. The monomyth—The Hero's Journey—may be understood as a

DOI: 10.4018/978-1-4666-9891-8.ch005

template and key to understanding reality-as-dream, and its principles of dream analysis can be applied to the dreamlike interactive metaverse.

Archetypes of the collective unconscious were defined and explained by Carl Gustav Jung. In his essays, "The archetypes and the collective unconscious," Jung employs illustrations from fairy tales, myths, mandalas, and clinical examples from his practice as a therapist in Zurich in order to illustrate the nature of symbolic patterns. The collective unconscious expresses itself as projected images embedded with archetypal patterns. Jung called the projections archetypal representations. In 1913 after a split with Sigmund Freud, Jung put his academic career on hold and devoted himself to the mythological exploration of his inner world of images. He said later that the next four years were the most important time of his life. Jung's statements are originally written in German. Rather than relying on translation and interpretation, quoting and paraphrasing the original words should provide a purposeful emphasis.

[...] führt [...] nämlich zur Erkenntnis einer Unterscheidung im Unbewussten. Wir haben nämlich ein persönliches Unbewusstes und ein un- oder überpersönliches Unbewusstes zu unterscheiden. Wir bezeichnen Letzteres auch als das absolute oder kollektive Unbewusste, eben weil es vom Persönlichen losgelöst und ganz allgemein ist, weil seine Inhalte in allen Köpfen gefunden werden können, was bei den persönlichen Inhalten natürlich nicht der Fall ist. (Jung, 1917, p. 86)

Jung states that the unconscious mind is divided into a personal unconscious and an impersonal or transpersonal unconscious (literal translation). This is also known as absolute or collective unconscious. The contents of the collective unconscious can be accessed as an integrated record of human experience, whereas the "personal unconscious" is more contextual—based on personal experiences. Jung is convinced that all humans share the content of the impersonal unconscious.

Die urtümlichen Bilder sind die āltesten und allgemeinsten und tiefsten Gedanken der Menschheit überhaupt. Sie sind eben sowohl Gefühl als Gedanke, man könnte sie darum auch ursprüngliches Fühldenken nennen. (Jung, 1917, p. 86)

The next paragraph focuses on Jung's visual approach. He points out that primeval images represent the most common and deepest experiences of human beings. He interprets these images on four functional levels (thinking, feeling, sensing, and intuiting) but emphasizes "Feelthinking"—a hybrid of feelings and thoughts. This term may be interpreted as emotional thinking that comes in the shape of visuals. A process of thinking evokes an emotional reaction and vice versa.

Damit haben wir nun auch das Objekt gefunden, das die Libido wählte, nachdem sie aus der persönlich infantilen Übertragungsform befreit war. Sie sinkt nämlich hinunter in das Tiefste des Unbewussten und belebt dort, was seit Uralters schlummerte. Sie hat den vergrabenen Schatz entdeckt, aus dem die Menschheit je und je schöpfte, aus dem sie ihre Götter und Dāmonen emporhob und alle jene stärksten und gewaltigsten Gedanken, ohne welche der Mensch aufhört, Mensch zu sein. (Jung, 1917, p. 86)

This visual "Feelthinking" consists of energy patterns that are expressed by the term Libido. Jungian libido means energy, and the term is not constricted to sexual implication as is Freudian libido. So, Libido has its source in the collective unconscious and is projected as archetypal representations that function as mirror images of archetypal energy patterns. The archetypal template is a trove of narrative mythological material. Jung says that it consists of gods and demons—the vast and powerful human roots without which the human reality cannot exist.

It is not difficult to tell from the material provided by dreams, fantasies, and visions to what degree they transcend the personal sphere and involve the contents of the collective unconscious. Mythological themes, symbols rooted in the universal history of mankind, or reactions of extreme intensity always indicate the participation of the deepest strata. These motifs and symbols exert a determining influence on psychic life as a whole; they have a dominant functional character and an extremely high energy charge, which is why Jung at first spoke of them as "primordial images" or "dominants" of the collective unconscious. (Jacobi, Jolande, 1973, p.39)

Hence Jung searched for common myths and developed his theory and typology of archetypes. Archetypes are part of the collective unconscious while the personal unconscious features complexes in their place. These archetypal representations are the material of our dreams and myths.

Since 1946 [Nature, pp. 159 ff], Jung has distinguished...between the "archetype per se" that is, the nonperceptible archetype which is present only potentially in every psychic structure, and the actualized archetype [archetypal representation] which has become perceptible and already entered into the field of consciousness, The actualized archetype appears as an archetypal image, representation, or process, and its forms may change continuously according to the constellation [context] in which it occurs. (Jacobi, p. 40)

Joseph Campbell built on Carl Jung's concept of the collective unconscious to encompass all the world's mythologies. Campbell studied the world's religions, art, and stories and discovered common threads throughout all, including the hero. Campbell believed that mythology represents the collective "dream" of mankind, the "song of the universe." Campbell's work highlights mankind's common search, both personally and socially, for meaning and truth through the ages. Campbell popularized the idea that "myth is psychology", and he denominated the fundamentally Jungian principle of individuation as the hero's journey. Campbell worked through Jung's theories and finally broke down Jung's archetypes to a limited number of stereotypes and mapped out an underlying structure for all mythological stories. In doing so, he developed the theory of the one and only story, the Journey of the Hero, that has always been told by human-kind over thousands of years. Today it is known as the monomyth. The book was titled *The Hero with a Thousand Faces (1949).* In it, Campbell provided examples of stories from different cultures around the world and showed how they were using similar structures and archetypes.

Campbell's remarkable book on the hero's journey made Jungian principle generally accessible to the minds of people all around the world. Accordingly, media representations of the hero's journey are understood in largely stereotypical narrative ways rather than in terms of the deeper significance of psychic self-realization and psychoanalytic therapeutic potential. The journey is perceived primarily as a vehicle for entertainment, rather than as a powerful vehicle for self-realization and healing. As Jung says:

The dream speaks in images, and gives expression to instincts, that are derived from the most primitive levels of nature. Consciousness all too easily departs from the law of nature; but it can be brought again into harmony with the latter by the assimilation of unconscious contents. By fostering this process we lead the patient to the rediscovery of the law of his own being. ...The way of successive assimilations reaches far beyond the curative results that specifically concern the doctor. It leads in the end to that distant goal (which may perhaps have been the first urge to life), the bringing into reality of the whole human being—that is, individuation. (Jung 1933, p 26)

BACKGROUND

Movies and games along with other emerging media in the 20th century have appropriated these ideas and adapted them to their own needs and limitations. A very obvious example is the superhero phenomenon of the 20th century. Comic books introduced the superheroes like Superman, Spider-Man, and Batman to growing fan communities and the movie industry gladly helps spread these modern day heroes across cultures. Essentially, these superheroes become the mythical gods and champions of modern culture. They are replacing the ancient myths of all cultures and serving as role models. Fans celebrate or even worship these role models not from a religious perspective with its deeper meaning, but from a superficial perspective that has less archetypal potential. Culture seems addicted—or at least habituated—to surface representations with little understanding of their deeper meaning. The models and their stories are escapist rather than healing. The characters and plots of these superhero fictions are generally characterized by over simplification of behavior and social actions within cultural patterns. Nevertheless, the potential for deep meaning is inevitable if understood—to a degree-by media designers.

Jung's seminal discovery about dreams is that they have dramatic structure.

Dreams form a self-contained whole, a dramatic action which can meaningfully be broken down into the elements of a Greek play. (1) Place, time, dramatis personae: this is the beginning of the dream, which often indicates the scene of action and the cast of characters; (2) Exposition or statement of the problem. Here is presented the central content: the unconscious frames the question to which it will reply in the course of the dream; (3) Peripety: this is the 'backbone' of the dream; the plot is woven, the action moves toward a climax, transformation, or catastrophe; (4) Lysis, the solution, the outcome of the dream, its meaningful conclusion and the disclosure of its compensatory message. (Jacobi, p. 83).

Jungian dream analysis as well as his principal of archetypes and archetypal projections can be framed within the dramatic context, and "This rough pattern, on which most dreams are constructed, forms a suitable basis for interpretation." (Jacobi, p. 83)

Campbell's journey of the hero is based on Jung's concept of dramatic dream structure, and the monomyth as plot has proven to be a very practical standard for media designers who have not been particularly interested in complex psychological theories. Instead, movie screenwriting and game writing has used the skeleton of psychology without focusing on the character implications of archetypes. Instead of breaking new ground, there is an overwhelming tendency to reduce the number of archetypes and to melt the plots down to simplified standards.

In 2005, the Internet did not show too many accurate results on the hero's journey, but during the past ten years, focus on the monomyth and Campbell's narrative theory have exploded. A search today retrieves hundreds of slides, diagrams, synopses, and videos on the topic. Some are very instructive with appropriate examples mostly from film. Very few are critical, and most rely on analyzing the 20th century epics of *Star Wars*, *Lord of the Rings* and *The Hobbit*.

The notion of Campbell's work *The Hero with a Thousand Faces (1949)* may be seen best in *J.R.R. Tolkien*'s novel *The Lord of the Rings (1954/55)*. Tolkien and Campbell simultaneously worked on similar ideas. Later on *George Lucas* brought it all together in his original *Star Wars* (Kurtz & Lucas, 1977) movie and its sequels. Lucas borrowed from Tolkien and some other popular sources like Flash Gordon (Comic and Film serial) and used the plot structure laid out by Campbell as a blueprint for his movie. Today, Lucas' original Star Wars trilogy serves as the most perfect example of a plot pattern of the hero's journey.

However, within the framework of literary criticism, many variations on plot theory exist. Over the decades scholars have come up with different plot theories and different conclusions. The momomyth may be the most popular, but it is by no means the only theory of narrative structure. Though theories of narrative structure may seem to diverge from Campbell's monomyth, they can be integrated into its psychological framework. Many of these theories rely on concepts like Jungian archetypes, and they only differ as to the number and names of steps in plot sequencing. Such variance can be understood as contextual perceptions of Campbell's vaguely defined "Road of Trials".

Christopher Booker researched the matter for thirty-four years before publishing his work on the theory of *The Seven Basic Plots* (2004). According to his Jungian-influenced analysis, there is a meta-plot that divides any story into five stages and basically comes as a stripped down version of the hero's journey. With this analysis, he is not far away from Campbell. The Basic Plots however are imperatives like "Overcoming the Monster", "Rags to Riches", "The Quest", etc. that may be well illustrated with examples of world literature and film (like Beowulf, Cinderella, The Wonderful Wizard of Oz). Much earlier in 1895, the French writer Georges Polti (1895) came up with a list of thirty-six plausible plots from supplication, pursuit, disaster and revolt all the way to remorse, recovery of a lost one and loss of loved ones. On the other hand, the stages of a night journey or a hero's journey are reminiscent of the thirty-one functions in Vladimir Propp's theory on the *Morphology of the Folk Tale* (1958). As a structuralist, Propp broke up Russian fairy tales into sections and came up with individual functions that occur repeatedly. These range from absentation, interdiction and trickery, mediation, pursuit and rescue all the way to punishment and wedding. Without sullying the basic concepts underlying the monomyth, such theoretical variations could be utilized to design narrative-psychological video games.

THE COGNITIVE UNCONSCIOUS AS CULPRIT

From time immemorial, humans have speculated about the universe within—the nature of consciousness and the human mind. Artifacts such as prehistoric cave pictures, calendars, and stone circles can be understood as records of the human search for meaning and the connections between humans and gods. The universal science of astrology may be understood as a sophisticated system for examining the universe within from the standpoint of the universal bodies "out there".

So-called "pre-scientific" psychology may be traced To Greece. Until the sixth century B. C., the Greeks borrowed much of their culture from Egypt, Mesopotamia, and neighboring countries that had developed an extensive ontology encoded in symbols. "But from the sixth to the fourth centuries [the Greeks] generated a stupendous body of new and distinctive cultural materials. (Hunt, Morton M., 1993, pp. 11-33) They asked such psychological questions as: What is mind? What is Soul? How are mind and body connected? Is human nature the product of inborn tendencies or of experience and upbringing?

How does perception work? Does the mind rule emotions, or vice versa? (Hunt, pp. 6-7) So, the search for answers about the universe within is longstanding.

But, in 1912, John B. Watson changed the study of psychology radically. Watson rejected all conjectures about invisible mental processes, and began to formulate a new psychology based entirely on observable behavior. Thus Behaviorism was born and has persisted for a century. Though its principles have been invalidated, it persists in the cultural unconscious and impedes more realistic approaches to cognition.

Freud vs. Jung

It remained to the pioneers of psychoanalysis—Sigmund Freud and Carl Jung—to reinstate study of the unconscious indirectly through analysis of dreams. Both employed much more ancient principles of psychology than Behaviorists. However, their theories about the nature and dynamics of the universe within varied significantly. Obviously, this chapter cannot delve deeply into these theoretical differences, but it may be stipulated that Freud viewed the collective unconscious as a dangerous culprit, whereas Jung viewed it as a source of meaning, healing, and ultimate individuation. In particular, Jung employed the ancient psychological-ontological symbolism in his compensatory analysis of dreams.

In psychological terms, the Jungian collective unconscious is not negative. As Jung explains:

The unconscious is not a demonic monster, but a thing of nature that is perfectly neutral as far as moral sense, aesthetic taste and intellectual judgments go…the overwhelming of consciousness by the unconscious—is most likely to occur when the unconscious is excluded from life by repressions, or is misunderstood and depreciated…It is always helpful, when we set out to interpret a dream, to ask: What conscious attitude does it compensate?" (Jung, 1933, p 17)

The Jungian understanding of the unconscious as revealed in dreams is that:

Dreams give information about the secrets of the inner life and reveal to the dreamer hidden factors of his personality. As long as these are undiscovered, they disturb his waking life and betray themselves only in the form of symptoms. This means that we cannot effectively treat the patient from the side of consciousness alone, but must bring about a change in and through the unconscious." (Jung, 1933, p 16)

The Freudian view of the collective unconscious—the Id—was well expressed in the 1956 film, the *Forbidden Planet*, in which the unconscious stars as culprit and becomes the main protagonist in the progression of the story plot. The movie is loosely based on William Shakespeare's The Tempest. The screenwriters were very imaginative and came up with an exciting science fiction setting. Spaceship Commander Adams and his crew are sent to faraway planet Altair-4 to find out what happened to a colony of settlers. They find two survivors, Dr. Edward Morbius and his daughter Altaira/Alta living in a kind of paradise that was created by Morbius. The scientist was able to use secrets from the Krell, a long-lost civilization that once inhabited the planet. The crew of the spaceship is not welcome and soon after their arrival, the crew faces an invisible force that puts them all in danger. Morbius calls this force: the Id.

Captain Adams: *What is the Id?*
Morbius: *It is an obsolete term. I am afraid once used to describe the elementary base of the subconscious mind.*

Captain Adams: *Monsters from the Id? – Monsters from the subconscious. Of course, that's what Doc meant. – Morbius! A big machine, 8000 cubic miles of Kleister relais, enough power for a whole population of creative geniuses, operated by remote control! Morbius! Operated by the electro-magnetic impulses of individual Krell brains.*

Morbius: *To what purpose?*

Captain Adams: *In return that ultimate machine would instantaneously point silent matter to any planet of the universe. In any shape or color they might imagine. For any purpose! Morbius! Creation by mere thought.*

Morbius: *Why haven't I seen this all along?*

Captain Adams: *But like you the Krell forgot one deadly danger: Their own subconscious hate and lust for destruction.*

Morbius: *The Beast. The mindless primitive. Even the Krell must have evolved from that beginning.*

Captain Adams: *And so those mindless beasts of the subconscious had access to a machine that could never be shut down. The secret devil of every soul of the planet all set free at once to loot and maim - and take revenge, Morbius, and kill! (Forbidden Planet, Nayfack & Wilcox, 1956, transcribed key scene)*

Indeed, the Invisible Id-Monster is a great and unexpected culprit in this movie. Its invisible presence and intrinsic threat is skillfully orchestrated, and its appearance in the crossfire of lasers is masterfully managed. The monster is never fully shown. Instead, spectators have to imagine how it appears. Sounds and music are very much responsible for creating a creepy feeling. Bebe Barron, the sound designer was told many times that her music for the Id sounds just like dreams people have had. "We were expressing our subconscious", she said in an interview. The Id in this case is modeled after Sigmund Freud's Id (German original: "Es") (Freud, 1923). The Id in Freud's theory is part of the unconscious. This unconscious is divided into the Superego and the Id. While as the Superego represents conscience, the Id represents instincts. The Id-monster therefore may represent the basic instincts of the creators of the sophisticated machine. If we apply this to Morbius who used the machine for creating a sort of paradise for him and his daughter, the Id may show his personal unconscious, which is worrying about his daughter, trying to protect her from the all-male crew and save his created paradise. But there is a more interesting layer of unconsciousness because the original creators of the thought machine were the Krell, a technologically advanced alien species. The machine represents all that's left from the Krell. It seems that while the Krell were using the machine to create by mere thought, they were overcome by their collective unconscious that was inadvertently also fed into the machine. According to Jung, the collective unconscious is the deepest level of the psyche. It contains all inherited psychic structures and archetypal experiences. The collective unconscious contains material of an entire species rather than of an individual. Captain Adams concludes that this collective unconscious is responsible for the destruction of the Krell culture. Thoughts became real and were instantly manifested. These unconscious thought patterns destroyed their creators—a whole species. The unconscious was the culprit.

As mentioned above, both Freud and Jung employed ancient symbolism in order to interpret dreams, so this somewhat forgotten movie seems to employ not only the well known narrative structure of the monomyth but enriches the psychological framework with archetypes like the innocent, anima, shadow, over-protective father, alter ego and creature (tiger) tamed by the virgin (as in medieval myth a unicorn only can be tamed by a virgin). The film is unique in its literal use of the collective unconscious as adversary and culprit. The invisible monster or force that turns out to be not only the evil side of the guardian

Morbius but also—in many respects—a model for science fiction movies to come: Stanley Kubrick's 2001: A Space Odyssey (Kubrick, 1968), Star Wars (Kurtz & Lucas, 1977) and the TV series Star Trek: the Original Series (Roddenberry, 1966), and many sequels and other movies of this genre thereafter.

Christopher Vogler's Stereotypical Adaptation of the Monomyth

It goes without saying that study of unconscious cognitive dimensions is problematic, so reducing complex metaphysics and subjective interpretation to stereotypes for use in film and video games is understandable.

While C.G. Jung set the psychological foundations and Joseph Campbell laid out the story pattern of the Hero's Journey, Christopher Vogler adapted this journey, reduced it, and standardized it for screenwriting. First, Vogler used Campbell's work to create the now-legendary 7-page company memo for Hollywood screenwriters, A Practical Guide to The Hero with a Thousand Faces (1985). This memo impressed Disney Studios so much, as we will see in the next paragraph. Later, Vogler expanded his summary of Campbell's theory in the book The Writer's Journey (1992). This text gave Hollywood a blueprint devoid of depth psychology, which it keeps using and reusing in most of its productions.

In his memo from 1985, Vogler introduces Campbell as a Jungian scholar of utmost importance: "Mythographer Joseph Campbell wrote what many consider to be the most influential book of the 20th century, *The Hero With a Thousand Faces*. The ideas in his book are often described as Jungian. The book is based on Jung's idea of the "archetypes," constantly repeating characters that occur in the dreams of all people and the myths of all cultures." (1985) Vogler goes on to say:

Jung believes that these archetypes are reflections of the human mind – that our minds divide themselves into these characters to play out the drama of our lives. The repeating characters of the hero myth, such as the young hero, the wise old man, the shape-shifting woman, and the shadowy nemesis, are identical with the archetypes of the human mind, as shown in dreams. That's why myths, and stories constructed on the mythological model, are always psychologically true. Such stories are true models of the workings of the human mind, true maps of the psyche. They are psychologically valid and realistic even when they portray fantastic, impossible, unreal events. (Vogler, 1985)

Vogler is perhaps the most influential force for integrating psychological structure into the film and game industries. For practical, industry examples of mythic stages in story development, Vogler emphasizes Star Wars made by George Lucas in 1977. There are two references to the movie E.T. the Extra-Terrestrial (Spielberg, 1982), one reference each to The Wonderful Wizard of Oz (Le Roy & Fleming, 1939), Casablanca (Wallis & Curtiz, 1942) and Witness for the Prosecution (1957). All other examples were added later on in extended versions or book versions.

Ultimately Vogler defines twelve stages of the Hero's Journey. First the story has to introduce the ordinary world (1) where the hero lives. He uses Dorothy's Kansas in the Wonderful Wizard of Oz and Planet Tattoine of Star Wars as examples. Then it is the call for adventure (2) in which the main character is presented with a problem, a challenge. That is the tornado in the Wizard of Oz and R2D2's cryptic message in Star Wars. Best represented maybe by the arrival of Gandalf in The Hobbit. Next is the refusal of the quest (3). The hero is reluctant and balks at the threshold of adventure. In Star Wars, Luke Skywalker doesn't want to take on the quest until he realizes that his aunt and uncle were killed by the emperor's troops. This continues with meeting the Mentor (4). The hero is encouraged by a wise figure. It is Gandalf in The Hobbit and Obi Wan Kenobi in Star Wars. That is the end of the first act.

In his second act, Vogler discusses crossing the threshold (5), the hero's entry into the special world from which the story is generated. In the Wonderful Wizard of Oz, Dorothy set off on the yellow brick road. Then it is Test, Allies and Enemies (6), which means the hero is forced to find allies and make enemies and pass challenges. In Star Wars, Luke Skywalker finds an ally in rebel pilot Han Solo and lots of enemies in the representatives of the Galactic Empire. In the Wonderful Wizard of Oz Dorothy is tested by the Tin, Woodman, Scarecrow and the lion, before they become allies. Then the hero reaches the Innermost Cave (the Approach) (7). He comes to a most dangerous place, often deep underground, where a Holy Grail or a fight with a dragon awaits. In Star Wars, Luke and his allies get sucked into the Death Star where they have to rescue Princess Leia. The Supreme Ordeal (8) is the place where the hero touches rock bottom. He faces death in a mostly hopeless situation and has to overcome it. This is likely the most important stage of the journey for bonding the viewers or readers with the hero. The hero may be literally brought back from death, which lets the public emotionally identify with him. In The Wonderful Wizard of Oz it is the death of the wicked witch. In Star Wars it is the scene when the Death Star gets blown up. Vogler calls the next stage The Hero seizes the Sword (9). The hero has survived, slain the dragon or monster. He now takes possession of the treasure. The sword may also be a metaphor for gaining knowledge or experience or rescue of a loved woman or man. This brings the main part of the story or second act to an end – conclusion.

The next stage leads into the last and short third act. The Road Back (10) may not be the quiet walk back home wished for. Often the hero is still pursued by the forces he has taken the treasure or elixir from. In Star Wars, Luke and his allies escape with Princess Leia from the exploding Death Star, but they are still being chased. The Resurrection (11) means that the hero finally escapes from the special world of his adventure. Often there is a replay of some of the Supreme Ordeal. The hero is transformed into a new being. And finally, there is the last stage, Return with the Elixir (12) that closes the circle of the story. The hero returns to his ordinary world. However, he needs to bring back something, the elixir or a treasure, just to make the whole adventure meaningful. Sometimes it is knowledge or experience or a loved one. If the hero didn't achieve the goal of the adventure, he would be doomed to repeat the whole ordeal.

Vogler's adaptation of the psychological journey must necessarily have strong impact on viewers at unconscious levels. However, its emphasis is superficial—based on simple characterizations, choices, and consequences. Obviously, these are enjoyable, valuable, and influential as entertainment, but they do not address contextual self-realization (Individuation) or even contextual (individual oriented) story-telling. Although Vogler has great respect for Campbell, the depth psychology underlying Campbell's hero journey does not translate to Vogler's stereotype.

Joseph Campbell's Hero Journey

Over time, Campbell changed the names of story levels, and this has become a source of confusion to film and game writers. What they do not realize is that the journey is contextual and can be applied—almost infinitely—to unique individuals and cultures. At their base, story levels are symbolic representations of psychological evolution—as represented by the process of Initiation in the world's Mystery Schools—including growth cycles that can be symbolized with planetary seasons and cosmic revolutions. This initiation process is analogous with the achievement of increasingly difficult levels in game design. In each case, details are not as important as understanding the overview. Campbell's seventeen stages of the journey are not absolute, but they provide a good beginning for psychological depth design. The names of the various stages should not be understood simply as overt sequence. Rather, they are symbolic of deeper psychological conflicts that—applied to game levels—may be contextualized (personalized). Following is a summary of the journey:

The mythological hero, setting forth from his common-day hut or castle, is lured, carried away, or else voluntarily proceeds, to the threshold of adventure. There he encounters a shadow presence that guards the passage. The hero may defeat or conciliate this power and go alive into the kingdom of the dark (brother-battle, dragon-battle; offering, charm), or be slain by the opponent and descend in death (dismemberment, crucifixion). Beyond the threshold, then, the hero journeys through a world of unfamiliar yet strangely intimate forces, some of which severely threaten him (tests), some of which give magical aid (helpers). When he arrives at the nadir of the mythological round, he undergoes a supreme ordeal and gains his reward. The triumph may be represented as the hero's sexual union with the goddess-mother of the world (sacred marriage), his recognition by the father-creator (father atonement), his own divinization (apotheosis), or—if the powers have remained unfriendly to him—his theft of the boon he came to gain (bride-theft, fire-theft); intrinsically it is an expansion of consciousness and therewith of being (illumination, transfiguration, freedom). The final work is that of the return. If the powers have blessed the hero, he now sets forth under their protection (emissary); if not, he flees and is pursued (transformation flight, obstacle flight). At the return threshold the transcendental powers must remain behind; the hero re-emerges from the kingdom of dread (return, resurrection). The boon that he brings restores the world (elixir). (Campbell 1949, p. 227 – 228)

His journey is structured as an Aristotelian play of three acts. The first act is called "The Departure". It features five stages – right away The Call for Adventure (I), The Refusal of the Call (II), Supernatural Aid (III), Crossing of the first Threshold (IV) and the Belly of the Whale (V). The start in the Ordinary World falls together with the Call for Adventure. The stage Meeting with the Mentor had a more magical touch as Supernatural Aid. Flexibility in sequencing and scene variations should be adjusted to contextual audiences (like target groups) rather than attempting to stereotype the story for all audiences.

The second act titled "Initiation" consists of The Road of Trials (VI), The Meeting with the Goddess (VII), Woman as the Temptress (VIII), Atonement with the Father (IX), Apotheosis (X) and The Ultimate Boon (XI).

The third act titled "Return" has considerably more stages. The Refusal of the Return (XII), The Magic Flight (XIII), Rescue from Without (XIV), The Crossing of the Return Threshold (XV), Master of the Two Worlds (XVI) and Freedom to live (XVII). All of these stages

Campbell's journey relies much more on his character's psychology than Vogler's, which emphasizes a simplified character arc. However, the character arc has produced a primary tool for media design.

Applications in Film and Video Games

Walt Disney Studios, as a bridge between films, animations and games was particularly impressed by Vogler's standardization. Vogler's seven-page memo on the hero's journey (1985) was copied, faxed and distributed within the studios. In 1988, the head of Disney asked Vogler to do research and development work for the animation movie, The Lion King. Vogler subsequently spent some years working on The Lion King (Hahn & Allers, 1994) and many other projects with Disney's Feature Animation division. The Lion King is a very good example for meticulously emulating the structure of the twelve hero stages, and it was one of the most successful movies produced by the Disney animation division, which seemed proof enough for Vogler's reduced concept of Campbell's theory.

Hollywood's relentless adoption of the hero's journey translated directly to narrative game structure, especially RPGs (Role Playing Games) like the *Final Fantasy* and the *Fire Emblem* series as well as Action and Shooter Games. Campbell, Tolkien, the Star Wars movie and Vogler played an important developmental role as catalysts for the structuring of narrative videogames.

However, use of archetypes in movies and games often means that Jungian archetypes get reduced to stereotypes. Whereas Campbell in his involvement with myths of different cultures and modern epics like *Star Wars* showed that the archetypal energies present themselves within the drama, due to the inflexibility of Vogler's template, the importance of the archetypes is weakened and they become concretized stereotypes. The dynamics of the archetypes get lost. The individual archetype becomes an image perpetuated with no change, a reduced and rigid imprint. Video game spaces attempt to apply the stereotype only to end up with a weak image, a "deadened archetype" void of its complex vibrancy and voice. The depth of the archetypal impulses is reduced to a convenient Hollywood package to be unfortunately delivered dead upon arrival. In such cases "the unconscious as the culprit" is unable to present itself.

Game experts that have realized the link between Jung's archetypes, Campbell's journey of a hero, and narrative video games, have been scarce. Authors, Andrew Rollings and Ernest Adams (2003), Lee Sheldon (2004), and Andrew Glassner (2004) point out this link in a few paragraphs in their articles. Sheldon is the only author that introduces Jung and Campbell together as background for storytelling in games and talks of symbolism as being used to invoke emotions and reactions in players. Glassner recounts Campbell's "twelve-step structure" which in fact is Vogler's reduced version of the hero's journey, but he does this well and provides good insight into other narrative tools such as character "premise". In contrast, Bob Bates (2004, p.267f) points out that video game production is a team project that—presumably—requires strict rules of development in order to stay focused. Therefore, the complexities of depth psychology have received less attention from the game design community. There are some exceptions, which will be looked at later.

Unfortunately, there does not seem to be a great deal of analytical thinking about archetypes and plot in video game development. Instead, the journey of a hero is presented as a convenient manual for storytelling in games. Adams and Glassner do a great job in describing Campbell's model through all of the segments in a hero's story (Rollings & Adams, 2003; Glassner, 2004). However, like Glassner, Adams does not use Campbell's writing other than in one introductory quote. Instead, he emphasizes Christopher Vogler's reduced version for screenwriting of movies. Adams says, Campbell's book is heavy going and may be overkill except for the most story-intensive games. Adams quotes Campbell once:

Whether we listen with aloof amusement to [a] ... witch doctor of the Congo, or read with cultivated rapture thin translations from the sonnets of the mystic Lao tse; now and again crack the hard nutshell of an argument of Aquinas, or catch suddenly the shining meaning of [an] ... Eskimo fairytale: it will always be the one, shape shifting yet marvelously constant story that we find, together with a challengingly persistent suggestion of more remaining to be experienced than will even be known or told. (Campbell, 1949)

Subsequently, Adams goes step-by-step through Vogler's journey of a hero. As examples Adams often uses the game Half-Life (1998) and enhances it with many other game examples of different genres. Any psychological game context is often restricted to a preamble that images the ordinary world as seen in the non-interactive opening scene such as Gordon Freeman riding the monorail to work at the beginning of Half-Life. Often, such a preamble is passed over by the player because s/he cannot interact with the character(s). A similar well-narrated opening scene is featured by the game *Red Dead Redemption* (Rockstar, 2011) where the main character, John Marston, is transferred to the Wild West desert town Armadillo via public steam train and listens in on conversations of fellow travelers. Adams suggests that games often use the ordinary world to foreshadow events. (In Jungian terms, foreshadowing would be like a "prospective" dream.)

The various Star Wars games [...] that feature the Death Star often use this technique. The Death Star appears as part of the background graphics a couple of levels before the player is called upon to destroy it. As soon as it appears, ominously hanging in the distance like a small moon, the player knows that sooner or later he will be there. (Rollings and Adams, 2003, p. 97)

The Call to Adventure is often a fairly simple task in games. The Super Mario games use the trope of rescuing the princess as call to adventure. The princess gets kidnapped in broad daylight. The hero, Mario, pursues and starts the adventure that he intends to end successfully with rescue. Or pursuit can be a more complex matter where the hero has to leave his real world and literally enter another world like Britannica in *Ultima VII* (Origin Systems, 1992) via an object like the Obelisk (departure).

Furthermore Adams describes the circular journey story model as a story vehicle and then he debates the divide between gameplay and narrative. He states that all the scenes that are non-interactive are narrative while as all the interactive scenes are non-narrative. Such arbitrary division cannot be supported. With improved technology, there are many mixed forms now where interaction goes on while story information gets delivered to the player at the same time. And the world itself, in which the player's avatar resides, is constructed as a narrative environment that reveals important information to the player. Adams has a view of narrative that is naïve and devoid of any psychology.

The raison d'être of all computer gaming is interactivity: giving the player something to do that he cannot do in the real world. The trick, then, is to provide enough narrative to create the game world and motivate the player, but not so much as to inhibit his freedom to meet the game's challenges in his own way. (Rollings and Adams, 2003, p. 115)

In later books about the fundamentals of game design, Adams and Rollings concentrate much more on the mechanics of games and omit discussions of plot structures of narration in games. This may be the result of the disappearance of classical adventure games. Only a couple of reference to Campbell remain. (Adams & Rollings, 2007, p. 207) and (2010, p. 181). In what has been termed the Luddite view of game narrative, dramatic structure is perceived as simply linear. The reference suggests that many adventure games use the journey and make it a linear story.

Without realizing it, in pointing out that Interactivity and good story can be bound together, Adams and Rollings (2003, p. 119) are referring to dramatic structure that allows for greater depth in psychological storytelling. They refer to Star Trek's idea of a Holodeck as a latent implementation of reenactments of our desires and dreams. This brings up an entire new field of research in cognitive psychology that has traced neural energy patterns resulting from experience. In this context, all experience is virtual, and it is perceived as real. It seems that this idea of transforming a fictional story into a realistic virtual experience becomes frames of the cognitive unconscious. (Lakoff, George, 2008)

The Unconscious as Culprit

There is an abundance of nightmarish monsters in videogames. They appear as single enemies or come in hordes. They lurk, they are sneaky, and they sometimes surprise and scare the player. Quite often they are oversized and come as characters for a boss battle. In videogames, a boss is a significant enemy that is controlled by the computer. Boss battles are the climax of a particular section of a game or the endgame. The bosses are mostly monsters that endure a lot more damage than any other character in a game. They usually assume an intimidating form, and they are well equipped as culprit/adversaries for the initiatory test at the end of a game level. They may grow in size and change form. Bosses are mostly Id monsters.

Often, due to intensive psychological immersion on the part of the player, this boss battle can represent a psychological dissociation which tends to be a negative experience. The term dissociation describes a wide array of experiences ranging from a mild detachment from immediate surroundings to a more severe detachment from physical and emotional experience. For our present purposes, the major characteristic of all dissociative phenomena involves a detachment from reality that accommodates varied maladaptive mental constructions of an individual's natural imaginative capacity. In other words, these potentially "transcendent" virtual experiences become nightmares.

As an interesting example for dissociation of consciousness, Jung (1964, p.7) suggests the fictional example of Dr. Jekyll and Mr. Hyde from the 1931 movie. In dreams, the physical transformation of such a character is in reality a symbolic change of the inner psychic state. According to Jung, anthropologists refer to "the loss of a soul" as the most common mental derangement of so-called primitive cultures. But the psychological potentials of such challenges as boss battles and their opportunities to change the experience from culprit to Mentor are ignored. Visually, it is much easier to convey shallow and meaningless imagery than to pursue deeper meaning.

An example of game experience with more psychological depth and, therefore, more positive potential is the genre known as god games that explore simple ethical decisions and let the player develop the main character (avatar) into a good or a bad role. Game designer Peter Molyneaux is well known for his game Black and White (2001), in which the player acts from a top-down perspective and arranges world objects and characters by means of a big oversized (godlike) hand. The player manages a protagonsit that shows slow physical changes. The player morphs him eventually from a regular animal form of monkey, cow, lion and polar bear into either a good creature or an oversized bad monster. Dissociation of Consciousness is initiated by the player's decisions and the main character grows into either a likeable or an unlikeable personality without scruples.

Consciousness is a very recent acquisition of nature, and it is still in an "experimental" state. (Jung 1964, p.6)

While Molyneaux intentionally experiments with split psyche in these characters from Black & White, when designing fantasy figures other game character designers rely on invoking instincts without caring about cognitive dynamics. This tends to the result of unconscious as culprit. The game developer community is very diverse, with many skilled and well-educated game developers and many specialized artists. Among them are many graphic game artists who may not be aware of archetypes and their psychological foundation. Often they do not have that much insight into narrative story patterns. Besides their obsession for games, they developed a love for drawing and try to make a living with creating characters for fantasy stories. Mainly they are modeling fantasy figures according to their gut feelings.

The result is a glut of stereotypical characters, elves, trolls, orks, monsters and horror characters with similar or the same attributes such as oversized horns and antlers or paws and claws or spikes and fur that could be the substance of nightmares. This is not necessarily evidence of a great deal of ingenuity. On the other hand, these Z-Brush Monsters seem to point to a subconscious as culprit. They are nightmarish without awareness on the part of artists nor agency on the part of game players.

This state of affairs is amplified with software that requires little skill and is available to many. *ZBrush* is a very popular software for creating 3d models of digital characters, monsters, and objects for games and animation film. Artists love to put their creations on the Internet, particularly as speed paintings and speed sculpting movies that are accessible to anyone via Youtube. There are many ZBrush tutorials out there where game aficionados can learn how to sculpt and texture a detailed monster. It always seems that the aim of those visual arts tutorials is to create a monster. One of these online courses (Fabrizio Bortolussi) states that throughout a series of lessons, the new artist will learn to "cover all aspects of designing a scary creature within ZBrush using alternative techniques." Further the tutor announces that the students "will see some examples of scary imagery as well as a sneak peek of an upcoming short film which is characterized by the word "fear"." At this point Bortolussi provides some technical details and ends with the prospect of texturing the monster "using just simple brushes and alphas and adding some quick fur" (Bortolussi, 2012).

Another classic 3d modeling task for a tutorial is the female antagonist in form of a centaur. The tutorial by Peter Minister illustrates the trend. The model demonstrates creation of the "monster" using the standard shape of a centaur and enhancing the female human part of the figure with a second bottom, attractive breasts, tattoos, jewelry and ornaments and a huge gold fight axe. The stereotypical Bikini-armor is there too. Consequently, she holds the decapitated head of an ugly troll in her other hand presumably alluding to the mythical Judith. (Minister, 2014).

The Australian resource site BadKing specializes in free ZBrush tutorials, 3D modeling, insert multi mesh brushes, alpha maps, concept art and more. Again this is a group of professional artists that work in the videogame, feature film, advertising and publishing industries. Over a few years, BadKing has managed to create a fair-size community of artists and novices. Upon request of the community, in 2014, BadKing created a Monster Parts Brush Set for the ZBrush software and pronounced it "the ultimate organic brush pack complete with dozens of monster parts." The twist was that the community was asked to chip in and submit suggestions for "the BIGGEST and BADDEST FREE Monster Brush Set EVER!!!" The response by the community was great. There were plenty of submissions. Today, the Monster pack is available for download. The editors of BadKing had to divide the pack into downloads for arms, legs, ears, torsos, heads, wings, teeth and horns. A sample showcase can be seen on the website. It features monster body parts designed by individual artists. An approach with more depth might include the classical idea of the symbolism imbedded in the human body. Ultimately the symbolism leads to the alchemical principle of correspondence, "As it is above, so it is below." This principle is fundamental to depth psychology as it was understood both in ancient and modern times.

Instead, artists and designers go no further than generating stereotypical images of 3D-monster-parts that support the culprit and have no understanding of psychological significance. The community-made package is teeming with horns, all looking rather similar, even if they differ in size and thickness. There is also an abundance of chicken or turkey legs, often with oversized thighs. Pig legs with pig trotters or devil's feet with two toes are very popular, and so are cow legs. The package features some short and spiky tails on human-like backbones and feet and hands with only three digits each. Claws of crabs or lobsters are quite popular; they come oversized and look rather dangerous. Most of the monster heads resemble animals like a bull turning into a Minotaur, a prehistoric tiger with saber teeth, or a giant terrifying bear. Skeletal bones often are very prominent or the monster comes with a practically bare skull. Some of the creature parts seem to be almost bare skeletons from spiny creatures with bony arms or legs. The teeth mostly refer to animals, to tigers, bears, snakes, piranhas and sharks. Or they refer to the imagery of bats and vampires and have spiky nail-like teeth. Ears can be just a little deformed like peaky elves ears, or they can take on completely different shapes not exactly recognizable as ears anymore. Female torsos seem to be preferred for extensions like wings and tails. Furthermore the packages contain sets of antlers, devil heads with goat horns, scary alien monster heads with no eyes--only a big mouth with scary spiky teeth (maybe referring to H.R. Giger's creatures), and several sets with crustacean limbs and oversized insect-like parts. (BadKing, 2013-14) It is all there, right out of nightmares, a mental imprint of archaic images with different sets that are made by different community artists and look very much alike. There is not a great variation in the depiction of a monster. The imagination is vague, a minimally enhanced reflection of the culprit as such mythical monsters as Minotaur, centaur, giant snake, squid flying fire-dragon, and so forth.

New Trends in Understanding the Potentials of a Benign Unconscious

But there are and have been developers that are well aware of the psychology of archetypes. One of the most brilliant examples is game designer *Tim Schafer* who was inspired by a university course on *C.G. Jung* and says that he formed his game *Psychonauts* (Double Fine Productions, 2005) after his dreams. It features the Unconscious as game hub for his main character Raz, a Psychonaut-in-training, who can enter minds of several people with their own secret memories, nightmares and demons and find out about their specific mental problem. By definition, a psychonaut is a person who explores activities by which altered states of consciousness are induced and utilized for spiritual purposes or exploration of human condition in order to gain deeper insights into the mind (Jünger, 1970). Ernst Jünger coined the term in the 1970s when he described his friend Arthur Heffter after experimenting with entheogenic drugs. Raz, short for Razputin, enters the collective unconscious via machines: a brain tumbler or a PSI Popper Generator. The first time Razputin enters the collective unconscious hub, he can only enter his own mind from there. All other doors are locked. But as the game progresses, one by one, other doors open up, leading to more worlds. Upon entering the door to his mind, Raz finds himself in a dreamlike world, a dark clearing covered in thick fog. There is a caravan where it turns out Raz was once born. When he enters the caravan he gets stuck in an egg-like glitch (disturbance). It seems the caravan represents the womb. He manages to punch his way out of there. Outside he spots a bunny-like creature that emits hearts. He eventually follows the cute thing and comes to a different clearing where a monster with glowing eyes awaits him. Fortunately he gets pulled back to the real world at that point. This may be as analogy to waking up suddenly from a dream.

In an interview, Schafer refers to the psychology class on Jung as motivation for his character walking around in other characters minds. He also explains that he used the premise as a fun way of making a sandbox to develop a game in:

Taking this example of Psychonauts, where you're a young psychic kid, and you're going into people's heads, it's that whole idea of making a fun sandbox to work in. Because you can go into anyone's head, so each level of the game can be as different as the characters in the world. We have a character who's obsessed with black velvet art, and you go into his world, and his entire world is made of black velvet. It's a radically different style than the conspiracy theory nut, whose whole mind is literally a web of streets, spreading out from his house in the center, like concentric circles of conspiracy all around him. His mental state is represented by the level design, so that the actual world that he's in expresses his personality. (Pearce, 2003)

Later on in the game, Raz comes back to face his monster, now equipped and better prepared. But after firing the first shot from his PSI blaster, the monster disappears. Instead he finds a new clearing (memory to face) with a huge tower of thorns rising from the fog. On top of the tower there seems to be his friend strapped to a chair and threatened by a dentist who wants to remove his brain. Raz tries to climb the tower but cannot get to the very top. Instead he has to leave for the real world again for some levitation training that might enable him to get to the top. The game continues this way as if Raz has to wake up from his dreams (or memories) in crucial moments and face some more braining (training) in the real world to ready him for the challenge. It seems as if he has to complete some dream work that enables him to progress through the game. Raz also has to face some more of his fears. For instance he is afraid of large bodies of water due to a curse on his family. Again, a bathtub in an earlier level symbolizes this. The strongest metaphor is the debraining of the bodies by coach Oleander who uses the brains of his students for experiments and naturally wants to take over the world (which is intended to be as much a pun on games as a plot). Raz is in constant fear of loosing his abilities (brain) and needs to save his friends, some having already lost their brains. These brains reappear in brain tank machines and engage Raz in fights. Another interesting topic shows up after Raz defeats the brain tank with coach Oleander's brain. The victory comes at the loss of his brain, so Raz puts his own brain and Oleander's brain in a tank and mixes the psyches. Thus Raz's childhood memories get mixed together with Oleander's childhood memories of his cruel father's butcher shop. Raz has to face these memories in personification of the two psychopathic fathers. After they are defeated and thrown into the meat-grinder, they emerge as a grotesque two-headed monster. At that point Raz's real father shows up and gives him special powers that enable him to defeat that monster. There is a good ending with everyone in the camp being recranialized.

Another striking example is Schafer's game, *Grim Fandango* (LucasArts, 1998) that was remastered for publication on PS4 and PC (Double Fine Productions, 2015). Schafer creates the Land of the Dead populated with skeletal characters (calacas); through which recently departed souls must travel before they reach their final destination, the Ninth Underworld. Characters and setting are inspired by Aztec and Mexican folklore as well as by themes of film noir and Greek mythology. The dark comedy's irony is always around the corner. The story follows travel agent "Manny" Calavera as he attempts to save "Meche" Colomar, a newly arrived but virtuous female soul, during her long journey. Here we literally have Jung's night journey that takes place in an in-between-world of reality and afterlife. Manny is the ferryman that symbolizes Charon of Greek mythology who ferries the dead across the river Styx--the boundary between earth and underworld (Hades). Styx circumflows Hades nine times. Manny is a travel agent that sends the souls across the land of the dead. Good deeds in life are rewarded by access to better travel packages. The best ticket lands the player on the Number Nine, a train that takes four minutes to reach the gate to the Ninth Underworld. But there are those that have to go by foot. It takes them a four-year journey through the underworld to reach The Land of Eternal Rest that is to be found in the Ninth Underworld.

Schafer's adventure game exemplifies a view of the unconscious as more than culprit. It combines Aztec beliefs of the afterlife and the underworld Mictlan as cultural background. The Aztec underworld Mictlan apparently consisted of nine distinct levels. And the journey from the first level to the ninth took four years. Aztec mythology even knew a psychopomp in the form of fire god Xolotl that escorts the newly deceased souls from real life to afterlife (Dundes, 1965; Wolinsky, 2015). Psychopomps exist in other culture's myths. Examples are Charon in Greek and Anubis in Egyptian mythology. Manny Calavera is a rather literal interpretation of Xolotl who simply provides safe passage for the deceased and does not have the task to judge them. Jungian psychology sees a psychopomp as a mediator between the unconscious and conscious realms. In dreams he is personified as a wise man or woman, or he can be a helpful animal, even a shaman. Main character Manny Calavera plays exactly the role of such a mediator. In interviews with Celia Pearce (2003) and Wolinsky (2015) Schafer says that he was very influenced by his fascination with folklore that stemmed from an anthropology class he took at the University of California Berkeley. He says, "Folklore is such a great place to mine for ideas and stories. There's such a rich body of work that people have, for no commercial reason, dragged from generation to generation, so it obviously resonates with people." (Pearce 2003)

While sitting in a psychology class, Schafer was intrigued with the mythical four-year journey of the soul. Later on when he was developing the idea for Grim Fandango, Schafer recognized that this four-year journey in the Mictlan afterlife could indeed be a fitting premise or stage for his adventure game.

Then I thought, what role would a person want to play in a Day of the Dead scenario? You'd want to be the grim reaper himself. That's how Manny got his job. Then I imagined him picking up people in the land of the living and bringing them to the land of the dead, like he's really just a glorified limo or taxi driver. So the idea came of Manny having this really mundane job that looks glamorous because he has the robe and the scythe, but really, he's just punching the clock. (Evenson, 1998)

Schafer combines Campbell's mentor with Jung's wise man to create the protagonist, Manny, as a hero archetype. As the grim reaper, death, Manny seems to be rather likable and the player starts identifying with him. This is an important spin on the archetype because usually Death is hard to identify with, and immersion of a player in a game depends on depth of immersion. (Implicitly, degree of immersion represents degree of immersion into unconscious dimensions). Anyway, as soon as the player is ready to accept the character, it turns out that the grim reaper is nothing more than a cab driver that is imprisoned in his role and can't escape his mundane job. This is the opposite of what is usually expected of a hero. In this respect the story adheres more closely to Jung's concept of the night journey where we navigate through unknown territory of the dark side of life. This is emphasized by the fact that Schafer was also inspired by film noir. He recounts the initial connection of the two themes found in Mexican folklore where the dead were buried with two bags of gold to be used in the afterlife. One bag was put on their chest, the other one was hidden somewhere in the coffin. If the first bag gets stolen, the dead could still buy his way through afterlife with the second hidden bag. This suggestion of a criminal element led to the idea of using a detective story atmosphere of a film noir setting as a style for the game world.

Inspiration was drawn from films like *Double Indemnity* (DeSilva & Sistrom, 1944), in which a weak insurance salesman finds himself entangled in a murder plot.

Right when we were starting Grim there was a huge film noir festival in town. It was a strange coincidence [reminiscent of Jungian synchronicity], and I saw every single film showing there. I think I used something from every single movie. Like in Gilda, there's this character who always bets on the number two and wins, and that's how he gets his payoff in the Casino, and that's in the game. I just looted those films. Casablanca was the biggest influence on Grim, and The Big Sleep, and Double Indemnity. (Pearce, 2003)

Another recent example of an emergent trend comes from a group of students that studied and embedded the archetypes of Jung, Campbell and Vogler step-by-step into their game story. For *Journey of a Roach* they literally used the structure of the hero's journey for their dramatic structure of an adventure game but broke it with different characters and some un-heroic rather comedian behavior: a cockroach as an antihero with a clumsy sidekick (a spider) that is not characterized as a life-threatening monster but as a caring mother of fly babies and ant soldiers (as enemies) that get converted from militaristic guards to peaceful creatures. (Koboldgames, 2013)

The designers were aware of the pattern of the hero's story and wanted to experiment with this pattern. Their intention was to develop a good game structure with suspense. The designers assumed that the structure of the hero's story could be used for a game, and indeed, it turned out to be very helpful for development. For further strengthening of the story pattern, the designers decided to use characters that usually are not used in the lineup of dramatic archetypal roles. Assigning the main role to a cockroach is a symbolically ironic. Basically, the protagonist cockroach is the guy next door that is projected into an adventure. He has a (taller) sidekick that is a clumsy fellow. And many of the other characters are not what one would normally expect. They are not stereotypical. Even the enemy soldier ants (with their armbands referring to Nazis) turn into happy friendly guys at the end of the game when life changes back from hero mode to daily reality mode. As mentioned above, the spider is not a monster but a caring and protective mother for the fly babies. Contrary to expectation, the firefly is not very active, sleeps in his hammock, and smokes ganja all the time. As a hippy, he is in an unlikely communal living arrangement with a retired general. The general, a wasp, is not a strong figure but an old, frail and weak creature that needs all the help that he can get to survive. The designers of Koboldgames work with contrasts, – as they say – they try to break the frameworks of expectation in order to foster a unique projection of unconscious reality.

The strange, ironic, and humorous world of *Journey of a Roach* lends itself to a positive reframing of the unconscious. Though the game story is full of accidents, misfortunes, and black humor, these characteristics provide a positive access to the archetypal unconscious of the player. Every effort was made to create an atypical game. The designers planned to integrate references to movies that work with the hero's journey pattern. A scene from *Mission Impossible* (Cruise & De Palma, 2000) is integrated as persiflage. There are other references to movies and games. In one of the game puzzles is a picture of the Three Headed Monkey from the adventure game *Monkey Island* (LucasArts, 1990). The prison break scene refers to the movie *The Rock* (Simpson, Bruckheimer & Bay, 1996), and there are important references to *Planet of the Apes* (Jacobs & Schaffner, 1968). Reminiscent of *Dr. Strangelove* (Kubrick, 1964), the insects worship a nuclear bomb, and toward the end the protagonist rides a nuclear bomb.

However, the end of the game has references to the archetypal elixir as the two roaches survive and find the first flower on the surface of the scorched earth.

The original concept of *Journey of a Roach* employs dramatic structure based on Vogler's framework, but attempts to use the more accurate symbolism of the hero's journey. Vogler's structure worked as a narrative backbone upon which deeper principles were attached. For example, instead of text icons are used as language of the insects. Narrative backbone and distinct setting divided into segments respectively rooms (as standard in adventure games) interlocked very well. There are thirteen rooms, and the adventure leads from room-to-room leading to the Deepest Cave and up again room-by-room until the characters reach the top--the surface of the earth. The designers made a level-map where they indicate the narrative segments of the journey. The comedic behavior of the insect characters culminates in the ride on the nuclear bomb, and their unlikely survival or reincarnation on the surface of the earth where they encounter the first glimpse of hope in a budding and blossoming flower. Story development is as follows:

1. **Premonition:** Intro with dream sequence as cut scene. Premonition of war, noise, destruction.
2. **Call to Adventure:** Bud pokes Jim and tells him about his discovery.
3. **Refusal:** Jim can hardly stand and is dazed. (Tutorial explaining control).
4. **Mentor:** Bud shows Jim the next room and wants to go further.
5. **Crossing the First Threshold:** Bud gets buried alive and Jim must get help. Jim is now on his own.
6. **Test, Allies, Enemies:** Several Puzzles, Jim learns of the humans' journey to the moon.
7. **Progress to the Deepest Cave:** The bunker is unstable, the puzzles dangerous, Jim is getting more injured. He wants out of the department store.
8. **Decisive Test:** Jim finds the place where he left Bud behind. Bud is no longer there.
9. **Reward, Grabbing the Sword:** Jim pulls himself together with his last strength and finds Bud's map to the Great Room with the Miracle.
10. **Way Back:** Jim follows the map.
11. **Showdown:** Jim finds Bud and the nuclear rocket. Together, they shoot out of the bunker on top of the bomb.
12. **Return with the Elixir:** The two have not died in the explosion, but at last they reach the earth's surface (Geiser and Woll, 2011).

Dreamlike Indie Games

Some of the more interesting Indie Games today concentrate on individual archetypes such as the Shadow, a selection of archetypes, or variations differing from stereotypes in the game setup. Good examples of imaginative environments are *Limbo* (Playdead, 2010), *Feist* (Bits & Beasts, 2008-15) and *Dear Esther* (The Chinese Room, 2008-12). *Dear Esther, Gone Home* (Fullbright Company, 2013) and *Kentucky Road Zero* (Cardboard Computer, 2013) belong to a new recently emerging genre among Indie Games. They are so-called Story Exploration Games that base their narratives on emotions, social and psychological backgrounds and relationship stories. Often limit physical interactivity in order to make more careful use of selective archetypes and journey segments in their projects.

The game *Feist* (Bits & Beasts, 2008-15) features a little fury ball as main character. The player quickly gets emotionally attached to it. A Jungian interpretation of the little furry ball as an archetype child (innocence) is indeed possible, yet at the same time the player experiences irony and distance. In

Southern American English, Feist is a term for a small mongrel dog. In this game, Feist is not a dog, but it is a mongrel of some kind. The furry ball has a weapon, but it is a pinecone. In many aspects, Feist is a fighting game. The cute character has to avoid traps and gets a weapon, but the weapon is different than any martial devices usually employed in fighting games. Thus the main weapon in Feist is a pinecone. Another weapon is a twig. Faller says, that cones and twigs are references to the things that we fought and played with as children.

Feist is reminiscent of Black Forest. It employs several graphic layers that might originate directly from dream environments. The creatures in the game are not recognizable as known animals, but as dreamlike hybrids. The same is true of plants which are not identifiable as real-world plants. In conversation (May 2014) with the author, artist Florian Faller relates his creatures more to Freud's idea of the uncanny. But a certain proximity to Jung's collective unconscious is evident in the symbolic portrayal of archetypes that shine through the obscure scenarios. As in dreams, archetypes remain vague and indefinable.

Feist deliberately operates with figurative references. There are no beings, no plants, that exist in the known world or which refer to a particular species. At the same time they should not be exotic; to the contrary, the plant and animal world is built with familiar characteristics. The inhabitants of this world always have elements that are deliberately emphasizing the characteristics of familiar animal species. This may be fur, horns, and tusks reminiscent of domestic mammals of Western and Central Europe. The designers, Florian Faller and Adrian Stutz state that they didn't try to create hybrid creatures because this would be too exotic for them. They fully intended to stay as familiar as possible. The same is true for plants and landscapes. Feist is a fairy tale world.

The Indie game *Limbo* (Playdead, 2011) refers to an imaginary place for lost, forgotten or unwanted children or people. The Catholic Church uses the term Limbo as an abode of the unbaptized or innocent souls, mostly infants. They have to live at the edge of hell. The game comes only in black and white and with minimal ambient sounds and puts the player in the role of a young boy travelling through an eerie and treacherous world in an attempt to discover the fate of his sister. The young boy wakes up in a forest and starts to explore a bizarre and increasingly disturbing world. As he progresses through the forest, he addresses obstacles that often kill in shockingly gruesome ways. The little boy gets decapitated by a bear trap, cut up, crushed, smashed or eaten by a crocodile. He dies many cruel deaths. But after each death the player restarts the game Just before the trap, and has a renewed opportunity to figure out how to get around the obstacle.

Story and ending are open to much interpretation and to depth analytics. The boy may look for his dead sister. At one point in the game, he sees a girl, but before he can get to her, she runs away and disappears. After completing the final puzzle, the boy is thrown through a pane of glass back into the forest. He walks a short distance until he encounters a girl, maybe his sister, or his alter ego. When he approaches the girl, she stands up, startled. At this point, the game abruptly ends. Is the boy now reunited with his sister? Are they both dead and have to remain in Limbo? Can they progress to hell together? Is the girl just the alter ego of the boy? Are they both dead? Players have come up with different interpretations for the end, but the players have all been deeply emotionally involved by their experience of the game.

The Indie game *Dear Esther* (The Chinese Room, 2008-12) remains at least as mysterious with its setup on an unnamed island of the Hebrides and no visible characters. The player explores the shadowy island in a first person perspective and needs to pick up fragments of stories on his way. A male voice reads parts of letters to him. It is not clear whom that voice belongs to, but they are all addressing Esther who is dead. The player himself may be her husband searching for memories. There are other characters that are important to the story told via voice-over letters, but the longer the operation goes on, the more blurred they become. At the end of the game, the player climbs a radio mast atop a peak and jumps off. He falls to the shore, but the shadow we see becomes that of a bird. The player flies along the bay and sees an array of paper boats in the water. Those may be the letters he had written to Esther. This is definitely an unusual videogame since it plays with a person's psyche and creates an inner world as an outer world; in this case it is a shadowy unpleasant island that does not offer anything but loneliness, isolation, and self-deprecation. And this is what the player, as the main character of the story experiences throughout the game.

Gone Home (Fullbright Company, 2013) is another exceptional story exploration game that works with fragments of information that have to be discovered and read or heard by the player. The player takes the role of 21-year-old Kaitlin who comes home from a long trip abroad to the family mansion in Portland but finds no one home. A note on the door from her sister tells her not to look for answers about where she has gone. The information hunt starts from there. Kaitlin finds more and more messages and notes from her sister and starts putting a story together. Some discoveries also lead to clues about the past and the whereabouts of her parents. Again, there is no other visible character in the game but we get to know a lot of intimate information about all of the family members. The main story is the one of sister, Samantha, who has a relationship with another girl and after a few turns of the story, has run away with her girl-friend for good.

These Indie games illustrate that successful narrative does not always need to involve a hero's journey and a full array of archetypes. Archetypes are imbedded in all drama waiting too be discovered by the contextual viewer. These games are very dreamlike and do not adhere to the rules of consciousness. They work with reduced virtual imagery of the unconscious and explorative structures that do not necessarily comport with established rules of narrative. They focus a more accurate understanding of archetypes as contextual patterns and bring them to the spotlight. This is the process of individuation that can heal. Healing and learning are personal (contextual), but archetypal symbols are employed to mirror the unconscious. While *Feist* creates a shadowy but playful forest world in which an innocent creature fights nightmarish creatures right out of our dreams, *Limbo* creates a horrific afterlife world with gruesome mechanics that arrange thousands of deaths. *Limbo* is basically a game about the sinister sides of life and trying to cope with death. Similarly, *Dear Esther* shows a more contemplative way of dealing with loneliness and isolation after the loss of a loved one. The outer world, in this case corresponds to the inner world of the main character. It is very symbolic and as the player works through this in the first person perspective, s/he gets emotionally involved in such a way as to heal the emotional pains of real life. Finally, *Gone Home* develops the story of characters that are not visible in the game. It is not about death but about relationships, desires, conformity, and secrecy. The house in which we explore the story functions as the virtual world in which the characters evolve from conformity to a nonconformity that reveals all their inner secrets and offers new revelations as to problem solving.

Changing Perceptions of the Unconscious from Culprit to Mentor

Finally, a renewal of interest in virtual realities is underway. *Birdly* (Team Max Rheiner, 2014), an experimental hardware for the VR-console *Oculus Rift* that tries to get us closer to our Dream of Flying. Its goal for the user is to fly through the sky like a bird. With the rise of the Oculus Rift and the advent of more VR-consoles (from Google, Microsoft and independent developers), new opportunities reveal themselves for the game industries. These possibilities prepare the ground for new ways to engage in immersive virtual realities. Birdly is one of the most recent innovative experiments that successfully enhances one of the virtual reality systems. Birdly is a full-body VR installation that explores the experience of a bird in flight. It tries to capture the mediated flying experience with several methods. Unlike a common flight simulator one does not control a machine – one embodies a bird. The bird simulator was developed for a bird sanctuary that wanted to familiarize visitors with the life of birds by taking on their perspectives on the world. To evoke this embodiment, Birdly relies primarily on neural sensory-motor coupling. The user or participant controls the simulator with her hands and arms which correlates to the wings and the primary feathers of the bird. The inputs are reflected in the flight model of the bird and displayed physically by the simulator (a padded chair or frame that accommodates a player lying flat on her belly) through nick, roll and heave movements. This goes far beyond the classical approach of (immersive) gaming. By wearing VR-goggles, the user is not only separated from the real world and experiences a possible 360-degree immersion into the game world but registers that there is also wind and scent. Olfactory feedback is used in immersing the player or flying person with more sensory input. The closer she flies to the forest the stronger the scent of fir trees become. The headwind comes from a ventilator that sits directly in front of the player and simulates natural breezes. Wind and scent change according to scenery and location of the player. The wind adapts its strength according to the speed at which the player is flying.

Max Rheiner's Team at the University of the Arts Zurich is developing game and narrative approaches for the new simulator. Like several other Virtual Reality technologies that are presently in development for games, Birdly brings the game world one step closer to the Holodeck of living and experiencing dreams, narratives and gaming in Virtual Reality. The head of project, Max Rheiner, says: "We did not exactly know how a bird flies and what his perceptions are, so we were trying to emulate a human dream. As human beings, we are often dreaming of flying. And we realized the dream of flying as a physical experience." (Max Rheiner in SRF Kulturplatz, 25.2.2015) This means that Birdly may be as much an embodiment of a bird flying through the sky, as it is an embodiment of man experiencing flying sensations in his dream—a sensation that may remain vague—generated from the unconscious. Like Icarus, the virtual reality contraption of Oculus Rift and Birdly manages to play out the dream of flying in a physical way or at least with some comparable physical activities and sensations that make the user believe that he or she really flies across San Francisco like a bird. In this respect, flying with Birdly is fulfillment of a dream, a primal image like Icarus right out of the collective unconscious. It causes anxiety, maybe even nausea when the user dives head down into town. And it causes amazement and sometimes, tremendous happiness (emotional involvement) in experiencing something that cannot be experienced in real life. There are many ways of applying Birdly. It may be used to overcome fears. It may be used for education. In history classes, students could be transferred into a specific historical time period. Or it could be used with infinite applications to film, theater and other interactive formats including games.

There are many more research projects underway to bring us all into a real virtual reality or bring the virtuality in the shape of holograms right into our world. Some of them are low-funded projects like Birdly, that work amazingly well. Others are big projects with huge financial contributions like Oculus Rift (https://www.oculus.com), essentially a VR-Headgear system that tries to establish a separated virtual world for the user. The user is completely separated from his real surrounding and acts in full virtual world immersion. Several visor-style VR-Headgear sets will soon (2016) appear as consumer products. Besides Oculus Rift, there will be the Sony Project Morpheus goggles, Valve's Steam VR under the name

HTC Vive, Razer's OSVR, and Avegant's Glyph that works with micro mirror arrays. Some VR-goggles like Samsung's Gear VR and Carl Zeiss' VR One, Archos VR, and Google's cardboard goggles use a smartphone as power unit. Somewhat unique is Fove VR, which offers interactive eye-tracking and a new method of control through eye movements that may be better suited virtual reality verisimilitude.

Microsoft's HoloLens takes a different approach. It tries to merge reality and virtuality by creating an augmented second layer on top of the real world environment. The user is not separated from the real space but registers virtual objects in his surrounding and may be able to physically move through his surrounding area. And there are other comparable big projects like *Magic Leap* (Magic Leap, 2015) that work on merging virtual objects, scenes and worlds as holograms with the real world. Here the user may be confronted with holograms of game characters, virtual human beings, or dinosaurs in his real space. This may enable a whole new way in dramatic storytelling, games, therapy, medicine, and education.

All of the mentioned projects may not prove successful, but all are extending possibilities and enhancing potentials for dealing with the collective unconscious as Mentor rather than as culprit. Experience has seen other innovative VR-projects fail: Virtuality Group's VR-System (1994) with stand-up arena and head-gear, i-Glasses from Virtual I/O (1995), Nintendo's Virtual Boy (1995), and the VFX-1 from Forte Technologies (1994). Nevertheless potential abounds.

The fictional concept of a Holodeck, where people can physically play out their dreams and desires in adapted fictional worlds, was conceived for *Star Trek: The Next Generation* (Roddenberry, 1987). However, the concept was developed in Gene Dogloffs Holography Lab in New York in the 1960s. Gene Roddenberry, writer for the Star Trek series took up the idea after meeting Dolgloff in 1973. He first tested it in 1974 in *Star Trek: the Animated Series* (Roddenberry, 1974). In both series a Holodeck is depicted as an enclosed room in which objects and people are simulated by a combination of transported matter, replicated matter, tractor beams, and shaped force fields. Holographic images are projected upon it. The user runs it in first person perspective. The holographic figures and the real humans cannot be distinguished from each other. However, the fictions are not generated by the users themselves; they are written by Holonovelists and can only be adapted in a certain way by the users.

In 1997 Janet Murray published her book on the Holodeck as an intriguing and provocative model for future storytelling. The book describes the then current formats of digital storytelling and illustrates very well, that the whole community working with or on electronic literature, games and virtual reality had the hope of being able to develop and play holodeck-like games very soon. Procedural authorship was the keyword for the change that had taken place in digital storytelling and was supposed to set a new paradigm for digital storytelling to come. Top of the line for dramatic cyber-storytelling then was, according to Murray, a rather impressive narrative game by Jordan Mechner called *The Last Express* (Smoking Car Productions, 1997), an adventure crime game reminiscent of the Orient Express that travelled in 1914 from Paris to Constantinople (Istanbul). A remastered version of the game was released for iPad in 2012. Over the years those hopes fizzled out, games progressed towards open worlds with many more possibilities of interacting and assembling narrative segments for the player. Also, MMORPGs and Open Sims (like SecondLife) offered new variants of identity and immersion for the player, but the separation between game world and real world has only been perforated--not permeated. Therefore, we may need to ask the question: Are the new and exciting developments in virtual reality gaming tending closer to the Holodeck or are they deceptive as in 1997?

CONCLUSION

The Indie game examples show that dramatic games based on psychological intentions and motifs are now possible, and there are many more to illustrate the point. For example *Papo &Yo* (Minority, 2012) in which the player plays a ten-year-old boy that escapes to his fantasy world from his alcoholic father who turns into a monster when he drinks. Clearly, the unconscious is the culprit here too when surreal things happen and define the game path. Or *Brothers: A Tale of Two Sons* (Starbreeze Studios, 2013) that is essentially a game that may help to cope with grief. Or *Braid* (Blow, 2008) in which the player tries to save a dysfunctional relationship but turns out to be the monster himself. *Never Alone* (Upper One Games, 2014) demonstrates how the hardships of nature can take control of of an Inuit community. In *Limbo* (Playdead, 2010), a reduced 2D environment with silhouetted characters and no text are enough to create a disturbing nightmarish game direct from the unconscious. The same goes for games like *Feist* (Bits & Beasts, 2008/15), *Dear Esther* (The Chinese Room, 2008/12), *Gone Away* (Fullbright Company, 2013) and others that successfully manage to lure the player into exploration of inner worlds of the archetypal unconscious. All the tools are available, but understanding how to use them is lacking.

REFERENCES

Adams, E., & Rollings, A. (2007). *Fundamentals of Game Design*. Upper Saddle River, NJ: Pearson Publishing.

Adams, E., & Rollings, A. (2010). *Fundamentals of Game Design* (2nd ed.). Berkeley: New Riders Publishing.

BadKing. (2013). BadKing's Mega Monster Brush Pack. *BadKing. ZBrush Development & Resources*. Retrieved from http://www.badking.com.au/site/badkings-mega-monster-brush-pack/

Bates, B. (2004). *Game Design* (2nd ed.). Boston: Thomson Course Technology PTR.

Bits & Beasts. (2008/15). *Feist. Zurich: University of the Arts (ZHdK)*. Austin: Finji.

Blow, J. (2008). *Braid*. San Francisco: Microsoft Studios.

Booker, C. (2004). *The Seven Basic Plots. Why we tell stories*. London: Bloomsbury.

Bortolussi, F. (2012). Designing Scary Film Monsters in ZBrush." *Digital-Tutors*. Retrieved from http://www.digitaltutors.com/tutorial/752-Designing-Scary-Film-Monsters-in-ZBrush

Campbell, J. (1949). *The Hero with a Thousand Faces*. New York: Bollingen Foundation.

Cardboard Computer, C. (2013). Kentucky Route Zero. Chicago: Cardboard Computer.

Cruise, T., & Wagner, P. (Producer), & De Palma, B. (Director). (1996). Mission: Impossible. United States: Paramount Pictures.

DeSilva, B., & Sistrom, J. (Producer), & Wilder, B. (Director). (1944). Double Indemnity. United States: Paramount Pictures.

Double Fine Productions. (2005). Psychonauts. Eddison, NJ: Majesco Entertainment, THQ.

Double Fine Productions. (2015). *Grim Fandango Remastered*. San Francisco: Double Fine Productions.

Dundes, A. (1965). *The Study of Folklore*. Upper Saddle River: Prentice Hall College.

Evenson, L. (1998, October 27). Fleshing Out an Idea. *San Francisco Chronicle*. Retrieved from http://www.sfgate.com/entertainment/article/Fleshing-Out-an-Idea-Day-of-the-Dead-inspires-2982510.php

Freud, S. (1919). Das Unheimliche. In Imago. Zeitschrift für Anwendung der Psychoanalyse auf die Geisteswissenschaften, 5, 297 - 324.

Freud, S. (1923). *Das Ich und das Es*. Leipzig: Internationaler Psychoanalytischer Verlag.

Geiser, M., & Woll, B. (2011). *Journey of a Roach. A Maze Adventure. Unpublished Game Concept*. University of the Arts Zurich.

Glassner, A. (2004). *Interactive Storytelling. Techniques for 21st Century Fiction*. Natick, Massachusetts: A.K. Peters.

Hahn, D. (Producer), & Allers, R. (Director). (1994). *The Lion King*. United States: Walt Disney Pictures, Buena Vista Pictures.

Hornblow, A., Jr. (Producer), & Wilder, B. (Director). (1957). Witness for the Prosecution. United States: Metro-Goldwyn-Mayer.

Hunt, M. M. (1993). *The story of psychology*. New York: Doubleday.

Jacobi, J. (1973). *The Psychology of C.G. Jung*. New Haven, London: Yale University Press.

Jacobs, A.P. (Producer), & Schaffner, F.J. (Director). (1968). *Planet of the Apes*. United States: 20th Century Fox.

Jung, C. G. (1917). *Die Psychologie der Unbewussten Prozesse: ein Überblick über die moderne Theorie und Methode der analytischen Psychologie*. Zürich: Verlag Von Rascher & Cie.

Jung, C. G. (1933). *Modern man in search of a soul*. USA: Harcourt Brace & Company.

Jung, C. G. (1964). *Man and His Symbols*. London: Aldus Books.

Jünger, E. (1970). *Annäherungen. Drogen und Rausch*. Stuttgart: Ernst Klett.

Kelly, M. (2015). The social contract. Retrieved from http://americanhistory.about.com/od/usconstitution/g/social_contract.htm

Koboldgames. (2013). *Journey of a Roach*. Hamburg: Daedalic Entertainment.

Kubrick, S. (Producer & Director). (1964). Dr. Strangelove or: How I Learned to Stop Worrying and Love the Bomb. United States: Columbia Pictures.

Kubrick, S. (Producer & Director). (1968). 2001*: A Space Odyssey*. United Kingdom and United States: Metro-Goldwyn-Mayer.

Kurtz, G. (Producer), & Lucas, G. (Director). (1977). Star Wars. United States: Lucasfilm Ltd., 20th Century Fox.

Lakoff, G. (2008). *The Political Mind. A Cognitive Scientist's Guide to Your Brain and Its Politics*. New York: Viking Adult.

Magic Leap (2015). Retrieved from www.magicleap.com

Leroy, M. (Producer), & Fleming, V. (Director). (1939). The Wonderful Wizard of Oz. United States: Metro-Goldwyn-Mayer.

Lionhead Studios. (2001). Black & White. United States: Electronic Arts.

Lucas Arts. (1990). *The Secret of Monkey Island*. San Francisco: Lucasfilm Games.

Lucas Arts. (1998). *Grim Fandango*. Marin County: Lucas Arts.

Mamoulian, R. (Producer & Director). (1931). Dr. Jekyll and Mr. Hyde. United States: Paramount Pictures.

Minister, P. (2013). Creating a Centaur in ZBrush. *Digital-Tutors*. Retrieved from http://www.digitaltutors.com/tutorial/1099-Creating-a-Centaur-in-ZBrush

Minority. (2012). *Papo & Yo*. Montreal: Minority.

Murray, J. (1997). *Hamlet on the Holodeck. The Future of Narrative in Cyberspace*. New York: The Free Press.

Nayfack, N. (Producer), & Wilcox, Fred M. (Director). (1956). Forbidden Planet. United States: Metro-Goldwyn-Mayer.

Pearce, C. (2003). Game Noir – A Conversation with Tim Schafer. Game Studies. The International Journal of Games research. 3(1).

Playdead. (2010). *Limbo*. Copenhagen: Microsoft, Playdead.

Polti, G. (1895). *Les 36 situations dramatiques*. Paris: Mercure de France.

Propp, V. (1958). *The Morphology of the Folk Tale*. Austin: University of Texas Press. (Original work published 1928)

Roddenberry, G. (1966). *Star Trek: The Original Series (TV Series)*. United States: NBC.

Roddenberry, G. (1973). *Star Trek: The Animated Series (TV Series)*. United States: Paramount Television and CBS.

Roddenberry, G. (1987). *Star Trek: The Next Generation (TV Series)*. United States: Paramount Television and CBS.

Rollings, A., & Adams, E. (2003). *On Game Design*. Indianapolis: New Riders Publishing.

Rockstar San Diego. (2010). Red Dead Redemption. New York: Rock Star Games.

Sheldon, L. (2004). *Character Development and Storytelling for Games*. Boston: Thomson Course Technology PTR.

Silver, J. (Producer), & The Wachowski Brothers (Director). (1999). The Matrix. United States: Warner Bros.

Simpson, D., & Bruckheimer. J. (Producers), & Bay, M. (Director). (1996). *The Rock*. Hollywood Pictures, Buena Vista Pictures.

Smoking Car Productions. (1997). *The Last Express*. Novato, CA: Broderbund.

Spielberg, S. (Producer & Director). (1982). E.T. the Extra-Terrestrial. United States: Universal Pictures.

Starbreeze Studios (2013). *Brothers: A Tale of Two Sons*. Stockholm: 505 Games.

OriginSystems, . (1992). *Ultima VII*. Manchester, NH: Origin Systems.

Team Max Rheiner. (2014). Birdly. Zurich: University of the Arts (ZHdK).

The Chinese Room. (2008/12). Dear Esther. Brighton: Chinese Room/ United States: Steam.

The Fullbright Company. (2013). *Gone Home*. Portland: The Fullbright Company.

Tolkien, J. J. R. (1983/1931). A Secret Vice. In The Monsters and the Critics and Other Essays (p. 198-219).

Tolkien, J. R. R. (1954). The Lord of the Rings (Vols. 1–3). London: George Allen & Unwin.

Upper One Games. (2014). *Never Alone. (Kisima Inŋitchuŋa)*. Anchorage: E-Line Media.

Valve Corporation. (1998). *Half-Life*. Los Angeles: Sierra Entertainment.

Vogler, C. (1985) *A Practical Guide to The Hero with a Thousand Faces*. Manuscript. Retrieved on 04.02.2015 from http://www.thewritersjourney.com/hero's_journey.htm

Vogler, C. (1992). *The Writer's Journey: Mythic Structures for Storytellers & Screenwriters*. Studio City, CA: Michael Wiese Productions.

Wallis, H. B. (Producer), & Curtiz, M. (Director). (1942). Casablanca. United States: Warner Bros.

Wolinksy, D. (2015). Exhuming Grim Fandango's Mexican Folklore Inspirations. In *Kill Screen*. Retrieved from http://killscreendaily.com/articles/exhuming-grim-fandangos-mexican-folklore-inspirations/

Chapter 6
Virtual Psyche in Play and Tending the Collective Unconscious:
An Archetypal Psychology Perspective of Digital Games

Susan Marie Savett
Pacifica Graduate Institute, USA

ABSTRACT

Knowingly or unknowingly, games manifest archetypal forces from the unconscious. Through play and fantasy, unconscious content of the psyche is able to express its deep longings. Hypnogogic landscapes of videogames provide immersive realms in which players enact psychological dramas. Game designers reside on a unique axis from which their work with the imaginary realm can create profound psychic containers. At this pivotal point in our culture, digital games hold tremendous influence over the creation of new myths, lore, and possibilities. This chapter investigates archetypal psychology concepts of Carl Jung and James Hillman for insight into 21st century realm of virtual play and its relationship to the collective unconscious. It focuses on how games provide a means for bringing individual and cultural unconscious impulses into consciousness through personification, pathologizing and meaning making within virtual play. It aims to introduce an alternative lens to bridge psychological dynamics with the video game design.

INTRODUCTION

Digital realms are unique vessels for the collective consciousness and unconsciousness of our times. As virtual realms are increasingly inhabited, not only is the phenomenological perspective of embodiment challenged, but also the psychological and evolutionary alteration of the individual to the collective and to the unconscious. The phenomenon of psychic life was previously held within the container of the physical body, but now there is a new vessel for psychic energy.

DOI: 10.4018/978-1-4666-9891-8.ch006

"Just as the body has its evolutionary history . . . so too does the psyche" (Jung, 1912/1956, p. 29 [CW 5, Para. 38]). Is psyche evolving within virtual space? Are virtual games vessels for psyche? Do virtual games provide landscapes for the virtual soul to wander? Are designers the current-day alchemists who transmute matter into digital "spirit" and mediate access for the collective unconscious? Just as the notion of a virtual world is an evolving concept, so too is the notion of its role as psychic container.

This virtual landscape for psyche begs for interdisciplinary attention of archetypal psychology and game studies to understand the shared symbolic meanings, ritual, and myth within virtual human sociality. Edward Castronova in *Exodus to the Virtual World: How Online Fun is Changing Reality* (2007), observed "Whatever our deepest shared fantasies may be, we will be able to pursue them in cyberspace together, all day, every day, world without end"(p. xv).

Virtual storytelling and gameplay offer so much more than mere interaction of player with game: it's a journey into rich psychical landscapes filled with collective unconscious content. For millennia, storytelling of dreams, myths, and fantasies has provided a vehicle for meaning–making, for informing the culture of the potential generative and destructive forces of archetypes. Now, through virtual games, these fictional realms are not merely passive but are dynamic and vivid encounters. Virtual designers yield more than a tale; through code, a dimension of immersion and transmutation of the unconscious occurs as players embody the role of enactment.

As gazes attend to images within virtual realms we are suspended between conscious and unconscious landscapes, caught in a binary world, between dream and reality. We are extended beyond the skin of our being into a collective drama – a form of a hypnogogic drama – along with crowds of other "dreamers" sharing the hero's quest – spending psychic energy to fill a void, within the images of the virtual game. There is something very profound as people migrate into these realms. Media theorist Mark Hansen in *Bodies in Code: Interfaces With Digital Media* (2006) noted in virtual space the human being is "endowed with a collective dimension" (p. 85).

Knowingly or unknowingly, games manifest archetypal forces from the unconscious. Game designers reside on a unique axis from which their work and their relationships with the imaginary realm can create profound psychic containers. At this pivotal point in our culture, digital games hold tremendous influence not only over the gaze, attention, problem-solving skills, and collaboration of players, but most importantly, over the creation and engagement of new myths, lore, expectations, and possibilities (Castronova, 2007).

Three billion hours a week are spent playing digital games, and by October 2010, over 5.93 million years of gameplay time had been spent in one virtual game, *World of Warcraft* (2001), with over 12 million subscribers, according to game studies theorist and activist, Jane McGonigal at the Game Developers Conference (GDC) 2011 Serious Game Summit. She places the time frame in perspective by citing that the first human ancestors stood up 5.93 million years ago. With such magnitude of hours and players, one has to pause to consider what is occurring to draw so many hours of attention within mythic realms of virtual games. Archetypal psychologist James Hillman explained, "The power of myth, its reality, resides precisely in its power to seize and influence psychic life" (Hillman & Kerenyi, 1991, p. 90). Gameplay in mythic realms is seizing and influencing 21st century psychic life on an epic scale.

Jung indicated "The secret of cultural development is *mobility and disposability of psychic energy*" (1912/1956, p. 16 [CW 5, Para. 17]). With estimates of well over 3 billion hours spent per week playing digital games (McGonigal, 2011), there begs the consideration of the ensoulment of virtual containers and personified "psychic presences" evoked within the gameplay.

In a realm of virtual games where image is primary, and fantasy is played out, soul (Psyche) is present in its various disguises. Soul is messy. It descends into darkness where we avoid casting our eyes, and yet through gameplay a theater for soul to present itself is created. Digital games are not merely a game to play but rather a place immersing souls, new arenas for mythical fantasies and psyche.

GAMES AS THEATRE FOR SOUL

Since the ancient times of Plato and Aristotle, the theater has been considered a "seeing place", full of spectacle. In the "seeing place," truths of the human soul are revealed. It is a place of reflection and reaction. Jung described the theatre "as an institution for working out private complexes in public" (1952/1976, p. 35 [*CW* 5, para. 48]). Today, other mediated realms have been born: game worlds on computers have created a new institution for engaging psychological complexes in a modern world.

Whether the participation consists of immersion within a theater or within a game, the players' agency—the enactment—enables the possibility of transformational experience Janet Murray observed with her students in the MIT Media Labs (2000). Donning the mask within the theater gives shape and form to the tension and anxiety as one navigates through the virtual maze, moving into "another order of perception" (p. 112).

The research, "Games as Theater for Soul", applies archetypal and depth psychology as an alternative means to reflect on games as a means of soul-making. It weaves together game study theory, depth psychology, and conversations with leading game narrative designers. Game narrative designers have a responsibility for the emotional content within the game and the blending of the story to the game mechanics within the design process. Their reflection of the key concepts of archetypal psychology in current video games provide fascinating insights to the dynamics within gameplay.

This chapter endeavors to be an introduction to a depth and archetypal psychological study of the expression of soul through personifying, pathologizing, and seeing through to gain new perspective within the play of the virtual game. It does not strive to be a complete process for soul-making interpretation of virtual games, but rather a beginning point in posing the questions of how, if any way at all, we might explore the role of psyche in game space. For each player there exist many levels of personal and collective meaning. Due to the dynamic nature of game play, each encounter differs.

Importance of Play

Digital play unearths our archaic nature—that which civilization has suppressed, tamed, caged for the good of civilization. In the immersion of virtual worlds our archaic nature is unleashed on a global scale. Digital play is a counter response to the cultural structures that have previously confined our roles to participate in a "civilized" responsible pattern. And yet, with dramatic disruptive pressures of current cultural and technological changes to traditional roles, former expectations of what it means to be human, to be a male, or to be a female within society begins to fall apart. Through the fantasy within play one grapples with the shifts within civilizations.

When the dominant vision that holds a period of culture together cracks, consciousness regresses into earlier containers, seeking sources for survival which also offer sources of revival . . . an escape from contemporary conflicts into mythologies and speculations of a fantasy world. (Hillman, 1992, p. 27)

The importance of play to civilization and its evolution is often overlooked. Something is transpiring as our culture shifts towards massive engagement in play. This dynamic merits exploration and consideration as to understanding the underlying implications as we migrate more and more into virtual realms – not only of play but of ways in which we do business, relate to others, learn, and participate in virtual landscapes of life. However, like all animals, we begin by learning through play.

Johann Huizinga's *Homo Ludens: A Study of the Play Element in Culture* (1938/1955) is the seminal book upon which current game study theorists turn to as the foundation for gaming discussions. *Homo Ludens,* which means "Man the Player," defines play as an essential nature of the human and that learning comes from the "primeval soil of play" (p. 23). Accordingly, the qualities and necessities of play shape culture. Huizinga states, "In play there is something 'at play' which transcends the immediate needs of life and imparts meaning to the action. All play means something" (p. 1).

Play has a power in the formation of civilization as a critical act of learning and defining reality. It appears to be irrational and yet it is primary to culture. According to Dutch historian Huizinga "the great archetypal activities of human society are all permeated with play from the start" (1938/1955, p. 4). He further explained the necessity of play in the process of evolving civilization:

Now in myth and ritual the great instinctive forces of civilized life have their origin: law and order, commerce and profit, craft and art, poetry, wisdom and science. All are rooted in the primaeval soil of play. . . . The fact that play and culture are actually interwoven with one another was neither observed nor expressed, whereas for us the whole point is to show that genuine, pure play is one of the main bases of civilization. (p. 5)

Play allows one to step out of 'real' life "into a temporary sphere of activity with a disposition all of its own" (p. 8). The enactment of play is a transformation into the imaginal. It is "an intermezzo, an interlude in our daily lives" (p. 9). And yet it is even more than an interlude. The child in fantasy, or the player within a videogame, is creating an image of self that is different from what one really is: more beautiful, more sublime, more dangerous, and more courageous. One is transported beyond oneself to "inhabit a world of marvels" (Jung, 1952/1976, p. 21 [*CW* 5, para. 24]). From an archetypal perspective, play's imaginal realm creates an image of future possibilities.

Elements within life become amplified through imaginal worlds. During the immersion of play, like a theater, the players become in essence actors dressing up in masks and disguising themselves from others and, more importantly, from their own selves. The theater, the arena, the movie screen, the video screen, the religious temple, and the ritual—each contains an element of isolation, a special place, forbidden, with special rules of entry and rules of participation stated Huizinga. The magic circle created through the rules and masks of play provides the vessel to enact the ritual of the "other" within oneself.

The enjoyment provided in play, game theorist Bernie De Koven observed, is a "healing part of the human psyche" (2013, p. xix). Players are given the opportunity and permission to enact in accordance with the theater of the game. In doing so, there is the ability to participate in a well played game, one in which each person is called to perform with excellence. Play, be it in the realm of the theater or in the magic circle of game play, is the arena for archetypes to perform.

The Lens of Archetypal Psychology

The transformation occurring to the collective psyche via virtual realms, particularly those of game play, necessitates a view through the lens of psychoanalysts and archetypal theorists Carl G. Jung (1875-1961) and James Hillman's (1926-2011) work to provide essential meaning-making to understanding psyche's movement. Archetypal psychology established its roots in psychoanalysis, however it connects to the wide collective imagination of the Western world by extending its application beyond the therapy room to all cultural products. Applying the theories of archetypal psychology to the cultural form of virtual games speaks to the importance of the role of fantasy images as expression of soul and provides a unique framework to investigate the psychological layers of virtual gameplay.

It is my belief that Jung's insights in *Symbols of Transformation* (1952) is applicable today and provides a fresh approach to the images and fantasies within 21st century virtual games, particularly when pertaining to the role of the imaginal realms of fantasy dream as vehicles for the expression of the unconscious content of the individual and the culture. By encountering the images of virtual gaming when viewed from the perspective of Jung's writings on the primordial images of the imagination, we acquire a broader view of the psychological dynamics.

What we seek in visible human form is not man, but the superman, the hero or god, that quasi-human who symbolizes the ideas, forms, and forces which grip and mould the soul. These . . . are the archetypal contents of the (collective) unconscious, the archaic heritage of humanity. (Jung, 1952, pp. 177-178 [CW 5, para. 259])

Could the roles of the characters and the virtual landscapes in virtual games be "extraordinarily potent" expressions of archetypal impulses? It is my belief that Jung's observations may provide a valid means by which to understand virtual games as potent carriers of not only cultural but also deeply instinctual archetypal content.

James Hillman, an American psychologist, was the founder of the post-Jungian school of thought archetypal psychology that integrates the fields of psychology, philosophy, mythology, cultural studies and art. Hillman studied with Jung at the C. G. Jung Institute and received his doctorate at University of Zurich in 1959. He served as the Director of Studies at C. G. Jung Institute in Zurich until 1969. His work examined historical, cultural, and archetypal roots emphasizing the role of imagination and the human soul.

Archetypal theory is central to Jungian traditions. Jung saw archetypes as constructing the foundation of the collective unconscious—a phylogenetic layer—"which incorporated the entire psychic potential of humankind" (Stevens, 2006, p. 75). The archetypes form a "dynamic substratum . . . developing a unique array of psychological characteristics. In other words, the archetypes of the collective unconscious provided the basic themes of human life on which each individual worked out his or her own set of variations" (p. 75).

Archetypal influences from the unconscious present themselves in symbolic language of image. Jung explained how the symbol points to "that which is not fully known, giving expression to the unknown in the world" (1952/1976, p. 157 [*CW* 5, para. 223]) . . . virtual games connect with those archetypal energies through the image within the binary world of gaming. Archetypal themes dominate the realm of digital gameplay: Anima and animus, war and violence, the hero's journey, alchemy, quests, shadow, mages, and psychic spells are cast within the virtual encounter. The myths of ancient past have resurrected within the collective throughout the virtual landscape. Virtual game space is a mediated realm between unconscious influences and conscious enactment through play.

Fantasy-images are considered by Jung and Hillman to be the privileged mode of access to knowledge of soul. By examining fantasy images both the unconscious raw materials and the finished products of psyche are revealed (Hillman, 1975, p. xviii). These images within imaginative encounters are fundamental archetypal forces present within the individual and the collective.

Archetypal psychology views the world with a metaphorical lens, through which new perspectives are created. It offers a way of seeing the underlying psychological functions. Metaphorical viewing of the world allows one to enter into new relationship, expands one's boundaries of perception, interpretation, and ultimately one's consciousness. "It means looking at the frames of our consciousness, the cages in which we sit and the iron bars that form the grids and defenses of our perception" (Hillman, 1992, p. 127). To re-vision our current perceptions through archetypal fantasy the psyche speaks imaginally about what our conscious mind defines as literal.

Metaphorical lenses of archetypes, as espoused in archetypal psychology, enhance the dimension and quality of being present in daily lives and create awareness of particular patterns of thinking and being which determine one's actions and responses to events. Those "patterns," the *archai,* may be called archetypal impulses, complexes, or instincts, but the essential nature of patterns of thought and behavior demonstrates the way they determine how one encounters the world and what choices of participation are considered as possibilities within the encounter. The archetypal metaphors are in essence the tools we use to comprehend the intangible.

When an archetype grips an individual or culture, reality is interpreted, or seen through, by that one angle with its particular limited set of options available. In essence, being in the grips of a given archetype or set of archetypes can blind one to other metaphorical views—other mechanics—to interpret the world at hand. One is in the narrow framework of an illusion, unable to view the event from other metaphorical perspectives.

In gaming terms, archetypes infuse the game rules, and other aspects of game mechanics. They establish the options available for action (agency) and what imaginal landscape will surround the psychological process within the game space. The metaphorical viewpoint is determined though and by the game mechanics, creating the patterns available to the player to resolve the problems and quests placed before them. It specifies the lens, the archetypal lens, and the metaphorical lens through which the player will enact.

Dark Fantasies

Virtual games confront our current cultural quilt of the "unthinkables": warring, apocalyptic destruction of earth, machines overtaking humans, instinctual death drives . . . basic survival. Archetypal psychology suggests that pathologies are not merely something to be cured but rather a means to increase insight into the workings of the human and cultural soul. Taking a polytheistic approach to envision the multiplicity of archetypal figures operative in present-day situations provokes the expansion of one's perspective. Jung astutely observed "The myth is a fragment of the superseded infantile psychic life of the race" (1952/1976, p. 24 [*CW* 5, para. 29]) and through the mechanics of fantasies "the conscious fantasy may be woven" into the mythological. In fact Jung noted that "Typical myths . . . serve to work out our racial and national complexes" (*CW* 5, Para. 45).

Jung's assistant Marie Von Franz explains in *The Interpretation of Fairy Tales* (1970/1996), that the images and archetypal stories within "fairy tales are the purest and simplest expression of collective unconscious psychic processes. . . . the archetypal images afford us the best clues to the understanding of the processes going on in the collective psyche" (p. 1). Many video game dramas are digital enactment of the fairy tales of past generation transferred into digital mediated realms. The rawness of dramatic gameplay within many games is not only the re-enactment of traditional fairy tales, but also a participatory engagement – an active imagination – directly with the archetypes rising up from the unconscious into consciousness.

Gameplay in mythic realms is seizing and influencing 21st century psychic life on an epic scale. However, unlike most previous encounters with the myth, fairy tales, which convey symbolic meaning – the gamer is not alone as he/she immerses into the landscape of the soul: all the while transpiring with the community of other players. Gameplay is a collective endeavor to journey together into the labyrinth of the collective psyche, into the maze of virtual decent to meet demons. Are these demons symbolic of the external or internal monsters? They are both. The binary realm is the negative and the positive. It is the nightmare and the dream. It is the reality and the illusion. It is evil and good. It is personal and collective, conscious and unconscious.

Exploring Soul within Virtual Game Space

When exploring soul within virtual game space, one must grapple with how to define, how to describe, and how to write about "soul." Soul's perspective, according to archetypal psychology, shows us "the imaginative possibilities . . . through reflective speculation, dream, image, and fantasy—that mode, which recognizes all realities as primarily symbolic or metaphorical" (Hillman, 1992, p. xvi). An archetypal lens on society demands the perspectives of who and what we are as humans in our culture, looking to the source of attitudes about self, religion, science, culture, art, and morality. The imagination of our culture drives our interpretation and attitudes toward our individual fantasies (p. 225). Conversely, the mediated fantasy realms of virtual games provide insight into the psyche of the collective unconscious.

The framework of archetypal psychology, as outlined in *Re-Visioning Psychology* (1992), provides excellent guideposts to investigate the phenomenon of psyche and soul within digital games and explore the notion of "games as theater for soul". Examination of virtual games through four key concepts -- personifying, pathologizing, psychologizing, and soul-making--tends to the unconscious content that lies below the surface, activated through the game mechanics and design. For purposes of this exploration of digital games, *Personifying* refers to the player and game elements donning the cloaks of archetypes. *Pathologizing* is the enactment of the archetypal drama. *Psychologizing* is seeing through the drama to the underlying story for meaning. *Soul-making* is integrating wisdom obtained within the immersion back into daily lives, shifting perspective away from ego goals towards the soul; in essence it is a "re-humanizing" or re-vivification of soul. Through the overarching experience of the four archetypal movements there is a way in which to envision living in an ensouled world.

Personifying: The Interior Commune

Archetypal personifying is inherently an extremely potent psychological move in which the player and game elements don the cloaks of conscious and unconscious archetypal influences. It enables putting that which is interior in the soul to be experienced externally. The act of personifying devises protections by forming a layer between the exterior and the interior content. The soul reveals itself, enabling new eyes to see, opening one's vision and temporal embodiment of alternative experiences. By living in a metaphorical relationship with the world, personifying "revivifies" the relationship. To personify, one meets the "individual fragmentation, [the] many rooms and many voices" within oneself (Hillman, 1992,

p. 3). Personifying entails employing the imagination to allow the soul to present itself. Personifying is not only a way of engaging on the imaginary stage of the theater; it is its way of soul-making (p. 3).

As in the theater, the rituals of theatrical encounters occur in videogames through the concrete actions of kinetic performance. The game player's performance enacts the game's ritual. Ritual deliteralizing events. "As we go into a ritual, the soul of our actions "comes out"; or to ritualize a literal action, we 'put soul into it'" *(Hillman, 1992, p. 137).* Game play is a "highly consequential ritual" observed game theorist Jane McGonigal (2006, p. 2). From an archetypal psychology perspective the enactment enlivens portions of the soul. Most importantly, the process of personification psychologically enables the dissolving of the literal event and divests it by the enactment of a different psychological style.

Games such as the *Grand Theft Auto* series (1997-2014) are systemic, open world, less of an authored story and more of a sandbox-type space where players create their own stories. Repeatedly in the interviews with game designers and in private conversations with many people, the *Grand Theft Auto* series was mentioned as one of the personal favorites. Whereas an outside observer of the game may focus on the apparent violence possible, the players within *Grand Theft Auto* focus on the agency they control; and it all happens when they move the thumbstick—it becomes their story.

Grand Theft Auto's success taps into the desire for freedom to move within the game space to create one's own mythic, dark world of repressed desires in an imaginary world that responds to the player. The level of agency within the space enhances the ability of the player, in an imaginal world, to step onto the stage. The player takes over the dramatic text and creates a unique performance. The notion of "you" within the gameplay blurs the lines of the player sitting in a room and the character within the game. Who is "you"? The game structure provides virtual realms into which one both splits off from reality into fantasy and simultaneously merges fantasy with reality. All the while, this state of being remains part of "your" story. The individual is both the player on the improv stage of the game and the person in the room watching the story unfold for the character on the screen. Thus, the experience is incredibly compelling.

Jung wrote in his book, *Symbols of Transformation,* about the symbolic imaginal realm, in which images upon images appear: Dionysian phallagogies, chthonic mysteries, and theriomorphic monsters, half animal and half human, give face and representation to the gods within (Jung, 1952/1976, p. 27 [*CW* 5, para. 36]). The personified images in contemporary gameplay bear a striking resemblance to Jung's description of the symbolic imaginal realm. Archaic thinking and feeling states continue to reside side by side with the modern state of mind. Through personified fantasy, the archaic mind is mirrored back.

Configurations of images within gameplay are larger than life, amplified in the compelling nature of the game, reflecting like a large mirror a magnificent display and intensity of life. The beauty of personification as described in archetypal psychology is its ability to hold space on a plane of consciousness that mediates the unconscious, not as fragmented, undefined pieces of the psyche but as whole components, in order to witness the unique voices clamoring within.

Games can be a rich reflecting pool for the fragmented persons within, giving the individual the ability "to find other persons within oneself, to be divided into several souls, a field of multiple personalities" (Hillman, 1992, p. 2). The diversification of interior personalities are often confined and suppressed and yet seeks ways to be vivified. Digitally mediated fantasy realms of games give way for the psyche to the return to mythic imagination. Mythic imagination "offers a way of coping when our centers cannot hold and things fall apart" (p. 27). To successfully enter into a mythic experience, accordingly, we must personify. Personification carries us into the immersion of myth.

The degree of immersion in virtual worlds is placed in perspective to the conceptual and emotional barriers, as explained by Richard Bartle, a creator of the first virtual world MUD1 (Multi-User Dungeon) and a pioneer of the massive multiplayer online game industry. Similar to that of personifying, "You're not role-playing a being, you *are* the being; you're not assuming an identity, you *are* the identity; you're not projecting a self, you *are* that self . . . .*You* are *there*" explains Bartle in *Designing Virtual Worlds* (2004, p. 155). This occurrence is the moment where the player and character merge. He contends that merging is the reason that people go to virtual worlds, for it is that moment that they not merely playing in the world but start living it. Bartle claims that "it's not immersion itself that is intoxicating; rather, it's what immersion helps deliver: identity" (p. 157). Without personifying immersion into the virtual world cannot exist.

Game worlds are worlds of personification in which the invisibles of the psyche are given form. The player donning masks in play enters into another psychological dimension as she personifies fragments of interior personalities, the multiple archetypal gods and personas who control psyche. The many personalities with the individual's psyche inhabit and meet in imaginal worlds of play.

Like anthropomorphism and animism, personification takes an internal event and puts it outside in the fantasy of play. Through the act of personifying, we experience the game world as a psychological field in which the game mechanics become experiences that touch us, move us, and appeal to us. Through personifying, we immerse and become part of the world.

Jung stated, "the unconscious spontaneously personifies" (1959/1990, p. 285 [*CW* 9i, para. 514]); unconscious personification erupting into the imaginal activity of gameplay decisions is similar to the images that have the free will to roam in dreams. Jung's notion that archetypal complexes, are in essence independent entities with feeling, autonomy, intention, and even consciousness. The way they can erupt in our normal lives are through behavior—sometimes irrational—and symptoms.

The psychic realm of an individual may best be described as a landscape of interior relationships of archetypes rather than individual forces. The interplay of members within the interior commune enacts mythical scenarios that are manifested in life. The psychic field is a battleground for the interior commune to engage and battle for submission and dominance. Games enable enacting these interior dramas.

The historian Huizinga elaborates on the significance of the personification within play as the necessity to become another being, it is more than merely wearing a mask. Play provides a realm of secrecy and "differentness" that allows the player to experience an "extra-ordinary" state of being. "The terrors, . . . mystic fantasy and sacred awe are all inextricably entangled in this strange business of masks and disguises" (1938/1955, p. 13) during the ritual of play.

Game designer Richard Dansky asserts that the creation of the game is intended to resonate with the player's fragmented aspects of the player's personality that he or she may not be able to express (personal communication on March, 27, 2013). Virtual game realms tap into and give access to, and vivifies the diversities of personalities, some of which may have been suppressed. Through personification, the player is able to select and enact the persona with self-agency, overriding the persona of anonymity. Personification helps sub-personalities within the internal commune devise new relations.

The player, through the mechanics of the game, is given space for the various internal archetypes to perform and address the conflict. The player, for example, chooses the warrior hero to take action against the sense of feeling like an undifferentiated other through the separation and clarification of the multiplicity of internal personalities. This is a very important psychological move; the distance is a way of gaining internal detachment "as if there were now more interior space for movement and for placing events, where before there was a conglomerate adhesion of parts or a monolithic identification with each and all, a sense of being stuck in one's problem" (Hillman, 1992, p. 31). In a well-designed game the player's internal psyche is able to detach from the feeling of disempowerment amongst the "sea of the undifferentiated" (Dansky) to become something more than that of an Other. The personified image possesses a willfulness to differentiate (p. 34). This would suggest that the game mechanic verb *"shoot"* within the game fantasy separates one internal aspect of the player—the warrior—from the many other internal persons.

Splitting individuals' images of themselves through imaginal play, as shown in the many forms of gameplay, results in multiplying the individual parts so that they are more manageable to witness and come into relationship. In other words, this archetypal concept suggests that the various forms of gameplay provide a vehicle for encountering the many fragments within the individual psyche on a one-by-one basis. The gameplay is able to amplify a particular element of the individual in order for it to play out within the free space of imaginal play. Mythic realms "become the multiple magnifying mirror in which the psyche can recognize its persons and processes in configurations which are larger than life" (Hillman, 1992, p. 30). Not only do these mythic representations present the internal persons within the individual but also the processes by which they view, interpret, and act within the given world through the amplifications of the deeds.

The importance of mythic imaginative realms as a means of coping resonates with game designer Richard Dansky's explanation that "in video games you actively take arms against the sea of troubles and more actively take arms against this sea of 9-5 or 8-6 or dead-end doldrums and anonymity" (personal communication on March 27, 2013). The "sea of troubles" within life becomes personified as the various challenges to overcome within the game, allowing the individual to address conscious and unconscious fears present in daily life. Dansky continues, "It is not so much an aspect of player personality I think that we are rising up against; *it is against the player's fear* in many ways". His observation lends itself to the notion that the personification is not merely a reflection of the personality of the player—as in the desire to directly express one's image in the game content, but rather an engagement in a fantasy in which the unremarkable structures of life are personified through characters or gameplay mechanics. The daily 9-5 sacrifices required from the average person, bearing the weight of the anonymity in modern society, is given expression archetypally through the avatar personifying the hero. Psychologist Glen Slater noted that the archetypal role of the hero is such that "the hero always has the relationship with the dead and the underworld because they are always sacrificing" (2008a).

Without the space allotted through imaginal personification, the individual could potentially remain in the state of undifferentiation, both internally within the self and externally in society. However, through personification, the player is able to select and enact the persona with self-agency, overriding the persona of anonymity. The shooter genre particularly provides the player's fantasy a means to "stay close to the raw experience" by personifying the nature of fear and being overwhelmed by the "sea of undifferentiated others." Dansky's insight correlates with the importance of how personification helps to externalize these experiences as a way to devise a new relation with the feeling of isolation through the act of gameplay.

At best, games allow players to enter into and live from "Other" through fantasy play; at worst, games reduce "Other" to either stereotypes or entities to eliminate in order to achieve a fantasy goal. In fantasy, the symbol is often grounded in the unconscious archetype but manifested outwardly. The importance is to understand and tend to the appropriate level of personification available during game design so as to enhance the movement of energy within the experience.

The character in play, as well as other elements conveyed within the ritual open space, is available for deliteralizing psychological events and come into relation with "Other". Ubisoft's *Freedom Cry: Assassins Creed IV* (2013), an historical action-adventure open world game about slavery, is an example of using the ritual of game space to create strong emotions and use of game mechanics to deliver a twist to achieve more evocative gameplay. The avatar's use of the machete has consequences. The action verbs of *run, jump,* and *shoot* were realigning in such a way as to deeply connect emotional content through personifying and pathos: the verbs of the archetype are given an additional lens of the slaves. The game mechanics employed seeing through the underlying drama beyond the action of the verbs in order to generate a meaningful resolution. Highly memorable moments in a game create the connective tissue weaving the player's psyche, the avatars actions, and the other members in the virtual world; in the case of this game, the slaves such as Adwale. Game reviewer Patrick Klepek (2014) summarizes the profoundness of his experience within *Freedom Cry: Assassins Creed IV,* "When the mission was over, I had to set the controller down. I was drained, and Adwale's pain was my own."

Pathologizing: Dramatic Text of Game Play

Pathologizing is intrinsic to soul. Pathologizing language is the psyche's way of expressing its lacking and suffering rather than of the ego's human perfection. Archetypal psychology asks to turn a new lens toward darker content to ask the question, "Why is this pathological symptom necessary?" (Hillman, 1992, p. 56) rather than to either immediately condemn the pathology or, at the other end, to blindly enact it without measure.

Whereas video games are repeatedly described by critics of video games as soulless and responsible for intensifying violent urges within individuals, pathologizing looks to the reflections of the inner world of the individual and society. Disturbing images within some game genres—particularly shooters, zombie, adventurer, and horror—did not arise with the invention of video games. Ironically the description below is of medieval woodcuts and drawings used by alchemists describes similar scenes to that which we see in modern games:

Processes of dismemberment, torture, cannibalism, decapitation, flaying, poisoning, images of monsters, dragons, unipeds, skeletons, hermaphrodites; operations called putrefaction, mortification, pulverizing, dissolution. The woodcuts and drawings of the alchemists display the processes with every sort of bizarre and obscene configuration. (Hillman, 1992, p. 90)

Like medieval alchemist attempting to understand the world's soul, game designers are modern day alchemists, through which the soul's language speaks of its suffering. There is a necessity for the soul's growth to speak of repressed content, allowing expression of bizarre and heretical fantasies for the alchemical process to have full freedom (p. 40). Each person experiences moments in life of emotional instability, depression, or imbalance. Pathologizing gives raw and spontaneous expression of emotions: sorrow and happiness, dejection and passion, fear and excitement, surprise and monotony.

Temporal worlds of such cathartic encounters are similar to the therapist's office that "offered the vessel into which our unconscious pathologizing could be poured and then cooked long enough for its significance to emerge" (Hillman, 1992, p. 71). The term *psychopathology* comes from the root *psyche-pathos-logos*: the study of the soul's suffering of meaning (p. 71). Although games provide an alchemical vessel for the cooking of pathological content, whether the significance of the meaning is achieved remains to be seen. Nonetheless, to acknowledge the power of pathological content, not as evil to eradicate from play, but rather as a necessity for our psyche. Games pave the way to locating meaningful relations to the symptoms of the world around and within.

The images within the games provide a window into cultural symptoms: symptoms such as illusions and depressions, overvalued ideas, manic flights and rages, anxieties, compulsion, and perversions. "The psyche uses complaints to speak in a magnified and misshapen language about its depths" (Hillman, 1992, p. 82). Through the images within the entertainment-mediated realms, one sees into the cultural soul. Jung indicated, "The constellated archetype is always the primordial image of the need of the moment" (1952/1976, pp. 293-294 [*CW* 5, para. 450]). Interpreting culturally mediated realms such as digital games within this frame of reference provides insight as to how unconscious content presents itself and guidance for reflecting upon primordial images within pathological content of digital games so as to consider what is the need of this moment in time.

Zombie, dystopian, and post-apocalyptic genres in particular represent a fundamental change in the American and global experience and collective psyche. Amplification of decomposition of the natural is grappled with in many fantasy worlds that directly personify the experience of death and decomposition. The game *State of Decay* (2013) does a powerful job personifying the decline with each small detail, as game designer Steve Williams pointed out as we watched the gameplay. "There is a fascination within the culture to come to terms with the decay" (personal communication on April 8, 2013). Within the game the player moves through what was once a charming small town in the Pacific Northwest, but everything is now in decay: rusted cars, abandoned homes, broken toys lying on the ground, even trees are in a state of decay with the season of fall. Life has declined towards death. Williams pointed out that this was once a world—a small town—that one would have wanted to live in. Now, the infestation of zombies relentlessly attacks, and nothing lasts; morbidity surrounds the player.

In *State of Decay* (2013) players may choose a character named Maya, a psychotic, bloodthirsty female, and she is having the time of her life killing zombies. Some players love to be that character, exploring and mastering her archetypal power. This is an example of how "pathologizing forces the soul to a consciousness of itself as different from the ego and its life—a consciousness that obeys its own laws of metaphorical enactment in intimate relation with death" (Hillman, 1975/1992, p. 89). In this particular game genre the designers are often pushing emotional buttons hard. Dansky observed that the power of the zombie genre with its pulverization and mortification, provides "death to the world as we know it, obliterates all the daily stuff. The ultimate simplification is death" (March 27, 2013).

Fantasy enactment within virtual games enables coming into relationship with either that which lies quietly in the shadows or that which erupts violently, demanding to be heard. Fantasy allows for the soul to process in a world that cannot take place in the natural world (Hillman, 1992, p. 91). Discovering the psychological necessity of pathologizing shifts the angle and gives value to the expression of the pathos as a means to understand what the soul is saying. In other words, we open the space for creative digestion of the dysfunction (Slater, 2008a). Games open up the opportunity for emotional relationship with images and different ways of seeing things.

The power of symbolic imagery and fantasy, according to Jung, balances psychic reality "by shifting the whole question on to another and less dangerous plane" (1952/1976, p. 156 [*CW* 5, para. 220]). At its best, pathological content in games allows one to reimage a difficult situation and discover multiple ways of dealing with the pathos. At their worst, games can fixate the psyche to remain stuck in an obsessive pathological disorder, furthering the suffering. Jung warned of such potential perils of the soul, of "a splitting of the personality ("loss of a soul") and reduction of consciousness, both of which automatically increase the power of the unconscious. The consequences of this are a serious danger (1952/1976, p. 169 [*CW* 5, para. 248]).

Becoming consumed in pathological hyperactivity without reflecting inward creates a one-sidedness of an archetypal impulse. Balancing the necessary pathologizing with psychologizing, the seeing through to the underlying meaning, is addressed later in the chapter.

During the course of research interviews, games the designers spoke about contained quite substantial amounts of violence and pathological content. Jung addressed the notion of how primordial content is drawn out of an individual through images (1952/1976, p. 157 [*CW* 5, para. 223]). The examples of moments within games that possessed a potent energy validate the importance of coming into relation with primordial urges. What appears to be overcompensation provides psychological value through the hyperdrama of the pathos within the images and action.

Pathos takes one into relationship with loss: the loss of childhood, dreams, ambition, calling, virility, and ultimately the loss of control. Games give personified shape to encountering a loss and, sometimes, mastery. Game theorists point out that game worlds are full of problem scenarios; that is inherently what makes them games (Schell, 2010; Salen & Zimmerman, 2004).

As in theater, there are no real life consequences for the actions within the game space. The game provides amplification of the pathological behavior of the deeply flawed characters or the other deviant persons of the internal commune, each of which give expression to that which is falling apart in the world of the individual, the culture, and the natural world. Escapism allows the struggling psyche to relocate from the oppression of daily life; games are an invitation for the amplification of the distress. Pathologizing within the fantasy realm of games, or even within the therapy room, is about coming into a relationship to that which destroys.

The care of soul necessitates tending to what destroys and is destroyed within psychopathology when one falls apart (Hillman, 1992, p. 56); the issue may be whether the space of the game is capable of "tending" the destroying impulse and enabling any care for the soul. Asking what is within the pathologizing and what is behind this distortion makes the important psychological move: "the distortion is at the same time an enhancement and a new clarification, reminding the soul of its mythical existence" (p. 99). The following scenario may have allowed one player to achieve that reminder of his mythical existence.

The hyperviolence served the story in BioShock. It is a little bit of a meditation to be the guy who kills a hundred men. A good friend who is 22 years old said when he finished the game he sat and stared at the wall for a while and started crying a little bit and then stared at the wall for an hour more. You are serving an atavistic impulse such as power. (Williams, personal communication on March, 27, 2013)

The critical component that may be missing in gameplay as opposed to a therapy room is the opportunity for guided reflection of the trauma. Well-designed games, however, may also provide a new clarification of the soul's mythical existence. "The soul is moved most profoundly" Hillman proclaimed, "by images that are disfigured, unnatural, and in pain" (1992, p. 95).

The powerful success in the game industry of such games as *BioShock Infinite* (2013) and *Gears of War* (2006) taps into accessing the pathos of the human soul as well as the complexity of one's relationship with the external fantasy of the goal of perfection within society. The allotment of pathologizing in games is intensely impactful. *BioShock* is appropriately named, for it "shocks" the player with the dissonance of both societal and personal actions, exposing the cracks and challenging players with confrontations of the psyche.

Pathologizing is a natural component of gameplay. Games have an intimate relationship with death: there are winners and losers in most gameplay. In even the mildest of game genres, the act of destroying is permissible and often integral to successful play. Recall *Pac-Man* (1980), where ghosts are eaten by a little benign-looking yellow character. The popular game entailed the challenge of survival, as the imaginal world of the labyrinth became increasingly more inhabited with ghosts who destroyed the player's little yellow character: ghosts are killing the apparently innocent character, and yet it is this benign yellow one who cannibalistically eats ghosts named Blinky, Pinky, Inky, and Clyde. Pathological content does not require the graphic action of shooters and horror genre to be present within games. Even games such as chess, checkers, and tick-tack-toe are played to eliminate the opponent. "The push of progress leaves corpses in its wake" (Hillman, 1992, p. 10), and game progress is often no exception. Death is inherent within play as it is also in intimate relationship with soul's movement. In fact, one of soul's key defining attributes is "its special *relation with death*" (p. xvi).

Games bear witness to emotional quicksilver—nakedly volatile and unpredictable. Games bear witness to pathology. Games transmute suffering into fun. With the provision for little restraint of full expression within the fantasy of the game world, one is able to discover the range and intensity of "the dark river where deep drives and forces flow" (Skolnick, personal communication on March 28, 2013). The tears and rage of unfulfilled expectations are countered with battle and mastery of the personified enemies who repeatedly attack: the undead and alive, machines and monsters, sinister melee weapons, and magic spells.

Psychologizing or Seeing Through

Psychologizing is the act of seeing through the divine dramas of life. Where games to date have been rich in the imaginative personification and pathologizing, there is a question as to the current level of seeing through the metaphorical into the meaning-making for soul's continued expansion and evolution to new imaginative possibilities.

The action of imaginal play within games has the potential through the process of seeing through (psychologized) to translate the action into meaningful content for the soul, and for the soul to be expressed through the action. Having a vessel for meaning-making is a necessity of the soul. This is a critical notion for the premise of games as a theater for soul. Fantasying activity is a means by which archetypal ideas are able to encourage speculation. Images grappling with core archetypal content are present not only within religions and in the arts, but also seeing into what dominates the culture and the personal turns events into soul's experiences. The nature of therapy teases out the internal fantasies that one may possess based on influencing mythic archetypes. The elusive and complex qualities of human experience are seen through a lens. Meaning-making occurs when the lens that is being used for the viewing, and hence creating a reality, is able to give the appropriate identification of the "fantasy." In essence, this lens provides a seeing through of the seeing through process itself. In essence, to begin to understand that which grips one's reality requires a stepping back to see through, to bring to light the archetypal lens through which reality is interpreted.

The fantasy image of the finished product results with the new imagined forms of archetypal presences and new relationships with them that inform the individual and the collective. The fantasy relationships within games have an ability to generate an alternative psychological perspective for the player achieved through the ability of seeing through the metaphorical to the underlying psychic energies and possibly controlling behavioral patterns present.

One must look through the story to the one behind it—to see through the obvious to the larger drama at hand. Where personification of the archetype gives form and shape to the particular archetypal attitudes, and pathologizing exposes the darker drama and wounds, it is psychologizing that sees through the dramas for making meaning, for understanding, and for envisioning the full story. The entire cycle brings the quests, the driving impulses, and the dramatic subtext of life from the recesses of the psyche into the light of consciousness.

It is critical for psychological development to emphasize the need for meaning-making within gameplay. One walks a fine line with personification and pathologizing in game play and becoming stuck in constellated archetypes, unable to see through to some form of meaning-making. The movement of "seeing through" is a re-turn of the elements witnessed in the previous turns of personification and pathologizing, so that they now will be explored for mythical patterns by re-examining the "parts" of the "falling apart" to see how they might be re-imagined or how the virtual game may move from the apparent to the unapparent unconscious content. Archetypal psychology calls this process "finding the hidden god" and unveiling further ideas for consideration. Seeing through provides an important step in which new questions and doubts emerge. It is a step towards the discovery.

An image or idea can change the psychic landscape. However, to simply participate in events, does not deepen one's capacity for understanding the archetypal drama (Hillman, 1992, p. 122). Reflection takes place whenever one attempts to understand and deepen the psychological landscape. Reflection inspects the interior intention. It sees with "another eye" the drama at play, seeing through to deeper meaning. By dissolving a problem, or a dominant archetype, into a fantasy, its content is loosened up and more available for conscious interaction.

The action of imaginal play within games has the potential through the process of seeing through (psychologized) to translate the action into meaningful content for the soul, and for the soul to be expressed through the action. Having a vessel for meaning-making is a necessity of the soul. This is a critical notion for the premise of games as a theater for soul. Fantasying activity is a means by which archetypal ideas are able to encourage speculation. The nature of therapy teases out the internal fantasies that one may possess based on influencing mythic archetypes. The elusive and complex qualities of human experience are seen through a lens. In essence, to begin to understand that which grips one's reality requires a stepping back to see through, to bring to light the archetypal lens through which reality is interpreted.

One motivating archetype to even begin to play a game is the heroic ego: the willingness to encounter challenges with the potential for failure. The inherent action of gameplay is to overcome the problem or problems at hand. By picking up a game, there is the possibility that the player will become a hero through encountering the tension of the game space. "Problems challenge the heroic ego, presenting it with projects and projections. By means of problem solving, the ego defines itself. Heroic ego and hard problems require each other; they toughen each other in the coping game called 'reality'" (Hillman, 1992, p. 135). Where many games are obviously patterned after the hero's journey, all games by nature carry tension (Huizinga, 1938/1955; De Koven, 2013; Schell, 2010). A game allows one to play, in a version of fantasy, the illusion of suffering and death—a theatrical enactment of which wants to be avoided in life and yet which constantly remains as a threat to the ease of one's life.

Unreflective Action

Entering mythic enactments offers a multiplicity of meanings inherent in our lives (Hillman, 1992, p. 158), but with unreflective participation, the opportunity for meaningful insight is lost. Without seeing through archetypal dramas, unreflective action results in an anemic psyche. "It has meager means for orientating itself as a soul in a psychological field. It also loses the ability of seeing through ideas that are imposed upon it. It asks the wrong questions and forgets itself as soul" (p. 118).

Game narrative designer Susan O'Connor shared how many current games often fail to provide the reflective moments to resolve the activated dramas within gameplay. "We don't get catharsis. Games don't listen and don't respond meaningfully. We are getting these emotional states that flare, they wind up but don't ever resolve" (Personal communication on April 9, 2013). The psyche without reflective moments can easily become a victim to dominant archetypal ideas imposed from external cultural forces or from a one-sided internal view of the world. We become stuck in roles, caught in a loop of typical problems and blindly miss the fantasy we are enacting. Personification and pathologizing begin the process of the psyche to enter imaginal space, but action without reflection results in a potential alienation of the soul.

There is a potential loss of valid and rich psychological perspectives for the soul of the individual, of a culture, and of a community. The possession of particular ideas is difficult to be witnessed by the self. The grips of an ideation or archetypal drama blind the psyche's vision. One loses a valid, balanced perspective when overcome by an archetype. When in the grips of a constellated archetype, unconscious projections, acting out, blindness, and libidinally charged activity occur. The archetypal energy possesses a one-sided aspect of the archetype until it is resolved through a more holistic experience of the archetype or through inviting in additional archetypes within the pantheon.

Jung warned how the misuse of symbolic fantasy could leave one in a split-off fantasy. He indicated "The constellated archetype is always the primordial image of the need of the moment" (Jung, 1952/1976, pp. 293-294 [*CW* 5, para. 450]). The basic problem is not to be possessed by an archetype, but to be in relationship to it. Sometimes a player's psyche just wants to be witnessed. "It is not about keeping people stuck where they are but to allow the imagination to open up, to open a little gap to allow something else to come in" (Slater, 2008a). This is a goal of therapy:

"Constellated" (i.e., activated) unconscious contents are, so far as we know, always projected; that is, they are either discovered in external objects, or are said to exist outside one's own psyche. A repressed conflict and its affective tone must reappear somewhere." (Jung, 1952/1976, p. 59 [CW 5, para. 92])

Video games could also provide such space. As O'Connor speculated, unresolved conflict and despair within some gameplay can result, due to the stories and game mechanics which do not resolve the game story tension: "the best we can do is get them angry and blow it out. We need to somehow return them to a neutral state" (April 9, 2013). The notion of falling into the grips of an impulse serves as insight to the predicament of some games which keep players within the psychological limitations of their avatar. Where many designers seek to achieve addictiveness in their games (Rousse, 2005, p. 27), well-designed games provide an interesting stream of decision points that move play through and beyond a limited archetypal perspective.

Soul-Making

Soul-making is a culmination of both seeing through the archetypal dramas, where the root metaphors and operations myths are discovered through reflection, and, as a result, altering the way in which one relates to the world (Hillman, 1992, p. 169). The psychological spectrum is broadened and shifts the relationship to the larger world. Soul-making occurs when the archetypal influences are beyond personal influence in service of something greater. One might refer to this as individuation. Within the nature of imaginal fantasy, the hero recovers something deeper as a result of the experience. Imaginative possibilities are activated. The purpose of soul-making is "an attempt to *re*-humanize" (1992, p. 193) to that which is deeply human (G. Slater, personal communications, September 4, 2014). Re-humanizing, soul-making, is to touch and activate the imaginative possibilities to create. The soul opens up to different ways of seeing things. An image or idea can change the psychic landscape.

When soul-making occurs, the space, such as a game, is infused with psychic energy. The players' psyches enter into a conversation, where both the person and the game listen and speak to one another. There is an alchemical moment with ensouling in which an exchange transpires and has the ability to deeply move the soul, creating a moment of pause, of reflection, and of transcendence to another state of being. For soul-making to occur requires coming into relationship and into integration with all of life: ego with the inner self, consciousness with unconsciousness, individual with collective.

Whether soul-making occurs within games—great games—there is a broad range of perspectives from "games fail and dehumanize people" to the notion that games are constantly teaching and therefore enriching the soul. While many designers are working to create meaning-making within gameplay, at times the language around game design tables to convey psychological affect is limited.

To discuss soul-making in context to video games it is helpful to distinguish between the notion of fantasy and imagination. Within fantasy the ego is the star of the stage in which the fantasy facilitates the ego's need to inflate (Raff, 2000, p. 42) by means of playing various archetypal patterns. Fantasy feeds the ego desires and quest for aggrandizement" (p. 45). Within the virtual game fantasy, the gamer becomes the super-hero, overcoming obstacles. Fantasy resides in the illusion and folly of play: enjoyable, satisfying, and fun. However, it also serves the purpose to provide understanding of what the individual ego longs for and points the way towards further psychological growth. Fantasy tends to be played over and over in one's head, within a dream, within a game, or even within daily behaviors. Gamification is one game technique which directly plays off of the ego.

Fantasy, however, is also the precursor state to the imaginal, the imagination, which is beyond the ego, beyond fun, and unlocks transformation. Imagination integrates the inner psyche and the conscious self to unlock latent possibilities. Imagination, through play, is seeing through and "imaging" a new pattern of being for the Self to which one lives reality. Imaging is the view of world coherency and one's capacity to create the image into reality. Fantasy most closely correlates to the process of personification and pathologizing in which the individual encounters the archetypal dramas, allowing the psyche to relate to the archetypal impulses at play. Imagination correlates to the process of psychologizing (seeing through) and soul-making.

The ability to distinguish between fantasy and imagination assists in clarifying the process within a game design where the player moves from the ego-based goals into deeper levels of play. This can occur as a cyclical process: Once the player moves into deeper psychological engagement of seeing through and deeper meaning-making, the functions of personifying and pathologizing may continue to be re-experienced but from a broader spectrum and, hence, create transformative experiences.

It might be argued that the goals of soul-making are not the same as the goals of playing games: That the goals of greater wisdom, liberation, potential are too forced—or too politically correct—for pure gameplay, or that one is enforcing an agenda onto fun. I argue that there is merit in this position, that the mere bliss of the moment within a game is exciting enough. And I would also argue that the play of a game in itself possesses latent forces—and taps into these latent forces on a regular basis—shaping the underlying creative capacity of the player: consciously or unconsciously. However, this attribute of game play does not preclude the exploration of considering the soul-making, the deeply moving and transformative experiences, is possible within the medium.

Researcher and video game scholar James Paul Gee and author of *Why Video Games are Good for Your Soul* (2005), explains how the pervasive role of digital gaming in our modern, complex society is helping us make meaning: "All of us in the complex modern world are frightened of risk and the unknown. But that, I argue, is the disease of the soul that good games can help alleviate," (p. 6). Gee continues by arguing that though some escapes lead to nothing, others like games can fuel the imagination to process and invent new levels of exploration. "Gaming that can lead to the imagination of new worlds, new possibilities to deal with those perils and pitfalls, new possibilities for better lives for everyone. Our emotions and imagination—our souls—need food for the journey ahead" (pp. 6-7.) This reflects archetypal psychology's understanding of the power of the imaginative realm for reflection. In fact, Gee's observations align with Jung and Hillman in that it is our imagination that comprises our souls.

For example, strategy games such as *Tetris* fulfill "one of our deepest human desires: to solve problems by finding patterns inside a safe world in which there is a clear and comforting underlying order" (Gee, 2005, p. 15). These patterns are the archetypal. This escape into a manifestation of the archetypal impulse within a game to compensate for daily life is just one example of how soul is being tended through the gameplay. While Gee does not specifically reference archetypal psychological principles of psychologizing, or "seeing through", in his argument, he does indicate the same wisdom when he lauds the game's ability to encourage people's reflective ability about themselves and their society.

Game Mechanics, Verbs, and Archetypes

The mechanics of the game design, reflecting the dramatic text of the theater, not only embodies the magic circle of play, the rules, and the verbs available within the game, it creates the alchemical vessel for archetypal performance. Mechanics set up the space, objects, attributes, rules, verbs of the alchemical vessel from the archetypal perspective engaged from the designers and the technical tools they elect to incorporate into the gameplay. With interactive imagery, designers are "allowing players to occupy an ontological position somewhere between incarnation and imagination" according to game theorist Mark Wolf (2009, p. 167).

Designers, in their own psychological processes, access the archetypal influences to mold the structure of the game through the mechanics. Like alchemists who mix tinctures within a vessel in order to transform the material into the non-material, game designers mix the elements of code —all the while under the influence of their own unique archetypal lenses—to generate a magic circle for the performance of archetypal gods. Each element of the game, every line of code bears meaning: "Every space, character, object, and action stands for another idea in a complex array of interrelationships" (Howard, 2008, p. xiii). In creating the environment, each element is infused with archetypal significance: The staircase leading up, the whip in hand, a touch on the game controller, all create a cacophony of the gods' dramas enacted in a virtual state of being. A well-designed game is a complex blend of personified forces to allow a drama of challenges—pathologies— to unfold. The archetypal drama reflects what the god is wanting to perform and to be witnessed, for the archetype's essence defines and determines the nature of the rules. It influences the events to be played out, the dramatic text to be played.

Although the game designers only directly influence the mechanics (LeBlanc, et. al., 2004), the dynamics of gameplay are the enactment of the codified simulation created by the design team with the personified projections of players donning the masks of their avatars. The avatars—the characters—are the enactment of personification and pathologizing.

Dynamics of the game as the theatrical performance deliver the moment of the imaginal enactment during which psyche performs. Gameplay dynamics produce personified behavior of the archetypes. The masks of the various gods perform according to the verbs of the archetype. Avatars are influenced from conscious and unconscious intent within a personified experience, and performance within the imaginal realm consists of a blending of both the content of the designers and the players. Avatars and the virtual world of code enact the performance of the archetypes. The role of verbs in game mechanics is intricately woven into the psychological experience of the player. The game mechanics create the structure for personification—the taking on the role of an archetype: for pathologizing—encountering and behaving with the darker content of psyche in play; for meaning-making (psychologizing)—reflecting and enacting with other archetypal verbs; and ultimately for soul-making—by giving a language to revision possibilities. A dynamic layer of technology resides within the interface. There is a complexity in the phenomenon of game mechanics and its relationship with psychic content.

Game mechanics are the interactions and relationships of the game. Where the game mechanics may appear on the surface as objective rules within the code, game theorist and designer Schell, in *The Art of Game Design: A Book of Lenses* (2010), indicates that on another level, it "involves something more mysterious" (p. 130). As a result, some elements within game mechanics are not easy to define, but, according to Schell, are part of what makes for great games: It is when the game designers activate latent forces that "exist largely in the darkness of the subconscious mind" (p. 130).

Game mechanics, explains Schell (2010), consist of six main categories: space; objects, attributes and states; action (the verbs); rules; skill of player; and chance (pp. 130-153). Verbs are the game mechanics that facilitate the actions available to the player which defines the performance of player's potential actions and his/her personality within the game space. As a result the programming action verbs most closely align with the archetypal dynamics present within the stage of the game.

Ultimately it is game mechanics that define the emotional experience and potential meaning-making, delivering psyche *through* the mechanics. Soul-making within the game experience is a result of the weaving of the game mechanics in a digital web of rules, movement, and space. In gaming terms, archetypes are the rules and other game mechanics that determine options available for action (agency) and what imaginal landscape surrounds the psychological process within the game space. The metaphorical viewpoint is determined though and by the game mechanics, determining the patterns available to the player to resolve the problems and quests placed before them. It specifies the archetypal and metaphorical lenses through which the player will enact. Game narrative designer O'Connor during an interview on April 9, 2013 defined the "story" of a game that provides the emotional connection as being "what the player *does*. That activity of gameplay is triggering an emotional connection to the player". The operative words she used were "connection to" and not "reaction from," indicating a relationship that embodies a psychological relationship between player and digital code.

Just as actors point the way in deliteralizing events through performance of the theater, so do game designers with creation of ritualized spaces; they perform alchemical transformations of psyche. Hence, it is the game mechanic verbs—the kinetic drama—within the game that generates the psychological experience, tells the story, and constructs a vehicle of personification of the archetypal drama. Thus, theatrical encounters enacted in digital games through the concrete actions of kinetic performance are personifications.

The core mechanics of problem solving and mastery is in essence the same as a psychological moment where one gains better understanding of that which has gripped us in the past. There is inherently a re-visioning within gameplay that occurs when the perspective shifts. Whether it is solving a maze within a game or resolving a maze within one's interior psychic space, the underlying process of discovery is similar. "Aha!" moments occur with the opening of new layers and levels within gameplay. In essence, this is an unveiling of a limited archetypal perspective to see something new, something fresh, or something present but previously unrecognizable from the old lens. That is a moment of seeing through and potential movement of psyche into a new vision of possibilities.

SUMMARY

Prior to the advent of the digital age, Hillman suggested that we need to "build new imaginal arenas . . . theaters for the images . . . new imaginal processions for the driving mythical fantasies that now over-run us" (1992, p. 225). When envisioning theaters for the images in 1975, pervasive virtual game worlds were not yet a cultural medium. The 21st century is a ludic century in which the current age of games and play within the mass culture are a "part of the fabric of our time" (Zimmerman, in De Koven, 2013, p. x).

One probably would not mistake a game studio for a therapist's office (O'Connor, March 27, 2013), and yet the work within game studios possesses an effect upon the psychological states of players as expressed within and through the gameplay. Like the therapist analysis room games are in essence "the vessel into which our unconscious pathologizing could be poured and then cooked long enough for its significance to emerge" and for the soul to make meaning of its suffering (Hillman, 1992, p. 71). At times gameplay has the potential to be cathartic, and at times it has the potential to constellate archetypal impulses, stunting the psyche's progress; it has the potential of seeing through to the underlying metaphors and tending to the possibilities presented by the many voices personified in the gameplay.

Virtual games provide space for engagement with internal psychological forces – both conscious and unconscious. They provide a way in which psyche talks. One can envision a different relationship with pathological content such that it is possible to see the work of game designers as providing not only fun, but also cathartic psychic release and potentially even therapeutic engagement. Play, as mentioned in previous chapters, is an important vehicle for grappling with societal challenges (Huizinga, 1938/1955) and for engaging internal archetypal forces (Jung, 1961/1989). The first step is to step into the imaginary realm through personification and then to encounter pathos through mashing buttons. Play can present moments to see through to the underlying patterns and metaphors for meaning-making. What looks like play can be learning. What looks like gameplay can be soul's performance.

From an archetypal perspective, I propose that the value of gameplay comes down to the essential nature of meaning-making and that which resides within the unconscious longing to come forward into consciousness. The value cannot reside solely within the game experience without some form of psychic release. The integrated skills and touchstone moments move beyond the virtual magic circles, resembling a Venn diagram that extends beyond the boundary of gameplay. There is strategy, collaboration, pathological content, failure, victory, laughter and guilt. These are valid encounters through which soul moves. The issue is not whether soul is present, but, rather, whether we listen into the voices expressed on the virtual stage and whether we witness the rifting of dramas. Every time a game console is picked up to enter into a game world, there is a readiness and willingness to encounter potential failure and defeats as well as a commitment to develop mastery (Juul, 2013). This in itself is archetypal movement.

To willingly play with mercurial Hermes, trickster at heart, is a clear face-to-face confrontation with the gods: it is a battle of wits and mastery. To don the mask, body, and tool of this primary archetypal drama again and again, is the drama of soul being performed. Call it personified, pathologized, psychologized, or just call it fun; it is a game of soul.

Designers are creating substantial realms—places of distinction—for psyche to reside. Jung indicated that whoever speaks in the voice of an activated archetype "stirs us because it summons up a voice stronger than our own. Whoever speaks in a primordial image speaks for a thousand voices" (Jung, 1923/1978 p. 82 [*CW* 15, para. 129]). This is the powerful world of virtual gameplay.

The enhancement of the archetypal psychological lens to the understanding of games as psychological containers, lends itself to bringing fragmented parts of the psyche together within the creation process—vivifying the mechanics of inventions into creations that move life forward. Critics of video games miss the power of the need for regression in order to encounter and develop problem-solving skills that evolve the psyche. The issue of gameplay holds far greater consideration than to merely label it as culturally stultifying. If play evolves civilization as according to historian Huizinga and reflects back our cultural soul's compulsions, then great virtual games can potentially evolve our humanity into the virtual realms of existence as it reflects back into consciousness the soul's struggles and imaginations of new possibilities to re-humanize the world.

ACKNOWLEDGMENT

Portions of this paper appeared in an earlier version of the author's dissertation, *Games as Theater for Soul: An Archetypal Psychology Perspective of Virtual Games* (2014).

REFERENCES

Bartle, R. A. (2004). *Designing virtual worlds*. Berkeley, CA: New Riders.

BioShock [Computer software]. (2007). Novato, CA: 2K Games.

BioShock Infinite [Computer software]. (2013). Novato, CA: 2K Games.

Castronova, E. (2007). *Exodus to the virtual world: How online fun is changing reality*. New York, NY: Palgrave Macmillan.

De Koven, B. (2013). *The well-played game: A player's philosophy*. Cambridge, MA: The MIT Press.

Gears of War [Computer software]. (2006). Redmond, WA: Microsoft Studios.

Gee, J. P. (2005). *Why video games are good for your soul: Pleasure and learning*. Melbourne, Australia: Common Ground.

Grand Theft Auto [Computer software]. (1997-2014). New York, NY: Rockstar Games.

Hansen, M. (2006). *Bodies in code: Interfaces with digital media*. New York, NY: Routledge.

Hillman, J. (1992). *Re-visioning psychology*. New York, NY: Harper Perennial. (Original work published 1975)

Hillman, J. (2004). Archetypal psychology, volume 1. Putnam, CT: Spring. (Original work published 1983).

Hillman, J., & Kerenyi, K. (1991). Oedipus variations: Studies in literature and psychoanalysis. Dallas, TX: Spring.

Howard, J. (2008). *Quests: Design, theory, and history in games and narratives*. Wellesley, MA: Peters. doi:10.1201/b10929

Huizinga, J. (1955). *Homo Ludens: A study of the play element in culture*. Boston, MA: Beacon Press. (Original work published 1938).

Hunicke, R., LeBlanc, M., & Zubek, R. (2004). MDA: A formal approach to game design and game research. Retrieved from http://www.cs.northwestern.edu/~hunicke/MDA.pdf

Jung, C. G. (1953). Psychology and alchemy. In *The collected works of C. G. Jung* (Vol. 12). (R. F. C. Hull, Trans.). Princeton, NJ: Princeton University Press. (Original work published 1952).

Jung, C. G. (1976). Symbols of transformation. In *The collected works of C. G. Jung* (Vol. 5). (R. F. C. Hull, Trans.). Princeton, NJ: Princeton University Press. (Original work published 1952).

Jung, C. G. (1978). *The spirit in man, art,* and *literature*. In *The collected works of C. G. Jung* (Vol. 15). (R. F. C. Hull, Trans.). Princeton, NJ: Princeton University Press. (Original work published 1923).

Jung, C. G. (1989). *Memories, dreams, reflections* (R. Winston & C. Winston, Trans.). New York, NY: Vintage. (Original work published 1961).

Jung, C. G. (1990). The archetypes and the collective unconscious. In *The collected works of C. G. Jung* (Vol. 9, Part 1 (R. F. C. Hull, Trans.). Princeton, NJ: Princeton University Press. (Original work published 1959).

Juul, J. (2013). *The art of failure: An essay on the pain of playing video games*. Cambridge, MA: The MIT Press.

Klepek, P. (2014). Assassin's creed: Freedom cry review. Retrieved from http://www.giantbomb.com/reviews/assassin-s-creed-iv-freedom-cry-review/1900-626/

McGonigal, J. (2006). *This might be a game: Ubiquitous play and performance at the turn of the twenty-first century* (Doctoral dissertation).

McGonigal, J. (2011). *Reality is broken: Why games make us better and how they can change the world*. New York, NY: Penguin Press.

McGonigal, J. (2011, March 9). *We don't need no stinkin' badges: How to re-invent reality without gamification*. Paper presented at Serious Game Summit, Game Developers Conference, San Francisco, CA.

Murray, J. H. (2000). *Hamlet on the holodeck: The future of narrative in cyberspace*. Cambridge, MA: The MIT Press.

Pac-Man [Computer software]. (1980). Tokyo, Japan: Namco.

Perron, B., & Wolf, M. (Eds.). (2009). *The video game theory reader 2*. New York, NY: Routledge.

Raff, J. (2000). *Jung and the alchemical imagination*. Berwick, ME: Nicholas-Hays.

Rousse, R. III. (2005). *Game design theory and practice*. Plano, TX: Wordware.

Samuels, A., Shorter, B., & Plaut, F. (2000). *A critical dictionary of Jungian analysis*. New York, NY: Routledge. (Original work published 1986)

Schell, J. (2010). *The art of game design: A book of lenses*. Boston, MA: Morgan Kaufmann.

Slater, G. (2008a, February). *Archetypal psychology*. Lecture conducted from Pacific Graduate Institute, Carpinteria, CA.

Slater, G. (2008b, March). *Archetypal psychology*. Lecture conducted from Pacific Graduate Institute, Carpinteria, CA.

State of Decay [Computer software]. (2013). Redmond, WA: Microsoft Studios.

Tetris [Computer software]. (1984). Honolulu, HI: Tetris.

Von Franz, M.-L. (1996). *The interpretation of fairy tales*. Boston, MA: Shambhala. (Original work published 1970).

World of Warcraft [Computer software]. (2001). Irvine, CA: Blizzard Entertainment.

Zimmerman, E. (2013). Foreword. In *B. De Koven, The well-played game: A player's philosophy* (pp. vi–xx). Cambridge, MA: The MIT Press.

KEY TERMS AND DEFINITIONS

Archetypal Psychology: Archetypal psychology is a lens within depth psychology that facilitates understanding of the archetypal forces that reside beneath our conscious world. It seeks to acknowledge the universality, the timelessness, the irreducibility, the emotionality, and the animation of soul (Hillman, 1983, p. 70). Archetypal psychology is a derivative of the Jungian school of depth psychology. The foundational roots of archetypal psychology include the work of Sigmund Freud (1856-1939), the Swiss psychologist Carl Gustav Jung (1875-1961), the French philosopher Henri Corbin (1903-1978), and American psychoanalyst James Hillman (1926-2011).

Archetype: As defined Jung, archetypes are the agency that organizes and structures psychic energy into specific patterns to inform psychic life. They are the deepest patterns of psychic functioning and the patterns of energy affect both individual and collective behavior.

Depth Psychology: The word *psychology* literally means the word (logos) of the psyche (soul). Depth psychology, like its practice of psychoanalysis, is an investigation of unconscious phenomena and tends to explore what lies below the surface of behaviors, conflicts, dreams, social dynamics, and cultural aesthetics. One of the major differences of depth psychology from the behavioralist and cognitive psychologies is the belief that the understanding of human behavior cannot be reduced to mere measurable behavioral and cognitive responses. Freud and Jung worked extensively to establish the field of psychology as a component of the scientific medical community. Their work centered on the understanding and development of theories of "the unconscious." Jung furthered the theories of the unconscious to include the "collective unconscious."

Metaphor: For archetypal psychology, metaphor is soul's language. It reveals the underlying content to gain meaning and perspective.

Myth: "Myths are stories of archetypal encounters" (Samuels, Shorter, & Plaut, 2000, p. 95). The myth reflects archetypal structures, themes, and experiences. Myths provide a metaphorical expression of lived experiences, conscious or unconscious.

Psyche: Psyche has been translated within Western psychology to imply the "mind"; however, the etymological root of the Greek word is "soul." Jung and Hillman's use of the word *psyche* expands the meaning to be the totality of both conscious and unconscious psychic phenomena. The words *soul* and *psyche* are interchangeable in this study.

Soul: For the purpose of this paper, I defer to archetypal psychologist Hillman's definition of soul as a reflective perspective rather than a thing. Soul "mediates events and makes differences between ourselves and everything that happens" (1992, p. xvi).

Soul-Making: The manifestation of imaginative possibilities in our natures.

Symbol: Symbols are a manifestation of archetypes; they are a representation, or a language, of the unconscious. Through symbols, potential transformation may occur by bringing awareness to unconscious content.

Virtual Games: For the purposes of this research, I used the term *virtual games* to designate digital gaming—which may also be referred to as video games, computer games, virtual worlds, social networking games, and other forms of digitally mediated games using image, sound, and interactivity to create immersive worlds of play.

Chapter 7
Vision Quest:
Recreating the Mountaineering Experience through Digital Media

Doug Emory
Lake Washington Institute of Technology, USA

ABSTRACT

One source for consideration in the quest to develop media that are truly educational and therapeutic is to examine activities that rely on a high and prolonged sense of physical and psychological coherence. The concept of sense of coherence can be broadly defined as a view of life that allows people "to consider their external and internal resources, to identify and mobilize them, to promote effective coping by finding solutions, and to resolve tension in a health-promoting manner" (Mayer and Thiel, 2014, p.1), and is related to Jung's transcendent function—the removal of the separation between the conscious and unconscious mind (as cited in Campbell, p. 273). Paradoxically, enough, such an examination might profitably be directed toward activities such as extreme sports that, on their surface, appear to be primarily physical in nature.

INTRODUCTION

One source for consideration in the quest to develop media that are truly educational and therapeutic is to examine activities that rely on a high and prolonged sense of physical and psychological coherence. Sense of coherence can be broadly defined as a view of life that allows people "to consider their external and internal resources, to identify and mobilize them, to promote effective coping by finding solutions, and to resolve tension in a health-promoting manner" (Mayer & Thiel, 2014, p.1), and is related to Jung's transcendent function—the removal of the separation between the conscious and unconscious mind (as cited in Campbell, p. 273). Its possible benefits to personal and social health are described by Rollin McCraty, who writes, "this state is directly associated with increased intuition, improved health and cognitive functioning" (n.d., p. 2). Paradoxically enough, an examination of how individuals can achieve psychological coherence might profitably be directed toward activities such as extreme sports that, on their surface, appear to be primarily physical in nature. The sport of mountaineering stands as

DOI: 10.4018/978-1-4666-9891-8.ch007

a noteworthy example of this—although alpinism requires a high level of physical fitness, it ultimately involves all four aspects of human health—physical, mental, emotional, and spiritual.[1] During the days and hours a mountaineer spends in what is often an unforgiving environment, the alignment of these aspects achieves paramount importance. Obviously, the ability to approximate the sense of coherence essential for mountaineers would be beneficial to individuals in any setting. This, then, raises the following questions for research: by what mechanisms might we bring lessons from alpinism to what is becoming an increasingly urban population? Can interactive, media-based analogies be developed that reflect the physical and psychological techniques mountaineers use to maintain a sense of coherence? Drama-based video games, built on objective correlatives drawn between the direct climbing experience and a mediated reality, may provide avenues worth further exploration.

BACKGROUND

Interactive media attempts to recreate both the physical and emotional requirements of alpine sports have been limited. In video games, when climbing is built into the plot, it appears primarily as a type of stunt that must be performed, with one example of this being designer Naughty Dog's, 2009 *Uncharted 2: Among Thieves*, which features glorious settings in the Himalayas and the mythological mountain setting of Shambhala, but uses the mountains as a device in the action platforming genre, with the character leaping from hold to hold as the plot requires Historically, mountaineering has been described as a literary sport, having been the subject of numerous critically well-regarded books such as Heinrich Harrer's 1959 *The White Spider*, James Salter's 1988 *Solo Faces*, and David Robert's 1991 *The Mountain of my Fear.* To date, however, efforts to recreate the mountaineering experience through mainstream media, particularly digital media, have been both limited and generally unsuccessful. The majority of films that involve mountaineering have most often used climbing as an aspect of setting, with plot being driven by conflict other than the "man versus nature" frame that would be expected in the attempt to portray an ascent of a challenging peak. Of the few major productions that do at least place their characters in a mountain setting, many seem to find that climbing itself requires the addition of other risk factors in order to make the experience thrilling enough for a mainstream audience. Two egregious examples of this type of film include Columbia Pictures 2000 production, "Vertical Limit", which drew this comment from "Three Film Buffs" reviewer Scott Nash: "In fact, if you ever have the choice of being trapped, halfway up a mountain, or of having to watch this movie, then I advise you to don that parka and long underwear" (2000, Dec.10). In this film, the mere ascent of K-2, probably the world's most dangerous major peak, is deemed not to be challenging enough in itself, so characters are, by a plot device, required to climb while carrying jugs of nitroglycerine in their backpacks. Similarly, Tri-Star Picture's 1993 "Cliffhanger", drops a team of Uzi-wielding thieves into the mountains, where they discover a true mountaineer (played by Sylvester Stallone) and spend much of the time requiring him to scale dangerous cliffs without his shirt. While there have been several excellent films devoted to at least the attempt to recreate the climbing experience, these films, such as 2008's "North Face" and especially 2004's "Touching the Void" (discussed in more detail below), have been smaller budget, independent productions.

Other forms of media have not been particularly successful in capturing the climbing experience either. Even ostensibly objective media have difficulty representing the climbing experience. News coverage of accidents is frequently so garbled that climbers themselves have to interpret stories in order to ascertain what actually happened. On occasion, climbers return to publish books that directly contradict one another, with perhaps the most obvious instance of this being the controversy that arose from Jon Krakauer's highly successful book "Into Thin Air" (1997), which described the tragic events on Mount Everest in 1996 and ascribed blame to several climbers, notably guide Anatoli Boukreev. Boukreev responded with a book of his own, *The Climb (*1997), providing his own version of events and initiating a debate that is ongoing in climbing circles.

The reasons behind media's ongoing failure to accurately portray mountaineering are immediately evident. The areas in which the activity occurs are generally remote. In addition, the landscapes and atmospheric conditions through which climbers move are rife with opportunities for perceptual distortion. At times, simply the configuration of the landscape itself can produce confusion. For example, climbing guidelines for both Mount Rainier and Mount Hood list the ending stages of the descent as being especially dangerous. While one would expect that simply following the fall line (the straightest course downhill) would lead one back to the lodge and safety, the reality is that, in both cases, trusting one's instincts leads into difficulty. The Mount Hood National Forest, "Mount Hood Detailed Climbing Information" webpage says the following: "Poor visibility, particularly when descending, can pull you off route. Use your compass and/or GPS. Following the fall line from Crater Rock will pull you down into Zigzag Canyon - not back to Timberline Lodge." (U.S. Forest Service, n.d.). The same disorienting effect occurs on the descent from Camp Muir to Paradise Lodge on Mount Rainer, where a failure to retain focus leads one onto either the Paradise or Nisqually Glaciers rather than to safety. One of many examples is described in *Accidents in North American Mountaineering 1991*, which recounts a situation in which three highly trained soldiers from a Special Forces unit had to spend two unplanned nights on the mountain before making their way back to the lodge, with one soldier suffering from frostbite and another from a back injury. The cause of the accident was given as follows: "The three became disoriented and descended Paradise Glacier instead of the [safer] Muir Snowfield "(The Mountaineers, p. 48).

The disorientation caused by whiteouts as an atmospheric condition is especially severe. Again, multiple media definitions of the condition are in themselves inaccurate, describing the effect as being limited only to conditions involving falling snow. A more exact definition can be found in the *Cambridge Dictionaries Online:* "a weather condition in which snow and clouds change the way light is reflected so that only very dark objects can be seen." In essence, under whiteout conditions, earth, air and sky all are one uniform color, and visibility becomes limited to several feet, in severe cases to the point at which even other climbers on a rope team disappear. This form of sensory deprivation not only makes navigation difficult—it frequently also leads to hallucinations. An article by Hadley Leggett in *Wired* quotes psychiatrist Paul Fletcher's comments on a sensory deprivation study: "This is a pretty robust finding….It appears that, when confronted by lack of sensory patterns in our environment, we have a natural tendency to superimpose our own patterns" (2009). Alpinists move through these conditions for hours, often while extremely fatigued, and they frequently face the challenge of maintaining their focus and staying on route while dealing with what are essentially high-elevation mirages. As Wallace R. Hansen noted in his book *Greenland's Icy Fury,* "Weird side effects [of whiteouts] include hallucinations, or at least strange illusory images" (1994, p. 158). Climber Todd Wiggins, when recounting his descent of Nepal's Mera Peak, reported that he unclipped from the team's rope because he saw the team entering the safety of a grove of trees, when in reality they were on a narrow, rocky ridge far above tree line (Personal communication, April 12, 2015). In essence, mountaineers in these conditions must navigate treacherous areas while deprived of almost any reliable sensory information.

While all of these factors—the public's limited direct experience with the terrain and the confusion brought on by disorienting landscapes and the climber's exhaustion—play a role in the media's limited capacity to recreate the alpine experience, the central cause of the disconnection arises from the fact that mountaineering, which superficially appears to be a physical activity, is in reality grounded in the psychology of individual climbers, each of whom functions in relative isolation for a great portion of any climb. Mountaineers are guided not only by conscious decisions regarding any summit attempt, but also by internal motivation, mental tricks, subconscious drives, and archetypal frames based on the often-unstated narratives of why climbers climb. As an unnamed female climber says in Maria Coffey's *Explorers of the Infinite*, "The scariest thing for climbers….is having to look at why they climb" (2008, p. 3). The internal nature of climbing and the mystery of what motivates climbers presents the primary source of the difficulty the media faces in attempting to recreate the positive benefits of a mountaineering mentality.

RECREATING THE MOUNTAINEERING EXPERIENCE THROUGH DIGITAL MEDIA

In order to identify qualities from the climbing mindset that can be recreated in media, one needs first to identify and describe the mental environment in which mountaineers function. Physical skill plays a necessary but not sufficient role in climbing, and though one might expect that risk and adrenalin are the predominate factors in developing a certain state of mind, the reality is that climbing involves long periods that can only be described as drudgery. Although the sense of team is extremely important, mountaineers often cannot hear one another, and at times cannot even see one another, so they travel vast distances over large periods of time in isolation. As noted above, at times they traverse disorienting landscapes, made even more so by sensory deprivation and exhaustion. In a sense, climbers frequently move locked entirely within their own minds, a state of mind more akin to dreaming than waking. Viewed from the perspective of our ordinary, day-to-day cognition, the task of climbing a serious mountain seems almost impossible. One's judgement and one's awareness of the surrounding environment may mean the difference between life and death, but this extremity of focus must be maintained under sensory and emotional conditions that would seem certain to produce its opposite.

Although alpinists often function in isolation, their responses when asked how they manage in these challenging environments are relatively uniform. Climbers need to be intrinsically motivated, and they need to exercise self-discipline from the onset of any journey. Pace becomes extremely important because climbing by the "dash and gasp" method—charging ahead until one is breathless—is too physically taxing to carry a mountaineer forward over long distances. In order to avoid this, it becomes important to fall into a rhythm, and climbing "how to" guides provide explicit direction on how to move through steep terrain. According to *Mountaineering, the Freedom of the Hills*, "The most valuable technique is setting the right pace" (The Mountaineers, 1992, p. 81). Pacing on steep terrain is achieved through techniques such as the rest step, a movement which deliberately slows pace by adding a pause between steps and by synchronizing one's breathing with one's movements. When climbing steep glacial terrain, alpinists frequently adopt the French step, a method intended to keep all of one's crampon points on the slope, but which does so with a movement much like a dance step, a diagonal maneuver in which one foot swings in around the other, with that two-step sequence punctuated by the placement of the ice ax. Again, especially at higher elevations, each of those steps in the sequence is tied to one's breathing.

In addition to these formal techniques on which mountaineers are trained, every climber adopts methods of self-motivation. These range from mantra-like exhortations--"this is necessary" or "it's business time"--to counting, to singing and to the repetition of jokes and stories close-knit climbing teams have shared over period of years. Washington climber Jon Karpoff says that at the onset of trips his mind is filled with "lots of floating thoughts and concerns", but as the trip continues, his mind empties, and he becomes conscious primarily of elemental points such as his breathing and heart rate (Personal communication, April 12, 2015). In essence, mountaineers use rhythmic movements and repeated phrases, all of which are tied to their breathing, in order to enter a meditative state that, while looking inward, also makes them intensely aware of their surroundings in the present movement. In doing so, they are relying on ancient techniques such as pranayama (yoga breathing) that "rapidly bring the mind to the present moment and reduce stress" (Brown & Gerbarg, 2009). The repeated phrases or song lyrics, no matter how trivial or silly, provide the same type of focusing effect as is gained from any mantra.

The achievement of this highly-developed state of psychological coherence benefits alpinists in numerous ways. The extremity of focus on the present moment allows for sustained rhythmic physical movement at a level of precision rarely seen. Physiologically, it allows the climber to achieve what Rollin McCraty calls, "cross-coherence, which occurs when two or more of the body's oscillatory systems, such as respiration and heart rhythms, become entrained and operate at the same frequency" (p. 3). Through the maintenance of a sense of coherence, the mountaineer not only uses energy efficiently but also aligns body with mind, a necessity because, in certain situations, reactions need to occur so swiftly that time for thought followed by action simply does not exist. In retelling the story of a climb he and a partner made of the Isle of Skye's Cuillin Ridge, a 12-kilometer route along what is often a knife-edge geologic formation, Dave Cunningham, says that, when it became clear they were threatened with being benighted on the rock, he and his friend began moving wordlessly, without thinking, just reeling the rope back in and setting the next belay point, all in perfect harmony (Personal communication, April 12, 2015). His son, extreme snowboarder Russell Cunningham, in describing his descent down the heavily-crevassed 5000-foot North Face of Washington State's Mount Adams, said that he entered a new state of consciousness, one in which there was "no thinking, no waiting", only an understanding that each of his turns needed to be perfect: "When one's life depends on the placement of a single foot, or the direction of a single turn, there just isn't time to reflect on much else" (splitboardbindings.com, 2013, May 10).

A standard climbing saying is "to think about falling is the same as falling", because any contradiction between the conscious and unconscious mind, any discrepancy in thought, any doubt, erases the focus needed to stay on the slope. In extreme mountain settings, the mental imagery one carries and one's emotional state correspond directly to one's physical reality. Without a true state of coherence in which their mental, physical, and emotional aspects are aligned, climbers would immediately come into danger. While functioning within this necessary framework, one's emotions are controlled, neither rising too high or low, an important point in maintaining motivation in general but which acquires added significance in emergencies. In these cases, which often occur in seconds, time seems to stretch in duration, and despite an underlying realization of urgency, the mind works more or less logically through the steps necessary to prevent disaster. Karpoff, during a fall while skiing the Ptarmigan Traverse, remembers thinking, "I can't...believe I'm not stopping", a thought followed by his mind then walking logically through the steps needed to end a dangerous slide (Personal communication, April 12, 2015). Climber Nathan Vangor writes that, in emergency situations, it's "Like my brain just responds so fast that there isn't time to think about what has happened" (April 25, 2015). Joe Simpson, during the voice-over narration in the film version of his book *Touching the Void*, says that, at the moment when his rescue seemed impossible, "I could acknowledge that I was going to die in a very matter-of-fact way" (Pathe Pictures, 2004). Even having reached that conclusion, he then simply resumed moving toward the camp which offered his only possibility for salvation.

A final, less obvious benefit gained by the climber's achievement of a sense of coherence is the ability to monitor and react to changing situations and to maintain what are at first glance contradictory perspectives—a feature that has both physical and psychological benefits. Karpoff reports that he has navigated through the hallucinations caused by whiteouts by imagining himself playing a game of Tetris—laying a logical frame over a surreal landscape. Dave Cunningham, when asked to identify what he valued most about mountaineering, identifies the development of a sense of "perspective"—the way he aligns the seeming contradiction between his feelings of physical and technical competence, the sense that he is up to the task, against the reality that, in the vastness of the mountains, "You're literally an invisible speck" (Personal communication, April 12, 2015). As the Scottish poet Andrew Greig puts it beautifully in his book, *Summit Fever,* "We're so nearly nothing, but not quite. And that makes all the difference. The mountains teach us humility, but also how much we can achieve when we commit our all" (Grieg, 1998).

The commonality of these sensations among climbers occur at least in part because, though mountaineers so frequently function within their own internal world, the similarity of their techniques creates a shared psychological reality that manifests itself in value systems such as the "brotherhood of the rope". As renowned Yosemite Valley climber Royal Robbins noted during a speech at the 2000 Banff Mountain Film Festival:

Conflict and cross-purposes among climbers are a natural part of the human condition. But overall, and in the long run, the brotherhood of the rope has prevailed. Fellowship among comrades who share danger and who trust their lives in each other's hands has always been a powerful impulse in the climbing world... We have often heard of esprit de corps. What of Esprit de la Corde, that unseen thin line connecting climbers, through time and through space?

Clearly part of the value placed on team stems from the extreme dependence every rope team member has on his or her partners. One weak team member can prevent a team from reaching its goal, and at worst place the team at risk, a circumstance which leads mountaineers to be incredibly selective in choosing teammates. However, the bonds between climbers go beyond this simple avoidance of danger, arising from shared techniques, a joint achievement of peak experiences and possibly also from the changes in consciousness brought on by the meditative devices on which they rely, for it is possible that individuals whose minds are empty of self and open to the environment are equally open to the thoughts and feelings shared among team members. In describing his concerns while climbing, Nathan Vangor writes that "My values while climbing are to push myself as hard as I can, go as fast as I can, not endanger myself, and probably most important not endanger the group" (Personal communication, April 25, 2015). This value system goes beyond one's concern for one's team. The greatest ethical failing climbers can display is that of abandoning not only team members, but anyone else they find in distress on the mountain. The value system is such that any climber on any mountain accepts a level of responsibility for humanity as he/she finds encounters it in that unforgiving environment.

CORRELATIONS

The methods climbers use to ascend dangerous landscapes and the value system on which they rely, however, do not ultimately explain the source of their energy and motivation. Many sports rely on specific patterns of movement and on a team sensibility, and they do so without the element of risk mountaineers face. The amount of general psychic energy that is required to produce the outcomes climbers achieve seems to arise from a deeper source. This source may be related to "Jung's conception of the psyche…of a system which is dynamic, in constant movement, and at the same time self-regulating; he calls the general psychic energy, libido" (Fordham, 2013, Chapter 1, para. 7-11). This natural energy exists slightly in excess of what is necessary for ordinary purposes, but it is not channeled directly into conscious activities: after a "period of gestation in the unconscious a symbol is produced, which can attract the libido and also serve as a channel diverting its natural flow. The symbol is never thought out consciously, but comes usually as a revelation or intuition" (Fordham, 2013, Chapter 1, para. 7-11). One method for identifying possible sources for the energy that motivates mountaineers can be found in interviews about the narratives they relate to the climbing experience, with the stories cited giving insight into the symbols that are developed within a climber's subconscious and that drive his or her actions. When asked the question, "When you think back, can you think of any stories—history, fiction, fantasy—that made climbing as an activity resonate with you? If so, what were those stories?" climbers came up with common answers. While some made comments in the vein of, "I just put my boots on and started walking," the majority contacted had narratives from their childhoods that connected them to the experience. Several said that views of the open wilderness and tundra reminded them of great 19th-century expeditions to the poles; others similarly said they felt the urge to fill in the blank places on the maps as previous explorers had, in the sense of exploring untouched, undiscovered wilderness. Others related the experience to a sense they were going to war. The most common response was related to hero myths and fantasies. As writer and *Alpinist* magazine editor Katie Ives said: "Reading Narnia obsessively as a child probably created some of those myth-narratives in my mind--that, and parents who taught my sister and myself to believe that life had to include 'adventures'" (Personal communication, April 15, 2015). This comment is echoed by climbing writer Jacob Smith: "Looking for glory is definitely central. I always saw it like a quest from a medieval legend or a fantasy novel, slaying dragons or fighting in the revolution or whatnot" (Personal communication, April 14, 2015).

Because the desire to climb arises primarily from intrinsic motivations, the stories mountaineers view as analogous to their experiences are of extreme significance. One can assume these stories serve, as Jung outlined the function of dreams, as symbols that guide a climber's conscious activities. This correlation becomes even clearer when one focuses on the types of stories chosen—many of which are based in myth, fairytales, and historic adventures. Great climbs become mythic quests, with the narrative of those quests being repeatedly told within the community of climbers, within groups of mountaineering friends, and occasionally with the general populace. In essence, every climb reenacts the basic narrative of the hero's journey as outlined in Joseph Campbell's *The Hero with a Thousand Faces*. The fact that the archetypal hero's adventure served as the impetus for many mountaineers to take up their sport may explain the ultimate source of the energy that motives them.

Campbell makes the connection between the stories of myth and collective psychology explicit, calling them the: "spontaneous productions of the psyche" (2008, p. 2) and saying that "It is not difficult for the modern intellectual to concede that the symbolism of mythology has a psychological significance" (p. 219). He sharpens this connection and relates it to individual "quests" by saying, "Freud, Jung, and their followers have demonstrated irrefutably that the logic, the heroes, and the deeds of myth survive into modern times. In the absence of an effective general mythology, each of us has his own private, unrecognized, rudimentary, yet secretly potent pantheon of dream" (2008, p. 2). It is possible that alpinists attain their personal sense of coherence through the physical reenactment of the hero's journey and the archetypal symbols underlying it. They interact with the unknown lands outside of their communities, entering this new world of their own volition. In a physical way, they initiate themselves into a reenactment of the archetype the monomyth represents and give it a palpable reality.

The connection between Campbell's monomyth and the activity of climbing becomes even more explicit when one examines the stages into which the hero's journey are divided. "The adventure of the hero normally follows the pattern of...a separation from the world, a penetration to some source of power, and a life-enhancing return," as Campbell notes (2008, pp. 27-28). In other words, the journey can be classified into general steps of separation, initiation, and return. The initial stage often involves movement away from an established community and then the crossing of a threshold into wilderness, often toward a distant mountaintop—"a passage beyond the veil of the known into the unknown." (2008, p. 67). For mountaineers, these steps can be related to the opening stages of leaving home, with the crossing of the threshold being that stage at which the established trails end and climbers begin following faint "climber's trails" or forging their own route entirely. In myth, the crossing of the threshold often involves a passage between opposites—between fear and desire, between logic and intuition—with the hero transcending that duality. Analogously, climbers cross the threshold simultaneously holding what appears to be the contradictory perspective discussed above—they must become utterly self-reliant, confident in their training and their companions while simultaneously remaining cognizant of the irresistible power of the forces surrounding them.

For Campbell, the initiation step begins with "the road of trials", with the hero moving "in a dream landscape of curiously fluid, ambiguous forms." (2008, p. 81). It is a road of tests and ordeals, and one can, without exercising much imagination, relate this to a climber's moving more or less alone for periods of hours, often with limited consciousness of his or her self, through a surreal and often confusing environment, expending a vast amount of energy while avoiding hazards posed by weather as well as avalanches, crevasses, and rock fall—all of the objective hazards presented by the mountain itself.

Aspects of the final stage of the mythological hero's adventure, the return, are again reflected by the conclusion of any successful climb. In myth, the adventurers often receive aid from outside in order to successfully complete their quest. They may find that the time in which they felt their quest occurring proves to be mismatched with the passage of time in their community of origin—either no time has passed or great periods of time have passed in what seemed brief moments to the adventurer. Finally, they bring their community a gift, fire, a healing balm, or perhaps a wisdom on the hero's part that can be used to benefit society.

Again, correlations can be drawn between these characteristics of myth and aspects of mountaineering. Because of the intensity of the climbing experience, particularly in emergency situations, time does suffer from distortions, often being perceived, as philosopher Henri Bergson described it, more like lived time—Bergson's "real duration"—than time as measured by a stop watch. During safe but arduous uphill climbs, when a mountaineer is absorbed in the moment, time may appear to pass very quickly. In contrast, during emergencies the opposite occurs. As Nathan Vangor noted, "In dangerous situations, time slows down dramatically and what seems like minutes is actually just 30 seconds or so" (Personal communication, April 25, 2015). In regard to the physical attempt to return, as Ed Viesturs, perhaps America's finest high-altitude mountaineer, says at his presentations, coming home is the most important part of any climb. While attaining a summit would appear to be the greater challenge, the descent is generally considered among climbers to be the most dangerous portion of any climb since individuals may lose focus after attaining their objective, may be exhausted, and may face the reality that climbing downhill is simply more difficult than is ascending. The hazards involved in returning have even, in some cases, led some mountaineers to experience visits from their own "guardian angel"—a phenomenon known as the Third Man Syndrome. Mount Everest climber Doug Scott describes "the third man syndrome: [as] imagining there is someone else walking beside you, a comforting presence telling you what to do next". Scott's story and a comprehensive list of other such experiences is included in the book *The Third Man Factor*, published in 2009 by Royal Canadian Geographical Society member John Geiger. Geiger found that "the syndrome was endemic among climbers" and that "it's not highly unusual or freakish. It's an experience that people have had in all sorts of environments and conditions and that lends it a lot of power" (as cited in Porter, L., 2009). Something in the psychology of climbers desperately attempting to return home has, then, provided them with a guardian spirit like those found in fairy tales and myths, appearing to them at desperate moments to lead them to safety.

The question of whether or not climbers return with a wisdom that is of benefit to society is open to debate. Certainly climbers believe the experience provides them with knowledge that others lack. As Russell Cunningham eloquently describes the sensation:

The process following a mountain venture is a complex one. This is the essential recovery phase in which not only the body begins to rebuild the damaged muscle proteins and add bone density, but the brain itself finally has a chance to make sense of the experience, making sense of not only what it meant to live in the wilderness, but also what it meant to go through the process of changing identities– To be a modern human who has been touched by ancient wilderness. (splitboardbindings.com, 2013, May 10)

The knowledge gained from this contact can be as basic as understanding one's physical capabilities and a honing of one's reaction times, but it can involve a number of cognitive and emotional factors as well. In general, most climbers believe their sport has improved their decision-making skills and built their self-confidence. Others believe that it has given them an enhanced perspective on events and their day-to-day lives since they have the ability to compare serious, life-threatening emergencies with items that may be irritating but lack the need for an urgent response. In this way, their reactions tend to align with the situation, without the unnecessary conflict that often results when the trivial is mistaken for the significant.

Perhaps the most compelling type of knowledge with which alpinists return is, however, that of "flow" experiences which at times seem to touch on the spiritual. At its most general level, flow can be defined as "a state of concentration so focused that it amounts to absolute absorption in an activity" (Csikszentmihalyi, M.). It is related to intrinsic motivation in that it arises from rewards deeper than those most psychologists commonly rank within the hierarchy of needs and may stem from a desire to feel total ownership of one's behavior. Mihaly Csikszentmihalyi identified ten characteristics that are generally present in individuals experiencing a flow state:

1. *Clear goals that, while challenging, are still attainable.*
2. *Strong concentration and focused attention.*
3. *The activity is intrinsically rewarding.*
4. *Feelings of serenity; a loss of feelings of self-consciousness.*

5. *Timelessness; a distorted sense of time; feeling so focused on the present that you lose track of time passing.*
6. *Immediate feedback.*
7. *Knowing that the task is doable; a balance between skill level and the challenge presented.*
8. *Feelings of personal control over the situation and the outcome.*
9. *Lack of awareness of physical needs.*
10. *Complete focus on the activity itself.*

The benefits of achieving a flow state are obvious to mountaineers, with one profound reward being the ordering sensation it provides to an alpinist's consciousness:

Disorder in consciousness, also called psychic entropy, occurs whenever: 'Information ... conflicts with existing intentions or distracts us from carrying them out' (Csikszentmihalyi, 1990, p. 36). We use labels such as anxiety, fear, jealousy, or rage to describe disordered experiences. Entropy drains our psychic energy, fragments our attention, and compromises the integrity and effectiveness of the self. (Parr, G. D., Montgomery, M., & DeBell, C. 1998)

In other words, achieving a sense of coherence results in a flow state that anchors one in the moment, focuses attention, and reduces the distraction caused by anxiety, which in turn enhances one to respond positively and efficiently to any number of situations.

The benefits of flow state to climbers are so compelling that some authors view the primary attraction to extreme adventure as being the opening of a door to a sense of "spiritual transcendence" (Coffey xiii). Carlos Carsolio, perhaps the greatest Mexican high-altitude climber, says in regard to transcendent flow experiences "You open the channel. I looked for such moments in every expedition. It's why I wanted to climb alone and to do such hard routes. It's a kind of spiritual addiction." (Coffey, 2008, p. 17). Climbers frequently describe an intensity of focus so profound that they no longer sense a mind/body duality or even a Self differentiated from the wilderness surrounding them. Their connection with the environment around them has to be extreme given that "Their survival depends on their maintaining a constant focus and paying close attention to all the forces of nature, becoming hyperaware of the slightest breeze, a change in temperature, the way snow feels under their boots or rock on their fingers." (Coffey, 2008, p. xii). The wilderness has been viewed as a place of not only of risk but of spiritual discovery since the dawn of human history, with literary representations of this concept present in the Bible, the writings of the Romantic and Transcendental movements, and the products of the environmental movement. This sense of transcendence—the sense that climbers frequently speak of—is perhaps best captured in Ralph Waldo Emerson's essay "Nature":

In the woods, we return to reason and faith. There I feel that nothing can befall me in life, — no disgrace, no calamity, (leaving me my eyes,) which nature cannot repair. Standing on the bare ground, — my head bathed by the blithe air, and uplifted into infinite space, — all mean egotism vanishes. I become a transparent eye-ball; I am nothing; I see all; the currents of the Universal Being circulate through me; I am part or particle of God." ("Nature" Chapter 1, 1836)

The above is not intended to argue that alpinists are immune to all of the personality flaws and neuroses that afflict other individuals. It does, however, lead to a conclusion that, while engaged in the act of climbing, mountaineers attain a level of focus and coherence that allow them to function under what would otherwise be impossible conditions. These abilities are gained through training in techniques involving rhythm and breathing, through self-motivation and discipline, and through the alignment of the conscious and unconscious parts of the psyche, with that latter capacity grounded in narratives and images gathered from myth and symbol. The outcomes of these features are clear. In order to climb successfully, one must have the following characteristics:

- A high level of physical fitness and a deep ability to monitor one's physical capacity in any given moment.
- An ability to focus for prolonged periods, remaining highly aware of the external environment.
- An ability to interpret a situation and adapt to a changing reality.
- An ability to motivate oneself without reliance on external rewards.
- A sense of optimism and confidence that distant goals will be achieved.
- An ability to be comfortable with one's self and to become absorbed in the moment.
- A sense of team-focused values, being concerned with other team members and with one's role on the team.
- A capacity to manage one's emotional state and avoiding the distractions brought on by anxiety or panic.
- An ability to think clearly and react quickly under potentially disastrous circumstances.

Mountaineers with these abilities return having at times experienced a perfect alignment of their consciousness—remembering every step in a long journey, having action follow thought with absolute precision, and perhaps having attained a state of flow that borders on the transcendent. However, the community of climbers is small, and so these benefits are limited in scope. Mountaineering has, not without justification, been criticized as a selfish activity, one that has little social point and that has caused climbing families to be broken apart, with children losing parents and one spouse losing another. (An example of this viewpoint appeared in the June 13 *Globe and Mail*, in an article that contrasts climbers with victims of the recent Nepal earthquake by saying: "At the end of the day, the only reason you have chosen this otherwise pointless place to exert yourself is because it is All About You." (Saunders, D.)) Part of this common charge against the sport would be diminished were the benefits more visible and more widely disseminated. When viewed from the perspective of what climbers gain through the experience of climbing, it appears those lessons could be immensely beneficial to society if they could be presented in a format accessible to non-mountaineers. In an increasingly urbanized world, and in schools in which growing percentages of children lack the ability to focus and to delay gratification, is it possible to take the psychological characteristics one develops in alpine settings and broadcast them across a society? Could this be the healing balm that alpinists deliver to their community at their quest's end?

SUGGESTIONS FOR FUTURE WORK

Aspects of coherence as a concept have been discussed by a variety of researchers using different terminology and different research methodologies, with many of these theories directly applicable to the climbing experience. Jungian theory would hypothesize that mountaineers, through reenactment of a key archetype, amplify and gain energy and motivation through the use of a structural element of the human psyche. Maslow would refer to the attainment of important summits as indicating (no pun intended) a peak experience, filled with triumph and transcendence. Rollin McCraty would say that the benefits to climbers accrue from their alignment of systems, and he would note benefits to an individual's physiology and psychology alike. As has been discussed above, nearly all of the aspects of flow as outlined by Csikszentmihalyi, and through the positive psychology movement exist in mountaineering experiences. Each of these theories illustrates the relevance of the climbing mantra that "to think of falling is the same as falling," because each indicates how image and thought intervene in and influence outcomes in the physical world, That reality, taken one step further, indicates a possibility that qualities gained from mountaineering may be replicable without one physically entering an alpine environment.

Research into positive psychology (a movement that takes as its goal "fostering excellence through the understanding ad enhancement factors that lead to growth" (Berman, 2005, p.1) and its application to outdoor education suggests that transmitting the lessons learned from mountaineering would be beneficial, so a search for a mechanism by which to deliver this type of education is worth undertaking. Martin Seligman, in his compilation of essays *Positive Psychology: An Introduction* writes:" A science of positive subjective experience, positive individual traits, and positive institutions promises to improve quality of life and prevent the pathologies that arise when life is barren and meaningless.... Hope, wisdom, creativity, future mindedness, courage, spirituality, responsibility, and perseverance are ignored or explained as transformations of more authentic negative impulses" (2000, p.1). This point is echoed in Bolier et all's comment that, "it is recognized that mental health is more than just the absence of mental illness, as expressed in the World Health Organization's definition of mental health: "Mental health is a state of well-being in which the individual realizes his or her own abilities, can cope with the normal stresses of life, can work productively, and is able to make a contribution to his or her community" (Bolier et al, 2013). Mountaineers demonstrate many of the personality features for which positive psychology aims; they are autonomous and self-motivated; they trust in their skill level; they regulate their emotions; and they are optimistic.

Although its students are not commonly exposed to the risks of scaling major peaks, outdoor education is analogous in that it takes place in the wilderness, and it too has become increasingly concerned with a focus on positive activities that promote coherence rather than on older models which were grounded in the theory that people learn best by being placed in situations that move them "beyond their comfort level" and into activities that create anxiety and disequilibrium. The contrasting model proposed by Dene Berman et al runs by channels more like those used by mountaineers, who essentially achieve coherence by taking on summits with a high level of challenge, but summits matched to their skill level. Correspondingly, Berman suggests that, in order to have students gain from wilderness experiences, they should not be placed in situations that frustrate and terrify them. Instead, they should be placed in a "healthy, supportive community in which people can act on their personal strivings. Communities are created when there is an emergence of conditions such as working with nature, experiencing the outdoors because of an appreciation of the environment, and safety and sharing with a focus on group members' strengths. (p. 18). Essentially, this version of outdoor education corresponds with the type of community one sees on a well-structured climbing team. Outdoor education, which has traditionally catered to troubled youth and special populations, could provide a therapeutic function by structuring community and managing the level of challenge just as a climbing team does. Even traditional education is developing an interest in examining how qualities like those developed by climbers may improve student learning. Teaching in context and in authentic settings has received a great deal of recent attention as a mechanism for developing intrinsic motivation because the material presented to students possesses an immediate relevance to them. A concept such as teamwork, which seems only vaguely relevant in most academic settings, would attain an immediate and compelling relevance if approached from the stance taken by Royal Robbins and his ode to Esprit de la Corde. J.B. Mackinnon, writing for *Orion Magazine,* discusses how he overcame teenage anxiety through becoming a rock climber, saying, "we can also learn to regulate nihilistic despair, and it's important to note that this appears to improve with practice. It [rock climbing] was a forum in which fears are not abstract or pathological, but instead are acknowledged as reasonable and expected" (2015).

The controversial and fairly new development of the field of "character" education is based around the formation of seven non-cognitive characteristics in children: grit, zest, self-control, optimism, gratitude, social intelligence and curiosity—and it again aligns well with the characteristics climbers demonstrate in the mountains. "Grit", is defined by University of Pennsylvania professor and MacArthur Genius Award Winner Angela Duckworth as "perseverance and passion for long term goals. Grit entails working strenuously toward challenges, maintaining effort and interest over years despite failure, adversity, and plateaus in progress. The gritty individual approaches achievement as a marathon; his or her advantage is stamina" (Duckworth, A., Peterson, C., Matthews, M. & Kelly D. 2007). Parr and Debell, in their article "Flow theory as a model for enhancing student resilience", (1998) again point toward the use of high challenge/high skill tasks as a way of improving student focus, maintaining their interest, and assisting them in overcoming alienation.

These research discoveries all support the thesis that mountaineering creates a set of psychological conditions that, if replicated, could be useful both in therapy and in education. However, the logistical difficulties in moving mass numbers of students into the foothills or mountains become immediately evident. The world's population is increasingly urban, and the expenses involved in traditional outdoor education would be a disincentive in themselves. Additionally, in order to adequately recreate the psychological experience of an alpinist, the duration of any such experience, both in terms of training and the activity itself, would be daunting. A direction worthy of further research is whether a mechanism by which this experience can be delivered virtually could be designed, using techniques that would serve as objective correlatives to recreate the mountaineering experience.

Visual media such as film and interactive drama-based video games clearly have the capacity to recreate certain aspects of the climber's adventure. Both media are based in the image, and as is noted at several points above, in a mountain setting scant difference exists between one's emotion, one's perception and one's physical circumstances. At heart, both media are grounded in narrative, so each has the potential to outline the story of a climb, and both have the ability to convincingly recreate elements of mountaineering. Each can present the stunning scenery and the sense of immensity of the mountain wilderness as well as the confusion and perceptual distortion created by weather and cataclysmic events such as avalanches. They can also use special visual effects to capture certain elements of a mountaineer's psyche. One only has to turn to a video game such as *Uncharted 2: Among Thieves*, to see how well a drama-based game can graphically recreate the Himalayas. The excellent 2003 documentary, *Touching the Void,* provides stunning footage of climbers Joe Simpson's and Simon Yates' assault on the Andean peak Siula Grande, but at the same time it uses extreme close-ups to reflect the isolation brought on by the severe storm through which they had to descend, a situation in which they could neither hear nor see one another. The film uses both voice-over narration to convey the climbers' emotions as well as special effects to illustrate how Simpson, badly injured, regressed from a state of controlled despair, in which he was able to cry but still think logically enough to prepare his escape from the crevasse into which he had fallen, to one of complete psychological disequilibrium, a sensation recreated by the filmmaker through the use of spinning images superimposed over one another. At this point in the narrative, Simpson's voice-over commentary indicates that he had lost hold on himself as a distinct being: "At one point I had this weird sensation that I had lain there for centuries…becoming part of the rocks that I was never going to move from" (MacDonald, K., 2004).

What neither film nor gaming media have commonly addressed to this point are techniques analogous to the psychological self-management tools used by climbers to calm themselves, motivate themselves, and ultimately achieve the state of flow in which mind and body are aligned. The role repetition plays in developing a sense of grit or resilience as well as the feelings of confidence and mastery necessary to achieving a flow state seem extremely difficult to replicate in film, and thus would seem more suited to delivery through interactive video games. Although most games remain fixated on impressive, immediate gratification—*Uncharted 2*, for all of its gorgeous mountain graphics, still revels in the immediate enjoyment of its main character making superhuman leaps from climbing hold to climbing hold--.one can easily envision a much different version of even such a mainstream game. *Uncharted* contains elements of myth and, as with many games, moves its character through several stages of the hero's journey.

While few popular media steps have been taken in regard to teaching or enhancing these elements in individuals, some encouraging projects are currently underway. *Sina sprite*, a video game marketed by the Seattle-based company Litesprite, recently won a Robert Wood Johnson award for its creative attempt to help individuals overcome anxiety and depression. One element of the game involves players breathing along with the cartoon fox who becomes their avatar, in this way controlling their breathing as climbers do and calming the flight or fight reflex. The goal of the game is for the player to help the fox achieve the ranking of Zen master through its evolving ability to control and managing its emotions. (Radke, B., 2014). In its work toward this objective, the game aligns with MCraty's research into coherence-building techniques that create "self-regulation of emotions and stress responses" so that these methods then become "increasingly familiar and, eventually, automatic" (p. 14).

Potentially the single greatest lesson from climbing that video games could adopt would be a change in the manner in which the archetypal story from which climbers draw their energy is presented. Although hundreds of video games are based on the mythic quest motif that underlies any climb, they differ in that the ultimate goal of many games becomes one not of flow and transcendence but rather of control. As Dr. Laura Toussaint notes, a well-known game like *Grand Theft Auto* brings a character from humble beginnings to a position of mastery, but it does so through providing that character with an increasingly powerful set of tools with which he can dominate his community (Personal correspondence, April 21, 2015). The lesson from mountaineering is much different and is based on the incorporation of a key duality—mountaineers must be equal to the challenges they face, but they must at the same time accept the fact that they are ultimately powerless in the face of nature's force—they are, as Dave Cunningham says, "literally an invisible speck" (Personal correspondence, April 12, 2015). In recognition of this context, any underlying narrative would need to include the concepts of acceptance and surrender rather than simply being a tale of individual triumph. Climbing at its best touches on all four of the elements of character—mental, physical, emotional, and spiritual—and serious educational games would need to expand their focus to include this range of perspectives.

Again, video games have been developed that do touch more fully on themes reflecting the scope of human characteristics —the game *"Never Alone"*, created by E-Line Media and the Cook Inlet Tribal Council which serves the Inupiat and other Alaskan Native tribes, has been justifiable praised for its attempts to preserve Inuit culture and spirituality. An additional lesson from the game is that humanity, in its quests and adventures, needs to accept the natural forces surrounding us and as part of a team. In

Never Alone, "Each character has a different set of skills, and ...must work together to overcome obstacles on a journey that mirrors the one taken by Kunuuksaayuka, the blizzard investigator. This theme of interdependence is central to Iñupiat stories, no doubt born of the need to help one another in order to survive the harsh Alaskan conditions" (Parkin, S., 2014). In its narrative, then, the game provides analogies to the "brotherhood of the rope" and the need for even the most skilled climbers to recognize how they must work to accommodate the extreme conditions through which their quest progresses.

The unlikely pairing of an extreme physical activity with a media-based analogy could, then, produce a unique social good. Further research into games that correlate with the qualities outlined above could allow individuals who will never have the time or the fiscal or physical resources to climb a mountain come away with the best portions of climbing psychology: a reliance on intrinsic motivation, the ability to persevere in difficult conditions, a reduction of psychic disharmony and the achievement of a sense of coherence and flow, with many of these qualities achieved through an amplification of the energy provided through the symbols embedded in the myth of the hero's adventure. Gaming, and media in general, have too often been relegated to the day-to-day and the trivial, but climbing at its best focuses on the deepest of issues—an individual's relationship to his community, to the natural world, and to life itself. As Campbell writes, "The effect of the successful adventure of the hero is the unlocking and release again of the flow of life into the body of the world" (2008, p. 32). The archetype of this adventure is the foundation from which alpinism takes its genesis, and a conveyance of the sports' best qualities into our urban communities could unlock the door to the "flow of life" so many individuals would never otherwise experience.

REFERENCES

Berman, D. & Davis-Berman, J. (2005). Positive Psychology and Outdoor Education. *The Journal of Experiential Education,* 28(1), 17-24.

Bolier, L., Haverman, M., Westerhof, G. J., Riper, H., Smit, F., & Bohlmeijer, E. (2013). Positive psychology interventions: A meta-analysis of randomized controlled studies. *BMC Public Health, 13*(1), 1–20. doi:10.1186/1471-2458-13-119 PMID:23390882

Brown, R & Gerbarg, P. (2009). Yoga Breathing, Meditation, and Longevity. *Annals of the New York: Academy of Sciences* (Vol. 1172).

Campbell, J. (2008). *The Hero with a Thousand Faces*. Novato, California: New World Library.

Cherry, K. (n. d.). What is Flow? Understanding the Psychology of Flow. Retrieved from psychology. about.com/od/positive psychology/a/flow.htm

Coffey, M. (2008). *Explorers of the Infinite*. New York: Jeremy P. Tarcher/Penguin Books.

Csikszentmihalyi, M. (2000). *Flow: The Psychology of Optimal Experience*. Global Learning Communities. doi:10.1037/10518-188

Cunningham, R. (2013, May 10). Alaskan Dreams: My Wilderness Experience. Retrieved from http:// www.splitboardbindings.com

Duckworth, A., Peterson, C., Matthews, M., & Kelly, D. (2007). Grit: Perseverance and Passion for Long-Term Goals. *Journal of Personality and Social Psychology*, *92*(6), 1087–1101. doi:10.1037/0022-3514.92.6.1087 PMID:17547490

Emerson, R. (2009, September). *Nature, Chapter One.* Retrieved from www.emersoncentral.com

Fordham, F. (2013, October). *Introduction to Jung's Psychology, Chapter One.* Retrieved from http://www.cgjungpage.org

Geiger, J. (2010). *The Third Man Factor*. New York: Weinstein Books.

Graydon, D. (Ed.), (1992). *Mountaineering: The Freedom of the Hills (5th ed.).* Seattle: The Mountaineers Books.

Greig, A. (1998). *Summit Fever*. Seattle: Mountaineers Books.

Hansen, W. (1994). *Greenland's Icy Fury*. College Station: Texas A&M University Press.

Jung, C. The Transcendent Function. In J. Campbell (Ed.), *The Portable Jung* (pp. 273–300). New York: Penguin Books.

Leggett, H. (2009). Out of LSD? Just 15 Minutes of Sensory Deprivation Triggers Hallucinations. [Electronic Version] *Wired.* Retrieved from http://www.wired.com

MacDonald, K. (Director). (2004). *Touching the Void* [Motion picture]. United Kingdom: Pathe.

Mackinnon, J. B. (2015), "Facing Fear." [Electronic Version] *Orion Magazine.* Retrieved June 20, 2015 from https://orionmagazine.org

Mayer, J., & Thiel, A. (2014). Health in Elite Sports from a Salutogenetic Perspective: Athletes' Sense of Coherence. *PLoS ONE*, *9*(7), 1–11. doi:10.1371/journal.pone.0102030 PMID:25014085

McCraty, R. (n.d.). *Coherence: Bridging Personal, Social and Global Health.*

Nash, S. (2000, December 10). Review of the film *Vertical Limit.* Three Film Buffs. Retrieved from http://www.threemoviebuffs.com

Parkin, S. (2014, Nov. 17). Never Alone: Could a Video Game Help Preserve Inuit Culture? *The New Yorker.* Retrieved from http://www.newyorker.com

Parr, G. D., Montgomery, M., & DeBell, C. (1998). Flow theory as a model for enhancing Student resilience. *Professional School Counseling, 1*(5), 26.

Porter, L. (2009, June 28). Mystery of the Third Man. *The Sydney Morning Herald.* Retrieved from http://www.smh.com.au

Radke, B. (Interviewer). (2014, October). *Feeling Blue? Play this Game with Socks the Fox* [Radio broadcast]. Seattle: KUOW.

Robbins, R. (2000). *Standing on the Shoulders: A Tribute to my Heroes* (Speech). Proceedings of the 2000 Banff Mountain Film Festival. Retrieved from http://www.frostworksclimbing.com

Saunders, D. (2015, June 13). Mountain Climbing is the Height of Empty Egotism. *The Globe and Mail.* Retrieved from www.theglobeandmail.com

Seligman, M. E. P., & Csikszentmihalyi, M. (2000, January). Positive psychology: An introduction. *The American Psychologist*, *55*(1), 5–14. doi:10.1037/0003-066X.55.1.5 PMID:11392865

U.S. Forest Service. (n. d.). *Mount Hood Detailed Climbing Information.* Retrieved from http://www.fs.usda.gov

Williamson, J.E. (Ed.), (1991). *Accidents in North American Mountaineering* (pp. 46–47). Seattle: Mountaineers Books.

KEY TERMS AND DEFINITIONS

Campbell: Joseph Campbell, author of the seminal work, *The Hero with a Thousand Faces*, which analyzes mythology of heroes and their quests using Jung's theories of archetypes and the collective unconscious.

Coherence: A state in which one's mind (the conscious and unconscious components of the psyche) and physiological systems work in alignment, allowing one to be self-reliant, to be fully aware of one's resources, and to encounter and resolve problems without anxiety.

Drama-Based Video Games: Interactive video games which have a narrative structure. In many cases, the choices the player makes guide the manner in which the story unfolds.

Flow: Related to coherence, a state in which one is so fully absorbed in a task that one seems to be functioning outside of time, with little awareness of oneself as differentiated from surrounding environment. This state of mind often produces a state of spiritual transcendence.

Monomyth: According to Campbell, the core myth common across cultures in which the hero separates from his or her community on a quest, reaches a source of power and overcomes any obstacles, and then returns with knowledge beneficial to the world.

Motivation: The impetus that leads one to undertake and potentially complete a task. Motivations may be extrinsic (external to an individual) or intrinsic (developed within an individual). Mountaineering relies, for the most part, on intrinsic sources of motivation.

Mountaineering: Mountaineering includes such sports as mountaineering, extreme skiing and snowboarding, and backcountry skiing so long as the person ascends under his/her own power. For purposes of this essay, the terms "mountaineering", "climbing", and "alpinism" are used interchangeably.

Positive Psychology: A psychological theory grounded in the concept that individuals best gain skills through a focus on positive activities that promote coherence rather than through a focus on an analysis of their psychological deficits.

ENDNOTE

1 Mountaineering for purposes of this essay includes such sports as mountaineering, extreme skiing and snowboarding, and backcountry skiing so long as the person ascends under his/her own power. I use the terms "mountaineering", "climbing", and "alpinism" interchangeably.

Chapter 8
Jungian Reflections on South African Cinema
An Exploration of Cinema and Healing

Chris Broodryk
University of Pretoria, South Africa

ABSTRACT

This chapter explores how, in the aftermath of apartheid, Oliver Hermanus' film Skoonheid (2011) can serve as a healing fiction by inviting an engagement with present and past political and personal conflicts and resisting a type of cultural amnesia. In particular, this chapter draws on Jungian film studies to explore key scenes in Skoonheid that demonstrate the effects of a frustrated individuation process that nonetheless offers possibilities for the viewer to consider ways of healing. To position Skoonheid as healing fiction, the chapter utilises the work of James Hillman, amongst others, to conceptualise notions of healing. The chapter also locates the film against the historical backdrop of an Afrikaans-language cinema that traditionally privileged an inflexible white male subjectivity. In contrast, Skoonheid shows the Afrikaans-speaking white male as inhabiting a space of perceived disempowerment and loss, where the soul should still strive towards meaningful acts within a collective, within a community.

INTRODUCTION

In presenting a contribution to Jungian film studies, especially insofar as correlations between psyche and politics are concerned, this chapter provides a Jungian critical reading of Oliver Hermanus' Afrikaans film *Skoonheid* (2011) by way of positioning the film as a healing fiction. In this sense, a healing fiction is a film that provokes a psychological reading of and response to the film in its capacity to transform the viewer. Transformation in this context has specific psycho-symbolic dimensions that are facilitated by a healing fiction's specific presentation of characters grappling with themes of a personal-political and cultural nature.[1] In the virtual age, so-called traditional media such as the feature film can be access by a myriad of viewers across the world. The technology is often affordable and in the developed world, ample bandwidth allows for swift downloads. As this chapter is located within a larger conversation

DOI: 10.4018/978-1-4666-9891-8.ch008

about media and the exploration of the unconscious, it demonstrates the capacity of feature films, even from a minority cinema such as Afrikaans-language cinema, to provoke or stimulate the viewer's psychological reflections on matters of individuation as part of unconscious content becoming conscious on an individual as well as collective level.

The discussion of healing fiction in reference to *Skoonheid* takes on a dual purpose: to address the frustrated healing for the main character, Francois (played by Deon Lotz), and to illuminate possibilities of healing on a cultural level for viewers still slowly emerging from a history of psychological violence. This chapter demonstrates how, as Beebe (2011) explains it, the film *Skoonheid* precisely "[depicts] forms of unconsciousness that challenge the more conscious characters with life's threats, dangers, and complications, as well as their own defenses against moving forward" (p. 311); that is, mechanisms to sustain a psychological status quo by way of a frustrated individuation.

This chapter is located in Jungian film studies, which over the past fifteen years has experienced a clear increase given the rise in publications on Jung and film. Christopher Hauke and Luke Hockley (2011, p. 11), themselves key figures in the promulgation and practice of Jungian interrogations of cinema, cite the work of John Izod (2001; 2006), John Beebe (2008), Terrie Waddell (2006; 2010) and Greg Singh (2009) in this regard. The publications *Jung and Film*, in two volumes published in 2001 and 2011, offer stimulating critical readings of films to open up numerous provocative possibilities for how the viewer's affective, intuitive and intellectual responses to a film can be deepened. As Hauke and Ian Alister (2001) state in the introduction of the first volume, cinema offers opportunities "for the psyche to come alive, to be experienced and be commented upon" (p. 2), indicating that there is a level of psychological engagement or interaction between film and viewer: the film provokes or stimulates, and the viewer reflects and comments.

Kenevan (1999, p. 9) suggests that a film audience can connect with a film on two levels: a "personal emotional" level and also an "abstract intellectual" level. "The *organised information* of the film gives *coherence* to the viewer's mental energy; in a reciprocal way, the film is *brought alive* – 'amplified' by the energy from the spectators" (emphasis in original) (Hauke, 2014, p. 163). The core role of narrative is at the heart of human expression, of the implications the narrative holds for those who encounter it (Hauke, 2014, p. 125). A film must be an emotional experience in order to move its audience. Here, 'move' refers to a film as an emotionally moving experience as well as an experience that moves the individual viewer towards a psychologically introspective engagement that in all likelihood differs vastly from viewer to viewer. Movie watching is a personal (individual) and mass (collective) experience, an experience that invites, as Hauke (2014, p. 4) explains, comparisons to church and psychotherapy. In this sense, the experience of watching a film can be an engagement with processes of transformation located in a contained space (2014, p. 4).

The *Jung and Film* books demonstrate the capacity of a Jungian reading of film to invite meaning, as opposed to 'explaining away' a film's themes, motifs and symbolism. This chapter hopes to foster a symbolic attitude to film (see Fredericksen, 2001, p. 32) in relation to *Skoonheid* (2011) and its apparent capacities as healing fiction. In general, film serves as an ideal form of healing fiction in that film remains a dominant cultural form of expression (consider the multiple platforms through which one can obtain or stream a feature film) and offers a space to present narratives about individuals and the community and society they inhabit (Miller, 2011, p. 195).

In presenting a narrative of an individual grappling with socio-political transformation as well as his own psychological repression, *Skoonheid* offers a visually precise, almost visually clinical demonstration of Francois' psycho-political trajectory as he struggles with his homosexual desire, and the film was awarded the so-called 'Queer Palme' at the Cannes Film Festival in 2011.[2] More than a queer film shedding light on South African-specific manifestations of sexual desire repressed in public but practiced in private, *Skoonheid* addresses issues of cultural concern that illuminate some of the complexities of being white, male and Afrikaans speaking in post-apartheid South Africa.

Socio-political transformation is seen to pose particular challenges to the Afrikaans-speaking white male. There is a perception that the Afrikaans-speaking white male has experienced a betrayal of his ideal of whiteness (Straker, 2004, p. 409) and that whiteness has become associated with melancholia (p. 411). The transition from apartheid to democracy signified a sense of dislocation for white Afrikaans-speaking males (Steyn, 2004, p. 150), which necessitated a renegotiation of identities in the social imaginary. In *Skoonheid*, the character of Francois embodies pervasive anxieties about racial and cultural identity (2004, p. 153), where Afrikaans-speaking white males may see themselves as "[a]liens in a now foreign and disintegrating land" (p. 156). With this in mind, it is no wonder that the position of the victim – with its accompanying Afrikaans-speaking perception of a lack of agency and socio-political importance – has been prominent in discussions of white males.

Insofar as the film uses Francois' sense of political disempowerment to explore whiteness and masculinity in a South African minority known for its (religious) conservatism, *Skoonheid* serves as an example of how filmed fiction can offer possibilities of healing. Joseph Henderson first introduced the notion of the cultural unconscious – as opposed to the collective unconscious – in 1984. The cultural unconscious is a valuable notion, as Izod (2006) explains: "it points to an intermediate zone from which unconscious or semi-conscious arousals disturb and sway consciousness but without the potentially cataclysmic consequences which can occur when contents irrupt from the collective unconscious" (p. 18). The cultural unconscious makes itself known, like the collective unconscious, on an individual and collective level so that its contents may be integrated into both spheres of existence (Hauke, 2001, p. 154). A healing fiction can serve as a gateway to the cultural unconscious for the viewer insofar as they viewer becomes aware of possibilities of psychological growth in witnessing a narrative that stimulates such a coming to consciousness.

In providing the following critical reading of *Skoonheid* as a film that offers possibilities to engage the cultural unconscious, the author is cognizant that no text can control how it is read and is responded to, and this chapter does not suggest an intentionality on Hermanus' behalf as filmmaker. In addition, it does not assume the existence of a homogenous audience of like-minded individuals. Instead, the author suggests how a hypothetical viewer may use a Jungian framework to experience the film as a healing fiction, especially as the film sharply comments on and draws energy from South Africa's apartheid past in which the Afrikaner male enjoyed a particular position of socio-political privilege. The author will discuss selected Afrikaans films in this regard for contextual purposes, aligning the discussion with Elsaesser's (2005, p. 19) position that film that provides some sort of symptomatic revelation about itself or that serve as a kind of cultural event.

BACKGROUND

Reflecting on the country's volatile past, De Kock (2004) explains that South Africa "has been a fertile ground for foundational binary inscription, a place of blatant dualisms, such as civilized and savage, settler and indigene, White and Black, oppressed and privileged, rich and poor" (p. 18). In grappling with remembering, processes of selection (inclusion and exclusion) and a palimpsest of binaries, De

Kock (2004) suggests the notion of the seam as "the place where difference and sameness are hitched together – where they are brought to self-awareness, denied, or displaced into third terms" (p. 12). This notion of the seam, and its possibilities of self-awareness or negation, offers a point of entry for a Jungian approach to psychologically make sense of what De Kock (2004) is describing: that apartheid was a psychologically destructive system to all involved in different ways, and that living in post-apartheid South Africa requires a psychological shift to make sense of individuals' new statuses in a changed political landscape and within a radically different social order. So damaging was apartheid to individuals' psyches that Olivier (2009, p. 53) recounts how one psychologist was required to 'normalise' black political prisoners to accept and inscribe themselves into the absurd socio-political realities of late apartheid South Africa. In addition to the renegotiation of blackness as legitimately human, white South Africans, but particularly the white Afrikaans-speaking male, have had to renegotiate their own identities as these new identities are often framed by a perception of the loss of personal as well as political power.

As Flanery (2009) asks, "why has South African film failed to come of age? Why are its products so often either aesthetic, narrative, critical, or commercial failures, both within South Africa and in the global marketplace and mediascape?" (p. 239). If "South African" is substituted with the more specific "Afrikaans", Flanery's (2009) comments on failure ring even clearer. Absent from a type of cinematic political engagement aimed at excavating issues of race, class and gender is Afrikaans-language cinema, which was the dominant film in South African cinema for decades and now exists as a minority cinema located in slippery understandings of so-called post-transition cinema, transnational cinema and even problematic notions of third cinema, or the cinema of the developing world. In Olivier's (2009, p. 147) view, it is necessary to discuss images because it has 'Everything' to do with the socio-political realities of contemporary twenty first century existence. The socio-political realities of life in South Africa as represented in Afrikaans-language films have been historically shaped and manipulated by conservative cultural figures and their focus on maintaining a 'purely' Afrikaans-language cinema.

Much of Afrikaans language cinema's ideological and structural components and its sense of political engagement (or lack thereof) can be traced back to the work of Hans Rompel, a film critic and prominent figure in South African film history, who articulated certain ideals about Afrikaans cinema and how to preserve its cultural purity. According to Keyan Tomaselli (2008), "Rompel claimed that Afrikaners *reflect* their true God-given orientation in film" (p. 136); for Rompel, there is only a single reality, "a God-given set of conditions, a pre-existent state of being, uncluttered by ideological (or even theological) interpretations" (p. 136). In keeping with the idea of a God-given state of privilege, Rompel argued that Afrikaans film could resist cultural influences seen as *volksvreemd* (alien) and *volksgevaarlik* (national threats) (2008, p. 136). Originally, an Afrikaner cinema was established as an intervention to resist the ascendancy of Anglo-American cinema in South African cinema before World War II.

Rompel's concerns about a 'pure' Afrikaans cinema in South Africa translated into the creation of loyal white Afrikaans audiences to sustain such an industry. During the 1950s, as Botha (2012, p. 43) explains,

[t]he white Afrikaans audience for this local cinema was relatively large and very stable, guaranteeing nearly every Afrikaans-language film a long enough run to break even as long as it provided light entertainment, basically escapism, and dealt with Afrikaner reality and beliefs in an idealistic way. It meant that Afrikaners wanted their ideals visualized in these films. This idealistic conservatism was characterized by an attachment to the past, to ideals of linguistic and racial purity and to religious and moral norms.

Two key ideas emerge from the above description of 1950s Afrikaans cinema. Firstly, financially successful Afrikaans films were films that provided audiences with an escapism and idealism removed from the socio-political reality of South Africa at that time. Secondly, this cinema is best described as conservative, given its preference for (often nostalgic) notions of ethnic and sexual purity. The contemporary Afrikaans films mentioned above do not offer healing fictions. These films are much too focused on constructions of the South African past, the idealization of a pastoral Eden that fails to meaningfully psychologically engage the viewer (see Tomaselli, 1989). In addition, these films are populated by redundant symbols that have become, in my view, psycho-culturally outdated and, much like Afrikaans films from previous decades, aesthetically unremarkable.

Escapist filmmaking was endemic to 1960s and 1970s Afrikaans language cinema and was characterized by modes of sentimental excess and melodrama. Seldom did a film peel the veneer of social coherence away to reveal a deeply divided South Africa (Botha, 2012). The damaging effects of apartheid on the black majority population of the country was culturally negated by the specifically Afrikaans-language films, particularly those in 1960s and 1970s which were thematically and aesthetically unremarkable. Botha (2012, p. 12) observes that South African films made during this time were aimed at conservative Afrikaans audiences. These films presented their audiences with idealizations of their culture, and did not question or challenge the legitimacy of white minority power in South Africa.

South African films that did address the socio-political tensions during the 1970s and 1980s were either banned outright, or did not receive distribution. A lack of distribution meant that those films were not screened in public spaces for public consumption, except possibly at certain film festivals (2012, p. 13). There was much emphasis on racial purity, religious values and moral norms at the expense of an exploration of what Botha (2012, p. 51) refers to as the "national [collective] cultural psyche". There were exceptions; some Afrikaans filmmakers, such as Jans Rautenbach, did attempt to make sense of a white Afrikaans-speaking collective's shadow side. Rautenbach's feature film *Jannie Totsiens* (*Goodbye Johnny,* 1970), for instance, "uses a mental institution as an allegory of South Africa society under apartheid" (Botha 2012, p. 66), where the apartheid government is represented as an asylum (2012, p. 68) where dissident behavior among citizens is addressed. The film represents one of the historically few instances in Afrikaans cinema where the film is aware of itself, that is, of the processes of manipulation that characterize cinema (2006:71). Tomaselli (1989, p. 85) highlights the "allegorical implications" of *Jannie Totsiens*. Given the film's setting in a mental institution, Tomaselli (1989) reads it as representative of South Africa's political ruination: "[t]he insane run the asylum while the ineffectual doctor in charge represents the Prime Minister who tries to justify his position" (p. 86). Botha (2006, p. 75) agrees with Tomaselli's reading, summarizing the film's symbolic meaning (seeing as the film has such a vivid allegorical dimension) as commenting on the insanity of white Afrikaans-speaking minority in sustaining the apartheid project.

In his interrogation of selected Rautenbach films, South African film critic Barry Ronge comments that *Jannie Totsiens* is characterized by a story that is "archetypal in its simplicity", emphasising the film's allegorical and symbolic potency, yet has "great depth and poignancy" (Tomaselli, 1989, p. 121). Importantly, Rautenbach uses *Jannie Totsiens* to "[pose] a set of allegorical questions ... He does not provide answers, and has removed the film from his audience to the point where only an intellectual is able to decipher it" (1989, p. 128). Rautenbach's use of film language here is significant: the film is "full of nervous, swirling, vertiginous camera movements which create a deep sense of menace and dislocation between people and their environment and between each other" (1989, p. 129). Given the aesthetic innovation and self-awareness that characterizes the film, Botha (2006, p. 5) justifiably refers to *Jannie Totsiens* as an avant-garde milestone in Afrikaans-language cinema.

In contrast to milestones such as *Jannie Totsiens*, contemporary Afrikaans-language cinema is far less invested than South African cinema in general in addressing socio-political issues in narratively and visually innovative ways. The vast majority of Afrikaans language films aim mainly to blatantly position themselves within consumer culture. As Olivier (2009) explains: "[T]he dominant culture, globally, is consumer culture, and it has proved to be unparalleled in the efficacy with which it anaesthetizes 'consumers' – the masses of spectators ... absorbed in the imaginary world of soapies – in this way effectively dulling the potential for revolt that still exists in the recesses of people's psyches" (pp. 169-170).

Fu and Murray (2007) explain that "[w]ith the end of apartheid, film-makers have struggled with finding their voice to express the ambiguities, contradictions, and nuances of the 'new South Africa'" (p. 127), and the films mentioned above foreground these ambiguities, contradictions and nuances. As these films indicate, after South Africa's official transition to democracy in 1994, South African films would often address key socio-political issues of the country's past that inform its present. In this context, consider the how Ian Gabriel's *Forgiveness* (2004) explore individual and collective redemption in post-apartheid South Africa, with an Afrikaans-speaking policeman (played by Arnold Vosloo) seeking atonement for the committing acts of torture under instruction of the apartheid-era South African Police Force. In addition, Jason Xenopolous' *Promised Land* (2002) demonstrates the challenges in coming to terms with land ownership and apartheid's patriarchal legacy. *Forgiveness* already in its title highlights its most prominent theme, and shows that forgiveness must be central to processes of cross-racial reconciliation.

Of the above two films, *Promised Land* is more cynical as a commentary on how a certain Afrikaans-speaking minority on the political far right deliberately exclude themselves from racial integration, and how such individuals are willing to take up arms to defend their narrative of a conquering, God-fearing nation.[3] Similar to *Skoonheid, Forgiveness* and *Promised Land* offer explorations of being white, male and Afrikaans-speaking (or at least coming from an Afrikaans background) in a new social order in which both "white" and "male" have lost their socio-political primacy. However, where these feature films are made in English, *Skoonheid* is an almost exclusively Afrikaans-language film and asks of primarily (though not exclusively) Afrikaans viewers to respond to it as Afrikaans-speaking individuals, with all the political and cultural associations such a position implies.

While most contemporary Afrikaans-language films suggest an uncomfortable mix of denial and amnesia about the South African past and the psychological price paid by all involved, Elsaesser (2009) uses the term "double occupancy" rather than similar notions like 'diversity' or 'multi-culturalism' to position "discursive as well as geopolitical territories as 'always already occupied'" (p. 50). Elsaesser (2009) explains double occupancy is a "condition of possibility, as the conditions of entry, even, into the European political space" (p. 51). Double occupancy thus facilitates a presence in a designated political space. In elaborating on Europe's political situation, Elsaesser (2009, p. 51) views Europe as doubly occupied by its history (including the Holocaust and more contemporary historical events) and its colonialist activities and consequences. For Elsaesser (2009, p. 54), double occupancy can also be an aesthetic strategy. There has been "a shift from realism versus illusionism towards a different pair of alternatives: from *claiming* the real to *performing presence*", which requires "a different way of thinking about cinema's relation to fiction, to the mode of 'as if'" (Elsaesser 2009, p. 55). Insofar as an Afrikaans film such as *Skoonheid* performs presence, it acknowledges its position as one of not double but triple occupation: the film occupies a political space both as film text and in its depiction of South

African spaces such as ruralized Bloemfontein and tourist hub Cape Town. In addition, the film occupies a psychological space in offering images that evoke the cultural unconscious of the minority white Afrikaans-speaking population in South Africa.

Double occupancy here also evokes multiple psychological 'presences' (some known to the ego, some repressed) that are articulated in response to the process of socio-political transition following 1994. In addition, Elsaesser (1989, p. 254) also refers to Baudrillard's notion of retro-scenarios to refer to history films. In Baudrillard's view, "contemporary societies, locked into political stasis, nostalgically dream and imagine through the cinema – the traditional refuge for myths – a time where history still involved human agents and individual victims, forces and causes that mattered and decisions involving questions of life and death" (Elsaesser, 1989, p. 254). Such films invent a time of agents and victims clothed first and foremost in fiction. What Elsaesser (1989) describes here by way of Baudrillard is a complex system of film fictions that often revert to nostalgia and victimhood, and may inhibit processes of healing (where healing indicates a coming-to-terms-with the past in the socio-psychological and political present). Within the South African and Afrikaans contexts articulated above, healing fiction commenting on the Afrikaans speaking minority position must discourage regressive claims to victimhood and invite the viewer to become conscious of the necessity of certain psychological process, such as the need for individuation.

SKOONHEID AS HEALING FICTION

Botha (2012, p. 203) positions post-apartheid South African cinema as a cinema of marginality, where issues and mechanisms of marginality are exposed and the marginalised (black women; homosexual filmmakers) have a filmic voice. *Skoonheid* (2011) offers a disempowered, disenfranchised and self-less middle-aged Afrikaans white male, Francois, as the main character. At his age, Francois would have seen the effects of apartheid and benefitted from its policies. In addition, he would have been present for the transition from apartheid to democracy. At his eldest daughter's wedding, Francois sees the young, charismatic and handsome Christian (Charlie Keegan) from across the room. Francois is evidently infatuated with the younger man, an infatuation absent from his marriage to Elena (Michelle Scott). His domestic life is composed of routine and habit; a swimming pool that needs cleaning, a timber mill that needs to be restocked.

Against the backdrop of these environments, the film makes Francois' sexual desire for men explicit in a MSM (men-who-have-sex-with-men) scene set at a farm house on the outskirts of Bloemfontein, an all-male group sex scene that seems mechanical and rehearsed.[4] The men involved in the group sex are all middle-aged, male and Afrikaans-speaking. When one of the group members arrives with a young coloured male, he is told in no uncertain terms that the non-white man is not welcome in their circle, and that he should leave. Such is the ideological weight upon these men – first imposed by apartheid, then introjected by the individuals – that even after the fall of apartheid they cannot bring themselves to integrate a 'different' member of society into their private space. The colored male evidently embodies the shadow for the white Afrikaans-speaking collective in the film: to be seen at a distance, to be acknowledged in public, but never to be included in intimate spaces. The shadow figure of apartheid has still not been integrated; he remains outside, othered, in a world separate from the white male desire depicted in the film, and still a reminder of the processes of psycho-political repression that the men are subjected to (or subject themselves to).

Beyond clandestine group sex, Christian seems to offer a gravitational pull away from Francois sense of work and mundane domesticity, so much so that the older man travels from his home town of Bloemfontein in the Free State to the much more cosmopolitan city of Cape Town, where Christian lives. His interest in Christian can be pursued under family auspices since Christian is his nephew. After a series of events that increasingly force Francois to acknowledge the repressed homosexual urges he possesses which ends with a drunken evening's excesses in a Cape Town gay bar, Francois phones Charlie to pick him up. The two men end up in Francois' hotel room, where Christian formally asks his uncle for money to invest in an upcoming project. Once Christian confirms that he has no interest in Francois other than those of a financial nature, the older man violently forces himself upon Christian in an attempted rape. In the moment where the object of his desire meets his sexual intent, Francois cannot get an erection, as if finally obtaining his desired object has rendered him impotent because Francois still sees Christian as representing what is 'outside' of him, and remains unaware of his own shadow projections. As conceptualized by Alfred Adler, organ inferiority can feature prominently in awakening the individual to consciousness for the development of the psyche. Organ inferiority indicates that the unconscious becomes part of a felt experience of inferiority in which the unconscious points to the individual's inadequacies in a psychic situation where individuals will consistently attempt to negate this feeling of inferiority (Hillman, 2012). Francois' impotence as literal articulation of organ inferiority, demonstrates the individual's inability at a crucial moment to come to consciousness, to heed the unconscious' demand for awareness.

Francois returns to Bloemfontein, and the film does not offer any knowledge about Christian's well-being or status (not even Francois' daughter has had any recent contact with him) except for opening up the possibility that Christian might be extorting money from Francois in return for his silence over the attempted rape. The film continually privileges Francois' point of view, his subjectivity. He receives a letter at work and goes to a local mall where he sits down at the Spur restaurant, a large envelope filled with a substantial amount of cash in his hand, ostensibly waiting for someone (possibly Christian, or some sort of representative of Christian). Across from him sits a gay couple, two young men who have no inhibition to physically show their affection for each other. The viewer is not privy to any of the events that then transpire. We do not see what happens with the money. The final image in the film is of Francois leaving the parking lot, driving down the dark architectural spiral towards the exit, in all likelihood back to resuming his work at a timber mill where he never touches the material or brings it to life, and to the domestic life that often literally keep his repression and quietly seething anger invisible from public view.

Skoonheid (2011) offers images and scenes that can be amplified in a Jungian manner to make psychological sense of the film as healing fiction. If "[Freudian and psycho-analytical] association provides a way of developing meaning from spontaneous imagery and dream motifs by allowing linked images and meaningful associations to the original stimulus to be found" (Hauke 2014, p. 186), the Jungian practice of amplification enters into the image to make the image more richly detailed (2014, p. 186). Hauke (2014, p.156-157) discusses the use of film in therapy, which includes how "[m]ovie scenes are as able to unfold unconscious contents, and stir affects, just as the dream or transference events can" (p.157). Hauke (2014) helpfully refers to a third image that "arises out of the *negotiation between the viewer and the screen*" (emphasis in original) (p. 158). This third image, while very much the product of a series of image-viewer-psyche intersections, "*returns something to the movie itself*, causing it to grow beyond the bounds of its original conception" (emphasis in original) (2014, p. 159). This third image allows for the amplification of images that have a resonance for the viewer, and brings the cultural unconscious to the consciousness of the viewer who may make sense of it on an individual level (as contribution to individuation) as well as a collective level (foregrounding the significance of the cultural unconscious on a community level). There are a number of striking images and scenes that require amplification in order to highlight their significance – as symbolic or as archetypal events – in the sense that *Skoonheid* is positioned as a healing fiction. These scenes include:

- The opening shot of Francois gazing at Christian.
- Francois cleaning the pool, looking past his own reflection in the water's surface.
- Francois' evening in the gay bar, alcohol-fuelled and receding his attempted rape of Christian.

The above scenes and images (consider figures 1 and 2 in this regard) stimulate an engagement with possibly symbolic and archetypal content. A considerable amount of Jungian film scholarship emphasizes the amplification of symbols. Symbols can relate an individual's story on the level of activity of the ego (Broodryk, 2006, p. 55). The Jungian framework allows for a specific reading and interpretation of a film (Izod 2006, p. 217). The symbol has a numinous quality which functions towards psychological unification instead of opposition (Hockley, 2001, p. 57). A brief overview of scholarship on the archetypes offers the Hero archetype as a primary archetype, held to be the best-known myth – the myth of the Hero – in the world (Henderson, 1964, p. 101). The Hero is a powerful figure (even a "god-man" (Jung, 1977, p. 228) who confronts a figure or form of evil, and vanquishes it. In ostensible opposition to the Hero, yet entangled with the Hero in functional, even psychologically positive ways, is the Shadow, a dark figure or form who exists in opposition to the Hero's light and whose existence demonstrates that one's enemy is firstly located in oneself (Jung, 1947, p. xvii). In addition to the personal shadow is the collective shadow, such as the Shadow of apartheid cast by the 'civilized' white minority government on the majority black population (Broodryk, 2006, p. 71; see Von Franz, 1974).

Hermanus, a devotee of Alfred Hitchcock, establishes obsession as the film's main theme as early as the film's opening scene (Broodryk 2013, p. 31). Indeed, Hermanus describes Francois as having – or being possessed by? – an "electric affinity" for Christian (2013, p. 32). Similar to auteurs such as Hitchcock and Michael Haneke, Hermanus can be said to occupy a position of filmmaker-as-shaman, as Rountree (2008, p. 123) describes it. Such filmmakers exhibit a "heightened accessibility and responsiveness to the inner landscape of the self as well as to the physical and emotional cartography that surrounds them" (2008, p. 123). These figures occupy, then, a near Apollonian position of illuminating the psyche (or indulging its shadows (Rountree, 2008, p. 123). Provocatively, Hermanus describes editing the film as "a strange incubation period" (Broodryk 2013, p. 32). A Jungian approach to the film reveals the extent of Francois' projection early in the film, where the projection is the cause of a fascination with another person (Von Franz, 1980, p. 117). In such in instance, it is possible that the individual is projecting his shadow onto another person (1980, p. 35), and Francois, the Hero of the narrative, projects onto Christian a variety of repressed contents.

Francois is not a traditional Hero as much as an Afrikaans-speaking white male in search of a new identity in a dynamic political context in which his agency is called into question, and as an individual within a specific, complex socio-political landscape who has started the process of individuation. Individuation is an individual's tendency towards becoming wholly itself (Hauke 2014, p. 187). Indeed, the task of individuation is to move towards knowing the self – "the whole personality, including the ego" – as much as possible (Hauke 2014, p. 188). For Hall (1983, p. 14) 'natural' individuation - that is, individuation that occurs organically and not through the intervention of an analyst – takes place in instances "where there seems to be a need for the formation of a strong and reliable ego with which to establish oneself in the world". In the second half of life, from 40 years onward or so, the rejuvenated and consolidated ego works towards greater vitality (Jacobi, 1965, p. 42). En route to such greater vitality, Marie-Louise von Franz (1980, p. 208) explains that the process of working towards the Self through individuation is characterized by a certain malaise, a psychological imbalance. *Skoonheid* regularly reminds viewers of the malaise and imbalance in Francois' life.

Francois' marriage is a conflation of recycled statements about house maintenance and petty family squabbles, far from the psychologically nourishing *coniunctio oppositorum* or royal marriage (Izod, 2006, p. 77) that helps to cultivate an existence rich in meaning. Francois' malaise is further evident in the film as Hermanus shows us Francois' life of habit and routine as a cycle of hand-to-mouth gestures and actions lacking in a psychological dynamism that has been eroded by social convention and conservatism. Francois is aware of this malaise and seeks ways to disrupt it (if not end it), such has having sex with other men. Another indication of Francois' malaise is his lack of response at what he (and the audience) suspect to be his wife's infidelity, and his disproportionately aggressive reaction to his daughter taking his car to Cape Town to see 'his' Christian. While Francois is unaware of the psychological dynamic behind his infatuation with Christian, the younger man possesses some of the aspects typical to the *puer* in that "[he] is dangerous because he *knows* the truth, as opposed to struggling with uncertainty" (Bortz, 2009, p. 70) and knows to possibly manipulate someone as psychologically vulnerable as Francois into certain positions. It is also likely that Francois, in projecting his desire and shadow onto Christian, also sees in the younger man the figure of Dionysus, in touch with all his emotions (2009, p. 73) whereas Francois simply represses them (Francois' repressive nature is foregrounded early in the film when his general medical practitioner asks about his anger issues).

Francois' home life is literally dark. During scenes set inside his house – one hesitates to call it a 'home' – the setting is darkly lit only, suggesting the constant presence of shadows that lurk and threaten to engulf Francois. The psycho-visual darkness of the house setting contrasts with the sharply lit exteriors much of the rest of the film provides. Indeed, the film is colour coded to suggest *mortification*, signifying a form of death as indicated by the color black, and often experienced by a sense of defeat and failure, which often involves the shadow (Edinger, 1985, p. 111). The shadow, Hauke (2014) explains, is "[that] part of the personality that one does not identify with or wishes to disown" (p. 188), including negative aspects but also positive aspects that for whatever reason remain unavailable to the individual.

Humans operate within certain spatial parameters, such as the confines of the domestic sphere and spaces of labor. Hillman (1987, p. 29) explains that humans can separate physical distance from psychological distance, yet "the problem of distance, of how near to get, comes into every meeting" (p. 29). Significantly, "[d]istance is very often confused with coldness, just as closeness and nearness with warmth" (Hillman 1987, p. 33). Hillman (1987) foregrounds how human interaction is often coded by convention, and not by intent or meaningful connection. Distance does not always equal coldness, just as closeness does not always equal warmth – consider Francois' faraway infatuation with Christian, contrasted to his stasis when he is in the company of his family, especially Elena.

As the film ends, Francois is ostensibly no closer to psychological growth and awareness than when the film started. His malaise seems set to continue, just as his psychological development remains in stasis in spite of numerous moments that call him to consciousness, a call that Francois repeatedly denies or neglects. In Cape Town, Francois' prolonged visit to a gay club is his version of the night sea journey, or *nekyia*, which takes him into his version of the underworld where he publically comes face to face with the repressed contents and desire he only occasionally indulges in private. In a conversation in a diner with Christian (preceding the scene where Christian takes Francois to his hotel room), Francois prides himself on his capacity for self-control, his ability to "make things work". Contemporary existence, as Hauke (2014) explains, is characterized by a dominant consciousness of an over-reliance on "over-rational, linear, hierarchical and pragmatic thinking" (p. 5), an exaggerated extension of Enlightenment thinking's emphasis on the primacy of Reason. Using Reason alone to make meaning of the world lacks the meaning-making forces and processes that the unconscious, the irrational, provides (Hauke, 2014, p. 5). Francois inflated reliance on the efficacy of being able to "make things work" mirrors his inability or unwillingness to answer the call to consciousness. Francois does experience a major human encounter with Christian that leaves him wounded ("The human encounter is difficult, because it leads to that wounding experience, that *mania*, that exhaustion of the only-human", says Hillman (1987, p. 35)), but his failure to integrate shadow aspects of himself into his psyche means that these aspects will always be 'controlled' and remain at the fringes of his home town as well as of his psyche.

In the aftermath of Francois' attempted rape of Christian in the hotel room, the final scene in the film shows Francois as he is exiting the parking lot of the local mall, the road shaped as a downward spiral that should lead to a way out of the darkness. As Von Franz (1964, p. 176) explains, the unconscious is often represented by mazes, networks or passages, all of which visually suggest the difficulty (and often impossibility) of exploring the unconscious. Not once does Francois seem to be experiencing anything numinous. Instead, he experiences only the superficial pleasure of looking (at Christian) and desiring (projecting onto) what/who he cannot have. The downward spiral at the end suggests a type of arrested development and psychological stasis for Francois, who will continue to live a life of repression and mundane conservatism which stands in relative opposition to the changed socio-political landscape he inhabits. Socio-politically and psychologically, Francois is a remnant of a former cultural and ideological framework that refuses to fade into obscurity and persists at all costs, even if it includes Self-neglect or Self-negation to the point of Self-petrification.

If *Skoonheid* does not present a narrative of a character's psychological healing or at least his individuation as indicative of psychological progress, then how is it a healing fiction? In *Healing Fiction*, Hillman (2012) highlights contrasts and intersections in the work of Jung, Sigmund Freud and Alfred Adler. He explores the role of, and therapists' approaches to, case histories. Against the frameworks provided by Jung, Freud and Adler, Hillman (2012) explains that the soul pursues a sense of psychic purpose, where the process of individuation's aim of wholeness is a response to the soul's desire for purpose. Hillman (2012) regularly revisits the question, what does the soul want? Drawing on Adler, Hillman finds a dynamic response to the question that foregrounds the necessity of psyche's development to connect the individual to the collective: the soul wants community, where the soul strives to make each act significant in the sense that each act contributes to communal and cosmic life. *Skoonheid* is a healing fiction because it highlights the necessity of individuation, and of the significance of the individuating individual in the community where the individual can, in public and not in private, contribute to the community in a way that makes the individual's actions into meaningful acts.

In light of Hillman (2012) and the rest of the discussion of the film above, *Skoonheid* can be framed as a healing fiction as it offers a sequence of psychic events that offers possibilities of psychic integration. Firstly, *Skoonheid* offers viewers a tale of a man who encounters the possibility of healing, of assimilating shadow aspects of himself as part of his individuation. Secondly, the film frustrates these possibilities as the man fails, at least for now, to continue onwards toward perpetual psychological integration. Thirdly, although the character's possibilities of individuation do not materialize, these possibilities are now available to the viewer to amplify and to explore the film's individuation motif as well as its images for themselves in ways that are psychologically resonant. Hillman, as a founding figure of the archetypal school of post-Jungian studies, posits that the "individual can identify any image as being archetypal", which attributes to such a selected image a certain value and typicality (Izod 2006, p. 23). In dealing with such an image, the analyst will work with and focus on the image and not guide the individual away from the image towards identifying prior archetypes. Izod (2006, p. 25) nonetheless finds analytical value in the classical school of post-Jungian studies; here, "the interpretation of films seems to me to be justified, after their emotional and numinous impact have been afforded due time and attention so that they resonate in the psyche". Within *Skoonheid*'s narrative parameters, there are numerous possibilities for such amplification. A key image that invites amplification is that of Francois cleaning the swimming pool.

Given the film's individuation narrative, this chapter frames Francois cleaning the swimming pool as a profoundly psychological moment wherein Francois uses the pool net to remove leaves and other sorts of debris from the water as a tentative, superficial dabbling in the unconscious. Repeatedly Hermanus shows us Francois reflected in the water, as if to suggest the character's proximity to the unconscious. Through this repetition, the irony of the image becomes manifest: Francois manages to scoop out a lot of leaves and even some items of clothing from the bottom of the swimming pool, yet he refuses to appreciate the psychological significance of his actions even as he sees himself reflected in the dark water. The pool is appropriately unclear and green, suggesting a sense of bottomlessness as well as Francois' inability to penetrate it. Significantly, this image occurs in the aftermath of Francois' violation of Christian in Cape Town, of Francois' impotence in the presence of the object of his desire. As Zanardo (2011) states, "one must consciously suffer the losses (the sacrifice must be wrought in me) that 'undo' and disorder our sense of ourselves if we are to try to recover the enigma hidden in the recesses of our losses" (p. 57). Such is the requirement of engaging the unconscious, and neither violence (the attempted rape) nor quiet reflection (cleaning the swimming pool) guides Francois' apprehensive consciousness towards this realization. Not even a discussion with a friend and client who had recently left his wife and admits to being ecstatic because of it, can sway Francois from an existence that responds mostly to external cues and convention by way of unilateral thinking rather than internal feelings that suggest otherwise.

As Hillman (1987) explains, the ego "keeps us independently intact, uncontaminated, our lenses clean"; however, "[h]ealing comes from our unguarded side, from where we are foolish and vulnerable" (p. 22). The image thus indicates a possibility of individuation and an engagement with the contents of the unconscious as they break through the surface into consciousness, but Francois remains psychologically unaware of this possibility. For the hypothetical viewer of this film, *Skoonheid* makes these possibilities of individuation and psychological growth visually and thematically explicit, and invite the viewer to be conscious of such possibilities in a psycho-cultural sense. *Skoonheid* is a healing fiction on a psychological level as well as a socio-political (post-apartheid) level.

By not actualizing the possibility of individuation, Francois remains imprisoned in a life that seems to be not his own, a life devoid of actual libidinal energy. His life remains shaped by a rigid ego intent on maintaining the psychological *status quo*. As the viewer weighs the possibilities of individuation and coming to consciousness against Francois' resistance to psychological integration in the face of his frustrated desire, the viewer is made aware or reminded of, through Francois' constructive failure, the notion that "*the purpose of human life is the creation of consciousness*. The key word is 'consciousness'" (emphasis in original) (Edinger 1984, p. 17, 57). Edinger (1984) explains consciousness as "the experience if *knowing together with an other,* that is, in a setting of twoness" (emphasis in original) (p. 36), where the process of coming to consciousness "requires both seeing and being seen, knowing and being known" (p. 53). Francois' arrested psychological development becomes an imagistic counter to the viewer's own consideration of consciousness and particularly an awareness of repressed contents and desires.

CONCLUSION

In an unbalanced world, a world that continuously issues interruptions to individual and collective psyches, Mackey-Kallis (2003) observes that films can "offer us dreams and therapeutic visions of the collective journey necessary for us to re-establish right relations" (p. 166); that is, the rebalancing of the relationship between consciousness and the cultural unconscious. In this sense, film is an important component in engaging the world around us, as well as unconscious content. If the activity of psychotherapy is to "[bring consciousness] to bear on the images psyche presents us with" (Hauke, 2014, p. 164), then *Skoonheid* provides images that can be read as psychologically symbolically meaningful for the viewer. If the "assimilation of the symbol is marked by the liberation of unconscious energy … [the viewer] can [now] use this energy consciously" (Broodryk, 2006, p. 59; see Ellenberger, 1994, p. 704). Such an assimilation is often followed by the viewer's experience of feelings of transcendence, and even a deeper understanding of an issue that is central to the individual's existence (2006, p. 59).

Skoonheid further reveals Hermanus to be a shamanic filmmaker insofar as his film shifts the consciousness of the viewer, resulting in a different world view (Rountree, 2008, p. 129). As Beebe (2001) explains it, the director's function in making a film is "not unlike that of the Self in creating dreams" by stimulating the ego through images affectively and symbolically evocative of the psyche (p. 208), images derived from "anxieties generated by current concerns" (p. 212). The film offers visual and thematic motifs of transformation, consciousness and imagination that, even if they elide the characters in the film, seem to call out to the viewer with intensity. As such, the film offers, as Fredericksen (2011) describes it, "*a psychologically meaningful critique we find ourselves and [the film] nested within*" (emphasis in original) (p. 101).

For all of its visual and thematic emphasis on mundane domesticity, then, *Skoonheid* is almost paradoxically transcendent in using its fictional narrative to demonstrate the dangers of psycho-political repression and offering itself as a healing fiction for viewers grappling with similar questions about psychological growth. As viewers finish watching the film, they may recall events in the film in a highly narrativized way, accompanied by a discussion of the film's meaning and its impact on the viewer (Singh, 2011, p. 164). Finally, *Skoonheid* functions as a healing fiction because it is a cautionary tale of privileging thinking at the expense of feeling, and of attributing exorbitant worth to the idea of self-control and the notion that one can control one's environment and rationally manage one's desire. As an example of a minority cinema, *Skoonheid* cautions against the ease of assuming the position of victim where there are multiple opportunities for psycho-political growth.

As a country still struggling with apartheid's psychological residue, the notion of double occupancy, as illuminated by a Jungian approach as proposed above, allows for psychological meaning making with a film that demonstrates that a failure to functionally adjust to a dynamic socio-political context correlates with an inability for the individual to individuate.

REFERENCES

Beebe, J. (2001). The anima in film. In C. Hauke & I. Alister (Eds.), *Jung & Film: Post-Jungian takes on the moving image* (pp. 208–225). Hove, East Sussex: Brunner-Routledge.

Beebe, J. (2011). 'The Wizard of Oz'. A vision of development in the American political psyche. In C. Hauke & L. Hockley (Eds.), *Jung & Film II: the return. Further post-Jungian takes on the moving image* (pp. 302–327). London: Routledge.

Bortz, M. (2009). Tomorrow belongs to me. *Jung Journal: Culture & Psyche*, *3*(4), 69–77. doi:10.1525/jung.2009.3.4.69

Botha, M. P. (2006). *Jans Rautenbach: dromer, baanbreker en auteur. Parklands: Genugtig! Botha, MP. (2012). South African cinema 1896-2010*. Bristol: Intellect.

Broodryk, C. (2013). A cinema of exploration: In conversation with Oliver Hermanus. *International Journal of Cinema*, *1*, 31–33.

Broodryk, C. W. (2006). *The moving image: contemporary film analysis and analytical psychology*. (Unpublished master's thesis). University of Pretoria, Pretoria.

Costet, D. (Producer) & Hermanus, O. (Director). (2011). *Skoonheid* [Motion Picture]. South Africa: Swift Productions.

De Kock, L. (2003). South Africa in the global imaginary: an introduction. In L. de Kock, L. Bethlehem, & S. Laden (Eds.), *South Africa in the global imaginary*. Pretoria: University of South Africa Press.

De Kock, L., Bethlehem, L., & Laden, S. (Eds.). (2003). *South Africa in the global imaginary*. Pretoria: University of South Africa Press.

Edinger, E. F. (1984). *The creation of consciousness. Jung's myth for modern man*. Toronto: Inner City Books.

Edinger, E. F. (1985). *Anatomy of the psyche: alchemical symbolism in psychotherapy*. Chicago, Illinois: Open Court.

Ellenberger, H. F. (1994). *The discovery of the unconscious: the history and evolution of dynamic psychiatry*. London: Fontana Press.

Elsaesser, T. (1989). *New German cinema: a history*. London: Palgrave MacMillan.

Elsaesser, T. (2005). *European cinema: face-to-face with Hollywood*. Amsterdam: Amsterdam University Press. doi:10.5117/9789053566022

Elsaesser, T. (2009). Real location, fantasy space, performative place: double occupancy and mutual interference in European cinema. In T. Trifonova (Ed.), *European Film Theory* (pp. 47–62). New York, NY: Routledge.

Flanery, P. D. (2009). What national cinema? South African film cultures and the transnational. *Safundi: the Journal of South African and American Studies*, *10*(2), 239–253. doi:10.1080/17533170902793174

Fredericksen, D. (2001). Jung/sign/symbol/film. In C. Hauke & I. Alister (Eds.), *Jung & Film: Post-Jungian takes on the moving image* (pp. 17–55). Hove, East Sussex: Brunner-Routledge.

Fredericksen, D. (2011). Jungian film studies. The corruption of consciousness and the nurturing of psychological life. In C. Hauke & L. Hockley (Eds.), *Jung & Film II: the return. Further post-Jungian takes on the moving imag* (pp. 99–108). London: Routledge.

Fu, A., & Murray, M. J. (2007). Cinema and the edgy city: Johannesburg, carjacking, and the post-metropolis. *African Identities*, *5*(2), 279–289. doi:10.1080/14725840701403606

Gabriel, C. (Producer), & Gabriel, I. (Director). (2004). *Forgiveness*. South Africa: Giant Films, DV8 Films.

Hauke, C. (2001). "Let's go back to finding out who we are". Men, *Unheimlich* and returning home in the films of Steven Spielberg. In C. Hauke & I. Alister (Eds.), *Jung & Film: Post-Jungian takes on the moving image* (pp. 151–174). Hove, East Sussex: Brunner-Routledge.

Hauke, C. (2014). *Visible mind: movies, modernity and the unconscious*. London: Routledge.

Hauke, C., & Alister, I. (Eds.). (2001). *Jung & Film: Post-Jungian takes on the moving image*. Hove, East Sussex: Brunner-Routledge.

Hauke, C., & Alister, I. (2001). Introduction. In C. Hauke & I. Alister (Eds.), *Jung & Film: Post-Jungian takes on the moving image* (pp. 1–13). Hove, East Sussex: Brunner-Routledge.

Hauke, C., & Hockley, L. (Eds.). (2011). *Jung & Film II: the return. Further post-Jungian takes on the moving image*. London: Routledge.

Hauke, C., & Hockley, L. (2011). Introduction. In C. Hauke & L. Hockley (Eds.), *Jung & Film II: the return. Further post-Jungian takes on the moving image* (pp. 1–14). London: Routledge.

Henderson, J. L. (1964). Ancient myths and modern man. In C. G. Jung (Ed.), *Man and his symbols* (pp. 97–156). New York, NY: Dell.

Hillman, J. (1987). *Insearch: psychology and religion*. Dallas: Spring Publications.

Hillman, J. (2012). *Healing fiction* (Kindle ed.). Thompson, Connecticut: Spring Publications. Retrieved from http://www.amazon.com/Healing-Fiction-James-Hillman-ebook/dp/B0079LCEN4/ref=tmm_kin_swatch_0?_encoding=UTF8&sr=1-1&qid=1435641664

Hockley, L. (2001). *Cinematic projections: the analytical psychology of CG Jung and film theory*. Luton: University of Luton Press.

Izod, J. (2006). *Screen, culture, psyche. A post-Jungian approach to working with the audience*. London: Routledge.

Jacobi, J. (1965). *The way of individuation* (R. F. C. Hull, Trans.). New York, NY: Hodder & Stoughton.

Jung, C. G. (Ed.). (1964). *Man and his symbols*. New York, NY: Dell.

Jung, C. G. (1977). *The symbolic life*. London: Routledge.

Kenevan, P. B. (1999). *Paths of individuation in literature and film: a Jungian approach.* Boston, MA: Lexington Books.

Mackey-Kallis, S. (2003). Who would have dreamed that movies mattered so much? *Review of Communication, 3*(2), 161–166. doi:10.1080/ 0308385

Miller, C. (2011). 'Twilight'. Discourse theory and Jung. In C. Hauke & L. Hockley (Eds.), *Jung & Film II: the return. Further post-Jungian takes on the moving image* (pp. 185–205). London: Routledge.

Nathan, J. (Producer), Wheatley, M. (Producer), & Hermanus, O. (Director). (2009). *Shirley Adams* [Motion Picture]. South Africa: DV8 Films, Centropolis Entertainment, London Film School.

Olivier, B. (2009). *Philosophy and psychoanalytic theory. Collected essays.* Oxford: Peter Lang.

Rautenbach, J. (Producer), & Rautenbach, J. (Director). (1970). *Jannie Totsiens* [Motion Picture]. South Africa: Sewentig.

Rountree, C. (2008). Auteur film directors as contemporary shamans. *Jung Journal: Culture & Psyche, 2*(2), 123–134. doi:10.1525/jung.2008.2.2.123

Shaw, H. (Director). (1916). *De Voortrekkers* [Motion Picture]. South Africa: African Film Productions.

Singh, G. (2011). Cinephilia, Or, looking for meaningfulness in encounters with cinema. In C. Hauke & L. Hockley (Eds.), *Jung & Film II: the return. Further post-Jungian takes on the moving image* (pp. 163–184). London: Routledge.

Sonnekus, T. (2013). 'We're not faggots!': Masculinity, homosexuality and the representation of Afrikaner men who have sex with men in the film 'Skoonheid' and online. *South African Review of Sociology, 44*(1), 22–39. doi:10.1080/21528586.2013.784446

Steyn, M. E. (2004). Rehabilitating a whiteness disgraced: Afrikaner 'white talk' in post-apartheid South Africa. *Communication Quarterly, 52*(2), 143–169. doi:10.1080/01463370409370187

Straker, G. (2004). Race for cover: Castrated whiteness, perverted consequences. *Psychoanalytical Dialogues: The International Journal of Relational Perspectives, 14*(4), 405–422. doi:10.1080/10481881409348795

Tomaselli, K. G. (1989). *The cinema of apartheid: race and class in South African film.* Sandton, Transvaal: Radix.

Tomaselli, K. G. (2008). Paradigms in South African cinema research: Modernity, the New Africa Movement and beyond. *Communicatio, 34*(1), 130–147. doi:10.1080/02500160802144611

Trifonova, T. (Ed.). (2009). *European Film Theory.* New York, NY: Routledge.

Von Franz, M. L. (1964). The process of individuation. In C. G. Jung (Ed.), *Man and his symbols* (pp. 157–254). New York, NY: Dell Publishers.

Von Franz, M.L. (1974). *Shadow and evil in fairy tales.* New York: Spring.

Von Franz, M. L. (1980). *Alchemy: an introduction to the symbolism and the psychology.* Toronto: Inner City Books.

Wicht, D. (Producer), & Xenopoulos, J. (Director). (2002). *Promised land* [Motion Picture]. South Africa: Film Afrika Worldwide, Khulisa Productions.

Zanardo, A. (2011). Love, loss, imagination and the 'other' in Soderbergh's *Solaris*. In C. Hauke & L. Hockley (Eds.), *Jung & Film II: the return. Further post-Jungian takes on the moving image* (pp. 49–65). London: Routledge.

KEY TERMS AND DEFINITIONS

Amplification: The Jungian practice of creating meaning out of the symbolism in images in mostly dreams, but also in films.

Apartheid: The South African mode of racial segregation from 1948 to 1994 during which time a white Afrikaans-speaking minority exercised excessive rule over a black majority.

Double Occupancy: The notion that a space is at least double or even triple occupied in a geopolitical as well as a psychological manner.

Healing: A process of psychological integration and a coming-to-terms with aspects of the Self following a perceived or real traumatic event such as severe loss.

Healing Fiction: A work of art such as a film that stimulates or provokes the viewer into recognizing possibilities for healing through the potency of its images.

Individuation: The continuous psychological trajectory of the individual who is called to consciousness in the pursuit of psychological wholeness.

Shadow: An archetypal representation of the repressed or hidden content of the Self that is often projected onto other people on an individual as well as collective level.

ENDNOTES

1 The author acknowledges the research assistance of Micia de Wet in developing this chapter.

2 Hermanus' feature debut was *Shirley Adams* (2009), a family drama set in the Cape Flats coloured community and featuring a strong female protagonist who cares for her disabled son. *Skoonheid* is his second film. Both Hermanus' films address positions of marginality in a country where forms of marginality were deliberately politically, culturally and religiously entrenched.

3 The narrative of the God-fearing conquering white South Africans was cinematically established in the infamous *De Voortrekkers* (Shaw, 1916). The film detailed the historical event of the Great Trek in which some inhabitants of the Cape Province relocated to the Transvaal.

4 See Sonnekus (2013) for an interrogation of MSM culture in relation to white Afrikaans masculinity.

Chapter 9
The Group Hero: An Archetype Whose Time Has Come

Claudia Hall
California Institute of Integral Studies, USA

ABSTRACT

The Group Hero is an emerging archetype of the Hero story that differs from lone hero stories in five specific ways. These are: 1) Heroism is about participation in the larger cause, 2) Heroism is team based, 3) Each team member is different and everyone's contributions are important, 4) The cause takes precedence over personality conflicts, and 5) Leadership is dynamic and team based. Using mass media examples of movies, comic books, and MMO games, this chapter explores each of these themes and how they differ from the presentation of heroism in more traditional lone hero stories. The Group Hero archetype template is then applied to the problem of school bullying, and the chapter ends by challenging digital storytellers of all kinds to apply the Group Hero archetype in new and creative ways to effect positive social changes.

INTRODUCTION

The group hero is an emerging psychological archetype of the hero found in stories where heroic exploits are credited to the actions of the entire group, not a single individual. Throughout Western history, the primary definition of "hero" has been solitary: "a person who is admired for great or brave acts or fine qualities" (Merriam-Webster, 2014, online). The stories cultures tell, known as myths, reflect common patterns within human experience. Jung (1959) called these patterns archetypes, writing often about these patterns and their specific expressions in people's lives (as cited in Jacobi, 2007). Campbell (2008) took the idea of archetypes and applied it to mythology, most notably in his work on the hero archetype. In the case of the hero archetype, every culture has stories about brave people who overcame great challenges. In *The Hero with a Thousand Faces*, Campbell (2008) wrote of the lone hero archetype, the person who might have help along the way, but in the end acquires success on his or her own merits.

This lone hero archetype is the primary hero story told in mythology throughout time, including in the modern myth stories told in popular literature and through cinema. The lone hero archetype is so

DOI: 10.4018/978-1-4666-9891-8.ch009

prevalent that Campbell (2008) presented it in many ways as the only hero archetype. However, in a minority of stories within cinema and literature, the entire group is credited with the heroic action. In the last few decades, this minority has gained strength, and today, it is arguably at a tipping point where this minority archetype may be coming into prominence as the primary type of hero story.

According to Box Office Mojo (2014), a website dedicated to tracking movie statistics, in 2014, group hero movies were the primary type of hero story watched by American moviegoers. Six of the top ten grossing films in America in 2014 were full or partial group hero stories (Box Office Mojo, 2014). Two of these, *The LEGO Movie* and *Big Hero 6*, might be argued to be solo hero tales because there is a distinct lead character. However, an argument can equally be made that they are at least partially group hero stories because of the critical necessity of the team for the mission's success. In lone hero movies, the hero receives help from others but ultimately success or failure rest on them (Campbell, 2008). In group hero stories, success is dependent on the performance of the entire team. Thus, *The LEGO Movie* and *Big Hero 6* might be seen as group stories because the main characters could not succeed without their team. Regardless of which side of the hero line those two movies are placed on, the other four, *Guardians of the Galaxy*, *The Hobbit: The Battle of the Five Armies*, *Transformers: Age of Extinction*, and *X-Men: Days of Future Past*, are purely group based hero stories, offering cinematic examples of the emerging group hero archetype defined in this chapter.

Comic books, movies, and MMOs are multigenerational genres, offering a wide variety of people access to stories of the group hero archetype. In all cases, people looking to utilize the group hero themes as the basis for social change will find rich material for application. However, one of the main arguments against viewing comic and movie hero stories is that they are very violent (Signorielli, 2012). This is true, and the creators of heroic tales need to address the impact of violent messages, whether lone hero or group hero stories (Parham-Payne, 2014). While it is currently true that the dominant means of overcoming problems in hero stories is violence, there is nothing in the archetype of the group hero that demands violence to succeed.

One question faced by the storytellers of every generation is whether or not to tell stories of violence, and that is equally true for those telling stories of group heroism. Society is shaped by the stories it tells itself, so if it wants to change, it must change the stories told. Wales (2013) has explicitly begun using comic books to teach anti-bullying behavior, using student's own storytelling skills to create novel, peaceful solutions to bullying. This is one immediately available model for utilizing hero stories to combat bullying. In each educational context, a nonviolent group story can be told, one which utilizes the skills and talents of all students, whatever their previous role(s) may have been.

In this chapter the group hero archetype is defined and explored, using various kinds of mass media presentations to explore the nuances of the archetype. The chapter then discusses the problem of school bullying from the perspective of the group hero, and it ends with a challenge to digital storytellers of all kinds to consider the group hero when choosing what kinds of heroic stories to tell.

BACKGROUND

The group hero archetype, like all archetypes, is a creation of the collective unconscious of humanity and is not restricted to American stories (Jacobi, 2007). In fact, some cultures have included this archetype in their hero stories for some time. In the Latin American world, group hero stories, such as *El Eternauta*, have existed for decades (Ferreira, 2012). In Native American writing, group heroics have been portrayed in many ways, including as a multigenerational matter (Helstern, 2013). In Japan, group hero stories have been told in cinematic form since the beginnings of anime in World War II (WWII) (Schodt, 1986). These are a few examples of the way the group hero is found across human storytelling as one possible manifestation of the hero archetype. The group hero archetype is still gaining prominence in larger American culture, but it is not new, even in America. As early as 1940, comic book superheroes banded together in a group hero format, tackling larger and larger threats to Earth (Moore, 2014).

Comic books are a medium for telling all kinds of archetypical hero stories, from lone hero tales to stories about groups of heroes, where the relationships between the characters is as central to the story as their battles with villains. As a major literary medium, comic books provide a wealth of material when discussing archetypes and their expression in American culture for the last century (Kuskin, 2008). During the 1940s, a time known as the "Golden Age of Comics", comic titles exploded in popularity, offering readers a dizzying array of stories involving superheroes engaged in epic battles of good and evil (Petty, 2006).

After the defeat of Nazi Germany, the McCarthy-era censorship drove superhero comics into near-obscurity (Petty, 2006). The genre languished until the late 1950s/early 1960s, and one of the titles that pulled superhero comics back into the mainstream was *The Fantastic Four* published in 1961 (Petty, 2006). This superhero group was also a family and much of the character interest came from their interactions with each other as much as the action sequences (Krensky, 2008). Since that time, many comic superhero stories have focused on the relationships and psychology of the heroes, in addition to the action, integrating social issues into the storylines (Krensky, 2008).

Along with this resurgence of comic book sales was another phenomenon that told a group hero story: the publication of Tolkein's *The Lord of the Rings* trilogy in the United States (Flowers, 2014). While the books were published in 1954–55, they did not gain much in the way of mainstream American attention until a copyright dispute in 1965 brought the books to media prominence (Duriez, 2012). Tolkien's group hero story is one of the most enduring examples of the archetype, and the contribution of Tolkien to the current American mythology of the group hero would be hard to overestimate. One of the many results of this series' popularity was people wanting to go from being merely passive observers of the group hero story to being participants in group hero tales.

This desire to enact heroic roles gave rise to an entire subculture, and for the past 40 years Tabletop Role-Playing Games (TRPGs) have offered small groups of people structured ways to immerse themselves in the group hero archetype in intensely social and creative ways (Cover, 2010). TRPGs are inherently social games, requiring people to work together to overcome the challenges of the story (Fine, 1983). They are immersive in nature, allowing people the chance to enact a wide variety of heroic roles (MacKay, 2001). Instead of being dependent on story writers to tell people what the heroes are like, TRPGs give individuals the chance to write their own heroic story, always in the company of others (Cover, 2010). As such, TRPGs are one of the main ways to tell group hero stories in ways that can offer lasting psychological and sociological change.

While millions of people have played TRPGs in the last 40 years (Brace, 2012), the most easily accessible examples of the group hero archetype for mainstream American audiences remain movies, such as *The Avengers* or *Guardians of the Galaxy* where it takes the entire team's effort to defeat the villain. These movies make people passive recipients of the story, rather than active players in the way TRPGs do. However, their larger appeal makes them more accessible for presenting the themes of the group hero archetype to a general audience. As such, the main focus of this chapter is an analysis of group hero themes using *The Avengers* and *Guardians of the Galaxy* as examples.

Please note that the following analysis is limited to movies based on super groups from the Marvel Comics line. This is not because that comic publisher is superior to others but because, although DC Comics created the superhero group with the 1940 introduction of the Justice Society of America and while they remain a powerhouse in the comic industry, as of this writing, they have not translated the super group story to mass theater audiences in the same way as Marvel has (Box Office Mojo, 2015).

THE GROUP HERO ARCHETYPE: FIVE THEMES

Stories of group heroism, including the two movies being discussed, *The Avengers* and *Guardians of the Galaxy*, have five common themes that emerge which distinguish them from other types of hero stories. In stories about the archetypical group hero, these five themes form the core of the story:

1. Heroism is about participation in the larger cause.
2. Heroism is team-based.
3. Each team member is different, and unique contributions are important.
4. The cause takes precedence over personality conflicts.
5. Leadership is dynamic and skills-based.

Heroism is about participation in the larger cause. In group hero stories, the emphasis is on the overall contributions of the group to the story, instead of a focus on specific actions. In other words, as long as the goal is achieved, those who participate are considered equal heroes. In *The Avengers*, Loki converts the character Hawkeye is for a time, yet he is still considered a vital part of the group for his role in helping defeat Loki. At several points in the movie, Loki tricks characters, at other times, individuals fail to prevent various major problems. At the end, however, they are considered a team of heroes because their working together saved Earth from an alien invasion.

There can be a great deal of tension in group hero stories between the motivations and actions of the individual and the fulfillment of the team goal. The character of Nick Fury is ruthless in his willingness to do whatever is necessary to protect Earth and is shown throughout the film as a morally complex character. While he is not portrayed as a direct member of the Avengers team, he is the person responsible for their assembly and direction, at least in the beginning. Other members of the group have equally complex moral lives, specifically Iron Man (aka Tony Stark), who is an alcoholic playboy whose fortune originated from arms-dealing. He is a narcissist who demonstrates excessive anti-social tendencies and an unwillingness to accept others as equals. His motivation for joining the cause seems to be less about helping others and more about his ego-driven need to be superior.

Group hero stories offer complex conceptions of people, to the point that some members of the team might not be considered heroic at all except for their participation in the group. The movie, *Guardians of the Galaxy*, is based on this idea. The entire team consists of murderers, swindlers, opportunists, and other criminals. Yet, as a team, they overcome an even worse evil and in the process find a purpose and a cause to serve. Each individual member begins the story out for themselves, looking for revenge, for profit, or simply to survive. In fact, two of the characters, Rocket and Groot, are introduced as bounty hunters trying to capture the character of Star Lord. Star Lord is a thief who has stolen an important artifact, something so critical that the behind-the-scenes villain sends his daughter, Gamora, to retrieve it.

These four characters come together in an action scene that culminates in them all being captured and sent to jail. There they meet the fifth member of their developing team, Drax. A fighter of great renown, he has a personal vendetta against the main villain and so joins the team to fight him. Faced with a foe that will destroy them, they set aside their differences and work together to overcome the problem. None of them could handle the challenge on their own, and at different times in the movie, their differences threaten to split them apart. Only at the final moment, when they join together, do they succeed at saving the world.

Returning to *The Avengers*, each member of the group is split on motivations and methods. Hulk, Thor, and Iron Man are loners, while Captain America, Hawkeye, and Black Widow are soldiers who work well as a unit. Thor has a personal vendetta against his brother, while the humans seek to save their world. Black Widow is not primarily a fighter; unlike the others, she specializes in information gathering, using violence as a last resort. None of them begins the movie working well together, and much of the movie plot revolves around the rocky path the group takes while learning to work together.

Group hero stories such as these may be more morally muddled than lone hero stories, since each addition to the group provides an exponential layer of challenges, conflicts, and morality issues. Each character on the team has different reasons for being there, different motivations for their actions, and different methods for addressing the problem. In a group hero story, it can sometimes seem as though the members are heroes in spite of themselves. As expressions of an archetype, the mythological nature of group hero stories leaves the recipient with many unresolved tensions (Campbell and Moyers, 1991).

Questions raised by group hero stories include whether or not there can there be a universally recognized group hero, or if one group's noble cause is another group's moral decay. As an archetype, the group hero reflects timeless symbols of humanity, but the particular stories told about an archetype are always reflections of their culture (Jacobi, 2007). Thus, the cultural norms of the day dictate the shape and form of how heroism is defined and perceived. In fact, this shifting perception of heroism has created the expression of the hero archetype under examination.

Many lone hero stories are defined by the individual resisting larger causes that they perceive as unjust (Campbell, 2008). Conversely, group hero stories revolve around the group coming together to participate in a larger cause, for reasons that may or may not involve a higher personal morality. This is the first major difference between the group hero expression of the hero archetype and its lone hero expression.

Heroism is team-based. The second major difference between group hero stories and their lone hero counterparts is that in group hero stories, heroism is not attributed to one individual. The Avengers save the world, not Thor or Hulk or Iron Man. Each of them does heroic things, but the sum total of their efforts is what matters. When they fail to work as a team, they fail to prevent the invasion. Only when they begin to work together are they able to overcome the challenges and succeed at their goals. Because of the large, sometimes insurmountable differences between group members, teamwork can be a fragile and often broken thing.

In *The Avengers* there is constant tension between the team members that is not resolved even after the epic battle to save the world from alien invasion. Thor and Hulk are rivals, while Captain America and Iron Man are about as opposite as personalities get. The team repeatedly fractures, and each time that happens, their enemy gains the advantage. Only when the team acts together, putting egos aside for the common cause, are they able to overcome Loki's plot and save the world.

In *Guardians of the Galaxy*, the members have active cause to hate each other, and the only issue that brings them together initially is their larger cause. None of them is especially heroic during most of the movie. Major action sequences include four of the characters destroying a city center while fighting among themselves, the five of them coming together to break out of prison after starting a riot, and several of the group being drunk and disorderly (fighting and causing a scene) on what was supposed to be a clandestine mission. Over the course of the movie, they slowly begin to learn how to work together, focusing on using each of their strengths to achieve their goal of stopping the villain from obtaining the artifact.

In group hero stories such as *Guardians*, figuring out how to work as a team in spite of large differences is a major part of the story. Dealing with the social pressures and psychological factors within the team is just as important as dealing with epic battles and external deeds. In group hero stories, being a team does not happen instantly. Rather, the creation of the team and their learning to work together are a vital part of the story. Rigid roles make it easier, since individual team members can immersive themselves in their role, but personal differences cannot be eliminated.

As an example of this, Captain America is a solider from WWII and he is used to taking orders and fighting as commanded. His role of soldier usually allows him to suspend his personal problems with the others and get the job done. But it is not a perfect immersion, so when there is no immediate action, the role fractures and differences well up. Captain America also has conflicts with the others of the team who do not fall into this role.

In one scene, Captain America and Iron Man are fighting over what to do after the death of Agent Coulson. Captain America asks Iron Man if this is the first time he has ever lost a soldier, to which Iron Man snaps back that he is NOT a soldier. Captain America is completely immersed in the role, but Iron Man is not, and the difference in how they perceive their roles is a deep part of the conflict between them. This happens in *Guardians of the Galaxy*, as everyone but Groot is used to acting independently, and there are repeated conflicts about how the characters will work together, or even if they can.

Learning to act as a team in spite of differences is one aspect of the group hero that deserves special attention when discussing real world applications of this archetype. In many causes today, people are willing to come together for a purpose, but the social problems faced by America are not causes with easy solutions. Being able to sustain teamwork when there is no crisis is one of the major challenges faced by group organizers, and something group hero stories grapple with (Wollschleger, 2013). Mass media, especially visual media, is recognized as an important influence on perceptions of reality (Parham-Payne, 2014).

Movies like *The Avengers* and *Guardians of the Galaxy* are not just escapism; they offer mass media portrayals of dynamic interpersonal relationships that group organizers can draw from when creating teams. They can be a shared cultural experience that can be called on for inspirational or pedagogical purposes (Phaire, 2013). When perceived as cultural tools for teaching values and developing teams to enact positive social change, group hero stories such as these go from simple entertainment to truly mythical stories that engage eternal themes of the human condition (Phaire, 2013).

Each team member is different, and unique contributions are important. This is one of the most unusual elements of the group hero archetype. In these stories, no one hero can do it alone, and no one hero can be good at everything. In lone hero stories, the hero might get assistance from mentors or gods in the beginning, but the majority of the adventure is about their solo abilities and their personal journey (Campbell, 2008).

Continuing the example of *The Avengers*, the character of Black Widow is a spy. She is not super human, nor is she exceptionally good at combat compared with other members of the team. However, her ability to gather information makes it possible for the team to even assemble in the first place. Without her skills and talents, the Hulk would not have been found or convinced to join the team. Additionally, she is the one who saves Hawkeye. Ironically, Black Widow's lack of superpowers saves him. If the super-strong Thor or Hulk had hit Hawkeye, they probably would have killed him, not just broken him loose from Loki's power. Her skills are mainly useful away from the action, but without them the team would not exist.

In group hero stories, every person has something vital that they bring to the group which allows the story to be told. In *The Avengers*, each member has moments where their unique perspectives or skills are what allow for success. Even flaws can be useful for telling a group hero story. Iron Man's egotistical nature provides insight at a critical moment, allowing the group to determine where the alien attack will happen.

In *Guardians of the Galaxy*, Rocket is the genetically engineered brains of the group, and Star Lord is the face character, able to bluff the team's way out of several situations. Drax and Gemora are the fighters, able to hold their own in combat of various kinds in ways that the weak Rocket or the half-human Star Lord could not. Groot appears at first as a comic figure, a walking plant with limited speech who provides physical might that Rocket cannot. However, despite his lack of verbal communication, he demonstrates abilities to fight, to heal, and to protect the team, eventually saving them all.

In a group hero story like this, the recognition that each member brings important and different things to the group aids the team in overcoming obstacles and becoming victorious. Teamwork, at least in part, is being honest about the abilities each member brings and using those abilities creatively to achieve the common cause. Creative thinking is required to utilize the talents, flaws, limits, and gifts of team members. One way group hero stories can inspire is by presenting complex characters with clearly defined limits who are able to achieve larger goals through creative use of their skills in combination with others.

The cause takes precedence over personality conflicts. The Avengers provides a very good example of this theme. Most of the members do not get along. Iron Man is an egotistical loner, while Hulk alternates between being withdrawn and depressed and being so full of rage that nobody can reason with him. Captain America is from another time and faces culture clashes with the rest of the team. Thor truly does not understand humanity. Black Widow is rarely treated as an equal, and Hawkeye does not have the powers or the personal skills to fit in very well with the group. Despite this and the constant manipulations of Nick Fury, when a larger threat is posed the group focuses their attention and energy on overcoming the problem at hand.

The idea that the larger purpose can bring together people who otherwise do not agree is another critical theme of the emerging group hero. Again, this is of importance when discussing applying this archetype to social issues. In today's interconnected society, being able to form teams from disparate, even conflicting, groups of people is a necessary skill if global issues are to be overcome. Coming together around a common cause is the first step. Raising awareness of the necessity of the team to accomplish the goal is next, followed by finding ways for each participant to be vital based on honest evaluation and creative application of skills. But who is best equipped to make that call, and whether or not particular team members get along are points of contention that inevitably arise when dealing with human groups. Group hero stories can provide examples of disparate groups learning to work together in novel ways, offering ideas in stories that address real-world problems.

In *Guardians of the Galaxy*, the team is less motivated by heroism than by self-interest, at least in the beginning. Each of the members is made aware of what the villain will do if he obtains the artifact, and despite their bickering and infighting, they all risk their lives to stop him from taking this power. Their heroism is evident in the fact that earlier in the movie, it is made quite clear that mortals cannot touch the artifact and survive. But, to try and stop the villain, they all join together to grab the artifact, each thinking they will die in the attempt. It is only when they are willing to come together in great sacrifice that they succeed. This does not happen right away, but is the result of the shared heroes' journey that enables each member to participate willingly in the climactic event.

While both *The Avengers* and *Guardians of the Galaxy* end with the team succeeding in their task, none of the characters, in either of the movies, has their full story told. Unlike the typical lone hero journey, where the story is about the hero and their achievements, in a group hero story the mission is emphasized. At the end of *The Avengers*, the group is battered and bruised, and questions about whether they will remain a team loom large. At the end of *Guardians of the Galaxy*, there are more questions than answers about the future of each character. However, the story is complete because it is not about the individuals, it is about the goal and telling the story of how the group worked together to accomplish the goal. In group hero stories, each member has time to shine, but the emphasis is on how they use their skills to achieve the larger goal. At the end, the important part of a group hero story is that the goal was achieved, not who did what part or who had superior talents.

Leadership is dynamic and Skill-Based. In *The Avengers*, Nick Fury is the director of SHIELD, supposedly in charge of events. Yet he is rarely seen as a leader by the group. There is little direct, hierarchical chain of command in this movie. This causes conflict among the group, as egos and tempers flare. In fact, it takes the death of a sidekick (Agent Coulson) before the group is willing to start learning to truly work together. Despite the conflict, without this shifting leadership, the goal of repelling the alien attack would not have been a success.

Nick Fury gets the Avengers together, while Thor provides knowledge of his brother's actions. Hulk is responsible both for figuring out how to fight the weapon, and for subduing Loki. Black Widow saves Hawkeye and inspires him to keep going, while figuring out how to close the portal. Captain America coordinates rescue efforts, while Iron Man turns Loki's tactics against him, fighting Loki's egotism, trickery, and narcissism with his own.

In *Guardians of the Galaxy*, Star Lord is voted in as leader of the group, but not until after Gamora comes up with a plan for profiting from the artifact and after Rocket's plans succeed in helping them escape from prison. Groot's plan and self-sacrifice enable the group to survive the shipwreck and thus enables them to defeat the villain. Drax is the only member of the team who does not have a concrete leadership role at some point during the movie.

Throughout both these movies, the action and the focus shift fluidly between characters. In group hero stories, the focus is on the group, not any particular individual. This is true for the action and for the leadership, each shifting depending on what talents and skills are needed at that moment. In a group hero story, the elements of the hero archetype are divided among the members of the group instead of focused on any one individual. Rather than attach one name to a successful cause, group hero stories acknowledge the necessity of many participants to overcome the great challenges humanity faces. To date many of these stories have been about fantastic, larger-than-life mythic characters, but there is no compelling need to limit group hero stories to such tales.

Various kinds of group hero stories are being told in American culture today, ranging from the staple of comic book super hero groups to the emergence of Massively Multiplayer Online Role-Playing Games (MMOs), which bring together millions of people around the world to participate in immersive visual worlds where group heroes gather together to overcome fantastic villains and challenges on a daily basis. This essay now will open the door to these worlds, glancing in to see how the five themes play out in different kinds of stories. The themes are then examined in light of the current focus on anti-bullying campaigns, ending with recommendations for further applications of the archetype to promote positive social change.

MODERN EXAMPLES OF GROUP-CENTERED HEROISM

This section of the chapter deals with how the archetype of the group hero is manifesting in current American literature and immersive computer role-playing game (CRPG) play, looking briefly at how each of the themes is treated in these genres.

Comic Book Super Hero Groups

The Golden Age of super hero comics began in 1938 with the publication of Superman (Krensky, 2008). All throughout WWII, noble heroes with larger-than-life abilities fought against the evil Axis powers (Petty, 2006). This included the *Justice Society of America* (*JSA*), started in 1940 as the first super hero group comic (Serchay, 2010). After WWII, comics came under fire for their content, with public pressure leading to the industry self-censoring their titles (Krensky, 2008). Many titles, including the *JSA*, were shelved during this period, and a number of publishers closed down completely (Krensky, 2008). In what has been dubbed the Silver Age of Comics, two comic book publishers—Marvel and DC—came to the front of the pack as industry leaders, a position they have maintained ever since (Petty, 2006). DC reinvented the *JSA* in 1960, changing their name to the *Justice League of America* (*JLA*) (Serchay, 2010). The JLA was very popular, and in 1961, Marvel Comics responded with the debut of *The Fantastic Four*, a team of heroes who spent as much time dealing with their relationships to each other as they did dealing with taking down the bad guys (Petty, 2006).

Stan Lee, one of the designers of *The Fantastic Four*, continued his success, releasing *The X-Men* in 1963 (Darowski, 2014). *The X-Men* is a comic series about a group of people who have altered genetic structures, giving them abilities very different from ordinary humans. Some of these are incredibly powerful, while others are quite disfiguring or disabling, making it virtually impossible for the mutant to live among the general populace (Darowski, 2014). Since their debut, the X-Men comics have consistently tackled social issues, such as Communism, race relations, class issues, sexuality, and feminism, and what it means to belong to a society (Darowski, 2014).

Whether the *JLA* or *The X-Men*, comic book super heroes serve an important purpose in the furthering of the group hero archetype. Across the different eras of their writing, both the *JLA* and *The X-Men* have offered a group hero solution to problems. In both cases, these comics have provided generations of Americans with examples of group centered heroism. As such, they are important works for looking at the group hero archetype as applied in literary form.

Massively Multiplayer Online Game Role-Playing Groups

Massively Multiplayer Online Role-Playing Games (MMORPGs or MMOs) are virtual worlds created and shaped by the scripts of the game designers and the interaction between players and those scripts. Virtual worlds have been described as "an automated, shared, persistent environment with and through which people can interact in real time by means of a virtual self" (Bartle, 2010, p. 24). Virtual worlds are a multi-billion dollar business engaging millions of people across the world (Statista, 2014). As such, they are one of the primary ways people engage with the archetype of the group hero on a regular basis (Bartle, 2010). Unlike a movie, which may only be watched once or twice, players of MMOs are often online for hours each day (Kelly, 2007). In most MMOs, players team up to tackle larger challenges, and when that occurs, the five principles of the group hero come into play in a dynamic and immersive environment where the players become the group heroes.

In an MMO group, like other forms of role-playing game, the goal is to overcome the challenges presented to the players by the game designers. These challenges usually require a diverse team of players to succeed (Yee, 2006). The success of the group is based on the ability of the members to work together, and if the group does not work together, the goal is much harder (or impossible) to achieve. Members of the group need to perform well at their assigned role, but how the role is assigned is a complex matter of socially negotiated leadership combined with the particular skill set of any given character filtered through the player's experience level. Additionally, members of the group must be able to remain aware of the larger dynamic aspects of the environment, acting in concert with all the other members, if the group is to be successful. MMOs offer players the ability to immersive themselves in a dynamic virtual world where interdependence is normative (Yee, 2006). By creating worlds where group hero stories are the norm, MMOs provide a valuable source for people looking to use this emerging archetype to address social problems, such as the final focus of this chapter: the problem of bullying.

Applying Group Hero Themes in a School Setting: Anti-Bullying Efforts

This section applies the five themes from the archetype of the group hero to a serious problem in America: bullying. There are a wide variety of initiatives, nonprofit groups, school trainings, and classroom activities designed to address the problem of bullying behavior, but few have met with even limited success (Brown, Low, Smith, & Haggerty, 2011). One of the identifiable factors in the failure of anti-bullying programs is the current inability of programs to combat the social norms of the classroom (Pozzoli, Gini, & Vieno, 2012). The majority of anti-bullying programs have focused on changing individual behavior, rather than addressing the cultural issues that influence social interactions (Brown et al., 2011). When the culture of the classroom is considered, there are much greater correlations in student behavior than when students are examined solely as individuals (Pozzoli et al., 2012).

From a social constructionist standpoint, this makes sense. Individuals are not separate from their environment, rather they are a complex interwoven matrix of experiences and unconscious influences created and sustained by their environment (Gergen, 2009). The culture of the classroom, and of the school as a whole, influences whether or not children feel that bullying behavior is appropriate, acceptable, encouraged or devalued. The culture of the school influences whether or not children feel they are alone when they face problems, or whether they feel that there is a support network to help them deal with their concerns. The culture of the school, combined with the other cultures the children experience, dictates what values and social norms they hold valid (Ryalls, 2011). Reality is created by human interactions and the narratives told about those interactions; thus, questioning basic assumptions is one way to begin the process of social change (Gergen, 2009). In the paragraphs below, the hypothesis extended is that the archetype of the group hero offers students a way to understand and prevent bullying behavior by reconstructing the culture from one of individualism to one of participation in a group cause.

Applied Themes: Bullying as Cause

Group hero stories express the potential for heroism and villainy to exist in unlikely and ordinary places, sometimes simultaneously. In The Avengers, Loki is brilliant, charming, energetic, creative, and dynamic. He loves his mother, works hard to achieve his goals, and possesses a great deal of determination. In some ways he is more appealing than his brother, yet he is the villain because he has no cause larger than himself. Guardians of the Galaxy ends with the team deciding not to do something good or bad, but a bit of both. While they were heroes in the movie, their future is undecided, and only their actions will determine if they remain heroes.

The first theme of the group hero archetype reminds us that labels can, and should change. In other words, even bullies can be heroes. Not every bully will become a hero. But the potential exists in every person to act as part of a heroic team. One of the cultural shifts that happens in both *The Avengers* and *Guardians of the Galaxy* is that people who are not on the same side in the beginning come together to overcome greater problems. Every member of *Guardians of the Galaxy* is a villain to one extent or another; thieves, spies, murderers, and pirates banding together to stop an even bigger problem. In *The Avengers*, Iron Man is a narcissistic loner with addiction problems, while Hulk has severe anger management issues. Captain America is from a different culture, and Thor is not even remotely human. These are not necessarily what would traditionally be called heroic figures, when you examine them individually. What makes them heroes is that they come together to serve a greater cause. In American schools, what is the greater cause?

For many children, school is a mandatory sentence, not a place that serves a higher purpose. Even parents often seem more interested in after-school social programs than educational achievement (Bishop et al., 2004). What sorts of goals or greater causes could be appropriate for a school, or even a classroom, to adopt? Would it make more sense to sort students out not by grade level, but by their interest in a cause? In group hero stories, the cause is what brings a diverse and unruly group together, and forges them together into a functional team. What would education look like if dedication to social change was the motivating force behind attendance?

Instead of asking how to raise achievement scores on standardized tests, the deeper question is what does society desire children to become? The rising level of student debt compared with earning potential suggests that the purpose of education needs to be revisited in light of the many changes occurring in the workforce (Kingkade, 2013). For many in America, the goal of education has become clouded (Sloan, 2012). Determining a team goal is the center point around which group hero stories can be used to emphasize the necessity of a team to reach that goal. The group hero archetype teaches that no one person can do everything well; perhaps it is time to apply that to schools, focusing on what society wants children to become, then portioning off the parts of that ideal which schools can assist with. However society decides to organize education, the first theme of the group hero, applied to education, reminds society that there must be a clear goal before the team can assemble to achieve it.

Applied Themes: Teams Opposing Bullying

Nobody can do it alone. This is one of the core messages of group hero stories, and one that is often forgotten when trying to combat complex social issues. Anti-bullying campaigns are often targeted toward individual behavior (such as stopbullying.gov, 2014). Bullies are not created in a vacuum. Neither are heroes. Zimbardo (2007) spoke of the 'banality' of both evil and good, and about how most actions we perceive as good or bad stem from larger problems with the group. In emphasizing individual achievement, to what extent have the group factors been ignored in schools? How can classrooms become teams, where members are able to rely on one another for support and aid in overcoming larger social issues?

Returning to the first theme, the group hero story teaches that without a clear goal, teams have no way to measure their progress. In both *The Avengers* and *Guardians of the Galaxy*, the teams only learn to work together when a clear purpose brings them together. Several members could easily be considered bullies, but they are redeemed by participation in a greater cause. How can schools offer greater causes to those students who would otherwise participate in bullying behavior? In both movies, the group comes together for a common cause, but their motivations are diverse. What methods or practices could uncover the motivations underlying bullying behavior and channel those toward a greater goal?

Applied Themes: Unique Opposition to Bullying

Group hero stories teach that every person brings something to the table, no matter what their mental or physical limitations might be. In Guardians of the Galaxy, Rocket is physically weak, Groot is nonverbal, and Drax could be considered autistic (Merryweatherblue, 2014). Yet each of these characters plays a role in making the mission a success.

In the case of bullying, one question to be asked is how can an entire classroom be evaluated for their skills and be brought together to use those skills? Group hero stories teach that every member has skills and not all have to be involved in the climactic confrontations to be effective team members. As examples, some people are more empathetic and could be peer listeners. Some are more charismatic and could be the outspoken ones. Some are more creative and could come up with solutions and plans that others would not have thought of.

Group hero stories teach us that everybody can play a role on the team. All skills have value and are needed at different times. Conversely, when used at the wrong time, they become detriments to the cause, such as when Drax summons the villain before the group is ready for him. Yet his same stubborn determination is later an asset, as it allows him to aid the others in overcoming the villain at the end of the movie.

Even bullies have talents; it is the lack of dedication to a team and the mistimed or misplaced use of their talents that makes them a bully instead of a hero. How can schools work to channel skills and talents into times and places where the outcome will be more positive? What stories need to be told to make it more acceptable and respected to be a listener than a bully? Should dedication to nonviolence be an important goal? If so, how can digital storytellers tap into the mythological and archetypical themes of humanity in nonviolent ways, telling and emphasizing stories of heroism that do not require physical or emotional violence to propel the plot? American culture finds violence exciting, making this difficult to accomplish, but not impossible. There is a great deal of group heroism to be found in medical teams, scientific exploration, social justice workers, and more. Typically thought of as feel-good stories, not action thrillers, how could these nonviolent examples be reframed to fit the mold of exciting action required for profitable mass media storytelling?

Applied Themes: The Cause Takes Precedence over Personality Conflicts

Use of this theme requires a group purpose to be defined in such a way that diversity becomes an asset not a liability. It is a mark of maturity to be able to set aside personal differences to serve a common cause, and as such, this is perhaps the most difficult theme to translate into school settings. Ideas for doing so will be as varied as the groups who come together, but one of the ways this can work is dedication to a cause. Students and families must buy-in to the educational process so that teams can develop and larger goals be achieved.

Children are socialized from birth into cultural constructs that determines their level of participation in and adherence to group norms (Tam, Kee, Kim, Li, & Chao, 2012). One part of this socialization happens through the stories they are exposed to (Egan, 1986). When group hero stories emphasize how different people work together in spite of their problems, it is one step toward socializing children away from violent conflicts and toward useful negotiations. Conversely, when group hero stories utilize violence, cultural norms of aggression are reinforced (Bond, 2004). Indeed, education needs a clear goal for instilling nonviolence in children. However, as long as coercive violence of all kinds is considered normative in the larger culture, this goal will be difficult to attain (Bond, 2004). When the culture shifts, so too will the behavior of its children (Bond, 2004).

One way to enact this shift is by telling new stories (Gergen, 2009). For storytellers, the question is how to present stories where diversity is valued and important, and where the group can achieve their goal without resorting to violence. Even more nuanced is the question of if or when violence is appropriate, and of how to make that judgment in a society where there are conflicting answers (Ryalls, 2011).

Applied Themes: Leadership Is Dynamic and Skills-Based

This theme may be more appropriate for older children, but even young children can learn by participating in situations of flexible leadership. Rather than accepting bullying from a young age, stories told to even the youngest children can discuss how to build teams and ways to work together, along with nonviolent methods for resolving conflict when others are not willing to come together (Egan, 1986). In group hero stories, one person is not the only leader, as every member of the team has the potential for leadership depending on whether they have the skills or perspective necessary for the situation. The right skills to accomplish the goal, rather than coercive power, are at the heart of leadership in the group hero model. Unlike traditional leadership models that focus on the exchange of rewards, transformational leadership, like what is found in group hero stories, focuses on the way the leader helps the followers change internal values, thus improving performance (Molero, Cuadrado, Navas, & Morales, 2007). In group hero stories, leadership is shared because each member can contribute to achieving the goal in a different way, and thus, everyone can shine. Leadership is less about the power to coerce behavior than it is about the ability to present a plan to the group persuasively.

RECOMMENDATIONS

Taken together, the five themes found in group hero stories comprise the basis for an emerging archetype that has a different focus from the lone hero figure so traditionally predominant in mythology and storytelling. All the essential qualities of the hero figure are present, including traits, such as leadership, inner strength, special abilities, people skills, and an epic cause. All the traditional failings of the hero are also present, like egotism and hubris, arrogance, and narrow-mindedness (Davis, 1997). Instead of being focused on only one person, the group hero story focuses on a cause and the outcome of a group's actions on that cause. This emerging archetype could be applied to everyday social situations to inspire groups to create heroic outcomes, just as lone hero stories are used as examples of inspiring individual behavior.

In identifying themes of this archetype, the goal of this essay is to produce a template that can be deliberately applied to a variety of situations to promote positive social changes. Zimbardo (2007) wrote of the way small ordinary actions combine to create either heroism or evil. Today's world is complex and interconnected on a level previously unknown (Archer & Cameron, 2009). Mass media impacts people's perceptions of reality (Strasburger, Donnerstein, & Bushman, 2014). Media portrayals of human interaction act as models for behavior, for better or worse, meaning the archetypical stories presented by the media create direct social changes. As digital storytellers, readers of this book are uniquely situated to identify and tell group hero stories that entertain and inspire. Humanity constructs the world through the conscious and unconscious stories told by a culture to justify the status quo (Gergen, 2009). Storytellers are offered the chance to deliberately craft a different world, one where group heroism is the norm and teamwork is routine. Stories are the foundation of perceived reality, so if the stories change, reality can change (Gergen, 2009). Explicit attention to group hero themes in storytelling has the potential to overcome many social challenges by articulating an alternate reality in fun and exciting, even attractive, fashion (Gergen, 2009).

As storytellers, creating complex and richly nuanced characters is important, but equally important is the realization that stories create reality. If change is desired, stories about change must be told. Cynicism and apathy are at an all-time high (Longo & Meyer, 2006). Stories that combat this by presenting positive group heroes who succeed at their causes are an important part of shaping a more positive future.

FUTURE RESEARCH DIRECTIONS

The five themes of the group hero provide a template that could be applied in a wide variety of media and social settings. Comic books, computer games, and educational settings were discussed here, but any situation in which groups work together to achieve a higher purpose could benefit from application of this template. Workplaces, volunteer organizations, and higher educational settings could all provide locations to test out applications of the group hero template in cross-cultural settings. Additional research that tests the themes of the group hero in anti-bullying programs would be welcomed as a demonstrable application of the archetype in creating social change. From a storytelling perspective, this chapter seeks to inspire creators of mass media entertainment to utilize the group hero template to deliberately create heroic stories which will inspire positive social changes.

CONCLUSION

This essay notes five themes that tell a group based heroic story. First, that heroism comes from participation in a larger cause. Second, that heroism is team-based. Third, that every member of the team is different, and that their contributions are important for success. Fourth, that success happens when the cause takes precedence over personality conflicts. Finally, that heroic leadership is dynamic and changes depending on who has the right skills for a situation.

As a psychological archetype, the group hero reflects psychosocial processes occurring within humanity, in this case the emerging awareness of interconnectedness and the need for groups to unite to overcome current social problems. Looking at the archetype as it has emerged in mainstream American storytelling, it appears to be coming into prominence as a type of hero story being told across media forms. Tracing the archetype through current mass media presentations, both passive and active, it is readily apparent that presentations of this archetype in our society are generally violent. However, the group hero is an archetypical template, how it is applied is for storytellers to decide. In examining the issue of bullying, it becomes obvious that the archetypal themes of the group hero beg for nonviolent expressions where students can learn transformative group processes, rather than the idea that coercive violence is acceptable (Wales, 2013).

Thus, this essay ends with a challenge to its readers, the leaders and game designers and scriptwriters of our new millennium: Will you continue to tell stories in which violence propels the plot, or will you work together as a team to provide examples of nonviolent, group based heroism that will encourage positive changes in our culture?

REFERENCES

Archer, D., & Cameron, A. (2009). *Collaborative Leadership: How to Succeed in an Interconnected World*. Burlington, MA: Elsevier, Ltd.

Bartle, R. A. (2010). From MUDs to MMORPGs: The History of Virtual Worlds. In J. Hunsinger, L. Klastrup, & M. Allen (Eds.), *International Handbook of Internet Research*. Netherlands: Springer.

Bendis, B. M., McNiven, S., & Pichelli, S. (2014). *Guardians of the Galaxy*. New York, NY: Marvel Worldwide, Inc.

Bishop, J., Bishop, M., Bishop, M., Gelbwasser, L., Green, S., Peterson, E., & Zuckerman, A. et al. (2004). Why we harass nerds and freaks: A formal theory of student culture and norms. *The Journal of School Health*, *74*(7), 235–251. doi:10.1111/j.1746-1561.2004.tb08280.x PubMed doi:10.1111/j.1746-1561.2004.tb08280.x PMID:15493701

Bond, M. H. (2004). Culture and aggression- From context to coercion. *Personality and Social Psychology Review*, *8*(1), 62–78. http://psr.sagepub.com/content/8/1/62.short doi:10.1207/s15327957pspr0801_3 PMID:15121540

Box Office Mojo. (2014). *2014 Domestic Grosses*. Retrieved from http://www.boxofficemojo.com/yearly/chart/?yr=2014

Box Office Mojo. (2015). *DC Comics Movies*. Retrieved from http://www.boxofficemojo.com/franchises/chart/?view=main&id=dccomics.htm&sort=date&order=DESC&p=.htm

Brace, C. S. (2012). *Of dice and men: An ethnography of contemporary gaming subculture* [Master's thesis]. University of Arkansas.

Brown, E. C., Low, S., Smith, B. H., & Haggerty, K. P. (2011). Outcomes from a school-randomized controlled trial of Steps to Respect: A bullying prevention program. *School Psychology Review*, *40*(3), 423–443.

Campbell, J. (2008). *The hero with a thousand faces*. Novato, CA: New World Library.

Campbell, J., & Moyers, B. (1991). *The Power of Myth. New York: Anchor Books.*

Cover, J. G. (2010). *The creation of narrative in tabletop role-playing games*. Jefferson, NC: McFarland & Company, Inc.

Darowski, J. (2014). *The Ages of the X-Men: Essays on the Children of the Atom in Changing Times*. Jefferson, NC: McFarland & Company, Inc.

Davis, B. M. (1997). *The Archetypal Hero in Literature, Religion, Movies, and Popular Culture* Retrieved from http://www.tatsbox.com/hero

Duriez, C. (2012). *Amazing & Extraordinary Facts: J.R.R. Tolkien*. Devon, UK: David & Charles.

Egan, K. (1986). *Teaching as storytelling: an alternative approach to teaching and curriculum in the elementary school*. London, Ontario: The University of Western Ontario.

Feige, K., Penn, Z., & Whedon, J. (2012). *Marvel's The Avengers*. Burbank, CA: Distributed by Buena Vista Home Entertainment.

Ferriera, R. (2012). Oesterheld's Iconic and Ironic Eternautas. In M. E. Ginway & J. A. Brown (Eds.), *Latin American Science Fiction: Theory and Practice* (pp. 155–184). New York: Palgrave Macmillan. doi:10.1057/9781137312778.0015

Fine, G. A. (1983). *Shared fantasy: Role-playing games as social worlds*. Chicago, IL: University of Chicago Press.

Flowers, M. (2014). *J.R.R. Tolkien Timeline*. Retrieved from http://www.tolkiensociety.org/author/timeline/

Gergen, K. (2009). *An Invitation to Social Construction* (2nd ed.). Thousand Oaks, CA: SAGE Publications, Inc.

Helstern, L. (2013). Thriller Survivance: The Subversive Resistance of Louis Owens. In A. R. Velie & A. R. Lee (Eds.), *The Native American Renaissance: Literary Imagination and Achievement*. Norman, OK: University of Oklahoma Press.

IMDB. (2014). *The Avengers: Synopsis*. Retrieved from http://www.imdb.com/title/tt0848228/synopsis

IMDB. (2014). *Guardians of the Galaxy: Synopsis*. Retrieved from http://www.imdb.com/title/tt2015381/synopsis?ref_=ttpl_ql_3

Jacobi, J. (2007). *Complex/Archetype/Symbol in the Psychology of C G Jung*. London: Routledge.

Jung, C. G. (1959). *The Archetypes and the Collective Unconscious* (R. F. C. Hull, Trans.). New York: Princeton University Press.

Kelly, J. (2007). *Play Time: An Overview of the MMORPG Genre*. Retrieved from http://www.anthemion.org/playtime_over.html

Kingkade, T. (2013). *Student loan debt: New reports find 'unsustainable' trend dragging economy*. Retrieved from http://www.huffingtonpost.com/2013/01/31/student-loan-debt-unsustainable_n_2593303.html

Krensky, S. (2008). *Comic Book Century: The History of American Comic Books*. Minneapolis, MN: Twenty-First Century Books.

Kuskin, W. (2008). Continuity in Literary Form and History. *English Language Notes*, *46*(2), 5–13.

Longo, N. P., & Meyer, R. (2006, May). *College Students and Politics: A Literature Review*. Kettering Foundation, CIRCLE Working Paper 46. Retrieved from http://www.civicyouth.org/PopUps/WorkingPapers/WP46LongoMeyer.pdf

Mackay, D. (2001). *The fantasy role-playing game: A new performance art*. Jefferson, NC: McFarland & Company, Inc.

Merriam-Webster. (2014). *Definition of "Hero"*. Retrieved from http://www.merriam-webster.com/dictionary/hero

Merryweatherblue. (2014, August 13). *Just Keep Swimming, Swimming, SwimmingP"{* (Tumblr Blog). Retrieved from http://merryweatherblue.tumblr.com/post/94638266248/i-took-my-little-brother-who-falls-on-the-autism

Molero, F., Cuadrado, I., Navas, M., & Morales, J. F. (2007). Relations and Effects of Transformational Leadership: A Comparative Analysis with Traditional Leadership Styles. *The Spanish Journal of Psychology*, *10*(02), 358–368. doi:10.1017/S1138741600006624 PMID:17992962

Moore, S. S. (2014). *History of the Justice Society*. Retrieved from http://www.cosmicteams.com/jsa/

Parham-Payne, W. (2014). The role of the media in the disparate response to gun violence in America. *Journal of Black Studies*, *45*(8), 752–768. doi:10.1177/0021934714555185

Petty, J. (2006). *A Brief History of Comic Books*. Retrieved from http://www1.heritagestatic.com/comics/d/history-of-comics.pdf

Phaire, D. W. (2013). *Linking character strengths and learning with films: A content analysis of films for adolescents*.

Pozzoli, T., Gini, G., & Vieno, A. (2012). The Role of Individual Correlates and Class Norms in Defending and Passive Bystanding Behavior in Bullying: A Multilevel Analysis. *Child Development*, *83*(6), 1917–1931. doi:10.1111/j.1467-8624.2012.01831.x PMID:22880944

Ryalls, E. D. (2011). *The culture of mean: Gender, race, and class in mediated images of girls' bullying*.

Schodt, F. (1986). *Manga! Manga! The World of Japanese Comics*. New York: Kodansha America, Inc.

Serchay, D. (2010). Justice Society of America. In M. K. Booker (Ed.), *Encyclopedia of Comic Books and Graphic Novels*. Santa Barbara, CA: ABC-CLIO, LLC.

Signorielli, N. 2012. Violent Content on US Television. The International Encyclopedia of Media Studies, 3(2), 16.

Sloan, W. M. (2012). What is the purpose of education? *Educator's Update*, *54*(7). Retrieved from http://www.ascd.org/publications/newsletters/education-update/jul12/vol54/num07/What-Is-the-Purpose-of-Education%C2%A2.aspx

Statista. (2014). *Number of World of Warcraft Subscribers from 1st Quarter 2005 to 4th Quarter 2014*. Retrieved from http://www.statista.com/statistics/276601/number-of-world-of-warcraft-subscribers-by-quarter/

Stopbullying.gov. (2014). *What is Bullying?* Retrieved from http://www.stopbullying.gov/what-is-bullying/definition/index.html

Strasburger, V., Donnerstein, E., & Bushman, B. (2014). Why is it so hard to believe that media influence children and adolescents? *Pediatrics, 133*(4), 571–573. doi:10.1542/peds.2013-2334 PMID:24590743

Tam, K., Lee, S., Kim, Y., Li, Y., & Chao, M. (2012). Intersubjective model of value transmission: Parents using perceived norms as reference when socializing children. *Personality and Social Psychology Bulletin, 38*(8), 1041–1052. doi:10.1177/0146167212443896 PMID:22539215

Wales, A. (2013). *Peaceful panels: Using comics to teach anti-bullying to junior high school students.*

Wollschleger, J. (2013). Church Government and Religious Participation. *Rationality and Society, 25*(4), 470–400. doi:10.1177/1043463113504449

Yee, N. (2006). The Demographics, Motivations and Derived Experiences of Users of Massively-Multiuser Online Graphical Environments. *Presence (Cambridge, Mass.), 15*(3), 309–329. doi:10.1162/pres.15.3.309

Zimbardo, P. (2007). *The Lucifer Effect: Understanding How Good People Turn Evil.* New York: Random House.

KEY TERMS AND DEFINITIONS

Archetype: A descriptive expression of a common pattern of behavior within human experience. Roles like "mother," "hero," or "teacher" are archetypes. These expressions may take very different forms across time and culture.

Bullying: Behavior that causes a person or group to feel unwelcomed, threatened, or unsafe. There are overt and covert forms of bullying.

Comic Books: Paper or digital storytelling media characterized by graphic images and dialogue that combine to create the story.

Group Hero: An expression of the larger hero archetype, the Group Hero is created when multiple people gather together to tackle a larger social problem. Group hero stories are distinguished from other hero tales by their focus on the group's actions.

Lone Hero: An expression of the larger hero archetype, the Lone Hero is the form of the hero most well known in mythology and storytelling, described in books such as *The Hero With a Thousand Faces* (Campbell, 2008).

Role-Playing Game: An interactive game rooted in character-driven storytelling.

Team: A group of people working together for a common cause. Teams may be more or less cohesive, and function more or less effectively.

Chapter 10
The Media-Sphere as Dream
Researching the Contextual Unconscious of Collectives

Stephen Brock Schafer
Digipen Institute of Technology, USA

ABSTRACT

The psychological nature of the electronic media environment is a virtual reality that—according to Jungian principles—is dreamlike. Perhaps it can be analyzed with Jung's Analytical Psychology. Science is experiencing a paradigm shift into a reality of mediated illusion, and psychological research on this illusion has become the human imperative. It may be stipulated that physics has abolished matter, conceding that "reality is organized mind stuff." If cosmos is structured holographically and the brain is structured holonomically, it is probable that "mind stuff" is structured holographically. The Jungian concept of Psyche is a good place to begin researching the Media-sphere as mind stuff. Cognitive sciences are probing the brain and nervous system in search of the template for cognitive organization, and the salient features have already emerged. It appears that both conscious and unconsciousness cognitive dimensions have dramatic form. This dreamlike structure can be employed to analyze the media dream, and to foster coherent psychological states in contextual collectives.

INTRODUCTION

Carl Jung used symbolic patterns occurring in dreams to promote understanding of contextual meaning residing in a patient's unconscious. Jung equated the patterns of the unconscious with atomic structure and called them archetypes. Dream symbols were understood to be projections from unconscious dimensions, but because they were relatively conscious, Jung called the projections archetypal representations which—as projections—mirrored their source. In this way, discovery of unconscious meaning not only becomes possible, it becomes measurable according to degrees of coherence. Based on a number of correlations between Jungian dreams and media dreams, the hypothesis of this chapter is that the metaverse constitutes a dreamscape, and its holographic images constitute contextual media dreams.

DOI: 10.4018/978-1-4666-9891-8.ch010

As this chapter will document, according to Jungian depth analysis, a series of dreams will disclose unconscious patterns of meaning of which a patient is unaware. The psychiatrist can use principles of Analytical Psychology to extrapolate the meaning of dream symbols for the purpose of providing feedback to the patient as to the meaning of dream symbols. Given this feedback, the patient is positioned to gain meaningful insight that can have healing affect—much like biofeedback. Though Jung's research was empirically based, more recent cognitive research on heart-rate coherence—to be documented later—has verified that media dreams are susceptible to scientific measurement. Therefore, just as a psychiatrist provides feedback to a patient and as advanced algorithms provide feedback as to a computer user's preferences, research addressed to specific (contextual) target groups could provide mediated feedback designed to foster healing insight to contextual collectives

According to Jung, dream sequences (Jung, 1933, p 14) provide a medium for communication between conscious and unconscious cognitive dimensions:

Dreams give information about the secrets of the inner life and reveal to the dreamer hidden factors of his personality. As long as these are undiscovered, they disturb his waking life and betray themselves only in the form of symptoms. This means that we cannot effectively treat the patient from the side of consciousness alone, but must bring about a change in and through the unconscious. (Jung, 1933, p. 16)

So—in Jungian practice—dreams are not negative. Even if they are nightmares, dreams have a benign function because they hold the keys to meaningful insight that can result in multi-functional (physical, mental, emotional, spiritual) healing. Accordingly, even if the mediated dreams of the metaverse—psychologically multi-functional images—are symbolically saturated with sex, violence, and nightmarish threat, these patterns must be understood as positive, potentially therapeutic messages from the contextual unconscious. If recognized as such, these "dreams" can promote meaningful insight that could lead to unprecedented healing of collective personae. Contextual collectives are much like target groups and come in many formats—great and small—such as Rockets fans, Coca Cola drinkers, stay-at-home-pops, African Americans, white supremacists, environmentalists, Republicans, Buddhists, females, Germans, etc..

It would be safe to say that technological media research in the context of holographic cognitive function—though incipient—is advancing apace. The technological media has long been the prime mover in the creation of modern human reality, but now it becomes clear that using that immense power wisely will not be easy. There can be no doubt that this media power is rooted in the capacity to reach into the *cognitive unconscious* of individuals and demographic groups in order to alter their perceptions of reality by reframing archetypal patterns. The fact that commercial and political motives have skewed the programming of mass media for at least half a century need not be argued.

In advertising, politics, and education, though much is already known about the psychological power of the mass media, proportional efforts to manifest positive potentials for the power of psychological mass media have not been forthcoming. The primary purpose of this chapter is to discuss these potentials in necessarily innovative terms: Dreams, functional coherence, learning, healing, and even transcendence.

Taking a prospective view of benign media purposes, Internet potentials for education, healing, and maintaining coherent states in dimensions of the cognitive unconscious are just beginning to emerge. In *Amusing Ourselves to Death*, (1995) Neil Postman argued that any research on media should recognize that each medium has its own personality, its deficits, and its potentials. In *The Media Equation*, (1996)

Stanford researchers Byron Reeves and Clifford Nass concluded that at unconscious levels and in all demographics, people perceive media as "real"—that is to say—unconsciously—all people experience media in terms of personality and psychological experience based in social interaction. These incipient works began to establish parameters for a millennial study of the media dream. More recently, the Immersive Education Initiative, an offshoot of MediaGrid (2015), continues a global effort to advance understanding of the uses of technological media in educational contexts.

Jung says that "dreams have a purpose" (Jacobi, 1973), so if the media dream has Jungian veracity, the media dreamscape is imbedded with the holographic patterns of that purpose in fractal form. Most importantly, the path to Jungian *Individuation*—symbolized by the archetypal Journey of the Hero as process—consummation of which may be understood as the ultimate purpose of all human evolutionary (transcendent) experience, lies latent in the digital/virtual field that is energetically correlated with the Jungian collective unconscious.

In other words, if the mathematics of Fourier transforms can demonstrate recursive correlation between energy configurations (archetypes) in the collective unconscious and the energy images they project in dreams (archetypal representations) energy patterns in digital programs (algorithms) can be correlated with images in the metaverse (dreamscape). How would this be accomplished? With research, of course! The chapter will argue that the use of psychecology games as dream analogs allows for the use of Fourier transforms to interrogate correlations between real-time neuro-biological images (EEG, ECG, MEG, fMRI, etc) and images on the game monitor. Even in 1991, research had already confirmed that some human sensory perceptions are based on Fourier mathematics (Talbot, 1991, pp. 27-29; Lashley, 1950, pp 454-82; Collier, Burkhardt, & lin, 1971; Pollen & Tracktenberg, 1972, p. 109; DeValois, Karen K. & DeValois, Russel L., 1979, pp. 483-505; Chopra) and it is well known that *Fourier Transforms* serve as transducers in the digital dreamscape.

If the correlation between dreams and monitor images stands, all the benefits of Jungian dream analysis may accrue to analysis of the media dream. Then what? Ultimately, such analysis could lead to a documentable understanding of unconscious dimensions of collective personae including a definition of contextual purpose—collective *self realization*—as well as discovery of contextual psychological obstacles that obscure and block that state of harmonious self-realization. Analyzing the media dream "successfully" could eventually lead to harmonization of Earth's psyche and the literal introduction of the vaunted "Golden Age."

If correlates can be established between the holographic-dramatic structure of dreams and the holographic-dramatic structure of mediated images, that structure provides a framework for research with which to analyze digital "dream" illusions as if they were "psychic" dream images. In the emergent reality of psychological electronic media, a *Psych*ecology (an ecology of psyche) may be contemplated as a dreamscape. Ample research evidence exists (see below) in order to hypothesize that—like Jungian Psyche—the *metaverse* is holographic and that its computational patterns correspond to archetypal patterns of Psyche. The terms psychecology and metaverse are similar, but the metaverse is manmade and increasingly digital, while the psychecology is primordial. If this is so—and this is why we must refer to myth—archetypal images projected from the psychecology become archetypal representations in the metaverse. Because projections are essentially recursive, the patterns imbedded in archetypal representations can be used like patterns imbedded in dream images. So archetypal patterns can be employed to discover meaning, to diagnose collective mental disorder, and to apply therapy using media feedback targeted to fostering coherent states in contextual subject groups.

BACKGROUND

It may be stipulated that psychological dynamics of advertising and propaganda have been very successful, but that the profit motive underlying advertising and the power motive underlying propaganda have been largely responsible for fostering the horrors of the nuclear age, the arms race, wars and rumors of wars, the insanity of the Cold War, black ops and covert political action, fear-based dehumanization, genocide, and devaluation of natural life. (Curtis, 2009; Moyers, 1987)

It may be argued that advertising and political agendas have monopolized the technological media. Notwithstanding the power of all media as catalysts for human evolution, the modern media have functioned as prime movers throughout the latter half of the twentieth century and have amply demonstrated their psychological power to alter human values, choices, and behaviors using psychological tools. (Curtis, 2009) Increasingly, sub-optimization, power-lust, and profit have characterized media policy to a catastrophic degree, and political advertising has intruded itself on national governance. Though opinions vary, the recent Supreme Court decision known as Citizens United—a U. S. constitutional case dealing with the regulation of campaign spending by organizations—is having a profoundly detremental influence on U. S. elections because wealthy corporations can now buy unlimited advertising.

For a variety of reasons—well argued by Adam Curtis (2009)—psychological media power has been closely held by the elites of academia, industry, and government, but these entities—apparently preferring the negative Freudian perspective and fear of the collective unconscious (Curtis)—have refused to embrace many of the positive evolutionary neuro-cognitive potentials of mass media. Even the Public Broadcasting System has been cannibalized and exists in a constant state of attack. One consequence of this sub-optimizing stance is that media potentials for learning and healing have neither been supported nor trickled down and been assimilated by the general populace.

There can be no doubt that today incipient human "cognition"—including thoughts, feelings, memories, and perceptions—that expresses itself through language, science, art, law, technology, and all things cultural—has a powerful influence upon the course of planetary evolution. Due to cognitive plasticity, the digital media have a profound and evolving influence on human perceptions of reality, morality, ethics, and learning. Meanwhile, the Internet provides a constant stream of intelligence relative to the nearly incredible advances in computer technology. The MIT Review is especially adept at reviewing new intelligence. Recently, The Review reported that large corporate entities like Face Book have begun expending vast sums in order to better understand cognitive process for neuro-marketing purposes. The rapidly evolving ecosystems associated with personal data is creating an entirely new field of scientific study, (Geril, Philippe, 2014c; Claes, Zane, 2014; Simonite, Tom, 2015d & 2014; 2015; Demers, 2015)

Industrial-governmental interest in "mapping" the brain is becoming pervasive. Based on a twelve year effort involving dozens of research institutes using supercomputers to create a simulation of how the human brain works, the European Union agreed last year to invest more than one billion Euros in the Human Brain Project (HBP). However, a letter from dissenting scientists has charged that the project employs opaque management and the pursuit of goals not widely shared by neuroscientists. The letter says, "We believe the HBP is not a well-conceived or implemented project and that it is ill suited to be the centerpiece of European neuroscience." (Regaaldo, Antonio, 2014; Simonite, Tom, 2014c)

The European Union is not alone. Governments, including those of the United States and China, have all launched large neuroscience projects to study the brain. But having roughly 86 billion neurons and trillions of connections, the brain is so massively complex that there is little consensus on how to study it. (Human brain project, 2014) Related to this interest in cognitive dynamics is Microsoft's heavy investment in Holographic research and the dynamics of machine intelligence. (Simonite, Tom, 2014) A new trajectory of research on deep cognitive dynamics in the metaverse is the modern human mandate.

EVOLUTION OF THE MEDIA AS DREAM CONCEPT

Long ago, in *The Tempest*, Shakespeare observed that, "We are such stuff as dreams are made on." More recently, Sir Arthur Eddington said, "The stuff of the world is mind-stuff," (Foster, 1985, p7-12) Deepak Chopra has argued that, "We are experiencing the final stages of the overthrow of the superstition of materialism," (Chopra, 1995) and Lewis Carroll asked, "Is all our life, then, but a dream? Taken together, these statements sound a keynote not only for study, but for survival in the emergent age of virtual illusions.

The importance of dreams has reverberated from time immemorial, and characteristics of the dreamscape resound in the metaverse that is synonymous with the media dream. Primary correlates between dreams and media are language, metaphor, and symbolism. In this regard, myth provides important precedent not to be ignored by scientists. Not withstanding Fritjof Capra in his *Tau of Physics*_(1976), many physicists including Arthur Eddington, James Jeans, Bertrand Russell, Alfred North Whitehead, and J. Robert Oppenheimer have made note of the correlations between quantum physics and myth. (Foster, 1985) According to most myth, the source of dreams is other-dimensional—a "spiritual" dimension that employs symbolic language as a medium between humans and spirit. The Bible Hub quotes John 1:1 (The Holy Bible), "In the beginning was the Word, and the Word was with God, and the Word was God." That's saying a lot, and one commentator, Mathew Henry, accurately clarifies the matter saying, "The plainest reason why the Son of God is called the Word, seems to be, that as our words explain our minds to others, so was the Son of God sent in order to reveal his Father's mind to the world." (Bible Hub, 2015) Without going into great theological commentary and analysis, if they are understood as symbols, words are the quintessential media. This principle is basically true of the trinities in most myths. As documented by Manley T. Hall (2003), Huston Smith (1958), and Joseph Campbell (1968), it is safe to say that all myths are based on symbolic systems, and the "Word" takes many oracular forms including Odinian runes, the Confucian I Ching, the Cabalistic Sephiroth, Pythagorean numbers, Alchemical symbolism, Hermetics, Tarot cards, the Zodiac, ad infinitum.

What the ancients understood as creation by Spirit, moderns may understand as creation with energy. Not coincidentally, the two pillars upon which Jungian theory are based—psychic totality (coherence) and psychic energism—are also consistent with fundamental principles of physics including the unified field, non-locality/synchronicity, and interactivity. Such factors constitute fundamental correlations between physics and myth. As to cognitive correlation among individuals and collective personae, Jung says:

For every piece of conscious life that loses its importance and value—so runs the law—there arises a compensation in the unconscious. We may see in this an analogy to the conservation of energy in the physical world, for our psychic processes have a quantitative aspect also. No psychic value can disappear without being replaced by another of equivalent intensity. This is a rule which finds its pragmatic sanction in the daily practice of the psychotherapist; it is repeatedly verified and never fails. Now the doctor in me refuses point blank to consider the life of a people as something that does not conform to psychological law. A people, in the doctor's eyes, presents only a somewhat more complex picture of psychic life than the individual. (Jung 1933, p 209-210)

For purposes of digital knowledge engineering, Jungian dreams appear to be holographic. Though opinions differ, as mentioned above, exploration of the holographic model has been comprehensively researched by Michael Talbot. (Talbot, 1991) If the basic principles of Psyche are unity and energy (Jacoby, 1973, p. 2), and if dreams are the archetypal representations of archetypal energy and information patterns, the "conversation" between archetypal patterns and projected images as archetypal representations may be understood as the basic form of mediation. Relative to discovery of the meaning embedded in dreams, that meaning may be divulged—as in any conversation—with insight and an understanding of the contextual language—the Word. If the media-sphere may be understood as a holographic conversation in contextual-symbolic dream language between unconscious and conscious dimensions, archetypal patterns of the collective unconscious may be understood to correspond with unconscious algorithmic patterns of digital software articulated as Fourier Transforms. The structure and purpose of projected images in the metaverse can then be correlated with dreams that Jung defined as archetypal representations.

Like film projections, archetypal representations are recursively structured and constitute a symbolic language between conscious and unconscious dimensions of Psyche. In other words, the dream is an accurate projection of unconscious multifunctional patterns. The term multi-functional refers to the four classical human functions (physical, emotional, mental, spiritual) that Jung called Sensing, Feeling, Thinking, and Intuiting. Because they consist of frequencies of energy, these functions cannot actually be separated. Human functions can be correlated with Aristotle's dramatic functions. The psychological functions constantly influence one another in ways consistent with Aristotle's definition of "dramatic unities," and these dramatic structures and unities can be used as a fundamental point of reference for cognitive research. For example, George Lakoff explains the chemical processes in the nervous system relative to semantic "scripts". (Lakoff, 2008) Lakoff cites Roger Shank and Robert Abelson (Lakoff, 2008, p. 249) in his paraphrase, "Complex narratives—the kinds we find in everyone's life story, as well as in fairy tales, novels, and dramas—are made up of smaller narratives with very simple structures." Lakoff says:

The neural circuitry needed to create frame structures is relatively simple [neural binding circuitry, neural signatures, event structures] and so frames tend to structure a huge amount of our thought...Each frame has roles (like a cast of characters), relations between the roles, and scenarios carried out by those playing the roles." (Lakoff, 2008, p. 22; Goffman, 1974) There is a protagonist, the person whose point of view is being taken. The events are good and bad things that happen. And there are appropriate emotions that fit certain kinds of events in the scenarios. (Lakoff, 2008, p. 23)

Citing Goffman, Dr. Lakoff also observes that words are all defined relative to conceptual frames: "Groups of related words, called 'semantic fields,' are defined with respect to the same frame. Thus words like 'cost,' sell,' 'goods,' price,' buy,' and so on are defined with respect to a single frame," (Lakoff, 2008, p 22; Goffman) and the roles of Buyer, Seller, Goods, and Money, form a narrative field context for the frame. Sounding remarkably like Jung who observed that dreams have dramatic action that can meaningfully be broken down into the elements of a Greek play (Jacoby, 1973, p. 83), both Jung and Lakoff understand the importance of the functional unities of cognition.

Symbolic patterns in dreams can be analyzed to discover their message—their purpose—so perhaps, digital images in the media-sphere can be analyzed like dream images in order to diagnose and treat collective mental disorder. Diagnosis would depend on "engineering" the knowledge management software according to principles of cognitive framing, and treatment would involve multifunctional mediated biofeedback based on extensive research. By employing the compensational processes Jung calls the Amplification Method, a Jungian psychiatrist can mentor a patient by providing feedback as to the meaning of dream symbols. If successful, the process leads to meaningful (healing/coherent) insight on the part of the patient. In cognitive terms, unconscious cognitive frames can be adjusted into more coherent frames by providing media feedback. The psychological feedback/association process has been validated by advertising and propaganda, but the process of Jungian feedback is much different, more sophisticated, and differently motivated.

Adjusting cognitive frames in the collective unconscious of targeted personae with feedback in the form of interactive media content could foster meaningful insight and the achievement of coherent states among contextual collectives. The Jungian process of compensation is essentially a process of metaphorical extension, but it is based upon intense empathy with the patient on the part of the psychiatrist. The question of whether such empathy can be incorporated into digital simulations must be addressed with research, and such research lies within the realm of dramatic unities, their integrated archetypal functionality, and their degree of coherence. Because the psychiatrist must have extensive and empathetic knowledge about the patient, s/he is enabled to provide feedback to the dreamer relative to the dreamer's contextual psychic state. Feedback takes the form of suggestions about the meaning of symbolic patterns in the patient's dreams. When a patient (or learner) has insight as to the meaning of a dream, insight becomes learning and healing. According to this same process, media content targeted to contextual subject groups could foster a collective state of coherence (meaningful insight).

The dream speaks in images, and gives expression to instincts, that are derived from the most primitive levels of nature. Consciousness all too easily departs from the law of nature; but it can be brought again into harmony with the latter by the assimilation of unconscious contents. By fostering this [amplification] process we lead the patient to the rediscovery of the law of his own being. ...The way of successive assimilations reaches far beyond the curative results that specifically concern the doctor. It leads in the end to that distant goal (which may perhaps have been the first urge to life), the bringing into reality of the whole human being—that is, individuation. (Jung 1933, p 26)

A fundamental assumption in the chapter is that the *Psych*ecology and--as archetypal representation—the media-sphere function in accordance with the rules of dream dynamics observed by Carl Jung. Directly relevant to this media dream-likeness is that humans have finally verified that so-called "material reality" is—in fact—illusion. Therefore, the universal axiom of myth and philosophy has also become scientific fact verified by quantum physics, and echoed by cognitive neuroscience. So, hypothetically, the *Media Dream* can be researched from the perspective of its curative potential. (Schafer & Yu; 2011) It may be understood that precisely like Jungian dreams, mediated digital dreams arise from the collective *unconscious* that is directly correlated with the digital unconscious and ultimately exists as a unified field of energy and information where human functions are unified according to principles of dramatic unity. Both cognitive and digital patterns take the form of frequencies of energetic force that, according to cognitive-psychiatric research, clothe themselves in linguistic-dramatic images and are projected as "dreams" (illusions).

During the past twenty years, research in neurological plasticity has reached a degree of agreement about the existence of this narrative-metaphorical structure of Psyche by studying the electro-chemical dynamics of the nervous system, integrating them with principles of physics, and researching neurobiological processes with technologies such as EEG, ECG, fMRI, MEG, etc. Drama is a more accurate term than narrative for cognitive-linguistic structure because drama is electro-chemically interactive; i.e., actors on the stage and people in the audience perceive drama according to a fourfold matrix of functional components that have always been used to gauge human behavior and experience. To reiterate, Carl Jung called these functions reason, emotion, sensing, and intuition. Jung observed that dreams have dramatic structure, and modern cognitive researchers like George Lakoff have observed that the cognitive unconscious has dramatic structure to which we all refer our projected realities. The roles we play in life have their origin at unconscious levels and provide us with a template for understanding ourselves, our context, our exposition (statement of the problem), and our *lysis* (resolution of the problem). In other words, we live out our unconscious narratives, and—for example—we use the same part of our brains to see, imagine we are seeing, remember seeing, and understand language about seeing. (Lakoff, 2008, p. 39) The four functions are integrated in drama, and this dynamic explains why—when people have vicarious experience such as dreams, film, and video games—they experience emotions appropriate to the film/game story and access unconscious moral patterns. (Lakoff, 2008, p. 63) This effect is usually understood as immersion or suspension of disbelief.

While research on this emergent reality is yet in its infancy, it is certainly apparent that it constitutes a paradigm shift. Therefore, a better understanding of psychological health, morality, ethics, and laws appropriate to the shift become the human mandate. Researching the reality of the media dream according to dream dynamics becomes the human imperative. Though the most recent cognitive research seems to be entirely consistent with the principles of psyche and dream analysis established by Carl Jung, his research opus is more comprehensive and has provided a universal (and often unattributed) framework for computer engineering—memory—and analysis of cognitive research (neural networks, connectionism, holographic computing, etc.). As a recommendation and suggestion of future prospects, this paper addresses the Media Dream primarily from the standpoint of its potential for discovery of unconscious meaning at psychological levels of cultural collectives. Such meaning resides in the imbedded symbolism of mediated images.

Contextual Dream Patterns in War and Entertainment

A significant trend in current virtual reality research is sponsored by the military, and battlefield training courses are intended to be as realistic as possible—a clear example of the paradigm shift into the reality of the metaverse. From the cognitive perspective addressed above, these battle exercises are perceived by trainees as real (Reeves & Nass). Being "immersive" they also impact trainees at unconscious functional cognitive levels. In other words, the contextual group of trainees experiences virtual training exercises as real experience, and this experience changes unconscious "archetypal" cognitive frames at all functional levels including values. Presently, these training "dreams" are being programmed precisely for these reasons. The military wants its trainees to have "warfigher" values.

Warfighters

Just one example of this may be found online at the Naval Office of Research site as reported by EUROSIS, "ARLINGTON, Va.—Marines were able to turn a lush golf course into a hostile battleground complete with tanks, mortar fire and smoke. (Crawford, Katherine H., 2015) This "dream" was made possible by a newly developed augmented reality technology. "The Augmented Immersive Team Trainer (AITT) moved one step closer to its ultimate goal of giving warfighters glasses that can be worn to enhance augmented reality training scenarios." (Crawford) The reporter makes a distinction between the terms "augmented reality" and "virtual reality". The former refers to "a live environment onto which virtual images are superimposed. Think of watching a football game on television and seeing the yellow first-down line added to the screen you're watching." (Crawford) A "virtual reality" is different because it "is a wholly computer-generated environment in which users immerse themselves." However, according to Peter Squire, a program officer with ONR's Expeditionary Maneuver Warfare and Combating Terrorism Department, says that the AITT system, "which can support a wide array of live, virtual and constructive training scenarios, is 'only limited by the imaginations of those using it,'" (Crawford) For the purposes of this chapter, this is a clear sign of the trend that employs virtual reality to alter unconscious cognitive frames.

Virtual Humans

Another example of the trend to employ contextual dreams to alter experience-based cognitive frames at unconscious levels is the following. Online, we find that: "Research and technology are essential for providing the best capabilities to our warfighters." (Bellman, Orli, 2015) An online article, Researchers Create Virtual Humans, quotes Dr. Laurel Allender, director of the ARL Human Research and Engineering Directorate as saying, "This is especially so for the immersive and live-training environments we are developing to achieve squad overmatch and to optimize Soldier performance, both mentally and physically." The Army and USC are, "exploring the potential of developing a flexible multi-modal human-robot dialogue that includes natural language, along with text, images and video processing." (Bellman)

If this online article is analyzed as part of a more general dream sequence, it may disclose unconscious meaning. The more general sequence has to do with the scientific passion for virtual realities and robotics. We should be asking the question, "Where will this passion lead?" With the emergence of the brave new world of illusion being created by technological media, "virtual humans" are just one form of the denizens projected to inhabit the Metaverse. In the Metaverse, "real" people are expected to express themselves increasingly as avatars—in the same way as game players project their persona into a video game protagonist. The implicit concept underlying the Metaverse is that real life is a metaphor and that virtual life is reality. The term is being used to describe the concept of a future iteration of the internet, made up of persistent, shared, 3D virtual spaces linked into a perceived virtual universe—a virtual reality-based successor to the Internet. (Smart, J.M., Cascio, J. and Paffendorf, J., 2007) Whether "reality" is metaphorical or virtual, both are illusions, and the symbolism in the dreams can promote meaningful insight.

Artificial Intelligence and Robotics

Virtual humans and avatars exemplify the explosion of artificial intelligence applications which are enabling an incipient virtual age. Artificial intelligence algorithms underlie research on *robotics*, so Artificial intelligence and robotics are essentially synonymous. As suggested above, much AI research is being sponsored by governments—with research done by universities—for purposes of waging war. A conclusion is implicit; Just as the video game genre called *First-Person-Shooters,* in which the game player's avatar is first person, have achieved overwhelming popularity in video games, virtual realities based on warfare and "warfighters" have become a priority aspect of media age illusion. Because a basic assumption of this chapter is that all experience, including virtual experience, alters the cognitive patterns in the personal and collective unconscious, the following example of the explosive trajectory of research in robotics becomes a prospective dream that is susceptible to analysis.

The US Defense Advanced Research Projects Agency (DARPA) has launched a new program to help small businesses, and individuals who have not previously worked with the federal government, develop new robotics capabilities. Dubbed Robotics Fast Track (RFT), the program aims to enable rapid, cost-effective development of new robotics capabilities designed to respond to, and even anticipate, quickly emerging warfighter requirements. (Geril, 2015a)

More ominous than the DARPA project is the following report from The U.S. Army that computer simulations improve lethality by understand the effects different caliber ammunition will have on targets. The research center at Picattiny Arsenal in New Jersey, "handles nearly 90 percent of the Army's lethality projects and all conventional ammunition for joint warfighters." (Kowal, Eric, 2015) The research center works with organizations like the U.S. Army Research Laboratory and the Survivability/Lethality Analysis Directorate at Aberdeen Proving Ground, Maryland.

Kowal points out that though large caliber system analysis has taken advantage of computational simulation tools for years, in order to improve consistency and performance with newly released smaller caliber enhanced performance rounds (EPR) a combination of modeling, simulation and testing was employed. "The use of newer, faster computers made critical portions of that effort possible. Some data was statistical, some physical and some probabilistic, but all done using physics-based models to simulate ballistics on soft targets" (Kowal). An "up-side" of simulating soft-target wounds might be that many who study survivability and lethality such as program executive officers and program managers, users, testers, the Army's independent evaluator and other "customers" would not see this as ominous because the research supports milestone decisions that might save lives. Another aspect of the "up-side" is that prototypes can cost millions of dollars a piece. "Modeling and simulation can save money by avoiding costly prototypes and testing" (Kowal).

Obviously, DARPA is not the only government agency interested in warfighters. "Several US government agencies including the army, navy, the department of homeland security, and the National Aeronautics and Space Administration have expressed interest in validating successful RFT projects and performers for use in their operations" (Geril, 2015a).

Research on robotics is not all about warfare. The Europe 2020 Initiative: Digital Agenda for Europe, "Scientists have created underwater robot swarms that function like schools of fish, exchanging information to monitor the environment, searching, maintaining, exploring and harvesting resources in underwater habitats." (Cocoro, anon., 2015) In ten experimental demonstrations, autonomous robots interact with each other and exchange information, resulting in a cognitive system that is aware of its environment. The European Union supported the COCORO project that explored and developed collective cognition in autonomous robots. COCORO's scientists used nature as a model. For example, observing how honeybees cluster, helped scientists develop the BEECLUST algorithm that they used to aggregate robots at a specific location. "Robot swarms not only look like schools of fish, they behave like them" Cocoro, par. 2).

Increasingly, the research on "robotics" involves the use of algorithms based on cognitive function. (Simonite, Tom, 2015b). As Neil Jacobstein, head of the Singularity University told the BBC:

Artificial intelligence agents are already involved in every aspect of our lives - they keep our inboxes free of spam, they help us make our web transactions, they fly our planes and if Google gets its way will also soon drive our cars for us. "AI's are embedded in the fabric of our everyday lives. They are used in medicine, in law, in design and throughout automotive industry." And each day the algorithms that power away, making decisions behind the scenes, are getting smarter. It means that one of the biggest quests of the modern world - the search to make machines as intelligent as humans - could be getting tantalizingly close. (Wakefield, Jane, 2014)

In another recent report, the MIT Technology Review reports on an algorithm that can help robots heal themselves without human intervention. Researchers say that:

The robots learn with an "evolutionary algorithm.' This means that it will run repeated trial and error steps—building on a list it created before being deployed that details the things it can do and how valuable each one is—to determine a new way to get around. It's like a simplified version of what humans do: if you sprain an ankle, you use memory and experimentation to figure out how to hobble around in the most efficient and least painful way. (Garling, 2015, par. 6)

Though researchers' examples such as the Mars Rover or search and rescue robots are still far from real-world scenarios such as fighting fires or rescuing people, they are a significant aspect of the metaverse. Researchers Jean-Baptiste Mouret and Antoine Cully say these learning algorithms will soon be tested outside the lab on bigger robots. Perhaps they will be tested on virtual humans; this raises considerable ontological, epistemological, and ethical questions relative to the reality of the metaverse. "While watching the six-legged robot figure out a new method of movement inevitably brings about visions of the Terminator and evil robots, Mouret says researchers have plenty of time to build in proper safeguards to prevent robots from implementing behaviors that could harm people" (Garling).

Thinking of contextual collectives in terms of target groups is more a hop than a quantum leap. The use of focus groups in advertising to tap buy buttons in target groups is longstanding and very successful procedure. Now, AI research on demographics—from virtual humans to autonomous robot swarms—employs smart algorithms based on cognitive mapping. The Virtual Worlds Report for March 2015 defines "contextual" demographics, attitudes, and preferences: "The aim of this study was to enhance our understanding of demographics, attitudes, activities and play preferences across a variety of non-game, social virtual worlds, also referred to as metaverses" (Geril, 2015b).

Entertainment

In another framework of the psychological media sphere, the entertainment industry has always been about illusion addressed to contextual collectives. From musicals to war films, drama is based on appeal to contextual collectives, and these collectives are multi-faceted. For example, films of the WWII era were propagandistic and appealed to entire cultures as well as to subsidiary collectives. It may be stipulated that entertainment—to use a vastly general term—has always been a powerful source for acculturation. The idea that the entertainment industry has enormous influence on culture at large: cultural values, individual & cultural choices, and behaviors, need not be extensively documented. (Curtis, 2009)

Entertainment and the Internet are becoming ever more closely linked as the age of illusion unfolds in a kaleidoscopic phantasmagoria of wireless applications. In answer to the question, "Where is the entertainment industry going?" we discover that Star Trek has provided the pre-eminent paradigm, in the form of the 'holodeck', the virtual reality facility on the Starship Enterprise. The holodeck was a box of a room where crewmembers could immerse themselves in an array of virtual illusions, like distant planets, and interact with aliens without ever leaving their spacecraft. However, mapping consumer demand against industrial innovation is questing beyond the holodeck:

Producing immersive entertainment experiences will require a whole suite of tools and underpinning technologies: in computer vision, positional and spatial audio, smart content creation, compression and real time rendering. Other advances will be needed in capabilities outside the range of even the leading audio-visual production studios. These will include 3-D display, augmented reality, holography, surround sound and haptic technologies. (Geril, 2015b)

Whether a virtual reality is a dream, a memory, a fantasy, a film, television, the Internet, or a video game, the research-based understanding of virtual-cognitive reality is that it has dramatic structure—even at quantum levels. According to Jung and Lakoff, the cognitive structures in unconscious dimensions are *projected* into so-called "real-life" contexts. (Jacobi, 1973; Lakoff, 2008; Goffman, Erving, 1974; Schafer & Yu, 2011) As already mentioned, Jung called the structural patterns of the unconscious *archetypes*, and Lakoff calls them *cognitive frames*. Cognitive-level processes that explain precisely *why* dramatic structure is important for an understanding of virtual illusion—of both conscious and unconscious (immersive) dimensions of *reality*— are not well-known except in fields of cognitive research. Nevertheless, researchers have been exploring linguistic issues of the unconscious for decades. Whether understood from cognitive levels or not, in diverse fields ranging from law enforcement to psychiatry, the value of narrative is practical and well known. Always interested in the poetic dimensions of drama, now the entertainment industry—especially the game industry—is becoming interested in cognitive dimensions as well. For example:

21st century storytelling will require not just enabling technologies, but also story tellers: professionals with expertise in interaction, human experience and story design to create content and experiences to be developed and consumed on these platforms. This in turn may necessitate new organizational structures, management systems and business models to enable innovations and the merging of technologies across films, games and media industries. (Boyd, Frank, 2015)

Recursive Holography and the Metaverse

From these brief references to massive cultural trends, contemplating the media illusion as a dreamscape and using dream analysis to psychoanalyze collective personae for purposes of harmonization and healing does not seem entirely crazy. An increasingly popular term for the media dream is the metaverse which is the global holographic projection of interactive images including Internet, film, video games, television and all the technological paraphernalia presently available. Our fundamental hypothesis is that the digital software (AI) sources of mediated *dream images* is analogous to the archetypal energy/information that is the cognitive source of dreams. Accordingly, the holographic projections of computer engineered archetypes (programs) are analogous to what Carl Jung calls "archetypal representations." As discussed above, an important aspect of such representations—especially images—is that they are essentially recursive; i.e. they have the same dramatic structure as "archetypes" that inhabit the personal and collective unconscious. Though research is necessary to verify, the translation from archetype to archetypal representation appears to be based on recursive frequency analyzers known as Fourier transforms (Talbot, 1991, p. 27). It has been verified that human sensory mechanisms are based on Fourier mathematics (Talbot, p. 27; DeValois, Karen, DeValois, Russell L., Yund W. W., 1979 pp. 483-505), but the specific connection to archetypal-quantum structure remains to be validated.

The term "recursive" may be understood in terms of the "fractal" forms of physics, or in terms of the Gestalt perceptual principle of "Invariance". Invariance is the property of perception whereby simple geometrical objects are recognized independent of rotation, translation, and scale. Another psychological aspect of recursion includes such perceptions defined by Gestaltists as "Multistability" or multistable perception (the tendency of ambiguous perceptual experiences to pop back and forth unstably between two or more alternative interpretations), and "Reification" (the *constructive* or *generative* aspect of perception, by which the experienced percept contains more explicit spatial information than the sensory stimulus on which it is based).

This recursive dynamic of perception allows for the computational modeling of what appears to be randomly fluctuating symbols and pixilated images in both dreams and computer monitors. In other words, a quantum flux of archetypes that inhabit the personal and collective unconsciousness as defined by Carl Jung are projected as recursive archetypal representations in a neurobiological-holographic media-sphere. (Schafer & Yu, 2011; Schafer, 2011; Schafer, 2012)

Research on issues of the relationship between the holographic cosmos and the holonomic (holographic) brain is longstanding, and it's early proponents (Penfield, Wilder, 1975; Lashley, Karl, 1950, pp.454-82; Pribram, Karl, 1977, p. 75; Pribram, Karl, 1977, p. 123 & 169; Goleman, Daniel, 1971, pp. 71-72; Collier, J., Burckhardt, C. B.,& lin, L. H., 1971; van Heerden, Pieter, 1970, pp. 410-11; Pietsch, Paul, 1981, p. 78; Pollen, Daniel A. & Tractenberg, Michael C., 1972, p. 109; DeValois, Karen K., DeValois, Russell L., & Yund, W.W., 11979, pp. 483-505; Dossey, Larry, 1982, pp. 108-9; Restak, Richard, 1981, p. 19; Restak, Richard, 1979, p. 253; et al.) are well documented in Michael Talbot's *The Holographic Universe* (1991)

Holographic Coherence

The most recent research evidence that verifies this connection between quantum dimensions and their projections as "consciousness" is the discovery by Stuart Hameroff and Sir Roger Penrose of quantum vibrations in "microtubules" inside brain neurons. "They suggest that EEG rhythms (brain waves) also derive from deeper level microtubule vibrations, and that from a practical standpoint, treating brain microtubule vibrations could benefit a host of mental, neurological, and cognitive conditions." (Hameroff & Penrose, 2014) These researchers based their discovery on two decades of previous research on "orchestrated objective reduction" (Orch Or) which suggests that quantum vibrational computations (microtubules) are orchestrated by synaptic inputs and memory stored in microtubules. (Hameroff & Penrose, 2014) The term "orchestration" suggests the potential to harmonize conscious patterns with archetypal patterns according to the principle of coherence. Coherence is a measurable harmonious neurobiological state that has been studied extensively by the Heartmath Institute. (McCraty, Rollin & Childre, Doc (2010); McCraty, Deyhle, & Childre (2012).

Coherent states appear to have the same characteristics as Carl Jung's "Compensational" states and "Flow". (Csíkszentmihályi, 1990) Compensation is the fundamental Jungian principle that makes discovery of unconscious meaning possible using the process of symbolic analysis on projected archetypal energy patterns in dream images. As images, dreams and computer graphics have structural correlates. The entirety of Carl Jung's psychiatric theory and practice is based on symbolic images in dreams, so interpretation of the underlying meaning in dream-computer images measured in terms of coherence has identical potential.

Correlated Images

Dream images and computer monitor images are directly correlated as to structure, perception, and leaning-healing potential. These correspondences are a primary component for qualifying psychecology games as a dream analog. (Schafer, 2011; Schafer, 2012) Therefore, psychecology games can be used as a cognitive research instrument in conjunction with MEG, EEG, ECG, fMRI, etc. for measuring real-time neurobiological activity in subject game players. (Schafer & Yu, 2011; Schafer, 2011; Schafer, 2012; Trafton, Anne, 2014) Research methodologies must be contextualized to various media and to myriads of demographics, but the dynamics of dream analysis remain constant. Though the media dream includes multi-functional sensory data that is integrated at levels of the unconscious, this chapter emphasizes the primarily visual symbolism in images.

Jung is not the only observer to say that the changing human perceptions of reality—what he calls the Spirit of the Age (Jung, 1933, pp. 175,196-220)—have been thrust upon us so rapidly that throughout the twentieth century it has disoriented and traumatized human collectives throughout the world. At base, the changes derive from discoveries in the realms of physics, psychology, and computer science. It is a well established fact that the psychological dynamics and structure of advertising and propaganda entail utilizing unconscious demographic patterns to sell their "products". This chapter develops the hypothesis that because the discoveries in these sciences have been incorporated into the holographic, psychological metaverse, its contextual projections can be analyzed like dreams.

THE MEDIA DREAM: REALITY AS ILLUSION

Researching the nature and dynamics of this illusory paradox of human beingness, human creativity, and human responsibility is critical to planetary survival. The arguments and details of why human existence—specifically material existence—is an illusion and a paradox is an issue of physics and psychology that has been well developed by many of humanity's ablest exemplars. Our argument emphasizes Jungian dream parameters as a basis for addressing the importance of the media dream as illusion that appears real. Based on the two pillars of Jungian psychiatry—psychic totality and psychic energy—this chapter postulates correlations among the unified fields of physics, psyche, and the technological media-sphere. (Schafer & Yu, 2011; Schafer, 2012) Though ongoing research constantly adds to the verification of the hypothesis, it is already an authentic premise in diversified scientific fields and is being addressed by an increasingly evolutionary neuroscience. Moreover, scientists and scholars including Eddington, Jeans, Whitehead, Capra, Radins, Oppenheimer, and many others have observed the connections that exist between myth and physics and which are central to Jungian principles of symbolic-metaphorical dream analysis and the process of Compensation through Amplification. Many have recognized the correlations between physics and psychology. Perhaps the most prominent of these is the scholar of myth, Joseph Campbell who asserted that, "Myth is psychology." Campbell was referring specifically to Jungian psychology.

Functional Interactivity

Based in physics, the most promising candidate for dream dynamics and structure is holography—a science that is just coming into its own. (Talbot, 1991) Accordingly, because of their corresponding structure and dynamics, it may be argued that both dreams and media dreams are holographic. Both realities share the principles of energy patterns, wholeness, linguistic structure, functionality, and—most importantly—interactivity. (Schafer & Yu, 2011) The entire framework of Jungian analysis and treatment is founded on his observation that dreams are interactive. (Jacoby, 1973) In other words, the symbolism and context of dreams change according to a patient's evolving need for psychic meaning. These changing patterns resulting from interactive experience manifest as bio-energetic phenomena in the nervous system. We will detail this research in a later chapter. For now, this same bio-energetic interactivity can be imaged and measured in real time as a player makes choices leading to a game-win while playing drama-based video games.

Because non-local bio-energetic processes are now being applied to research using a plethora of electronic devices that contribute to understanding the cognitive connection to holographic media, the collective unconscious is being impacted with the digital unconscious generated by complex algorithms. The fundamentally interactive nature of dreams has already become nearly pervasive—though not recognized—in the media dream. In ways that are correlated, increasing interactivity in media domains allows people to use the Internet, television, smart phones, and a growing array of apps to access contextual meaning from almost anywhere in the virtual domain of the holographic media dream—action at a distance. The electro-chemical neural processes associated with this pervasive interactivity may be calculated mathematically employing sophisticated engineering sets and components such as finite element analysis, fluid dynamics, Discreet Fourier Transforms, efficient algorithms of fast Fourier Transforms, and a variety of other calculations for articulating the paradigm shift. (Schafer, 2011) To reiterate, for decades, scientists from various fields have speculated that the human brain and the universe itself are holographic. (Talbot, 1991; Bohm, 1951; Mishlov, 1998) So holography becomes an increasingly relevant metaphorical model that has the potential to verify the media dream hypothesis.

Deepak Chopra has explained reality is "a socially programmed hypnosis," and promised that ours is an age of the "overthrow of the superstition of materialism." (Chopra, 1995) In a scientific environment where Wilder Penfield has searched for the "thinker of the thought," and others have researched "cellular memory," we have made important strides in the aggressive study of cognition and consciousness, (Chopra, 1995), but we have not yet accepted the ramifications or the psychological impact of the media dream as a primary aspect of human reality. Our research has studied this premise from a variety of angles including the enhancement of psychological coherence in contextual collectives (Schafer, 2011), serious games for articulating the paradigm shift (Schafer, 2011), ethical design of social influence marketing (Schafer & Palamedes, 2011), the use of drama-based video games as a research instrument for creation of meaningful media (Schafer & Yu, 2011), and optimizing cognitive coherence and learning in contextual collectives. (Schafer & Yu, 2011) The arguments in these publications and many conference presentations assert the concept that the technological media-sphere is dynamically and structurally analogous with the unified field of energy and information known to physics and has virtually the same dynamics as dreams defined by the Analytical Psychology of Carl Jung.

As mentioned above, this analog extends to the structure and dynamics of psychecology games. Defining target groups with subjective data for advertising purposes has been very successful. Using more sophisticated personality profiling like Myers-Briggs and Big 5 profiles to define game player functionality would contribute greater scientific authenticity to the process of defining target (contextual) groups. During drama-based video game play, player choice patterns could be stored and studied using sophisticated headsets or virtual reality technologies to track electro-magnetic and chemical activity in the nervous system. Such research will then contribute to understanding of distributive functions and unconscious motivations in collective personae. Correlating neuro-linguistic dynamics experienced by game players with neuro-linguistic dynamics experienced by users of the media dream could lead to a much better understanding of the "positive" uses of media content, media policy, and media education. This would provide a key that could open the portal of opportunity. Opening the door and crossing the threshold of opportunity would constitute a critical initiation in the human perception and understanding of what is real. We would begin to appreciate the reality of illusion as portrayed in the Media Dream. This would be our crisis of departure from the superstition of materialism. Now we have an opportunity to address the psychological crisis of the media age before we lose track of reality and become immersed in psychotic reaction to illusion—the symbols and symptoms of which are now rampant in the Media Dream. (Schafer, 2012)

According to the dynamics of holography, our technological media provide insight—like a hall of mirrors—to the collective unconscious, while video games have the potential to provide highly specific access to neurobiological function. If neural processes can be correlated with archetypal states of the cognitive unconscious where archetypes form a magnetic field and energy center recursive with the projection of images, a wealth of Jungian principle and research will become available for timely use. "The dream is a statement, uninfluenced by consciousness, expressing the dreamer's inner truth and 'reality as it really is.'" (Jacoby, 1973) "Thus for Jung the manifest content of a dream is not a façade but a fact which always reveals what the unconscious has to say about the situation and which always says exactly what the unconscious means." (Jacoby, 1973) Therefore, the imbedded symbolism in images can be analyzed—as it is in Jungian dream analysis—to access contextual meaning that resides in both the cognitive unconscious and the digital unconscious. (Schafer, 2011) Such access to the personal and collective unconscious can be employed to reinforce cognitive coherence. (Schafer, 2012)

In today's reality of statistics and target groups, it may be stipulated that—at least metaphorically—human groups have "personalities," (ethnic, religious, political, corporate) that are defined by normative-conceptual cognitive structures imbedded in the energy and information fields of the collective unconscious. Jung discusses cognitive structures in terms of archetypal patterns, and George Lakoff discusses them in terms of "neural recruitment" which is a process for strengthening neural synapses. (Lakoff, 2008) Employing the process of Jungian Amplification (symbolic-metaphorical extension), these energy/information patterns of the unconscious are susceptible to harmonization (measured in terms of heart rate variability as a signifier of coherence).

By all indications, Jungian Compensation is synonymous with "coherence". It is our contention that with the application of Jungian principles to the Media Dream, coherent psychological states can be induced in collective personae by pre-measuring how target groups can be predisposed to functionally coherent states. McCraty and Childre discuss the nature of coherence, how it can be measured and reinforced with biofeedback, and applied to harmonization of psyche in all its functions—physical, emotional, rational, and spiritual. "In globally coherent systems such as human beings, there is an incredible amount of activity at every level of magnification or scale that spans more than two-thirds of the 73 known octaves of the electromagnetic spectrum." (McCraty & Childre, 2010) The functions cited by McCraty and Childre correspond to the Jungian functions of psyche—sensing, feeling, thinking, and intuiting. It is these functions that can be integrated into experimental design in order to foster cognitive coherence. As cited by Michael Talbot in *The Holographic Universe*, researchers (DeValois, 1979 pp. 483-505) have discovered that the brain uses Fourier mathematics to translate patterns of the sensory function. For example, the visual cortex responds to frequencies of various wave forms. (Talbot, p. 28) Subsequently, their research has been expanded to confirm that the other sensory functions are based on Fourier mathematics (Talbot, 1991). Moreover, though much more research is necessary to expand our understanding of the dynamic, Lakoff confirms that the functions are integrated by the process of narrative and metaphor. "There is a protagonist, the person whose point of view is being taken. The events are good and bad things that happen. And *there are appropriate emotions* that fit certain kinds of events in the scenarios (italics mine)." (Lakoff, 2008, p. 23)

Characteristics of compensation and coherence are also consistent with characteristics of the "Flow" phenomenon researched by Mihály Csíkszentmihályi. "Flow is the mental state of operation in which the person is fully immersed in what he or she is doing by a feeling of energized focus, full involvement, and success in the process of the activity." (Csíkszentmihályi, 1990) Components of flow include clear goals, concentration and focus, diminished self-consciousness, loss of the sense of time passage, and a sense of personal control and intrinsically rewarding action are aspects of immersion in games and—perhaps—suggestions of contact with an altered cognitive state.

As this dynamic of functionally coherent, compensational, flow becomes more generally accepted—making it a global fact of everyday reality—the human reality will shift in benign ways. Emergent changes in human perceptions of reality and human responsibility will evoke the imperative to generate coherent patterns relative to morality, law, responsibility, privacy, and an entire gamut of social interactions that are presently obscure. Gradually, as we achieve this new understanding of the "real", we will mark a breakthrough in the human sense of responsibility for the direct power humans wield with the energy of their thought and desires. Certain oft-reiterated truths will be clarified: "Thoughts are things." (Plato); "As a man *thinketh* in his heart, so is he." (Christ); "A man is what he thinks." (Buddha); "Our thoughts are epochs in our lives." (Thoreau); "Nurture your minds with great thoughts. To believe in the heroic makes heroes." (Disraeli); "The greatest events of an age are its best thoughts. Thought finds its way into action." (Boice). Greater understanding of the media dream may mark a crossing of the initiatory threshold comparable to the discovery of fire.

From these brief references to massive cultural trends, contemplating the media illusion as a dreamscape and using dream analysis to psychoanalyze collective personae for purposes of harmonization and healing does not seem entirely crazy. A popular term for the media dream is the metaverse which is the global holographic projection of interactive images including Internet, film, video games, television and all the technological paraphernalia presently available. Our fundamental hypothesis is that the digital software, AI, sources of mediated *dream images* is analogous to the archetypal energy/information that is the cognitive source of dreams. Accordingly, the holographic projections of computer engineered archetypes (programs) are analogous to what Carl Jung calls "archetypal representations." An important aspect of such representations—especially images—is that they are essentially recursive; i.e. they have the same dramatic structure as "archetypes" that inhabit the personal and collective unconscious. Though research is necessary to verify, the translation from archetype to archetypal representation appears to be based on recursive frequency analyzers known as Fourier transforms (Talbot, 1991, p. 27). It has been verified that human sensory mechanisms are based on Fourier mathematics (Talbot, p. 27; DeValois, Karen, DeValois, Russell L., Yund W. W., 1979 pp.483-505), but the specific connection to archetypal-quantum structure remains to be validated.

The term "recursive" may be understood in terms of the "fractal" forms of physics, or in terms of the Gestalt perceptual principle of "Invariance". Invariance is the property of perception whereby simple geometrical objects are recognized independent of rotation, translation, and scale. Another psychological aspect of recursion includes such perceptions defined by Gestaltists as "Multistability" or multistable perception (the tendency of ambiguous perceptual experiences to pop back and forth unstably between two or more alternative interpretations), and "Reification" (the *constructive* or *generative* aspect of perception, by which the experienced percept contains more explicit spatial information than the sensory stimulus on which it is based).

This recursive dynamic of perception allows for the computational modeling of what appears to be randomly fluctuating symbols and pixilated images in both dreams and computer monitors. In other words, a quantum flux of archetypes that inhabit the personal and collective unconsciousness as defined by Carl Jung are projected as recursive archetypal representations in a neurobiological-holographic media-sphere. (Schafer & Yu, 2011; Schafer, 2011; Schafer, 2012)

Research on issues of the relationship between the holographic cosmos and the holonomic (holographic) brain is longstanding, and it's early proponents (Penfield, Wilder, 1975; Lashley, Karl, 1950, pp.454-82; Pribram, Karl, 1977, p. 75; Pribram, Karl, 1977, p. 123 & 169; Goleman, Daniel, 1971, pp. 71-72; Collier, J., Burckhardt, C. B.,& lin, L. H., 1971; van Heerden, Pieter, 1970, pp. 410-11; Pietsch, Paul, 1981, p. 78; Pollen, Daniel A. & Tractenberg, Michael C., 1972, p. 109; DeValois, Karen K., DeValois, Russell L., & Yund, W.W., 11979, pp. 483-505; Dossey, Larry, 1982, pp. 108-9; Restak, Richard, 1981, p. 19; Restak, Richard, 1979, p. 253; et al.) are well documented in Michael Talbot's *The Holographic Universe* (1991).

The most recent research evidence that verifies this connection between quantum dimensions and their projections as "consciousness" is the discovery by Stuart Hameroff and Sir Roger Penrose of quantum vibrations in "microtubules" inside brain neurons. "They suggest that EEG rhythms (brain waves) also derive from deeper level microtubule vibrations, and that from a practical standpoint, treating brain microtubule vibrations could benefit a host of mental, neurological, and cognitive conditions." (Hameroff & Penrose, 2014) These researchers based their discovery on two decades of previous research on "orchestrated objective reduction" (Orch Or) which suggests that quantum vibrational computations (microtubules) are orchestrated by synaptic inputs and memory stored in microtubules. (Hameroff & Penrose, 2014) The term "orchestration" suggests the potential to harmonize conscious patterns with archetypal patterns according to the principle of coherence. Coherence is a measurable harmonious neurobiological state that has been studied extensively by the Heartmath Institute. (McCraty, Rollin & Childre, Doc (2010); McCraty, Deyhle, & Childre (2012).

Coherent states appear to have the same characteristics as Carl Jung's "Compensational" states and "Flow". (Csíkszentmihályi, 1990) Compensation is the fundamental Jungian principle that makes discovery of unconscious meaning possible using the process of symbolic analysis on projected archetypal energy patterns in dream images. As images, dreams and computer graphics have structural correlates. The entirety of Carl Jung's psychiatric theory and practice is based on symbolic images in dreams, so interpretation of the underlying meaning in dream-computer images measured in terms of coherence has identical potential.

This chapter argues that dream images and computer monitor images are directly correlated as to structure, perception, and leaning-healing potential. These correspondences are a primary component for qualifying psychecology games as a dream analog. (Schafer, 2011; Schafer, 2012) Therefore, psychecology games can be used as a cognitive research instrument in conjunction with MEG, EEG, ECG, fMRI, etc. for measuring real-time neurobiological activity in subject game players. (Schafer & Yu, 2011; Schafer, 2011; Schafer, 2012; Trafton, Anne, 2014) Research methodologies must be contextualized to various media and to a myriad demographics, but the dynamics of dream analysis remains constant. Though the media dream includes multi-functional sensory data that is integrated at levels of the unconscious, this chapter emphasizes the primarily visual symbolism in images.

Jung is not the only observer to say that the changing human perceptions of reality—what he calls the Spirit of the Age (Jung, 1933, pp. 175,196-220)—have been thrust upon us so rapidly that throughout the twentieth century it has disoriented and traumatized human collectives throughout the world. At base, the changes derive from discoveries in the realms of physics, psychology, and computer science. It is a well established fact that the psychological dynamics and structure of advertising and propaganda entail utilizing unconscious demographic patterns to sell their "products". This chapter develops the hypothesis that because the discoveries in these sciences have been incorporated into the holographic, psychological metaverse, its contextual projections can be analyzed like dreams.

CONCLUSION

Jungian Dream Analysis

The unconscious aspect of *psyche* is much like a *unified field of physics*. According to Jung:

Sooner or later nuclear physics and the psychology of the unconscious will draw closer together as both of them, independently of one another and from opposite directions, push forward into transcendental territory, the one with the concept of the atom, the other with that of the archetype. (Aion, p. 69; from Jacoby, 1973)

Dreams employ a symbolic language that communicates messages between that part of the dreamer's brain that is conscious and that part that is unconscious. Psychecology games are structurally analogous with the structure of Psyche. Due to the interactive loop between conscious-unconscious player choices a complex cognitive process becomes a recursive monitor image—the interactive process articulates the psychological process. This interactivity represents an important breakthrough that incorporates total functionality in the mediating process.

Functionality should be understood in terms of agency and the consequences of action. In the sense that players make psychological choices that are both conscious and unconscious and take action based on the images (and other sensory data) in their perceived reality, video games can be understood as an authentic simulation of a "real" existence in which causal behavior is generated and consequences of the behavior seem to materialize as images. So doing, players are creating their functional four-dimensional reality based largely on unconscious memories of psychological experiences. Using perceptions of images, they are employing cognitive alchemy and symbolic language to translate the unknown into the known. Imbedded unconscious meaning is translated into meaningful insight—precisely the compensational objective of Jung's Amplification Process.

RECOMMENDATIONS FOR FUTURE RESEARCH

An abundance of current research on Artificial Intelligence, psychological dynamics of global target groups, and robotics is underway. However, the frameworks of research are generally antiquated; i.e. they do not employ a comprehensive understanding of dream dynamics at work in the virtual media-sphere.

Contextual Ecosystems

As reported by EUROSIS—The European Multidisciplinary Society for Modeling and Simulation Technology—and directly relevant to analyzing contextual groups with digital technology, we hear that Facebook has "Like Farms". Emiliano De Cristofaro and colleagues (2014) from the University College London, targeted Facebook users in the US, France, India, Egypt, and worldwide. By measuring "likes" activity on an array of Facebook pages, researchers correlated user profiles with measures of page-popularity. Data relative to understanding "likes" of Facebook users translates to traditional personality profiling of target groups, but does not sufficiently factor unconscious dynamics into conclusions. Though an intuitive sense of the scope of unconscious issues exists, the importance of data relative to page popularity has commercial motivation and is being applied primarily to promote business opportunities. Such studies of contextual collective personae should be employed in more profound ways to promote cognitive coherence.

The study of online social networks has revolutionized the way social scientists understand human interaction on a grand scale. It is based on the assumption that the fundamental unit of interaction is the social tie that exists between individuals. This tie can be a message that one person has sent to another, that one person follows another, that one person "likes" another and so on. (8/1/2014)

The MIT Technology Review (1-11-2015) reports that computer scientists in the emergent science of human-data interaction say, "The rapidly evolving ecosystems associated with personal data are creating an entirely new field of scientific study." (Ecosystems, 2015) Again, the article goes on to illustrate the marketing potentials of this new science instead of the more significant potentials for addressing cognitive coherence:

Back in 2013, the UK supermarket giant, Tesco, announced that it was installing face recognition software in 450 of its stores that would identify customers as male or female, guess their age and measure how long they looked at an ad displayed on a screen below the camera. Tesco would then give the data to advertisers to show them how well their advertising worked and allow them to target their ads more carefully. (Ecosystems, 2015)

A remarkable online article defines three neuromarketing lessons derived from video games. The article explains that:

Games are uniquely adept at leveraging human psychology to motivate behavior. We play them for hours on end and enter into a state of flow with an ease not found in other fields. This is no accident: during my time studying game design and working in the field, neurological language like "dopamine hits" and "social proof" were commonplace. In this post, I'll examine some of the common tools used by video game designers in order [to] insure engagement and ultimately drive sales. (Claes, 2014)

Another recent article is about *The New Statistics*. In their abstract, authors say that, in response to heightened concern that our published research literature is incomplete and untrustworthy, "We need to make substantial changes to how we conduct research." The article goes on to explain that null hypothesis significance testing (NHST) has recognized flaws, and recommends preferred techniques including estimation based on effect sizes, confidence intervals, and meta-analysis (Cumming, 2013).

Robotics and Artificial Intelligence

Recent advances in robotics research constantly confirm the functional interactivity of physics, mathematics, and cognition. In another fascinating article from the MIT Review (Sept 22, 2014), "Eugene Izhikevich thinks you shouldn't have to write code in order to teach robots new tricks. "It should be more like training a dog," he says. "Instead of programming, you show it consistent examples of desired behavior." For example, to teach a robot to pick up trash, a mentor uses a remote control to repeatedly guide the robot's gripper to perform that task. After just minutes of repetition, the robot takes the initiative and starts doing the task for itself. Izhikevich's startup, *Brain Corporation*, based in San Diego, has developed an operating system for robots called *BrainOS* to make that possible. (Simonite, 2014)

Global Coherence Initiative

Perhaps the most exciting and relevant development in the vast arena of current research is the Global Coherence Initiative (GHI) spearheaded by the Institute of HeartMath. There is strong support for the existence in the earth's ionosphere of a global information field that connects all living systems and consciousness. "Every cell in our bodies is bathed in an external and internal environment of fluctuating invisible magnetic forces that can affect virtually every cell and circuit in biological systems." (McCraty, Deyhle, & Childre, 2012). Progress on the establishment of a global network of monitoring stations for studying these electro magnetic fluctuations portends a quantum leap in the direction of understanding of the media dream and how humans interact with it to create reality.

The scope of integration among all earth's inhabitants is becoming a conscious fact throughout the human population. Though vested interests seem always to marginalize the importance of the natural environment, the pervasiveness and popularity of media paraphernalia must eventually lead to a widespread appreciation of their dynamic impact and integration at all functional levels of human reality. We know something about the sun's influences on the earth—like the fact that without the sun, all life on earth would disappear. However, scientists have been expanding our knowledge with regularity. "The most likely mechanism for explaining how solar and geomagnetic influences affect human health and behavior are a coupling between the human nervous system and resonating geomagnetic frequencies called Schumann resonances, which occur in the earth-ionosphere resonant cavity and Alfvén waves. (McCraty, et al 2012) HeartMath researchers say that, "It is well established that these resonant frequencies directly overlap with those of the human brain and cardiovascular system" (McCraty, et al 2012).

This section on the need for further research is rather long in order to emphasize the vast scope and significance of the subject. The scope of necessary research is ontological, and research must be framed to contemplate the very nature of the paradigm shift into a virtual reality. The chapter takes the perspective—as does Joseph Campbell--that "mythology is psychology", that the Jungian archetypes of mythology are the selfsame energy and information patterns of physics, that the media-sphere or metaverse is analogous with psyche, and that it constitutes a holographic projection of media dreams from the collective unconscious.

Relative to more research, the scope of the chapter is both metaphysical and practical. Realization of the existence of a virtual *correspondence* between individuals and collectives—a sort of fractal bio-energetic relationship between the individual and the group as illustrated in such phenomena as focus groups, target groups, or statistical entities—marks the beginning of a more positive scientific understanding of the cognitive reality of the mediated dream. Many scientists have addressed this subject, and David Foster has provided an excellent overview. (Foster, 1985) Today, the marketing industry applies the correspondence principle constantly. Carl Jung understood the correspondence between individual and collective psyche as a fundamental principle of his therapeutic method. Accordingly, with appropriate adjustments in research methodology, therapy that works on individual levels may also be hypothesized to work at collective levels.

Now the doctor in me refuses point blank to consider the life of a people as something that does not conform to psychological law… "A people, in the doctor's eyes, presents only a somewhat more complex picture of psychic life than the individual," to quote Swedenborg. And so we can draw a parallel: just as in me, a single human being, the darkness calls forth the helpful light, so does it also in the psychic life of a people. (Jung 1933, p 209-210)

The therapeutic efficacy of narrative/drama is ancient and well-documented. (White, 2000) Phenomena such as catharsis have long been studied, so—given the robust interest in the technologies of the media-sphere—drama-based video games and Massively Multi-Player Online Games (MMOG) may provide a portal relative to collective healing and such new-paradigm experiences as epiphany, "metanoia" (Markley, 1972) or psychological critical mass.

REFERENCES

Bellman, O. (2015). Researchers create virtual humans. Playa Vista, CA: USC Institute for Creative Technologies. Retrieved from http://www.army.mil/article/147822

Bohm, D. (1989). Quantum Theory. New York: Prentice Hall. (Original work published in 1951). Retrieved from http://en.wikipedia.org/wiki/David_Bohm

Boyd, F. (2015). Immersive Media: To the Holodeck and Beyond. Retrieved from https://www.linkedin.com/grp/post/1039687-6004890688691453955

Campbell, J. (1973). *The hero with a thousand faces.* Princeton, NJ: Princeton University Press.

Capra, F. (1976). *The tau of physics.* Boulder, CO: Shambhala Publications, Inc.

Chopra, D. (1995). Body, Mind, and Soul: The mystery and the magic (VHS). Public Broadcasting Service/Turner Home Entertainment: Atlanta, GA.

Claes, Z. (2014). Three neuromarketing lessons derived from video games. *Neuromarketing*. Retrieved from http://www.neurosciencemarketing.com/blog/articles/neuromarketing-video-games.html

COCORO. anon. (2015). COCORO: robot swarms use collective cognition to perform tasks.European Commission: Digital Agenda for Europe. Retrieved from https://ec.europa.eu/digital-agenda/en/news/cocoro-robot-swarms-use-collective-cognition-perform-tasks

Collier, J., Burckhardt, C. B., & Lin, L. H. (1971). *Optical Holography*. New York: Academic Press.

Crawford, K. H. (2015). Here's looking at you: ONR tests new glasses for augmented reality system with Marines. *Office of Naval Research.* Retrieved from http://www.onr.navy.mil/en/Media-Center/Press-Releases/2015/Augmented-Reality-Demo-With-Marines.aspx

Csíkszentmihályi, M. (1990). *Flow: The Psychology of Optimal Experience*. New York: Harper and Row.

Cumming, G. (2013). *Substantial changes to how we conduct research needed.* Statistical Cognition Laboratory, La Trobe University. Retrieved from http://pss.sagepub.com/content/25/1/7.full

Curtis, A. (2009). *Century of the self: Happiness machines for free.* British Broadcasting Corporation, Freedocumentaries.com. Retrieved from http://freedocumentaries.org/film.php?id=140

De Cristofaro, E. (2014). Facebook "Likes". *The European Multidisciplinary Society for Modeling and Simulation Technology.* Retrieved from http://www.technologyreview.com/view/530961/the-hidden-world-of-facebook-like-farms/

Demers, T. (2014). Using gamefication to drive brand awareness. *Small Business Trends.* Retrieved from http://smallbiztrends.com/2014/03/using-gamification-brand-awareness.html

DeValois, Karen, & DeValois, Russell, and Yund, W. W. (1979). Responses of striate cortex cells to grating and checkerboard patterns. *The Journal of Psychology*, *291*, 483–505. PMID:113531

Dossey, L. (1982). *Space, time, and medicine* (pp. 108–109). Boston: New Science Library.

Ecosystems associated with personal data is creating an entirely new field of scientific study (2015). The MIT Technology Review. Retrieved from http://www.technologyreview.com/view/533901/the-emerging-science-of-human-data-interaction/)

Eddington, A. (1935). *The Nature of the physical world.* Cambridge University Press.

Foster, D. (1985). *The philosophical scientists*. USA: Dorset Press.

Garling, C. (2015). An algorithm that can help robots walk off injuries. MIT Technology Review. Retrieved from http://www.technologyreview.com/news/537791/an-algorithm-that-can-help-robots-walk-off-injuries/?utm_campaign=newsletters&utm_source=newsletter-daily-all&utm_medium=email&utm_content=20150528#

Geril, P. (2014c). Startup Europe- Capacity building for Business Angels (BAs) in ICT/ A digital Agenda for Europe. *Newsroom*. Retrieved from https://ec.europa.eu/digital-agenda/en/news/startup-europe-capacity-building-business-angels-bas-ict

Geril, P. (2015b). The virtual worlds 2015 survey report. *EUROSIS, The European Multidisciplinary Society for Modelling and Simulation Technology*. Retrieved from https://www.linkedin.com/grp/post/1039687-5988685234479075329

Goffman, E. (1974). *Frame analysis: An essay on the organization of experience*. New York: Harper and Row.

Goleman, D. (1979, February). Holographic memory: interview of Karl Pribram. *Psychology Today*, *12*(9), 71–72.

Greitemeyer, T., & Mügge, D. (2014). Video games do affect social outcomes: A meta-analytical review of the effects of violent and prosocial video game play. *Sage Publishing*. Retrieved from http://psp.sagepub.com/content/40/5/578.full

Hall, M. P. (2003). *The Secret Teachings of All Ages*. New York: Jeremy P. Tarcher/Penguin.

Hameroff, S., & Penrose, S. R. Discovery of quantum vibrations in 'mocrotubules' corroborates theory of consciousness. Retrieved 1/16/2014 http://phys.org/news/2014-01-discovery-quantum-vibrations-microtubules-corroborates.html)

How Yahoo Research Labs Studies Culture as a Formal Computational Concept (2014). *MIT Technology Review*. Retrieved from http://www.technologyreview.com/view/529521/how-yahoo-research-labs-studies-culture-

Hubb, B. (2015). John 1:1. Retrieved from http://biblehub.com/john/1-1.htm

Human behavior as a formal computational concept (2015). *MIT Technology Review*. Retrieved 1/25/2015 http://www.technologyreview.com/view/529521/how-yahoo-research-labs-studies-culture-as-a-formal-computational-concept/

Human Brain Project. (2014). *MIT Technology Review* July 7, 2014. http://www.technologyreview.com/news/528796/neuroscientists-object-to-europes-human-brain-project/

Jacobi, J. (1973). *The psychology of CG Jung*. London, USA: Yale University Press.

Jung, C. (1933). *Modern man in search of a soul*. Orlando, Fl: Harcourt Brace & Co.

Kleinman, Alexis (2014). Man successfully controls 2 prosthetic arms with just his thoughts.

Kleinman, A. (2014). Man successfully controls 2 prosthetic arms with just his thoughts. *Huffington Post*. Retrieved from http://www.huffingtonpost.com/2014/12/18/prosthetic-arms-thoughts_n_6348026.html

Kowal, E. (2015). Computer simulations improve lethality. The Official Home Page of the United States Army. Retrieved fromwww.army.mil

Lakoff, G. (2008). *The political mind* (pp. 83–84). USA: Viking Penguin.

Lashley, K. (1950). In search of the engram. In *Physiological Mechanisms in Animal Behavior* (pp. 454–482). New York: Academic Press.

Makuch, E. (2015). Microsoft has invested heavily in Holographic research and the dynamics of machine intelligence. *Gamespot.com*. Retrieved from http://www.gamespot.com/articles/windows-holographic-revealed/1100-6424791/

Markley, O. W. (1972). *Unity with diversity: Toward Social Policies for a future world order*. Center for the Study of Social Policy: Stanford Research Institute.

McCraty, R., & Childre, D. (2010). Coherence: bridging personal, social, and global health. Alternative Therapies, 16(4).

McCraty, Deyhle, & Childre (2012). The Global Coherence Initiative: Creating a coherent planetary standing wave. *Global Advances in Health & Medicine*, 1(1). Retrieved from www.gahmj.com

MediaGrid, Immersive Education Initiative. (n. d.). Retrieved from http://immersiveeducation.org/

Mishlove, J. (1998). The Holographic Brain with Karl Pribram, MA; Ph.D. *TWM.co.nz*.

Mortier, R. (2015). *The emerging science of human-data interaction*. MIT Technology Review.

Moyers, B. (1987). The secret government: The constitution in crisis. *Public Broadcasting System*. Retrieved from https://search.yahoo.com/search?fr=mcafee&type=B011US739D20150419&p=The+Secret+Government,+Bill+Moyers

Myers, M. (2015). Augmenting Agriculture with Social Impact Games has produced a digital prototype of a new social impact board game Bumper Crop. *The Arts Humanities Research Council research project Play to Grow*. Retrieved from https://play.google.com/store/apps/details?id=foam.bumpercrop

Pattern recognition in Go (2014). *MIT Technology Review 12-15-2014*. Retrieved from http://www.technologyreview.com/view/533496/why-neural-networks-look-set-to-thrash-the-best-human-go-players-for-the-first-time/

Penfield, W. (1975). *The mystery of the mind; a critical study of consciousness and the human brain*. Princeton, N.J.: Princeton University Press.

Philippe, G. (2015a). The AI Revolution: The Road to Superintelligence. *EUROSIS, TheEuropean Multidisciplinary Society for Modelling and Simulation Technology*. Quoted from Private Group DARPA seeks non-traditional entities to develop new robotics capabilities. *Army Technology.com*. Retrieved from http://www.army-technology.com/news/newsdarpa-seeks-non-traditional-entities-to-develop-new-robotics-capabilities-4580219?WT.mc_id=DN_News#.VVtNUbpwZLQ.linkedin

Pietsch, P. (1972, May). Shufflebrain. *Harper's Magazine* 244, p. 66.

Pietsch, P. (1981). *Shufflebrain: The quest for the hologramic mind* (p. 78). Boston: Houghton Mifflin.

Pister, K. (2015). Smart Dust. *The European Multidisciplinary Society for Modeling and Simulation Technology*. Retrieved from https://medium.com/war-is-boring/smart-dust-is-getting-smarter-4b062abd7769

Pollen, D. A., & Tractenberg, M. C. (1972, May 12). Alpha rhythm and eye movements in eidetic imagery. *Nature*, *237*(5350), 109–112. doi:10.1038/237109a0 PMID:4555444

Postman, N. (1985). *Amusing ourselves to death*. USA: Viking Penguin Inc.

Pribram, K. (1969, January). The neurophysiology of remembering. *Scientific American, 220*(1), 75. doi:10.1038/scientificamerican0169-73 PMID:4972532

Pribram, K. (1977). Language of the brain (pp. 123 & 169). Monterey, CA: Wadsworth Publishing.

Reeves, B., & Nass, C. (1996). The media equation. Stanford: Center For the study of Language and Information & Cambridge University Press.

Regaaldo, A. (2014). Neuroscientists Object to Europe's Human Brain Project. *MIT Technology Review.* Retrieved from http://www.technologyreview.com/news/528796/neuroscientists-object-to-europes-human-brain-project/

Restak, R. (1979). *The brain* (p. 253). New York: Warner Books.

Restak, R. (1981). Brain power: A new theory. *Science Digest*, (March): 19.

Schafer, S. (2011). Articulating the paradigm shift: Serious games for psychological healing of the collective persona. In M.M. Cruz-Cunha (Ed.), *Handbook of Research on serious games as educational business and research tools* (Ch. 19). Hershey, PA, USA: IGI Global. Retrieved from www.igi-global.com

Schafer, S. (2012). Optimizing Cognitive Coherence, Learning, and Psychological Healing with Drama-based Games. In J. Gackenbach (Ed.), *Video Game Play and Consciousness.* Nova Science Publishers.

Schafer, S., & Palamides, T. (2011). Designing an Ethical structure for Social Influence Marketing. In M.M. Cruz-Cunha, P. Gonçalves, N. Lopes, & G.D. Putnik (Eds.), *Handbook of research on Business Social Networking: Organizational, Managerial, and Technological Dimensions*. Hershey, PA, USA: IGI Global. Retrieved from www.igi-global.com

Schafer, S., & Yu, G. (2011). *Meaningful video games: drama-based video games as transformational experience*. Hershey, PA, USA: IGI Global. doi:10.4018/978-1-60960-567-4.ch019

Schroeder, R. (2014). Big data and the brave new world of social media research. *Big Data & Society*. Retrieved from http://bds.sagepub.com/content/1/2/2053951714563194.abstract

Simonite, T. (2014). Digital Summit: Microsoft's Quantum Search for the "Next Transistor". MIT Technology Review. Retrieved from http://www.technologyreview.com/news/528256/digital-summit-microsofts-quantum-search-for-the-next-transistor/

Simonite, T. (2014a). Robots That Learn Through Repetition, Not Programming. *MIT Technology Review.* Retrieved from http://www.technologyreview.com/news/530871/robots-that-learn-through-repetition-not-programming/

Simonite, T. (2014c). Google's Brain-Inspired Software Describes What It Sees in Complex Images. *MIT Technology Review.* Retrieved from http://www.technologyreview.com/news/532666/googles-brain-inspired-software-describes-what-it-sees-in-compleximages/?utm_campaign=newsletters&utm_source=newsletter-daily-all&utm_medium=email&utm_content=20141119

Simonite, T. (2015b). A Better Way to Build Brain-Inspired Chips. *MIT Review*. Retrieved from http://www.technologyreview.com/news/537211/a-better-way-to-build-brain-inspired-chips/

Simonite, T. (2015d). A startup's neural network can understand video. *MIT Review*. Retrieve from http://www.technologyreview.com/news/534631/a-startups-neural-network-can-understand-video/

Smart, J. M., Cascio, J., & Paffendorf, J. (2007). Metaverse Roadmap Overview, 2007. *Accelerated Studies Foundation*. Retrieved from http://en.wikipedia.org/wiki/Metaverse

Smith, H. (1991). *The World's Religions*. New York: Harper Collins.

Stoupel, E. (1993). Sudden cardiac deaths and ventricular extrasystoles on days of four levels of geo-magnetic activity. *J Basic Physiol Pharmacol.*, *4*(4), 357–366. PMID:8664252

Talbot, M. (1991). *The holographic universe*. New York: Harper.

Cumming, G. (2013). The New Statistics. *Psychological Science*, 25(1), 7-29. Retrieved from http://pss.sagepub.com/content/25/1/7.full

The rapidly evolving ecosystems associated with personal data is creating an entirely new field of scientific study (2015). *MIT Technology Review*. Retrieved from http://www.technologyreview.com/view/533901/the-emerging-science-of-human-data-interaction/)

Toma, C., & Hancock, J. (2013). Self-affirmation underlies Facebook use. *Pers. Soc. Psychol. GBull.*, 39(3), 321-331. Retrieved from http://psp.sagepub.com/content/39/3/321.abstract

Trafton, A. (2014). New brain-scanning technique allows scientists to see when and where the brain processes visual information. *Medicalxpress.com*. Retrieved from http://medicalxpress.com/news/2014-01-brain-scanning-technique-scientists-brain-visual.html

Twist, J. (2004, March 24). Brain waves control video game. *BBC News*. Retrieved from http://news.bbc.co.uk/2/hi/technology/3485918.stm

Understanding human behavior as a Formal Computational Concept (2014). *MIT Technology Review & Yahoo Research Labs*. Retrieved from http://www.technologyreview.com/view/529521/how-yahoo-research-labs-studies-culture-as-a-formal-computational-concept/

VanHeerden, P. (1970, July 25). Models for the brain. *Nature*, *227*(5256), 410–411. doi:10.1038/227410b0 PMID:5428449

Wakefield, J. (2014). Singularity: The robots are coming to steal our jobs. *BBC News*. Retrieved from http://www.bbc.com/news/technology-25000756

White, M. (2000). *Narrative Means to Therapeutic Ends; Maps of Narrative Practice. Reflections on Narrative Practice*. Adelaide, South Australia: Dulwich Centre Publications.

Why Neural Networks Look Set to Thrash the Best Human Go Players for the First Time. *MIT Technology Review*. Retrieved from http://www.technologyreview.com/view/533496/why-neural-networks-look-set-to-thrash-the-best-human-go-players-for-the-first-time/

KEY TERMS AND DEFINITIONS

Archetypal Representations: Jungian archetypes of mythology are the selfsame energy and information patterns of physics that constitute the source of the media-sphere or metaverse and are analogous with psyche. Archetypes are the psychoenergetic, generative source of holographic projections (archetypal representations) of media dreams from the collective unconscious.

Archetype: Jungian archetypes of mythology are the selfsame energy and information patterns of physics that constitute the source of the media-sphere or metaverse and are analogous with psyche. Archetypes are the psychoenergetic, generative source of holographic projections (archetypal representations) of media dreams from the collective unconscious.

Artificial Intelligence (AI): This field overlaps with electronics, computer science, robotics, mechatronics, nanotechnology, and bioengineering.

Avatar: The doctrine of avatars is a mythical concept in which a deity takes incarnation in human form that embodies a cosmic concept or philosophy in a person; i.e. Jesus embodies the concept of Love, and the Buddha embodies the concept of Compassion. In in the computer world, an avatar specifically refers to a character that represents an online user. Avatars are commonly used in multiplayer gaming, online communities, and Web forums.

Coherence: A single wavelength or frequency with all the waves in phase.

Collective Personae: According to Carl Jung, the persona is the social face the individual presents to the world—a kind of mask that is projected into the world and serves as a mirror of unconscious psychic patterns of individuation. A primary function of the persona is the evolutionary development of a viable, adaptive social persona. Jung was explicit as to the existence of collective personae (much like target groups in advertising) that are functional correspondences to individual personalities.

Compensation: A natural process aimed at establishing or maintaining balance within the psyche. The activity of consciousness is selective and requires direction, but direction requires the exclusion of everything irrelevant. According to Jung, the conscious orientation is one-sided. The psychic contents that are excluded and inhibited by the chosen direction sink into the unconscious, where they form a counterweight to the conscious orientation. As a rule, the unconscious compensation does not run counter to consciousness, but is rather a balancing or supplementing of the conscious orientation. In dreams, for instance, the unconscious supplies all those contents that are constellated by the conscious situation but are inhibited by conscious selection, although a knowledge of them would be indispensable for complete adaptation.

Contextuality: Jung's principle of compensation demands that dream interpretation must incorporate significant familiarity and understanding of the individual or patient who is doing the dreaming. In order for game software to provide authentic compensation, the game must be specifically programmed to the psychological profile or "context" of the player.

Holography: A method of reproducing a three-dimensional image of an object by means of light wave patterns recorded on a photographic plate or film. Holography is sometimes called lensless photography because no lenses are used to form the image. The plate or film with the recorded wave patterns is called a *hologram.* The light used to make a hologram must be coherent, i.e. of a single wavelength or frequency and with all the waves in phase. A coherent beam of light can be produced by a laser. The term is often used as a metaphorical model; i.e. "holographic universe" and "holographic brain".

Interactivity: In computers, interactivity is the dialog that occurs between a human being and a computer program. Programs that run without immediate user involvement are not interactive, but video games are usually thought of as fostering a great amount of interactivity. In the context of the chapter, interactivity extends to the four psychoenergetic Jungian functions (thinking, feeling, sensing, and intuiting). However, order entry applications, channel changing, and many other business applications are also interactive.

Media Dream: The media dream, a term coined by the author, goes beyond the technologically generated virtual realities called the metaverse and provides a comprehensive framework for correlating fundamental dimensions of reality by including multi-functional dynamics of Jungian dreams. The dreamscape of the holographic media-sphere that has the same psychoenergetic structure as Jungian dreams; i.e. dramatic, multifunctional structure.

Metaverse: The Metaverse is a virtual shared space—a collective—created by the convergence of virtually enhanced physical reality and "physically persistent virtual space, including the sum of all virtual worlds, augmented reality, and the internet. The word *metaverse* is a portmanteau of the prefix "meta" (meaning "beyond") and "universe" and is typically used to describe the concept of a future iteration of the internet, made up of persistent, shared, 3D virtual spaces linked into a perceived virtual universe. The term was coined in Neal Stephenson's 1992 science fiction novel *Snow Crash*, in which humans, as avatars, interact with each other and software agents, in a three-dimensional space that employs the real world as metaphor. Stephenson used the term to describe a virtual reality-based successor to the Internet. Concepts similar to the Metaverse have appeared under a variety of names in the cyberpunk genre of fiction as far back as 1981 in the novella *True Names*, Stephenson stated in the afterword to *Snow Crash* that after finishing the novel he learned about *Habitat*, an early MMORPG which resembled the Metaverse" (Smart, J.M., Cascio, J. and Paffendorf, J., 2007).

***Psych*ecology:** The unified field ecology of psychoenergetic, multidimensional reality.

***Psych*ecology Video Games:** These drama-based, psychoenergetic games should not be unduly associated with video games in their present state of development. Rather, they constitute an emergent game genre that is characterized by advanced principles of cognitive dynamics and story-telling art. These games have all the components of dreams, physics, the media, and interactivity with which to research the fourth dimension.

Psychological Functions: The classical four dimensions of human reality are 1) sensory/material, 2) emotional, 3) mental/rational and 4) spiritual. Jung called them 1) Sensing, 2) Feeling, 3) Mental, and 4) Intuitive. These dimensions are symbolized by 1) earth, 2) water, 3) air, and 4) fire.

Recursion: The process of repeating items in a self-similar way. For example, when the surfaces of two mirrors are exactly parallel with each other, the nested images that occur are a form of infinite recursion. The term has different meanings specific to a variety of disciplines ranging from linguistics to logic. The most common application of recursion is in mathematics and computer science, in which it refers to a method of defining functions. The term function refers to a relation between a set of inputs and a set of permissible outputs in which the function being defined is applied within its own definition. The functional relationship between Jungian archetypes and archetypal representations (projections) is analyzed in dreams according to symbolic images that are projections of unconscious psychoenergetic patterns. Recursion may also apply to metaphorical resonance that can be coded mathematically.

Robotics: A branch of engineering that involves the conception, design, manufacture, and operation of robots. This field overlaps with electronics, computer science, artificial intelligence, mechatronics, nanotechnology, and bioengineering.

Glossary

Adventure Games: Essentially, these are drama-based games; i.e. they have dramatic structure as defined by Aristotle, but the dramatic structure is based primarily on stereotypical templates of the Hero's Journey—such as Christopher Vogler's twelve act play—rather than the more complex psychological context of functional *Psych*ecology games.

Alpha Waves: Alpha Brain Waves are a sign of relaxed activity in your brain. Alpha brainwaves are defined as brain waves that cycle between the frequency 8 Hz – 12 Hz. They are commonly produced when both hemispheres of the brain are synchronized (coherence), though they can also be found solely in the right hemisphere. The alpha state can be produced with such practices as meditation, yoga, or the focused activity that is known as the Flow state.

Amplification: The Jungian practice of creating meaning out of the symbolism in images in mostly dreams, but also in films. Metaphorical amplification—essentially metaphorical extension—is the quantifiable basis for Jungian method (Amplification Method) in dream analysis.

Apartheid: The South African mode of racial segregation from 1948 to 1994 during which time a white Afrikaans-speaking minority exercised excessive rule over a black majority.

Archetypal Psychology: Archetypal Psychology—a movement initiated by James Hillman—focuses on what it calls the *psyche*, or *soul*, and the deepest patterns of psychic functioning, "the fundamental fantasies that animate all life". Archetypal psychology likens itself to a polytheistic mythology which recognizes the myriad of fantasies including gods, goddesses, demigods, mortals and animals - that shape and are shaped by our psychological lives. Hillman reports that Archetypal Psychology emerged partly from the Jungian tradition while also drawing from other traditions and authorities such as Henry Corbin, Vico, and Plotinus. In this framework the ego is but one of an assemblage of psychological fantasies.

Archetypal Representations: Jungian archetypes of mythology are the selfsame energy and information patterns of physics that constitute the source of the media-sphere or metaverse and are analogous with psyche. Archetypes are the psychoenergetic, generative source of holographic projections (archetypal representations) of media dreams from the collective unconscious.

Archetype: The term, archetype, was coined by Carl Jung to represent electrophysiological patterns of the cognitive unconscious. Jungian archetypes of mythology are the selfsame energy and information patterns of physics that constitute the source of the media-sphere or metaverse and are analogous with psyche. They are the generative source of what Jung called archetypal representations that are recursive projections existing primarily as sensory functions—especially images in dreams, memory, television, computer monitors, and so-called "real life". Unconscious archetypal content and meaning may be accessed by analyzing the symbolic content of relatively conscious archetypal representations. Archetypes are unconscious descriptive expressions of common patterns of behavior within human experience. Roles like "mother", "hero", or "teacher" are archetypes. These expressions may take very different forms across time and culture.

Artificial Intelligence (AI): This field overlaps with electronics, computer science, robotics, mechatronics, nanotechnology, and bioengineering.

Avatar: The doctrine of avatars is a mythical concept in which a deity takes incarnation in human form that embodies a cosmic concept or philosophy in a person; i.e. Jesus embodies the concept of Love, and the Buddha embodies the concept of Compassion. In in the computer world, an avatar specifically refers to a character that represents an online user. Avatars are commonly used in multiplayer gaming, online communities, and Web forums.

Bioenergetic Function: The ability of the cell to generate sufficient energy through oxidative phosphorylation and to maintain healthy pools of mitochondria are critical for survival and maintenance of normal biological function, especially during periods of increased oxidative stress.

Broadcast: The dissemination of frequency modulated electrical field into extracellular and extracorporeal space outside the point of origin. To transmit programs or signals from a radio or television station. To disseminate or make something known widely. To cast or scatter abroad over an area, as seed in sowing.

Bullying: Behavior that causes a person or group to feel unwelcomed, threatened, or unsafe. There are overt and covert forms of bullying.

Campbell: Joseph Campbell, author of the seminal work, *The Hero with a Thousand Faces,* which analyzes mythology of heroes and their quests using Jung's theories of archetypes and the collective unconscious.

Cognition: Cognition is a term referring to the mental processes involved in gaining knowledge and comprehension. These processes include thinking, knowing, remembering, judging, and problem-solving. These are higher-level functions of the brain and encompass language, imagination, perception, and planning. *Psychology Today* adds: Quite simply, cognition refers to thinking. There are the obvious applications of conscious reasoning—doing taxes, playing chess, deconstructing *Macbeth*—but thought takes many subtler forms, such as interpreting sensory input, guiding physical actions, and empathizing with others. The old metaphor for human cognition was the computer. If this bee true, the computer-as-cognitive-analog implies the participation of unconscious dimensions as well as conscious ones. In the analog, computer software equates to unconscious states, while the projections created by the software equate to conscious states.

Coherence: A state in which one's mind (the conscious and unconscious components of the psyche) and physiological systems work in alignment, allowing one to be self-reliant, to be fully aware of one's resources, and to encounter and resolve problems without anxiety. A single wavelength or frequency with all the waves in phase.

Collective Personae: According to Carl Jung, the persona is the social face the individual presents to the world—a kind of mask that is projected into the world and serves as a mirror of unconscious psychic patterns of individuation. A primary function of the persona is the evolutionary development of a viable, adaptive social persona. Jung was explicit as to the existence of collective personae (much like target groups in advertising) that are functional correspondences to individual personalities.

Collective Unconscious: Perhaps the best way to understand the Jungian collective unconscious is to apply a correspondence with the unified field of physics. "The microphysical world of the atom exhibits certain features whose affinities with the psyche have impressed themselves even on the physicists." (Education, p. 89) Just one example of the correspondence is that, "For every piece of conscious life that loses its importance and value—so runs the law—there arises a compensation in the unconscious. We may see in this an analogy to the conservation of energy in the physical world, for our psychic processes have a quantitative aspect also. No psychic value can disappear without being replaced by another of equivalent intensity. This is a rule which finds its pragmatic sanction in the daily practice of the psychotherapist; it is repeatedly verified and never fails. Now the doctor in me refuses point blank to consider the life of a people as something that does not conform to psychological law. A people, in the doctor's eyes, presents only a somewhat more complex picture of psychic life than the individual." For Jung, archetypes constitute the structure of the collective unconscious. They are based on basic human behavior and situations, and they predispose behavior in much the same way as what today are called frames of the cognitive unconscious (George Lakoff). For example the relationship between mother and child is governed by the mother archetype: Father-child - by the father archetype, and powerful dynamics such as birth, death, religion, mystical experience, and evolution (individuation), are predisposed by archetypes.

Comic Books: Paper or digital storytelling media characterized by graphic images and dialogue that combine to create the story.

Compensation: A natural process aimed at establishing or maintaining balance within the psyche. The activity of consciousness is selective and requires direction, but direction requires the exclusion of everything irrelevant. According to Jung, the conscious orientation is one-sided. The psychic contents that are excluded and inhibited by the chosen direction sink into the unconscious, where they form a counterweight to the conscious orientation. As a rule, the unconscious compensation does not run counter to consciousness, but is rather a balancing or supplementing of the conscious orientation. In dreams, for instance, the unconscious supplies all those contents that are constellated by the conscious situation but are inhibited by conscious selection, although a knowledge of them would be indispensable for complete adaptation.

Consciousness: The experience of experiencing, the knowledge of knowing, the sense of sensing.

Contextuality: Jung's principle of compensation demands that dream interpretation must incorporate significant familiarity and understanding of the individual or patient who is doing the dreaming. In order for game software to provide authentic compensation, the game must be specifically programmed to the psychological profile or "context" of the player.

Depth Psychology: Historically, *depth psychology* refers to psychoanalytic approaches to therapy and research that take the unconscious into account. The term was rapidly accepted by Sigmund Freud to cover a topographical view of the mind in terms of different psychic systems. Depth psychology has since come to refer to the ongoing development of theories and therapies pioneered by Pierre Janet, William James, and Carl Jung as well as Freud which explore the relationship between the conscious and the cognitive unconscious.

Digital Physics: In physics and cosmology, *digital physics* is a collection of theoretical perspectives based on the premise that the universe is susceptible to description with information, and is therefore computable. According to this theory, the universe can be conceived of as either the output of a deterministic or probabilistic computer program, a vast, digital computation device, or mathematically isomorphic to such a device.

Distortion: Distortion is the alteration of the original shape (or other characteristic) of something, such as an object, image, sound or waveform--a lack of proportionality in an image resulting from defects in the optical system or a falsified reproduction of an audio or video signal caused by change in the wave form of the original signal. Theoretically, due to contextuality, archetypal representations all display a degree of distortion from perfect proportionality with the generating archetypal psychoenergetic patterns. In this context, distortion is not necessarily bad because it represents unique (personal) patterns within san overarching absolute.

Double Occupancy: The notion that a space is at least double or even triple occupied in a geopolitical as well as a psychological manner.

Drama-Based Video Games: DBG are hypothesized to have the same dramatic-functional structure as Jungian dreams. That structure adheres to Aristotle's definition of good drama. According to Jung this structure provides the fundamental framework within which multifunctional dreams (thinking, feeling, sensing, & intuiting) may be analyzed for the purpose of meaningful discovery.

Dreams: The presence of consciousness during sleep. The Australian Aborigines believe that what we consider the realm of dreams is the real world (the Dreamtime), and the world we experience with our senses is a dream. C.G. Jung put forth a theory of dreams which is quite popular today. Following in the footsteps of Sigmund Freud, Jung claimed that dream analysis is the primary way to gain knowledge of the unconscious mind. He says that the dream is a natural phenomenon which we can study, thereby gaining knowledge of the hidden part of our mind—the personal and collective unconscious. Jung calls dream images archetypal representations or projections of unconscious electromagnetic patterns. The images are symbolic of conscious and unconscious mental processes, so understanding symbolic patterns in dreams allows for discovery of unconscious meaning.

Electrophysiological: 1) There is strong and convincing evidence for physiological frequency based electrical fields being an important and active functioning component of CNS processing during wake and sleep. These fields clearly affect the potentials of neurons to fire, affect ion-equilibrium at the cell membranes and intra-cellular kinetics. Extracellularly, these fields define the activity of widely separated neural networks such as the default systems. 2) This electrophysiological system is affected and altered by externally applied chemicals and electrical fields. Psychoactive medications and disease processes produce consistent alterations in these fields. The induced changes in these physiologic fields are associated with changes in wake and sleep functioning. 3) These electrophysiological systems can be affected and altered by biofeedback and training in different approaches of meditative practice. These alterations can be frequency specific, based on the technique utilized in training. Such induced alterations in this system can be used to affect waking cognitive function and performance. These induced alterations may affect some disease processes. 4) When applied in the supra-physiologic range electrically as ECT or magnetically as TMS, alterations in memory and sensory systems can be induced. The application of electrical fields in this manner is known to alter cognitive processing and the course of a variety of psychiatric illnesses. 5) Externally applied electrical fields in the physiological range can be demonstrated to induce alterations in this system as determined by electrophysiological monitoring. These fields are likely to affect neural electrolyte equilibrium and cellular kinetics. 6) Externally applied cognitive interventions (hypnotherapy and hypnopedia) have been shown to induce alterations in sleep electrophysiology. During the lighter stages of sleep, some cognitive stimuli (name-calling and sounds) as well as aversive physical stimuli, can incorporated into dream content.

Ethics: For the purposes of the book, ethics may be understood to have similar structure to Jungian dreams. For example, ethics are "contextual"—based on the variable parameters of personal, cultural, and moral/religious understanding. However, ethics may be analyzed in ways similar to Jungian analysis of dreams.

Film: For the purposes of this book, film may be understood to have identical structure as Jungian dreams with the exception of interactivity.

Flow: Also known as being in the zone, Flow is the cognitive state of operation in which a person performing an activity is fully immersed in a feeling of energized focus, full involvement, and enjoyment in the process of the activity. In essence, flow is characterized by complete absorption in what one does. Named by Mihály Csíkszentmihályi, the concept has been widely referenced across a variety of fields. However the state of Flow has been described for thousands of years under other guises. Flow may be equated to transcendence as understood in Eastern religions. For our purposes, Flow seems identical to Jungian Compensation and to states of coherence. According to Csikszentmihalyi, flow is completely focused motivation. It is a state of single-minded, coherent immersion and represents the ultimate experience in harnessing the mind and emotions in the service of performing and learning.

Frequency: as applied to oscillating physiological electrical fields of the CNS.

Gameplay: The interactive process of playing video games goes beyond play. The game industry thinks of gameplay in terms of the platform and software involved.

Gamma: Gamma radiation, also known as gamma rays, and denoted by the Greek letter γ, refers to electromagnetic radiation of an extremely high frequency and therefore consists of high-energy photons. Gamma rays typically have frequencies above 10 exahertz (or $>10^{19}$ Hz), and therefore have energies above 100 keV and wavelengths less than 10 picometers (10^{-12} meter), which is less than the diameter of an atom.

Group Hero: An expression of the larger hero archetype, the Group Hero is created when multiple people gather together to tackle a larger social problem. Group hero stories are distinguished from other hero tales by their focus on the group's actions.

Healing: A process of psychological integration and a coming-to-terms with aspects of the Self following a perceived or real traumatic event such as severe loss.

Healing Fiction: A work of art such as a film that stimulates or provokes the viewer into recognizing possibilities for healing through the potency of its subjectively meaningful images.

Hermanus, Oliver: A South African film director. His graduation film, 'Shirley Adams', premiered in competition at the Locarno International Film Festival in 2009. In 2011 his film 'Skoonheid' was invited to compete in the Un Certain Regard competition at the 64th Cannes film festival. 'Skoonheid' won the Queer Palm on May 24th 2011.

Heroism: In the context of this book, heroism is personified by the hero protagonist as archetype in video games.

Hillman, James: The American psychologist, James Hillman studied at the C.G. Jung Institute in Zurich, and founded a movement toward archetypal psychology. Archetypal psychology is a polytheistic psychology that recognizes the myriad fantasies and myths—including the myth of the ego—that shape and are shaped by our psychological lives.

Holodeck: Derived from the television series *Star Trek*, a holodeck is a simulated reality facility located on starships and starbases. The holodeck is said to function by combining holography with magnetic force fields and energy-to-matter-forcefields. For the purposes of the book, the holodeck provides a popular metaphor for simulations of psychological reality and for the Metaverse.

Holography: A method of reproducing a three-dimensional image of an object by means of light wave patterns recorded on a photographic plate or film. Holography is sometimes called lens less photography because no lenses are used to form the image. The plate or film with the recorded wave patterns is called a *hologram*. The light used to make a hologram must be coherent, i.e. of a single wavelength or frequency and with all the waves in phase. A coherent beam of light can be produced by a laser. The term is often used as a metaphorical model; i.e. "holographic universe" and "holographic brain".

Image: In the Jungian context, images are "archetypal representations". Whether they are dream images, memory images, fantasy images, computer monitor images, television images, or the images we call "real" life, they are illusory projections that have their source in unconscious psychoenergetic patterns that Jung called archetypes.

Indie Games: Short for Independent Games, these are video games developed by unofficial game developers—individuals or small teams generally without video game publisher financial support.

Individuation: The continuous psychological trajectory of the individual who is called to consciousness in the pursuit of psychological wholeness. The ideal is synonymous with transcendental experience.

Interactivity: In computers, interactivity is the dialog that occurs between a human being and a computer program. Programs that run without immediate user involvement are not interactive, but video games are usually thought of as fostering a great amount of interactivity. In the context of the chapter, interactivity extends to the four psychoenergetic Jungian functions (thinking, feeling, sensing, and intuiting). However, order entry applications, channel changing, and many other business applications are also interactive.

Interface: The shared boundary and interconnection between systems and equipment and human beings.

Interactivity: Human communication is the basic example of interactive communication which involves two different processes; human to human interactivity and human to computer interactivity. Many fields are concerned with interactivity, including information science, computer science, human-computer interaction, communication, and industrial design. For the purposes of this book, the term alludes to psychological-functional interaction in a unified field of electro-magnetic frequencies.

Jung, C. G.: Often referred to as C. G. Jung, was a Swiss psychiatrist and psychotherapist who founded analytical psychology. His work has been influential not only in psychiatry but also in philosophy, anthropology, archeology, literature, and religious studies. He was a prolific writer, though many of his works were not published until after his death. The central concept of analytical psychology is individuation—the psychological process of integrating the opposites, including the conscious with the unconscious, while still maintaining their relative autonomy. Jung considered individuation to be the central process of human evolution. Jung created some of the best known psychological concepts, including the archetype, the collective unconscious, the comples, and extraversion and introversion. His work is at the basis of Myers-Briggs personality profiling and the work of Joseph Campbell who said, "Mythology is psychology." More specifically, Campbell meant Jungian psychology.

Jungian Psychology: The essence of Jungian psychology is that: "Dreams give information about the secrets of the inner life and reveal to the dreamer hidden factors of his personality. As long as these are undiscovered, they disturb his waking life and betray themselves only in the form of symptoms. This means that we cannot effectively treat the patient from the side of consciousness alone, but must bring about a change in and through the unconscious." (Jung, 1933, p. 16) "The unconscious is not a demonic monster, but a thing of nature that is perfectly neutral as far as moral sense, aesthetic taste and intellectual judgments go...the overwhelming of consciousness by the unconscious—is most likely to occur when the unconscious is excluded from life by repressions, or is misunderstood and depreciated...It is always helpful, when we set out to interpret a dream, to ask: What conscious attitude does it compensate?" (Jung, 1933, p. 17) "Every dream is a source of information and a means of self-regulation...In reality, the relation between consciousness and the dream is strictly causal, and they interact in the subtlest of ways." (Jung, 1933, p. 18-19)

League of Legends (LoL): This has grown in popularity to become the most-played game in North America and Europe. In terms of the number of hours played, as of January 2014, over 67 million people play League of Legends per month, 27 million per day, and over 7.5 million concurrently during peak hours. In terms of psychoelectrical impact on the geosphere, of all media such video games are unprecedented.

Lone Hero: An expression of the larger hero archetype, the Lone Hero is the form of the hero most well known in mythology and storytelling, described in books such as *The Hero With a Thousand Faces* (Campbell, 2008).

Lucid Dreaming: The awareness of dreaming while dreaming, most often associated with capabilities of controlling dream content and the ability to consciously awake from sleep.

Media Dream: The media dream, a term coined by the author, goes beyond the technologically generated virtual realities called the metaverse and provides a comprehensive framework for correlating fundamental dimensions of reality by including multi-functional dynamics of Jungian dreams. The dreamscape of the holographic media-sphere that has the same psychoenergetic structure as Jungian dreams; i.e. dramatic, multifunctional structure.

Media-Sphere: A term synonymous with media dream, the unified field of physics, and the Metaverse.

Meditation: Engagement in the act of continued or extended contemplation. Meditation is a practice of concentrated focus upon a sound, object, visualization, the breath, movement, or attention itself in order to increase awareness of the present moment, reduce stress, promote relaxation, and enhance personal and spiritual growth. Meditation cultivates an emotional stability that may be understood as a coherent state that allows the meditator to experience intense emotions fully while simultaneously maintaining perspective on them. The meditative state has often been related to the "Flow" state of harmony.

Metaverse: The Metaverse is a virtual shared space—a collective—created by the convergence of virtually enhanced physical reality and "physically persistent virtual space, including the sum of all virtual worlds, augmented reality, and the internet. The word *metaverse* is a portmanteau of the prefix "meta" (meaning "beyond") and "universe" and is typically used to describe the concept of a future iteration of the internet, made up of persistent, shared, 3D virtual spaces linked into a perceived virtual universe. The term was coined in Neal Stephenson's 1992 science fiction novel *Snow Crash*, in which humans, as avatars, interact with each other and software agents, in a three-dimensional space that employs the real world as metaphor. Stephenson used the term to describe a virtual reality-based successor to the Internet. Concepts similar to the Metaverse have appeared under a variety of names in the cyberpunk genre of fiction as far back as 1981 in the novella *True Names*, Stephenson stated in the afterword to *Snow Crash* that after finishing the novel he learned about *Habitat*, an early MMORPG which resembled the Metaverse." (Smart, J.M., Cascio, J. and Paffendorf, J., 2007)

MMOs: As explained in Wikipedia, A massively multiplayer online game (MMO or MMOG) is a multiplayer video game which is capable of supporting large numbers of players simultaneously. By necessity, they are played over a network, such as the Internet. MMOs usually have at least one persistent virtual world, however some games differ. These games can be found for most network-capable platforms, including the personal computer, video game console, and other mobile devices. MMOGs can enable players to cooperate and compete with each other on a large scale, and sometimes to interact meaningfully with people around the world. They include a variety of gameplay types, representing many video game genres. The most popular type of MMOG, and the subgenre that pioneered the category, is the massively multiplayer online role-playing game (MMORPG).

Monomyth: According to Campbell, the core myth common across cultures in which the hero separates from his or her community on a quest, reaches a source of power and overcomes any obstacles, and then returns with knowledge beneficial to the world. Joseph Campbell's Monomyth (*Hero With A Thousand Faces*) has become the standard formula for storytelling in the media. Campbell based the Monomyth on Jungian psychology of psychological evolution leading to "Individuation". The template is widely used by storytellers in all media, but the stages of the journey vary. The standard path of the journey is almost exclusively stereotypical—as is the case with Christopher Vogler's twelve step version of the Monomyth. However, even as a stereotype, the standard path of the mythological adventure of the hero is a formula for expression of the psychological rites of passage that are universal in human experience: *separation--initiation—return.* As Campbell pointed out, the journey is a universal archetype that exists in the personal and collective unconscious where it serves s a framework for conscious behavior.

Motivation: The impetus that leads one to undertake and potentially complete a task. Motivations may be extrinsic (external to an individual) or intrinsic (developed within an individual). Mountaineering relies, for the most part, on intrinsic sources of motivation.

Mountaineering: includes such sports as mountaineering, extreme skiing and snowboarding, and backcountry skiing so long as the person ascends under his/her own power. For purposes of this essay, the terms "mountaineering", "climbing", and "alpinism" are used interchangeably.

Movie Heroes: For the purposes of the book, these role models usually adhere to the archetypal definition of the hero.

Mythology: Mythology can refer to the collected stories shared by contextual groups of people—their body of drama which they tell or enact to explain nature, history, and customs. Though approaches to the discussion of myth vary, this book emphasizes the psychological nature of myth as defined by Joseph Campbell and the archetypal nature of myth defined by Carl Jung. As a collection of such stories, mythology is a vital feature of every culture. In each contextual culture, the stories are unique. However, the underlying patterns in the mythic dramas are universal (archetypal), and they represent the collective-cultural personae that is projected in myth as it is in personal dreams.

Nightmares: Vividly realistic and disturbing dreams, nightmares are usually multisensory. According to Carl Jung, dreams are symbolic messages from the psychic unconscious. The purpose of all dreams is to discover meaning in their symbolic content. The more intense the dream, the more urgent is the message which must be discovered in order to compensate for dissonance between the conscious and unconscious aspects of the dreamer's life. Nightmares are generally the most intense of dreams, so they signify the urgent need to understand their message.

Pathology: The term pathology is a broad term for the study of disease in general. The term incorporates a wide range of bioscience research fields and medical practices.

Perception: The organization, identification, and interpretation of sensory information in order to represent and understand the environment. All perception involves signals in the nervous system, which in turn result from physical or chemical stimulation of the sense organs. For example, vision involves light striking the retina of the eye, smell is mediated by odor molecules, and hearing involves pressure waves. Psychological factors such as learning, memory, expectation, and attention shape contextual perceptions.

Positive Psychology: A psychological theory grounded in the concept that individuals best gain skills through a focus on positive activities that promote coherence rather than through a focus on an analysis of their psychological deficits.

Psyche: In psychology, the psyche is the totality of the human mind, conscious and unconscious. For Carl Jung, the psyche can be directly and fully experienced and observed. "It is a word of its own governed bylaws, structured, and endowed with its own means of expression." (Jacoby, 1973, p. 1) Psyche consists of two complementary but antithetical spheres: consciousness and unconsciousness that are self-regulating oppositions which provide a basis for psychoelectric dynamics.

Psychecology: The term Psychecology alludes to the existence of an ecology of psyche that exists both macrocosmically and microcosmically. The implication is that—based on research in diverse scientific fields—the universe can be understood in terms of bio-energetic life-forms and extrapolated to dimensions not usually considered biological. This ontology that has its roots in the mythologies of most cultures, is re-emergent—a sort of scientific pantheism. New media technologies have begun generating a paradigm shift in human understanding of reality—and life—through advances in Artificial Intelligence (AI), robotics, and a whole array of super intelligences within the "singularity". The term suggests a vital reality in which mathematics, the media, the unified field of physics, and the unified field of Jungian Psyche can be researched using the most advanced cognitive parameters and technology.

***Psych*ecology Video Games (PEG):** These drama-based, psychoenergetic games should not be unduly associated with video games in their present state of development. Rather, they constitute an emergent game genre that is characterized by advanced principles of cognitive dynamics and story-telling art. These games have all the components of dreams, physics, the media, and interactivity with which to research the fourth dimension.

Psychological Functions: The classical four dimensions of human reality are 1) sensory/material, 2) emotional, 3) mental/rational and 4) spiritual. Jung called them 1) Sensing, 2) Feeling, 3) Mental, and 4) Intuitive. These dimensions are symbolized by 1) earth, 2) water, 3) air, and 4) fire.

Psychological Growth: The process of functional evolution leading to transcendence of the human condition as symbolized in the archetype known as the Hero's Journey.

Reality: For the purposes of this book, reality is an illusion based on contextual (unique) human perceptions that has all the structural-functional elements of Jungian dreams.

Recursion: The process of repeating items in a self-similar way. For example, when the surfaces of two mirrors are exactly parallel with each other, the nested images that occur are a form of infinite recursion. The term has different meanings specific to a variety of disciplines ranging from linguistics to logic. The most common application of recursion is in mathematics and computer science, in which it refers to a method of defining functions. The term function refers to a relation between a set of inputs and a set of permissible outputs in which the function being defined is applied within its own definition. The functional relationship between Jungian archetypes and archetypal representations (projections) is analyzed in dreams according to symbolic images that are projections of unconscious psychoenergetic patterns. Recursion may also apply to metaphorical resonance that can be coded mathematically.

Robotics: A branch of engineering that involves the conception, design, manufacture, and operation of robots. This field overlaps with electronics, computer science, artificial intelligence, mechatronics, nanotechnology, and bioengineering.

Role-Playing Game: An interactive game rooted in character-driven storytelling.

Russian Woodpecker: A Soviet over-the-horizon (OTH) radar system used as part of the Soviet ABM early-warning network.

Shadow: An archetypal representation of the repressed or hidden content of the Self that is often projected onto other people on an individual as well as collective level.

Simulation: According to Wikipedia, Simulation is the imitation of the operation of a real-world process or system over time. The act of simulating something first requires that a model be developed; this model represents the key characteristics or behaviors/functions of the selected physical or abstract system or process. The model represents the system itself, whereas the simulation represents the operation of the system over time. Simulation is used in many contexts, such as simulation of technology for performance optimization, safety engineering, training, education, and video games. Often, computer experiments are used to study simulation models. Simulation is also used with scientific modeling of natural systems or human systems to gain insight into their functioning. Simulation can be used to show the eventual real effects of alternative conditions and courses of action. Simulation is also used when the real system cannot be engaged, because it may not be accessible, or it may be dangerous or unacceptable to engage, or it is being designed but not yet built, or it may simply not exist.

Skoonheid: A South African film story of a man who is the product of apartheid and feels excluded from the new South Africa. Raised within the confines of conservatism, the protagonist carefully constructs his life to achieve societal approval, but experiences a sterile existence that fills him with profound regret and the conviction that his is a wasted life.

Sleep: A reversible state of perceptual isolation.

Social Media: Wikipedia explains Social media as computer-mediated tools that allow people to create, share or exchange information, ideas, and pictures/videos in virtual communities and networks. *Social media* is defined as "a group of Internet-based applications that build on the ideological and technological foundations of Web 2.0, and that allow the creation and exchange of user-generated content." For the purposes of this book, virtual communities—like target groups—are excellent examples of contextual personae.

Soul: "The *soul,* in many religious, philosophical and mythological traditions, is the incorporeal and, in many conceptions, immortal essence of a living thing. According to most of the Abrahamic religions, immortal souls belong only to human beings. For example, the Catholic theologian Thomas Aquinas attributed "soul" (anima) to all organisms but argued that only human souls are immortal. Other religions (most notably Jainism and Hinduism teach that all biological organisms have souls, and others teach that even non-biological entities (such as rivers and mountains) possess souls. This latter belief is called animism. Greek philosophers such as Socrates, Plato, and Aristotle understood the psyche (ψυχή) to be crowned with the logical faculty, the exercise of which was the most divine of human actions. At his defense trial, Socrates even summarized his teachings as nothing other than an exhortation for his fellow Athenians to excel in matters of the psyche since all bodily goods are dependent on such excellence (The Apology, 30a–b)." *Anima mundi* is the concept of a "world soul" connecting all living organisms on the planet.´ (Wikipedia: https://en.wikipedia.org/wiki/Soul). In this book, relative to humans, the term connotes transcendent or "coherent cognitive states. However, the concepts of "world soul" and animism are both implicit and explicit in a number of chapters.

Team/Teamwork: A group of people working together for a common cause. Teams may be more or less.

Virtual Reality: An artificial environment which is experienced through sensory stimulation (also called multi-functional--as sights and sounds) provided by a computer and in which one's actions partially determine what happens in the environment. The technology used to create or access a virtual reality has evolved at great speed in terms of both agency and immersion. The Holodeck of the television classic, Star Trek, was an early conceptual metaphor that today has become technology such as Oculus Rift. Increasingly, the technology of the Metaverse and the mediated universe are becoming an interactive virtual reality.

Vogler, Christopher: Vogler was inspired by the writings of mythologist Joseph Campbell, particularly *The Hero with a Thousand Faces*. He used Campbell's work to create the now-legendary 7-page company memo for Hollywood screenwriters, *A Practical Guide to The Hero with a Thousand Faces*.

Waking State: The cognitive state behaviorally characterized by the integration and utilization of perceptual input.

Compilation of References

Abernethy, G. L., & Langford, T. A. (1970). *Introduction to Western philosophy: Pre-Socratics to Mill.* Belmont, CA: Dickenson.

Adams, E., & Rollings, A. (2007). *Fundamentals of Game Design.* Upper Saddle River, NJ: Pearson Publishing.

Adelson, J. (1974). The dreams of creative college girls. In R. Woods & H. Greenhouse (Eds.), *The new world of dreams.* New York: Macmillan.

Alexander, C. N., Davies, J. L., Dixon, C. A., Dillbeck, M. C., Ortzel, R. M., Muehlman, J. M., & Orme-Johnson, D. W. (1990). Higher stages of consciousness beyond formal operations: The Vedic psychology of human development. In C. N. Alexander & E. J. Langer (Eds.), *Higher stages of human development: Adult growth beyond formal operations.* New York, NY: Oxford University Press.

Alexander, C., Boyer, R., & Alexander, V. (1987). Higher states of consciousness in the Vedic psychology of Maharishi Mahesh yogi: A theoretical introduction and research review. *Modern Science and Vedic Science, 1*(1), 89–126.

Anastassiou, C., Perin, R., Markam, H., & Koch, C. (2011). Emphatic coupling of cortical neurons. *Nature Neuroscience, 14*(2), 217–223. doi:10.1038/nn.2727 PMID:21240273

Andrews-Hanna, J. (2011). The brain's default network and its adaptive role in internal mentation. *The Neuroscientist, XX*, 1–20. PMID:21677128

Arbib, M. A. (1985). In Search of the Person: Philosophical Explorations in Cognitive Science (November 1, 1985)

Arbib, M. A., & Hesse, M. B. (1986). *The Construction of Reality.* Cambridge Studies in Philosophy. doi:10.1017/CBO9780511527234

Archer, D., & Cameron, A. (2009). *Collaborative Leadership: How to Succeed in an Interconnected World.* Burlington, MA: Elsevier, Ltd.

Aristotle (350 B.C.E.). *Poetics.* Translated by S. H. Butcher. Retrieved April 22, 2015 from http://classics.mit.edu/Aristotle/poetics.1.1.html

Arndt, M., Nairz, O., Vos-Andreae, J., Keller, C., Van der Zouw, G., & Zeilinger, A. (1999, October 14). Nature: Wave–particle duality of C_{60} molecules.

Aronne, L. J., Mackintosh, R., Rosenbaum, M., Leibel, R. L., & Hirsch, J. (1997). Cardiac autonomic nervous system activity in obese and never-obese young men. *Obesity Research, 5*(4), 354–359. doi:10.1002/j.1550-8528.1997.tb00564.x PMID:9285844

Axmacher, N., Mormann, F., Fernandez, G., Elger, C., & Fell, J. (2006). Memory formation by neuronal synchronization. *Brain Research. Brain Research Reviews, 52*(1), 170–182. doi:10.1016/j.brainresrev.2006.01.007 PMID:16545463

Baars, B.J. (1997). In the theatre of consciousness: global workspace theory, a rigorous scientific theory of consciousness. *Journal of Consciousness Studies*, 4(4), 292.

BadKing. (2013). BadKing's Mega Monster Brush Pack. *BadKing. ZBrush Development & Resources.* Retrieved from http://www.badking.com.au/site/badkings-mega-monster-brush-pack/

Barker, C. (2005). *Cultural Studies: Theory and Practice* (p. 448). London: Sage.

Barker, R., & Longman, C. (1992). *Case Method: Function and Process Modeling.* Addison-Wesley Professional.

Barr, A., & Winkler, R. (2015). Can Google Outsell Amazon and eBay? Company will launch buy buttons on its search-results pages in coming weeks. *Wall Street Journal.* Retrieved from http://www.wsj.com/articles/can-google-outsell-amazon-and-ebay-1431730741

Bartle, R. A. (2004). *Designing virtual worlds.* Berkeley, CA: New Riders.

Bartle, R. A. (2010). From MUDs to MMORPGs: The History of Virtual Worlds. In J. Hunsinger, L. Klastrup, & M. Allen (Eds.), *International Handbook of Internet Research.* Netherlands: Springer.

Bartsch, H., Bartsch, C., Mecke, D., & Lippert, T. H. (1994). Seasonality of pineal melatonin production in the rat: Possible synchronization by the geomagnetic field. *Chronobiology International*, *11*(1), 21–26. doi:10.3109/07420529409057227 PMID:8013047

Baselli, G. et al.. (1994). Model for the assessment of heart period variability interactions of respiration influences. *Medical and Biological Engineering and Computing*, 32(2), 143-152.

Bates, B. (2004). *Game Design* (2nd ed.). Boston: Thomson Course Technology PTR.

Beebe, J. (2001). The anima in film. In C. Hauke & I. Alister (Eds.), *Jung & Film: Post-Jungian takes on the moving image* (pp. 208–225). Hove, East Sussex: Brunner-Routledge.

Beebe, J. (2011). 'The Wizard of Oz'. A vision of development in the American political psyche. In C. Hauke & L. Hockley (Eds.), *Jung & Film II: the return. Further post-Jungian takes on the moving image* (pp. 302–327). London: Routledge.

Bell, J. S. (1987). *Speakable and Unspeakable in Quantum Mechanics.* CERN.

Bellman, O. (2015). Researchers create virtual humans. Playa Vista, CA: USC Institute for Creative Technologies. Retrieved from http://www.army.mil/article/147822

Belov, D. R., Kanunikov, I. E., & Kiselev, B. V. (1998). Dependence of human EEGsynchronization on the geomagnetic activity on the day of experiment. *Rossiiskii Fiziologicheskii Zhurnal Imeni I. M. Sechenova*, *84*(8), 761–774.

Bendis, B. M., McNiven, S., & Pichelli, S. (2014). *Guardians of the Galaxy.* New York, NY: Marvel Worldwide, Inc.

Berger, H. (1931/1969). On the electroencephalogram of man: Third report. *Electroencephalography and Clinical Neurophysiology. Supplement*, *28*, 95–132. PMID:4188920

Berger, R. (1963). Experimental modification of dream content by meaningful verbal stimuli. *The British Journal of Psychiatry*, *109*(463), 722–740. doi:10.1192/bjp.109.463.722 PMID:14080566

Bergiannaki, J.-D., Paparrigopoulos, T. J., & Stefanis, C. N. (1996). Seasonal pattern of melatonin excretion in humans: Relationship to day length variation rate and geomagnetic field fluctuations. *Experientia*, *52*(3), 253–258. doi:10.1007/BF01920718 PMID:8631397

Berk, M., Dodd, S., & Henry, M. (2006). Do ambient electromagnetic fields affect behaviour? A demonstration of the relationship between geomagnetic storm activity and suicide. *Bioelectromagnetics*, *27*(2), 151–155. doi:10.1002/bem.20190 PMID:16304696

Berman, D. & Davis-Berman, J. (2005). Positive Psychology and Outdoor Education. *The Journal of Experiential Education,* 28(1), 17-24.

Besserve, M., Jerbi, K., Laurent, F., Baillet, S., Martinerie, J., & Garnero, L. (2007). Classification methods for ongoing EEG and MEG signals. *Biological Research*, *20*, 415–437. PMID:18575676

Biocca, F., Kim, T., & Levy, M. R. (1995). The vision of virtual reality. In F. Biocca (Ed.), *Communication in the age of virtual reality* (pp. 3–14). Hillsdale, NJ: Erlbaum.

BioShock [Computer software]. (2007). Novato, CA: 2K Games.

BioShock Infinite [Computer software]. (2013). Novato, CA: 2K Games.

Bishop, J., Bishop, M., Bishop, M., Gelbwasser, L., Green, S., Peterson, E., & Zuckerman, A. et al. (2004). Why we harass nerds and freaks: A formal theory of student culture and norms. *The Journal of School Health*, *74*(7), 235–251. doi:10.1111/j.1746-1561.2004.tb08280.x PubMed doi:10.1111/j.1746-1561.2004.tb08280.x PMID:15493701

Bits & Beasts. (2008/15). *Feist. Zurich: University of the Arts (ZHdK).* Austin: Finji.

Blackmore, S. (2012). *Consciousness: An introduction* (2nd ed.). Oxford, UK: Oxford University Press.

Blaha, S. (2000). *Cosmos and Consciousness*. New Hampshire: Price Hill Publishing.

Blow, J. (2008). *Braid*. San Francisco: Microsoft Studios.

Blume, W. (2006). Drug effects on EEG. *Journal of Clinical Neurophysiology*, *23*(4), 306–311. doi:10.1097/01.wnp.0000229137.94384.fa PMID:16885705

Bohm, D. (1989). Quantum Theory. New York: Prentice Hall. (Original work published in 1951). Retrieved from http://en.wikipedia.org/wiki/David_Bohm

Bohm, D., & Hiley, B. J. (1993). *The Undivided Universe*. London: Routledge.

Bolier, L., Haverman, M., Westerhof, G. J., Riper, H., Smit, F., & Bohlmeijer, E. (2013). Positive psychology interventions: A meta-analysis of randomized controlled studies. *BMC Public Health*, *13*(1), 1–20. doi:10.1186/1471-2458-13-119 PMID:23390882

Bond, M. H. (2004). Culture and aggression- From context to coercion. *Personality and Social Psychology Review*, *8*(1), 62–78. http://psr.sagepub.com/content/8/1/62.short doi:10.1207/s15327957pspr0801_3 PMID:15121540

Booker, C. (2004). *The Seven Basic Plots. Why we tell stories*. London: Bloomsbury.

Born, M. (1926). Zur quantenmechanik der stoßvorgänge. *Zeitschrift fur Physik*, *37*(12), 863–867. doi:10.1007/BF01397477

Bortolussi, F. (2012). Designing Scary Film Monsters in ZBrush." *Digital-Tutors*. Retrieved from http://www.digitaltutors.com/tutorial/752-Designing-Scary-Film-Monsters-in-ZBrush

Bortz, M. (2009). Tomorrow belongs to me. *Jung Journal: Culture & Psyche*, *3*(4), 69–77. doi:10.1525/jung.2009.3.4.69

Bostrom, N. (2011). *World Science Festival Video Are We Living in a Simulation?* Retrieved from https://www.youtube.com/watch?v=iq1vly0HHo

Bostrom, N. (2003). Are you living in a computer simulation? *The Philosophical Quarterly*, *53*(211), 243–255. doi:10.1111/1467-9213.00309

Botha, M. P. (2006). *Jans Rautenbach: dromer, baanbreker en auteur. Parklands: Genugtig! Botha, MP. (2012). South African cinema 1896-2010.* Bristol: Intellect.

Box Office Mojo. (2014). *2014 Domestic Grosses*. Retrieved from http://www.boxofficemojo.com/yearly/chart/?yr=2014

Box Office Mojo. (2015). *DC Comics Movies*. Retrieved from http://www.boxofficemojo.com/franchises/chart/?view=main&id=dccomics.htm&sort=date&order=DESC&p=.htm

Boyd, F. (2015). Immersive Media: To the Holodeck and Beyond. Retrieved from https://www.linkedin.com/grp/post/1039687-6004890688691453955

Boyes, A., & Gackenbach, J. I. (2014, June). Nightmare protection hypothesis and female gamers. *Paper presented at theannual meeting of the International Association for the Study of Dreams*, Berkley, CA.

Brace, C. S. (2012). *Of dice and men: An ethnography of contemporary gaming subculture* [Master's thesis]. University of Arkansas.

Bradley, R. T., Gillin, M., McCraty, R., & Atkinson, M. (2011). Nonlocal Intuition in Entrepreneurs and Non-entrepreneurs: Results of Two Experiments Using Electrophysiological Measures. *International Journal of Entrepreneurship and Small Business*, *12*(3), 343–372. doi:10.1504/IJESB.2011.039012

Bradley, R. T., McCraty, R., Atkinson, M., & Gillin, M. (2007). Reducing Test Anxiety and Improving Test Performance in America's Schools: Results from the TestEdge National Demonstration StudyBoulder Creek, CA: HeartMath Research Center, Institute of HeartMath, Publication No. 07-09-01.

Bradley, R. T., McCraty, R., Atkinson, M., & Gillin, M. (Eds.). (2008). Nonlocal Intuition in Entrepreneurs and Nonentrepreneurs: An Experimental Comparison Using Electrophysiological Measures. Regional Frontiers of Entrepreneurship Research, Hawthorne, Australia.

Bradley, R. T., McCraty, R., Atkinson, M., Tomasino, D., Daugherty, A., & Arguelles, L. (2010). Emotion Self-Regulation, Psychophysiological Coherence, and Test Anxiety: Results from an Experiment Using Electrophysiological Measures. *Applied Psychophysiology and Biofeedback*, *35*(4), 261–283. doi:10.1007/s10484-010-9134-x PMID:20559707

Broodryk, C. W. (2006). *The moving image: contemporary film analysis and analytical psychology.* (Unpublished master's thesis). University of Pretoria, Pretoria.

Broodryk, C. (2013). A cinema of exploration: In conversation with Oliver Hermanus. *International Journal of Cinema*, *1*, 31–33.

Brown, R & Gerbarg, P. (2009). Yoga Breathing, Meditation, and Longevity. *Annals of the New York: Academy of Sciences* (Vol. 1172).

Brown, E. C., Low, S., Smith, B. H., & Haggerty, K. P. (2011). Outcomes from a school-randomized controlled trial of Steps to Respect: A bullying prevention program. *School Psychology Review*, *40*(3), 423–443.

Buckner, R., Andrews-Hanna, J., & Schacter, D. (2008). The brain's default network – Anatomy, function and relevance to disease. *Annals of the New York Academy of Sciences*, *1124*(1), 1–38. doi:10.1196/annals.1440.011 PMID:18400922

Buckner, R., & Carroll, D. (2007). Self projection and the brain. *Trends in Cognitive Sciences*, *11*(2), 49–57. doi:10.1016/j.tics.2006.11.004 PMID:17188554

Burch, J. B., Reif, J. S., & Yost, M. G. (1999). Geomagnetic disturbances are associated with reduced nocturnal excretion of a melatonin metabolite in humans. *Neuroscience Letters*, *266*(3), 209–212. doi:10.1016/S0304-3940(99)00308-0 PMID:10465710

Buzsaki, G. (2005). Theta rhythm of navigation: Link between path integration and landmark navigation, episodic and semantic memory. *Hippocampus*, *15*(7), 827–840. doi:10.1002/hipo.20113 PMID:16149082

Buzsaki, G. (2006). *Rhythms of the Brain*. Oxford: Oxford University Press. doi:10.1093/acprof:oso/9780195301069.001.0001

Cacioppo, J. T., Tassinary, L. G., & Berntson, G. G. (Eds.). (2007). *Handbook of psychophysiology* (3rd ed., p. 121). New York: Cambridge Univ. Press. doi:10.1017/CBO9780511546396

Cahn, B., Delorme, A., & Polich, J. (2010). Occipital gamma activation during Vipassana meditation. *Cognitive Processing*, *11*(1), 39–56. doi:10.1007/s10339-009-0352-1 PMID:20013298

Campbell, J. (1949). *The Hero with a Thousand Faces*. New York: Bollingen Foundation.

Campbell, J. (1973). *The hero with a thousand faces*. Princeton, NJ: First Princeton/Bolingen.

Campbell, J., & Moyers, B. (1991). *The Power of Myth. New York: Anchor Books.*

Campbell, T. (2007). *My big TOE: The complete trilogy*. Huntsville, AL: Lighting Strike Books.

Cantero, J., & Atienza, M. (2005). The role of neural synchronization n the emergence of cognition across the wake-sleep cycle. *Reviews in the Neurosciences*, *16*(1), 69–83. doi:10.1515/REVNEURO.2005.16.1.69 PMID:15810655

Cantero, J., Atienza, M., Stickgold, R., Kahana, M., Madsen, J., & Kocsis, B. (2003). Sleep dependent theta occilations in the human hippocampus and neocortex. *The Journal of Neuroscience*, *23*, 10897–10903. PMID:14645485

Capra, F. (1976). *The tau of physics*. Boulder, CO: Shambhala Publications, Inc.

Cardboard Computer, C. (2013). Kentucky Route Zero. Chicago: Cardboard Computer.

Cartwright, N. (1983). *How the Laws of Physics Lie*. Oxford University Press. doi:10.1093/0198247044.001.0001

Cash, S., Halgren, E., Dehghani, N., Rossetti, A., Thesen, T., Wang, C., & Ulbert, I. et al. (2009). The human K-complex represents an isolated cortical down state. *Science*, *324*(5930), 1084–1087. doi:10.1126/science.1169626 PMID:19461004

Castronova, E. (2007). *Exodus to the virtual world: How online fun is changing reality*. New York, NY: Palgrave Macmillan.

Cernouss, S., Vinogradov, A., & Vlassova, E. (2001). Geophysical Hazard for Human Health in the Circumpolar Auroral Belt: Evidence of a Relationship between Heart Rate Variation and Electromagnetic Disturbances. *Natural Hazards*, *23*(2/3), 121–135. doi:10.1023/A:1011108723374

Chalmers, R. (2015). *Summary of scientific research on Maharishi's Transcendental Meditation and Transcendental Meditation-Sidhi program.* Retrieved from http://www.truthabouttm.org/truth/TMResearch/TMResearchSummary/index.cfm

Chan, A., Han, Y., & Chueng, M. (2008). Electroencephalographic (EEG) measurements of mindfulness-based Trirchic body-pathway relaxation technique: A pilot study. *Applied Psychophysiology and Biofeedback*, *33*(1), 39–47. doi:10.1007/s10484-008-9050-5 PMID:18214668

Cheek, T. R. (1989). Spatial aspects of calcium signaling. *Journal of Cell Science*, *93*, 211–216. PMID:2613762

Cherry, K. (n. d.). What is Flow? Understanding the Psychology of Flow. Retrieved from psychology.about.com/od/positive psychology/a/flow.htm

Cherry, N. (2002). Schumann Resonances, a plausible biophysical mechanism for the human health effects of Solar/ Geomagnetic Activity. *Natural Hazards*, *26*(3), 279–331. doi:10.1023/A:1015637127504

Chiesa, A. (2009). Zen meditation: An integration of current evidence. *Journal of Alternative and Complementary Medicine (New York, N.Y.)*, *15*(5), 585–592. doi:10.1089/acm.2008.0416 PMID:19422285

Cho, B., & Lee, J. K. U. J Jang D, et al. (2002), Attention Enhancement System using Virtual Reality and EEG Biofeedback. *Proceedings of the IEEE Virtual Reality*.

Chopra, D. (1995). Body, Mind, and Soul: The mystery and the magic (VHS). Public Broadcasting Service/Turner Home Entertainment: Atlanta, GA.

Chopra, D. (1995). Body, mind, and soul: The mystery and the magic. Atlanta, GA: Turner Home Entertainment; Public Broadcasting Service.

Christakos, C. N. (1986). The mathematical basis of population rhythms in nervous and neuromuscular systems. *The International Journal of Neuroscience*, *29*(1-2), 103–107. doi:10.3109/00207458608985640 PMID:3699995

Christoff, K., Gordon, A., Smallwood, J., Smith, R., & Schooler, W. (2009). Experience sampling during fMRI reveals default network and executive system contributions to mind wandering. *Proceedings of the National Academy of Sciences of the United States of America*, 106(21), 8719-8724. PMID:19433790

Claes, Z. (2014). Three neuromarketing lessons derived from video games. *Neuromarketing*. Retrieved from http://www.neurosciencemarketing.com/blog/articles/neuromarketing-video-games.html

Clarke, D. S. (2004). *Panpsychism: Past and recent selected readings*. New York, NY: State University of New York Press.

Coburn, K., Lauterbach, E., Boutros, N., Black, K., Arciniegas, D., & Coffey, C. (2006). The value of quantitative electroencephalography in clinical psychiatry: A report by the committee on research of the American Neuropsychiatic Association. *The Journal of Neuropsychiatry and Clinical Neurosciences*, *18*(4), 460–500. doi:10.1176/jnp.2006.18.4.460 PMID:17135374

COCORO. anon. (2015). COCORO: robot swarms use collective cognition to perform tasks.European Commission: Digital Agenda for Europe. Retrieved from https://ec.europa.eu/digital-agenda/en/news/cocoro-robot-swarms-use-collective-cognition-perform-tasks

Coffey, M. (2008). *Explorers of the Infinite*. New York: Jeremy P. Tarcher/Penguin Books.

Cole, M., & Derry, J. (2005). We have met technology and it is us. In R. J. Sternberg & D. D. Preiss (Eds.), *Intelligence and technology: The impact of tools on the nature and development of human abilities* (pp. 209–228). Mahwah, NJ: Erlbaum.

Collier, J., Burckhardt, C. B., & Lin, L. H. (1971). *Optical Holography*. New York: Academic Press.

Cornelissen, G., Halberg, F., Schwartkopff, O., Delmore, P., Katinas, G., & Hunter, D. et al.. (1993). Chronomes, Time Structures, for Chronobioengineering for "A Full Life". *Biomedical Instrumentation & Technology*, *1999*(33), 152–187. PMID:10194568

Corsi-Cabrerra, M., Guevara, M., & Rio-Portilla, Y. (2008). Brain activity and temporal coupling related to eye movements during REM sleep: EEG and MEG results. *Brain Research*, *1235*, 82–91. doi:10.1016/j.brainres.2008.06.052 PMID:18625213

Costet, D. (Producer) & Hermanus, O. (Director). (2011). *Skoonheid* [Motion Picture]. South Africa: Swift Productions.

Cover, J. G. (2010). *The creation of narrative in tabletop role-playing games*. Jefferson, NC: McFarland & Company, Inc.

Crawford, K. H. (2015). Here's looking at you: ONR tests new glasses for augmented reality system with Marines. *Office of Naval Research.* Retrieved from http://www.onr.navy.mil/en/Media-Center/Press-Releases/2015/Augmented-Reality-Demo-With-Marines.aspx

Crick, F. (1994). *The Astonishing Hypothesis: The Scientific Search for the Soul.* New York: Charles Scribner's Sons.

Cruise, T., & Wagner, P. (Producer), & De Palma, B. (Director). (1996). Mission: Impossible. United States: Paramount Pictures.

Csíkszentmihályi, M. (1990). *Flow: The Psychology of Optimal Experience.* Harper & Row.

Cumming, G. (2013). *Substantial changes to how we conduct research needed.* Statistical Cognition Laboratory, La Trobe University. Retrieved from http://pss.sagepub.com/content/25/1/7.full

Cumming, G. (2013). The New Statistics. *Psychological Science*, 25(1), 7-29. Retrieved from http://pss.sagepub.com/content/25/1/7.full

Cunningham, R. (2013, May 10). Alaskan Dreams: My Wilderness Experience. Retrieved from http://www.splitboard-bindings.com

Curtis, A. (2002). The century of self. *BBC.* Retrieved from http://topdocumentaryfilms.com/the-century-of-the-self/

Curtis, A. (2009). *Century of the self: Happiness machines for free.* British Broadcasting Corporation, Freedocumentaries.com. Retrieved from http://freedocumentaries.org/film.php?id=140

Curtis, A. (2009). Century of the self: Happiness machines for free. *Freedocumentaries.com.* Retrieved from http://freedocumentaries.org/film.php?id=140

Daoust, A., Lusignan, F., Braun, C., Mottron, L., & Godbout, R. (2008). EEG correlates of emotions in dream narratives from typical young adults and individuals with autistic spectrum disorders. *Psychophysiology, 45*(2), 299–308. doi:10.1111/j.1469-8986.2007.00626.x PMID:18047484

Darowski, J. (2014). *The Ages of the X-Men: Essays on the Children of the Atom in Changing Times.* Jefferson, NC: McFarland & Company, Inc.

Davis, B. M. (1997). *The Archetypal Hero in Literature, Religion, Movies, and Popular Culture* Retrieved from http://www.tatsbox.com/hero

Davis, M. (1965). *The undecidable, basic papers on undecidable propositions, unsolvable problems and computable functions.* New York, NY: Raven Press.

De Cristofaro, E. (2014). Facebook "Likes". *The European Multidisciplinary Society for Modeling and Simulation Technology.* Retrieved from http://www.technologyreview.com/view/530961/the-hidden-world-of-facebook-like-farms/

De Kock, L. (2003). South Africa in the global imaginary: an introduction. In L. de Kock, L. Bethlehem, & S. Laden (Eds.), *South Africa in the global imaginary.* Pretoria: University of South Africa Press.

De Kock, L., Bethlehem, L., & Laden, S. (Eds.). (2003). *South Africa in the global imaginary.* Pretoria: University of South Africa Press.

De Koven, B. (2013). *The well-played game: A player's philosophy.* Cambridge, MA: The MIT Press.

deBoer, R. W., Karemaker, J. M., & Strackee, J. (1987). Hemodynamic fluctuations and baroreflex sensitivity in humans: A beat-to-beat model. *The American Journal of Physiology, 253*(3 Pt 2), H680–H689. PMID:3631301

DeLuca, M., Beckmann, C., DeStafano, N., Matthews, P., & Smith, S. (2006). fMRI resting state networks define distinct modes of long-distant interactions in the human brain. *NeuroImage*, *29*(4), 1359–1367. doi:10.1016/j.neuroimage.2005.08.035 PMID:16260155

Dement, W., & Wolpert, E. (1958). The relation of eye movements, body motility, and external stimuli to dream content. *Journal of Experimental Psychology*, *55*(6), 543–553. doi:10.1037/h0040031 PMID:13563767

Demers, T. (2014). Using gamefication to drive brand awareness. *Small Business Trends*. Retrieved from http://smallbiztrends.com/2014/03/using-gamification-brand-awareness.html

DeSilva, B., & Sistrom, J. (Producer), & Wilder, B. (Director). (1944). Double Indemnity. United States: Paramount Pictures.

DeValois, Karen, & DeValois, Russell, and Yund, W. W. (1979). Responses of striate cortex cells to grating and checkerboard patterns. *The Journal of Psychology*, *291*, 483–505. PMID:113531

Deyhle, A. (2010) Interconnectedness. *Global Coherence Initiative Commentary*. Retrieved from http://www.glcoherence.org/monitoring-system/commentaries.html

Deyhle, A. (2013). Solar Activity, Global Coherence Monitoring System and Saudi Arabia HRVStudy. *Global Coherence Initiative Commentary*. Retrieved from http://www.glcoherence.org/monitoring-system/commentaries.html

Dimitrova, S., Stoilova, I., & Cholakov, I. (2004). Influence of Local Geomagnetic Storms on Arterial Blood Pressure. *Bioelectromagnetics*, *25*(6), 408–414. doi:10.1002/bem.20009 PMID:15300726

Ditner, A. (2015, January). Female gamers and the nightmare protection thesis: A further exploration. *Paper presented at the MacEwan Student Research Showcase*, Edmonton, Alberta.

Ditner, A., Hakopdjanian, S., & Gackenbach, J. (2015, June). Video game play and nightmare protection hypothesis: A cross cultural analysis. *Poster presented at the International Association for the Study of Dreams conference*, Virginia Beach, VA.

Dolgato, K. M., & Kholodov, Y. A. (1987). Magnetic fields and brain. *Future Science*, *20*, 133.

Domhoff, G. W. (2007). Realistic simulation and bizarreness in dream content: Past findings and suggestions for future research. In D. Barrett & P. McNamara (Eds.), The new science of dreaming: Vol. 2. *Content recall, and personality characteristics* (pp. 1–27). Westport, CT: Praeger Press.

Domhoff, W. (2003). *The Scientific Study of Dreams*. Washington, DC: American Psychological Association.

Dooley, R. (2015). Repeat, repeat, repeat…and sell. *Neuromarketing*. Retrieved from http://www.neurosciencemarketing.com/blog/articles/repetition.htm

Doronin, V. N., Parfentev, V. A., & Tleulin, S. Zh., Namvar, R.A., Somsikov, V.M., Drobzhev, V.I. & Chemeris (1998). A.V. Effect of variations of the geomagnetic field and solar activity on human physiological indicators. *Biofizika*, *43*(4), 647–653. PMID:9783072

Dossey, L. (1982). *Space, time, and medicine* (pp. 108–109). Boston: New Science Library.

Double Fine Productions. (2005). Psychonauts. Eddison, NJ: Majesco Entertainment, THQ.

Double Fine Productions. (2015). *Grim Fandango Remastered*. San Francisco: Double Fine Productions.

Drinkwater, B. A. (1976). Visual memory skills of medium contact aboriginal children. *Australian Journal of Psychology*, *28*(1), 37–43. doi:10.1080/00049537608255261

Duckworth, A., Peterson, C., Matthews, M., & Kelly, D. (2007). Grit: Perseverance and Passion for Long-Term Goals. *Journal of Personality and Social Psychology*, *92*(6), 1087–1101. doi:10.1037/0022-3514.92.6.1087 PMID:17547490

Duggan, M., & Smith, A. (2014, December 30). Social media update 2013. Retrieved from http://pewinternet.org/Reports/2013/Social-Media-Update.aspx

Dundes, A. (1965). *The Study of Folklore*. Upper Saddle River: Prentice Hall College.

Duriez, C. (2012). *Amazing & Extraordinary Facts: J.R.R. Tolkien*. Devon, UK: David & Charles.

Durkheim, E. (1961). *The elementary forms of the religious life*. New York, NY: Collier Books.

Ecosystems associated with personal data is creating an entirely new field of scientific study (2015). The MIT Technology Review. Retrieved from http://www.technologyreview.com/view/533901/the-emerging-science-of-human-data-interaction/)

Eddington, A. (1935). *The Nature of the physical world*. Cambridge University Press.

Edinger, E. F. (1984). *The creation of consciousness. Jung's myth for modern man*. Toronto: Inner City Books.

Edinger, E. F. (1985). *Anatomy of the psyche: alchemical symbolism in psychotherapy*. Chicago, Illinois: Open Court.

Egan, K. (1986). *Teaching as storytelling: an alternative approach to teaching and curriculum in the elementary school*. London, Ontario: The University of Western Ontario.

Einstein, A., Podolsky, B., & Rosen, N. (1935). Can Quantum-Mechanical Description of Physical Reality Be Considered Complete? *Physical Review*, *47*(10), 777–780. doi:10.1103/PhysRev.47.777

Ellenberger, H. F. (1994). *The discovery of the unconscious: the history and evolution of dynamic psychiatry*. London: Fontana Press.

Elsaesser, T. (1989). *New German cinema: a history*. London: Palgrave MacMillan.

Elsaesser, T. (2005). *European cinema: face-to-face with Hollywood*. Amsterdam: Amsterdam University Press. doi:10.5117/9789053566022

Elsaesser, T. (2009). Real location, fantasy space, performative place: double occupancy and mutual interference in European cinema. In T. Trifonova (Ed.), *European Film Theory* (pp. 47–62). New York, NY: Routledge.

Elul, R. (1971). The genesis of the EEG. *International Review of Neurobiology*, *15*, 227–272. doi:10.1016/S0074-7742(08)60333-5 PMID:4949975

Emerson, R. (2009, September). *Nature, Chapter One*. Retrieved from www.emersoncentral.com

Ertel, S. (1996). Space weather and revolutions: Chizhevsky's heliobiological claim scrutinized. *Studia Psychologica*, *39*, 3–22.

Evenson, L. (1998, October 27). Fleshing Out an Idea. *San Francisco Chronicle*. Retrieved from http://www.sfgate.com/entertainment/article/Fleshing-Out-an-Idea-Day-of-the-Dead-inspires-2982510.php

Fable 2. (n. d.). *Microsoft Corporation*. Retrieved from http://www.lionhead.com/Fable2/About.aspx

Facebook, Inc. (2014). Stats. Retrieved from http://newsroom.fb.com/company-info/

Fairbanks, A. (1898). *The first philosophers of Greece*. London, UK: Kegan Paul, Trench, Trübner & Co. Ltd.

Feige, K., Penn, Z., & Whedon, J. (2012). *Marvel's The Avengers*. Burbank, CA: Distributed by Buena Vista Home Entertainment.

Feldman, J. (2006). From molecule to metaphor. Cambridge, MA: MIT ress.

Fell, J., Axmacher, N., & Haupt, S. (2010). From alpha to gamma: Electrophysiological correlates of meditation-related states of consciousness. *Medical Hypotheses*, *75*(2), 218–224. doi:10.1016/j.mehy.2010.02.025 PMID:20227193

Ferriera, R. (2012). Oesterheld's Iconic and Ironic Eternautas. In M. E. Ginway & J. A. Brown (Eds.), *Latin American Science Fiction: Theory and Practice* (pp. 155–184). New York: Palgrave Macmillan. doi:10.1057/9781137312778.0015

Fine, G. A. (1983). *Shared fantasy: Role-playing games as social worlds*. Chicago, IL: University of Chicago Press.

Finglehurts, A., & Finglehurts, A. (2011). Persistent operational synchrony within brain default-mode network and self processing operations in healthy subjects. *Brain and Cognition*, *75*(2), 79–90. doi:10.1016/j.bandc.2010.11.015 PMID:21172727

Flanery, P. D. (2009). What national cinema? South African film cultures and the transnational. *Safundi: the Journal of South African and American Studies*, *10*(2), 239–253. doi:10.1080/17533170902793174

Flowers, M. (2014). *J.R.R. Tolkien Timeline*. Retrieved from http://www.tolkiensociety.org/author/timeline/

Fordham, F. (2013, October). *Introduction to Jung's Psychology, Chapter One*. Retrieved from http://www.cgjungpage.org

Foster, D. (1985). *The philosophical scientists*. USA: Dorset Press.

Foulkes, D. (1985). *Dreaming: A Cognitive-Psychological Analysis*. Hillsdale, NJ: Lawrence Erlbaum Associates.

Fox, M., & Raichle, M. (2007). Spontaneous fluctuations in brain activity observed with functional magnetic resonance imaging. *Nature Reviews. Neuroscience*, *8*(9), 700–711. doi:10.1038/nrn2201 PMID:17704812

Fredericksen, D. (2001). Jung/sign/symbol/film. In C. Hauke & I. Alister (Eds.), *Jung & Film: Post-Jungian takes on the moving image* (pp. 17–55). Hove, East Sussex: Brunner-Routledge.

Fredericksen, D. (2011). Jungian film studies. The corruption of consciousness and the nurturing of psychological life. In C. Hauke & L. Hockley (Eds.), *Jung & Film II: the return. Further post-Jungian takes on the moving imag* (pp. 99–108). London: Routledge.

Freud, S. (1903). The Interpretation of Dreams. In J. Strachey (Ed.), The Standard Editions of the Complete Psychological Works of Sigmund Freud (Vol. IV and V). London, England: Hogarth Press (1953).

Freud, S. (1919). Das Unheimliche. In Imago. Zeitschrift für Anwendung der Psychoanalyse auf die Geisteswissenschaften, 5, 297 - 324.

Freud, S. (1899). *The interpretation of dreams*. Bellingham, WA: Barnes & Noble.

Freud, S. (1923). *Das Ich und das Es*. Leipzig: Internationaler Psychoanalytischer Verlag.

Frie, R. (2008). Psychological agency: Theory, practice, and culture. Cambridge, MA: The MIT Press; Retrieved from http://mitpress.mit.edu/books/psychological-agency

Frigg & Hartman. (2009). Models in Science. In E.N. Zalta (Ed.), The Stanford Encyclopedia of Philosophy (Summer 2009 ed.).

Frysinger, R. C., & Harper, R. M. (1990). Cardiac and respiratory correlations with unit discharge in epileptic human temporal lobe. *Epilepsia*, *31*(2), 162–171. doi:10.1111/j.1528-1167.1990.tb06301.x PMID:2318169

Fu, A., & Murray, M. J. (2007). Cinema and the edgy city: Johannesburg, carjacking, and the postmetropolis. *African Identities*, *5*(2), 279–289. doi:10.1080/14725840701403606

Gabriel, C. (Producer), & Gabriel, I. (Director). (2004). *Forgiveness*. South Africa: Giant Films, DV8 Films.

Gackenbach, J. I., & Flockhart, C. (2013). Nightmare protection thesis of video game play in first responders. *International Journal of Dream Research: Supplement* (pdf). doi: 10.11588/ijodr.2013.0.10874

Gackenbach, J. I. (2006). Video game play and lucid dreams: Implications for the development of consciousness. *Dreaming*, *16*(2), 96–110. doi:10.1037/1053-0797.16.2.96

Gackenbach, J. I. (2008). Video game play and consciousness development: A transpersonal perspective. *Journal of Transpersonal Psychology*, *40*(1), 60–87.

Gackenbach, J. I. (2009). Electronic media and lucid-control dreams: Morning after reports. *Dreaming*, *19*(1), 1–6. doi:10.1037/a0013781

Gackenbach, J. I. (2012). Video game play and dreams. In D. Barrett & P. McNamara (Eds.), *Encyclopedia of sleep and dreams* (pp. 795–800). Santa Barbara, CA: ABC-CLIO.

Gackenbach, J. I., & Bosveld, J. (1989). *Control your dreams*. New York, NY: Harper and Row.

Gackenbach, J. I., & Bown, J. (2011). Mindfulness and video game play: A preliminary inquiry. *Mindfulness*, *2*(2), 114–122. http://www.springerlink.com/content/p26n3h1uq1w00771/ doi:10.1007/s12671-011-0049-2

Gackenbach, J. I., & Boyes, A. (2014a). Non-gaming computer use relationship to type of dream. *International Journal of Dream Research*, *7*(2), 95–104.

Gackenbach, J. I., & Boyes, A. (2014b). Social media versus gaming associations with typical and recent dreams. *Dreaming*, *24*(3), 182–202. doi:10.1037/a0037616

Gackenbach, J. I., Darlington, M., Ferguson, M. L., & Boyes, A. (2013). Video game play as nightmare protection: A replication and extension. *Dreaming*, *23*(2), 97–111. doi:10.1037/a0032455

Gackenbach, J. I., & Dopko, R. (2012). The relationship between video game play, dream bizarreness, and creativity. *International Journal of Dream Research*, *5*(1), 23–36.

Gackenbach, J. I., Ellerman, E., & Hall, C. (2011). Video game play as nightmare protection: A preliminary inquiry in military gamers. *Dreaming*, *21*(4), 221–245. doi:10.1037/a0024972

Gackenbach, J. I., & Gahr, S. (2015). Media use and dreams associations between Canadians of differing cultural backgrounds. *International Journal of Dream Research*, *8*(1).

Gackenbach, J. I., Heilman, N., Boyt, S., & LaBerge, S. (1985). The relationship between field independence and lucid dreaming ability. *Journal of Mental Imagery*, *9*, 9–20.

Gackenbach, J. I., & Hunt, H. (2014). A deeper inquiry into the association between lucid dreams and video game play. In R. Hurd & K. Buckeley (Eds.), *Lucid dreaming cross cultural understandings of consciousness in the dream state*. Santa Barbara, CA: ABC-CLIO.

Gackenbach, J. I., & Kuruvilla, B. (2008). The relationship between video game play and threat simulation dreams. *Dreaming*, *18*(4), 236–256. doi:10.1037/a0013782

Gackenbach, J. I., Kuruvilla, B., & Dopko, R. (2009). Video game play and dream bizarreness. *Dreaming*, *19*(4), 218–231. doi:10.1037/a0018145

Gackenbach, J. I., Matty, I., Kuruvilla, B., Samaha, A. N., Zederayko, A., Olischefski, J., & Von Stackelberg, H. (2009). Video game play: Waking and dreaming consciousness. In S. Krippner & D. Ellis (Eds.), *Perchance to dream* (pp. 239–253). Hauppauge, NY: Nova Science Publishers.

Gackenbach, J. I., & Rosie, M. (2011). Presence in video game play and nighttime dreams: An empirical inquiry. *International Journal of Dream Research*, *4*(2), 98–109.

Gackenbach, J. I., Sample, T., & Mandel, G. (2011). The continuity versus discontinuity hypotheses: A consideration of issues for coding video game incorporation. *International Journal of Dream Research*, *4*(2), 63–76.

Gackenbach, J. I., Swanston, D., & Stark, H. (in press). Effects of video game play versus meditation/prayer in waking and dreaming experiences. Paper under editorial consideration. *Journal of Transpersonal Psychology*.

Gackenback, J., & Kurville, B. (2013). Cognitive structure associated with the lucid features of gamer's dreams. *Dreaming*, *23*(4), 256–267. doi:10.1037/a0034817

Gahr, S. (2015, June). The relationship between dreaming and self-construals, sex role orientation and media use in Canadians of differing ethnic backgrounds. Paper to be presented at the International Association for the Study of Dreams, Virginia Beach, VA.

Garling, C. (2015). An algorithm that can help robots walk off injuries. MIT Technology Review. Retrieved from http://www.technologyreview.com/news/537791/an-algorithm-that-can-help-robots-walk-off-injuries/?utm_campaign=newsletters&utm_source=newsletter-daily-all&utm_medium=email&utm_content=20150528#

Gears of War [Computer software]. (2006). Redmond, WA: Microsoft Studios.

Gee, J. P. (2005). *Why video games are good for your soul: Pleasure and learning*. Melbourne, Australia: Common Ground.

Geiger, J. (2010). *The Third Man Factor*. New York: Weinstein Books.

Geiser, M., & Woll, B. (2011). *Journey of a Roach. A Maze Adventure. Unpublished Game Concept*. University of the Arts Zurich.

Georgopoulos, A. P., Karageorgiou, E., Leuthold, A. C., Lewis, S. M., Lynch, J. K., Alonso, A. A., & Westermeyer, J. J. et al. (2007, December). Synchronous neural interactions assessed by magnetoencephalography: A functional biomarker for brain disorders. *Journal of Neural Engineering*, *4*(4), 349–355. doi:10.1088/1741-2560/4/4/001 PMID:18057502

Gergen, K. (2009). *An Invitation to Social Construction* (2nd ed.). Thousand Oaks, CA: SAGE Publications, Inc.

Geril, P. (2014a). Startup Europe- Capacity building for Business Angels (BAs) in ICT/ A digital Agenda for Europe. Retrieved from https://ec.europa.eu/digital-agenda/en/news/startup-europe-capacity-building-business-angels-bas-ict

Geril, P. (2014b). Crowdfunding innovative ventures in Europe - The financial ecosystem and regulatory landscape (SMART 2013/0074) Digital Agenda for Europe. Retrieved from https://ec.europa.eu/digital-agenda/en/news/crowdfunding-innovative-ventures-europe-financial-ecosystem-and-regulatory-landscape-smart

Geril, P. (2014c). Project proposal: Image Recognition to Distinguish Foods inside Refrigerator. *EUROSIS - The European Multidisciplinary Society for Modelling and Simulation Technology* Retrieved from https://www.linkedin.com/grp/post/1039687-5902320911746375684

Geril, P. (2014c). Startup Europe- Capacity building for Business Angels (BAs) in ICT/ A digital Agenda for Europe. *Newsroom*. Retrieved from https://ec.europa.eu/digital-agenda/en/news/startup-europe-capacity-building-business-angels-bas-ict

Geril, P. (2015b). The virtual worlds 2015 survey report. *EUROSIS, The European Multidisciplinary Society for Modelling and Simulation Technology.* Retrieved from https://www.linkedin.com/grp/post/1039687-5988685234479075329

Ghione, S., Mazzasalma, L., Del Seppia, C., & Papi, F. (1998). Do geomagnetic disturbances of solar origin affect arterial blood pressure? *Journal of Human Hypertension, 12*(11), 749–754. doi:10.1038/sj.jhh.1000708 PMID:9844945

Ginsberg,, J.P., Berry, M.E., & Powell, D.A. (2010). Cardiac Coherence and PTSD in CombatVeterans. *Alternative Therapies in Health and Medicine, 16*(4), 52–60. PMID:20653296

Glassner, A. (2004). *Interactive storytelling.* Natick, Massachusetts: A.K. Peters.

Glassner, A. (2004). *Interactive Storytelling. Techniques for 21st Century Fiction.* Natick, Massachusetts: A.K. Peters.

Goffman, E. (1974). *Frame analysis: An essay on the organization of experience.* New York: Harper and Row.

Goleman, D. (1979, February). Holographic memory: interview of Karl Pribram. *Psychology Today, 12*(9), 71–72.

Goodman, B., & Rushkoff, D. (2004). *The Persuaders.* Arlington, VA: WGBH Educational Foundation & PBS Home Video.

Gordon, C., & Berk, M. (2003). The effect of geomagnetic storms on suicide. *South African Psychiatry Review, 6*, 24–27.

Gousheva, M. N., Georgieva, K. Y., Kirov, B. B., & Antanasov, D. (Eds.), (2003, November 20-22). On the relation between solar activity and seismicity. *Proceedings of International Conference on Recent Advances in Space Technologies RAST '03.* doi:10.1109/RAST.2003.1303913

Grand Theft Auto [Computer software]. (1997-2014). New York, NY: Rockstar Games.

Grasse, R. (1996). *The waking dream.* Wheaton, IL: The Theosophical Publishihng House.

Graydon, D. (Ed.), (1992). *Mountaineering: The Freedom of the Hills (5th ed.).* Seattle: The Mountaineers Books.

Green, C. S., & Bavelier, D. (2003). Action video games modifies visual selective attention. *Nature, 423*(6939), 534–537. doi:10.1038/nature01647 PMID:12774121

Greenfield, P. M. (1996). Video games as cultural artifacts. In P. M. Greenfield & R. R. Cocking (Eds.), *Interacting with video: Advances in applied developmental psychology* (Vol. 11, pp. 85–94). Norwood, NJ: Ablex.

Greig, A. (1998). *Summit Fever.* Seattle: Mountaineers Books.

Greitemeyer, T., & Mügge, D. (2014). Video games do affect social outcomes: A meta-analytical review of the effects of violent and prosocial video game play. *Sage Publishing.* Retrieved from http://psp.sagepub.com/content/40/5/578.full

Grigoryev, P., Rozanov, V., Vaiserman, A., & Vladimirskiy, B. (2009). Heliogeophysical factors as possible triggers of suicide terroristic acts. *Health, 1*(4), 294–297. doi:10.4236/health.2009.14048

Gröblacher, S., Paterek, T., Kaltenbaek, R., Brukner, C., Zukowski, M., Aspelmeyer, M., & Zeilinger, A. (2007). An experimental test of non-local realism. *Nature, 446*(7138), 871–875. doi:10.1038/nature05677 PMID:17443179

Gusner, D., & Raichle, M. (2001). Searching for a baseline: Functional imaging and the resting human brain. *Nature Reviews. Neuroscience, 2*(10), 685–694. doi:10.1038/35094500 PMID:11584306

Hacking, I. (1983). *Representing and Intervening. Introductory Topics in the Philosophy of Natural Science.* Cambridge University Press. doi:10.1017/CBO9780511814563

Hahn, D. (Producer), & Allers, R. (Director). (1994). *The Lion King.* United States: Walt Disney Pictures, Buena Vista Pictures.

Halberg, F., Cornelissen, G., McCraty, R. A., & Al-Abdulgader, A. (2011). Time Structures (Chronomes) of the Blood Circulation, Populations' Health, Human Affairs and Space Weather. *World Heart Journal*, *3*(1), 1–40. PMID:24511305

Halberg, F., Cornelissen, G., Otsuka, K., Watanabe, Y., Katinas, G. S., & Burioka, N. et al.. (2000). Cross-spectrally coherent ~10.5- and 21-year biological and physical cycles, magnetic storms and myocardial infarctions. *Neuroendocrinology*, *21*, 233–258. PMID:11455355

Halberg, F., Cornélissen, G., Sothern, R. B., Katinas, G. S., Schwartzkopff, O., & Otsuka, K. (2008). Cycles Tipping the Scale between Death and Survival (="Life"). *Progress of Theoretical Physics Supplement*, *173*, 153–181. doi:10.1143/PTPS.173.153

Hall, M. P. (2003). *The Secret Teachings of All Ages*. New York: Jeremy P. Tarcher/Penguin.

Hamer, J. R. (1965). Biological entrainment of the human brain by low frequency radiation. *Northrop Space Labs.*, *1965*, 65–199.

Hameroff, S., & Penrose, S. R. (2014). Discovery of quantum vibrations in 'mocrotubules' corroborates theory of consciousness. Retrieved from http://phys.org/news/2014-01-discovery-quantum-vibrations-microtubules-corroborates.html)

Hameroff, S., & Penrose, S. R. Discovery of quantum vibrations in 'mocrotubules' corroborates theory of consciousness. Retrieved 1/16/2014 http://phys.org/news/2014-01-discovery-quantum-vibrations-microtubules-corroborates.html)

Hand, M. M., Thomas, D., Buboltz, W. C., Deemer, E. D., & Buyanjargal, M. (2013). Facebook and romantic relationships: Intimacy and couple satisfaction associated with online social network use. *Cyberpsychology, Behavior, and Social Networking*, *16*(1), 8–13. doi:10.1089/cyber.2012.0038 PMID:23101932

Hangya, B., Tihanyi, B., Entz, L., Fabo, D., ErFss, L., Wittner, L., & Ulbert, I. et al. (2011). Complex propagation patterns characterize human cortical activity during slow-wave sleep. *The Journal of Neuroscience*, *31*(24), 8770–8779. doi:10.1523/JNEUROSCI.1498-11.2011 PMID:21677161

Hansen, M. (2006). *Bodies in code: Interfaces with digital media*. New York, NY: Routledge.

Hansen, W. (1994). *Greenland's Icy Fury*. College Station: Texas A&M University Press.

Harold, F. M. (1986). *The vital force: A study of Bioenergetics*. New York: WH Freeman & Co.

Hartmann, E. (1998). *Dreams and Nightmares – the New Theory on the Origin and Meaning of Dreams*. New York: Plenum Trade.

Hartmann, E., & Kunzendorf, R. G. (2006-2007). Boundaries and dreams. *Imagination, Cognition and Personality*, *26*(1-2), 101–115. doi:10.2190/HK76-038K-407M-8670

Hauke, C. (2001). "Let's go back to finding out who we are". Men, *Unheimlich* and returning home in the films of Steven Spielberg. In C. Hauke & I. Alister (Eds.), *Jung & Film: Post-Jungian takes on the moving image* (pp. 151–174). Hove, East Sussex: Brunner-Routledge.

Hauke, C. (2014). *Visible mind: movies, modernity and the unconscious*. London: Routledge.

Hauke, C., & Alister, I. (2001). Introduction. In C. Hauke & I. Alister (Eds.), *Jung & Film: Post-Jungian takes on the moving image* (pp. 1–13). Hove, East Sussex: Brunner-Routledge.

Hauke, C., & Alister, I. (Eds.). (2001). *Jung & Film: Post-Jungian takes on the moving image*. Hove, East Sussex: Brunner-Routledge.

Hauke, C., & Hockley, L. (2011). Introduction. In C. Hauke & L. Hockley (Eds.), *Jung & Film II: the return. Further post-Jungian takes on the moving image* (pp. 1–14). London: Routledge.

Hauke, C., & Hockley, L. (Eds.). (2011). *Jung & Film II: the return. Further post-Jungian takes on the moving image*. London: Routledge.

Headrick. (1990). Looking over the horizon (HF radar). *IEEE Spectrum*, 27, 36-39.

Heisenberg, W. (1927). Über den anschaulichen inhalt der quantentheoretischen kinematik und mechanik. *Zeitschrift fur Physik*, *43*(3–4), 172–198. doi:10.1007/BF01397280

Heisenberg, W. (1958). *Physics and philosophy: The revolution in modern science*. New York, NY: Harper & Row Publishers, Inc.

Helstern, L. (2013). Thriller Survivance: The Subversive Resistance of Louis Owens. In A. R. Velie & A. R. Lee (Eds.), *The Native American Renaissance: Literary Imagination and Achievement*. Norman, OK: University of Oklahoma Press.

Henderson, J. L. (1964). Ancient myths and modern man. In C. G. Jung (Ed.), *Man and his symbols* (pp. 97–156). New York, NY: Dell.

Herrmann, W. M., & Schaerer, E. (1986). Pharmaco-EEG: Computer EEG analysis to describe the projection of drug effects on a functional cerebral level in humans. In Lopes et al. (Eds.), Clinical application of computer analysis of EEG and other neurophysiological signals, EEG Handbook (Vol. 2, Rev. ed., pp. 385-445). Amsterdam: Elsevier.

Hillman, J. (2004). Archetypal psychology, volume 1. Putnam, CT: Spring. (Original work published 1983).

Hillman, J. (2012). *Healing fiction* (Kindle ed.). Thompson, Connecticut: Spring Publications. Retrieved from http://www.amazon.com/Healing-Fiction-James-Hillman-ebook/dp/B0079LCEN4/ref=tmm_kin_swatch_0?_encoding=UTF8&sr=1-1&qid=1435641664

Hillman, J., & Kerenyi, K. (1991). Oedipus variations: Studies in literature and psychoanalysis. Dallas, TX: Spring.

Hillman, J. (1987). *Insearch: psychology and religion*. Dallas: Spring Publications.

Hillman, J. (1992). *Re-visioning psychology*. New York, NY: Harper Perennial. (Original work published 1975)

Hiriyanna, M. (2000). *The essentials of Indian philosophy*. Delhi, India: Motilal Banarsidass.

Hobson, J. A. (1999). *Consciousness*. New York: Scientific American Press.

Hobson, J. A., Pace-Schott, E. F., & Stickgold, R. (2000). Dreaming and the brain: Toward a cognitive neuroscience of conscious states. *BBS*, *23*(6), 793–842. doi:10.1017/S0140525X00003976 PMID:11515143

Hobson, J., Pace-Schott, E., & Stickgold, R. (2003). Dreaming and the brain: Toward a cognitive neuroscience of conscious states. In E. Pace-Schott, M. Solms, M. Blagrove, & S. Harnad (Eds.), *Sleep and Dreaming: Scientific Advances and Reconsiderations* (pp. 1–50). Cambridge, UK: Cambridge University Press.

Hockley, L. (2001). *Cinematic projections: the analytical psychology of CG Jung and film theory*. Luton: University of Luton Press.

Hodges, A. (2012). *Alan Turing: The enigma*. Princeton, NJ: Princeton University Press. doi:10.1515/9781400844975

Hodgkin, A., & Horowicz, P. (1959). The influence of potassium and chloride ions on the membrane potential of single muscle fibers. *The Journal of Physiology*, *148*(1), 127–160. doi:10.1113/jphysiol.1959.sp006278 PMID:14402240

Holzel, B., & Ott, U. (2006). Relationships between meditation depth, absorption, meditation practice, and mindfulness: A latent variable approach. *Journal of Transpersonal Psychology*, *38*(2), 179–199.

Holzinger, B., LaBerge, S., & Levitan, L. (2006). Psychophysiological correlates of lucid dreaming. *Dreaming*, *16*(2), 88–95. doi:10.1037/1053-0797.16.2.88

Hornblow, A., Jr. (Producer), & Wilder, B. (Director). (1957). Witness for the Prosecution. United States: Metro-Goldwyn-Mayer.

Hoskovek, J. (1966). Hypnopedia in the Soviet Union: A critical review of recent major experiments. *The International Journal of Clinical and Experimental Hypnosis*, *14*, 305–315. PMID:5977010

How Yahoo Research Labs Studies Culture as a Formal Computational Concept (2014). *MIT Technology Review*. Retrieved from http://www.technologyreview.com/view/529521/how-yahoo-research-labs-studies-culture-

Howard, J. (2008). *Quests: Design, theory, and history in games and narratives*. Wellesley, MA: Peters. doi:10.1201/b10929

Huang, H., & Lo, P. (2009). EEG dynamics of experienced Zen meditation practitioners probed by complexity index and spectral measure. *Journal of Medical Engineering & Technology*, *33*(4), 314–321. doi:10.1080/03091900802602677 PMID:19384707

Hubb, B. (2015). John 1:1. Retrieved from http://biblehub.com/john/1-1.htm

Huizinga, J. (1955). *Homo Ludens: A study of the play element in culture*. Boston, MA: Beacon Press. (Original work published 1938).

Human behavior as a formal computational concept (2015). *MIT Technology Review*. Retrieved 1/25/2015 http://www.technologyreview.com/view/529521/how-yahoo-research-labs-studies-culture-as-a-formal-computational-concept/

Human Brain Project. (2014). *MIT Technology Review* July 7, 2014. http://www.technologyreview.com/news/528796/neuroscientists-object-to-europes-human-brain-project/

Hunicke, R., LeBlanc, M., & Zubek, R. (2004). MDA: A formal approach to game design and game research. Retrieved from http://www.cs.northwestern.edu/~hunicke/MDA.pdf

Hunt, H. (1989). *Multiplicity of dreams: Memory, imagination, and consciousness*. Westford, MA: Yale University Press.

Hunt, H. (1989). *The Multiplicity of Dreams: Memory, Imagination, and Consciousness*. New Haven: Yale University Press.

Hunt, M. M. (1993). *The story of psychology*. New York: Doubleday.

Iber, C., Ancoli-Israel, S., Chesson, A., & Quan, S. (2007). *The AASM Manuel for the Scoring of Sleep and Associated Events. Westchester, Il.* American Academy of Sleep Medicine.

IMDB. (2014). *Guardians of the Galaxy: Synopsis*. Retrieved from http://www.imdb.com/title/tt2015381/synopsis?ref_=ttpl_ql_3

IMDB. (2014). *The Avengers: Synopsis*. Retrieved from http://www.imdb.com/title/tt0848228/synopsis

Ioannides, A., Kostopoulos, G., Liu, L., & Fenwick, P. (2008). MEG identifies dorsal medial brain activations during sleep. *NeuroImage*, *44*(2), 455–468. doi:10.1016/j.neuroimage.2008.09.030 PMID:18950718

Itil, T. M. (1981). The discovery of psychotrophic drugs by computer analyzed cerebral bioelectrical potentials (CEEG). *Drug Development Research*, *1*(4), 373–407. doi:10.1002/ddr.430010407

ITU (International Telecommunication Union). (2011). *World Telecommunication/ICT Indicators Database*. Retrieved from http://www.itu.int/ITU-D/ict/statistics/

Izod, J. (2006). *Screen, culture, psyche. A post-Jungian approach to working with the audience*. London: Routledge.

Jacobi, J. (1965). *The way of individuation* (R. F. C. Hull, Trans.). New York, NY: Hodder & Stoughton.

Jacobi, J. (1973). *The Psychology of C.G. Jung*. New Haven, London: Yale University Press.

Jacobi, J. (1973). *The psychology of CG Jung*. London, USA: Yale University Press.

Jacobi, J. (1973). *The Psychology of CG Jung*. London, USA: Yale University Press.

Jacobi, J. (2007). *Complex/Archetype/Symbol in the Psychology of C G Jung*. London: Routledge.

Jacobs G.D., Friedman R. (2004). EEG spectral analysis of relaxation techniques. Appl Psyclophysiol biofeedback 29,245-54

Jacobs, A.P. (Producer), & Schaffner, F.J. (Director). (1968). *Planet of the Apes*. United States: 20th Century Fox.

Jobson, C. (2014). An Aerial Laser Display Capable of Projecting 3D Objects in Mid-Air. *EUROSIS - The European Multidisciplinary Society for Modelling and Simulation Technology*. Retrieved from http://www.thisiscolossal.com/2014/11/an-aerial-laser-display-capable-of-projecting-3d-objects-in-mid-air/

John, E. (1968). Mechanisms of Memory (Vol. 1 & 2). New York: Academic Press.

Jung, C. (1965). *Memories, Dreams, Reflections*. New York: Vintage.

Jung, C. G. (1917). *Die Psychologie der Unbewussten Prozesse: ein Überblick über die moderne Theorie und Methode der analytischen Psychologie*. Zürich: Verlag Von Rascher & Cie.

Jung, C. G. (1933). *Modern Man in Search of a Soul*. Oxon: Routledge.

Jung, C. G. (1933). *Modern man in search of a soul*. USA: Harcourt Brace & Company.

Jung, C. G. (1953). Psychology and alchemy. In *The collected works of C. G. Jung* (Vol. 12). (R. F. C. Hull, Trans.). Princeton, NJ: Princeton University Press. (Original work published 1952).

Jung, C. G. (1959). *The Archetypes and the Collective Unconscious* (R. F. C. Hull, Trans.). New York: Princeton University Press.

Jung, C. G. (1964). *Man and His Symbols*. London: Aldus Books.

Jung, C. G. (1976). Symbols of transformation. In *The collected works of C. G. Jung* (Vol. 5). (R. F. C. Hull, Trans.). Princeton, NJ: Princeton University Press. (Original work published 1952).

Jung, C. G. (1977). *The symbolic life*. London: Routledge.

Jung, C. G. (1978). *The spirit in man, art,* and *literature*. In *The collected works of C. G. Jung* (Vol. 15). (R. F. C. Hull, Trans.). Princeton, NJ: Princeton University Press. (Original work published 1923).

Jung, C. G. (1989). *Memories, dreams, reflections* (R. Winston & C. Winston, Trans.). New York, NY: Vintage. (Original work published 1961).

Jung, C. G. (1990). The archetypes and the collective unconscious. In *The collected works of C. G. Jung* (Vol. 9, Part 1 (R. F. C. Hull, Trans.). Princeton, NJ: Princeton University Press. (Original work published 1959).

Jung, C. G. (Ed.). (1964). *Man and his symbols*. New York, NY: Dell.

Jung, C. The Transcendent Function. In J. Campbell (Ed.), *The Portable Jung* (pp. 273–300). New York: Penguin Books.

Jünger, E. (1970). *Annäherungen. Drogen und Rausch.* Stuttgart: Ernst Klett.

Juul, J. (2013). *The art of failure: An essay on the pain of playing video games.* Cambridge, MA: The MIT Press.

Kahan, T. L., & LaBerge, S. (1996). Cognition and metacognition in dreaming and waking: Comparisons of first and third-person ratings. *Dreaming*, *6*(4), 235–249. doi:10.1037/h0094459

Kahan, T., & LaBerge, S. (1994). Lucid dreaming as metacognition: Implications for cognitive science. *Consciousness and Cognition*, *3*(2), 246–264. doi:10.1006/ccog.1994.1014

Kaplan, D. (2015). Facebook, Oculus, and the future of virtual reality. *TechCrunch.* Retrieved from http://techcrunch.com/2015/03/15/facebook-oculus-and-the-future-of-virtual-reality/

Katayama, H., Gianotti, L., Isotani, T., Faber, P., Sasada, K., Kinoshita, T., & Lehmann, D. (2007). Classes of multichannel EEG microstates in light and deep hypnotic conditions. *Brain Topography*, *20*(1), 7–14. doi:10.1007/s10548-007-0024-3 PMID:17587166

Kay, R. W. (1994). Geomagnetic Storms: Association with Incidence of Depression as Measured by Hospital Admission. *The British Journal of Psychiatry*, *164*(3), 403–409. doi:10.1192/bjp.164.3.403 PMID:8199794

Kay, R. W. (2004). Schizophrenia and season of birth: Relationship to geomagnetic storms. *Schizophrenia Research*, *66*(1), 7–20. doi:10.1016/S0920-9964(02)00495-4 PMID:14693348

Kelly, J. (2007). *Play Time: An Overview of the MMORPG Genre.* Retrieved from http://www.anthemion.org/playtime_over.html

Kelly, M. (2015). The social contract. Retrieved from http://americanhistory.about.com/od/usconstitution/g/social_contract.htm

Kenevan, P. B. (1999). *Paths of individuation in literature and film: a Jungian approach.* Boston, MA: Lexington Books.

Kiebel, S., Garrido, M., Moran, R., Chen, C., & Friston, K. (2009). Dynamic causal modeling for EEG and EMG. *Human Brain Mapping*, *30*(6), 1866–1876. doi:10.1002/hbm.20775 PMID:19360734

Kingkade, T. (2013). *Student loan debt: New reports find 'unsustainable' trend dragging economy.* Retrieved from http://www.huffingtonpost.com/2013/01/31/student-loan-debt-unsustainable_n_2593303.html

Kirk, T. (2014). Superconducting spintronics pave way for next-generation computing. *Nature Communications.* Retrieved from http://phys.org/news/2014-01-superconducting-spintronics-pave-next-generation.html

Kleimenova N, Kozyreva O. (2005). Daytime quasiperiodic geomagnetic pulsations during the recovery phase of the strong magnetic storm of May 15, 2005. *Geomagnetism and Aeronomy,* 47(5), 580-7.

Kleinman, A. (2014). Man successfully controls 2 prosthetic arms with just his thoughts. *Huffington Post.* Retrieved from http://www.huffingtonpost.com/2014/12/18/prosthetic-arms-thoughts_n_6348026.html

Kleinman, Alexis (2014). Man successfully controls 2 prosthetic arms with just his thoughts.

Klepek, P. (2014). Assassin's creed: Freedom cry review. Retrieved from http://www.giantbomb.com/reviews/assassin-s-creed-iv-freedom-cry-review/1900-626/

Knox, E. G., Armstrong, E., Lancashire, R., Wall, M., & Haynes, R. (1979). Heart attacks and geomagnetic activity. *Nature*, *281*(5732), 564–565. doi:10.1038/281564a0 PMID:492317

Koboldgames. (2013). *Journey of a Roach*. Hamburg: Daedalic Entertainment.

Konvalinka, I., Bauer, M., Stahlhut, C., Hansen, C. K., Roepstorff, A., & Frith, C. D. (2005). Frontal alpha oscillations distinguish leaders from followers: Multivariate decoding of mutually interactive brains. *NeuroImage*, *94*, 79–88. doi:10.1016/j.neuroimage.2014.03.003 PMID:24631790

Koriat, A. (2007). Metacognition and consciousness. In P. D. Zelazo, M. Moscovitch, & E. Thompson (Eds.), *The Cambridge handbook of consciousness* (pp. 289–325). Cambridge, NY: Cambridge University Press. doi:10.1017/CBO9780511816789.012

Kosslyn, S. (1994). *Image and brain*. PA: Massachusetts Institute of Technology.

Koulack, D. (1969). Effects of somatosensory stimulation on dream content. *Archives of General Psychiatry*, *120*, 71–80. PMID:4306322

Kowal, E. (2015). Computer simulations improve lethality. The Official Home Page of the United States Army. Retrieved fromwww.army.mil

Krensky, S. (2008). *Comic Book Century: The History of American Comic Books*. Minneapolis, MN: Twenty-First Century Books.

Kubrick, S. (Producer & Director). (1964). Dr. Strangelove or: How I Learned to Stop Worrying and Love the Bomb. United States: Columbia Pictures.

Kubrick, S. (Producer & Director). (1968). 2001*: A Space Odyssey*. United Kingdom and United States: Metro-Goldwyn-Mayer.

Kurtz, G. (Producer), & Lucas, G. (Director). (1977). Star Wars. United States: Lucasfilm Ltd., 20th Century Fox.

Kuskin, W. (2008). Continuity in Literary Form and History. *English Language Notes*, *46*(2), 5–13.

LaBerge, S. & DeGracia, D.J. (2000). Varieties of lucid dreaming experience. *Individual Differences in Conscious Experience*, 269-307.

Laberge, S. (1980). Lucid dreaming: An exploratory study of consciousness during sleep [PhD thesis]. Stanford University.

LaBerge, S. (1985). *Lucid Dreaming*. Los Angeles, CA: JP Tarcher.

LaBerge, S., Nagel, L., Dement, W., & Zarcone, V. Jr. (1981). Lucid dreaming verified by volitional communication during REM sleep. *Perceptual and Motor Skills*, *52*(3), 727–732. doi:10.2466/pms.1981.52.3.727 PMID:24171230

Lagopoulos, J., Xu, J., Rasmussen, I., Vik, A., Malhi, G., Eliassen, C., & Ellingsen, O. et al. (2009). Increased theta and alpha activity during nondirective meditation. *Journal of Alternative and Complementary Medicine (New York, N.Y.)*, *15*(11), 1187–1192. doi:10.1089/acm.2009.0113 PMID:19922249

Lakatos, P., Karmos, G., Mehta, A., Ulbert, I., & Schroeder, C. (2008). Entrainment of neuronal occilations as a mechanism of attentional selection. *Science*, *320*(5872), 110–113. doi:10.1126/science.1154735 PMID:18388295

Lakoff, G. (2002). *Moral Politics*. University of Chicago Press: Chicago

Lakoff, G., & Narayanan, S. (2010). *Toward a Computational Model of Narrative*. Association for the Advancement of Artificial Intelligence. Retrieved from http://www1.icsi.berkeley.edu/~snarayan/narrative-aaai-fs2010.pdf

Lakoff, G. (2008). *The political mind* (pp. 83–84). USA: Viking Penguin.

Lakoff, G. (2008). *The Political Mind. A Cognitive Scientist's Guide to Your Brain and Its Politics*. New York: Viking Adult.

Lakoff, G. (2008). *The Political Mind.* New York, NY: Viking Penguin.

Lakoff, G. (2008). *The political mind. Viking Penguin, USA.*

Lakoff, G., & Narayanan, S. (2010). *Toward a computational model of narrative. Association for the Advancement of Artificial Intelligence.* Berkeley, CA: International Computer Science Institute and University of California at Berkeley.

Lashley, K. (1950). In search of the engram. In *Physiological Mechanisms in Animal Behavior* (pp. 454–482). New York: Academic Press.

Laswell, H. (1948). *The structure and function of communication and society: The communication of ideas* (pp. 203–243). Institute for Religious and Social Studies.

Laszlo, E.(1995). The Interconnected Universe: Conceptual Foundations of Transdiciplinary Unified Theory. Singapore: World Scientific.

Laszlo, E. (1995). *The Interconnected Universe: Conceptual Foundations of Transdiciplinary Unified Theroy.* Singapore: World Scientific.

Laszlo, E. (2008). *Quantum Shift in the Global Brain: how the new scientific reality can change us and our world.* Rochester, VT: Inner Traditions.

Leblanc, M. (1880, December 1). Etude sur la transmission électrique des impressions lumineuses (Study on electrical transmission of luminous impressions). *La Lumière électrique* (Electric light).

Leggett, H. (2009). Out of LSD? Just 15 Minutes of Sensory Deprivation Triggers Hallucinations. [Electronic Version] *Wired.* Retrieved from http://www.wired.com

Lehmann, D., Faber, P., Achermann, P., Jeanmonod, D., Gianotti, L., & Pizzagalli, D. (2001). Brain sources of EEG gamma frequency during volitionally meditation-induced, altered states of consciousness, and experience of the self. *Psychiatry Research, 108*(2), 111–121. doi:10.1016/S0925-4927(01)00116-0 PMID:11738545

Lehrer, P. M., Vaschillo, E., Vaschillo, B., Lu, S.-E., Eckberg, D. L., Edelberg, R., & Hamer, R. M. et al. (2003). Heart rate variability biofeedback increases baroreflex gain and peak expiratory flow. *Psychosomatic Medicine, 65*(5), 796–805. doi:10.1097/01.PSY.0000089200.81962.19 PMID:14508023

Leopold, D., Murayama, Y., & Logothetis, N. (2003). Very slow activity fluctuations in monkey visual cortex: Implications for functional brain imaging. *Cereb Cortex, 13*(4), 423–433. doi:10.1093/cercor/13.4.422 PMID:12631571

Leroy, M. (Producer), & Fleming, V. (Director). (1939). The Wonderful Wizard of Oz. United States: Metro-Goldwyn-Mayer.

Levin, R., & Nielsen, T. A. (2009). Nightmares, bad dreams, and emotional dysregulation: A review and new neurocognitive model of dreaming. *Current Directions in Psychological Science, 18*(2), 84–88. doi:10.1111/j.1467-8721.2009.01614.x

Levitan, L. & LaBerge, S. (1993). Testing the limits of dream control: The light and mirror experiment. *Nightlight, 5*(2).

Levy, B. R., Slade, M. D., Kunkel, S. R., & Kasl, S. V. (2002). Longevity increased by positive self-perceptions of aging. *Journal of Personality and Social Psychology, 83*(2), 261–270. doi:10.1037/0022-3514.83.2.261 PMID:12150226

Linden, M., Habib, T., & Radojevich, V. (1996). A controlled study of the effects of EEG biofeedback on cognition and behavior of children with attention deficit disorder and learning disabilities. *Biofeedback and Self-Regulation, 21*(1), 35–49. doi:10.1007/BF02214148 PMID:8833315

Lindmark, S., Buren, J., & Eriksson, J. W. (2006). Insulin resistance, endocrine function and adipokines in type 2 diabetes patients at different glycaemic levels: Potential impact for glucotoxicity in vivo. *Horumon To Rinsho*, *65*(3), 301–309. doi:10.1111/j.1365-2265.2006.02593.x PMID:16918948

Lindmark, S., Lönn, L., Wiklund, U., Tufvesson, M., Olsson, T., & Eriksson, J. W. (2005). Dysregulation of the autonomic nervous system can be a link between visceral adiposity and insulin resistance. *Obesity Research*, *13*(4), 717–728. doi:10.1038/oby.2005.81 PMID:15897481

Lindmark, S., Wiklund, U., Bjerle, P., & Eriksson, J. W. (2003). Does the autonomic nervous system play a role in the development of insulin resistance? A study on heart rate variability in first-degree relatives of Type 2 diabetes patients and control subjects. *Diabetic Medicine*, *20*(5), 399–405. doi:10.1046/j.1464-5491.2003.00920.x PMID:12752490

Lindsay, R. (2015). Google to add "buy" buttons to some research. *Christian Science Monitor* Retrieved from http://www.csmonitor.com/Technology/2015/0517/Google-to-add-buy-buttons-to-some-search-results-video

Lionhead Studios. (2001). Black & White. United States: Electronic Arts.

Lisman, J. E., & Idiart, M. A. (1995). Storage of 7 + 2 short term memories in oscillatory subcycles. *Science*, *267*(5203), 1512–1515. doi:10.1126/science.7878473 PMID:7878473

Liu, C., & Reppert, S. M. (2000). GABA synchronizes clock cells within the suprachiasmatic circadian clock. *Neuron*, *25*(1), 123–128. doi:10.1016/S0896-6273(00)80876-4 PMID:10707977

Lloyd, A., Brett, D., & Wesnes, K. (2010). Coherence Training Improves Cognitive Functions and Behavior In Children with ADHD. *Alternative Therapies in Health and Medicine*, *16*(4), 34–42. PMID:20653294

Lochtefeld, J. (2002). Maya. In *The illustrated encyclopedia of Hinduism* (Vol. 1, p. 433). New York, NY: Rosen Publishing.

Locke, J. (1991). A Letter Concerning Toleration (p. 5) [Introduction]. New York: Routledge.

Lock, T. (1995). Stimulus dosing. In C. Freeman (Ed.), *The ECT Handbook* (pp. 72–87). London: Royal College of Psychiatrists.

Longo, N. P., & Meyer, R. (2006, May). *College Students and Politics: A Literature Review*. Kettering Foundation, CIRCLE Working Paper 46. Retrieved from http://www.civicyouth.org/PopUps/WorkingPapers/WP46LongoMeyer.pdf

Lucas Arts. (1990). *The Secret of Monkey Island*. San Francisco: Lucasfilm Games.

Lucas Arts. (1998). *Grim Fandango*. Marin County: Lucas Arts.

Luthar, S. S., Cicchetti, D., & Becker, B. (2000). The construct of resilience: A critical evaluation and guidelines for future work. *Child Development*, *71*(3), 543–562. doi:10.1111/1467-8624.00164 PMID:10953923

Lutz, A., Greischar, L., Rawlings, N., Richard, M., & Davidson, R. (2004). Long-term meditators self-induce high-amplitude gamma synchrony during mental practice. *Proceedings of the National Academy of Sciences of the United States of America*, *101*(46), 16369–16373. doi:10.1073/pnas.0407401101 PMID:15534199

MacDonald, K. (Director). (2004). *Touching the Void* [Motion picture]. United Kingdom: Pathe.

Mack, A., & Rock, I. (2000). *Inattentional Blindness*. Cambridge, MA: MIT Press.

Mackay, D. (2001). *The fantasy role-playing game: A new performance art*. Jefferson, NC: McFarland & Company, Inc.

Mackey-Kallis, S. (2003). Who would have dreamed that movies mattered so much? *Review of Communication*, *3*(2), 161–166. doi:10.1080/ 0308385

Mackinnon, J. B. (2015), "Facing Fear." [Electronic Version] *Orion Magazine.* Retrieved June 20, 2015 from https://orionmagazine.org

Magic Leap (2015). Retrieved from www.magicleap.com

Mair, V. H. (1998). Chuang-tzu. In W. Nienhauser (Ed.), *The Indiana companion to traditional Chinese literature* (Vol. 2, pp. 20–26). Bloomington: Indiana University Press.

Makuch, E. (2015). Microsoft has invested heavily in Holographic research and the dynamics of machine intelligence. *Gamespot.com.* Retrieved from http://www.gamespot.com/articles/windows-holographic-revealed/1100-6424791/

Malin, S. R. C., & Srivastava, B. J.Malin SRCaS. (1979). B.J. (1979). Correlation between heart attacks and magnetic activity. *Nature, 277*(5698), 646–648. doi:10.1038/277646a0 PMID:423962

Mamoulian, R. (Producer & Director). (1931). Dr. Jekyll and Mr. Hyde. United States: Paramount Pictures.

Mandema, J. W., & Danhof, M. (1992). Electroencephalogram effect measures and relationships between pharmackinetics and pharmacodynamics of centrally acting drugs. *Clinical Pharmacokinetics, 23*(3), 191–215. doi:10.2165/00003088-199223030-00003 PMID:1511536

Marcer, P., & Schempp, W. (1998). The brain as a conscious system. *International Journal of General Systems, 27*(1-3), 231–248. doi:10.1080/03081079808962066

Markley, O. W. (1972). *Unity with diversity: Toward Social Policies for a future world order.* Center for the Study of Social Policy: Stanford Research Institute.

Markoff, J. (2014). Microsoft Makes Bet Quantum Computing Is Next Breakthrough. *The New York Times* retrieved from http://www.nytimes.com/2014/06/24/technology/microsoft-makes-a-bet-on-quantum-computing-research.html

Marzano, C., Ferrara, M., Mauro, F., Moroni, F., Gorgoni, M., Tempesta, D., & DeGennaro, L. et al. (2011). Recalling and forgetting dreams: Theta and alpha oscillations during sleep predict subsequent dream recall. *The Journal of Neuroscience, 31*(18), 6674–6683. doi:10.1523/JNEUROSCI.0412-11.2011 PMID:21543596

Mason, L., Alexander, C. N., Travis, F., Gackenbach, J. I., & Orme-Johnson, D. (1995). EEG correlates of "higher states of consciousness" during sleep. *Sleep, 24*, 152.

Mavrematis, A. (1987). *Hypnogogia: The Unique State of Consciousness Between Wakefullness and Sleep.* Routledge, Chapman & Hall, Incorporated.

Mayer, J., & Thiel, A. (2014). Health in Elite Sports from a Salutogenetic Perspective: Athletes' Sense of Coherence. *PLoS ONE, 9*(7), 1–11. doi:10.1371/journal.pone.0102030 PMID:25014085

McCarley, R., & Hobson, J. (1975). Neuronal excitability modulation over the sleep cycle: A structural and mathematical model. *Science, 189*(4196), 58–60. doi:10.1126/science.1135627 PMID:1135627

McCraty, Deyhle, & Childre (2012). The Global Coherence Initiative: Creating a coherent planetary standing wave. *Global Advances in Health & Medicine*, 1(1). Retrieved from www.gahmj.com

McCraty, R., & Childre, D. (2010). Coherence: bridging personal, social, and global health. Alternative Therapies, 16(4).

McCraty, R. (n.d.). *Coherence: Bridging Personal, Social and Global Health.*

McCraty, R., Atkinson, M., Lipsenthal, L., & Arguelles, L. (2009). Arguelles aL. (2009). New Hope for Correctional Officers: An Innovative Program for Reducing Stress and Health Risks. *Appl Psych and Biofeedback, 34*(4), 251–272. doi:10.1007/s10484-009-9087-0

McCraty, R., Atkinson, M., Tomasino, D., & Bradley, R. T. (2009). The coherent heart: Heart-brain interactions, psychophysiological coherence, and the emergence of system-wide order. *Integral Review.*, *5*(2), 10–115.

McCraty, R., & Childre, D. (2004). The grateful heart: The psychophysiology of appreciation. In R. A. Emmons & M. E. McCullough (Eds.), *The Psychology of Gratitude* (pp. 230–255). New York: Oxford University Press.

McCraty, R., & Childre, D. (2010). Coherence: Bridging Personal, Social and Global Health. *Alternative Therapies in Health and Medicine*, *16*(4), 10–24. PMID:20653292

McCraty, R., Deyhle, A., & Childre, D. (2012). The Global Coherence Initiative: Creating a Coherent Planetary Standing Wave. *Global Advances in Health and Medicine*, *1*(1), 64–77. doi:10.7453/gahmj.2012.1.1.013 PMID:24278803

McGonigal, J. (2006). *This might be a game: Ubiquitous play and performance at the turn of the twenty-first century* (Doctoral dissertation).

McGonigal, J. (2011, March 9). *We don't need no stinkin' badges: How to re-invent reality without gamification.* Paper presented at Serious Game Summit, Game Developers Conference, San Francisco, CA.

McGonigal, J. (2011). *Reality is broken: Why games make us better and how they can change the world.* New York, NY: Penguin Press.

MediaGrid, Immersive Education Initiative. (n. d.). Retrieved from http://immersiveeducation.org/

Merriam-Webster. (2014). *Definition of "Hero"*. Retrieved from http://www.merriam-webster.com/dictionary/hero

Merryweatherblue. (2014, August 13). *Just Keep Swimming, Swimming, SwimmingP"{* (Tumblr Blog). Retrieved from http://merryweatherblue.tumblr.com/post/94638266248/i-took-my-little-brother-who-falls-on-the-autism

Metaverse. (2011, May 1). *Wikipedia.* Retrieved from http://en.wikipedia.org/wiki/Metaverse

Mikulecký, M. (2007). Solar activity, revolutions and cultural prime in the history of mankind. *Neuroendocrinology Letters*, *28*(6), 749–756. PMID:18063926

Miller, C. (2011). 'Twilight'. Discourse theory and Jung. In C. Hauke & L. Hockley (Eds.), *Jung & Film II: the return. Further post-Jungian takes on the moving image* (pp. 185–205). London: Routledge.

Mill, J. S. (1909). *On Liberty, Harvard Classics* (Vol. 25, p. 258). New York: PF Collier & Sons Company.

Minister, P. (2013). Creating a Centaur in ZBrush. *Digital-Tutors.* Retrieved from http://www.digitaltutors.com/tutorial/1099-Creating-a-Centaur-in-ZBrush

Minority. (2012). *Papo & Yo.* Montreal: Minority.

Minsky, M. (1961). Steps toward Artificial Intelligence. *Proceedings of the IRE*, *49*(1), 8–1. doi:10.1109/JRPROC.1961.287775

Mishlove, J. (1998). The Holographic Brain with Karl Pribram, MA; Ph.D. *TWM.co.nz.*

Molero, F., Cuadrado, I., Navas, M., & Morales, J. F. (2007). Relations and Effects of Transformational Leadership: A Comparative Analysis with Traditional Leadership Styles. *The Spanish Journal of Psychology*, *10*(02), 358–368. doi:10.1017/S1138741600006624 PMID:17992962

Montez, T., Poil, S.-S., Jones, B. F., Manshanden, I., Verbunt, J. P. A., van Dijk, B. W., & Linkenkaer-Hansen, K. et al. (2009). Altered temporal correlations in parietal alpha and prefrontal theta oscillations in early-stage Alzheimer disease. *Proceedings of the National Academy of Sciences of the United States of America*, *106*(5), 1614–1619. doi:10.1073/pnas.0811699106

Moore, S. S. (2014). *History of the Justice Society*. Retrieved from http://www.cosmicteams.com/jsa/

Mortier, R. (2015). *The emerging science of human-data interaction*. MIT Technology Review.

Moyers, B. (1987). The secret government: The constitution in crisis. *Public Broadcasting System*. Retrieved from https://search.yahoo.com/search?fr=mcafee&type=B011US739D20150419&p=The+Secret+Government,+Bill+Moyers

Murray, J. (1997). *Hamlet on the Holodeck. The Future of Narrative in Cyberspace*. New York: The Free Press.

Murray, J. H. (2000). *Hamlet on the holodeck: The future of narrative in cyberspace*. Cambridge, MA: The MIT Press.

Myers, M. (2015). Augmenting Agriculture with Social Impact Games has produced a digital prototype of a new social impact board game Bumper Crop. *The Arts Humanities Research Council research project Play to Grow*. Retrieved from https://play.google.com/store/apps/details?id=foam.bumpercrop

Myers-Briggs Type Indicator. (2015, February 21). Wikipedia. Retrieved from http://en.wikipedia.org/wiki/Myers%E2%80%93Briggs_Type_Indicator

Nairz, O., Arndt, M., & Zeilinger, A. (2003, April). Quantum interference experiments with large molecules. *American Journal of Physics*, *71*(4), 319–325.

Nash, S. (2000, December 10). Review of the film *Vertical Limit*. Three Film Buffs. Retrieved from http://www.three-moviebuffs.com

Nathan, J. (Producer), Wheatley, M. (Producer), & Hermanus, O. (Director). (2009). *Shirley Adams* [Motion Picture]. South Africa: DV8 Films, Centropolis Entertainment, London Film School.

Nayfack, N. (Producer), & Wilcox, Fred M. (Director). (1956). Forbidden Planet. United States: Metro-Goldwyn-Mayer.

Nelson, R. (2004). Questions and explorations probing the GCP database: What matters, what doesn't, what questions we can ask. *Paper presented at theannual meeting of the Society for Scientific Exploration*, Las Vegas, NV.

New Player Guide. (2014). *League of Legends*. Riot Games.

New Player Guide. (2014). League of Legends. *Riot Games*. Retrieved from http://en.wikipedia.org/wiki/League_of_Legends

Nielsen, M., & Chuang, I. (2000). *Quantum Computation and Quantum Information*. Cambridge University Press.

Nikolaev, Y. S., Rudakov, Y. Y., Mansurov, S. M., & Mansurova, L. G. (1976). Interplanetary magnetic field sector structure and disturbances of the central nervous system activity. Reprint N 17a, Acad Sci USSR. *IZMIRAN, Moscow*, *1976*, 29.

O'Donnell, M. (2010). *The dramatic structure of dreams*.

Oak Ridge Associated Universities Panel for the Committee on Interagency Radiation Research and Policy Commission. (1992). Health Effects of Low-Frequency Electric and Magnetic Fiels. Washington, D.C., Oak Ridge Associated Universities (US Government).

Odintsov, S., Boyarchuk, K., Georgieva, K., Kirov, B., & Atanasov, D. (2006). Long-period trends in global seismic and geomagnetic activity and their relation to solar activity. *Physics and Chemistry of the Earth Parts A/B/C*, *31*(1–3), 88–93. doi:10.1016/j.pce.2005.03.004

O'Flaherty, W. D. (1986). *Dreams, Illusion, and Other Realities*. Chigaco, IL: University of Chicago Press.

Olgivie, R., Hunt, H., Tyson, P., Lucescu, M., & Jeankin, D. (1978). Searching for lucid dreams. *Sleep Research*, *7*, 165.

Olivier, B. (2009). *Philosophy and psychoanalytic theory. Collected essays*. Oxford: Peter Lang.

Oppenheimer, S., & Hopkins, D. (1994). Suprabulbar neuronal regulation of the heart. In J. A. Armour & J. L. Ardell (Eds.), *Neurocardiology* (pp. 309–341). New York: Oxford University Press.

Oraevskii VN, Breus, T.K., Baevskii, R.M., Rapoport, S.I., Petrov, V.M., Barsukova, Zh.V., Gurfinkel' IuI, & Rogoza, A.T. (1998). Effect of geomagnetic activity on the functional status of the body. *Biofizika*, 43(5), 819-826.

Orhm-Johnson, D., Alexander, C., Davis, J., Chandler, H., & Larimore, W. (1988). The international peace project in the Middle East: The effects of the Maharishi technology of the unified field. *The Journal of Conflict Resolution*, *32*(4), 776–812. doi:10.1177/0022002788032004009

OriginSystems, . (1992). *Ultima VII*. Manchester, NH: Origin Systems.

Orme-Johnson, D. W. (2002). Quantifying the field effects of consciousness: From increased EEG coherence to reduced international terrorism. In R.A. Chez (Ed.), Proceedings of Bridging Worlds and Filling Gaps in the Science of Healing. Corona del Mar, CA: Samueli Institute for Informational Biology (pp. 326-346).

Orme-Johnson, D. W. (2002). Quantifying the field effects of consciousness: From increased EEG coherence to reduced international terrorism. *Proceedings: Bridging.*

Ortiz de Gortari, A. B. (2007). Psychosocial implications of online video gaming. *Paper presented at Game in Action*, Gothenburg, Sweden.

Ortiz de Gortari, A. B., & Griffiths, M. D. (2012). An introduction to game transfer phenomena in video game playing. In J. I. Gackenbach (Ed.), *Video game play and consciousness* (pp. 217–244). NY: Nova Science Publishers.

Ortiz de Gortari, A. B., & Griffiths, M. D. (2014). Auditory experiences in Game Transfer Phenomena: An empirical self-report study. *International Journal of Cyber Behavior, Psychology and Learning*, *4*(1), 59–68. doi:10.4018/ijcbpl.2014010105

Otsuka, K., Cornelissen, G., Norboo, T., Takasugi, E., & Halberg, F. (2008). Chronomics and "Glocal" (Combined Global and Local) Assessment of Human Life. *Progress of Theoretical Physics Supplement.*, *173*, 134–152. doi:10.1143/PTPS.173.134

Pac-Man [Computer software]. (1980). Tokyo, Japan: Namco.

Pagel J. (2013). Lucid Dreaming as Sleep Offset Waking – Sleep 34- Abstract supplement.

Pagel, J. F. (2011). REMS and Dreaming – Historical Perspectives. In B.N. Mallick, S.R. Pandi Perumal, R.W. McCarley, A.R. Morrison (Eds.), Rapid Eye Movement Sleep – Regulation and Function (pp. 1-14). Cambridge University Press.

Pagel, J. F. (2014). Dream Science: Exploring the Forms of Consciousness. Oxford UK: Academic Press (Elsiever).

Pagel, J. F. (1990). *Proposing an Electrophysiology for State Dependent Sleep and Dream Mentation*. APSS Abstracts.

Pagel, J. F. (1993). Modeling drug actions on electrophysiologic effects produced by EEG modulated potentials. *Human Psychopharmacology*, *8*(3), 211–216. doi:10.1002/hup.470080307

Pagel, J. F. (1996). Pharmacologic alteration of sleep and dreams - a clinical framework medications. *Human Psychopharmacology*, *11*, 217–224. doi:10.1002/(SICI)1099-1077(199605)11:3<217::AID-HUP790>3.0.CO;2-0

Pagel, J. F. (2003). Non-dreamers. *Sleep Medicine*, *4*(3), 235–241. doi:10.1016/S1389-9457(02)00255-1 PMID:14592328

Pagel, J. F. (2005). Neurosignals – Incorporating CNS electrophysiology into cognitive process. *Behavioral and Brain Sciences*, *28*(01), 75–76. doi:10.1017/S0140525X05330020

Pagel, J. F. (2008). *The Limits of Dream: A Scientific Exploration of the Mind/brain Interface.* Oxford, UK: Academic Press. doi:10.1016/B978-012374215-5.50033-7

Palva, J., Palva, S., & Kaila, K. (2005). Phase synchrony among neuronal oscillations in the human cortex. *The Journal of Neuroscience, 24*(15), 3962–3972. doi:10.1523/JNEUROSCI.4250-04.2005 PMID:15829648

Parham-Payne, W. (2014). The role of the media in the disparate response to gun violence in America. *Journal of Black Studies, 45*(8), 752–768. doi:10.1177/0021934714555185

Parkin, S. (2014, Nov. 17). Never Alone: Could a Video Game Help Preserve Inuit Culture? *The New Yorker.* Retrieved from http://www.newyorker.com

Parr, G. D., Montgomery, M., & DeBell, C. (1998). Flow theory as a model for enhancing Student resilience. *Professional School Counseling, 1*(5), 26.

Pascalis, V. (1999). Psychophysiological correlates of hypnosis and hypnotic susceptibility. *The International Journal of Clinical and Experimental Hypnosis, 47*(2), 117–143. doi:10.1080/00207149908410026 PMID:10208074

Pascual-Leone, A., Davey, N., Rothwell, J., Wassermann, E. M., & Puri, B. K. (2002). *Handbook of Transcranial Magnetic Stimulation.* London: Edward Arnold.

Pattern recognition in Go (2014). *MIT Technology Review 12-15-2014.* Retrieved from http://www.technologyreview.com/view/533496/why-neural-networks-look-set-to-thrash-the-best-human-go-players-for-the-first-time/

Pearce, C. (2003). Game Noir – A Conversation with Tim Schafer. Game Studies. The International Journal of Games research. 3(1).

Penfield, W. (1975). *The mystery of the mind; a critical study of consciousness and the human brain.* Princeton, N.J.: Princeton University Press.

Penrose, R. (2004). *The Road to Reality: A Complete Guide to the Laws of the Universe* (p. 603). London.

Perron, B., & Wolf, M. (Eds.). (2009). *The video game theory reader 2.* New York, NY: Routledge.

Persinger MA. (1998). Sudden unexpected death in epileptics following sudden, intense, increases in geomagnetic activity: prevalence of effect and potential mechanisms. *Int J Biometeorol.* 43(5), 819-826.

Persinger, M. A. (1987). Geopsychology and geopsychopathology: Mental processes and disorders associated with geochemical and geophysical factors. *Experientia, 43*(1), 92–104. doi:10.1007/BF01940360 PMID:3792507

Persinger, M. A. (1999). Wars and increased solar-geomagnetic activity: Aggression or change in intraspecies dominance? *Perceptual and Motor Skills, 88*(3 Pt. 2), 1351–1355. doi:10.2466/pms.1999.88.3c.1351 PMID:10485122

Petty, J. (2006). *A Brief History of Comic Books.* Retrieved from http://www1.heritagestatic.com/comics/d/history-of-comics.pdf

Phaire, D. W. (2013). *Linking character strengths and learning with films: A content analysis of films for adolescents.*

Philippe, G. (2015a). The AI Revolution: The Road to Superintelligence. *EUROSIS, TheEuropean Multidisciplinary Society for Modelling and Simulation Technology.* Quoted from Private Group DARPA seeks non-traditional entities to develop new robotics capabilities. *Army Technology.com.* Retrieved from http://www.army-technology.com/news/newsdarpa-seeks-non-traditional-entities-to-develop-new-robotics-capabilities-4580219?WT.mc_id=DN_News#.VVtNUbpwZLQ.linkedin

Pietsch, P. (1972, May). Shufflebrain. *Harper's Magazine* 244, p. 66.

Pietsch, P. (1981). *Shufflebrain: The quest for the hologramic mind* (p. 78). Boston: Houghton Mifflin.

Pister, K. (2015). Smart Dust. *The European Multidisciplinary Society for Modeling and Simulation Technology*. Retrieved from https://medium.com/war-is-boring/smart-dust-is-getting-smarter-4b062abd7769

Playdead. (2010). *Limbo*. Copenhagen: Microsoft, Playdead.

Pobachenko, S. V., Kolesnik, A. G., Borodin, A. S., & Kalyuzhin, V. V. (2006). The Contigency of Parameters of Human Encephalograms and Schumann Resonance Electromagnetic Fields Revealed in Monitoring Studies. *Complex Systems Biophysics.*, *51*(3), 480–483.

Poels, K., IJsselsteijn, W. A., & de Kort, Y. A. W. (2010). Digital games, the aftermath: Qualitative insights into post game experiences. In R. Bernhaupt (Ed.), *Evaluating user experience in games* (pp. 149–164). Berlin, Germany: Springer. doi:10.1007/978-1-84882-963-3_9

Poels, K., IJsselsteijn, W. A., & de Kort, Y. A. W. (2014). World of Warcraft, the aftermath: How game elements transfer into perceptions, associations and (day) dreams in the everyday life of massively multiplayer online role-playing game players. *New Media & Society*. doi:10.1177/1461444814521596

Pollen, D. A., & Tractenberg, M. C. (1972, May12). Alpha rhythm and eye movements in eidetic imagery. *Nature*, *237*(5350), 109–112. doi:10.1038/237109a0 PMID:4555444

Polti, G. (1895). *Les 36 situations dramatiques*. Paris: Mercure de France.

Porter, L. (2009, June 28). Mystery of the Third Man. *The Sydney Morning Herald*. Retrieved from http://www.smh.com.au

Postman, N. (1985). *Amusing ourselves to death*. USA: Viking Penguin Inc.

Pozzoli, T., Gini, G., & Vieno, A. (2012). The Role of Individual Correlates and Class Norms in Defending and Passive Bystanding Behavior in Bullying: A Multilevel Analysis. *Child Development*, *83*(6), 1917–1931. doi:10.1111/j.1467-8624.2012.01831.x PMID:22880944

Preiss, D. D., & Sternberg, R. J. (2005). Technologies for working intelligence. In R. J. Sternberg & D. D. Preiss (Eds.), *Intelligence and technology: The impact of tools on the nature and development of human abilities* (pp. 183–208). Mahwah, NJ: Erlbaum.

Pribram, K. (1977). Language of the brain (pp. 123 & 169). Monterey, CA: Wadsworth Publishing.

Pribram, K. (1969, January). The neurophysiology of remembering. *Scientific American*, *220*(1), 75. doi:10.1038/scientificamerican0169-73 PMID:4972532

Pribram, K. (1991). *Brain and perception: holonomy and structure in figural processing*. Hillsdale, N.J.: Lawrence Erlbaum Associates.

Pribram, K. H., & Bradley, R. T. (1998). The brain, the me and the I. In M. Ferrari & R. Sternberg (Eds.), *Self-Awareness: Its Nature and Development* (pp. 273–307). New York: The Guilford Press.

Propp, V. (1958). *The Morphology of the Folk Tale*. Austin: University of Texas Press. (Original work published 1928)

Radin, D. (2009). The conscious universe: The scientific truth of psychic phenomena. New York: Harper One.

Radin, D. (2006). *Entangled minds: Extrasensory experiences in a quantum reality*. New York: Paraview Pocket Books.

Radin, D. I. (2009). *The conscious universe: The scientific truth of psychic phenomena* (1st ed.). New York, NY: HarperOne.

Radin, D., Michel, L., Galdamez, K., Wendland, P., Rickenbach, R., & Delorme, A. (2012). Consciousness and the double-slit interference pattern: Six experiments. *Physics Essays Publication*, *25*(2), 157–171. doi:10.4006/0836-1398-25.2.157

Radke, B. (Interviewer). (2014, October). *Feeling Blue? Play this Game with Socks the Fox* [Radio broadcast]. Seattle: KUOW.

Raff, J. (2000). *Jung and the alchemical imagination*. Berwick, ME: Nicholas-Hays.

Raichle, M., MacLeod, A., Snyder, A., Powers, W., Gusnard, D., & Shulman, G. L. (2001). A default mode of brain function. *Proceedings of the National Academy of Sciences of the United States of America*, *98*(2), 676–682. doi:10.1073/pnas.98.2.676 PMID:11209064

Rapoport, S. I., & Blodypakova, T. (1998). D., Malinovskaia, N.K., Oraevskii, V.N., Meshcheriakova, S.A., Breus, T.K. and Sosnovskii, A.M. (1998). Magnetic storms as a stress factor. *Biofizika*, *43*(4), 632–639. PMID:9783070

Rapoport, S. I., Malinovskaia, N. K., Oraevskii, V. N., Komarov, F. I., Nosovskii, A. M., & Vetterberg, L. (1997). Effects of disturbances of natural magnetic field of the Earth on melatonin production in patients with coronary heart disease. *Klinicheskaia Meditsina*, *75*(6), 24–26. PMID:9273394

Rautenbach, J. (Producer), & Rautenbach, J. (Director). (1970). *Jannie Totsiens* [Motion Picture]. South Africa: Sewentig.

Rechtschaffen Kales. (1968). *AASM Manual for Sleep and Associated Events*. Rochester, Minnesota: American Academy of Sleep Medicine.

Reeves, B., & Nass, C. (1996). The media equation. Stanford: Center For the study of Language and Information & Cambridge University Press.

Regaaldo, A. (2014). Neuroscientists Object to Europe's Human Brain Project. *MIT Technology Review*. Retrieved from http://www.technologyreview.com/news/528796/neuroscientists-object-to-europes-human-brain-project/

Rescher, N. (1991). *G. W. Leibniz's Monadology*. Pittsburgh, PA: University of Pittsburgh Press.

Restak, R. (1979). *The brain* (p. 253). New York: Warner Books.

Restak, R. (1981). Brain power: A new theory. *Science Digest*, (March): 19.

Revonsuo, A. (2006). *Inner presence: Consciousness as a biological phenomenon*. Cambridge, MA: MIT Press.

Revonsuo, A., & Salmivalli, C. (1995). A content analysis of bizarre elements in dreams. *Dreaming*, *5*(3), 160–187. doi:10.1037/h0094433

Revonsuo, A., & Valli, K. (2000). Dreaming and consciousness: Testing the threat stimulation theory of the function of dreaming. *Psyche*, *6*, 1–25.

Rincon, P. (2014). Study doubts quantum computer speed. *BBC News website*. Retrieved from http://www.bbc.com/news/science-environment-25787226

Rinpoche, T. W. (1998). *The Tibetian Yogas of Dream and Sleep*. Ithaca, NY: Snow Lion Publications.

Robbins, R. (2000). *Standing on the Shoulders: A Tribute to my Heroes* (Speech). Proceedings of the 2000 Banff Mountain Film Festival. Retrieved from http://www.frostworksclimbing.com

Rockstar San Diego. (2010). Red Dead Redemption. New York: Rock Star Games.

Roddenberry, G. (1966). *Star Trek: The Original Series (TV Series)*. United States: NBC.

Roddenberry, G. (1973). *Star Trek: The Animated Series (TV Series).* United States: Paramount Television and CBS.

Roddenberry, G. (1987). *Star Trek: The Next Generation (TV Series).* United States: Paramount Television and CBS.

Rollings, A., & Adams, E. (2003). *On Game Design.* Indianapolis: New Riders Publishing.

Rountree, C. (2008). Auteur film directors as contemporary shamans. *Jung Journal: Culture & Psyche, 2*(2), 123–134. doi:10.1525/jung.2008.2.2.123

Rousseau, J.-J. (1754). *Discourse on the Origin of Inequality, Part Two. The Basic Political Writings.* Hackett Publishing Company.

Rousse, R. III. (2005). *Game design theory and practice.* Plano, TX: Wordware.

Ryalls, E. D. (2011). *The culture of mean: Gender, race, and class in mediated images of girls' bullying.*

Salinas, E., & Sejnowski, T. (2001). Correlated neuronal activity and the flow of neural information. *Nat Rev Neuroscience, 2*(8), 539–550. doi:10.1038/35086012 PMID:11483997

Samuels, A., Shorter, B., & Plaut, F. (2000). *A critical dictionary of Jungian analysis.* New York, NY: Routledge. (Original work published 1986)

Saunders, D. (2015, June 13). Mountain Climbing is the Height of Empty Egotism. *The Globe and Mail.* Retrieved from www.theglobeandmail.com

Schack, B., Klimesch, W., & Sauseng, P. (2005). Phase synchronization between theta snd upper alpha occilations in a working memory task. *International Journal of Psychophysiology, 57*(2), 105–114. doi:10.1016/j.ijpsycho.2005.03.016 PMID:15949859

Schafer, S. (2006). Curriculum and The dream Paradigm. Retrieved from http://www.gmecareerguide.com/features/288/curriculum_and_the_dream_paradigm.php

Schafer, S. (2006, October). Curriculum and the dream paradigm. *Gamasutra.* Retrieved from http://www.gmecareerguide.com/features/288/curriculum_and_the_dream_paradigm.php

Schafer, S. (2007). Premise: The Key to Interactive Storytelling. *Game Career Guide.* Retrieved from http://www.gamecareerguide.com/features/357/premise_the_key_to_interactive_.php?page=1

Schafer, S. (2007, April). Premise: The key to interactive storytelling. *Gamasutra.* Retrieved from http://www.gamecareerguide.com/features/357/premise_the_key_to_interactive_.php?page=1

Schafer, S. (2008). The *Psych*ecology Game I-V; Using Story-based Video Games to Capture Veridical Data on Subliminal States of Being. (The computational Resonance of Jungian Synchronicity) *Toward a Science of Consciousness 2008*, sponsored by the Consciousness Center & the University of Arizona. Retrieved from https://bandura.sbs.arizona.edu/login/consciousness/pubreport.aspx?aid=2761

Schafer, S. (2011). Articulating the paradigm shift: Serious games for psychological healing of the collective persona. In M.M. Cruz-Cunha (Ed.), *Handbook of Research on serious games as educational business and research tools* (Ch. 19). Hershey, PA, USA: IGI Global. Retrieved from www.igi-global.com

Schafer, S. (2011). *Book Chapter: Articulating the paradigm shift: Serious games for psychological healing of the collective persona.* Business Social Networking: Organizational, Managerial, and Technological Dimensions. IGI Global. Retrieved from http://www.igi-global.com/book/handbook-research-serious-games-educational/5

Schafer, S. (2012). Optimizing Cognitive Coherence, Learning, and Psychological Healing with Drama-based Games. In J. Gackenbach (Ed.), *Video Game Play and Consciousness.* Nova Science Publishers.

Schafer, S. (2012). Optimizing Cognitive Coherence, Learning, and Psychological Healing with Drama-based Games. In J. Gackenbach (Ed.), *Video Game Play and Consciousness.* Nova Science Publishers. http://www.facebook.com/insights/?sk=po_261980910540561#!/pages/Video-Game-Play-and-Consciousness/261980910540561?sk=wall

Schafer, S., & Palamides, T. (2011) Designing an Ethical structure for Social Influence Marketing. In M.M. Cruz-Cunha, P. Gonçalves, N. Lopes, & G.D. Putnik (Eds.), *School Handbook of Research on Business Social Networking: Organizational, Managerial, and Technological Dimensions.* Hershey, PA, USA: IGI Global. Retrieved from www.igi-global.com

Schafer, S., & Palamides, T. (2011). Designing an Ethical structure for Social Influence Marketing. In M.M. Cruz-Cunha, P. Gonçalves, N. Lopes, & G.D. Putnik (Eds.), *Handbook of research on Business Social Networking: Organizational, Managerial, and Technological Dimensions.* Hershey, PA, USA: IGI Global. Retrieved from www.igi-global.com

Schafer, S., & Yu, G. (2011) Meaningful Video Games: Drama-Based video Games as transformational experience. In M.M. Cruz-Cunha, & V.H. Varvalho, & P. Tavares (Eds.), *Business, Technological, and Social Dimensions to Video Games: Multidisciplinary Approach.* Hershey, PA, USA: IGI Global. Retrieved from http://resources.igi-global.com/Marketing/discountforms/FillableGenericBookDiscountForm.pdf

Schafer, S. (2012). *Optimizing cognitive coherence, learning, and psychological healing with drama-based video games. Video game play and consciousness.* New York: Nova Science Publishers, Inc.

Schafer, S. (2015). *The Mediasphere as Dream: Exploring the media dream.* Hershy, PA: IGIGlobal.

Schafer, S., & Yu, G. (2011). *Meaningful video games: drama-based video games as transformational experience.* Hershey, PA, USA: IGI Global. doi:10.4018/978-1-60960-567-4.ch019

Schafer, S., & Yu, G. (2011). Meaningful video games: drama-based video games as transformational experience. In M. M. Cruz-Cunha, V. H. Valvalho, & P. Tavares (Eds.), *Business, Technological, and Social Dimensions of Computer Games: Multidisciplinary Developments* (pp. 312–329). Hershey, PA, USA: IGI Global.

Schecter, N., Schmeidler, G. R., & Staal, M. (1965). Dream reports and creative tendencies in students of the arts, sciences, engineering. *Journal of Consulting Psychology, 29*(5), 415–421. doi:10.1037/h0022463 PMID:5827514

Schell, J. (2010). *The art of game design: A book of lenses.* Boston, MA: Morgan Kaufmann.

Schempp, W. (1992). Quantum holography and neurocomputer architectures. *Journal of Mathematical Imaging and Vision, 2*(4), 279–326. doi:10.1007/BF00121876

Schmidhuber, J. (2002). Algorithmic theories of everything. *International Journal of Foundations of Computer Science, 13*(4).

Schmidt, M. B. (2002). *Thinley Norbe Rinpoche in the Dzogchen Primer.* Boston, MA: Shambala.

Schodt, F. (1986). *Manga! Manga! The World of Japanese Comics.* New York: Kodansha America, Inc.

Schredl, M. (2003). Continuity between waking and dreaming: A proposal for a mathematical model. *Sleep and Hypnosis, 5*(1), 26–39.

Schrödinger, E. (1926). Quantisation as an eigenvalue problem. *Annalen der Physik, 81*(18), 109–139. doi:10.1002/andp.19263861802

Schrödinger, E., & Born, M. (1935). Discussion of probability relations between separated systems. *Mathematical Proceedings of the Cambridge Philosophical Society, 31*(4), 555–563. doi:10.1017/S0305004100013554

Schroeder, R. (2014). Big data and the brave new world of social media research. *Big Data & Society*. Retrieved from http://bds.sagepub.com/content/1/2/2053951714563194.abstract

Schultes, R. E., Hofmann, A., & Rätsch, C. (2001). *Plants of the Gods: Their sacred, healing and hallucinogenic powers*. Rochester, VT: Inner Traditions/Bear & Company.

Searle, J. R. (1998). *The Rediscovery of the Mind*. Cambridge, Massachusetts: The MIT Press.

Seligman, M. E. P., & Csikszentmihalyi, M. (2000, January). Positive psychology: An introduction. *The American Psychologist*, *55*(1), 5–14. doi:10.1037/0003-066X.55.1.5 PMID:11392865

Serchay, D. (2010). Justice Society of America. In M. K. Booker (Ed.), *Encyclopedia of Comic Books and Graphic Novels*. Santa Barbara, CA: ABC-CLIO, LLC.

Shapiro, J. (2014). Games Can Advance Education: A Conversation With James Paul Gee. *MindShift*. Retrieved from http://ww2.kqed.org/mindshift/2014/07/03/games-can-advance-education-a-conversation-with-james-paul-gee/

Shaw, H. (Director). (1916). *De Voortrekkers* [Motion Picture]. South Africa: African Film Productions.

Sheer, I. (2014). Player Tally for 'League of Legends' Surges. *Wsj.com*. Retrieved from http://en.wikipedia.org/wiki/League_of_Legends

Sheer, I. (2014, January 27). Player Tally for 'League of Legends' Surges. *Wsj.com*.

Sheldon, L. (2004). *Character Development and Storytelling for Games*. Boston: Thomson Course Technology PTR.

Shultz, H. (2008). Rethinking sleep analysis: Comment on the AASM manual for the scoring of sleep and associated events. *Journal of Clinical Sleep Medicine*, *15*, 99–103.

Siegel, J. M. (2000). Brainstem Mechanisms generating REM sleep. In M.H. Kryger, T. Roth, W.C. Dement (Eds.), Principles and Practice of Sleep Medicine (3rd ed., pp.112-114). Philadelphia: WB Saunders.

Signorielli, N. 2012. Violent Content on US Television. The International Encyclopedia of Media Studies, 3(2), 16.

Silver, J. (Producer), & The Wachowski Brothers (Director). (1999). The Matrix. United States: Warner Bros.

Simonite, T. (2014). Digital Summit: Microsoft's Quantum Search for the "Next Transistor". MIT Technology Review. Retrieved from http://www.technologyreview.com/news/528256/digital-summit-microsofts-quantum-search-for-the-next-transistor/

Simonite, T. (2014a). An experiment involving a chip on a small drone shows how hardware modeled on the brain could provide useful intelligence. *MIT Technology Review*. Retrieved from http://www.technologyreview.com/news/532176/a-brain-inspired-chip-takes-to-the-sky/?utm_campaign=newsletters&utm_source=newsletter-daily-all&utm_medium=email&utm_content=20141111

Simonite, T. (2014a). Robots That Learn Through Repetition, Not Programming. *MIT Technology Review*. Retrieved from http://www.technologyreview.com/news/530871/robots-that-learn-through-repetition-not-programming/

Simonite, T. (2014b). Digital Summit: Microsoft's Quantum Search for the "Next Transistor". *MIT Technology Review*. Retrieved from http://www.technologyreview.com/news/528256/digital-summit-microsofts-quantum-search-for-the-next-transistor/

Simonite, T. (2014c). Google's Brain-Inspired Software Describes What It Sees in Complex Images. *MIT Technology Review*. Retrieved from http://www.technologyreview.com/news/532666/googles-brain-inspired-software-describes-what-it-sees-in-complex images/?utm_campaign=newsletters&utm_source=newsletter-daily-all&utm_medium=email&utm_content=20141119

Simonite, T. (2014c). Google's Brain-Inspired Software Describes What It Sees in Complex Images. *MIT Technology Review*. Retrieved from http://www.technologyreview.com/news/532666/googles-brain-inspired-software-describes-what-it-sees-in-compleximages/?utm_campaign=newsletters&utm_source=newsletter-daily-all&utm_medium=email&utm_content=20141119

Simonite, T. (2015). A startup's neural network can understand video. *MIT Technology Review.* Retrieved from http://www.technologyreview.com/news/534631/a-startups-neural-network-can-understand-video/

Simonite, T. (2015b). A Better Way to Build Brain-Inspired Chips. *MIT Review*. Retrieved from http://www.technologyreview.com/news/537211/a-better-way-to-build-brain-inspired-chips/

Simonite, T. (2015d). A startup's neural network can understand video. *MIT Review*. Retrieve from http://www.technologyreview.com/news/534631/a-startups-neural-network-can-understand-video/

Simpson, D., & Bruckheimer. J. (Producers), & Bay, M. (Director). (1996). *The Rock*. Hollywood Pictures, Buena Vista Pictures.

Sims, V., & Mayer, R. (2002). Domain specificity of spatial expertise: The case of video game players. *Applied Cognitive Psychology*, *16*(1), 97–115. doi:10.1002/acp.759

Singer, W. (1999). Neuronal synchrony: A versatile code for the definition of relations? *Neuron*, *24*(1), 49–65. doi:10.1016/S0896-6273(00)80821-1 PMID:10677026

Singh, G. (2011). Cinephilia, Or, looking for meaningfulness in encounters with cinema. In C. Hauke & L. Hockley (Eds.), *Jung & Film II: the return. Further post-Jungian takes on the moving image* (pp. 163–184). London: Routledge.

Sinyard, A. (2015, June). Emerging implications of virtual reality game play on dreams. *Paper to be presented at Towards a Science of Consciousness*, Helsinki, Finland.

Slater, G. (2008a, February). *Archetypal psychology*. Lecture conducted from Pacific Graduate Institute, Carpinteria, CA.

Slater, G. (2008b, March). *Archetypal psychology*. Lecture conducted from Pacific Graduate Institute, Carpinteria, CA.

Sloan, W. M. (2012). What is the purpose of education? *Educator's Update*, *54*(7). Retrieved from http://www.ascd.org/publications/newsletters/education-update/jul12/vol54/num07/What-Is-the-Purpose-of-Education%C2%A2.aspx

Sloman, A. (2008). Why scientists and philosophers of science should teach intelligent design alongside the theory of evolution.

Smart, J. M., Cascio, J., & Paffendorf, J. (2007). Metaverse Roadmap Overview, 2007. *Accelerated Studies Foundation*. Retrieved from http://en.wikipedia.org/wiki/Metaverse

Smart, J. M., Cascio, J., & Paffendorf, J. (2007). Metaverse Roadmap Overview. *Accelerated Studies Foundation*. Retrieved from http://en.wikipedia.org/wiki/Metaverse

Smith, H. (1991). *The World's Religions*. New York: Harper Collins.

Smoking Car Productions. (1997). *The Last Express*. Novato, CA: Broderbund.

Solms, M. (2003). Dreaming and REM sleep are controlled by different brain mechanisms. In E. Pace-Schott, M. Solms, M. Blagrove, & S. Harnad (Eds.), *Sleep and Dreaming: Scientific Advances and Reconsiderations* (pp. 51–58). Cambridge, UK: Cambridge University Press.

Solms, M. (2011). Neurobiology and the neurological basis of dreaming. In P. Montagna & S. Chokroverty (Eds.), *Handbook of clinical neurology* (3rd ed., pp. 519–544). New York, NY: Elsevier. doi:10.1016/B978-0-444-52006-7.00034-4

Sonnekus, T. (2013). 'We're not faggots!': Masculinity, homosexuality and the representation of Afrikaner men who have sex with men in the film 'Skoonheid' and online. *South African Review of Sociology*, *44*(1), 22–39. doi:10.1080/21528586.2013.784446

Spielberg, S. (Producer & Director). (1982). E.T. the Extra-Terrestrial. United States: Universal Pictures.

Starbreeze Studios (2013). *Brothers: A Tale of Two Sons.* Stockholm: 505 Games.

StarCraft 2: Legacy of the Void [YouTube video]. (2014). YouTube.com. Retrieved from https://www.youtube.com/watch?v=cML814JD09g&feature=share

State of Decay [Computer software]. (2013). Redmond, WA: Microsoft Studios.

Statista. (2014). *Number of World of Warcraft Subscribers from 1st Quarter 2005 to 4th Quarter 2014.* Retrieved from http://www.statista.com/statistics/276601/number-of-world-of-warcraft-subscribers-by-quarter/

Steriade, M. (2001). *The Intact and Sliced Brain.* Massachusetts: MIT Press.

Steriade, M. (2006). Grouping of brain rhythms in corticothalamic systems. *Neuroscience*, *137*(4), 1086–1106. doi:10.1016/j.neuroscience.2005.10.029 PMID:16343791

Sternberg, R. J., & Lubart, T. I. (1999). The concept of creativity: prospects and paradigms. In R. J. Sternberg (Ed.), *Handbook of creativity* (pp. 3–15). Cambridge, UK: Cambridge University Press.

Sternberg, R. J., & Preiss, D. D. (2005). *Intelligence and technology: The impact of tools on the nature and development of human abilities.* Mahwah, NJ: Erlbaum.

Steyn, M. E. (2004). Rehabilitating a whiteness disgraced: Afrikaner 'white talk' in post-apartheid South Africa. *Communication Quarterly*, *52*(2), 143–169. doi:10.1080/01463370409370187

Stopbullying.gov. (2014). *What is Bullying?* Retrieved from http://www.stopbullying.gov/what-is-bullying/definition/index.html

Stoupel, E. (1993). Sudden cardiac deaths and ventricular extrasystoles on days of four levels of geomagnetic activity. *J Basic Physiol Pharmacol.*, *4*(4), 357–366. PMID:8664252

Straker, G. (2004). Race for cover: Castrated whiteness, perverted consequences. *Psychoanalytical Dialogues: The International Journal of Relational Perspectives*, *14*(4), 405–422. doi:10.1080/10481881409348795

Strasburger, V., Donnerstein, E., & Bushman, B. (2014). Why is it so hard to believe that media influence children and adolescents? *Pediatrics*, *133*(4), 571–573. doi:10.1542/peds.2013-2334 PMID:24590743

Strickland, D. (2015). FeelReal brings sense of smell to virtual reality. *VR World.* Retrieved from http://www.vrworld.com/2015/03/11/feelreal-brings-sense-of-smell-to-virtual-reality/

Strickland, J. (2014). What is predictive modeling? *LindedIn Pulse.* Retrieved from https://www.linkedin.com/pulse/what-predictive-modeling-jeffrey-strickland-ph-d-cmsp-asep

Subrahmanyam, K., & Greenfield, P. M. (1994). Effect of video game practice on spatial skills in girls and boys. *Journal of Applied Developmental Psychology, 15*(1), 13–32. doi:10.1016/0193-3973(94)90004-3

Subrahmanyam, S., Narayan, P., & Srinivasan, T. (1985). Effect of magnetic micropulsations on the biological systems — A bioenvironmental study. *International Journal of Biometeorology, 29*(3), 293–305. doi:10.1007/BF02189660 PMID:3902670

Sun, R., & Bookman, L. (1994). Computational Architectures Integrating Neural and Symbolic Processes. Needham, MA: Kluwer Academic Publishers. Retrieved from http://www.cogsci.rpi.edu/~rsun/book2-ann.html doi:10.1007/b102608

Susskind, L. (1995). The world as a hologram. *Journal of Mathematical Physics, 36*(11), 6377–6396. doi:10.1063/1.531249

Talbot, M. (1991). *The Holographic Universe*. New York, NY: Harper Collins Publishers.

Talbot, M. (1991). *The holographic universe*. New York: Harper.

Tam, K., Lee, S., Kim, Y., Li, Y., & Chao, M. (2012). Intersubjective model of value transmission: Parents using perceived norms as reference when socializing children. *Personality and Social Psychology Bulletin, 38*(8), 1041–1052. doi:10.1177/0146167212443896 PMID:22539215

Team Max Rheiner. (2014). Birdly. Zurich: University of the Arts (ZHdK).

Tetris [Computer software]. (1984). Honolulu, HI: Tetris.

The Chinese Room. (2008/12). Dear Esther. Brighton: Chinese Room/ United States: Steam.

The Fullbright Company. (2013). *Gone Home*. Portland: The Fullbright Company.

The Hidden World of Facebook "Like Farms". (n. d.). *MIT Technology Review*. Retrieved from http://www.technologyreview.com/view/530961/the-hidden-world-of-facebook-like-farms/

The rapidly evolving ecosystems associated with personal data is creating an entirely new field of scientific study (2015). *MIT Technology Review.* Retrieved from http://www.technologyreview.com/view/533901/the-emerging-science-of-human-data-interaction/)

Tholey, P. (1983). Relation between dream content and eye movements tested by lucid dreams. *Perceptual and Motor Skills, 56*(3), 875–878. doi:10.2466/pms.1983.56.3.875 PMID:6877973

Tiller, W. A., Dibble, J. W. E., & Kohane, M. J. (2001). *Conscious Acts of Creation: The Emergence of a New Physics. 2001* (pp. 201–202). Walnut Creek, CA: Pavior Publishing.

Tiller, W. A., McCraty, R., & Atkinson, M. (1996). Cardiac coherence: A new, noninvasive measure of autonomic nervous system order. *Alternative Therapies in Health and Medicine, 2*(1), 52–65. PMID:8795873

Timmins, L. R., & Lombard, M. (2005). When 'real' seems mediated: Inverse presence. *Presence (Cambridge, Mass.), 14*(4), 492–500. doi:10.1162/105474605774785307

Tolkien, J. J. R. (1983/1931). A Secret Vice. In The Monsters and the Critics and Other Essays (p. 198-219).

Tolkien, J. R. R. (1954). The Lord of the Rings (Vols. 1–3). London: George Allen & Unwin.

Toma, C., & Hancock, J. (2013). Self-affirmation underlies Facebook use. *Pers. Soc. Psychol. GBull.*, 39(3), 321-331. Retrieved from http://psp.sagepub.com/content/39/3/321.abstract

Tomaselli, K. G. (1989). *The cinema of apartheid: race and class in South African film*. Sandton, Transvaal: Radix.

Tomaselli, K. G. (2008). Paradigms in South African cinema research: Modernity, the New Africa Movement and beyond. *Communicatio*, *34*(1), 130–147. doi:10.1080/02500160802144611

Trafton, A. (2014). New brain-scanning technique allows scientists to see when and where the brain processes visual information. *Medicalxpress.com*. Retrieved from http://medicalxpress.com/news/2014-01-brain-scanning-technique-scientists-brain-visual.html

Trifonova, T. (Ed.). (2009). *European Film Theory*. New York, NY: Routledge.

Twist, J. (2004, March 24). Brain waves control video game. *BBC News*. Retrieved from http://news.bbc.co.uk/2/hi/technology/3485918.stm

U.S. Forest Service. (n. d.). *Mount Hood Detailed Climbing Information*. Retrieved from http://www.fs.usda.gov

Umetani, K., Singer, D. H., McCraty, R., & Atkinson, M. (1998). Twenty-four hour time domain heart rate variability and heart rate: Relations to age and gender over nine decades. *Journal of the American College of Cardiology*, *31*(3), 593–601. doi:10.1016/S0735-1097(97)00554-8 PMID:9502641

Understanding human behavior as a Formal Computational Concept (2014). *MIT Technology Review & Yahoo Research Labs*. Retrieved from http://www.technologyreview.com/view/529521/how-yahoo-research-labs-studies-culture-as-a-formal-computational-concept/

Upper One Games. (2014). *Never Alone. (Kisima Inŋitchuŋa)*. Anchorage: E-Line Media.

Valve Corporation. (1998). *Half-Life*. Los Angeles: Sierra Entertainment.

Van de Castle, R. L. (1994). *Our dreaming mind*. New York: Random House.

van Lommel, P. (2011). Near-death experiences: The experience of the self as real and not as an illusion. *Annals of the New York Academy of Sciences*, *1234*(1), 19–28. doi:10.1111/j.1749-6632.2011.06080.x PMID:21988246

VanHeerden, P. (1970, July25). Models for the brain. *Nature*, *227*(5256), 410–411. doi:10.1038/227410b0 PMID:5428449

Vernon, D. (2005). Can Neurofeedback Training Enhance Performance? *An Evaluation of the Evidence with Implications for Future Research Applied Psychophysiology and Biofeedback*, *30*, 165–205. PMID:16385423

Vialatte, F., Bakardjian, H., Prasad, R., & Cichocki, A. (2009). EEG paroxysmal gamma waves during Bhramari Pranayama: A yoga breathing technique. *Consciousness and Cognition*, *18*(4), 977–988. doi:10.1016/j.concog.2008.01.004 PMID:18299208

Villoresi, G., Ptitsyna, N. G., Tiasto, M. I., & Iucci, N. (1998). Myocardial infarct and geomagnetic disturbances: Analysis of data on morbidity and mortality[In Russian]. *Biofizika*, *43*(4), 623–631. PMID:9783069

Vogler, C. (1985) *A Practical Guide to The Hero with a Thousand Faces*. Manuscript. Retrieved on 04.02.2015 from http://www.thewritersjourney.com/hero's_journey.htm

Vogler, C. (1992). *The Writer's Journey: Mythic Structures for Storytellers & Screenwriters*. Studio City, CA: Michael Wiese Productions.

Von Franz, M.L. (1974). *Shadow and evil in fairy tales*. New York: Spring.

Von Franz, M. L. (1964). The process of individuation. In C. G. Jung (Ed.), *Man and his symbols* (pp. 157–254). New York, NY: Dell Publishers.

Von Franz, M. L. (1980). *Alchemy: an introduction to the symbolism and the psychology*. Toronto: Inner City Books.

Von Franz, M.-L. (1996). *The interpretation of fairy tales*. Boston, MA: Shambhala. (Original work published 1970).

Voss, U., Holzmann, R., Tuin, I., & Hobson, J. A. (2009). Lucid dreaming: A state of consciousness with features of both waking and non-lucid dreaming. *Sleep*, *32*, 1191–1200. PMID:19750924

Wakefield, J. (2014). Singularity: The robots are coming to steal our jobs. *BBC News*. Retrieved from http://www.bbc.com/news/technology-25000756

Wales, A. (2013). *Peaceful panels: Using comics to teach anti-bullying to junior high school students.*

Walker, M. P. (2005). A refined model of sleep and the time course of memory consolidation. *Behavioral and Brain Sciences*, *28*(01), 51–104. doi:10.1017/S0140525X05000026 PMID:16047457

Wallace, B. A. (2006). *The Attention Revolution: Unlocking the power of the Focused Mind*. Boston: Wisdom Publications.

Wallis, H. B. (Producer), & Curtiz, M. (Director). (1942). Casablanca. United States: Warner Bros.

Weinstein, M., & Smith, J. (1992). Isometric squeeze relaxation (progressive relaxation) vs. meditation: Absorption and focusing as predictors of state effects. *Perceptual and Motor Skills*, *75*(12), 63–71. PMID:1484796

Wheeler, J. A. (1990). Information, physics, quantum: The search for links. In W. H. Zurek (Ed.), *Complexity, Entropy, and the physics of information*. Redwood City, CA: Addison-Wesley.

White, M. (2000). *Narrative Means to Therapeutic Ends; Maps of Narrative Practice. Reflections on Narrative Practice*. Adelaide, South Australia: Dulwich Centre Publications.

Why Neural Networks Look Set to Thrash the Best Human Go Players for the First Time. *MIT Technology Review*. Retrieved from http://www.technologyreview.com/view/533496/why-neural-networks-look-set-to-thrash-the-best-human-go-players-for-the-first-time/

Wicht, D. (Producer), & Xenopoulos, J. (Director). (2002). *Promised land* [Motion Picture]. South Africa: Film Afrika Worldwide, Khulisa Productions.

Williamson, J.E. (Ed.), (1991). *Accidents in North American Mountaineering* (pp. 46–47). Seattle: Mountaineers Books.

Wlassoff, V. (2015). Brains aren't fooled by virtual reality. *ISPR Presence News*. Retrieved from http://ispr.info/2015/03/

Wolfram, S. (2002). *A New Kind of Science*. Champaign, IL: Wolfram Media, Inc.

Wolinksy, D. (2015). Exhuming Grim Fandango's Mexican Folklore Inspirations. In *Kill Screen*. Retrieved from http://killscreendaily.com/articles/exhuming-grim-fandangos-mexican-folklore-inspirations/

Wollschleger, J. (2013). Church Government and Religious Participation. *Rationality and Society*, *25*(4), 470–400. doi:10.1177/1043463113504449

World Bank. (2012). *International Internet bandwidth (bits per person)*. Retrieved from http://www.tradingeconomics.com/country-list/international-internet-bandwidth-bits-per-person-wb-data.html

World of Warcraft [Computer software]. (2001). Irvine, CA: Blizzard Entertainment.

Wright, W. R. (1960). Functional analysis and mass communication. *Public Opinion Quarterly*, (24): 610–613.

Yee, N. (2006). The Demographics, Motivations and Derived Experiences of Users of Massively-Multiuser Online Graphical Environments. *Presence (Cambridge, Mass.)*, *15*(3), 309–329. doi:10.1162/pres.15.3.309

Zaitseva SAaP. (1995). M. I. (1995). Effect of solar and geomagnetic activity on population dynamics among residents of Russia[In Russian]. *Biofizika*, *40*(4), 861–864. PMID:7495913

Zanardo, A. (2011). Love, loss, imagination and the 'other' in Soderbergh's *Solaris*. In C. Hauke & L. Hockley (Eds.), *Jung & Film II: the return. Further post-Jungian takes on the moving image* (pp. 49–65). London: Routledge.

Zimbardo, P. (2007). *The Lucifer Effect: Understanding How Good People Turn Evil*. New York: Random House.

Zimmerman, E. (2013). Foreword. In *B. De Koven, The well-played game: A player's philosophy* (pp. vi–xx). Cambridge, MA: The MIT Press.

Zuckerberg, M. (2014). Blog message. Retrieved from https://www.facebook.com/zuck

Zuse, K. (1967). Rechnender Raum. *Elektronische Datenverarbeitung*, *8*, 336–344.

Zyga, L. (2013). Maxwell's demon can use quantum information to generate work. *Phys.org*. Retrieved from http://phys.org/news/2013-12-maxwell-demon-quantum.html

About the Contributors

Stephen Schafer's interest is on communications research relating to media influence on cultural transformation. He has been developing a theoretical analog between cognitive models and video game structure. The analog is based on a multidimensional common denominator—narrative-metaphorical linguistic structure—that operates as an affective transducer between conscious and unconscious cognitive dimensions. Accordingly, a genre of drama-based video games (DBG) may be used as a research instrument to access robust data relative to unconscious cognitive states. Schafer is Principal Lecturer and Past Chairman of the Humanities & Social Sciences Department at Digipen Institute of Technology where he taught from 2000 to 2015. In addition to teaching at several colleges and universities, he has twenty-five years of experience that includes senior management in both the public and private sectors, social and environmental activism, marketing, and journalism. The unusual breadth and depth of his practical experience supports his research on the media dynamics of cultural evolution. Conference presentations and professional affiliations include such events as PAX 2009, GDC Austin 2008 & 2009, Toward a Science of Consciousness 2008 & 2009, Social Approaches to Consciousness, Game Education Summit (GES) North America 2009, GES North America 2010, and GES Europe 2010. He was invited to co-organize an international invitational workshop on Meaningful Media at the Asia Festival 2009, is a Senior Fellow of the Video Games & Human Values Initiative, an invited member of The Society of Industry Leaders, a member of the Immersive Education Initiative (MediaGrid), The C. G. Jung Foundation, and others. He teaches an array of classes that emphasize mythology, symbolism, and Jungian psychological dynamics of dream interpretation in order to train game-story writers to apply the principles to interactive narrative.

* * *

Chris Broodryk, PhD, teaches Drama and Film Studies at the University of Pretoria. He is working towards his PhD in Film Studies at the University of Cape Town.

Doug Emory has been the Dean of Academics at Lake Washington Institute of Technology since 1997. He is also an active mountaineer who has climbed well over 200 different peaks in the United States and Mexico.

Jayne I. Gackenbach received her Ph.D.in 1978 in Experimental Psychology from Virginia Commonwealth University. She is currently an Associate Professor at MacEwan University. She has taught at the post-secondary level both in the US and in Canada for over 30 years. As well as being a past-president of the International Association for the Study of Dreams, she has numerous professional publications on dreams and in the last decade on video game play. Dr. Gackenbach is editor of "Sleep and Dreams: A Sourcebook" (1986) for Garland Publishers. She co-edited "Conscious Mind, Sleeping Brain: Perspectives on Lucid Dreaming" (1988) for Plenum Publishers; "Dream Imagery: A Call to Mental Arms" (1991) for Baywood Publishers. Her first authored book is "Control Your Dreams" (1989; 2012) for Harper-Collins. She was invited in 1992 to present her work on lucid dreaming to the Dalai Lama at a conference on sleeping, dreaming, and dying. Dr. Gackenbach's interests have shifted to computer-mediated communications. In this regard she has edited a book from Academic Press (1998; 2007), "Psychology and the Internet: Intrapersonal, Interpersonal, and Transpersonal Implications" and co-wrote a book called "cyber.rules" for Norton publishers (2007) with examines healthy and unhealthy internet use. Dr. Gackenbach's most recent research interest combines her dream and technology interests examining the dreams of video game players. She has released two related books. One was co-written with her gamer son, Teace Snyder, on the effects of video game play, "Play Reality". She also has an edited book "Video Game Play and Consciousness" from NOVA publishers. Both books came out in 2012. She has pursued an active research program into gaming and dreams expanding it in recent years to include social media usage. Over her 35 year career she has 46 peer reviewed articles, 26 book chapters and nine books with two translated into Chinese, one into German and one into Arabic.

Sarkis Hakopdjanian is an honors student in psychology at MacEwan University working in the video game and dreams laboratory under the direction of Dr. Gackenbach. He previously received a bachelor's degree at the University of Alberta.

Claudia Hall is a PhD candidate at California Institute of Integral Studies, Transformative Studies Department. Her areas of interest include interfaith religion and spirituality, the integration of sexuality and spirituality, polyamory and the family, Tabletop Role-Playing Games, and the interplay between social construction theory and depth psychology. She lives in St. Louis with her family.

Rollin McCraty, Ph.D. is Director of Research of the HeartMath Research Center at the Institute of HeartMath. He is also a Professor at Florida Atlantic University. A psychophysiologist, Dr. McCraty's research interests include the physiology of emotion, with a focus on the mechanisms by which emotions influence cognitive processes, behavior, and health as well as the global interconnectivity between people and the earth's energetic systems. Findings from this research have been applied to the development of simple, user-friendly mental and emotional self-regulation tools and techniques that people of all ages and cultures can use in the moment to relieve stress and break through to greater levels of personal balance, stability, creativity, intuitive insight and fulfillment. Dr. McCraty has acted as Principal Investigator in numerous research studies examining the effects of emotions on heart–brain interactions and on autonomic, cardiovascular, hormonal, and immune system function. He is a member of the American Autonomic Society, the Pavlovian Society, National Association for Psychological Science, the Association for Applied Psychophysiology and Biofeedback, and Society for Scientific Exploration. His research team regularly participate in collaborative studies with U.S. and international scientific, medical and educational institutions; they have worked in joint partnership with research groups at Stanford University, Claremont Graduate University, Dalhousie University (Halifax, Nova Scotia), Prince Sultan Cardiac Center (Saudi Arabia), University of Lithuania, among many others. Dr. McCraty has been interviewed for numerous feature articles in publications such as Prevention, Natural

Health, Men's Fitness and American Health magazines, and has appeared on television segments for CNN-Headline News, ABC-World News Tonight, ABC-Good Morning America, NBC-Today Show, PBS-Body & Soul and Discovery Channel- and has been featured in a number of documentary films such as I am, The Truth, The Joy of Sox move, The Power of the Heart, Solar Revolution, and The Living Matrix among many others.

James Pagel, MD, MS Basic Medical Science (Neuropharmacology) UAB, Board Certification - Family Medicine, Sleep Medicine, Behavioral Sleep Medicine. Associate Professor University of Colorado School of Medicine. 170 publications in the fields of sleep and dream study. Books: The Limits of Dream: A Scientific Exploration of the Mind/Brain Interface (Academic Press 2008), Primary Care Sleep Medicine: A Practical Guide (Co-ed. Humana, 2007; Springer 2014), Dreaming and Nightmares (Ed. Saunders 2010), Dream Science: Exploring the Forms of Consciousness (Academic Press 2014).

Susan Marie Savett, PhD, Pacifica Graduate Institute. Dr. Susan M. Savett is an Archetypal Psychology consultant and researcher focusing on the application of Jungian and archetypal theories to the field of game studies. Her work focuses on game developers design processes and the unconscious influences present on game developers, archetypal transference to game mechanics, and the realm of play as a vessel for players' conscious and unconscious content. Dr. Savett is certified in Embodied Imagination and Dream Therapy, a therapeutic and creative form of working with dreams, imagination, and creative process. Working with its founder, Jungian analyst Robert Bosnak, she is researching the role of embodied imagination within game design and virtual reality.

Beat Suter received his Ph.D. in Literature from the University of Zurich in 2000. In 2004 he was hired to found a curriculum for Game Design at the University of the Arts Zurich, Switzerland. He currently works there as a lecturer and researcher for game design and he manages the GameLab together with René Bauer. He has been working as publisher and independent scholar of electronic literature, storytelling and game design. He is founding member of the art group AND-OR, specializing in media art and game art. Over the years the group has been able to show its media art and artgames worldwide. He is chairman of gameZfestival, an annual festival for the game design and game culture community.

Index

G

H

I

J

L

M

N

P

R

S

T

V

W

www.ingramcontent.com/pod-product-compliance
Lightning Source LLC
LaVergne TN
LVHW060420300926
849162LV00006B/1485
9781466698918